the city seeking to destroy it... ...ing to dissolve the Union, and... ...gotiation. Both parties deprecated war; but one of them would make war rather than let the nation survive; and the other would accept war rather than let it perish. And the war came.

One eighth of the whole population were colored slaves, not distributed generally over the Union, but localized in the Southern part half of it. These slaves constituted a peculiar and powerful interest. All knew that this interest was, somehow, the cause of the war. To strengthen, perpetuate, and extend this interest was the object for which the insurgents would rend the Union, even by war; while the government claimed no right to do more than to restrict the territorial enlargement of it. Neither party expected for the war, the magnitude, or the duration, which it has already attained. Neither anticipated that

ABRAHAM LINCOLN
Redeemer President

> *Original manuscript of second Inaugeral presented to Major John Hay.*
>
> *A Lincoln*
>
> *April 10. 1865*

*Reproduced on the endsheets is one of the
original manuscripts of Lincoln's second inaugural address,
presented by Lincoln to one of his private secretaries, John Hay.*

Abraham Lincoln

Redeemer President

Allen C. Guelzo

WILLIAM B. EERDMANS PUBLISHING COMPANY
GRAND RAPIDS, MICHIGAN / CAMBRIDGE, U.K.

© 1999 Wm. B. Eerdmans Publishing Co.
255 Jefferson Ave. S.E., Grand Rapids, Michigan 49503 /
P.O. Box 163, Cambridge CB3 9PU U.K.

Printed in the United States of America

04 03 02 01 00 99   7 6 5 4 3 2 1

Library of Congress Cataloging-in-Publication Data

Guelzo, Allen C.
    Abraham Lincoln: redeemer president / Allen C. Guelzo.
    p.   cm.
    Includes bibliographical references and index.
    ISBN 0-8028-3872-3 (alk. paper)
    1. Lincoln, Abraham, 1809-1865 — Philosophy.   2. Lincoln, Abraham,
1809-1865 — Political and social views.   3. Lincoln, Abraham,
1809-1865 — Religion.   4. Presidents — United States Biography.
I. Title.
E457.2.G88   1999
973.7′092 — dc21
  [B]   99-38021
                                           [CIP]

For Jack Kemp

Contents

CONTENTS

Acknowledgments

The writing of acknowledgments is one of the more deliciously selfish pleasures an author can enjoy, since it allows a one-by-one recollection of the entire circle of friends, contributors, and critics from whom he has been allowed to borrow reflected glory and wisdom. The work was actually born in the Charles Warren Center for American Studies at Harvard University, where some of the preliminary research work was carried out in the Widener Library's quite-considerable collection of Lincolniana. But it has continued in many other Lincolnian places, as well including Springfield, Galesburg, Peoria, Chicago, Gettysburg, and numerous points in between.

Organizationally, I must single out for recognition the encouragement I have received from the Abraham Lincoln Association, the Lincoln Studies Institute at Knox College, the Civil War Institute at Gettysburg College, and the Abraham Lincoln Institute of the Mid-Atlantic. Michael Burlingame has been chief among those who have devoted time and effort to this project, and I have benefited from both his work and personal friendship. But I must also single out Thomas F. Schwartz (Secretary of the Abraham Lincoln Association), Rodney O. Davis and Douglas L. Wilson (Lincoln Studies Institute, Knox College), Ronald Rietveld (California State University/Fullerton), John

ACKNOWLEDGMENTS

Patrick Diggins (City University of New York), David Hein (Hood College), Scott Sandage (Carnegie-Mellon University), Kim Bauer (Illinois State Archives), Mark E. Steiner (University of Houston), Cullom Davis (Lincoln Legal Papers Project), Paul Verduin (Abraham Lincoln Institute of the Mid-Atlantic), William E. Gienapp (Harvard University), Lucas Morel (John Brown University), and James A. Rawley and Kenneth Winkle (University of Nebraska/Lincoln) for their special acts of comment and generosity. In particular, Burlingame, Rietveld, Diggins, Wilson (and Mark Noll) all read and criticized parts of this manuscript; Burlingame, Schwartz, Sandage, Davis, and Wilson all shared freely manuscript sources they themselves have been working upon. In thanking them, I attempt no shifting of interpretive blame onto their shoulders for any of the ideas or arguments offered herein.

I am grateful to Roger Lundin and Thomas O. Kay of Wheaton College, George Marsden and James Turner of the University of Notre Dame, William R. Hutchison of the Harvard Divinity School, and Bernard Bailyn of the Charles Warren Center for the opportunity to present some of the first pieces of this work in Wheaton, South Bend, and Cambridge. Charles Van Hof, Jennifer Hoffman, Amanda Dombek, and Anita Eerdmans of Wm. B. Eerdmans Publishing have exhibited, more than patience, a sense of Lincolnian "Highlarity" in the long gestation of this book.

Thanks are also due to the editors of the *Lincoln Herald* for permission to reprint material from "That All Men Are Created Equal: Lincoln's Declaration of Independence" (Winter 1995) and to the editors of the *Journal of the Abraham Lincoln Association* for permission to reprint material from "Abraham Lincoln and the Doctrine of Necessity" (Winter 1997) and "Come-Outers and Community-Men: Abraham Lincoln and the Idea of Community in 19th-Century America" (Winter 2000). Among the manuscript collections used in this study, I should acknowledge the permission of the New York Public Library for the use of the Josiah Gilbert Holland Papers, the University of Chicago Library for citations from the papers of William E. Barton, the Firestone Library at Princeton University for citations from the papers of Josiah Royce, and Allegheny College for citations from the papers of Ida M. Tarbell. I am grateful to Mr. James A. Mundy, the Archivist of the Union League of Philadelphia, for obtaining the League' s permission to reproduce on the cover Edward Dalton Marchant's portrait of

Lincoln, which Marchant painted from life between February and August, 1863, on commission from John W. Forney. The portrait hung in Independence Hall from 1863 till 1866, when it was hung in the League House. Today, it occupies the place of honor in the Union League's Lincoln Hall.

This book represents more than simply a new way of speaking about Abraham Lincoln. For this and for so much else, only my beloved wife and children know how peculiar but how comforting it was to have this strange friend, and friendly stranger, take up prolonged, if metaphorical, residence with them. These thanks are for them, too.

The dedication is for you, Jack, in salute of a common interest in our nation's most uncommon man.

Allen C. Guelzo
The Villas
Cape May, New Jersey
June 21, 1999

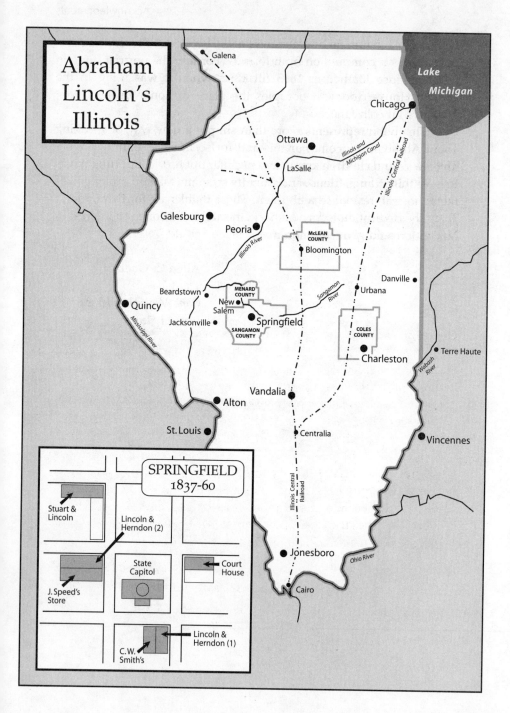

Abraham
Lincoln's
Illinois

Galena

Lake
Michigan

Chicago

Ottawa

LaSalle

Illinois and Michigan Canal

Illinois Central Railroad

Galesburg

Peoria

McLEAN
COUNTY

Bloomington

Illinois River

Danville

Beardstown

MENARD
COUNTY

New
Salem

Sangamon River

Urbana

Quincy

Jacksonville

Springfield

SANGAMON
COUNTY

COLES
COUNTY

Charleston

Terre Haute

Mississippi River

Wabash River

Vandalia

Alton

St. Louis

Centralia

Vincennes

Illinois Central Railroad

SPRINGFIELD
1837-60

Stuart &
Lincoln

Lincoln &
Herndon (2)

State
Capitol

Court
House

J. Speed's
Store

Lincoln &
Herndon (1)

C. W.
Smith's

Jonesboro

Ohio River

Cairo

Pensive by Nature, he had gone of late
To those who preached of Destiny and Fate,
Of things fore-doomed, and of Election-grace,
And how in vain we strive to run our race;
That all by Works and moral Worth we gain,
Is to perceive our Care and Labour vain;
That still the more we pay, our Debts the more remain;
That he who feels not the mysterious Call,
Lies bound in Sin, still grovelling from the Fall. . . .
For ever to some evil Change inclined,
To every gloomy thought he lent his Mind,
Nor rest would give to us, nor Rest himself could find. . . .

George Crabbe, The Borough (1810)

Civil War. . . . What did the words mean? Was there any such thing as 'foreign war'? Was not all warfare between men warfare between brothers? Wars could only be defined by their aims. There were no 'foreign' or 'civil' wars, only wars that were just or unjust. . . . Outside the sacred cause of justice, what grounds has one kind of war for denigrating another? . . . Are we to condemn every resort to arms that takes place within the citadel, without concerning ourselves with its aim? What cause can be more just, what war more righteous, than that which restores social truth, restores liberty to its throne, restores proper sovereignty to all men . . . reasserts the fullness of reason and equity, eliminates the seeds of antagonism by allowing each man to be himself, abolishes the hindrance to universal concord represented by monarchy and makes all mankind equal before the law.

Victor Hugo, Les Miserables (1862),
trans. Norman Denny

Southerners knew full well that the Constitution's heart was a moral commitment to equality and hence condemned segregation of blacks. The Constitution was not just a set of rules of government but implied a moral order that was to be enforced throughout the entire Union. Yet the influence, which has not been sufficiently noted, of Southern writers and historians on the American view of their history has been powerful. They were remarkably successful in characterizing their "peculiar institution" as part of a charming diversity and individuality of culture to which the Constitution was worse than indifferent. The idea of openness, lack of ethnocentricity, is just what they needed for a modern defense of their way of life against all the intrusions of outsiders who claimed equal rights with the folks back home.

Allan Bloom, *The Closing of the American Mind* (1987)

———————

It is very common in this country to find great facility of expression and less common to find great lucidity of thought. The combination of the two in one person is very uncommon; but wherever you do find it, you have a great man.

Abraham Lincoln to Edward Dicey,
Macmillan's Magazine (May, 1862)

———————

Introduction: The Strife of Ideas

It had taken a good deal of trawling through old, downstate newspapers, but during the first week of September, 1860, the *Chicago Times* finally found something from the past that could embarrass Abraham Lincoln.

It was a speech the *Times'* editors exhumed from a dusty 1844 issue of the obscure Macomb *Eagle*, when Lincoln had been campaigning for Henry Clay's last presidential bid, a speech that dared to attack the father of American independence, Thomas Jefferson. "The character of Jefferson was repulsive," the speech declared, and the chief evidence of Jefferson's degradation was the long-whispered story of Jefferson's liaison with his slave, Sally Hemings, and the slave children he had sired by her. "Continually puling about liberty, equality, and the degrading curse of slavery, he brought his own children to the hammer, and made money of his debaucheries."

This was not usually the stuff out of which serious political embarrassments are made, but when Anson Chester passed a copy of the article to Lincoln, the tall Springfield lawyer's reply crackled with irritation. Lincoln was now in the midst of his own campaign for the presidency of the United States, and over the last six years, he had made Jefferson's Declaration the moral touchstone of his argument against the extension of slavery in the American republic. He had gone out of his way to praise Jefferson as one of "those noble fathers — Washington, Jefferson, and Madison," and in 1859 he had pinpointed "the principles of Jefferson" as "the definitions and axioms of free society."

> All honor to Jefferson — to the man who, in the concrete pressure of a struggle for national independence by a single people, had the coolness, forecast, and capacity to introduce into a mere revolutionary document, an abstract truth, applicable to all men and all times, and so embalm it there, that to-day, and in all coming days, it shall be a rebuke and a stumbling-block to the very harbingers of re-appearing tyranny and oppression.

Lincoln's response to the *Chicago Times* accusation was a sharp, harsh denial, published in the *Illinois State Journal* on September 6, 1860. "This is a bold and deliberate forgery. . . . Mr. Lincoln never used any such language in any speech *at any time.*"

Oddly, the denial was not signed by Lincoln. "I wish my name not to be used," Lincoln wrote back to Chester, "but my friends will be entirely safe in denouncing the thing as a forgery, so far as it is ascribed to me." And he may have had good reason, for in fact, as William Henry Herndon (Lincoln's law partner and biographer) wrote years later, "Mr. Lincoln hated Thomas Jefferson as a man" as well "as a politician." In Jefferson, Lincoln saw a compound of hypocrisy and aristocracy, a commitment to freedom in words but not in deeds, the champion of an agrarian order that concealed an elite class agenda within a fog of solidarity with farmers and laborers. At the same time, though, Jefferson by the 1850s had become an American icon, and it ill-behooved Lincoln to air his "hatred" too publicly. Besides, icons can be used for more purposes than their designers plan. Lincoln upended the Jeffersonian icon by embracing Jefferson's words on freedom and equality, and then using them as a way of highlighting how Jefferson's own party now seemed to be deserting them in favor of protecting the political interests of the slaveholding South. During the great debates he held in 1858 with his Democratic rival, Stephen A. Douglas, Lincoln delighted in drawing as vast a gulf as he could between Jefferson's declarations and the justifications Jefferson's political heirs were now weakly uttering in defense of slavery, as if to make the founder of the

Democratic party a useful convert to Lincoln's anti-slavery Republicanism. But behind the tactical shrewdness of wrenching Thomas Jefferson out of his opponents' hands, the editors of the *Chicago Times* had been right to see Abraham Lincoln as sitting far from Jefferson's seat, and shrewd in their own way in digging up old speeches that would prove it.

Lincoln was born only three weeks before Jefferson finished his second and last term as the third president of the United States. But for all of his life, Lincoln would stand uneasily in the shadow of the great Virginian. His life was entwined around a pattern of cultural values that parted sharply from Jefferson's. Jefferson carefully pared apart his political principles from his personal life, demanding public virtue from office-holders but pursuing his own hedonistic satisfactions in private, lauding liberty but holding between 150 and 200 African-Americans in slavery during his lifetime. By contrast, Lincoln was a moral rigorist who made a fetish of his own sincerity and honesty, who endured a difficult political marriage without ever arousing the slightest imputation of faithlessness, and who claimed that he was so "naturally anti-slavery" that "I can not remember when I did not so think, and feel." Jefferson was also notorious for his religious unorthodoxy. Lincoln, on the other hand, started in the 1830s from a position of unorthodoxy not much different from Jefferson's, but throughout his life he increasingly wrapped his political ideas around religious themes, appealing at the very end to a mysterious providence whose inscrutable and irresistible workings both baffled and comforted him. The moment the focus shifts from Thomas Jefferson the icon to Thomas Jefferson the political man — the anti-Federalist, the critic of Washington and avowed enemy of Alexander Hamilton, the patrician republican and slaveholder, the agrarian opponent of cities, of industry, of any form of wealth not tied to land — then it has to be said that Abraham Lincoln grew and matured as an American political thinker into an adversary of almost every practical aspect of Thomas Jefferson's political worldview.

When Jefferson spoke about freedom and equality, he spoke for a generation of classical patrician republicans who hoped to replace the artificialities of monarchy with a "natural" gentry aristocracy and a broad base of independent yeoman farmers who worked the land to provide for themselves rather than working for others, as dependents, for wages. Lincoln spoke for a later generation of middle-class Northern and Western merchants and professionals who came to see "natural" aristocrats as no different from any other kind. It was not the stability of a benign gentry-ruled republic that Lincoln prized, but the mobility of a self-interested liberal democracy. Like the great English liberals — James Mill, John Stuart Mill (whom Lincoln read and admired), Jeremy Bentham, Richard Cobden, John Bright — Lincoln glorified progress, middle-class individualism, and the opportunities for economic self-improvement which the new capitalist networks of the nineteenth century were opening up across the Atlantic world. "I hold that while man exists, it is his duty to improve not only his own condition, but to assist in ameliorating mankind," Lincoln said in 1861, and promptly explained this amelioration in terms of Bentham's famed utilitarian tag: "I am for those means which will give the greatest good to the greatest number."

To Jefferson and the Jeffersonians the opposite of stability was simply instability, not opportunity. Part of this fear grew from Jefferson's own desperate yearning for settledness, which in his case meant a world without creditors in which all republican citizens would plant themselves under their own vines and fig trees without fear of taxes or debt, free of manipulation and refusing all temptations to make themselves greater at someone else's expense. Nothing symbolized this more in Jefferson's mind than the image of the virtuous farmer. In one of his most famous *bon mots*, Jefferson rhapsodized on the link between political virtue and the life of the rural republican farmer:

> Those who labour in the earth are the chosen people of God, if ever he had a chosen people, whose breasts he has made his peculiar deposit of substantial and genuine virtue. It is the focus in which he keeps alive that sacred fire, which otherwise might escape from the face of the earth. Corruption of morals in the mass of cultivators is a phenomenon of which no age nor nation has furnished an example.

This was not merely a matter of rural sentimentality. In the 1790s, the United States was still overwhelmingly a nation of small-scale farmers, and unlike England, where by 1800 only 36 percent of the population was engaged in agriculture, the American republic had anywhere between 75 to 90 percent of its population still on the farm. What was more, the extraordinary availability of cheap land (especially after the Revolution had removed imperial restraints on settlement westward across the Appalachians) and the absence of an American aristocracy meant that American farmers usually owned their land outright, with no feudal obligations and only the most minimal taxation. In rural Hampshire County in western Massachusetts, 65 percent of all taxpayers owned their own land, and 92 percent of all the housing was owned — not rented or leased — by the people living in it. What indebtedness there was usually involved the widespread borrowing of small sums back and forth along kinship and neighbor networks, with interest often neither asked for nor given.

Since land titles were not usually jeopardized by indebtedness, taxation, or fees, the American farmer's chief incentive for production was household or local consumption. American farm households grew or produced by themselves as much as three-fourths of what they required, and then purchased the remainder with the surplus of their own agricultural production. In regions close to major seaports, a rather higher percentage of agricultural output was clearly intended for distant markets. But farmers in Hampshire County, who were sealed off from Boston by land distance and from Old Saybrook by falls and rapids on the Connecticut River, produced crops first for home consumption, and then for barter for goods — liquor, tea, farm tools — which a local storekeeper or another farmer might produce. Few farmers, except those within five miles of a river or coastline, grew single "staple" crops intended solely for sale or export.

The absence of large-scale commercial interests in the United States was, in Jefferson's mind, exactly what guaranteed the survival of liberty. Jeffersonian liberty was local rather than national, and its deadly enemy lay in too-great concentrations of power at the center — liberty, in fact, thrived only in inverse proportion to the presence of power, and so the more power could be broken up and distributed round to localities, the less danger there was to liberty. This meant that the great political Satan was either a central government, or big commercial centers, or a lethal combination of both. Big governments required big taxation, and taxation undermined the security of landholders in their property; big cities were sinkholes of corruption, influence-peddling, and suspicious forms of illusory wealth, like bank

7

notes, bonds, mortgages, and other symbols of debt that threatened the independence of the property holder. "I am the holder of no stock whatever, except livestock," boasted the most sharp-tongued of the Jeffersonians, John Randolph of Roanoke,

> and am determined never to own any, because it is the creation of a great and privileged order of the most hateful kind to my feelings and because I would rather be the master than the slave. If I must have a master let him be one with epaulettes, something that I could fear and respect, something I could look up to — but not a master with a quill behind his ear.

Not only liberty, but virtue was most likely to be found in the healthy atmosphere of rural agriculture. To Jefferson's fellow-Virginian, John Taylor of Caroline, "the ideal of a republican statesman" is "a skillful, practical farmer, giving his time to his farm and his books, when not called by an emergency to the public service — and returning to his books and his farm when the emergency was over." Let loose the genie of self-interest, and corruption was precisely what could be expected, as the pursuit of luxury would lead to competition and accumulation on the part of the successful, dependence and misery for the failures, and the end of stability in the republic. "I consider the class of artificers as the panders of vice," wrote Jefferson, "and the instruments by which the liberties of a country are generally overturned."

Stability, however, does not pay its own bills, which is why Jefferson's distaste for markets, manufacturing, and mobility was inextricably bound up with race. The agricultural wealth Jefferson relied upon (and spent his life vainly trying to shore up) was sustained by the coerced labor of black slaves, who may have constituted as much as 25 percent of the English-speaking population of North America on the eve of the Revolution. The number of people who actually owned these slaves and profited directly from their labor was always comparatively small in the American republic, but the Jeffersonians could always rally large numbers of nonslaveholding farmers and urban workers to their side with the whispered threat of what might happen to them if freedom and mobility were extended to blacks. The success of the Jeffersonian vision depended on the debasement and exploitation of blacks, which is why race legitimated and maddened the resistance of the Jeffersonians to capitalist mobility.

If Lincoln had only criticized slavery as one unpleasant oversight on Jefferson's part, nothing that he otherwise did with his life would have required his "hatred" of Jefferson. But Lincoln's opposition to slavery was rooted in a fierce resentment of everything that grew out of the slave system, up to the whole agrarian ideology itself. Although Lincoln's claims to have "always" opposed slavery have been skeptically discounted since the 1960s (because he showed little enthusiasm for abolition before the 1850s), Lincoln was not exaggerating in making this claim, since he defined *slavery* as any relationship which forestalled social dynamism and economic mobility, or obstructed "the paths of laudable pursuit for all." For Lincoln, his first experience of what he called *slavery* described how his own father, a Jeffersonian farmer, manipulated and exploited his labor as a young man. It would take only time and circumstances for Lincoln to expand his resentment at Jeffersonian "slavery" to include the blacks who were owned by Jefferson's heirs. Even though he harbored persistent racist doubts about whether blacks could be "equal" to whites "in color, size, intellect, moral developments, or social capacity," Lincoln came to see black slavery as synonymous with the denial of his own liberal aspirations for "improvement of condition."

On no other single point was the distance between Thomas Jefferson and Abraham Lincoln more apparent; on no better grounds did Jefferson and the Jeffersonians fear "the designs of ambition."

In 1800, when Jefferson was elected president in a triumphant landslide over the Federalist John Adams, the perspective had looked very different. Jefferson's defeat of Adams and the Federalist ascendancy in the early republic was interpreted by him as a mandate to bring the United States back onto the course he believed it had been created to follow in 1776. Curiously, there was less difference between Jefferson's "Democratic-Republicans" and the Federalists than there would later be between Lincoln and the Democrats of 1860. Both Jefferson and his Federalist enemies, Hamilton and Adams, agreed rather broadly that the American republic ought to be ruled by an enlightened, benevolent and gentlemanly elite. Hamilton, as a landless bastard with no family connections to rely upon, had a far higher estimate than Jefferson of commerce and merchandising as a means to wealth and independence, and for that reason Hamilton, as the first Secretary of the Treasury, offered a comprehensive economic blueprint to Congress which called for the establishment of a national bank (for federal funding of development projects), the full funding of the republic's Revolutionary War debts (which meant a windfall for Hamilton's financier friends who had held United States government securities since the 1780s, but bad news for landowners who would have to pay the taxes to fund the debts), and federal support for manufacturing interests.

But if to Jefferson this looked like selling the republic back to British commercial interests, it would be unwise to overdraw the distance between the Federalists and Jefferson's Democratic-Republicans. Hamilton's notion of a commercial economy was small-scale, and he ridiculed any notion of turning the United States into a free-trade zone; Jefferson, especially after the War of 1812, found moments to be friendly to various forms of manufacture and hoped that the products of American agriculture could be aggressively marketed in Europe. "He, therefore, who is now against domestic manufacture, must be for reducing us either to dependence on [Great Britain] or to be clothed in skins, and to live like wild beasts in dens and caverns," Jefferson wrote in 1816.

There was also a good deal of cultural common ground between Jefferson and Hamilton. Both read the same books and admired the same political theorists, and neither of them made any attempt to link virtue with Christianity or any other form of religious morality. Jefferson was a deist who believed that traditional Christianity was little more than "an engine for enslaving mankind . . . a mere contrivance to filch wealth and power," while Hamilton was a milk-and-water Episcopalian. Unlike more radical American deists in the 1790s like Thomas Paine and Ethan Allen, Jefferson at least professed some respect for Jesus of Nazareth as an ethical thinker of great value, and twice proceeded to assemble an edition of the New Testament from parts of it that he thought worth salvaging. But such differences as there were between Jefferson and Tom Paine's crude but effective attacks on the Bible as "a book of lies, wickedness and blasphemy" were lost on pious observers in the new republic, and when Jefferson was put forward as the Democratic-Republican nominee for president, New England divines prophesied that should America "impiously declare for JEFFERSON — AND NO GOD," the Jeffersonian victory would provoke "the just vengeance of insulted heaven." Notwithstanding, Jefferson took 53 percent of the electoral vote in the election of 1800, and the world did not end.

If anything looked like being close to its end in 1800, it was orthodox Christianity in America. Although many of the British North American colonies were settled by religious communities — such as the Quakers of Pennsylvania or the Puritans of Massachusetts Bay — the potential of these groups for developing any kind of stable religious culture in America turned out to be severely limited. Most of the émigré religious communities (and the Puritans and Quakers are prime examples) belonged to the radical fringes of English Christianity, with deep grudges against the English state church, the Church of England, and an almost suicidal hostility to formal assertions of authority by their own leaders. The Puritans of Massachusetts Bay imported a fairly straitlaced predestinarian Calvinism as their official theology, but they also imported a highly decentralized and well-nigh uncontrollable Congregational church order which licensed any individual congregation to revise Calvinist theology as it saw fit. And revise it they did, as the intellectual allure of Enlightenment rationalism persuaded New England's established leadership to shuck off Calvinism for the more prestigious and "rational" religion of the deists and unitarians.

The home government in England, which was supposed to support and foster the establishment of Christianity through the Church of England, might have done more to straighten out these irregularities, but regulation was an expensive proposition. For almost a century the British government, in order to save administrative costs, preferred to let the colonial governments run their own shows; it was just as inclined to continue the savings by letting the colonial religious dissenters do what they liked. This meant that in the better-developed colonial settlements, the Church of England installed only a few token outposts. In other places, where English colonists had settled with no particular religious motive in view at all, there was liable to be little or no formal Christianity.

Not until the 1690s did British imperial planners decide to end this era of benign neglect and begin the strategic organization of Church of England parishes in the colonies. But it turned out to be too

11

little, too late. In 1739, a major revival of religion known as the Great Awakening swept through large parts of New England and the mid-Atlantic colonies, preaching a hard-hitting but radically personalized "new birth" of spiritual transformation and redemption through Christ. It lasted only a comparatively short time — it was effectively over by 1742 — but it successfully managed to reawaken all of the most radical, individualistic, and anti-authoritarian urges of the radical religion that the colonies had started out with.

Then, in 1775, came the Revolution, which completed the religious disruptions the Awakening had begun thirty years before. The Anglican churches, torn by their loyalty to the mother country, fell to pieces; but the "New Lights" of the Awakening were too preoccupied with their own brands of spiritual radicalism to have much hope of claiming the allegiance of the gentleman revolutionaries who populated the Continental Congress. New Lights might support the Revolution, but their support was received without enthusiasm and without much reward. The new federal Constitution of 1787 made no provision for public funding or even recognition of any Christian church. Everywhere, the "natural" religion of Enlightenment deism seemed a more appropriate religion for the natural aristocracy of the new republic, and in state after state — New Jersey in 1776, New York in 1777, Jefferson's Virginia in 1785 — all public support for Christian churches was eliminated. As late as 1822, Jefferson did not hesitate to predict that in his agrarian republic, every young man then alive would die a unitarian.

But this was not what happened. In the first place, no one doubted that Jefferson was a great writer and talker, but his mismanagement of his own financial affairs at Monticello suggested that he had substantially fewer gifts as an administrator. Although he promised that the "revolution of 1800" would be "as real a revolution in the principles of our government as that of 1776 was in its form," reversing the tide of Federalist government proved much harder than he had thought. He struggled from the first to pay off the remaining federal debt from the Revolution so that he could cancel the taxes Hamilton imposed for funding the debt, but not even Jefferson's scrimping and saving could reduce the debt by more than a third. Jefferson also hesitated to tamper with Hamilton's pet creation, the federally chartered Bank of the

12

United States, since the Bank of the United States had turned out to be the primary engine for establishing good American credit ratings in Europe.

Jefferson's most serious embarrassment grew directly out of his serene conviction that self-sufficient agriculture and home-shop manufacture were all that the American republic needed. From 1806 onwards, Britain and Napoleon Bonaparte's France declared mutual blockades on the North Atlantic, and caught in the middle were American merchant ships. Jefferson would have preferred to blame his ancient enemies, the British, for all this havoc, but not even Jefferson could turn a blind eye to the outrages of Bonaparte. So, in the absence of an effective American navy to fend off interference by the British and French, Jefferson proposed a universal boycott: the United States would break off all trade with the warring powers and self-sufficient American farmers would simply keep their produce for themselves. In December, 1807, an overwhelmingly Jeffersonian Congress approved an Embargo Act, and sat back to applaud the results.

The results were anything but worthy of applause. American exports plunged from $108 million in 1807 to $22 million in 1808, in the process bankrupting seaport merchants, then flattening the banks that lent them money, and flinging dock workers, artisans, and the trades that depended on them into unemployment. Jefferson thus learned that, whatever the virtues of rural agriculture, the American economy was more dependent on the international web of imports and exports than he had thought. Although he would not admit it, by the time he left office, in the early spring of 1809, the embargo was a dead letter. "We can never get rid of [Hamilton's] financial system," Jefferson moaned. "It mortifies me to be strengthening principles which I deem radically vicious, but this vice is entailed upon us by the first error."

What Jefferson thought he was encountering was a corruption of American virtue. What he was actually encountering was the leading edge of an economic transformation that was only just beginning to impact the American republic in a large way as he was leaving office and as Abraham Lincoln was born. And that transformation was itself only part of the far larger story of how European-based capitalism emerged in the late eighteenth and nineteenth centuries as the most successful pattern in the world for creating and exchanging goods. Unhappily, defining capitalism can be a very slippery business, since it forms a pattern involving four disparate factors: the entrepreneurial drive for profit, the use of cash as the means of exchange (so that all economic relationships can be painlessly converted into paper, and made rational, impersonal, and long-distance), markets (any location, literal or abstract, where goods and services are exchanged), and governments (which could, after all, shut down all forms of capitalist exchange if they wished).

What gave capitalism its luster was how neatly its claims for being a natural economic order gelled with the eighteenth-century Enlightenment's passion for rational and natural orders of things. Capitalism also thrived on how perfectly its valences suited the political shape of liberalism, so that capitalism (as an economic theory) and liberalism (as a political one) became a potent engine for mutual promotion throughout Western Europe. Commerce, wrote Richard Cobden, was "the great panacea" for political oppression, and he could not sympathize in the slightest with those who "seem bent on destroying manufacturers in order to restore the age of gothic feudalism."

Looked at in this way, the dramatic expansion of capitalist patterns of exchange involved more than merely rewriting the rules of the economic game. It amounted to a transformation of human relationships in which cash, merchandising, and markets could open up vast new personal alternatives to the agrarian economy, and even transform the agrarian economy itself into a competitive, mobile enterprise. Land, the source of all wealth for the Jeffersonians, would cease to be the prime factor in social and economic relationships, and be replaced by markets.

This kind of transformation was what the Jeffersonians dreaded. Although Jefferson was himself a man of the Enlightenment, it was not the liberal Enlightenment of Locke and Adam Smith he espoused so much as the critical Enlightenment of Rousseau. The liberal Enlightenment prided itself on reason's conquest of nature, including the various forms of traditional "natural" society; the critical Enlightenment replied that conquering nature also alienated humanity from it, and that the only solution to this experience of alienation was a lapse back into nature. This endowed agrarianism in the Jeffersonian mind as a quasi-religious axiom as much as an economic idea, and it undergirded the Jeffersonian contempt for economic rationalism as a kind of disease. The ideal society was an exercise in unity and stability, the free

14

play of the passions, the glorification of culture rather than commerce as a form of community (a glorification which for the Jeffersonians only further underscored the impossibility of considering whites and blacks as political or economic equals). Even though Jefferson himself never once cited Rousseau in his vast assemblage of writings, he hardly needed to. As Conor Cruise O'Brien writes, "The intellectual inheritance here is quite clear, and it is a heritage of awesome import."

But at least economic transformation represented the kind of threat the Jeffersonians could recognize and understand, even as they deplored it. There was another kind of transformation at work in the early republic, and this one would have surprised Jefferson beyond telling, and that was the extraordinary revitalization of evangelical Protestant Christianity in the decades after the Revolution. Instead of fading into a unitarian future, the trinitarian Christian denominations embarked on a voyage of evangelistic expansion and empire building that easily outstripped the overall growth of the entire American population, building 10,000 new churches between 1780 and 1820, quadrupling that number again by 1860, and making church building into "a ubiquitous feature of the early national and antebellum landscape."

The most obvious reason for this astonishing growth was the resiliency of evangelical revivalism, based on the model of the colonial Great Awakening. Between 1812 and 1830, a second Great Awakening erupted in New England, only this time the revivalist heirs of the "New Lights" spilled over into upstate New York and Ohio, and joined hands with evangelical Baptists from the upper South and a new wave of imported evangelical fervor in the form of John Wesley's Methodists, and carried the preaching of the new birth across the Appalachians.

In numbers alone, the second Great Awakening was a formidable achievement: one revivalist, Asahel Nettleton, was credited with the conversion of "above thirty thousand souls." But what made the revivals culturally formidable was the extent to which the temperamental profile of the revivals coincided with the new economic language of liberal capitalism. Both were based on the promise of personal self-transformation: in the market of exchanges, personal identities became fluid and could be adopted or shuffled off as the demands of a cash economy dictated, while in the fires of revival old sinful identities could be regenerated by the power of the Spirit and all things made new. "These two programs, the improvement of the nation and that of the individual," writes Daniel Walker Howe, "were mutually reinforcing."

The revivalists were not the only ones at work to redeem the republic. The remnants of the old Congregational and Episcopal church establishments, and their near-kin among the "Old School" mid-Atlantic Presbyterians looked almost as dimly on "New School" revivalism as they did on Jefferson. But they had been pulled back at almost all points by the impact of the revivals from the pre-revolutionary dalliance with deism and unitarianism to create a "rational" synthesis of confessional orthodoxy and Enlightenment epistemology which could talk about the new birth but without the emotional radicalism of the revivalists. They, too, sought to turn the flank of Jeffersonian infidelity by criticizing the weakest link in the liberal ideology, *virtue*. Every good liberal knew that republics were politically fragile and, unlike monarchies, depended for their existence on the virtue of their peoples. But the excesses of the French Revolution had demonstrated that the ethical formulas of Jefferson's deism did not offer much protection from anarchy and the guillotine. The alternative, as proposed by John Witherspoon and Samuel Stanhope Smith (two presidents of Old School Presbyterianism's intellectual citadel, Princeton), was to define religion as the necessary virtue-component of the republic: "to promote religion as the best and most effectual way of making a virtuous and regular people."

In making religion synonymous with virtue, Witherspoon was not so unwise as to insist that religion was also synonymous with Presbyterianism or even revivals, and for that reason Old Schoolers who shared Jefferson's suspicion of instability and accumulation tended in the nineteenth century to gravitate toward the Democratic party, while the New School revivalists went elsewhere. But if it was true, as Samuel Stanhope Smith insisted, that virtue was best secured when religion was publicly supported by "laws for the punishment of profanity and impiety," then Old Schoolers and New Schoolers alike could hardly miss garnering precisely the public sponsorship of Christianity that Jefferson hoped to avoid. This, then, became the refrain sung through the American republic's colleges (which were mostly church-owned) and through the high intellectual discourse of its moral philosophy textbooks: that new public order required virtue,

16

that virtue required belief in God, and that the Christian God was the most obvious nominee.

This allowed Charles Hodge, Francis Wayland, Mark Hopkins, Francis Bowen, James Haven, Archibald Alexander, and other academic moral philosophers to speak in general, nonsectarian terms about the need for a public theism as the basis for republican virtue, while at the same moment subtly securing a Protestant "influence" on American culture. By the 1840s, Protestant churches, whether through Old School persuasion or New School revival, commanded an overall audience (when we combine both the official membership numbers and the penumbra of "hearers" who were associated with them) of almost 40 percent of the American population, and in the estimate of Richard Carwardine, nine out of ten of that audience were pledged to a Protestant orthodoxy that Jefferson had overconfidently thought obsolete.

The great danger of this Protestant return was that it might choke on the very virtues that had made it so irresistible. This was especially true of the New Schoolers. The great moral demand of the revivalists, based upon the strenuous Calvinist scheme of Jonathan Edwards, was for a religion of absolute submission to a sovereign God, in which everyone was understood to be helpless and in need of redemption, but which everyone was obliged to seize for themselves as an expression of their own moral responsibility. The tension between these two ideas was artfully framed by Edwards's heirs to promote an atmosphere of almost unbearable tension, leading to a shattering emotional conversion of purpose and intention, even to the point of embracing absolute "disinterested benevolence." "Pure, disinterested, universal benevolence is a plain and infallible criterion, by which men may determine whether they truly love God, or not," preached Nathanael Emmons. To do anything less than this suggested that in fact one's claim to conversion was a hypocrisy, and the slightest tinge of hypocrisy leavened the whole lump.

This was all well and good for the morally heroic, and it gave the republic Charles Finney, Harriet Beecher Stowe, and John Brown. But for those who, after self-searching, found themselves in any way shy of the mark, it produced devastation and alienation. Emily Dickinson, who tried to put herself in the way of conversion and failed, could only mourn the distance that separated her and God. "God's Hand is

17

amputated now / And God cannot be found," she would write, and her mingled sense of loss and inability to put the loss to rights would chart an eerie parallel to Abraham Lincoln's half-antagonistic, half-wistful loss of his own youthful Calvinism.

But the Old Schoolers also were in danger of promising more than could be easily delivered. Just as New School moralists set the bar of expectations higher than many people could hurdle, so too the moral philosophers rashly predicted that virtue was a matter of paying attention to self-evident intuitions. This seemed to offer no problem, until the problem was slavery, at which point the moral philosophers fell to quarreling and hesitating, and the whole enterprise of a common-front of liberal virtue began to flunk. Even the American Bible Society could not be persuaded to sponsor a program of free Bible distribution to slaves for fear of alienating Southern contributors to the society. But for the time being, the Protestant return made the United States the most apparently Christianized polity in the world, the nation with the soul of a church. "Never afterward," writes Alfred Kazin, "would Americans North and South feel that they had been *living* Scripture."

These were not the only surprises American society could have offered Jefferson, but they were the ones that were already starting to cut through Jefferson's confidence as he left office in the spring of 1809. They were also the ones that would most decisively distance Lincoln from the Jeffersonian legacy. Abraham Lincoln would become, personally and publicly, one of the most determined and eloquent apostles of liberal capitalism, and a stalwart of the Whig party, the enemies of the Jeffersonian legacy. At the same time, Lincoln would also become the president best known through the nineteenth century for pouring public policy into the molds of religious thought, the one most often claimed after his death as "the Christian president"; and he would conduct a lifelong dalliance with Old School Calvinism which attempted to acknowledge the significance of religion in a republic's character without surrendering to the fiery agenda of New School evangelicalism.

Yet, his place in these contexts was complex, shifting, and not always consistent. His life was a pursuit of transformations in his rise from the son of a Baptist dirt-farmer to a cultured corporate lawyer, but he sought transformation while all the while denying that he had sought anything, that he was "an accidental instrument, temporary"

18

and "a piece of floating driftwood." While liberal capitalism was supposed to expand the horizons of one's choices and opportunities, Lincoln insisted all through his life that he did not believe in free choice, but rather in a "doctrine of necessity." Intellectually, he was stamped from his earliest days by the Calvinism of his parents. But he rebelled vigorously against that influence in adolescence, declined to join his parents' church, and turned instead toward the Enlightenment as his intellectual guide, toward "infidelity," "atheism," and Tom Paine in religion, to Benthamite utilitarianism in legal philosophy, and to "Reason, all-conquering Reason" in everything else.

Taking these as the principal guideposts for understanding Abraham Lincoln asks that we do something with Lincoln which virtually no modern Lincoln biographer has managed to do, which is to read Lincoln seriously as a man of ideas. As Mark Neely has complained, Lincoln biography tends to travel either the road of personality-history (as blazed by William Henry Herndon) in which Lincoln's achievements are explained in terms of temperament or genealogy; or else the road of public-history (the model for this being the ten-volume biography by Lincoln's White House secretaries, John G. Nicolay and John Hay) in which Lincoln is lauded mostly for his public management skills as a president, a politician, or a commander-in-chief. The fruits beside these roads are not inconsiderable; nor is it going to be claimed here for the sake of difference that Lincoln was a philosopher, a theologian, a mystic (all of which have been tagged on Lincoln for reasons that have more to do with self-interested authors than with Lincoln). In particular there is no intention here to add to the delusive mythology that seeks to baptize (literally or figuratively) Abraham Lincoln as an evangelical Protestant (which he was not) or as a devout believer in Swedenborgianism, Universalism, Presbyterianism, or even Freemasonry (he was not any of those, either).

What is sought here is to take Lincoln at his own word when he declared in the spring of 1860 that great political questions could not be answered by mere political solutions. "Whenever this question shall be settled," Lincoln wrote about slavery, "it must be settled on some philosophical basis. No policy that does not rest upon some philosophical public opinion can be permanently maintained." For Lincoln, a "philosophical basis" was not a school-philosophy; but it was certainly a coherent intellectual scheme of things which transcended mere policies.

19

Lincoln, it is true, was a professional politician, and not an intellectual; but he was not a mere politician. Poorly schooled (by his own definition) and too poor in his youth to afford either college training or even the law-office tutoring which educated most of his fellow lawyers in the 1830s and 1840s, he was gifted with an amazingly retentive memory and a passion for reading and learning. "A capacity, and taste, for reading, gives access to whatever has already been discovered by others," Lincoln believed, and his reading provided three large-scale contexts for his intellectual maturation. The first of these was the rigid Calvinism in which he was raised during his early years in Kentucky and Indiana. It was, as William Barton once wrote, "a Calvinism that would have out-Calvined Calvin." It was also a Calvinism which Lincoln rejected, partly because it was his father's religion, partly because he could make no ultimate intellectual sense of it; and yet it was ingrained so deeply into him that his mental instincts would always yield easily to any argument in favor of determinism or predestination, in favor of the helplessness of humanity to please God, in favor of melancholy as the proper estimate of the human condition.

The second of these contexts was the Lockean Enlightenment, which made Lincoln religiously skeptical, suspicious of the Rousseau-ean passions (he confessed that he had never read a novel, and failed to get more than halfway through that paragon of Romantic novels, *Ivanhoe*), convinced of the supremacy of individual rights over community conventions. And yet, whatever skeptical nourishment Lincoln derived from reading religious "infidels" like Tom Paine and Robert Burns, he also arrived chronologically at the very end of the "long Enlightenment" and lived most of his life as a Victorian. This meant that, like Carlyle and Mill and George Eliot, the loss of faith was not for Lincoln a triumphant emancipation but instead the source of what A. N. Wilson calls a "terrible, pitiable unhappiness" and a wearying sense of "metaphysical isolation" that could be stanched only by submission to "impersonal and unrecompensing law."

The last of these contexts was classical liberalism, especially the economic liberalism which in Lincoln's decades seemed so full of promise of liberation and mobility for the talented and morally self-restrained, and the Benthamite utilitarianism which he accepted as finding a rational — and thoroughly deterministic — cause for human conduct in self-interest. And yet he would come at the end of his liberal's progress to see that liberalism could never achieve its highest goal of liberation and mobility without appealing to a set of ethical, even theological, principles that seemed wholly beyond the expectations and allowances of liberalism itself. While he would hold organized religion at arm's length, he would come to see liberalism's preoccupation with rights needing to be confined within some public framework of virtue, a framework he would find in a mystical rehabilitation of his ancestral Calvinism and an understanding of the operations of divine Providence.

Looking at Lincoln in this way, we may address Neely's complaint about the bifurcation of Lincoln biography by understanding Lincoln's ideas, and the cultural scaffolding that emerged around them, as the bridge by which we can reunite the mysterious fascination we have with Lincoln's inner personality with the public life that guided the republic through its direst political crisis.

Part of our difficulty in beholding Abraham Lincoln as a man of ideas is that he wrote nothing more sustained than a speech or a lecture or a public letter. (A small book or essay on "infidelity" which he wrote in his youth was destroyed by well-intentioned friends who feared the trouble it would make for him.) But a larger part stems from the difficulty we have had in conceding that the American republic has any intellectual history at all. We are too numbed by fanfares for the Common Man, by Ralph Waldo Emerson's sniffling laments about the absence of American scholars, by Hollywood glorifications of sharpshooting hillbillies in coonskin caps, to hear the frantic solemnity with which the most isolated patriarch on the most godforsaken acre of wiregrass would sit up all the night alongside a wandering evangelist to discuss the intricacies of predestination and free will, or to hear a Scottish free thinker and an itinerant elder hold two thousand people in Cincinnati spellbound for a week in 1829 debating the possibility of intelligent design in the universe. From our images of hard cider and log cabins, we have assembled an impression of the American mind as the ultimate exercise in pragmatism, unconcerned with larger realms of ideas and deficient in any culture but popular culture, the Sahara of the Bozarts. Within this, Lincoln appears only as the Great Fixer, the political moralizer, the policymaker who made it his policy to have no policy.

21

The antebellum United States would scarcely recognize itself in this mirror. In the English-speaking world of the new republic, writes John Brewer, "There were not only more books in circulation than ever before, but new and more varied means by which the reader could secure them. . . . Even those who could not read lived in an unprecedented degree in a culture of print." Although the United States was still an intellectual province of Western Europe after the Revolution, it was a self-conscious and vital province all the same; and even if it lacked its own philosophical tradition, it developed what Bruce Kuklick has called a "speculative tradition," especially in moral and intellectual philosophy, which was shared impartially among college presidents, divines in their parishes, and public professionals. "Drank Tea," wrote a New England lawyer, "and spent the whole Evening, upon original sin, Origin of Evil, the Plan of the Universe, and at last, upon Law." And its colleges, for all their ties to religious denominations and their dominance by clergy with theology at the forefront of their concerns, teemed with commentary on the same epistemological questions that animated Kant, Berkeley, Reid, and Hutcheson over the "dead-end of British empiricism."

Despite the absence of great universities and an established literary tradition, republicanism infected Americans with the conviction that "everyone should have access to learning," while the commodification of writing and printing which the markets made possible presented Americans in the early republic with a varied range of intellectual choices. Over Lincoln's lifetime, writes David Newsome, "The Victorian consumption of books reached a peak never even contemplated before and probably never exceeded since." The riotous urban theaters where workers and artisans lounged, guffawed, and argued with the stage players also produced more Shakespeare than any other playwright in the 1830s, to the point where James Fenimore Cooper named him "the great author of America." "When foreigners accuse us of extraordinary love for gain," wrote an irritated Josiah Royce twenty years after Lincoln's death, "they fail to see how largely we are a nation of idealists."

> Wherever you go, you find the typical American sensitive to ideas, curious about doctrines, concerned for his soul's salvation, still more concerned for the higher welfare of his children, willing to hear

about great topics, dissatisfied with merely material objects, seeking even wealth rather with a view to more ideal uses than with a mere desire for its sensuous gratifications. . . . He pauses in the midst of the rush of business to discuss religion, or education, or psychical research, or mental healing, or socialism. . . . In our country it is extraordinarily easy, and as one may at once admit, it is too easy, to get a hearing for any seemingly new and large-minded doctrine relating either to social reform or to inspiring change of creed.

Even as Lincoln was first establishing himself in law practice, cheap pirated editions of Dickens, Bulwer-Lytton, Wilkie Collins, Thomas De Quincy, George Eliot, and Frederick Marryat were regularly serialized in urban weeklies, alongside a series of new literary quarterlies like *The Knickerbocker* (1833), the *North American Review* (1823), the *Southern Literary Messenger* (1834), the *Southern Literary Journal* (1835), the *Boston Quarterly Review* (1839), *The Dial* (1840), the *Western Literary Messenger* (1835), *Burton's Gentleman's Magazine* (1839), and *DeBow's Review* (1846). American science already had long roots into the eighteenth century, and it supported publication of the *Transactions* of the American Philosophical Society, the *American Journal of Science and the Arts* (1818), the *New England Journal of Medicine* (1812), and the *American Farmer* (1819). Behind the journals stood the scientific institutions, including the Sheffield Scientific School at Yale, the Lawrence Scientific School at Harvard, the Philadelphia Academy of Natural Sciences, the American Geological Society, the New York Lyceum of Natural History, and even, in 1831, the Historical and Philosophical Society of Ohio (which had only become a state in 1803). English ballad opera was supplanted on New York stages by Rossini as early as 1818, Weber in 1825, and a complete *Don Giovanni* in 1826, not to mention Meyerbeer, Flotow, Balfe, and (by the 1850s) Verdi. In 1855, *Musical World* editor Richard Willis boasted that his magazine was read by the president, vice president, members of the cabinet, and seventy members of Congress.

Those who lacked science, the arts, or philosophy at their doorsteps could get it on wheels. The 200 newspapers printed in the United States in 1800 rocketed to over 2,500 by mid-century (subsidized by free exchanges of newspapers and free local delivery of weeklies through the post office), magazine circulation rose from 125 in 1825 to

600 in 1850, and the American book trade exploded from $2.5 million worth of books in 1820 to $16 million by 1856, and by 1850 employed 22,000 men. Private book collections of over a thousand volumes became frequent rather than rare. Touring soloists like Louis Moreau Gottschalk traveled over 50,000 miles to give over 900 concerts in three years, while popular collections of parlor piano music featured *bel canto* operatic arias — Rossini, Donizetti — side-by-side with "The Wood-Up Quickstep."

In 1826, Josiah Holbrook launched a plan for an "Association of Adults for Moral Education" in the pages of the *American Journal of Education*, and ended up creating a system of 3,000 lecture associations across the republic known as the American Lyceum, with Daniel Webster and Ralph Waldo Emerson as the star attractions. Holbrook's Lyceum was only the largest of these associations: in 1828, even a village as small as Utica, New York, with only 8,000 inhabitants, contained forty-one "Benevolent and Charitable Institutions." A young Philadelphia law student in 1841 could be a member of "The Washington Library, the Henry Institute, and the Camden Literary Association."

> By paying four dollars a year to the last of these I have access to about twenty-five of the best periodicals of this country and England. The newspapers which are taken by our family of three, are *The Saturday Courier* and *Pennsylvanian;* the Trenton *Emporium;* and the *Mail* and *Democrat,* of Camden: weekly; Kendall's *Expositor,* Washington: irregularly; and *The Spirit of the Times,* Philadelphia. In addition to these I receive every few days from some old schoolmate papers from all parts of the country.

And none of this begins even to touch the mania for social experimentation staged at Brook Farm, New Harmony, Hopedale, Northampton, and elsewhere by "come-outers and community-men" like Robert Owen, George Rapp, and John Humphrey Noyes. This is, enthused Yale professor Benjamin Silliman in 1821, "the *intellectual age of the world.*"

Without in any way trying to obscure other ways of stating the case of Abraham Lincoln, the work we have to do here is an intellectual biography about a man not usually thought of as an intellectual in an era which, unfortunately, is not often thought of as an arena of ideas. Modern Americans, standing on this side of pragmatism, are not used to seeing antebellum America as a cornucopia of ideologies, and modern American pragmatists like Richard Rorty reinforce that prejudice by suggesting that ideas may actually be dangerous for democracy. "A liberal democracy," wrote Rorty in 1988, "will not only exempt opinions on such matters from legal coercion, but also aim at disengaging discussions of such questions from discussions of social policy."

Or else, what is more likely, we are too afraid now to think of what ideology might do if we let it loose across the land the way it was let loose between 1800 and 1860. The conventional genealogy of American ideas, which runs us from Franklin to Emerson to Dewey, is *ipso facto* a confession of failure, an "American evasion of philosophy" (in the words of Cornel West). But it has this virtue: it provides a conveniently harmless backdrop to a bland and undisturbing secularism, shorn of religious debate and principled acrimony, and oblivious to its connections to the world at its margins. We know, however dimly, that once in the past the strife of ideas brought us civil war, and it is not comfortable to reflect on what it might bring us in the future in the form of "culture wars."

But then again, the strife of ideas also brought us Abraham Lincoln.

1 The American System

The American Revolution was a revolt against restraint. And one of the first restraints to collapse was the one that had been imposed by British imperial authorities, in the decade before the Revolution, on new colonial settlements beyond the Appalachian Mountains. Once the stiff hand of British confinement was removed, curious American adventurers began pushing through the mountain gaps to spill out into the vast Ohio River valley, unlicensed land companies sprang up to sell title to tracts of land they had hardly bothered to investigate themselves, and, in 1780, a Shenandoah Valley farmer named Abraham Lincoln sold off the 210 acres of valley farmland he owned in Virginia and bought 1,200 new acres in the wilderness of what was already known as Kentucky.

The Lincoln family had actually been on the move ever since the first of the Lincolns arrived in Hingham, Massachusetts, in the 1630s, as part of the out-migration of disaffected Puritans fleeing an English church and an English government they had lost all hope of purifying. One of these Lincolns, Samuel, set up as a weaver in Hingham and died there in 1690; one of his sons, Mordecai, promptly began moving again, first to Hull, then to Cohasset; and then his sons, Abraham and another Mordecai, left New England entirely for northern New Jersey

26

in the 1720s and Berks County in eastern Pennsylvania in 1730. This second Mordecai died prematurely in 1735, leaving land amounting to over a thousand acres in both New Jersey and Pennsylvania to be divided among his four sons, John Lincoln (from a first marriage in New Jersey), Thomas, and the by-now-predictable Mordecai and Abraham. As the oldest son, John Lincoln had been singled out in his father's will to inherit the family's 300-acre tract in New Jersey. But the Lincolns seem to have had a notorious reluctance to backtrack from ground they had already covered, and so John Lincoln remained in Pennsylvania, and then in 1758 followed a new stream of Pennsylvania emigrants south to Virginia's Shenandoah Valley, where he bought a 600-acre tract north of Harrisonburg, in the valley's center.

For all their rootlessness, the Lincoln clan had not done badly. The Lincolns who were left behind in Hingham prospered, and one of them, Levi Lincoln (a distant cousin of "Virginia John"), helped write Massachusetts's revolutionary constitution, and served as Thomas Jefferson's attorney general. John Lincoln's youngest brother, Abraham, married into the family of Daniel Boone, and John's father had actually held a number of minor public offices before his death. John's 600 acres in the Shenandoah was land enough to boost him into the ranks of the Virginia squireage, and when the Revolution came, one of his sons went into the Revolutionary army as an officer, while another, Abraham, married into one of the première families of the county and served in the Virginia militia as an ensign during Lord Dunmore's War (1774) and as a captain in the 1778 expedition to Ft. Laurens. Still, even 600 acres was not a great deal when it would come to be divided after John's death among his five sons. And so, even though John deeded a tract of 210 acres to his son Abraham in 1773, this newest Abraham took the first opportunity the Revolution presented, and in 1780 bolted over the Appalachians into Kentucky.

No Lincoln move looked less likely than this one. In the absence of British control during the Revolution, Virginia claimed Kentucky as its western province, and it was from Virginia's hastily contrived land offices that Abraham Lincoln bought his Kentucky domain. Virginia was still fighting the Revolution, and so Abraham Lincoln entered into what was, for the most part, an almost uncleared forest where many of the main routes of travel were controlled by British-allied Indians. It was a raiding party of one of these Indian tribes which caught Abra-

27

ham in the open in 1786 while he was clearing ground with his three sons, and killed him. They might have killed the boys, too, and it appears that one of the raiders picked up the youngest, eight-year-old Thomas, to carry him off as a captive. But the oldest, Mordecai, snatched up a rifle and shot the raider dead, leaving his dazed younger brother miraculously safe.

The death of Abraham Lincoln was, remarkably, the first violent blow the Lincolns had received in their long march from Massachusetts. Its greatest weight was felt by young Thomas, since his father had died without a will, and control of the family's property seems to have fallen to his oldest brother Mordecai. "I have often said that Uncle Mord ran off with all the talents of the family," his presidential nephew said ruefully, and Mordecai Lincoln was often admired in later years as a man of "great good Common sense" and "Entitled to genius." But Mordecai was evidently not quite that selfish with either the talents or the family property. Mordecai Lincoln was "quite a story-teller . . . and, to the last degree charitable and benevolent." Although Thomas Lincoln left for Tennessee to work as "a wandering laboring boy" for an uncle in 1798 and was then apprenticed as a cabinetmaker and carpenter in Elizabethtown, Kentucky, he came up with enough money in 1803 to buy 238 acres of land just north of Elizabethtown on Mill Creek and two forty-dollar lots in Elizabethtown; and it is likely that the money came from his older brother.

Three years later, at age 26, Thomas Lincoln married Nancy Hanks, a relative (possibly a niece) of the Elizabethtown carpenter from whom he had learned his trade. They lived briefly in Elizabethtown, where their first child, Sarah, was born in February, 1807, and then in 1808, they moved to a 300-acre farm on Nolin Creek, in Hardin County, Kentucky. There, on February 12, 1809, yet another Lincoln was born to the name of Abraham.

Abraham Lincoln remembered nothing of the place of his birth. The tillage was meager, and, what was worse, Thomas Lincoln's title to the property proved embarrassingly defective. To Thomas Lincoln's surprise, the farm turned out to have a lien against it from an earlier owner, and in 1813 that owner sued the subsequent owners (including Thomas Lincoln) for recovery of the property. A year later, Lincoln was forced to sell his other property on Mill Creek at a loss because, once again, there were problems with the title. Neither of these losses was entirely Thomas Lincoln's fault. Having been first settled under Virginia law, Kentucky land boundaries were laid out under the old English system of "metes and bounds," which reckoned boundaries from prominent landmarks and physical features. But in Kentucky, where an uncleared forest had yet to be leveled and where careful mapping of the ground was still unfinished, what was a prominent physical feature one day might disappear by the next. In the case of the Mill Creek property, the original survey line "would not close" (would not create a continuous boundary) and so Thomas Lincoln lost thirty-eight acres and a good deal of money.

Giving up on both the Nolin Creek and Mill Creek farms, Thomas Lincoln purchased a new farm of only thirty acres on Knob Creek, still in Hardin County. This farm was the stuff of Abraham Lincoln's "earliest recollection," although what he remembered in 1864 was not particularly encouraging: "it lay in a valley surrounded by high hills and deep gorges" where flash floods "coming down through the gorges washed ground, corn, pumpkin seeds and all clear off the field." It could not have been much sunnier for Thomas or Nancy Lincoln, either. A third child was born to them there, named Thomas, but the infant "did not live three days." And then, in September, 1815, Kentucky's unstable land titles struck again. "Mr. Thomas Lincoln, tenant in possession," was sued by the heirs of a wealthy land speculator, Thomas Middleton, whose ten-thousand-acre tract was suddenly discovered to include the Lincolns' thirty acres.

It would take until 1818 for this suit to be resolved, and Lincoln would actually win this one. But even before that point, Thomas Lincoln had decided he was sick of the uncertainties of Kentucky land titles, and uprooted his family yet again, this time to cross the Ohio River into the Indiana Territory. Crossing the Ohio brought the Lincolns into what amounted to a new world, since the Indiana Territory had been established, not by state authorities in Virginia, but under the aegis of the new national government as part of the great land ordinances of 1785 and 1787. Starting in Ohio and working westward by 1804 to Illinois, the federal government had undertaken a comprehensive land survey, which divided the geography of the Northwest into neat one-square-mile sections of 640 acres, with the price of these government lands pegged by the federal Land Law of 1800 at two dollars an acre.

Because Congress regarded land sales as a revenue device, initial sales were limited to the 640-acre sections, which meant that only the wealthiest speculators could hope to buy them. But in 1804 public pressure forced Congress gradually to reduce the minimum acreage to quarter-sections of 160 acres, and then to 80 acres. Even then, cashless squatters often took up occupation on their own, and it proved so difficult to evict them that Congress finally granted "pre-emption" to long-time squatters who had "improved" their lands and could pay the original "Congress price."

The genius of the system from the point of view of settlers like Thomas Lincoln was that the federal government guaranteed both clean surveys and indisputable title. What was more, territorial governor William Henry Harrison had successfully cleared Indiana of the dangerous Tecumseh Indian confederation in 1811, and the great chief Tecumseh himself had been killed in Canada at the battle of the Thames in 1813. Neither the Indians who had killed his father nor the speculators who had subverted his titles need threaten Thomas Lincoln in Indiana, and so in December, 1816, just as Indiana was being admitted as a full-fledged state in the Federal Union, Thomas Lincoln crossed over into southern Indiana and led his family to a site Thomas had selected on Little Pigeon Creek, in what was then Perry County near what became the crossroads hamlet of Gentryville. "This contry at that time was a perfect wilderness with out roads or bridges," remembered one neighbor of the Lincolns, "so that Thomas Lincoln and his little family had to cut a road throu heavy forrests of timber." Within a year he had made his first payment of sixteen dollars on a quarter-section of 160 acres of land.

But even in Indiana, Thomas Lincoln could not find shelter from one more dreadful reckoning. In the autumn of 1817, Nancy Lincoln's aunt and uncle, Elizabeth and Thomas Sparrow, arrived on Pigeon Creek, trailing Nancy's illegitimate cousin, Dennis Hanks, with them. Thomas Lincoln hospitably put them up in a small cabin on his property until spring came when they could set about clearing their own land. But the following summer, southern Indiana broke out with what was known simply as "the milk sickness," which the settlers understood dimly as a poison that contaminated cows' milk. Actually, it came from the poisonous white snake-root plant, which cows often grazed upon; but it was passed through the cows' milk to whoever drank it, and the results were a slow paralysis, nausea, and death. The Sparrows came down with the milk sickness first, and both died of it; Nancy Lincoln, who may have drunk the Sparrows' cows' milk while nursing them in their death throes, collapsed and then died on October 5, 1818. Thomas Lincoln buried her less than a mile from their cabin, leaving him with two motherless children of his own and the now-twice-abandoned Dennis Hanks.

There seems to have been a streak of dogged persistence in Thomas Lincoln, because rather than reeling under these setbacks, Lincoln waited only until the next year's crop was in before he returned to Kentucky and proposed marriage to Sarah Bush Johnston, the widow of Daniel Johnston, another Hardin County farmer who had died in 1816. Thomas Lincoln was not a man of subtleties: he briskly proposed marriage "right off," and after paying several of Sally Johnston's debts, married her before a local Methodist minister on December 2, 1819. He then crated up Sally's belongings — a bureau, a table, a clothes chest, a spinning wheel, "2 Beds & Bedding & other articles" — and along with her three Johnston children (Elizabeth, John, and Matilda), brought her back over the Ohio River and the rutted roads that led to Little Pigeon Creek.

The arrival of Sarah Lincoln was a minor watershed in young Abraham Lincoln's life. "Mr. Lincoln had erected a good log cabin, tolerably comfortable," but subsistence agriculture was deeply committed to a rigidly patriarchal division of labor between men and women, and with the death of his wife, Thomas Lincoln evidently had no idea of how to fill the vacuum of "womens work" left by Nancy Hanks. Sally Bush Lincoln was "astonished to find that there was no floor or Door to the House of her Husband, no furniture of any Kind, no Beds or Bedding," while the Lincoln children "were Sufring greatly for clothes," young Abraham and Dennis Hanks being "Dressed mostly in Buck Skins." She "at once had a floor Laid in the House, Doors & Windows put in," and "Dressed the children up out of the Large supply she had brought with her."

But more than simply making things "snug and comfortable," Sally Bush Lincoln "Knew exactly how to Manage children," and brought genuine maternal affection into young Abraham's life. Lincoln, almost from the first, reciprocated her kindness with an affection he never extended to another woman. "She had been his best friend in the world," he later told one of the Johnston children. "No man could have loved a mother more than he loved her." After his father's death, Abraham stepped in to protect her financial interests from his opportunistic step-relatives; and his last personal visit before leaving Illinois forever in 1861 would be to Sarah Bush Lincoln. "Abe was a good boy," she told William Henry Herndon after Lincoln's death, "and I can say what scarcely one woman — a mother — can say in a thousand: Abe never gave me a cross word or look, and never refused, in fact or appearance, to do anything I requested him. . . . His mind and mine — what little I had — seemed to run together."

This inverts the Grimm-fairy-tale version of what stepmother relationships were expected to be, but it parallels an even greater inversion of the relationship that ought to have prevailed between Abraham and his father, Thomas. Some of this was clearly Thomas's fault. "Thos. Lincoln never showed by his actions that he thought much of his son Abraham when a Boy," recalled one Lincoln relative in 1865. "He treated him rather unkindly than otherwise, always appeared to think much more of his stepson John D. Johnston than he did of his own son, Abraham." Thick-set and "low-slung," Thomas was touchy and uncomfortable ruling over "a Boy" who was already showing signs of "uncommon natural Talents," and he "treated him with habitual cruelty." Thomas liked to think of himself as a jokester, but neighbors remembered how easily irritated — and sometimes physically abusive — Thomas became when his son began displaying the same gift for mimicry, and trying it out in public. "When strangers would ride along & up to his fathers fence," recalled Dennis Hanks, "Abe always, through pride & to tease his father, would be sure to ask the stranger the first question." Enraged by this "rude and forward" challenge to his own status as patriarch of the family, Thomas "would sometimes knock him a rod" or lay on with a whip.

This eventually became more than a simple clash of personalities. Although Thomas Lincoln was hardly the "ne'er-do-well" or "poor white trash" that Lincoln's first biographers painted the father as being in order to greater magnify his son's achievements, what is true is that he was a classic subsistence farmer who was, on the model of Jefferson's ideal "husbandman," "a piddler" who was ambitious mostly to produce by himself no more than what his household required. One of his neighbors remarked simply that Thomas Lincoln "was satisfied to live in the good *old* fashioned way; his shack kept out the rain; there was plenty of wood to burn . . . the old ways were good enough for him." He "was happy — lived Easy — & contented" and "had but few wants and Supplied these . . . Easily." The Lincoln farm "was well Stocked with Hogs, Horses & cattle," and once Sally Bush Lincoln had taken charge of the homestead, Thomas "raised a fine crop of Wheat, corn & vegetables." The Lincolns even "taned there own Leather," and young Dennis Hanks "made them Shoes out of their rude Leather." Even the "clothing was all made at home . . . from cotton & Flax of there own raising." From a small store in Gentryville "they obtained many necessaries in life," but even then the "Legal tender" was really only barter, "Hogs and Venison hams . . . and Coon skins all so." Overall, Thomas Lincoln "Jest Raised a Nuf for his own use" and "Did Not Send any produce to any other place Mor than Bought his Shugar and Coffee and Such Like."

Thomas Lincoln saw no reason why his son would not follow him in these classic agrarian patterns. "I was raised to farm work," Lincoln remembered in 1859, which meant (as he explained to John Locke Scripps a year later) that "A. though very young . . . had an axe put into his hands at once; and from that till within his twentythird year, he was almost constantly handling that most useful instrument — less, of course, in plowing and harvesting seasons." It also meant that as Lincoln grew into adolescence, Thomas loaned his son out to neighboring farmers as part of the incessant borrowing-and-swapping of rural subsistence networks of exchange, and kept for family use whatever goods and kind were offered as barter-style pay for the boy's labor. At least as early as thirteen, Abraham was cutting and pitching hay, felling and splitting logs for fences and firewood, working at the Ohio River ferries, and mostly for "pay . . . in Store goods."

Instead of inuring the boy to the traditional patterns of Jeffersonian yeoman agriculture, the experience only embittered young Abraham. Lincoln often remarked in later years that "his father taught him to work but never learned him to love it" — or at least not the kind of work his father intended for him. What he did cherish was a memory of a very different sort of work, of two men hurrying down to the ferry-landing on the Ohio River where Lincoln kept a small cock-boat, dragooning him into rowing them out mid-stream to intercept an on-coming steamboat, and each rewarding him with "a silver half-dollar" which they "threw . . . on the floor of my boat."

> Gentleman, you may think it was a very little thing, and in these days it seems to me a trifle; but it was a most important incident in my life. I could scarcely credit that I, a poor boy, had earned a dollar in less than a day. . . . The world seemed wider and fairer before me.

Abraham Lincoln had met the cash economy.

The tensions he experienced with his father surfaced in other ways as Abraham Lincoln grew toward manhood. The demands of farm work left little time for schooling, and Lincoln never ceased to lament the fact that his own education was "defective." He remembered that he and his sister had briefly attended "some schools, so called," but he estimated in 1860 that "the agregate of all his schooling did not amount to one year" (which is echoed by one neighbor's estimate that Lincoln "went to school . . . about four winters"). The blame for this has usually been bestowed upon Thomas Lincoln, who his son disparagingly claimed "never did more in the way of writing than to bunglingly sign his own name," and who had the reputation for being frankly contemptuous of "eddication." (Sally Bush Lincoln agreed that "Mr. Lincoln could read a little & could scarcely write his name. . . .")

But Lincoln conceded to Leonard Swett in 1853 that "my father . . . determined at an early day that I should be well educated," and it is worth noticing that, since neither Kentucky nor Indiana had any publicly funded school systems while the Lincolns lived there, even the "A.B.C. schools" the Lincoln children attended had to be paid for by subscription, which was a sacrificial proposition for a less-than-wealthy farmer like Thomas Lincoln. And by all accounts, it was not a bad schooling either, to judge by the textbooks: Asa Rhoads's *An American Spelling Book, Designed for the Use of Our Common Schools* (1802) and possibly Noah Webster's *The American Spelling Book* (1783) for spelling; Nicholas Pike's *A New and Complete System of Arithmetic, Composed for the Use of the Citizens of the United States* (1788) for arithmetic; William Grimshaw's *History of the United States* (1820), David Ramsay's *Life of George Washington* (1807), and the more famous *Life of Washington* (1800) by "Parson" Mason Weems for history; *The Kentucky*

Preceptor, Containing a Number of Useful Lessons for Reading and Speaking (1812), *The American Speaker* (1811) and William Scott's *Lessons in Elocution, or a Selection of Pieces in Prose and Verse* (1779) for "Speeches & pieces to recite" from Shakespeare, Alexander Pope, Milton, William Cowper, and Thomas Gray; along with Americanized reprints (and bowdlerizations) of Bunyan's *Pilgrim's Progress*, Defoe's *Robinson Crusoe*, *The Oriental Moralist* (an American version of "The Arabian Nights"), and even "Aesop's Fables" (although apparently "No geography — nor grammar").

It was not so much on education itself that the two Lincolns differed as on what purpose education should serve. Thomas Lincoln's "idea of a thorough education . . . was to have me cipher through the rule of three." And much as he tried as "a rule never to aske him to lay down his book," Thomas Lincoln was easily irritated when Abraham began to bestow on reading time that his father might have better wanted to see him spend on hire-out labor, "his father having Sometimes to slash him for neglecting his work by reading." For Abraham, however, reading meant a catalyst for "Improvement," for self-transformation, for joining the ranks of the revolutionary soldiers on the pages of Parson Weems or of Henry V's bowmen at Agincourt (from Scott's *Elocution*), both of which "fixed themselves on my memory." He was "not Energetic Except in one thing," remembered his stepsister, Matilda Johnston, but "he was active & persistant in learning — read Everything he Could." Obstinately, he would rather work to obtain books than "Store goods," and he was "so attatched to reading" that eventually his father allowed him to hire himself out in order to get copies of Caleb Bingham's *The American Preceptor* (1794) and *Columbian Orator* (1797), which promised to "improve youth and Others in the Ornamental and Useful Art of Eloquence."

Nor was it that Lincoln's education was so bad, as that it could have easily been so much better, which fueled his later disappointment. Only fifty miles away to the west, Robert Owen opened the experimental colony of New Harmony where a cadre of a thousand intellectuals, free-thinkers, and education reformers — a "boatload of knowledge" — headed by William Maclure, Charles Lesueur, Marie Fretageot, and Joseph Neef planned to preside over the establishment of a new society of "universal charity, benevolence, and kindness." Owen, the quondam industrialist and bankroller of New Harmony, bought the colony's property from a hermitage of religious recluses in 1825, and then took Washington by storm with his blueprint for an avant-garde community where "PRIVATE, OR INDIVIDUAL PROPERTY" and "ABSURD AND IRRATIONAL SYSTEMS OF RELIGION" would be abolished. The project survived for only two years after Owen's flatboat, the *Philanthropist*, dumped its collection of professors on the lower Wabash, as New Harmony broke up into the usual old disharmony over who was giving the orders. But the Lincolns could hardly have been ignorant of New Harmony — Thomas Lincoln, in fact, briefly owned a small parcel of land close to New Harmony — and Dennis Hanks years later claimed that Abraham Lincoln had wangled copies of New Harmony's short-lived newspaper, the *New Harmony Gazette*, to study.

He certainly developed more in common with New Harmony's religious skepticism than with his father's religion; in fact, on no other point did Abraham Lincoln come closer to an outright repudiation of his father than on religion. Thomas and Nancy Lincoln had been members in Kentucky of the Little Mount Separate Baptist Church, a congregation linked to one of a plethora of rigidly predestinarian Calvinist Baptist congregations scattered throughout central Kentucky and Tennessee, and once in Indiana they associated with the Little Pigeon Creek Baptist Church, which was organized in 1816. Although these churches and their county-based associations found enough differences among themselves to split into Separate, Regular, and even "Two-Seed-in-the-Spirit" factions, they were all (according to James Ross) "staunch Predestinarians, and gloried in the doctrine they preached."

Predestination, in this case, meant "that long before the morning stars sang together, and the sons of God shouted for joy at the glories of the new creation, the Almighty looked down upon the ages yet unborn, as it were, in review before him, and selected one here and another there to enjoy eternal life and left the rest to the blackness of darkness forever." Hence, the condition of one "not elected from the foundation of the world was as changeless and as hopeless as if he were already in the bottomless pit." This also meant, in practical terms, that if an individual "were not of the elect, all the preaching in the world would do [him] no good, so far as salvation was concerned, since they believed Christ died for the elect only." Hence, many of the

Calvinist Baptist groups had no use for social reform movements, especially temperance and abolition. The Primitive Baptists in particular would, as the Primitive Baptist Gilbert Beebe declared in 1832, support "no Mission Boards for converting the heathen, or for evangelizing the world; no Sunday Schools as nurseries to the church; no schools of any kind for teaching theology and divinity, or for preparing young men for the ministry."

The attraction this ultra-predestination had for Calvinist Baptists lay in the confidence it gave that, "if he were of the elect, neither his wrong doings nor all the powers of darkness could prevent his salvation," and James Ross remembered how one of the veteran ministers of the Bethel Association (in central Tennessee) would "beam with delight and . . . say 'Glorious day for my soul'" whenever another "would preach one of their powerful discourses advocating" predestination. On the other hand, Ross remembered, "there was one dread thought that often brought these old Christians low even unto the dust."

"Am I, after all, one of the elect? May I not after all, be mistaken? And if so, then all my hope is gone!" The storm-tossed mariner, when his boat goes down, may find a plank or broken spar, and on it may reach the friendly shore; but for him who is not of the elect there is no plank or spar or friendly shore; he must sink in the deep, deep waters. There is ground for believing that by this dread apprehension the reason of many has been dethroned. . . .

Predestination set the threshold of acceptability with God exceptionally high, and for those who could get over it, and be somehow certain that they were of the elect for whom Christ died, it gave "the most exalted ideas, and no doubt many of them considered themselves as much superior, in these respects, to the surrounding Christian denominations as did the ancient Jews in comparing themselves with the heathen nations around them." But for those lacking the spiritual athleticism to vault over that bar, it could trigger a killing despair, "gloomy apprehensions . . . that they would ultimately be lost after all their fond hopes to the contrary," and a deep-seated and persistent melancholy.

This did nothing to stop the growth of Calvinist Baptist sects along the frontier, and by the 1840s, the Primitives (who were also known as the "Anti-Mission" or "Hardshell" Baptists) alone accounted for nearly 20 percent of all the Baptist congregations listed in the annual *Almanac and Baptist Register.* And although the Little Pigeon Creek congregation affiliated with the somewhat more moderate Separate Baptists, their articles of belief nevertheless affirmed that "we belive in Election by grace given in Christ Jesus Before the world began & that God Cawls regenerates & Sanctifies all who are made meat for Glory by his special grace." Sarah Bush Lincoln was particularly identified as a "hardshell Baptist." But even though he was "Raised under the predesternarin school," there is no evidence that Abraham Lincoln ever joined the rest of his family in the Separates' fellowship. Sarah Bush Lincoln conceded that Abraham "had no particular religion — didnt think of that question at that time, if he ever did — He never talked about it."

It was not that Lincoln was ignorant of his parents' ultra-Calvinism: "he went to meeting sometimes and was well-behaved," one neighbor remembered, and the first recorded scribblings of Lincoln's pen, four lines written in a copybook and preserved lovingly by Sarah Bush Lincoln, are some verses from the well-known Calvinist hymnwriter, Isaac Watts:

> Time what an emty vaper tis
> and days how swift they are
> swift as an indian arr[ow] fly
> or like a shooting star.

But Lincoln showed no flicker of interest in joining his father's church. "He Never would Sing any Religious Songs," Dennis Hanks remembered, but he would amuse his sister and half-siblings with parody performances "on a stump or log" of the previous Sunday's sermons, "and almost repeat it word for word" and "mimacing the Style & tone of the old Baptist Preachers," until Thomas Lincoln would "come and make him quit — send him to work." Matilda Johnston recalled that "When father & Mother would go to Church," the children would often stay home and "Abe would take down the bible, read a verse — give out a hymn — and we would sing." But otherwise, according to Nathaniel Grigsby, Lincoln "never made any profession while in Ind[iana] that I know of."

As Lincoln grew toward adulthood, the ties uniting Lincoln to his father and the rest of his awkwardly spliced family began to snap. In 1826, his sister Sarah married Aaron Grigsby, but within a year and a half, she died in childbirth. In the same year, 1828, Lincoln was hired by the local storekeeper, James Gentry, to help take a flatboat full of salted meat and produce down the Ohio River, and from the Ohio down the Mississippi to the great seaport of New Orleans. His wages, which amounted to the princely sum of eight dollars a month in cash, had to be dutifully turned over to Thomas. Old enough by now to earn his own living, and ever more determined to keep what he earned, Lincoln began looking for an opportunity to get away on his own, even trying to hire himself out to an Ohio River steamboat.

Thomas Lincoln, however, had one more job for his son. Tiring of Indiana and nearing fifty years old, the elder Lincoln decided to move once more, to the newer lands being thrown open for sale to the west, in Illinois.

The great weakness of Jefferson's dream of a nation of self-sustaining yeoman farmers was not in what it produced but what it reproduced. Large farm families were a necessity, not for the emotional values that a later middle-class urban culture would invest in them, but for carrying out the multitude of basic tasks that household production required. The difficulty with this was that it would never stand still: sons grew to adulthood and needed land of their own, daughters married sons-in-law with the same need, and the numbers overflowed the capacity of settled agricultural areas to accommodate them. By 1819 settlers from Indiana were venturing westward across the Wabash, and other adventurers from Mississippi, Tennessee, and Kentucky were spilling across the Ohio River, into what had once been the old French settlements of Illinois.

Once upon a time, France had ruled the Mississippi River valley. But French Illinois had never been thickly settled, and most of the French colonial settlements had clustered around Kaskaskia on the Mississippi or at Port Vincennes on the Wabash. All of this had passed to the British after the Seven Years' War, and Virginia had taken quick advantage of the Revolution to wrest the Illinois territory for herself, only to grudgingly cede it to Congress in 1784 so that it could be included under the organizational rubric of the post-revolutionary congressional land ordinances. Every layer of new ownership, however, had left unchallenged the slaves the French had first brought into the territory in the late 1600s, and even though the Northwest Ordinance of 1787 officially prohibited slavery in the Northwest Territory, both the British and the Virginians had given explicit legal recognition to French slave ownership, and Congress actually granted the crucial saltworks at Salines, near Shawneetown, an exemption from the Northwest Ordinance so that slaves could continue to be used there.

None of this much bothered the new immigrants into Illinois, since so many of them came from the upper South or the Carolinas, where slavery was taken for granted. "Our influential men, and all who held office, from the governor to the constable, were from slave-states," wrote one early immigrant. "Every sheriff and every clerk of the county were pro-slavery men." Most of these migrants were younger sons, seeking room for the farms that could no longer accommodate them; some were older farmers who had sold their lands in order to buy larger tracts at cheaper rates and thus provide for their sons and their own support in old age at the same time. Few of them came to Illinois out of any moral repugnance for slavery. And among this tide of yeoman immigrants was one of Thomas Lincoln's former in-laws, John Hanks.

John Hanks was a cousin of Nancy Hanks Lincoln, and he was very nearly the only member of the Hanks family that Abraham Lincoln would later rate as "beautiful, honest, and noble." He had followed the Lincolns to southern Indiana in 1822, lived briefly with his Lincoln in-laws, and then in 1826 returned to Kentucky. Two years later, he was on the move again, this time into Macon County in central Illinois, at the upward edge of Kentucky migration into Illinois; and at some point, Hanks wrote to Thomas Lincoln and urged the Lincolns to join him there. There is no way of telling what made John Hanks so persuasive, or even if it was Hanks's letters alone that turned the trick, since Mordecai Lincoln had also migrated to Illinois, establishing yet another piece of the Lincolns' westward itch. Also Congress had granted broad preemption rights to Illinois squatters in 1813, and after 1820, a mere hundred dollars in cash could get a farmer clear title to half a quarter-section in Illinois. What was more, Illinois levied no land taxes on occupied property for the first five years of ownership.

Whatever the reason, in the fall of 1829, Thomas Lincoln sold off the last few bits of Kentucky property he still owned, plus the eighty acres of Congress land he had finally paid off in Indiana, obtained a letter of dismissal from the Little Pigeon Creek Separate Baptists, and on March 1, 1830, set off with his own family (including twenty-one-year-old Abraham) and an extended collection of Johnstons, Hankses, and their new families — a party of thirteen in all. Coming out of the southwestern corner of Indiana, they moved northwards in a long arc that crossed the Wabash River into Illinois at Vincennes and then headed up into central Illinois and the Sangamon River country.

As they did so, the thick bower of forest that surrounded them in southern Indiana fell away and revealed the broad parti-colored carpet of prairie-land and prairie grasses of Illinois. It was "land of the richest soil, and of the most beautiful waving shape and smooth surface," according to the well-born Scot, James Stuart, who traveled through Illinois at about the same time as the Lincolns were arriving, "all laid out by the hand of Nature, as English parks are." Another Scot, Patrick Shirreff, was so amazed by "the beauty and sublimity of the prairies . . . interspersed with flowering plants of every hue . . . appearing like a sea," that it all offered a standing refutation to "Mr. Malthus's doctrine," that humanity's capacity for procreation was bound to exceed the earth's capacity to feed it. "If a considerable portion of mankind ever are in want of food, the cause will be found to arise from human agency, and not from nature refusing to do her part" — or at least not in Illinois.

Even the people teemed with both talk and trade. The Englishman Morris Birkbeck dismissed the pioneers he found in the first Illinois settlements in 1817 as "in a low state of civilization, about half-Indian in their way of life," but much of Birkbeck's distaste for the Illinois settlers was influenced by his aversion to slavery. One of Birkbeck's associates, John Woods, noticed more sharply that "most of them are well acquainted with law . . . a most determined set of republicans, well-versed in politics, and thoroughly independent . . . far from ignorant and much better informed than could be expected from their appearance."

It is not likely, though, that Thomas Lincoln had much of an eye for the prairies or the people. Years later, in retrospect, Abraham Lincoln explained his father's restless urges to move from Kentucky to Indiana and then to Illinois as "partly on account of slavery; but chiefly on account of the difficulty in land titles." Actually, the two causes

41

were identical for Thomas Lincoln. The older Lincoln never demonstrated much feeling over what slavery did to slaves; if so, both southern Indiana and Illinois were strange places to take that feeling. George Flower, another of Birkbeck's associates, noticed that both southern Indiana and southern Illinois were "chiefly peopled by Southerners, who hold property in higher esteem than liberty," and that included (to Flowers's chagrin) slave property. (Whatever the Northwest Ordinance had said about slavery, small-scale slavery had been actively condoned throughout Illinois's years as a federal territory, and in 1823, an effort to formally legalize slavery by rewriting the new state constitution came within an ace of succeeding.) What is more probable is that Thomas Lincoln disliked the prospect of competing with great slaveholding planters, and in fact slavery was turned down in Illinois in 1823 mostly by the votes of immigrant upper South yeomen (like Thomas Lincoln) who had no objection to slavery itself and no love for blacks, but who minded very much the idea of an influx of big plantations.

Thomas Lincoln was even less moved by the beauties of the unplowed prairie. The federal land surveys of Illinois evaluated the fertility of land by the variety of its vegetation, and by those standards, the immense expanses of prairie held little promise of worth for farmers. Time and experience would eventually prove this false, but even if time and experience had proven quicker in their testimony, many early Illinois farmers still found that the prairie grass, with its twisty root systems as much as three feet deep, could not be broken by anything but heavy prairie plows, pulled by five to ten yoke of oxen. This led most emigrants, including the Lincolns, to the easier, richer, timbered bottom-lands of Illinois's rivers, including the Sangamon River, where hogs and cattle could be let graze freely and where enough wood for firewood and fences was available.

John Hanks selected a site in Macon county, ten miles west of Decatur, "on the North side of the Sangamon river, at the junction of the timber-land and prairie," and there, Thomas and Abraham Lincoln "built a log cabin, into which they removed, and made sufficient of rails to fence ten acres of ground, fenced and broke the ground, and raised a crop of sow[n] corn upon it the same year." In the shade of the slow-moving Sangamon River's overhanging trees, the Lincolns found what must have seemed like the subsistence farmer's heaven.

"We raised cotton sufficient to supply . . . us with most of our wearing apparel," recalled an early Sangamon settler, and sixty acres could easily yield a thousand bushels of corn and two hundred of wheat, oats, and potatoes, while livestock fattened on the cool, unfenced riverbanks.

Rivers, however, had always promised something different to Abraham Lincoln. In the spring of 1831, with his father and stepmother set up near Decatur and his Johnston and Hanks kin "temporarily set up at other places in the county," Abraham Lincoln looked for his fortune down the Sangamon River. It was not a river that looked like promising much, at least on its own, but it was navigable for a good part of its length (depending on the season and the height of the river) by shallow-draft flatboats, and after curving in a long loop for some seventy miles downstream from Decatur, the Sangamon emptied into the Illinois River, which in turn finally joined the Mississippi just north of the village of Alton, with its splendid deep-draft docking, and St. Louis on the far Missouri side of the river. From there, the river highway led to New Orleans and the world, and to Lincoln that was enough. While still working for his father, Lincoln heard a local politician, John F. Posey, make a lackluster speech on the desirability of dredging the Sangamon River. Lincoln promptly mounted "a box or a Keg" and made a speech on "the navigation of the Sangamon river" which so surprised Posey that the older man "Encouraged Lincoln to persevere." And he did: Lincoln would be making that same speech for the next twenty years.

Perseverance did not make the rivers or flatboating an easy ticket to prosperity. Flatboating on the rivers was slow, and slowness made the value of whatever cargo was brought to St. Louis or New Orleans unpredictable. And then once there, there was no way to float a flatboat back up against the river currents, so a flatboat crew was left with only the options of walking home from New Orleans or poling and towing a slim, narrow keelboat back up the Mississippi. But there were always entrepreneurs willing to take what chances there were, and in the spring of 1831, a local hustler named Denton Offutt hired John Hanks, who had already taken flatboats down the Mississippi before, to take a load of Sangamon goods down to New Orleans for sale. And it was Hanks, knowing of Abraham Lincoln's earlier experience with James Gentry and knowing that Lincoln was "going about wherever he could get work," who recommended that Offutt hire Lincoln and Lincoln's stepbrother John D. Johnston as well.

It was not easy work. Lincoln, Hanks, and Johnston first had to canoe their way down the Sangamon to Offutt's storehouse at the village of Sangamon Town, build the flatboat ("Eighteen feet wide and Eighty feet long," by Hanks's recollection, "about 30 feet long and about 12 feet wide," by another witness), and afterward load it with Offutt's cargo of "barrell pork — Corn & live hogs" — and leave Sangamon Town. Below Sangamon Town, the flatboat came abreast of the little mill village of New Salem, perched high on massive bluffs overlooking the Sangamon River, and there it jammed itself, half-on, half-over the town milldam, and was nearly lost along with its cargo. It took another two months to get Offutt's cargo all the way to New Orleans and sold. In the process, though, Offutt's fancy had been taken by young Lincoln. It was Lincoln who ingeniously managed to float the stranded flatboat off the milldam at New Salem, and as Offutt had taken out a license to open "a store and Mill at New-Salem," he offered to hire Lincoln as his clerk.

New Salem exists today only as a recreated state historical park, but in 1829, when John Cameron and James Rutledge cast a canny eye on the site and constructed a mill there, it looked like it might become one of the most strategic commercial locations in central Illinois. The Sangamon River deepened there to provide enough water, not only for the mill, but perhaps, under the right conditions, enough depth for a steamboat landing.

The lure of the market might have meant little if there had been no means of access between rural agriculture and the real or abstract markets on the eastern seaboard or New Orleans. An ordinary stage-coach ride from Boston to New York cost between ten and eleven dollars in 1810, and the time involved (in the case of the stage-ride from Nashville to Washington City, four weeks) added a further hidden cost. There had been calls in Congress for the federal government to undertake the construction of a National Road, but so long as Jeffersonians like James Madison and James Monroe held the White House, the usual result of any national improvements bill was a veto. Some state governments funded turnpikes or chartered turnpike corporations to build roads within their own domains, but even the best of the revolutionary new macadamized roads remained slow and expensive.

In 1807, however, a Pennsylvania-born entrepreneur named Robert Fulton, who had prudently married into the wealth of the New York Livingstons, launched an experimental riverboat on the Hudson River, powered not by pole or sail but by a paddle wheel turned by a wood-fired steam engine. The use of compressed steam as a source of energy dated back to the primitive mine-pumps developed by Thomas Newcomen in Britain in the early 1700s, but it was not until 1765 that James Watt designed a steam engine so efficient that it could be harnessed to almost any need for massive, artificial power. One American, John Fitch, had tried his hand at building a steam-powered riverboat in 1787, and failed. Fulton, whose steamboat looked "precisely like a backwoods sawmill mounted on a scow and set on fire," drove 150 miles upriver from New York to Albany in only thirty-two hours, and within a month his boat was carrying ninety passengers on each trip.

Fulton's steamboat had the potential to turn every navigable river in the United States into a fast, cheap highway for moving goods and people — which meant, in effect, that the steamboat could annihilate the immovable physical distance that had insulated subsistence agriculture and bring the lure of a cash economy into regions where it could never before have penetrated. In 1811, a flat-bottomed, shallow-draft steamboat of 371 tons, built by a group of Pittsburgh investors and optimistically named *New Orleans*, was launched onto the Ohio River, and set off in the general direction of its namesake. It handily navigated the Falls of the Ohio, survived an earthquake that dumped acres of riverbank into the Mississippi, and finally fetched up at New Orleans three and a half months later; and though it was sunk two and a half years afterward by a monster snag in the river, the little boat had proved its easy superiority as a commercial carrier over anything else floating on the inland rivers.

Even before the *New Orleans* met its unhappy end, new experimental boats like Henry M. Shreve's *Enterprise* could make the *upriver* trip from New Orleans to Louisville in only twenty-five days; all the way to Pittsburgh took no more than fifty-four days. The riverboats not only slashed time, they slashed the costs of transportation and communication with the market. In 1810, it had cost five dollars to move a hundred pounds of freight downriver by flatboat from Louisville to New Orleans. By 1830 the steamboats had cut that to two dollars, and by 1850 it would cost about twenty-five cents. By 1820 there were thirty-one steamboats operating on the Mississippi and the Ohio; by the time the Lincolns arrived on the Sangamon River, there were 361 steamboats on the Mississippi and all of its tributaries, including the Wabash, the Monongehela, the Tennessee, the Missouri, the Cumberland, and the Arkansas.

This annihilation of time and distance became the key to the transformation of Jefferson's agrarian hinterland into a resource for east-coast markets, and it did not stop with steamboats. Steamboats could only go where natural rivers took them; but if a river did not flow someplace naturally, then it could be made to flow artificially in the form of a canal. Six years after the *New Orleans* made her maiden voyage down the Ohio, New York governor DeWitt Clinton floated a risky state bond issue for over seven million dollars to finance a gigantic canal to link Albany on the Hudson with Lake Erie, and so with the Great Lakes and the upper Northwest. Thomas Jefferson derided the canal as "little short of madness," but after seven years and 363 miles of digging, Clinton triumphantly opened the Erie Canal, and stood by to gloat as the cost of moving freight between Albany and Buffalo plummeted from $100 a ton to $6, while the time in transit fell from forty-five days to five. The spectacular success of the Erie Canal set off a canal mania that furiously dug up 3,300 miles of canals over the next fifteen years, and promoted schemes to circumvent Niagara Falls and, closer to New Salem, link the Illinois River with Lake Michigan and the Great Lakes.

Not even the canals, however, could match the power of extension of the railroads. First developed in England as simply one more adaptation of steam power, the first commercial rail line was laid in the United States in 1828 in Baltimore. By 1859, the railroads had pushed all the way over the Appalachians and slashed shipping costs to under three cents a ton per mile. Taken together, canals, turnpikes, steamboats, and railroads cut the cost of transporting goods to American markets by 95 percent and permitted the long fingers of the market to reach into what had once been the remote agrarian societies of independent patriarchal farmers. "The long shriek" of the railroad whistle, wrote Nathaniel Hawthorne in 1844, "harsh above all other harshness," tells a story of busy men, citizens, from the hot street, men of business; and no wonder that it gives such a startling shriek, since it brings the noisy world into the midst of our slumbering peace.

It brought more than noise. With the coming of the new transportation, "not only our homemade manufactures, but our homemade life and habits to a great measure disappeared," recalled Milton Hay, a Sangamon lawyer whose nephew, John Hay, would later serve as Abraham Lincoln's White House secretary.

> The ox . . . the spinning wheel and the loom, disappeared together. We began to build houses of a different style and with different materials. We farmed not only with different implements but in a different mode. Then we began to inquire what the markets were and what product of the farm we could raise and sell to the best advantage. The farmer enlarged his farm and no longer contented himself with the land that himself or his boys could cultivate, but he must have hired hands and hired help to cultivate his large possessions.

And no wonder: the steamboats with their little tea-kettle boilers and tin-pipe smoke-funnels cheerfully and diligently heaped cheap industrial textiles from England's cotton mills or their New England imitations onto the shelves of rural storekeepers in the Sangamon country and elsewhere, and for an exchange of cash or a polite loan, the new goods would supplant painstaking, laborious homespun. Or else they hauled in from New York or Baltimore steel plows strong enough to bite the prairie sod and cotton gins to pick raw cotton clean.

The surprising surpluses these new tools produced could, in turn, be marketed for cash to pay debts to the storekeepers, until finally, in the inevitable spiral of irresistible acquisition, the farm gradually produced nothing except the crops that could be most profitably sold in New Orleans or Louisville. There was a note of warning in this, that if a bad year struck a farmer whose crops were all in one kind or who had overextended himself on loans to buy new land, that farmer could end up dangling over a precipice with no cash to supply his needs or to pay debts owed to bankers whose rationalized calculations of interest permitted none of the old indulgences. "The market is a canker," warned a New England agricultural newspaper in 1829, "that will by degrees, eat you out, while you are eating upon it."

But that was not the voice being listened to in New Salem where, with its saloon, two other stores, a blacksmith, a tinner, a cooper, a few other artisanal enterprises, and a post office, a small town sprang up aggressively along with the grist mill. And it was drowned out entirely in January, 1832, when Vincent Bogue, who also owned a small mill on the Sangamon, began advertising up and down the Sangamon country that he intended to lease a steamboat, the *Talisman,* and bring it up the Sangamon River to New Salem to see if steamboat commerce on the Sangamon River was practicable. What was particularly titillating was Bogue's promise to "deliver freight from St. Louis . . . for thirty-seven and a half cents for 100 pounds," which was half of what the usual costs were. This was good news in particular for Denton Offutt, who hoped that gaining a cheap access to the St. Louis and New Orleans markets would make his New Salem general store into a success.

Offutt was discovering that he had already taken a step toward that success simply by hiring Abraham Lincoln. Although Lincoln had arrived in New Salem a "friendless, uneducated, penniless boy," he "rapidly made acquaintances and friends." He had grown from being "somewhat bony & raw" and a "long tall dangling awkward droll looking" adolescent into a "well and firmly built" young man: "His thighs were as perfect as a human being could be," remembered William Greene; he "weighed 214 [pounds]: his height was six feet four inches" and "He was more fleshy in Indiana than Ever in Ill[inoi]s." He was poorly dressed, in a suit of "blew Janes . . . a corse pare of Stoga Shoes" and a "low Crowned Brod-brimed Hat," but Caleb Carman soon found him "to be a very inteligent young man" whose "Conversation very often was about books — such as Shakespear & other histories. . . . He talked about politics Considerable."

As Offutt's clerk, he possessed exactly the virtues that Jeffersonian aristocrats like John Randolph of Roanoke sneered at: "attentive to his business — was kind and considerate to his customers & friends and always treated them with great tenderness — kindness & honesty." Henry McHenry described him as "a good — obliging clerk & an honest one: he increased Offuts business much by his simplicity." Henry Onstott remembered Lincoln in New Salem as "a man of temperate habits, truthful and honest, never addicted to profane language, to the use of Spirituous liquors, nor Tobacco, and had the good will of all who Knew him."

And he kept on reading. He picked up lessons in Samuel Kirkham's *A Compendium of English Grammar* (1823) from a local schoolmaster, and "also studied Natural Philosophy" — possibly Thomas Brown's *Lectures on the Philosophy of the Human Mind* (1820) or the more well-known theological utilitarian William Paley's *Principles of Moral and Political Philosophy* (1785) — as well as "Astronomy, Chemistry" from whatever other books he could find "from which he could derive information or knowledge." James Short remembered that "History and poetry & the newspapers constituted the most of his reading," and "[Robert] Burns seemed to be his favorite. . . . Used to sit up late of nights reading, & would recommence in the morning when he got up." Charles Maltby, who worked in the store with Lincoln, saw him "take up Burns' poems, which he read much and admired greatly . . . his favorite selections being Tom [Tam] O'Shanter, Address to the Dial, Highland Mary, Bonny Jeane and Dr. Hornbrook." The newspapers were usually political ones: the *Congressional Globe*, the Louisville *Journal*, the Sangamon *Journal*, and the St. Louis *Republican*. The poetry was fed to him in part by an amiable New Salem loafer and former schoolmaster named Jack Kelso, who was "well educated" and "loved Shakspear and fishing" and would "draw Abe . . . to sit on the bank of the river and quote Shakespear — criticize one another." But whatever he read, "He generally mastered a book quickly — as one who was simply reading — so comprehensive was his mind."

Lincoln also joined a small twice-a-month debating society "which met in an old store house," and it was there that his drift away from his parents' religion became more noticeable. Lincoln "was always skeptical, read [Constantin] Volney in New Salem and other books." According to Henry Rankin, Lincoln "used the language" of radical deism, "that, according to the history of the case in the New Testament, Christ was a bastard and his mother a base woman." He had no use for a doctrine of redemption through the death of Christ, or of a "new birth" through divine grace and repentance. But he took particular exception "to the belief in eternal punishment" for sin, not because he scoffed at either sin or punishment (he later told one friend that "he was not sure but the world would be better off if a little more punishment was

49

preached by our ministers, and not so much pardon for sin") but because of the injustice he saw in an arrangement where "doom" was the result for behavior that was already predetermined. Divine predestination rendered all talk of pardon and punishment irrational. He believed "that God predestined things." But Lincoln did not think, for that very reason, that it made any sense to believe "that the result of that would be Eternal damnation," and he at least once admitted that he could not believe in the personal immortality of the soul. "So you really believe there isn't any future state?" asked Parthena Hill. "Mrs. Hill, I'm afraid there isn't," Lincoln replied. "It isn't a pleasant thing to think that when we die that is the last of us."

This skeptical disillusion was what made Lincoln such an admirer of Burns, another free-thinking refugee from Calvinism. "Burns helped Lincoln to be an infidel," James Matheny recalled, or "at least he found in Burns a like thinker & feeler," particularly when Burns excoriated the justice of a predestinating God who nevertheless held people to account for the actions he had created them to perform: "And no for ony guid or ill/They've done afore thee!" There were moments when God ceased to be a person at all in Lincoln's thinking, but instead became simply "a Superintending & overuling Providence, that guides and controls the operations of the world" by "Law & Order, & not their violation or suspension." Under such a remote, almost mechanical God, it was better to resign oneself to circumstances, than to seek conversion or revival. As Burns wrote,

> Who made the heart, 'tis He alone
>   Decidedly can try us;
> He knows each chord, its various tone,
>   Each spring, its various bias.
> Then at the balance let's be mute,
>   We never can adjust it;
> What's done we partly may compute,
>   But know not what's resisted.

In 1834, Lincoln tried his own hand at writing "a little Book on Infidelity." This was probably no more than an essay written on foolscap "attacking the divinity of Christ — Special inspiration [of the Bible] — Revelation &c.," which he was thinking of sending to a newspaper for publication. The public fury that might descend on his head from such an essay persuaded Lincoln, or least some of his friends, to "burn it, which was done." Parthena Hill remembered that her husband actually "took it out of his hand and threw it into the fire." But in the same year, he did publish an anonymous attack on the Methodist preacher-turned-politician Peter Cartwright, belittling Cartwright's followers as "in some degree priest-ridden." And since "Tom Paine . . . used similar language, Lincoln was published in some of the papers as an infidel."

Whisperings about "infidelity" did nothing to interfere with Lincoln's scrupulous management of Offutt's ledger books, and for all his reading and debating, he superintended Offutt's store without becoming a self-important prig. Pioneer society in Illinois prided itself on what John Mack Faragher has called "familiarity," and Lincoln demonstrated his capacity for familiarity through his remarkable memory for rollicking stories and the physical strength his father's ax had built on his long frame. James Short recalled Lincoln being "full of Highlarity and fun, which made him Companionable, and rather Conspicuous among his associates," and another New Salemite recalled that Lincoln "Could Carry what 3 ordinary men would grunt & sweat at."

When Offutt began boasting that his new clerk could whip any rough-houser in New Salem, several of them put their champion, Jack Armstrong, up to wrestle Lincoln. Just how the match was fought, or even who exactly won, is probably unsure (Armstrong later admitted "that he threw L. but did not do it fairly"); what does seem sure is that Lincoln came away with the admiration, and probably the store business, of even New Salem's roughest lot and the lifelong loyalty of the Armstrongs. "He won us by his bearing and boldness," Royal Clary recalled, "Jack and [Lincoln] were the warmest friends during life."

It may have been Offutt who convinced Bogue to hire Lincoln as the *Talisman*'s river pilot when the *Talisman* arrived on the Illinois River from St. Louis in late February, 1832. "Offitt seemed to think that with Lincoln as Pilot or Captain there was no such thing as fail in the navigation of the Sangamon," recalled one New Salemite. Lincoln knew the Sangamon's tricks and shoals as well as anyone, but more obviously, putting Lincoln at the *Talisman*'s wheel would only draw more attention to Offutt's little enterprise and send land values in New

Salem through the roof. (Lincoln had also unwisely put something of his own meager savings into the venture.) No matter what Lincoln's talents as a river pilot might have been, though, the Sangamon River gave only barely enough depth for the *Talisman* to get past New Salem up to Bogue's sawmill, even with the river temporarily deepened with freshets of snow runoff. The tangle of river debris and overhanging branches along the Sangamon slowed even that progress down to a crawl, with Lincoln and other hired hands chopping and hacking with axes at the obstructions as they went along.

The *Talisman*'s master waited at Bogue's mill for a week, stalling to see if the river would rise; when it didn't, he swung the *Talisman*'s head about and it puffed slowly back to St. Louis. Bogue was stuck with the costs of the vessel's lease and no goods to market, and simply took French leave of his creditors. This also seems to have doomed Offutt's hopes, as well. The New Salem store "was failing — had almost failed" by the time the *Talisman* turned around, and the inability of the *Talisman* to open the path to the market probably finished it.

The *Talisman* had, however, taught Abraham Lincoln an enormously valuable lesson. Not all the new engines in the world could bring the market to the closed world of the yeoman farmers simply and purely on its own. A new economy would require government, and so even before the *Talisman* had disappeared glumly over the horizon and demonstrated the inequities of Nature in shaping the Sangamon, Abraham Lincoln had announced himself as a candidate for the Illinois legislature, with the express aim of "the improvement of Sangamo[n] river."

Walking onto the political stage in the spring of 1832 landed Abraham Lincoln in the midst of political pandemonium, not just in Illinois, but in the United States as a whole. Ever since the national election of 1800, Jefferson's Democratic-Republicans had ruled national politics without serious competition from the disgraced Federalist party. But it was not, as Jefferson had learned, as easy to impose the Jeffersonian vision on American life as he had supposed: the Federalists did not obligingly disappear, American merchants resisted embargoes, and suspicious Indian tribes in the west contested the advance of American farmers into the Northwest Territory. But the Jeffersonians only interpreted these frustrations as a sign that their vision of a virtuous republic was being undermined by a conspiracy older and darker than Federalism — the British. It was the British, after all, who had armed and encouraged the Tecumseh Confederacy in 1811, and it was the British navy that was boldly stopping American merchant ships on the high seas and seizing their cargoes and their sailors. And so a new cadre of radical Jeffersonians from the west — Henry Clay and Richard M. Johnson of Kentucky, John C. Calhoun from the uplands of South Carolina — began screeching for war with Great Britain as the solution to all the Jeffersonian frustrations.

Some of these new "War Hawks" were more Jeffersonian than Jefferson. Henry Clay, born in 1777 and elected to Congress in 1810 as an enemy of banks, corporations, and Federalist privilege, helped sink Alexander Hamilton's old Bank of the United States when it came up for rechartering before Congress in 1811. A national bank, announced Clay, "is a splendid association of favored individuals, taken from the mass of society, and invested with exemptions and surrounded by immunities and privileges." But his greatest fixation was on the conspiratorial threat of Great Britain, the mother of monarchy, aristocracy, and of course, international banking. "We have complete proof that [Britain] will do everything to destroy us — our resolution and spirit are our only dependence." The fact that Britain was now distracted by its life-or-death struggle with France, leaving British Canada vulnerable and undefended, seemed to Clay to offer the United States the chance of a lifetime to bring the British to heel. Invade Canada, the "War Hawks" chanted, and either hold it hostage to good British behavior on the high seas or add it to America's republican empire.

They got their chance in 1812, when President Madison finally sent Congress a request for a declaration of war against Great Britain. The result, however, was the severest humiliation the American republic would receive in international politics in that century. The small British garrison in Canada easily threw back ill-organized American invasions in 1812 and 1813, while the British navy clamped a close, mocking blockade on American seaports. Apart from a handful of scratch victories by American troops in Canada in 1814 and a successful but lame-duck defense of New Orleans two weeks after the signing of a peace treaty with the British at Ghent, the War of 1812 went down as a stupendous succession of calamities. The British raided the eastern seaboard with impunity, even burning Washington City; the New

England states met at Hartford, Connecticut, in October, 1814, with threats of leaving the Union in their mouths; the ill-timed closure of the Bank of the United States in 1811 left President Madison without a mechanism for financing the war, and reduced him, by 1814, to borrowing money from private financiers to keep the United States government from bankruptcy.

The War of 1812 was an immense shock to the leadership of Jefferson's Democratic-Republicans, and especially for Henry Clay. As if to atone for pushing the nation into a war which his own radical Jeffersonianism had left it utterly unprepared to wage, Clay now became the spokesman for what became known as *National* Republicanism. Clay, the former bank-killer, threw his weight behind a revival of the Bank of the United States, proposing the creation of a Second Bank of the United States which would be capitalized at $35 million and serve as the nation's central lending institution. And Clay, a gentleman farmer himself, now called for a new system of national import tariffs that would jack up the cost of importing European manufactured goods and give protection and encouragement to Americans to start up the manufacture of those same goods at home, capitalized, of course, with loans from the Second Bank. It was only by these means, argued Clay in Congress in 1816, that "national independence was . . . to be maintained . . . against foreign encroachments."

It marks how deeply the War of 1812 shook Jeffersonian confidence that James Madison in his last term as president, as well as James Monroe in his two terms as president from 1816 to 1824, allowed Clay and his allies to bolt forward in chartering the Second Bank of the United States, doubling the tariff rates, and funding a National Road that would connect Maysville, Maryland, with the Illinois territory. State legislatures followed Clay's cue and chartered 200 state banks in 1815, followed by another 392 new banks in the next three years, all of which dispensed loans and, along with the loans, paper bank notes to be used as easy paper currency. The state legislatures also began chartering corporations, which issued their own paper in the form of stocks and bonds in order to raise cash directly on major money markets. By 1817 a whole new financial profession — stock brokering — had appeared in New York City. A national market network, in the guise of what Clay would call "the genuine AMERICAN SYSTEM," would now become a government project.

What Henry Clay could not have predicted in this upsurge of market inventiveness was the liability of capitalism to cycles of collapse as well as expansion, and in 1819 collapse is precisely what happened. The plethora of state banks chartered by the legislatures were supposed to retain sufficient coin in their vaults to redeem the shower of paper bank notes they printed and dispensed, but in the great postwar development binge, it was all too easy for banks to ignore this. When British cotton prices fell from a high of 33 cents per pound to 14 cents, the drop in cotton income pulled the banks down with it, and by the spring of 1819 the collapse had turned into a national panic. The new Bank of the United States, which held title to huge collections of western property, foreclosed on mortgages and sold off land at less than half its pre-1819 value. "All the flourishing cities of the West are mortgaged to this money power," wailed Thomas Hart Benton. "They are in the Jaws of the Monster."

The economic panic set off a political stampede, and Clay was unable to prevent the stampede from trampling both his projects and the political coalition he had created within the Democratic-Republican party. The stampede reached Clay himself in 1824, when the Tennessee legislature bypassed the customary Democratic-Republican party caucus and nominated, not Clay, but Andrew Jackson for president. Jackson had commanded the American defense of New Orleans in 1815, and his victory there, even if it had no bearing on the peace settlement, still made him a national hero. As a Southerner and a slaveholder, he was also the darling of the old Jeffersonians, hating with an Old Testament hatred the entire scheme of bankers, speculators, and canal-diggers who, in his mind, were sapping the country of republican virtue. "Every one that knows me," Jackson claimed, "does know that I have been always opposed to the U. States Bank, nay all banks," and his solution to the panic of 1819 was for the people to return "to our former habits of industry and simplicity."

Clay at once saw that Jackson was his enemy, and both Clay and one of Clay's "National Republican" allies, John Quincy Adams, threw themselves into the 1824 presidential race to stop Jackson. But the nation was still seething with disaffection from the panic of 1819, and so Jackson swept the country with almost as many popular votes as his opposition combined. He lacked, however, a majority of electoral votes, and Clay took advantage of that constitutional technicality to strike a "corrupt bargain" with John Quincy Adams and arrange for the House of Representatives to elect Adams rather than Jackson as president.

Adams might as well not have shown up for his own inauguration. The "corrupt bargain" tainted his administration from the beginning and paralyzed every effort Adams made for federally sponsored "improvement of agriculture, commerce, and manufactures, the cultivation and encouragement of the mechanic, and of the elegant arts, the advancement of literature, and the progress of the sciences." In 1828, Jackson returned to the presidential contest and, to the howling dismay of Henry Clay, won a landslide victory. With no apologies, Jackson vengefully fired over one thousand federal officeholders who had any form of association with Adams or Clay, opened up 22 million acres of prime cotton land in Georgia and central Alabama for new agricultural settlement, vetoed further construction of the National Road, and in 1832, struck down a rechartering of the Second Bank of the United States. "Jackson played the tyrant to the last," groaned a despairing Henry Clay, and Clay looked forward only to escaping from Washington City "as soon as I decently can, with the same pleasure that one would fly from a charnel-house."

The election of Andrew Jackson destroyed all illusion that a single Republican party, the party of Jefferson and the party of the Revolution of 1800, still existed. In 1834, Clay bestowed on his National Republicans their own party name, a name dredged out of the English political past as the party of resistance to military aristocracy and political tyranny, the *Whigs*. "The Whigs of the present day," announced Clay in a speech on the floor of the Senate on April 14, 1834, "are opposing executive encroachment" — meaning Andrew Jackson — "and a most alarming extension of executive power and prerogative. They are ferreting out the abuses and corruptions of an administration, under a chief magistrate who is endeavouring to concentrate in his own person the whole powers of the government" and to protect the "one unextinguished light, steadily burning, in the cause of the people, of the constitution, and of civil liberty."

Although Clay strove to define "the Whigs of the present day" as simply good republicans, in fact Whiggism stood for a cluster of political and public values and ideas that sharply differentiated them from the Jacksonians. Primarily, the Whigs understood themselves to be the party of small-scale urban business and finance, and usually urban businessmen and financiers who were parts of transatlantic networks of investment and trade, or of trade that crossed state and regional boundaries. This did not mean that the Whigs were entirely a city-oriented party: in fact, the Whigs drew a large measure of their support from farmers. But Whig farmers tended to be large-scale commercial farmers, who produced agricultural products for distant markets, and who were tied to markets that benefited from the regulation of state or even national controls on trade. It was not, in other words, a party whose members identified themselves strictly with their state or their locality, either economically or socially. Most often, the Whigs looked to escape the restraints of locality and community, seeking to refashion themselves on the basis of new economic identities in a larger world of trade, based on merit, self-improvement, and self-control.

This is what attracted them to Clay's "American System," and led them to support high protective tariffs (to assist American business in competing with European products), subsidies for internal improvements (to help break down barriers to further trade), innovative transportation technology (primarily canals and railroads), and a national bank (to create a dependable and uniform system of national investment, currency, and finance). And although this opened the Whigs to the accusation that they were simply a party for the rich, the Whigs replied that what it really meant was that they were the party of economic opportunity. "Who are the rich men of our country?" asked a Whig newspaper. "They are the enterprising mechanic, who raises himself by his ingenious labors from the dust and turmoil of his workshop, to an abode of ease and elegance; the industrious tradesman, whose patient frugality enables him at last to accumulate enough to forego the duties of the counter and indulge a well-earned leisure." For the Whigs, the power of the markets was precisely what offered Americans liberty to remake and improve themselves.

The Whigs also described themselves as the "sober, industrious, thrifty people," which is a statement, not only about economic behavior, but about moral behavior as well. Whig economics depended upon regularity across the national economy, but the Whigs also relied upon regularity of moral behavior, and this led the Whigs into a close alliance with New School Protestantism. Not every evangelical would turn Whig, any more than every Whig would turn out to be an evangelical, but large numbers of them, like the fiery revivalist Charles Grandison Finney, or Nathaniel William Taylor of Yale and his lifelong friend Lyman Beecher, were persuaded to see in the market not a rival to oppose, but a force to harness. The Whig party offered Americans multiple opportunities for mobility and self-transformation — from agriculture to the professions, from backwoods to city, from rags to riches — and since self-transformation was what evangelical conversion was all about, many New Schoolers found it difficult to see the Whigs as an enemy. It was true, admitted Philadelphia pastor Henry Augustus Boardman in 1853, that "where war has slain its thousands, commerce has slain its tens of thousands." But to silence the banks or disrupt the corporations would be no solution: "The silence of death would replace the intolerable but productive clatter of the foundries and machine shops," and (what was more fatal to the public ambitions of the evangelicals) "our noble array of religious and charitable institutions would be shorn of their efficiency, if not annihilated."

The Whigs' harmonization of evangelical conversion and the energies of the market not only created a cultural congruence, it also opened up the possibility of creating a Protestant political consensus within America's secularized republican society. Lyman Beecher, for instance, wept on his rush-bottomed chair in 1819 when Connecticut voted to disestablish its Congregational churches, but he now sought by every possible angle consistent with republicanism to rebuild that establishment in the form of Christian "influence." He sponsored a series of voluntary reform societies that could carry on the work of Christian social activism when the churches could not (because of disestablishment and the "separation of church and state" dogma); and then he moved to Ohio to become the president of Lane Seminary and save the West from Roman Catholicism. Similarly, Henry Boardman deplored "our locomotives and steamboats" as "slaughtering machines," but he found them "inert and tame when compared to the grog-shop." In the ongoing quest for Christian influence over society, Beecher and Boardman happily struck up a close alliance with the Whigs, and the Whigs found in the broad band of evangelical power the ideal rule for promoting the kind of national unity necessary for the smooth operation of an "American System."

This meant that both secular Whigs and New School Protestants became, out of necessity, committed to the preservation of the Union over the persistent tendency of the republic toward democratic individualism. Clay, for instance, was a Kentucky slaveholder, which aligned him with Southern slaveholding interests; but he also publicly condemned the morality of slaveownership, actively sought to restrict the spread of slaveholding in the United States, promoted colonization schemes for freed slaves (not so much for the good of the slaves as to remove a potential irritant to national harmony), and was the architect of one compromise after another to hold the Southern slave states in the Union. Lyman Beecher, similarly, although a Connecticut Yankee and anti-slavery by persuasion, actively tried to suppress all discussion of slavery at Lane Seminary for fear of the disruptive effect it would have on the students and on his plan of national Christian influence. Together, both secular and evangelical Whigs believed that only a strong national Union could guarantee the triumph of prosperous markets and the establishment of Christian influence, and it became the great Whig agenda to suppress localism, private immorality, and secession at all costs.

Whiggism was thus a movement with wide intellectual connections. At the same time as it made common cause with evangelical Protestants, it also enjoyed clear links with European liberalism in the 1840s. Like liberalism, it was a movement based on reason, and especially the economic rationalism of the market. Like liberalism again, the Whig ideology glorified the individual, although in this case, it was not the anarchic, independent individual of the Jeffersonian imagination, but economic individuals who had been emancipated from the restraints of local community and set on the unfettered path of economic opportunity. The dark side of Whiggism, however, like the dark side of bourgeois liberalism, was its suspicion of popular democracy, and its conviction that only an enlightened but non-aristocratic elite was fitted to govern human society. "All the world out of doors is not so wise and patriotic as all the world within these walls," Daniel Webster reminded the Senate. This allowed Democrats to denounce their one-time fellows as "British-bought, bank-Federal-Whig gentry who wear ruffle shirts, silk stockings and Kid gloves." To that extent, although only to that extent, Andrew Jackson had been right: Clay and the Whigs were not the party of "the people."

But Jackson's Democrats (the more cumbersome double-formula of "Democratic Republicans" dropped out of usage when the National Republicans adopted "Whig" as their name) left a great deal to be desired as a party of "the people," too. Although Jackson thought of himself as the champion of "the *American Husbandman*, fresh from his plow," the Jacksonians transformed this into a political ideology fully as complex as the Whigs. In direct line from Jefferson's agrarianism, the Democrats believed that "The farmer is naturally a Democrat . . . untainted by the corruptions and contagions of the crowded city."

> Take a hundred ploughmen [wrote William Leggett] from their fields and a hundred merchants from their desks, and what man, regarding the true dignity of his nature, could hesitate to give the award of superior excellence, in every main intellectual, physical, and moral respect, to the band of hearty rustics, over that of the lank and sallow accountants, worn out with the sordid anxieties of traffic and the calculations of gain?

While the Whigs mixed economic opportunism and Protestant moralism, thereby blending public acquisitiveness and private ethics, the Democrats compartmentalized the public and the private, arguing for majoritarian democracy to rule in the public sphere and *laissez-faire* in the private. "Let the people do as it seemeth good unto them," became the Jacksonian banner. And as the Democrats made political virtue almost synonymous with the popular will, they neither needed or welcomed second opinions from Christian moralism or Christian influence. "The aim of religion is to regulate the conduct of man with reference to happiness in a future state of being," declared Leggett in his editorials for the *New York Evening Post* in the 1830s, while the purpose "of politics" was a quite different affair, "to regulate his conduct with reference to the happiness of communities."

This was not entirely an anti-religious stance, since there were important religious communities in the United States that found more comfort in the Democrats than the Whigs. Old School Presbyterians were split between Democrats and Whigs, usually because Southern Old Schoolers looked to the Democratic party as protection against interference with slavery, and because Northern Old Schoolers were often cultural Tories who yearned for Old World models of social organization that they did not find in the Whigs. High Church Episcopalians, similarly, snorted at the notion that their hierarchical Episcopal Church should make any attempt to involve itself with bourgeois republicanism. "The great practical feature of that system is subordination — a subordination based on principle and not convenience — existing in virtue and divine command, and not of human suggestion," boasted the High Church magazine *Churchman* in 1831, thus setting itself off decisively from the social-climbing, self-transformed world of Whig identity. At the same time, the most *ultra* of the evangelical Baptists and Methodists also found reason for aligning themselves with the Democrats, so that Lyman Beecher thought the Democratic party in Connecticut "included nearly all the minor sects, besides the Sabbath-breakers, rum-selling tippling folk, infidels, and ruff-scuff generally." Like the Southern Old Schoolers, Baptist and Methodist laypeople feared the social consequences of allowing political agendas to shape church policies, and the militant commitment of Jefferson and the Democrats to a complete separation of church and state sounded to them like a promise of security, rather than a diminution of "influence."

Methodists and Baptists also sympathized with the Democrats in their valorization of the passions over reason. Just as the Methodists and Baptists became marked for appealing loudly and unambiguously to emotion to justify religious belief, Democrats became renowned for their revivalistic appeal to the "passions" of the democracy, and speaking manuals recommended that Democratic orators adopt "rapidity, interruption, rant, harshness, and trepidation." For the Democratic stump campaigner, as well as the Methodist exhorter, "the neck is stretched out, the head forward, often nodding and shaken in a menacing manner against the object of the passion." Andrew Jackson, himself an Old School Presbyterian, shocked even Thomas Jefferson by his "passionate" behavior. "His passions are terrible," the aged Jefferson remarked after meeting Jackson. "He could never speak on account of the rashness of his feelings. I have seen him attempt it repeatedly and as often choke with rage." This might not have made Jefferson lie easy, but the glorification of the passions established a common rhetorical pattern between anti-religious Democrats and their religious allies. It also created a cultural pattern in which the farthest right and left of the religious spectrum — "passionate" sectarians and starch-shirt Old Schoolers — went to the Democrats, while middle-class New

Schoolers and the more evangelical Old Schoolers in the middle went to the Whigs.

While this established some common purpose among the radical fringes of American religion and the Jacksonians, it was far from being a blueprint to promote public "influence." In terms of religious substance, William Leggett wanted *"perfect free trade in religion,"* which meant no moral tariffs and no "government protection, regulation, or interference of any kind or degree whatever." And this extended, as far as Leggett was concerned, even to declaring an annual Thanksgiving day: "We regret that even this single exception should exist to that rule of entire separation of the affairs of state from those of the church. . . ." Even in the midst of the great cholera epidemic of 1832, Jackson threatened to veto any request emerging from Congress for a day of fasting and prayer. "Whenever religion leaves its proper home, the heart, to join in the noise and strife of the affairs of State," warned the Democratic national convention in 1835, "it is out of its province, and ever sullies its purity." Religious moralism was a matter of private conclusions; and political virtue was not to be judged by an abstract standard of moral behavior, but by whatever the common voice of the democracy called for. If the popular majority preferred to abolish banks, ignore Indian treaties, and sanction the immoral high-handedness of a "military chieftain," then they presumably had every right to do so.

Whigs and Democrats alike thought of themselves as champions of liberty, but it quickly became obvious that Whigs thought of liberty as freedom from the rednecked restraints of localism, whereas Democrats thought of freedom as the privilege of restraining large concentrations of wealth and power. John L. O'Sullivan's *Democratic Review* editorials in the 1830s cast liberty as a veto over "the strong influence" of "cities, where wealth accumulates, where luxury gradually unfolds its corrupting tendencies, where aristocratic habits and social classifications form and strengthen themselves, where the congregation of men stimulates and exaggerates all ideas . . ."; and the New York trade unionist Ely Moore preached liberty as a restraint on "an undue accumulation and distribution of wealth" which "we all know, constitutes the aristocracy of this country." Consequently, liberty was a negative, rather than a positive, idea to the Democrats, and it was to be used, not for achievement, but for protection.

Thus, while Whiggery found itself more and more resembling the confident and nationalistic middle-class liberalism of Europe, the Democrats found themselves more and more speaking for slave-based agriculture and for industrial workers who either resented the power of their bourgeois employers or resisted the imposition of bourgeois moral culture. As Daniel Walker Howe has put it, the Whigs promoted a society that would be economically diverse but culturally uniform; Democrats preferred economic uniformity and equality, but tolerated the spread of cultural, ethnic, and moral diversity. It would not be too much to say (as Marvin Meyers once remarked) that, in the context of the 1830s, the Whigs were the party of optimism, while the Democrats were the party of fear. "The [Democratic] Administration occupies a position of defence," wrote O'Sullivan in 1837. "It is . . . difficult if not impossible to preserve a perfect purity from abuse and corruption throughout all the countless ramifications of the action of such an executive system as ours, however stern may be the integrity and high the patriotism of the presiding spirit which, from its head, animates the whole."

For Abraham Lincoln, entering into his first political election in 1832, the world of Illinois politics must have seemed mired in "lobbies, local interests, and political adventurers." Throughout the 1820s, the single greatest political force in Illinois had been, not a party, but the family of the former territorial governor, Ninian Edwards. But by 1832 the patterns that were shaping the great national political contests were framing and confining state politics, as well. And given how deeply Lincoln's sympathies were with any ideology that preached emancipation from agricultural life, glorified social mobility, and agreed that wage labor actually guaranteed the ability "to improve one's condition," there could not have been much doubt with whom Lincoln would find his friends. "I have always been an old-line Henry Clay Whig," Lincoln told John Minor Botts in 1861, and he would be able to prove it from the first.

2 The Costs of Union

No one who read Abraham Lincoln's campaign platform when it was published in the newly founded *Sangamo Journal* on March 15, 1832 (and later distributed as a handbill), could have imagined that it was written by anything other than a thoroughgoing disciple of Henry Clay. "Time and experience have verified to a demonstration," he told his prospective constituents, "the public utility of internal improvements." The "improvement" he thought Sangamon County most needed was the deepening and dredging of the Sangamon River. "For the last twelve months I have given as particular attention to the state of the water in this river, as any other person in the country," and Lincoln was now convinced that widening and damming of old channels and cutting new channels for the river across the "zig zag" peninsulas that crooked its meandering length would make navigation of the Sangamon "completely practicable." He did not, he admitted, know what the cost of this work would be. But he was convinced that "the improvement of the Sangamo[n] river" would "be vastly important and highly desirable to the people of this county." It also went without saying that deepening the Sangamon River had to pay direct commercial dividends to New Salem, while a railroad or canal might just as easily be built somewhere else, to someone else's benefit.

This was a strong platform to run upon in New Salem, and Lincoln made it stronger by his blossoming talent for public speech-making. Just as he had once mounted stumps to imitate Baptist preachers and surprised John Posey two years before with his "Stump Speech" on "the navigation of the Sangamon," Lincoln now just as readily mounted wagon-beds and the porches of stores to promote his candidacy for the state legislature. His inaugural "Political Speech" was made at an auction at Pappsville, and it had already all the marks of Lincoln's mature political style: humor, a clear-cut Whiggish economic program, and an almost-apologetic self-deprecation. Thirty-three years later, James Herndon could almost piece it together from memory:

> Fellow Citizens: I have been solicited by many friends to become a candidate for the legislature. I have so concluded to do. I presume you all know who I am. My name is Abraham Lincoln. My politics is short and sweet, like an old woman's dance. I am in favor of a national bank, a high and protective tariff, and the internal improvement system. If elected, I will be thankful. If beaten, I can do as I have been doing, work for a living.

Despite looking "tall and gawky and rough," Lincoln possessed a "tenor intonation of voice . . . that Shrill monotone Style of Speaking, that enabled his audience, however large, to hear distinctly the lowest Sound of his voice." And whenever "he was asked a question and have an answer it was always characteristic, brief, pointed, *a propos*, out of the common way and manner, and yet exactly suited to the time, place, and thing."

All of this might have been more successful had not Lincoln's little campaign been interrupted by a call to arms. All through the 1790s, the United States government had struggled to clear the old Northwest Territory of Indian tribes, mostly by treaties but sometimes by force. Many of these tribes thought that the War of 1812 would give them a chance to strike back at the Americans, but instead it gave the United States an excuse to undertake massive Indian clearances, not only in the Northwest but also in the Mississippi and Alabama territories. By 1819, old Illinois tribes like the Kickapoo, Pottawatomi, and Chippewa had all grudgingly exchanged their Illinois lands for federal territory across the Mississippi. But in the spring of 1832, after a particularly difficult winter, a band of two thousand Sauk-and-Fox Indians under Black Hawk repudiated the treaties they had signed in 1804 and 1816 and recrossed the Mississippi back into northern Illinois to reclaim their old planting and hunting grounds. Federal troops were summoned, and on April 14, 1832, the state militia was called out for thirty days' service.

Illinois adopted a militia system in 1826 which mandated that "all free white male inhabitants" organize, train, and equip themselves in local companies. In most cases membership in these companies meant little more than showing up one day a year for some perfunctory training and the distribution of large numbers of honorific officers' commissions to the governor's friends. But for just that reason, it was also a significant opportunity for politicking and patriotic publicity-seeking, and it was probably with those objects uppermost in mind that Lincoln turned out for the militia and, to "his own surprise," was elected captain of the New Salem company. Thirty years and numerous elections later, Lincoln recalled that "he has not since had any success in life, which gave him so much satisfaction."

Even more important for the sake of his political advancement, Captain Lincoln was thrown together with some of the rising stars of Illinois politics: Elijah Iles, a central Illinois land speculator, Orville Hickman Browning, whose mounted company was brigaded together with Lincoln's, and John Todd Stuart, a dapper and well-connected Springfield lawyer who served as the brigade major and who was even now emerging as Sangamon County's most influential apostle for Henry Clay's "American System." Stuart, especially, took note of the gangling militia captain as a future political protégé. "I fell in with Lincoln first when he was captain," Stuart recalled. "He was then noted mainly for his great strength, and skill in wrestling and athletic sports . . . [but] he was also noted for being a kind genial and companionable man, a great lover of jokes and teller of stories."

None of Lincoln's summer soldiers were employed in much more than a clumsy chase of Black Hawk's half-starved band around the northwestern corner of Illinois. "Lincoln often expressed a desire to get into an engagement to see how that would meet Powder & Lead," remembered Benjamin Irwin, "but failed to do so." And it was just as well, since Lincoln "had the wildest company in the world" and any real collision with Black Hawk might have had unpleasant conclusions for them. Lincoln himself knew so little about maneuvering his undisciplined collection of New Salem roughnecks that he was at a loss to know even how to get them to shift from column into line. But after a few skirmishes, Black Hawk conveniently took off into Wisconsin, and the now-jaded militiamen seized this as a pretext for announcing that they had no obligation to follow Black Hawk out of Illinois. Lincoln's New Salem boys went home, but Lincoln stayed on to serve as an ordinary soldier in a ranger company. Even then, there was little real fighting to see. Black Hawk and his dwindling band were run to ground in a savage little fight at the Bad Axe River in southern Wisconsin that August, and Lincoln went back to New Salem and electioneering without having ever fired a shot in anger.

Lincoln's spell in the militia would pay many long-term political rewards, but for his legislative campaign that summer, it paid none at all. In his absence, the *Sangamo Journal* unintentionally left his name off its list of favored candidates and had to hurry an endorsement of "Capt. Lincoln, of New Salem," into its columns. Even with that, Lincoln had only two weeks left between his mustering-out and the election day to do any face-to-face vote-hustling. "Gentlemen, I have just returned from the Campaign," he apologetically told a hasty campaign gathering, "My personal appearance is rather shabby & dark. I am almost as red as those men I have been chasing through the prairies & forests on the rivers of Illinois." As a result, Lincoln garnered only 657 votes in Sangamon County, running a dismal eighth in a field of thirteen candidates. There was some consolation in the fact that his home precinct of New Salem had gone for him almost unanimously, but that must have paled beside the unhappier fact that Lincoln was now without employment. Offutt's store had given up the ghost, perhaps as early as Lincoln's original enlistment in the militia, and "he was now without means and out of business."

Offutt's failure should have been a signal to Lincoln that New Salem would never live up to its expectations as a market entrepôt, and that the little village was a dead end. But Lincoln had invested so much of himself socially in New Salem that he was reluctant to leave it to its end. He was (as he put it) "anxious to remain with his friends who had treated him with so much generosity, especially as he had nothing elsewhere to go to." Anxious not to be seen, or feel himself, a deserter of New Salem, Lincoln unwisely used the militia wages and state bounty money he had earned from his Black Hawk service and, together with a series of promissory notes, bought up half-interest in a store of his own, going into partnership with a militia chum, William Berry. "Of course," Lincoln wrote later, the partners "did nothing but get deeper and deeper in debt."

In desperation, Berry and Lincoln applied for a license to turn their store into a tavern — "a common grocery — *whiskey shop*" — despite the fact that Lincoln himself had an aversion to the kind of hard liquor a village tavern was expected to dispense. Business, in fact, was so bad that Lincoln's friends had to wangle him an appointment in May, 1833, as postmaster in New Salem just to provide him with some minimal income. And when even that "insignificant" position failed to pay enough, the same friends persuaded the Sangamon County surveyor to take Lincoln on as an assistant, despite the fact that Lincoln knew next to nothing about surveying. It was all to no avail. "The store winked out" in 1833, and when his alcoholic partner died in 1835, Lincoln found himself saddled with notes and debts amounting to over $1,100 — four or five times the annual earnings of an ordinary laborer. By the spring of 1834, he was back to clerking in another man's store in New Salem and performing whatever odd jobs came to hand, along with some occasional surveying.

And yet, for all these setbacks, Lincoln remained "a most ambitious man." Orville Hickman Browning admired him as "a man of very strong ambition," and William Herndon would later comment that "He was always calculating, and always planning ahead. His ambition was a little engine that knew no rest." Handed a surveying appointment that he knew little enough about, Lincoln determinedly "procured a compass and chain" and threw himself into studying the standard surveying texts, Abel Flint's little portable handbook, *A System of Geometry and Trigonometry: Together with a Treatise on Surveying* (1804), and Robert Gibson's substantial *The Theory and Practice of Surveying; Containing All the Instructions Requisite for the Skilful Practice of This Art* (1803). By January, 1834, he had begun his first surveys for the county road commission; over the next two years, he would stake out plats for the towns of Bath, Tallula, Petersburg, and New Boston, and perform surveys for an increasing number of well-paying private customers. Surveying was difficult outdoor work, since Lincoln had to supervise a team of chain-men, flag-men, and wood-choppers, and since land surveys had to conform to the relentless regular geometry of the federal land survey no matter what obstacles the physical lay of the land might present. But it was well paid (at three dollars a day by the county) and it gave nimble-witted surveyors a valuable preview of good lands they could buy up themselves for speculative resale. Town surveys often paid additional bonuses in the form of town lots in the proposed towns; and any town that proved a success would reward its surveyor by multiplying the value of his bonus lot. And by all accounts, Lincoln soon turned himself into a skilled surveyor: "Mr. Lincoln had the monopoly of finding the lines, and when any dispute arose among the Settlers, Mr. Lincoln's Compass and chain always settled the matter satisfactorily."

For Abraham Lincoln, however, the greatest bonus county surveying paid was the interaction it gave him with people all over Sangamon County. "He made friends everywhere he went," John Todd Stuart kept on noticing, and "acquired a reputation for candor and honesty, as well as for ability in speech-making." In the summer of 1834, he announced himself once again as a candidate for the state House of Representatives from Sangamon County, and this time, "because of the standing he had got in the county, and especially the prominence given him by his captaincy in the Black Hawk War," Lincoln came in second on a slate of thirteen candidates. He trailed the leader by only fourteen votes, and that was sufficient to get him a seat in the state House.

Another Sangamon representative remembered Lincoln as "Six feet and four inches high in his Stockings" and "Stoop Shouldered."

> His legs were long, feet large; arms long, longer than any man I ever knew. When standing Straight, and letting his arms fall down his Sides, the points of his fingers would touch a point lower on his legs by nearly three inches than was usual with other persons. . . . His eyes were a bluish brown, his face was long and very angular; when at ease [he] had nothing in his appearance that was marked or Striking, but when enlivened in conversation or engaged in telling, or hearing some mirth-inspiring Story, his countenance would brighten up the expression would light up . . . his eyes would Spar-

kle . . . all terminating in an unrestrained Laugh in which every one present willing or unwilling were compelled to take part.

He was too deep in debt to afford the fine clothing of an established politician. But he was able to borrow enough money to buy a "a very respectable looking suit of jeans" (since "Henry Clay once went to Congress in a suit of jeans" to illustrate "the protective idea of wearing home manufactures" and afterwards "it had become a sort of whig dress"), and on November 28th, he joined the other Sangamon County representatives on board a stagecoach taking them to a special session of the Ninth General Assembly called by the governor at the state capital at Vandalia.

"Nothing . . . has produced such deep-seated evil," wrote Andrew Jackson, as "the establishment of a national bank by Congress." It was not that Jackson hated only the institution known to its friends as the Second Bank of the United States. For Jackson, banks in general were a bad idea, since banks were only the tip of a threatening commercial iceberg that included state-chartered corporations, taxpayer-financed schemes of "internal improvements," federal meddling in state affairs, and the whole repulsive Henry Clay "system" which threatened to corrupt the integrity of the independent American farmer.

But in Jackson's imagination, the Second Bank of the United States had become an especially monstrous hydra. There, greedy private investors used the credit of the government to heap up unwholesome and suspicious concentrations of wealth, then converted that wealth into "the paper system," into bank notes (which were supposed to represent the true value of the banks' deposits of hard coin and which were lent out at interest to finance economic development), which were then turned into stocks and bonds by corporations (the corporations often receiving paper money in exchange for the stocks and bonds, thus creating a double fraud), and mortgages (which enticed simple farmers to reach for too much land or too many goods). "If your currency continues as exclusively paper as it now is, it will foster this eager desire to amass wealth without labor," Jackson intoned like an Old School prophet, "it will multiply the number of dependents on bank accommodations and bank favors; the temptation to obtain money at any sacrifice will become stronger and stronger, and inevitably lead to corruption which will find its way into your public councils and destroy, at no distant day, the purity of your Government." This was a passionate exaggeration, but at least he was right in this much: banks were the pumping-stations of capitalism. And he took the Second Bank of the United States as his particular target because it had presented itself to Congress so insolently for rechartering in 1832.

Jackson tried to decapitate as many of the heads of this banking monster as he could, beginning with an astounding veto of the charter Congress voted for the Second Bank. But the Whigs responded to Jackson's anti-bank campaign with hoots that the "military chieftain" and his party "would leave no man safe in the enjoyment of his property" and "substitute for a government of perfect freedom and perfect equality, a system of anarchy, corruption, and misrule, naturally terminating in absolute despotism." And to Jackson's dismay the state legislatures, over which he had substantially less control, promptly chartered two hundred new state banks to fill up the gap left by the Second Bank, and they casually issued so much paper money that the money supply shot up from $172 million to $276 million. On that fountain of cash, the creation of new corporations and the funding of internal improvement schemes proceeded willy-nilly.

It annoyed Jackson even more that the western state legislatures had been petitioning the federal government since the 1820s to sell or distribute federally owned land in the states to the state legislatures so that they could be sold by the states to charter still more banks and fund still more internal improvement projects. Jackson fumed: "With specious and deceitful plans of public advantages and State interests and State pride," the "paper money system and its natural associates, monopoly and exclusive privileges" will "besiege the halls of legislation in the General Government as well as in the States," and in the unfair struggle of power over liberty, "the agricultural, the mechanical, and the laboring classes" will be "in constant danger of losing their fair influence in the Government and with difficulty maintain their just rights."

On those terms, Andrew Jackson would not have liked what he saw in Abraham Lincoln when Sangamon County's newest state representative stepped out of the stagecoach in Vandalia at the end of November, 1834. Not only was Lincoln "as stiff as a man can be in his

Whig doctrines" and capable of making "powerful and convincing" arguments for "a National Currency, Internal improvements by the general government, and the encouragement of home manufactories," but he arrived under the wing of John Todd Stuart, "the ablest and most efficient jury lawyer in the State" and the political chief of Sangamon County's restless Whigs. Having kept an interested eye on Lincoln ever since the Black Hawk War, Stuart invited the gangly freshman politician to room with him and become a sort of legislative secretary for Stuart and the Whig interests in the state House. It may have been Stuart, too, who got Lincoln signed up as the Vandalia legislative correspondent for the *Sangamo Journal,* giving Lincoln a chance to turn his gift for mimicry into "hundreds" of unsigned (and virulently anti-Democratic) political editorials.

Above all, Stuart increasingly deployed Lincoln as a mouthpiece for the Whig agenda. "Lincoln was not worth a cent in caucus," William Butler remembered, but "Lincoln and [Usher] Linder [for the Democrats] were the two principal men we relied on in the Legislature to make speeches for us." In fact, Lincoln hardly warmed his chair in the state capitol before he was on his feet to offer a resolution "that our Senators be instructed, and our Representatives requested, to use their whole influence in the Congress of the United States" to push for the sale of the federal land holdings in Illinois and ensure that Illinois would be guaranteed 20 percent of the proceeds. Lincoln also knew what he wanted those proceeds spent upon. The first bill he introduced onto the floor was an internal improvements measure — an authorization for the construction of a toll bridge "across Salt Creek in Sangamon County" — and he followed that by supporting an "Act to incorporate the Beardstown and Sangamon Canal Company," five bills for state road extensions, and a new east-west state road to link the Wabash River with the Mississippi.

But the most extravagant internal improvements measure Lincoln supported was the centerpiece of the Ninth Assembly, the Illinois and Michigan Canal. For more than a decade, since the initial success of the Erie Canal, commercial entrepreneurs had been calling for the construction of a major canal that would link the town of LaSalle on the Illinois River with the village of Chicago on Lake Michigan, opening up a water highway between the Great Lakes and the Mississippi River, but, more important, opening access to east-coast markets over the Lakes and the Erie Canal to central Illinois farmers. Governor Joseph Duncan, a turncoat Jacksonian, was an outspoken advocate for the Illinois and Michigan Canal, and Duncan had called the special legislative session which included Lincoln largely to get legislative approval and land appropriations for the canal. He certainly got the support he wanted from Lincoln: when a bill to authorize the canal came to a vote in the House of Representatives on February 9, 1835, Lincoln, along with Stuart and two of the other Sangamon Country representatives, joined a pro-improvements majority in giving the canal bill's first reading a whopping 40-12 endorsement.

Lincoln's first stint as a lawmaker ended four days after the canal vote, when the legislature formally adjourned and Lincoln took the road back to New Salem. The contrast must have been painful: for two and a half months, Lincoln had been in the thick of high state politics, and he had even got a whiff of national political debate when he helped divert into committee a series of seven resolutions offered by an unrepentant Democrat, Jesse B. Thomas, calling for the destruction of the Second Bank and praising Andrew Jackson's campaign against this "soulless corporation." In New Salem, all that Lincoln had to anticipate was his dreary postmaster's job, more surveying work on the county roads, and the deadening weight of the money he owed his creditors from the failure of his store. Some of them were quick to remind him of that debt, too: he had only been back in New Salem a week when the county sheriff seized Lincoln's horse and surveying instruments to sell at auction to satisfy an impatient creditor. That might have left him without any means of support at all, had it not been for the $258 he had collected as a legislative salary, and had not a sympathetic neighbor bought his instruments back for him.

Lincoln spent most of the summer of 1835 performing surveys, almost to the neglect of the New Salem post office; and he might not have even had that, given General Jackson's freewheeling willingness to evict disloyal government employees from even the smallest offices, if his general friendliness had not persuaded local Democrats not to squeal on him. That favor did not weigh heavily on his mind, however, when the Ninth General Assembly was called back for its second session at Vandalia on December 7th. There, Lincoln not only voted for the third and final reading of the Illinois and Michigan Canal bill, but began feeding onto the floor of the House of Representatives a bill to incorporate a Sangamon Valley canal company, a number of corporate charters for central Illinois marketing and export companies, and a new north-south Illinois Central Railroad.

Lincoln made himself so clearly into a promoter of Sangamon County's connections to national markets that he experienced almost no trouble in getting re-elected to the legislature that summer on a platform which frankly called for "distributing the proceeds of the sales of the public lands to the several states, to enable our state, in common with others, to dig canals and construct railroads. . . ." Stuart, meanwhile, ran for Congress, leaving Lincoln as the head of the nine-member Sangamon delegation (who were all so tall that they were nicknamed "The Long Nine"). But Lincoln had learned well from his mentor, and he helped beat back assaults on the Illinois and Michigan Canal bill from truculent Democrats, and sponsored still more corporate charters.

Lincoln also stood up to defend the Illinois State Bank, which had been founded in Illinois's territorial days and which was flying in the face of Jacksonian anti-bank rage by extending across Illinois the commercial credits which the now-vetoed Second Bank of the United States could no longer offer. In his lengthiest formal speech yet, Lincoln assailed the Bank's Democratic critics. The Bank, Lincoln declared, had done the people of Illinois nothing but good: "It has doubled the prices of the products of their farms, and filled their pockets with a sound circulating medium" [i.e., paper bank notes]. "Injure the credit" of the state bank, warned Lincoln, and "you will depreciate the value of its paper in the hands of the honest and unsuspecting farmer and mechanic" — which was to say, the Whiggish commercial farmers and urban wage-earners that Lincoln now identified himself with.

Injuring the state bank would also cripple the largest legislative project Lincoln became involved with, an omnibus internal improvements bill that not only borrowed (through the sale of state bonds) $8.5 million for the financing of the Illinois and Michigan Canal, but an additional $10 million for the construction of the Illinois Central Railroad system and the dredging and deepening of the Wabash, Rock, Kaskaskia, and Illinois rivers, with $200,000 set aside for smaller projects in counties outside the reach of the canal and the railroad. "There was to be nothing but railroads," one Whig quipped. "Railroad meetings were held everywhere, and the State was to become a gridiron."

For Lincoln, the fight would be uphill most of the way. The Whigs were a numerical minority in the state House, and many legislators were uneasy at the prospect of committing such enormous sums to projects that would take years to complete before they could return a dime. But popular opinion in Illinois, fed by the success of the Erie Canal and the east-coast railroad companies, had turned "almost insane" with an "internal improvement mania" and demands for "a system of Internal Improvements for the State." A two-day "internal improvements" convention was held in Vandalia during the opening of the legislature's sessions, and even an otherwise Democratic-leaning newspaper like the Vandalia *State Register* had urged its readers to "elect representatives who will borrow money to make internal improvements." Still, it took a protracted session of the Tenth General Assembly, lasting into March, for Lincoln to secure a 61-to-25 vote in the House in favor of the omnibus improvements bill and then pass the enabling legislation for issuing the accompanying bonds. "I very much doubt if the bill could have passed as easily as it did without his valuable help," commented Gurdon Hubbard, one of the original promoters of the canal project.

But the victory, when it came for Lincoln, was sweet. His new-found skill in marshaling political power had marked Lincoln as "the acknowledged leader of the Whigs" in the House of Representatives (according to Jesse Dubois, who was then sitting in the Illinois senate), and earned him a place "among the recognized Whig leaders in the State." Moreover, as the *Sangamo Journal* promised, the passage of the omnibus internal improvements bill would guarantee that Lincoln and all the other Whigs "who had been conspicuous in bringing forward and sustaining this law will go down in the future as great benefactors." He would not return to New Salem. He had paid the dues of loyalty, and now the little village was collapsing helplessly into a ghost town. Instead, once the momentous first session of the Tenth Assembly was over, he packed his few belongings and in April of 1837, moved permanently to the Sangamon County seat of Springfield, the headquarters of his mentor, Stuart, and the Whig ascendancy in Illinois. And he would do no more surveying. His service in the legislature had thrown him together with men of law and the making of laws, and he had learned from both where power and advancement in Illinois lay.

On April 12, 1837, a brief advertisement in the *Sangamo Journal* announced that "J. T. Stuart and A. Lincoln, Attorneys and Counsellors at Law, will practice in the courts of this Judicial Circuit." With Stuart once more as his sponsor, Abraham Lincoln had become a lawyer.

As in so many other things, it was John Todd Stuart who, "in a private conversation" during Lincoln's first successful campaign for the state House in 1834, "encouraged A. [to] study law." Lincoln may have toyed with the idea of becoming a lawyer long before, even while still in Indiana, and he seems to have looked at the idea again when Offutt's store in New Salem failed. But he was convinced that "he could not succeed at that without a better education," and so nothing came of it before going off to the Black Hawk War. Stuart, both from some initial prompting in their Black Hawk days and from a serious urging in 1834, finally persuaded him to give lawyering a vigorous experiment as a profession, lack of "education" notwithstanding.

Lincoln lacked more education than he realized, although that might not have been apparent at first. Studying law in the 1830s only meant going to a law school in the seven schools in the country where law education had been formally organized; only three of those were in the west and none of them in Illinois. Formal professional education of any sort, much less law, was only just developing its own institutions, and adventuresome young students who wanted to enter lawyering, doctoring, or preaching received the bulk of their education first as college undergraduates and afterward took up apprenticeships of various sorts with the veteran practitioners of their professions. Only five out of forty-four lawyers practicing in Chicago between 1830 and 1850 had ever attended a law school.

What set Lincoln apart was not that he had no education — his schooling in his youth was not significantly less than many of his professional colleagues — but that he had never been "fitted" for college. ("That is what I have always regretted," Lincoln remarked in 1861.) And he got only the most minimal oversight from Stuart afterward. But, as William Herndon later wrote, Lincoln "had unbounded confidence in himself" and "thought that he could do anything that other men could or would try to do." Since he had learned surveying by reading, he went after law the same way. "He borrowed books of Stuart, took them home with him, and went at it in good earnest," and at an auction in Springfield "bought an old copy of Blackstone . . . and on his return to New Salem, attacked the work with characteristic energy."

Sir William Blackstone's *Commentaries* on English common law were the central text for all antebellum law students, and twenty-six years later, Lincoln was still advising inquirers to "begin with Blackstone's Commentaries" as they prepared for law studies. Blackstone's *Commentaries* had the great advantage of being written for the intelligent lay reader (they were actually a series of lectures, rather than a technical treatise); they had the disadvantage, however, of being addressed to a pre-Revolutionary English audience that assumed the sovereignty of a king, the supremacy of an established church, and the natural law of God. The American Revolutionaries, in their revolt against monarchy, were strongly tempted to replace English common law with new forms of popular statute law, and cast about for replacements for Blackstone. Nathaniel Chipman's *Sketches of the Principles of Popular Government* (1793) attacked Blackstone's ideas on sovereignty as "wholly inadmissible . . . in a democratic republic," and in 1821 Thomas Jefferson blamed the influence of Blackstone for the legal profession's "slide into toryism."

Abandoning both Blackstone and the English common-law tradition proved not to be so easy as it seemed, however. If getting rid of a British sovereign meant merely the substitution of thirteen individual sovereignties, then a major problem was posed, in both law and in government, for what sovereignty the American republic as a whole was supposed to have in law. The federal Constitution was one step toward asserting a form of national sovereignty in the federal government; and it was matched, beginning in 1790 with James Wilson's *Lectures on Law*, by an effort from national-minded lawyers to domesticate Blackstone and transfer his concept of sovereignty to the American people in general, irrespective of state identities. Jeffersonian lawyers like Charles Humphreys and Timothy Walker remained critical of the influence of Blackstone. But by the time Lincoln bought his auction copy of the *Commentaries* in 1834, sixteen Americanized versions of Blackstone, including those of Hugh Henry Brackenridge, St. George Tucker, and John Reed, were available, "with numerous alterations and additions" for American readers.

One significant alternative to the Americanization of Blackstone was the legal utilitarianism of the English liberal Jeremy Bentham, who died two years before Lincoln began his law studies. For Bentham, Blackstone's appeal to monarchy and natural law was an appeal to fiction, and he proposed the replacement of traditional common law with specific statutory codes adopted by legislatures on the purely secular basis of "utility": "the greatest happiness for the greatest number." But Benthamite utilitarianism also insisted that all governments must possess a central "authority that is absolute," since "*no* assemblage of men can subsist in a state of government, without being subject to some *one* body whose authority stands unlimited so much as by convention." For that reason, Benthamite utilitarianism had special appeal for secular Whigs like Richard Hildreth, who popularized Bentham's *Theory of Legislation,* William Beach Lawrence, and Edward Livingston (who authored a Benthamite law code for Louisiana, the one state in the Union that had never experienced English common law).

Secular Whigs like Hildreth, however, spoke for only a minority of the Whigs, and there is no evidence in the 1830s that Lincoln's reading of the Utilitarians had gone any deeper than William Paley. Consequently, Lincoln's first law study went into Blackstone, and probably into the treatises of two other Whig sympathizers with the Americanized Blackstone, Joseph Story and Joseph Chitty. (Story's *Commentaries on Equity Jurisprudence as Administered in England and America* and Chitty's *A Practical Treatise on Pleading* were among the five basic textbooks he recommended to aspiring lawyers in 1858 and 1860 which were in print in the early 1830s.)

This did not give Lincoln a very deep grasp of law, but it was enough for him to begin drawing up simple deeds and contracts from a book of legal forms, and in a year and a half he applied for a law license in Sangamon County. He needed to do nothing more than demonstrate a basic knowledge of the law and offer proof that he was not a felon, and on March 24, 1836, a certificate of "good moral character" was filed in the Sangamon County Circuit Court, followed by the issuing of a law license on September 9, 1836, just after his re-election to the Tenth General Assembly. (He was not, however, formally enrolled until March 1, 1837, when he was legally permitted to charge fees.)

In the meanwhile, Lincoln continued performing surveys and

waiting for the Tenth General Assembly to convene in Vandalia. And he might have stayed in surveys, too, had not Stuart suggested at the close of the legislative session in March, 1837, that Lincoln come up to Springfield and enter into a regular law partnership with him there. Stuart, who was already "in full practice of the law," had just lost his law partner since 1833, Henry E. Dummer (a Harvard law graduate) and since he had been grooming Lincoln politically, it must have seemed the natural next step for Stuart to help the fledgling lawyer onto his feet by getting him a secure start under his own wing in Springfield.

Springfield had only been laid out as a county seat for Sangamon County in 1821, with a twenty-foot-square log courthouse, a jail, and no more than a dozen inhabitants. When the Methodist evangelist Peter Cartwright rode into it for the first time in 1823, it possessed little more than "a few smoky, hastily-built cabins, and one or two little shanties called 'stores'. . . ." But having the court house at its center made Springfield a magnet for "enterprising men from Kentucky and the Atlantic States . . . Young Doctors, Lawyers, farmers, mechanics &c, who found towns, trade, speculate in land, and begin the fabric of Society." By 1835, Springfield had acquired nearly fifteen hundred inhabitants, along with all the trappings of a market town: nineteen dry goods stores, six groceries, four drug stores, clothing and shoe stores with glass, china, boots and hats from New Orleans, New York, and Philadelphia, eighteen doctors and eleven lawyers. A brick Presbyterian church had gone up with a Princeton Theological Seminary graduate as its minister, followed by a Second Presbyterian Church in 1835 and the founding of St. Paul's Episcopal Church by the energetic bishop of Illinois, Philander Chase. Readers of theology, law, politics, and fiction could be served by William Manning's bookstore; a circulating library managed by Birchall's bookstore offered "Scott, Cooper, Irving, Maryatt, Bulwer, Fielding and Smollett." What was read could be just as easily studied and debated, too, in the Springfield Academy, the Springfield Female Seminary, the Mechanics' Institute, the Sangamon County Lyceum, and the Springfield Young Men's Lyceum, where lectures "On the Responsibilities of the Medical Profession" (December 1833) alternated with debates on the question "Ought Capital punishment to be abolished?" (February 1836).

Small as it was, Springfield awed Lincoln. Less than a month after moving there, he admitted that "I am quite as lonesome here as [I] ever was anywhere in my life. . . . I've never been to church yet, nor probably shall not be soon. I stay away because I am conscious I should not know how to behave myself." But as one Springfield lawyer remarked, Lincoln "never went into any company or community that he did not do or say something which marked him as a popular man." And this was even more true in Springfield than it had been in New Salem. "He had always influential and financial friends to help him," William Herndon wrote many years later, "they almost fought each other for the privilege of assisting Lincoln." He walked into the store of Abner Y. Ellis on his first day in Springfield to ask about the purchase of bedding, and within an hour, Ellis's partner, an émigré Kentuckian named Joshua Speed, was offering Lincoln space to room with him in the store's second-floor loft. Speed soon became the closest friend Lincoln ever had, and since Lincoln's "Mind [was] of a metaphysical and philosophical order," a knot of ambitious young lawyers — James Matheny, deputy clerk of the county court, Milton Hay, a law clerk in Stuart's office, James C. Conkling, who joined the group in 1838 out of Princeton, Evan Butler "and other habitues of the courthouse" — gradually clustered around Speed and Lincoln. Since Stuart and Lincoln's office was in the same building as Matheny's (in "Hoffman's Row," a line of stores off the northwest corner of the state capitol square), it was Matheny's clerk's office that became the headquarters for "a Kind of Poetical Society" or "debating or literary society which met, usually in [Matheny's] office, once and sometimes twice a month." Lincoln seems to have written some poetry for the society's informal meetings, as well as debating law and politics.

But Lincoln had other subjects to discuss which were more sensational, and it soon became clear that Lincoln's absences from Springfield's five churches had little to do with social embarrassment. "I think that when I first knew Mr. L. he was skeptical as to the great truths of the Christian Religion," Speed recalled, and so "when all were idle and nothing to do," Lincoln (according to Matheny) "would talk about Religion — pick up the Bible — read a passage — and then Comment on it — show its falsity — and its follies on the grounds of *Reason*." Here was the voice of the Enlightenment, a voice that Abner Ellis was inclined to attribute to Lincoln's reading of "some of Tom Pains Works." "Lincoln was Enthusiastic in his infidelity," Matheny

80

continued. "Lincoln went further against Christian beliefs — & doctrines & principles than any man I ever heard: he shocked me." Matheny particularly remembered Lincoln calling "Christ a Bastard" and "always denied that Jesus was the Christ of God." If he had faith in anything, he "Had faith in laws — principles — causes & Effects — Philosophy." But he "Had no faith in the Christian sense of that term." Rumors of Lincoln's "infidelity" and "deism" became common in Springfield, and "Many Religious — Christian whigs hated to vote for Lincoln on that account," since Lincoln's unabashedly secular Whiggism threatened the core of the Whig political alliance with Protestant evangelicals.

What spared him any harsher reaction was his spirited defense of Springfield's civic interests in the legislature. Pressure had been mounting ever since 1832 to move the state capital out of the poorly constructed State House in Vandalia and out of Vandalia itself, and the rapidly increasing population and commercial power of Sangamon County gave weight to a call from the Sangamon County delegation to relocate the capital to Springfield. Vandalia vainly tried to stem the tide by constructing a new State House, but the work was hardly finished before the first session of the General Assembly (the same session that adopted the comprehensive internal improvements bill) repealed the statute that had fixed the capital in Vandalia and, after six weeks of debate, bestowed it on Springfield. The debate, from the Springfield side, was managed by Lincoln, who "was at the head of the project to remove the seat of government" and who had it "entirely trusted to him to manage." Lincoln not only fended off several subsequent efforts to repeal the move, but took a major hand in raising the $50,000 in public money that Springfield needed to erect a new State Capitol.

And so Lincoln prospered for the first time in his life. As John Todd Stuart's partner, Lincoln walked into an established and reasonably lucrative practice, and Stuart was unusually generous with Lincoln by agreeing to split the partnership's fee income equally. Although much of the Stuart and Lincoln case load involved small suits — trespasses, ejectments, nonpayments, slanders, divorces, pension suits — with relatively small fees ranging from $5 to $20, the size of the partnership's practice (twice the size of any other Springfield partnership) brought Lincoln a healthy income of about $800 a year and the prospect of finally paying off his New Salem debts. He even began to dabble in real estate speculation, buying forty-seven acres near the route of the proposed Beardstown Canal (north of Springfield) and two town lots in Springfield in 1836, and two more town lots in 1838.

On the other hand, earning those fees demanded a tremendous amount of work from Lincoln. No Springfield lawyer could hope to survive simply off the fees to be had trying cases during the two weeks each year that the Sangamon County Circuit Court sat in Springfield itself, and so Lincoln and Stuart were compelled to accompany the judges of the circuit court as they opened hearings in courthouses great and small across the vast Eighth Judicial Circuit.

Formed by the legislature in February, 1839, the Eighth Circuit was originally composed of Sangamon, Macon, McLean, Tazewell, Menard, Logan, Dane, and Livingston counties; it was periodically reorganized and expanded until by 1845 it included fifteen counties, nearly one-fifth of the entire state. The circuit judges were forced by the great distances between county seats to work in a ragged circle over the central Illinois prairie, "quite as desolate and almost as solitary as at Creation's dawn," riding from courthouse to courthouse over several weeks until the circuit had been completed. This process had to be completed twice a year, usually from mid-March (when the Federal court sessions in Springfield concluded) to mid-June, and then again from early September to the first of December, when winter would make the countryside impassable. As they moved, Eighth Circuit judges like Nathaniel Pope trailed lawyers after them, most of them traveling as a group "on horseback, with saddlebags" and "very frequently traversing uninhabited prairies of some 10 to 20 miles or more across."

This wandering flock of lawyers became its own little society, thrown together over the endless flat miles with no one's company but their own, pulling up in small court towns where in two or three days they had to connect with clients and take depositions or make declarations or interview witnesses, sharing meals and usually beds in flea-trap boarding houses. "They were not, as a general rule, highly cultured, but they had what was better and had it in large measure — a rude unpolished naturalness," William Herndon recalled. "They had great ambition and overflowed with manly spirit, health and strength; they came here to fight their way upward and they did so fight it; they met each other at the bar and on the stump and fought it out like strong brave men do fight it out." Yet, "these men were at all times personal friends, bearing no ill will," and it was in just this atmosphere of crude bonhomie, where "manners were rude, but genial kind, and friendly" and "relations between the bench and bar were familiar," that Lincoln felt most at home. He had found for the first time a society of equals that he could marvel at for its own respectability, and he would be remembered years later as the only Springfield lawyer who enjoyed circuit-riding so much that he rode both the spring and fall terms of the circuit. "I think Mr. Lincoln was happy — as happy as *he* could be, when on this Circuit," recalled Judge David Davis, "and happy no other place. This was his place of enjoyment."

It was not only the company, but the practice of law itself that fitted Lincoln perfectly. Lincoln's mind "ran to mathematical exactness about things," and Illinois common law pleadings, which required exhausting attention to detail, sharpened Lincoln into a rigorously logical thinker, with something close to a mania for terseness, consistency, and clarity of expression. "He had great natural clearness and simplicity of statement," recalled Joseph Gillespie, who sat in the legislature with Lincoln in the 1830s. "He despised everything like ornament or display and confined himself to a dry bold statement of his point and then worked away with sledge-hammer logic at making out his case." Lincoln's determination to reduce any problem to a concise and logical proposition could sometimes drive him past the point of obsession, and William Herndon remembered occasions when Lincoln would pace the floor, stare out of windows for hours, or withdraw into a tightly knotted and hostile concentration, searching for just the right words to state just the right idea. But the reward for this preoccupation, as Leonard Swett remembered from days riding the circuit with Lincoln, was that "when Lincoln had stated a case, it was always more than half argued and the point more than half won." "He excelled in the statement of his case," agreed Isaac Arnold. "However complicated, he would disentangle it, and present the real issue in so simple and clear a way that all could understand. Indeed his statement often rendered argument unnecessary, and frequently the court would stop him and say: 'If that is the case, Brother Lincoln, we will hear the other side.'"

Lincoln's passion for what Swett called the "clearness and the

perspicuity of his statements" was supported by his extraordinarily retentive memory, which allowed Lincoln to master easily the technicali-
ties of litigation. "If I like a thing," Lincoln said years later, "it just
sticks after once reading it or hearing it." On the whole, he once
warned Joshua Speed, he was "slow to learn," and most of his fellow
lawyers agreed that Lincoln "was never what might be called a very
industrious reader" of law books, preferring instead to bury his nose
in poetry or plays. Stuart remembered Lincoln "carrying around with
him on the Circuit . . . books such as Shakespear" and Edgar Allan Poe
(Lincoln "read and loved the Raven — repeated it over & over") and
both Davis and Stuart recalled Lincoln studying "Euclid — the Exact
Sciences" and even "Latin Grammar on the Circuit."

But if he was slow and unsystematic in his learning, he was also
"slow to forget that which I have learned . . . like a piece of steel, very
hard to scratch anything on it and almost impossible after you get it
there to rub it out." As a result, Lincoln had almost instant recall for
dates, names, places, and faces. (In 1855, he responded to a letter from
an inquirer by identifying Clardy Barnett, who had served in his New
Salem company in the Black Hawk War, as "a small man, with a scar
on his face, and not far from my own age.") And he could delight onlookers with his capacity to recognize long-distant acquaintances, recite long passages from Burns, Byron, or Shakespeare, or even (as
Herndon saw him do on one occasion) "write out a speech . . . and then
repeat it word for word, without any effort on his part." Rowan
Herndon believed that Lincoln "had the Best memory of any man I
Ever Knew, he Never forgot any thing he Read."

This "exceedingly retentive, tenacious, and strong" memory
made him a deadly cross-examiner, since he could carry the threads
of a witness's testimony in his head through a confusing labyrinth of
questioning, and then turn viciously when an inconsistency or contradiction betrayed the witness as a perjurer or liar. And in his early
years as a lawyer and politician, Lincoln developed a reputation for
single-minded aggressiveness. "I would not compromise the case at
any cost," he advised one client in 1845, "but let them sue if they
will. Even if the main point of the case is against you, there will be so
many little breakers in their way, as to prevent their ever getting
through safely."

His gift for ridicule made him something of a terror in political combat, using "wit, anecdote and ridicule, until his opponent was completely crushed." Stephen Logan recalled that Lincoln "was always very independent and had generally a very good nature," but "when he was roused," Lincoln could display "a very high temper . . . and at those times it didn't take much to make him whip a man." His ridicule of Jesse B. Thomas's virulent Jacksonianism in 1840 made Thomas "blubber like a baby, and [he] left the assembly." Listening to Edmund "Dick" Taylor, a Democratic merchant-turned-politician, rail against Whig "aristocracy," Lincoln reached over, tore open Taylor's vest, and out tumbled the frills of a very un-Democratic "ruffle shirt," and "gold watches with large seals hung heavily & massively down."

> Whilst Col. Taylor had his stores over the county [Lincoln declared], and was riding in a fine carriage, wore his kid gloves and had a gold headed cane, he was a poor boy hired on a flat boat at eight dollars a month, and had only one pair of breeches and they were of buckskin. . . . If you call this aristocracy, I plead guilty to the charge.

This, said James Matheny, "was too much for the good People — Democrat & Whig alike — and they burst forth in a furious & uproarious laughter."

Lincoln's skill at ridicule was just as useful in the courtroom. Horace White, a journalist, thought that "Nobody knew better how to turn things to advantage . . . and nobody was readier to take such advantage, provided it did not involve dishonest means." His gift for mimicry could lift "whole crowds off their seats," and "in the examination and cross-examination of a witness he had no equal," Isaac Arnold remembered. "He could compel a witness to tell the truth when he meant to lie, and if a witness lied he rarely escaped exposure under Lincoln's cross-examination." And if a witness or opposing counsel proved particularly difficult to crack, Lincoln would pick up some irrelevance to trigger laughter and humiliation in front of a jury. A Springfield attorney whose case had been laid down "with his accustomed acuteness and skill" had misbuttoned his collar, and Lincoln seized on that to ask "if it may not be possible that a lawyer who is so unmindful of the proprieties of this place as to come . . . with his standing collar on wrong-end-to, may not possibly be mistaken in his opinion of the law?" The courtroom roared. A witness who was sworn in as

J. Parker Green offered Lincoln no advantage at all except his name, which Lincoln seized happily:

> Why J. Parker Green? What did the J. stand for? John? Well, why didn't the witness call himself John P. Green? That was his name, wasn't it? Well, what was the reason he did not wish to be known by his right name? Did J. Parker Green have anything to conceal; and if not, why did J. Parker Green part his name in that way?

And so on, until Lincoln had the jury grinning and Green deflated.

Lincoln had other uses in the courtroom for humor than humiliation. He quickly learned how to turn the stories he had once enjoyed in New Salem for fun and familiarity into jury-winning illustrations and contradictions of opposing counsels' arguments. "If the case was a long, dry, tedious one and the jury got tired and showed signs of weariness, or of sleepiness, Lincoln would tell one of his fine stories and arouse them up to renewed attention," Herndon recalled, "and then he would take up the thread of his argument and proceed on to the end of it." Even after many years, Joseph Gillespie could still be amazed at Lincoln's "unfailing budget of genuinely witty and humorous anecdotes with which he illustrated every topic which could arise." And it was not just that Lincoln could riddle opposing counsel with laughter: "There was this about his stories," Milton Hay observed. "They were not only entertaining in themselves, but they were doubly interesting because they were always illustrative of some good point or hit." Any opposing lawyer who mistook Lincoln's storytelling as the mark of a courtroom yokel soon learned a lesson about the well-hammered logic that stood behind it. "That man who laughed at a contest with the clear head, the brave heart and the strong right arm of Abraham Lincoln always had to have his laugh first," wrote David Davis, "for after the contest had ended and the man woke up with his back in a ditch, laughing was too serious a matter." Leonard Swett agreed: "He was wise as a serpent in the trial of a case, but I have had too many scars from his blows to certify that he was harmless as a dove. . . . Any man who took Lincoln for a simple-minded man would very soon wake up with his back in a ditch."

But ultimately, lawyering suited Lincoln because lawyering suited the expansion of commercial capitalism and market exchange throughout the republic. "Lawyers," in Charles Sellers's memorable phrase, "were the shock troops of capitalism"; and by the early 1840s, legal magazines and legal directories were increasingly concerned with commercial law, bankruptcy, and land-title litigation. The very fact that market relations were, by virtue of banks and cash, now conducted over lengthy and impersonal distances meant that the old social reinforcements of face-to-face neighborliness were insufficient to guarantee adherence to agreements or contracts, and lawyers emerged as the bodyguard of the markets. Lawyering, which in colonial times had been a part-time gentrymen's affair for enforcing local moral codes about Sabbath observance and gambling, now became a middle-class profession aimed at protecting the sanctity and inviolability of market arrangements, no matter what the social costs or no matter what weight the testimony of community mores might bring against it.

The hand of that enforcement was strengthened by the ambitious series of legal commentaries that appeared between 1819 and 1835 from the pens of Nathan Dane, Peter Du Ponceau, Gulian Verplanck, James Kent, and Joseph Story. Verplanck's *Essay on the Doctrine of Contracts* (1825) rejected agrarian notions of just exchange and the inherent value of goods and reduced all transactions to the mere "agreement of the parties"; Joseph Story's *Equity Jurisprudence* (1836) dismissed equity as a recognition of fixed values in goods and declared that "The value of a thing . . . must be in its nature fluctuating, and will depend upon ten thousand different circumstances." Just as market relations ruthlessly rationalized commercial transactions, and excluded every nonrational consideration such as race, kinship, or religion, so the law retreated into rationalism and refused to countenance any other grounds for acting except the explicit rational choices of individual parties. The law, according to Story, acts "upon the ground, that every person . . . is entitled to dispose of his property in such manner and upon such terms, as he chooses; and whether his bargains are wise and discrete, or otherwise, profitable or unprofitable, are consideration, not for Courts of Justice, but for the party himself to deliberate upon." Indebtedness, which was once construed as a moral offense, was now a commercial obligation, to be calculated down to the last unyielding number. And if ensnared debtors and bankrupt farmers refused to comprehend that agreements struck up with "soulless corporations" admitted nothing less than exact satisfaction, the law would legitimate the use of force to bring sullen agrarians to heel.

Just how useful the courts could be in enforcing the power of market exchange appeared on the state level in cases like Kentucky's *Lexington & Ohio Railroad v. Applegate* (1839), where a local "nuisance" injunction against the railroad was overturned by the state court of appeals on the grounds that railroads ("the offsprings, as they will be also the parents, of progressive improvement") could not be barred simply because *"common law"* tradition gave local authorities a veto over nuisances. "The law is made for the times," the appeals court warned, "and will be made or modified by them." But nowhere was the alliance of law and market more visible than at the highest level, the United States Supreme Court, where John Marshall (an appointee of John Adams and the mortal enemy of Thomas Jefferson and Andrew Jackson alike) and Joseph Story struck down one challenge to the sacredness of commercial contract after another. In *Sturgis v. Crowninshield* in 1819, the Court upended a New York state law granting protection from debts; the same year, in *Dartmouth College v. Woodward,* it prevented the state of New Hampshire from canceling Dartmouth College's corporate charter, even though the state had written the charter.

To truculent Democratic yeomen and workers, this made lawyers appear as "the secret trades union" of the markets, bemystifying honest farmers and urban workingmen and winning "enormous fees" through "the multiplication of statutes, and the mysterious phraseology" of the law. But Lincoln regarded the markets as the poor man's road to success and accomplishment, and as a lawyer, not only could he walk that road himself, but he could police it from interference and obstruction by others.

It was just as well for Lincoln that he settled so well into lawyering, because he was now about to enter some of the roughest political water he would ever sail upon. Even while learning the basics of law and practicing it on the circuit, Lincoln remained a Sangamon County representative. Considering as the legislature sat, apart from special sessions, for only about three months of the year, this did not greatly disturb Lincoln's legal calendar. But that began to change abruptly in the spring of 1837. As the Jacksonians had been so glumly predicting, the international agricultural markets could not be relied upon to support the volume of farm commodities, especially cotton, which reckless American farmers, flush with bank-issued cash, were producing. Cotton prices began to fall on the British markets just as they had in 1819; and British investors in the American economy, fearing that a shortfall in cotton profits would mean a shortfall in American balance-sheets, began cashing in their American commercial paper.

This set off a spectacular run on American banks by American debtors who desperately needed hard coin — "specie" — to pay their British creditors. By May, the east-coast banks had been cleaned out: New York banks suspended all specie payments, and slow-footed lenders were left holding paper bank notes and bonds which the suspension of specie payments pretty strongly implied were worthless. Without a national bank to regulate the flow of paper and specie, the value of American money went into free fall. State banks frantically called in loans, hoping to scrape up enough specie to stay open; and when their debtors had none, the banks closed their doors, taking down with them their depositors and all the loans and businesses they had called in. Thousands of workers were unemployed — 50,000 in New York City alone — and the hunt for a political scapegoat commenced.

From the point of view of the Jacksonians, the fault lay clearly with the banks, and with the entire misbegotten commercial drive to enmesh the American economy with the ruthless patterns of the transatlantic market system. One Democratic writer attacked "the *banking system*" as the "fruitful mother of unutterable affliction to the sons of industry," bringing "us, at one fatal step, into the vortex of English aristocracy." A mass meeting of workers in Philadelphia's Independence Hall angrily attacked the banking system as "a system of fraud and oppression," while state and territorial legislatures in Iowa, Arkansas, and Louisiana actually moved to prohibit banking. In Illinois, the second session of the Tenth General Assembly opened in Vandalia to angry appeals from Democratic legislators for an investigation of the Illinois State Bank, for a law preventing it from suspending specie payments, and for the repeal of the internal improvements bill and its monstrous debt.

From the point of view of the Whigs, however, this panic of 1837 was nothing more than the predictably disastrous result one could have expected from Jackson's ill-tempered meddling with the economy. Jackson himself had just left office in March, 1837, but the Whigs found an equally suitable target in Jackson's anointed successor, Martin Van Buren. "Little Van" struggled to right the economic ship, but he could not restore a national bank without enraging his own Democratic party, and his best solution was to have the federal government hold or distribute its funds (in effect, to regulate and stabilize the national money supply) through the Treasury. This "independent Treasury" scheme would put most of the normal payments and receivables of the federal government back under the control of something like the Bank of the United States, but without the private credit or investment activities that had characterized the old bank. But instead of this placating both Jacksonians and Whigs, the Democrats went stiff with indifference, while the infuriated Whigs could not believe that the Jacksonians would prefer to let the government's money lie idle in the "independent Treasury" vaults rather than using it to stimulate the sagging economy.

In Vandalia, Lincoln fought back against any attempt to derail the state bank or the improvements bill. He made no extended speeches in the legislature, but he did use an opportunity provided in January, 1838, by the Young Men's Lyceum in Springfield to denounce the attack on the state bank and the improvements projects as part of a larger conspiracy of "increasing disregard for law which pervades the country" and a "growing disposition to substitute the wild and furious passions, in lieu of the sober judgement of the Courts." Unhappily, this disposition was "common to the whole country," but he was careful to point out special examples of lawlessness in Democratic strongholds — "in the State of Mississippi, and at St. Louis" — as "the most dangerous in example, and revolting to humanity." His invocation of "law" and the "courts" as the defenders of the commercial order was classic Whiggism, but so was his suggestion that the Democratic party was an expression of mere "furious passions," bent on satisfying irrational and uncontrolled personal preferences, in contrast to Whiggish self-discipline and reason which sought to develop personal potential. Charles Zane said that Lincoln "never allowed his natural emotions or the emotions of the heart to become agitated excited broken up and thrown out of their proper action. . . . They had the benefit of the light and wisdom of a great intellect, and the adminel stions of a great Conscience." And no wonder: the passions were the mark of the unimproved man, the reason the mark of the improved one, as much as railroads and canals were a mark of an "improved" state.

Self-government — "the capability of a people to govern themselves" — in both the constitutional and the psychological sense, was in jeopardy whenever the passions, or the Democrats, seized control, since the greatest danger a surrender to the "furious passions" posed was the ease with which it spilled over into the destruction of every other aspect of republican government. "Having regarded Government as their deadliest bane," the enemies of laws and courts "make a jubilee of the suspension of its operations" and "gather in bands of hundreds and thousands, and burn churches, ravage and rob provision stores, throw printing presses into rivers, shoot editors, and hang and burn obnoxious persons at pleasure." Let this go on, Lincoln warned, and "depend on it, this Government cannot last." Anarchy of this sort will eventually beckon to "some man possessed of the loftiest genius, coupled with ambition sufficient to push it to its utmost stretch," and this "towering genius" will not be content merely with occupying office within the inherited structure of the republic. "It sees *no distinction* in adding story to story, upon the monuments of fame . . . it thirsts and burns for distinction. . . ." Only "reverence for the laws," raised to the level of "the *political religion* of the nation," and the self-disciplined imposition of "Reason, cold, calculating, unimpassioned reason" on the "basest principles of our nature" could ensure the "establishing and maintaining civil and religious liberty."

The Young Men's Lyceum was not a political forum, and Lincoln refrained from direct political statements there (although few could have missed the sarcastic connection Lincoln was drawing between "Little Van" and the prospect of a dictatorial "towering genius"). He was more pointed on the floor of the state House, arguing that if the United States government would finally relent and allow the states to take over the sale of federal lands, the proceeds of the land sales would easily fund the internal improvements bill and save the state bank, too. But no Democratic administration in Washington was in a mood to listen to such pleas, and in the Twelfth General Assembly, even Lincoln's Whig allies in the Sangamon County delegation began to desert him. He angrily reminded them in February, 1839, that Sangamon County, more than any other, was "*morally*

91

bound, to adhere to that system [of internal improvements], through all time to come!" But it was all for nothing. Even the Sangamon Whigs began to slip away from Lincoln, one-by-one, and in December Lincoln gloomily notified Stuart that "the legislature is in session, and has suffered the Bank to forfeit its charter without *Benefit of Clergy.*" On January 28, 1840, the great internal improvements bill that Lincoln had lavished so much of his political reputation upon was repealed. Lincoln pleaded with the House "to save something to the State, from the general wreck," but he might as well have saved his words. In July, 1841, the state of Illinois defaulted on interest payments for its outstanding bond issues, and the value of Illinois paper securities tumbled as low as fourteen cents on the dollar. By 1842, when all work on the Illinois and Michigan Canal ceased, only 105 miles of canal had been dug; the Illinois Central Railroad project, which had managed to lay down only twenty-six miles of track, would have to wait for Congress to revive it in 1850.

The only satisfaction Lincoln could have drawn from this debacle was the bleak joy he saw in the collapse of the Van Buren administration. In November and December, 1839, Whigs and Democrats challenged each other to a series of debates in Springfield which pitted Stephen Logan, Edward Dickinson Baker, and Lincoln against John Calhoun, Josiah Lamborn, and the new star of the Illinois Democrats, Stephen A. Douglas. The issues were national, but the contest quickly became a warfare of personalities, especially between Lincoln and Douglas. Like Lincoln, Douglas was not an Illinois native (he was born in Vermont); he also had lost a parent (his father) early in life, and had drifted west to Illinois to find a future and to practice law. Thereafter, the similarities ended. Douglas was a foot shorter than Lincoln, eloquent and mannered, and a Jacksonian Democrat. He joined Lincoln in the legislature in 1836, but the following year accepted a patronage job from Van Buren as Register of the federal land office in Springfield. He was not a radical agrarian — a "Loco-foco" as the ultra-Jacksonians became known — but that made him no more palatable in Lincoln's Whiggish eyes. "Messr Lincoln and Douglas addressed the People of this County frequently" on "the Tariff question — the Bank question, Van Buren — and other democratic & whig measures." A particularly hard-hitting speech on the "independent Treasury" scheme which Lincoln delivered on December 26th was printed as a political pamphlet

— his first independent publication and a sign that the Whigs smelled political blood around Van Buren.

The possibility of a Whig revolution improved still more when, in December, 1839, the Whigs shrewdly nominated the old hero of the Indian wars, William Henry Harrison, for president for the 1840 national elections. (They balanced the ticket, as they then thought still more shrewdly, with a conservative Virginia Democrat, John Tyler, for vice president in order to swing hesitant Jacksonians behind the Whig banner.) "I have never seen the prospects of our party so bright in these parts as they are now," Lincoln wrote to Stuart on March 1, 1840. "Mr. Lincoln was merry," recalled Albert Taylor Bledsoe. "He entered into the very soul of the contest," helping "organize the whole State" for the Whig state committee "so that every Whig can be brought to the polls in the coming presidential contest." Lincoln set up a Harrison campaign newspaper, *The Old Soldier*, and took to the stump for Harrison through central Illinois from mid-August through October for the Whig state Central Committee, "discussing the principles of our party" and "ranging over the county for weeks before the election, begging, coaxing and commanding the voters to come out to the polls."

He was tagged by the Democrats as the Whigs' "travelling missionary": He debated John McClernand at Mount Vernon and Shawneetown, Josiah Lamborn in Equality (where Lincoln's "speeches were ingenious, and well calculated to command attention, and he was listened to, with so much patience, that the Whigs were in extacies"), Isaac Walker in Albion, and finally Stephen A. Douglas "in the Market house" in Springfield. Like "Dick" Taylor, Douglas tried to tag "the Whigs" as "federalists — Tories — Aristocrats &c. That the whigs were opposed to freedom, Justice & progress." This stung Lincoln, who "detested aristocracy in all its forms" and who looked on the Jacksonians as the real aristocrats. And as he had done with Taylor, Lincoln unhesitatingly stung back, reading aloud from an 1835 political biography of Van Buren to show "that Van had voted for Negro suffrage." This enraged and embarrassed Douglas, who "Snatched up the book and slung it into the crowd — saying damn such a book."

It was a personal triumph of sorts for Lincoln when Harrison carried nineteen states and swept into the presidency in November, 1840, on an electoral college landslide. But whatever joy Lincoln felt at the close of 1840 was tempered by the desertion of his Whig allies in the legislature, by the fact that Harrison had actually lost Illinois while winning the nation, and by the disheartening discovery, in the 1840 state legislative elections, that the once-popular leader of the Sangamon Whigs had finished next-to-last in Sangamon County in his bid for re-election to the state House.

By that time, though, Lincoln had an even greater dilemma on his hands. He had made the greatest promise of his life, and broken it. And what was worse, he had made his promise to no one less than John Todd Stuart's cousin, Mary Todd.

When Lincoln first came up to Springfield in the spring of 1837, according to Orville Hickman Browning, he "had seen very little of what might be called society and was very awkward, and very much embarrassed in the presence of ladies." A Whig newspaper in Quincy wrote him up in 1841 as "slender, and loosely built," but this was being politically generous. Henry Dummer, whose place Lincoln took in Stuart's law office, recalled more frankly that he "was the most uncouth-looking young man I ever saw." He cut no particularly romantic figure. Lincoln himself admitted in May of 1837 that "I have been spoken to by but one woman since I've been here, and should not have been by her, if she could have avoided it." He had been shy of women in New Salem, too. One New Salem neighbor remembered that Lincoln "didn't go to see the girls much. He didn't appear bashful, but it seemed as if he cared but little for them." John Hanks, Lincoln's flatboating cousin, agreed: "I never Could get him in company with woman; he was not a timid man in this particular, but did not seek such Company."

And yet, if he feared betraying his social awkwardness around women, Lincoln also envied the "excessive pleasure" of marriage, and he seriously contemplated marriage on at least two occasions in the 1830s. The first involved Ann Rutledge, "an amiable young Lady" and the daughter of one of New Salem's founders. Rutledge had actually been engaged to another New Salemite, John McNamar, but when McNamar left for the east and failed to return after two years, Rutledge and Lincoln "were engaged to be married absolutely." Rowan Herndon, among many other New Salemites, had "Know Dout he would have Maried," and years later, Lincoln told Isaac Cogdal that

"She was a handsome girl; would have made a good loving wife; was natural and quite intellectual, though not highly educated." But in August of 1835, she "took Sick and died," probably of typhoid fever. Lincoln, who had been "wofully in Love," took Rutledge's death "very hard, so much so that some thought his mind would be impaired." He was plunged into a "terrible Melancholy," a manic depression reminiscent of the hopeless torments of the predestinarian Baptists over the impossibility of controlling their futures. He moaned to William Greene, "I can never be reconciled to have the snow — rains & storms to beat on her grave," and his grieving became so frantic that "Mr. Lincolns friends were . . . Compelled to keep watch and ward" over him for "a week or two" to prevent "derangement or suicide."

One of his New Salem neighbors, Elizabeth Abell, tried to distract Lincoln by introducing him to her Kentucky-born sister, Mary Owens, and Lincoln found her sufficiently "intelligent and agreeable" to propose marriage on the rebound. "She was jovial, social, loved wit & humor — had a liberal English education & was considered wealthy," and above all she and Lincoln were Whigs who "in politics . . . saw eye to eye." But once he moved to Springfield in 1837 and focused his attention on the larger political and professional vista now opening up before him, Mary Owens rapidly lost appeal for him. But rather than bring on himself the onus of desertion, he struggled to offer her a way of backing out on him. In one of the most contorted letters he ever wrote, Lincoln suggested that Owens might be "mistaken in regard to what my real feelings towards you are" and therefore she should feel free to "drop the subject, dismiss your thoughts (if you ever had any) from me forever, and leave this letter unanswered, without calling forth one accusing murmur from me." He was, as he put it, eager "in all cases to do right, and most particularly so, in all cases with women," but he was clearly most eager to have Mary Owens do the deserting rather than himself. Owens was wise enough to read Lincoln's ambivalence for what it was. "I thought Mr. Lincoln was deficient in those little links which make up the great chain of womans happiness," she wrote thirty years later, and she finally refused any renewal of the engagement in the spring of 1838.

"I have come to the conclusion never again to think of marrying," Lincoln wrote after his breakup with Mary Owens. But it was exactly this loud affirmation of bachelorhood, together with his odd combination of raw intellectual talent and pathetic humility about his lack of education, which made Lincoln irresistible to Springfield's society matrons and match-makers. Once again, Lincoln had John Todd Stuart to thank. Two of Stuart's well-to-do Kentucky-born Todd cousins, Elizabeth and Frances, had married into the cream of the Springfield Whig Junto, Frances wedding the physician William Wallace and Elizabeth marrying Ninian Wirt Edwards, the son of the former territorial governor of Illinois and a well-heeled Whig who hated the Democrats "as the devil is said to hate holy water." It was a hatred Lincoln was happy to share, and Stuart drew him away from his fellow free-thinkers in Matheny's office and into the whirl of parties and dinners that cemented Whig political loyalties in Springfield. Ninian Edwards smilingly conceded that Lincoln was a "mighty rough man" to be part of the Edwards social circle, but Elizabeth Edwards and Eliza Browning "discovered his great merits" and so the Junto indulged Lincoln the way one might indulge an uncouth but interesting relative. And it was at one of the Edwards's galas in the fall of 1839, behind the flutter of fans and the Todd cousins' knowing glances, that Lincoln was first introduced to another Todd cousin, Mary.

Mary was Elizabeth and Frances's younger sister. Born in 1818, she was one of six children born to Robert and Eliza Todd, slave-holding plantation owners from Lexington, Kentucky. Unlike most of the landed gentry of the bluegrass, Robert Todd had made his fortune in merchandising, and he gave his personal and political allegiances to Henry Clay and the Whigs. Eliza Todd, however, died in childbirth in 1825, and a year later Robert Todd remarried. Eight-year-old Mary did not get along with her new stepmother, nor did her siblings, and Mary was bundled off to a series of boarding schools where she learned French and developed the high-strung assertiveness that marked her as her father's child. In 1837, Mary escaped to Springfield to visit with her married sisters, and two years later, emotionally mauled by "the relentless persecution of a stepmother," she took up Elizabeth Edwards's invitation to stay on in Springfield indefinitely. She was nineteen years old, "imperious, proud, aristocratic, insolent, witty, and bitter," but also petite and "very pretty" with "clear blue eyes, long lashes, light brown hair with a glint of bronze and a lovely complexion. Her figure was beautiful and no old master modeled a more perfect arm and hand." And she was clearly hoping to pick a husband from off the line of Springfield's eligible Whig bachelors.

That she might pick Abraham Lincoln must have seemed as remote as Neptune. Lincoln towered a foot over Mary's dainty figure, and "could not hold a lengthy conversation with a lady, was not sufficiently educated and intelligent in the female line to do so." But even knowing that, Elizabeth Edwards guessed that Lincoln "was . . . a rising man," and it was sister Elizabeth who probably first introduced the pair at an assembly ball shortly after Mary's permanent move to Springfield in 1839 and "advised Mary at first to marry L." Actually, they shared much more than met the eye: both had been scarred by the loss of mothers at an early age, both lacked fortunes of their own and were fired by ambition to get them, and both were ardent Whigs. And although Mary cheerfully flirted with all of the young Whig politicos who turned up at the Edwards's dinners, it was Lincoln she set her cap for. "Miss Todd was thoroughly in earnest [in] her endeavors to get Mr. Lincoln," recalled Orville Hickman Browning. "I always thought then and have thought ever since that in her affair with Mr. Lincoln, Mary Todd did most of the courting." Elizabeth Edwards remembered that "I have happened in the room where they were sitting often and often, and Mary led the conversation."

> He was charmed with Mary's wit and fascinated with her quick sagacity, her will, her nature, and culture. . . . Lincoln would listen and gaze on her as if drawn by some superior power, irresistibly so; he listened, never scarcely said a word.

The parlor conversations were followed by dinners and parties and excursions with friends and finally, by the fall of 1840, while Lincoln was stumping lower Illinois for the Harrison presidential campaign, some kind of understanding between the two was reached.

What happened next is one of the murkiest episodes in Lincoln's life, for sometime at the end of November or the beginning of December, Lincoln abandoned the agreement and plunged himself into another near-suicidal despair. There is good reason for the murkiness of this incident. The close of the year 1840 was a tempestuous one for Lincoln: the legislative program he had guided ever since 1837 was now in ruins; his roommate since 1837, Joshua Speed, sold off his interest in the Ellis store on January 1, 1841, and returned to Kentucky (his father had died and his relatives wanted him to take up the family business); and Stuart, who had been elected to Congress in 1838 and re-elected in 1840, was now proposing that he and Lincoln accept the obvious and dissolve their law partnership. With the partnership ending and Lincoln's political career in jeopardy, self-doubts about his "ability & Capacity to please and support a wife" were not surprising, especially with a wife who would expect to live on a level with her well-married sisters.

But there is other, darker evidence that suggests that Lincoln had in fact realized, once the prospect of marrying Mary Todd became a real one, that he had committed himself to a woman he did not love; that what he loved was the Edwards circle and the Whig coterie, not Mary, and that he had mistaken the one for the other; that he had been maneuvered into a promise he now dreaded. "In the winter of 40 & 41 — he was very unhappy about his engagement," recalled Joshua Speed, "not being entirely satisfied that his *heart* was going with his hand." To make matters worse, Lincoln returned from his electioneering for Harrison in November to meet yet another Edwards relative, Ninian Edwards's eighteen-year-old cousin, Matilda Edwards, who was in Springfield with her father, Cyrus Edwards of Alton, for a special session of the legislature. Speed was convinced that Lincoln was smitten with her. "During Lincoln's Courtship with Miss Todd," Speed wrote in 1865, "he, Lincoln, fell in love with a Miss Edwards." Orville Hickman Browning agreed that Lincoln "fell desperately in love" with Matilda Edwards; and Springfield neighbors whispered that Lincoln "fell desperately in love with her and found that he was not so much attached to Mary as he thought." Whatever the circumstances, this much is clear: Lincoln found himself poised between the enormity of a marriage he was no longer sure he wanted, and insulting the first family of Springfield's Whig aristocracy at just the moment when it could ruin his career permanently.

He grasped the second of those nettles, and confessing to Mary Todd that he "did love Miss Edwards," Lincoln begged for a release. The stress of the encounter had greatly disturbed Lincoln's equanimity, and "in his lunacy he declared he hated Mary and loved Miss Edwards." Mary agonizingly gave him the release, but Lincoln experienced no relief because of it. If anything, this set the stage for yet another round of "terrible Melancholy." Lincoln now found himself playing the worst of all roles in his dramatic imagination, the role of a capricious and willful deserter. Abandonment was exactly what the primitive Calvinism of his youth had taught him to fear the most; it was what he had suffered in the deaths of his mother, his sister, and Ann Rutledge; it was what he had tried hardest to avoid in the case of Mary Owens. Moreover, his Paine-ite "skepticism" suggested that this capriciousness was exactly what made belief in the Christian God unreasonable; a reasonable skeptic had to improve on Christianity, not fall below it. And the cultural logic of Whiggism had no other way to disarm Democratic criticisms of the profit-worship of the marketplace except by the imposition of the most rigid demonstrations of honesty and reliability, something that Lincoln now seemed to have forgotten.

His great speech the year before against the "independent Treasury" had concluded with a confession that nothing raised his spirits higher than the image of "the cause of my country, deserted by all the world beside, and I standing boldly and alone and hurling defiance at her victorious oppressors." Now, he realized that this was exactly the sin he had committed against Mary Todd, and Orville Hickman Browning became convinced that "his conscience troubled him dreadfully for the supposed injustice he had done, and the supposed violation of his word which he had committed." Lincoln sank into a despondency so deep that by the end of December "Lincoln went crazy," to the point where Speed "had to remove razors from his room" and "take away all knives and other such dangerous things." Another member of the Edwards circle thought Lincoln looked "reduced and emaciated in appearance and seems scarcely to possess strength enough to speak above a whisper." Even as late as the end of January, 1841, Lincoln still felt "that I am now the most miserable man living. If what I feel were equally distributed to the whole human family, there would not be one cheerful face on the earth."

By the spring, however, Lincoln was able to sign a new partnership agreement with one of the most prominent of Springfield's attorneys, Stephen Logan, and that August, Joshua Speed invited Lincoln to spend a restorative vacation with him on his family's plantation near Louisville. Now that Speed himself was engaged, Lincoln was able to bask in his friend's happiness and even dream of being "entirely happy" again. "But the never-absent idea, that there is *one* still unhappy whom I have contributed to make so," Lincoln added, "That still kills my soul." This was not so much for Mary Todd's sake as for the sake of his own rectitude. "Before I resolve to do one thing or the other, I must regain my confidence in my own ability to keep my resolves when they are made," Lincoln wrote to Speed in July. "In that ability, you know, I once prided myself as the only, or at least the chief, gem of my character; that gem I lost — how, and when, you too well know." There was, therefore, only one honorable path open, and little more than a year later, several mutual friends (including fellow-Whig John Hardin and the wife of his editor, Simeon Francis) began arranging delicate opportunities which threw Lincoln and Mary Todd "unexpectedly together" and produced a reconciliation.

Mary, for her part, was "greatly mortified by Mr. Lincoln's strange conduct," but unlike Mary Owens, she was unwilling to let Lincoln go. She "wanted L. Terribly and worked, played her cards, through Mrs. Francis's hands." Elizabeth Edwards doubted disapprovingly "that it was really a love affair between Mr. L. and Mary T, but think it was through mutual friends that the marriage was made up." Mary's most effective strategy, however, was Lincoln himself. "The question in his mind," recalled Turner King, "was 'Have I incurred any obligation to marry that woman,'" and Mary's blunt answer was to tell "L. that he was in honor bound to marry her." The result, from that point onward, was morally unavoidable. On November 4, 1842, Mary Todd and Abraham Lincoln were married in the parlor of the Edwards mansion by Charles Dresser, the rector of St. Paul's Church, where Mary and the Edwardses attended services.

But there would always remain some doubt in the minds of Lincoln's friends about what kind of marriage this was. At worst, it represented a cynical decision by Lincoln to shore up his access to Whig political power: John Todd Stuart was convinced that "the marriage of Lincoln to Miss Todd was a policy Match all around," and James Matheny, who was drafted by Lincoln to serve as best man at the wedding, recalled that Lincoln "looked and acted as if he were going to the slaughter — That Lincoln often told him directly and indirectly that he was driven into the marriage . . . by the Edwards family." At best, the marriage was a costly reaffirmation of Lincoln's pursuit of loyalty and fear of desertion. William Herndon claimed that "Lincoln self-sacrificed himself rather than be charged with dishonor," and Orville

Hickman Browning echoed that claim when he told John Nicolay that "his conscience was greatly worked up by the supposed pain and injury which this . . . had inflicted upon" Mary.

> In this affair of his courtship, he undoubtedly felt that he had made [a mistake] in having engaged himself to Miss Todd. But having done so, he felt himself in honor bound to act in perfect good faith towards her — and that faith compelled him to fulfill his engagement towards her. . . . I always have doubted whether, had circumstances left him entirely free to act upon his own impulses, he would have voluntarily made proposals of marriage to Miss Todd.

In the absence of any professed religion, the satisfaction of loyalty was the most obvious moral surrogate for Christianity, and loyalty was no small consideration to a Whig who ran his life on the niceties of reason and order. "I have always regarded him (Mr. L.) as one of the most conscientious men I have ever known," Browning recalled. "I have never in our intercourse known him to swerve one hair's breadth from what he considered the strict line of duty." Only in marriage to Mary Todd could he reassure himself that his lapse into "Melancholy" had been only a lapse, and not an indication that self-transformation was an illusion.

And it could not be denied that satisfying the expectations of loyalty was also important to a Whig who, notwithstanding the political reverses he had endured in the state legislature, still nursed ambitions for better things. Lincoln had already heard, on the basis of the 1840 census, that Illinois would go through a congressional redistricting which would create a new congressional seat in central Illinois, including not only Sangamon County but also the Whig-rich counties along the Illinois River. Two months after the wedding, Lincoln began delicately informing prominent Whigs in the newly proposed Seventh Congressional District that, since "your county and ours are almost sure to be placed in the same congressional district . . . I would like to be its Representative" in the United States Congress.

3 The Doctrine of Necessity

To all appearances, Lincoln's life settled down rapidly after the turmoil surrounding his marriage to Mary Todd. A daguerreotype made of Lincoln sometime in the late 1840s shows how laboriously Lincoln had scrubbed his image clean of any association with the farm: the look is confident, almost cocky, the hair is slicked glisteningly into place, the shirt and silk tie and vest are immaculate, the broad-lapelled frock coat appears fresh and uncreased. His new partnership with Stephen Logan linked him to another influential Whig politician and brought Lincoln a generous share of state supreme court appeals cases. A new federal bankruptcy law threw a tremendous amount of bankruptcy business their way — seventy-seven cases, one of the largest bankruptcy dockets in Illinois — and opened an inside track for them to buy up foreclosed lands for a fraction of their real value. "Few [people] appear at the sale of property, and the judgement creditor usually bids it in at half its value," Lincoln noted, and even if "the owner supposed that he would be able to redeem," he "was frequently unable, and his property was thus sacrificed. . . ." With a new family and the last of his New Salem debts still to pay off, Lincoln was chary of putting his hand too deeply into buying up foreclosed properties. As he told Joseph Gillespie, he "had no capacity whatever for speculation and never attempted it." But property did come his way all the same: his militia service in the Black Hawk War brought him a federal bounty in the form of 120 acres in Crawford County and another 40 acres in the Iowa Territory. And Lincoln did not mind offering his inside track to others: Joshua Speed, for instance, used Lincoln to buy up foreclosed houses and lots which "must be worth much more than the debt."

Lincoln also remained heavily involved in Whig politics. William Henry Harrison's great Whig victory in the 1840 presidential race quickly turned to ashes when the elderly Harrison contracted pneumonia after his inauguration, and died after only one month in office. His death exposed a ghastly Whig political mistake. Vice President John Tyler, although a Democrat, had only been added to the ticket to lure the votes of other Democrats disillusioned with Martin Van Buren. But he now became president and proceeded to stymie every Whig congressional initiative. The result was, as Lincoln remarked, that "by the course of Mr. Tyler the policy of our opponents has continued in operation." This only made clearer to the Whigs that the 1844 election had to be headed by Whig candidates in whom everyone could be confident, and so they turned for the third time to Lincoln's "beau-ideal of a statesman," Henry Clay.

The Illinois Whigs, as the minority party in the state, began laying out an election strategy for a Clay presidential victory as early as the spring of 1843, and Lincoln offered to a state Whig convention in Springfield the resolutions which became the Illinois Whigs' election banner: "That a tariff of duties on imported goods" was "indispensably necessary to the prosperity of the American people," that "a National Bank . . . is highly necessary and proper to the establishment and maintenance of a sound currency," and "That the distribution of the proceeds of the sales of Public Lands . . . accords with the best interest of the Nation, and particularly with those of the State of Illinois." He also composed (in collaboration with Logan and Albert Taylor Bledsoe) a public campaign circular which reinforced the call for "a tariff of duties upon foreign importations" and "the necessity and propriety of a National Bank" despite the "incomprehensible jargon . . . often urged against the constitutionality of this measure." At Whig organizing meetings around the state that fall, Lincoln rang the changes on "the three prominent principles of the Whig Party — The Tariff, a

103

sound and uniform National Currency and the Distribution of the proceeds of the Public Lands." And with an eye on voter mobilization, Lincoln vigorously endorsed a system of Whig district conventions, based on the Illinois congressional districts, to streamline the nomination of candidates, curtail factional infighting, and prevent desertions from the party standard. "When did the whigs ever fail," Lincoln confidently asked, as a man who understood all too well the consequences of desertion, "if they were fully aroused and united."

Even Lincoln's private life as a married man seemed to offer him a kind of domestic satisfaction he had only imagined to be "dreams of Elysium far exceeding all that any earthly thing can realize." His marriage, as he bashfully confessed to another lawyer, "is a matter of profound wonder to me." The newlyweds took over rented quarters in a new wing of the Globe Tavern which had just been vacated by Mary's sister, Frances Wallace, where boarding, to Lincoln's surprised satisfaction, "only costs four dollars a week." He cheerfully reported to Joshua Speed in February, 1843, that "Mary is very well and continues her old sentiments of friendship for you," but by March it was obvious that Mary was pregnant and Lincoln began hinting to Speed "about the prospect of your having a namesake at our house." In late July he told Speed that "We are but two, as yet," but on August 1, 1843, Mary gave birth to a son, who was named, not for Speed, but for her father, Robert Todd. Lincoln promptly moved them out of the Globe, first into a rented cottage on Fourth Street in Springfield, and then in January, 1844, into a one-and-a-half story frame house on the corner of Eighth and Jackson streets which would be the Lincoln family home for the next seventeen years. He had finally paid off all but a handful of his New Salem debts, and he now bought the house (from Charles Dresser, the Episcopal priest who had married him) for $1,200 in cash and a small town lot that Ninian Edwards had conveyed to Lincoln, probably to complete the sale. Two years later, a second son, named Edward Baker for Lincoln's long-time Whig ally in the legislature, was born. The Lincoln family circle seemed complete.

And yet, below this satisfying surface, Lincoln remained restless and unfulfilled. The old friends of his early Springfield days grumbled that Lincoln had married up into "a proud and eresticratic family, Meaning the Edwds & Todds." He tried to appear amused at the idea that he "had married in the aristocracy" ("he laughed Verry hartially" when Abner Ellis told him this), but it wounded him sufficiently to take James Matheny "to the woods and than and there Said in reference to L's marriage in the Aristocracy — 'Jim — I am now and always shall be the same Abe Lincoln that I always was — .'" He certainly did not feel born to a place in the aristocracy. His "want of a college education" weighed on him ("Those who have it should thank God for it," he told a New York reporter in 1861), and fear of backwoods mannerisms drove him to add advice books, like Mary G. Chandler's *The Elements of Character*, to his reading. (Some of Chandler's advice — "There is no station in life where there is not a constant demand for the exercise of charity" — evidently had long innings with Lincoln.) And he certainly did not feel that he was commanding an aristocratic income. Logan only awarded Lincoln one-third of the partnership's overall fee income, and while it netted Lincoln as much as $1,500 in a year, it was still a smaller proportion of the partnership's fees than Stuart had given him.

It did not help that Logan was an unlovable "little dried and shrivelled up man" and something of a legal prima donna who found Lincoln amateurish and pedestrian in his pleadings. "I don't think he studied very much," Logan sniffed, and "although he got to be a pretty good lawyer . . . his general knowledge of law was never very formidable." Logan also considered that Lincoln "was not much of a reader" and Logan later took credit for tutoring Lincoln, so that "after Lincoln went in with me he turned in to try to know more and studied how to prepare his cases." Logan's condescension must have grated on Lincoln, and therefore there was no argument from Lincoln when Logan proposed to dissolve the partnership in 1844 so that Logan could form a new one with his son, David. "Lincoln was perhaps by that time quite willing to begin on his own account," Logan remembered, "so we talked the matter over and dissolved the partnership amicably and in friendship."

Lincoln turned almost at once, not to another senior lawyer like Stuart or Logan, but to a promising younger attorney in Springfield named William Henry Herndon. Herndon, who had clerked for Lincoln and Logan and who had just been licensed to practice in Sangamon County that November, was a free-thinking, boozy bohemian whose excitableness and wild energy contrasted sharply with Lincoln's self-conscious intensity. But Herndon was also a Whig, and a leader of a younger generation of ambitious Sangamon Whigs that Lincoln wanted as allies. Herndon was also a tremendous reader, who although born (like Lincoln) in Kentucky, found his intellectual interests "turned *NewEnglandwards*." As such, Herndon became a walking review of books for Lincoln. "You have been a laborious, studious young man," Lincoln complimented him in 1848. "You are far better informed on almost all subjects than I have ever been."

Herndon returned the compliment by filling up the law office he and Lincoln shared on the second floor of the Tinsley store building (on the south side of the state capitol square) with his own dearbought copies of Thomas Carlyle's and Ralph Waldo Emerson's essays, Theodore Parker's and Henry Ward Beecher's sermons, the French "common-sense" realist Victor Cousin and his English counterpart Sir William Hamilton, the biblical criticism of D. F. Strauss and Ernst Renan, the left-Hegelianism of Ludwig Feuerbach, the materialist historical scholarship of Thomas Henry Buckle, and, later in the 1850s (when the office moved to the west side of the square, beside the store where Lincoln had once roomed with Joshua Speed), the evolutionary sociology of Sir Herbert Spencer. In addition to the books, Herndon stocked the office with the preeminent English liberal magazine, *The Westminster Review,* and its American counterparts, *The North American Review* and *The Southern Literary Messenger,* plus a sampling of major Whig newspapers, from the Richmond *Enquirer* to the weekly national edition of Horace Greeley's radical *New York Tribune.* This was the print culture "Lincoln had access to . . . and frequently read parts of the volumes." Lincoln was not, as Herndon found, "a general reader," but he was "a persistent thinker, and a profound analyzer of the subject which engaged his attention," and he readily slipped "into a philosophic discussion, and sometimes on religious questions and sometimes on this question and on that."

Lincoln lingered longest over books on political economy. "Theoretically, Mr. Lincoln was strong on financial questions," recalled Shelby Cullom. "On political economy he was great." "Lincoln, I think, liked political economy, the study of it," remembered Herndon, and Herndon noted Lincoln's special interest in John Stuart Mill's twovolume *Principles of Political Economy* (1848). Like Lincoln, Mill spoke for a generation of restless middle-class English intellectuals who sensed the power that commerce had placed in their hands and resented the deadening restraints the English landed aristocracy tried to place on that power through its lopsided dominance of Parliament and the restrictive agrarian legislation of the Corn Laws. Lincoln also found much to admire in Mill's religious skepticism, wedded as it was to a secularized Calvinistic belief in the overpowering influence of a "philosophical necessity" in human affairs. Neither could make sense of a world which was governed by "necessity" and yet also a world in which God judged men for the actions they took under necessity's influence. "I will call no being good, who is not what I mean when I apply that epithet to my fellow creatures," Mill wrote, "and if such a being can sentence me to Hell for not so calling him, to Hell I will go."

Yet, among American variations on Mill, Lincoln most admired the work of the evangelical Baptist and Brown University moral philosopher Francis Wayland. "Lincoln ate up, digested, and assimilated" Wayland's *Elements of Political Economy* (1837), finding in it an almost perfect marriage between Whig market economics and Protestant Whig moralism. In the marketplace of commodities, Wayland rejected any notion that objects have inherent values apart from "the *nature* and *the number* of the desires which [they] can gratify" and the labor that goes into the making of those objects. This creates an unpredictability in value which can swing drastically, but the unpredictability also involves opportunity for the nimble and talented to acquire wealth. Hence, in Wayland's most telling anti-agrarian illustration, a "farmer enters upon a new and untilled land," and after producing "the necessities of life," turns to commercial farming. "There would, therefore, arise a great demand for mechanical labor," and so "some portion" of the farmers "abandoned farming" and "must become merchants." Those who can amass that wealth can employ others for wages; and yet, because wage labor is only one stage on the path to commercial success, Wayland wanted there to be no anxiety that wage labor was in any way inferior to agricultural labor, or in conflict with the employers themselves. "One who owns the capital, unites in production with another or others, who perform the labor," Wayland wrote, "and there are just proportions to be observed between the wages of labor and the wages of capital."

This "harmonious co-operation" of capitalists and wage laborers was illustrated even more dramatically in another of Lincoln's preferred authors, the prolific Henry Carey, whose *Essay on the Rate of*

Wages (1835), *Principles of Political Economy* (1840), *The Past, the Present, and the Future* (1848), and *The Harmony of Interests, Agricultural, Manufacturing, and Commercial* (1850) were also Lincoln favorites. Like Lincoln, Carey espoused a labor theory of value, a high protective tariff, and the confidence of the Whigs that capital and labor could be economic partners rather than competitors. Association and competition were the natural facts of life, Carey argued: "The more power of association, the greater is the tendency toward development." Under the shield of a protective tariff, agriculture and industry could complement each other, and the payers of wages and the earners of them could coexist in "mutual advantage" and "improvements."

Alongside Whig political economy, Lincoln also "made Geology and other sciences a special study." Although geology might seem an odd prospect for an Illinois lawyer, geology had become a subject of particular intellectual anxiety in the Anglo-American world of the 1830s, especially after Sir Charles Lyell's three-volume *Principles of Geology* (1830-33) produced unsettling evidence from the record of fossils and erosion that the earth's geology was the product of long-duration build-ups rather than the sudden creation or the catastrophic flood described in the first book of the Bible. Lyell's conclusions, more than the scientific details of his geology text, may have piqued Lincoln's religious skepticism; it certainly would account for the interest Lincoln showed in Robert Chambers's *Vestiges of the Natural History of Creation* (1844), which took Lyell's notions of a steady, gradual development of the earth's geology and applied them to living organisms. "About the year 1846-47 Mr. Lincoln borrowed . . . and read, thoroughly read and studied, *The Vestiges of Creation*," Herndon recalled, and Chambers's willingness to use Lyell's steady-state notion of geological change as a model for explaining how organic life was also the product of gradual natural development, rather than a special creation by God, made Lincoln "a firm believer in the theory of development" — an evolutionist of sorts, in other words, even before Darwin's theory of evolution arrived in 1859.

Herndon's most practical contribution to Lincoln's reading touched on law. Like Logan, Herndon found that Lincoln was "not well read in the elementary" law textbooks and "never studied law books unless a case was on hand for contradiction," and then Lincoln would look only for specific citations he could use in that case.

Herndon took up the task of being Lincoln's citation-finder, and Lincoln relied on Herndon to "collect all sorts of cases and authorities for him" to use in trial pleadings. The basic resources Lincoln had for this research were a hefty collection of textbooks — over "200 volumes of law as well as miscellaneous books" according to one office visitor in 1858 — and several series of periodical case digests (like the *United States Digest* and the *Illinois Digest*) which gathered together short summaries of important cases on both the state and federal level, and which saved Lincoln and Herndon the forbidding task of trudging through volume after volume of full-text court reports. The textbooks included the cream of the Americanized Blackstone authors, especially James Kent and Joseph Story. Lincoln also used the state supreme court law library in the state Capitol, across the square from the law office, where Springfield's lawyers "were studying their cases and making abstracts and briefs," and where Lincoln would frequently "break up all reading, abstract, and brief business" in the evenings with story-telling.

It was usually only in appeals work, when he was not pressed for time, that Lincoln himself would "gather up the facts of the case, the issues and the law arising thereon, abstracts of the case." At the appellate level, Herndon believed, "Lincoln was great truly and indeed." Otherwise, in simple first-hearings, Lincoln preferred to "make his selections, and prepare his arguments" on the basis of citations supplied by Herndon, "to the great disgust often no doubt, of Mr. Herndon" (said one observer) "who saw so much of the material collected by him thrown aside as useless."

If there was such "disgust" on Herndon's part, he rarely showed it. Herndon frankly admired Lincoln as "a shrewd, sagacious, long-headed man," who managed to be "a cunning fox" while also possessing "unlimited integrity, always telling the exact truth, and always doing the honest thing at all times and under all circumstances." And Lincoln returned Herndon's loyalty in greater depth than Herndon could have at first imagined by praising his partner as "the one man who will stick to me to the end." But even Herndon, who thought Lincoln "as near a perfect man as God generally makes," acknowledged that this "perfect" man was also exceedingly difficult to understand. "He was not a very social man . . . not spontaneous in his feelings," Herndon admitted; there was always, even in his best moods, a shield

in Lincoln's manner, and from the time Herndon first became associated with Lincoln in 1841, he noticed an increasing tendency in Lincoln towards "melancholy" and withdrawal from even "his close and
intimate neighbors among whom he associated."

The appearance of "melancholy" was not a new feature in Lincoln's character, and it had cropped out before in near-suicidal depres-
sions over the death of Ann Rutledge and the crisis over his marriage.
Those who were close to him were aware that his "Highlarity," even in
the New Salem days, overlay a deep streak of despair, disappointment, and worthlessness. He told Robert Wilson while in the legislature that "although he appeared to enjoy life rapturously, Still he was
the victim of terrible melancholly" and "when by himself, he told me
that he was so overcome with mental depression, that he never dare
carry a knife in his pocket." But at least in his twenties, the melancholy
was sufficiently buried that it could escape notice by most observers.
One Indiana neighbor recalled that "While Abe was in Indiana he was
or seemed to be always cheerful and happy," and his almost-sister-in-
law in New Salem, Elizabeth Abell, thought he "was always social and
lively." He had usually impressed his Springfield circle in the 1830s as
being "a man of very uniform character and temper" who was "sometimes mirthful and sometimes sad, but both moods quickly passed
away and left him always the same man."

But after the early 1840s, this began to change. Henry C. Whitney,
who first met Lincoln in the mid-1850s, thought that no feature of Lincoln's character was "so marked, obvious and ingrained as his mysterious and profound melancholy," and even John Todd Stuart began to
see Lincoln as "a hopeless victim of melancholy." His sister-in-law,
Elizabeth Edwards, found him "a cold Man — had no affection — was
not Social — was abstracted — thoughtful." According to David Davis, even "his Stories — jokes &c." were done "to whistle off sadness
and are no evidences of sociality." Once having engineered the relocation of the state capitol to Springfield, Lincoln involved himself in
none of the local community-based societies and organizations — the
militia or the fire companies or fraternal societies such as the Masons.
"Mr. Lincoln I do not think belonged to any Secret Society," recalled
Abner Ellis, "neither Masonic nor Oddfellows." And when he was
asked "if he was not a Mason," Lincoln's answer was "I do not belong
to any society except it be for the Good of my Country" — which was

to say, the Whig party. Even out on the circuit, Lincoln became known for unpredictable withdrawals into depression. "On such occasions he was wont to sit by the fire," remembered Lawrence Weldon, "Muse, ponder and soliloquize, whisper no doubt by that strange psychological influence which is so poetically described by Poe in the raven."

Some of this melancholy, Herndon believed, arose simply from the habits of intense preoccupation with law matters Lincoln cultivated over almost a decade of legal practice. "Lincoln thought . . . that there were no limitations to the endurance of his mental and vital forces," and he would fling himself at cases or problems "with a severe, persistent, continuous, and terrible" concentration that produced "physical and mental exhaustion, a nervous morbidity and spectral illusions, irritability, melancholy, and despair." Stephen Logan agreed that practicing law pressed the high spirits out of Lincoln. "While he was down there at New Salem I think his time was mainly given to fun and social enjoyment and in the amusements of the people he came daily in contact with," recalled Logan, but "after he came here to Springfield however he got rid to a great degree of this disposition."

Others dared to put a finger on a more painful reason why Lincoln was developing into "a sad looking man" whose "melancholy dript from him as he walked," and that had to do with his life with Mary Todd Lincoln. Born and bred to a comfortable life, with slaves and servants on hand to perform menial tasks, Mary was ill-suited to take up life as the wife of a penny-wise middle-class lawyer who made a point of milking his own cow and sawing his own wood. "If Mr. Lincoln should happen to die," Mary was heard to complain, "his spirit will never find me living outside the boundaries of a slave state." Even though Robert Smith Todd actually handed enough money every year to hire domestic help, living with a man so abstracted and detached must have been a trial for the nervous and well-educated Mary, and it gradually degenerated into what Herndon called a "domestic *hell.*"

It did not help, either, that Lincoln's law practice took him out of Springfield and away from Mary for as much as twenty weeks of the year, that she found his new law partner wild and immature, and that even her own sisters in Springfield could not conceal their opinion that she had made a big mistake in marrying a man whom Elizabeth Edwards described as "odd and wholly irregular." Henry Whitney agreed that Lincoln "could not make any women happy . . . he was too much allied to his intellect to get down to the plane of domestic relations." "In her domestic troubles I have always sympathized with her," Herndon wrote years later. "The world does not know what she bore and the history of the bearing."

For all of this, Mary Todd Lincoln extracted her own measure of marital revenge. High-strung and easily irritated like so many of her Todd relatives, Mary soon displayed a temper that could turn her into what Herndon called "a tigress" and could turn the Lincoln marriage into "a domestic hell on earth." Turner King described her as "a hellion — a she devil" who "vexed — & harrowed the soul out of that good man." Her tantrums exceeded what might be otherwise thought of as simple outbursts of exasperation: Springfield neighbors "heard Mrs. L. yelling & screaming at L. as if in hysterics," saw her attempt to assault him, sometimes with stove wood or books or broom handles, or noticed that Lincoln would get up in the middle of the night "and went whistling through the streets & alleys till day" to escape her hectoring criticisms of his clothes or manners. Being "always rigidly frugal" in money matters, Lincoln inadvertently tipped Mary over into miserliness in bargaining with shopkeepers, and her early habits of dealing with servants as slaves made her an intolerable mistress to the string of immigrant Irish girls hired to do the kitchen chores.

With that reputation, Mary could hardly ever keep domestic help in the house for any length of time unless Lincoln surreptitiously slipped them bribes to endure his wife's abuse. When Lincoln hired an immigrant teenager named Margaret Ryan to help Mary, Lincoln "told her he would pay M. 75 cents more than Mrs. L. to stay there — not to fuss with Mrs. L." John Mendonza remembered Mary trying to haggle his father into offering three pints of blackberries for ten cents a pint rather than fifteen. "Mr. Lincoln put 15 cents in my hand and told Mrs. Lincoln to take them and put them away. Mrs. Lincoln did not like that." This was an evasion of the problem, rather than a solution. But it was of a piece with a larger pattern of Lincoln's responses to Mary. James Gourley remembered that when Mary flew into her rages, "Lincoln paid no attention — would pick up one of his Children & walked off — would laugh at her — pay no Earthly attention to her when in that wild furious condition." Between his own unwillingness to confront Mary's emotional problems and Mary's own inability to control her manic frenzies, the Lincoln household soon became what Herndon called "an ice cave" with "no soul, fire, cheer or fun in it."

Still, Lincoln's "burning, scorching hell" at home was not the only problem that preyed on his mind in the 1840s. His labors for the Whig party in the election of William Henry Harrison in 1840 not only failed to secure a Whig presidency and bring him the usual reward of salaried political office, but actually resulted in John Tyler and "the appointment of a set of drones . . . who have never spent a dollar or lifted a finger in the fight." The 1844 election was even more disappointing. Despite the nomination of Henry Clay, "our gallant HARRY OF THE WEST," and Lincoln's own efforts as a campaign speaker at Clay rallies in southern and central Illinois and southern Indiana, the Whigs were handed a close electoral defeat by James Knox Polk, a personal protégé of Andrew Jackson. Not only did his "beau ideal of a statesman" go down to defeat, but he became convinced that the defeat had been largely triggered by the defection of northeastern Whigs to an anti-slavery splinter party, the Liberty Party. Displays of political desertion infuriated him, since Lincoln treated them as one more example of the disloyalty his Whig soul abhorred. During an electioneering stump for Clay through Illinois, he singled out a turncoat Whig, William May, for savage sarcasm. May had complained that a local Whig "election pole," erected for Whig audiences to rally around, was as hollow as the Whigs' hearts. Lincoln snapped that "the hollow place at the butt of the pole was where Colonel May had crawled out of the Whig party, and his party friends now propose to close it up so that the colonel could never return."

The discouragement he felt over the 1844 campaign was magnified when he was recruited by Indiana Whigs to speak before Clay Whig clubs in southern Indiana, including his old neighborhood at Gentryville. He met many of his old acquaintances "at the cross-road voting place," but what struck him forcibly was how many more were long since dead and gone. "In the fall of 1844, thinking I might aid some to carry the state of Indiana for Mr. Clay, I went into the neighborhood in that State in which I was raised, where my mother and only sister were buried," Lincoln wrote a year and a half later. "That part of the country is, within itself, as unpoetical as any spot of earth; but still, seeing it and its objects and inhabitants aroused feelings in me which were certainly poetry. . . ." And certainly enough, he began writing an awkward but lengthy poem, fixed in ashen imagery, on death:

> The friends I left that parting day,
>   How changed, as time has sped!
> Young childhood grown, strong manhood gray,
>   And half of all are dead.
>
> I hear the loved survivors tell
>   How nought from death could save,
> Till every sound appears a knell,
>   And every spot a grave. . . .
>
> I range the fields with pensive tread,
>   And pace the hollow rooms,
> And feel (companion of the dead)
>   I'm living in the tombs.

Better still, a year afterward, in 1845, he came upon the Scottish poet William Knox's poem "Mortality," a poem he had probably read when he first arrived in New Salem, but which he now met "in a straggling form in a newspaper." It summed up Lincoln's darkening climb in life so well that it became his "favorite of favorites," to be recited over and over again for the rest of his life (so much so that some people actually thought Lincoln had written it himself). It, too, oozed a sense of melancholy and futility.

> O why should the spirit of mortal be proud!
> Like a swift flying meteor — a fast flying cloud —
> A flash of the lightning — a break of the wave,
> He passeth from life to his rest in the grave. . . .
>
> 'Tis the wink of an eye, tis the draught of a breath
> From the blossom of health to the paleness of death —
> From the gilded saloon to the bier and the shroud —
> O why sould the spirit of mortal be proud?

The death of old friends, of family, of his youth were matched by what looked like the death of his career in the state legislature. The influence he had wielded as architect of the great internal improvements program in the late 1830s had seriously ebbed. Squatter farmers on Illinois's federal lands bitterly resented Lincoln's calls for distribution of the public lands to the states, since this usually meant eviction by the state, while farmers with endangered mortgages or dangling credit remembered Lincoln only as the friend of banks. He made no effort to run for re-election for the state legislature in 1842, hoping as he did that the congressional redistricting which created the Seventh District would also make him the obvious Whig candidate to fill the district's seat in a late-term election in 1843. But the Sangamon County Whigs instead put forward Lincoln's ally, Edward Baker, and Lincoln was incensed when it turned out that Baker's people had been the ones responsible for whispering the word *aristocrat* behind Lincoln's back.

The Whig district convention decided to give their support to neither Lincoln nor Baker, but rather to John Hardin of neighboring Morgan County. All that Lincoln could salvage from these multiple losses was Hardin's pledge that he would run for only one term, and then, in the regular congressional election of 1844, yield the opportunity to Baker, while Baker promised to yield the opportunity to Lincoln for 1846. Given the electoral weight of the Whigs in the new Seventh District, Hardin had no trouble securing election in 1843, followed by Baker in 1844. But Lincoln's political standing was so insecure that when Baker returned from Washington at the end of 1845, Hardin began making noises about seeking the nomination again for himself. Only by earnestly appealing to the need for good party order did Lincoln finally persuade Hardin grudgingly to withdraw.

But Lincoln was no sooner nominated as the Whig candidate for the Seventh District on May 1, 1846, than he suddenly discovered that he had a much bigger problem on his hands than his standing with the Sangamon Whigs.

All of Lincoln's friends from his early days in Springfield — Speed, Matheny, even Stuart — united in describing Lincoln as a religious skeptic, and there is no evidence through the 1840s that Lincoln attended any church in Springfield. Nor did Mary: "her religion," ac-

115

cording to Herndon, "was like her husband's, rather infidel, agnostic, or atheistic," and though she may have attended ladies' meetings at the Episcopal and Presbyterian churches in Springfield, she never had her sons baptized. This failure to establish a recognizable religious profile had long been, as Lincoln knew, a major political liability: as early as 1837, he was aware that his political enemies were asking "an old acquaintance of mine" whether "he ever heard Lincoln say he was a deist," and in 1843 he acknowledged that as he "belonged to no church," he had suffered "a tax of a considerable per cent. upon my strength throughout the religious community." He sometimes replied, in religious self-defense, that "his parents were Baptists, and brought him up in the belief of the Baptist religion." But not even Noyes Miner, the minister of Springfield's First Baptist Church, who liked Lincoln and often borrowed the Lincoln family's horse and carriage for church work, could bring himself to suggest that Lincoln "was what is termed an experimental Christian." Lincoln frankly admitted to Thomas D. Jones, "My father was a member of the Baptist Church, but I am not."

In all except the most confidential company, Lincoln preferred not to talk about religion at all. And the more social and political prominence he acquired (or, in less friendly terms, the more he identified with the Whig Junto), the less "enthusiastic" he allowed himself to be "in his infidelity." James Matheny noted that "as he grew older he grew more discrete — didn't talk much before Strangers about his religion." And he would not have in 1846, either, if his Democratic opponent in the Seventh District congressional race had not decided to make an issue of it. The Democrats put up against Lincoln the Methodist circuit preacher Peter Cartwright, who still had Lincoln's editorial barbs in his skin from a decade before. Cartwright promptly began "whispering the charge of infidelity" against Lincoln through the Seventh District and urging pious Whigs to vote their piety and not their politics.

Nothing better illustrates just how sensitive Lincoln was about discussions of his "infidelity" than his decision on July 31, 1846, less than a week before the election, to issue a public handbill, replying to Cartwright's charges, which was distributed through the Seventh District and published three weeks later in the Tazewell *Whig*. (Handbills were a fairly common way of keeping current with charges and counter-charges in a political campaign; John Todd Stuart once complained that every day in a campaign he had to fend off a new Democrat accusation, only to find the next morning that another handbill with fresh accusations would appear.) The handbill is probably as revealing a statement of what Herndon called Lincoln's "philosophy" as Lincoln was ever persuaded to give in public, and it was clearly aimed at damping down Cartwright's "whispering" without trying to pretend that the "whispers" were entirely untrue.

The handbill began by noticing that "A charge" had been put "into circulation in some of the neighborhoods of this District, in substance that I am an open scoffer at Christianity." This Lincoln carefully denied. "That I am not a member of any Christian Church, is true," Lincoln admitted. But that did not mean that he was a "scoffer." Far from it: "I have never denied the truth of the Scriptures; and I have never spoken with intentional disrespect of religion in general, or of any denomination of Christians in particular." Forgetting for the moment whatever his New Salem "handbook on infidelity" might have implied about the "truth of the Scriptures," this allowed Lincoln to deny having any open hostility to Christianity, without actually affirming any preference for it.

Lincoln, in fact, made only one clear affirmation in the handbill, and although it is routinely short-changed in virtually all accounts of Lincoln's life, it was an affirmation that plunged straight to the core of Lincoln's own mind and character. "It is true," he conceded,

> that in early life I was inclined to believe in what I understand is called the "Doctrine of Necessity" — that is, that the human mind is impelled to action, or held in rest by some power, over which the mind itself has no control; and I have sometimes (with one, two or three, but never publicly) tried to maintain this opinion in argument. The habit of arguing thus however, I have, entirely left off for more than five years. And I add here, I have always understood this same opinion to be held by several of the Christian denominations.

What he was describing in this "Doctrine of Necessity" was, like J. S. Mill's "philosophical necessity," a belief that human beings possess neither free will nor the moral responsibility for the right or wrong actions that is supposed to follow the exercise of free choices. As Herndon had already discovered from law-office shop talk, Lincoln believed that "there was no freedom of the will," that "men had no free choice":

> things were to be, and they came, irresistibly came, doomed to come; men were made as they are made by superior conditions over which they had no control; the fates settled things as by the doom of the powers, and laws, universal, absolute, and eternal, ruled the universe of matter and mind. . . . [Man] is simply a *simple tool*, a mere cog in the wheel, a part, a small part, of this vast iron machine, that strikes and cuts, grinds and mashes, all things, including man, that resist it.

Lincoln, as Herndon went on to explain, believed that people do not choose on the basis of a free will, but because they are conditioned to respond to "motives." Motives were "the great leading law of human nature," and "moved the man to every voluntary act of his life." Motives possess that power because motives appeal, at the most basic level, to human self-interest. "His idea," recalled Herndon, "was that all human actions were caused by motives, and at the bottom of these motives was self."

> We often argued the question [Herndon remembered], I taking the opposite view. . . . I once contended that man was free and could act without a motive. He smiled at my philosophy, and answered that it was impossible, because the motive was born before the man. . . . He defied me to act without motive and unselfishly; and when I did the act and told him of it, he analyzed and sifted it to the last grain. After he had concluded, I could not avoid the admission that he had demonstrated the absolute selfishness of the entire act.

Lincoln seems to have been unconcerned that, in attributing all action to an impersonal cause like "motives," he might be subverting all moral sense of right or wrong, or any possibility of attributing blame or praise for human actions. On the contrary, Lincoln was inclined by his "fatalism" to soften or excuse what appeared to be the most obvious examples of human guilt or responsibility. He "quoted the case of Brutus and Caesar, arguing that the former was forced by laws and conditions over which he had no control to kill the latter, and vice versa, that the latter was specially created to be disposed of by the former."

The most obvious source for this "Doctrine of Necessity" was the Calvinistic atmosphere which pervaded his adolescence among the predestinarian Baptists in Indiana and which already governed much of his early religious skepticism. And the roots of his "melancholy" certainly have undeniable resemblance to the religious despair of those who feared they were not of the elect, and could not become that way by any effort of their own. But these Calvinistic origins and overtones, however, only lay the groundwork of Lincoln's "fatalism." His "Doctrine," with its intricate vocabulary of motives, necessity, and self-interest, contained elements that were clearly foreign to the discourse of the Baptists. What this vocabulary more nearly echoed, even more than Mill, was the determinism of Jeremy Bentham, whose comments on free will and necessity have, when set beside Lincoln's, an eerily familiar ring. Like Lincoln, Bentham believed that all human conduct was governed by *motives:* "on every occasion, *conduct* — the *course* taken by a man's conduct — is at the absolute command of — is the never-failing result of — the *motives*. . . ."

> It is an acknowledged truth, that every kind of act whatever, and consequently every kind of offence, is apt to assume a different character, and to be attended with different effects, according to the nature of the *motive* which gives birth to it. This makes it requisite to take a view of the several motives by which human conduct is liable to be influenced.

What gave these motives their power over human willing was, precisely as it had been for Lincoln, the self-interest to which they appealed. "On every occasion, [an act] is at the absolute command of *motives* and corresponding *interest*." Thus, every choice — and neither Bentham nor Lincoln made any exceptions — was a motivated one, and the fundamental characteristic of human nature to which motives played was a plain, bleak concern for one's own self-interest. "No human act ever has been or ever can be *disinterested*," wrote Bentham. "For there exists not ever any voluntary action, which is not the result of the operation of some *motive* or *motives*, nor any motive, which has not for its accompaniment a corresponding *interest*, real or imagined."

119

And not surprisingly, two of Bentham's American legal admirers, the Philadelphia lawyer John Allyn and the Louisiana Supreme Court jurist Henry Carleton, published treatises on free will, frankly hawking the Benthamite line on necessity. "Necessity varies with motive," wrote Carleton, and "when once the motive is fixed, it is no less certain in its effects than the forces of physical necessity."

Necessity, at first blush, might be supposed to be the companion of passivity, and from time to time Lincoln did speak as though he was only a passive observer of his own life. But those who knew him intimately, like Orville Hickman Browning, saw that what his "fatalism" produced was not a resigned passivity, but "a strong conviction that he was born for better things than then seemed likely or even possible. . . . I have no doubt that Mr. Lincoln believed that there was a predestined work for him in the world." It was not passivity, but charity which was the last fruit of Lincoln's "Doctrine of Necessity." Since Lincoln was a "thorough fatalist" and "believed that what was to be would be, and no prayers of ours could arrest or reverse the decree," then "men were but simple tools of fate, of conditions, and of laws," and no one "was responsible for what he was, thought, or did, because he was a child of conditions." This, Herndon believed, was the real spring of Lincoln's "patience" and "his charity for men and his want of malice for them everywhere." And though this does not seem like a very congenial attitude for a trial lawyer like Lincoln to adopt, it is worth remembering that Bentham had addressed the problem of blame and guilt by abandoning all idea of legal punishment for crimes as retributive justice and reconceiving imprisonment as an opportunity for moral exhortation and rehabilitation. Punishment, in John Allyn's *Philosophy of Mind* (1851), should not be "an expression of hatred, but a means of exciting in the mind of the delinquent a motive to do right, and thereby . . . remedying his deficient moral state."

Lincoln, who had arrived at precisely the same criticism of "punishment" from a belief in "necessity," often took that very line of argument in asking for the revision of sentences for criminals. "Punishment was parental in its object, aim and design, and intended for the good of the offender; hence it must cease when justice is satisfied," Lincoln told Isaac Cogdal. He could not believe in "Eternal punishment as the christians say," because "his idea was punishment as Educational." Otherwise, given "That men lived but a little while here," if it were the case that "eternal punishment were man's doom," the only prudent thing with so much at stake was to "spend that little life in vigilant & ceaseless preparation."

In 1846, however, Peter Cartwright made no demands for lengthy explications of Lincoln's "Doctrine of Necessity" or its sources. Lincoln carried eight of the eleven counties in the Seventh District on August 3, 1846, trouncing Cartwright by over 1,500 votes. Now looming before Lincoln were issues that made arguments about infidelity pale by comparison. For the first time, in any significant way, Abraham Lincoln would be compelled to confront the issue of slavery.

Slavery in America had always bothered Lincoln, but not exactly in the way we might expect. Although Lincoln insisted in 1858 that "I have always hated slavery" and that "the slavery question often bothered me as far back as 1836-40," what he meant by *slavery* before the 1850s was any relationship of economic restraint, or any systematic effort to box ambitious and enterprising people like himself into a "fixed condition of labor, for his whole life."

This slavery was what he experienced as a young man under his father, and he came to associate it with subsistence farming and the Jeffersonian ideology that glorified it, with a backwards-looking mentality that conveniently froze wealthy landholders in places of power while offering the placebo of subsidy and protection (especially in the form of cheap land) to bungling yeomen in order to pacify their disgruntlements. "I used to be a slave," Lincoln said in an early speech; in fact, "we were all slaves one time or another." Recognizing a face in the crowd, Lincoln said, "There is my old friend John Roll [who long before had helped him build Offutt's flatboat]. He used to be a slave, but he has made himself free, and I used to be a slave, and now I am so free that they let me practice law." As late as 1859, Adlai Stevenson was puzzled by the way Lincoln ended a brief self-description — "No other marks or brands recollected" — since this was the language "not infrequently employed in the South, especially Kentucky, for a notice of a 'runaway slave.'"

What appealed to Lincoln most deeply about Whig politics and the market economy was the sense of liberation it offered from the small-horizoned slavery of an agrarian economy. Like both Carey and Wayland, Lincoln believed that "*labor* is the source from which human

121

wants are mainly supplied." Labor imparted value to commodities, and was "prior to, and independent of, capital . . . in fact, capital is the fruit of labor, and could never have existed if labor had not first existed." Any attempt to deprive laborers of the full value of their productions was therefore (as Wayland put it) "robbery." Slavery, however, was exactly this kind of "robbery." Slavery, in this sense, included anyone, even a "freeman," who is "fatally fixed for life, in the condition of a hired laborer." What the market economy offered was mobility, a way around "fatal" fixations. "The man who labored for another last year, this year labors for himself, and next year he will hire others to labor for him."

This did not, however, keep "another class of reasoners" from claiming that "there is no *such* relationship between capital and labor." What the Jacksonians found suspicious in the market economy was the change it wrought in the nature of labor itself, from labor on one's own property to produce one's own goods, to labor on another's property for cash wages. Wage labor, in the Jacksonian imagination, created a relationship of dependency on the whims and fortunes of an employer little better than slavery, while subsistence agriculture was supposed to guarantee stability and well-nigh total independence. But Lincoln saw wage labor, not as a relationship of dependence, but as a ticket toward the kind of mobility and prosperity the agrarians could scarcely dream of. "What a mistaken view do these men have of Northern laborers!" Lincoln exclaimed in 1856. "They think that men are always to remain laborers here — but there is no such class." In subsistence agriculture, one might start poor and hope to gain ground only by digging oneself deeper into isolation and drudgery. In wage labor, anyone who "starts poor, as most do in the race of life," can hire himself out for wages, then "look forward and hope to be a hired laborer this year and the next, work for himself afterward, and finally to hire men to work for him!"

Lincoln did not try to pretend that wage labor always gave everyone their due. "It has so happened in all ages of the world, that *some* have laboured, and *others* have, without labour, enjoyed a large proportion of the fruits." This, he admitted, "is wrong." But the remedy the market offered to wage laborers was simply to withdraw their labor from such a situation and take it elsewhere. Workers whose wages fall below the value they impart to commodities can strike, and Lincoln was "glad to see that a system of labor prevails" in the North "under which laborers can strike when they want to, where they are not obliged to work under all circumstances, are not tied down and obliged to labor whether you pay them or not! . . . Then you can better your condition, and so it may go on and on in one ceaseless round so long as man exists on the face of the earth!"

What wage labor promised was a potential for betterment and self-improvement which the static, rigid system of both yeoman agrarianism and plantation slavery utterly lacked. A market system in which "the prudent, penniless beginner in the world, labors for wages awhile, saves a surplus with which to buy tools or land, for himself; then labors on his account another while, and at length hires another new beginner to help him" is "the just and generous, and prosperous system, which opens the way for all, gives hope to all, and energy, and progress, and improvement of condition to all."

It went without saying that Lincoln was describing his own experiences as much as prescribing for others, and the mobility one obtained by leaving the land and entering into the cash economy became the core of Lincoln's political philosophy as a Whig. But he never brought it closer to home than in 1848, when his stepbrother, John D. Johnston, wrote in desperation for a loan of eighty dollars to keep various creditors from his door. Johnston remained, like his stepfather, a small-time subsistence farmer, living on the same Coles County farm as the seventy-year-old Thomas Lincoln and surviving from season to season without much inclination to do better. And for that reason, Lincoln refused to lend him the money: it was not because he thought Johnston was *"lazy"* — not a congenital loafer — but because Johnston was content to be an "idler" who did "not work much, merely because it does not seem to you that you could get much for it" and who needed to see the virtues of working for cash wages.

Lincoln's advice was simple and blunt: get off the farm and out of subsistence agriculture, and find wage-paying labor in the market. "What I propose is, that you shall go to work, 'tooth and nails' for some body who will give you money [for] it." And just so that Johnston made no mistake about what he was recommending, Lincoln spelled out what Johnston had to do to satisfy him: "Let father and your boys take charge of things at home — prepare for a crop, and make the crop; and you go to work for the best money wages, or in discharge of any debt you owe, that you can get." Lincoln actually offered him the incentive of matching every dollar in wages Johnston earned, so that "you will have a habit that will keep you from getting in debt again." What he did not want Johnston to do was to throw himself into some get-rich-quick scheme, going off "to St. Louis, or the lead mines, or the gold mines in California, "but I mean for you to go at it for the best wages you can get close to home [in] Coles county." "Follow my advice," and, in effect, embrace wage labor, and "you will find it worth more than eight times eighty dollars to you."

From Lincoln's perspective, his stepbrother "was a slave," too, and the solution to his slavery was the mobility and self-transformative power of the market. And from that perspective, Lincoln was, as he claimed, a vehement opponent of slavery from the first, because all of his economic agendas in the Illinois legislature had been aimed at breaking up economic slavery of the Jacksonian sort. It did not, however, drive him into militant criticism of the American republic's most institutionalized version of slavery, and this has given rise to questions from many directions why Lincoln, in the 1830s and 1840s, failed to extend his rage against "slavery" to the literal enslavement of African-Americans.

It was certainly not from want of personal awareness of what black slavery was like. Even though Illinois voters rebuffed the movement in 1823 for a pro-slavery state constitutional convention, Illinois continued to permit slaves to be brought into the state as temporary workers under right-of-transit laws and, after 1827, the state fined Illinoisans who helped such slaves escape from their masters. Free blacks were burdened with a series of "black laws" that required them to carry a certificate of freedom and to post bond for good behavior, or else risk being arrested as a "runaway" and put out to service for a year. When Lincoln moved to Springfield, there were only 115 African-Americans listed among the town population, but six of them were slaves. His marriage into the Todd-Edwards connection brought him into a family network where the service of African-American slaves and servants was accepted as normal. At the time of the Lincoln marriage, Ninian Edwards held at least one "indentured servant" (a euphemism under Illinois law for what amounted to *de facto* slavery up until age eighteen) and the Lincolns employed at least two free African-American women, Maria Vance and Ruth Stanton, as domestic help. The house that Lincoln bought from Charles Dresser (who also held an "indentured servant" named Hepsey at the time of the sale) was in the middle of a neighborhood that had twenty-one African-Americans, in conditions ranging from free to slave, living in it.

Yet, close enough as black slavery remained to Lincoln in Illinois, there is no evidence before 1846 that the slavery of blacks seriously disturbed him. Slavery, considered strictly as an economic relationship, he disliked; slavery, considered as the badge of an agrarian planter class largely allied to the Democrats, he also disliked; but it is difficult to see that he had any corresponding concern up until the 1840s about slavery as a system of personal injustice when only blacks were on the receiving end of the injustice. When the Illinois General Assembly resolved in January, 1837, that "property in slaves, is sacred to the slave-holding states by the Federal Constitution," Lincoln and Whig judge Daniel Stone protested that "the institution of slavery is founded on both injustice and bad policy." But Lincoln and Stone waited to make their protest for more than a month after the original resolutions had been adopted by the legislature, long enough for Lincoln to slide the relocation of the state capital through the Assembly, and the protest bent obligingly in the other direction far enough to add that "the promulgation of abolition doctrines tends rather to increase than to abate its evils."

Lincoln, in fact, refused to lift a finger on behalf of abolition, even when it established a beachhead in central Illinois. In November, 1837, a pro-slavery mob in Alton attacked the print shop of an abolitionist newspaper owned by a New School Presbyterian named Elijah Lovejoy, smashing the press and shooting Lovejoy to death. This incident, which shocked the northern states, drew no more notice from Lincoln than a brief reference in his 1838 Lyceum address to mobs that "throw printing presses into rivers, shoot editors" — and even then, it was only to condemn mob rule (by which he meant, Democratic rule) and not to recommend Lovejoy. Far from sympathizing with abolitionists in the 1830s and 1840s, Lincoln believed that "the whig abolitionists of New York" had cost Henry Clay the 1844 presidential election by throwing away their votes on the abolitionist Liberty party. When the Illinois state legislature debated resolutions in January, 1839, to condemn the governor of Maine for refusing to extradite two Maine residents accused of helping a Georgia slave to run away, Lincoln "had inclined to vote in favor of concurring," on the grounds that the Constitution required such extradition. The same year, Lincoln successfully sued Nathan Cromwell on behalf of David Bailey, who had taken Cromwell's "indentured servant of color," Nance, as satisfaction for a debt Cromwell owed. Nance ran away from Bailey and claimed freedom on the grounds that this exchange constituted a slave sale, which was banned by Illinois law. Lincoln easily won the case, but not so much to enforce the ban on slavery as to assist Bailey's claim that he had been defrauded. When his father-in-law died in 1849 with a defective will, Lincoln apparently saw no problem in representing the claims of Mary and her sisters to the proceeds of an estate which included the auction of the Todd family slaves.

Nothing underscores Lincoln's indifference to slavery as an injustice to blacks more than his decision, shortly before leaving Illinois to begin his congressional term in Washington, to act as counsel for a Kentucky slaveowner, Robert Matson, when Matson's slave, Jane Bryant, filed a freedom suit for herself and her six children. In 1843, Matson purchased a farm in Coles County and, under Illinois transit laws, brought a group of slaves over the Ohio River every year for planting and harvest. These slaves included the enslaved wife and children of Matson's free black overseer, Anthony Bryant, who hoped eventually to purchase his family's freedom from Matson. But in the spring of 1847, Jane Bryant roused the ire of Matson's slatternly common-law wife, Mary Corbin, who threatened to see Jane and her children sold "way down south in the cotton fields." Anthony Bryant sought the help of two local abolitionists, Matthew Ashmore and Hiram Rutherford, and they counseled the Bryants to declare themselves free, on the grounds that Matson was in violation of the transit laws.

Matson promptly applied for a warrant under the 1793 federal fugitive slave law to recapture the Bryants, and hired Democratic lawyer Usher Linder to represent him. The county justice-of-the-peace in Charleston (the county seat) had the Bryants arrested, but the J.P. charged them, not with being runaways under the federal statute (since they had not crossed state lines) but with violating the Illinois "black laws," since they had no freedom papers. Jane and her children ended up, not with Matson, but in the county jail. Frustrated, Matson sued Ashmore and Rutherford in the circuit court, and in October

1847, while Lincoln was in Charleston defending a slander suit by one of Linder's clients, both Matson and Rutherford asked Lincoln to take their case. Matson (or perhaps Linder) evidently got to Lincoln first, and Lincoln and Linder appeared in the circuit court in Charleston on Matson's behalf on October 16th, arguing that Matson had clearly stated his intention to limit the service of Jane and her children only to seasonal labor under the transit laws. The circuit court judge — in this case, Illinois Supreme Court Chief Justice William Wilson — was unimpressed, and ruled that, notwithstanding all his declarations, Matson had kept Jane Bryant in Illinois for two years, and that was long enough to consider her "permanent" and free. There was nothing in the case for either Matson or Lincoln to be proud of, but nothing about Matson's case ever produced any regrets from Lincoln afterward that he had taken the case in the first place.

It is hard to escape the impression that Lincoln's indifference to black slavery had at least some roots in a racism not much different from that which ruled his Democratic counterparts, a racism which allowed him to feel that slavery was one thing when it pinned down ambitious whites, but another when it was fastened onto the necks of blacks. He certainly had few inhibitions about retailing vulgar racial jokes, like "the story of the old Virginian" he told Moses Hampton in 1849, "stropping his razor on a certain *member* of a young negro's body." And there is some suggestion, in a letter Lincoln wrote to Joshua Speed's sister in September, 1841, that Lincoln regarded blacks as being sufficiently inferior to whites as a race that slavery simply didn't mean the same thing to them. That summer, he told Mary Speed, he and Joshua Speed encountered "twelve negroes" on an Ohio River steamboat who had been "chained six and six together." Under such conditions, human happiness would normally be impossible, but "amid all these distressing circumstances, as we would think them, they were the most cheerful and apparently happy creatures on board." Far from being moved to anger, Lincoln was amused enough to compare them to "fish upon a trot-line." *They are not like us,* he implied to Mary Speed: "One whose offense for which he had been sold was an over-fondness for his wife, played the fiddle almost continually; and the others danced, sung, cracked jokes, and played various games with cards from day to day."

And yet racism cannot be the only reason why Lincoln turned a

127

blind eye to black slavery in the 1840s, if only because a genuinely consistent racist would scarcely have taken the risk in 1837 publicly to brand "the institution of slavery" as an "injustice and bad policy." There is actually a good deal of circumstantial evidence which suggests that Lincoln was more troubled by the enslavement of blacks than the Matson case or the Speed letter might indicate. John Hanks insisted that when he and Lincoln took Offutt's flatboat down to New Orleans in 1831, Lincoln's "heart bled" when he saw "Negroes chained, maltreated, whipped, and scourged" in the New Orleans slave markets, and "was silent from feeling . . . was thoughtful and abstracted." Hanks's recollection is a suspect one, since Lincoln remembered that Hanks had actually left the flatboat in St. Louis and never completed the trip to New Orleans. But Hanks may have been conflating this with an earlier 1828 flatboat trip, since Lincoln elsewhere made allusions to "horrid pictures" of the New Orleans slave market he had seen in his youth. Lincoln himself offered a significantly more intense version of the 1841 steamboat encounter in a letter written fourteen years later to Joshua Speed. "In 1841 you and I had together a tedious low-water trip, on a Steam Boat from Louisville to St. Louis," Lincoln reminded Speed, and "on board, ten or a dozen slaves, shackled together with irons." Now, Lincoln claimed, "that sight was a continual torment to me. . . . I confess I hate to see the poor creatures hunted down, and caught, and carried back to their stripes, and unrewarded toils." If in the 1840s Lincoln displayed little empathy for blacks in slavery, it was an exclusion he did not maintain for long.

Black slavery, in fact, had tremendous potential for aggravating Lincoln because the enslavement of blacks in the plantation South rested on a relationship of power and a denigration of labor which offended both Lincoln's cultural Whiggism and his Whiggish economics. Even Thomas Jefferson had seen in the 1780s that the virtually absolute control the slaveowner held over the slave encouraged an atmosphere of hedonism and passion on the part of the slaveholder, and nothing was better calculated to violate the Whiggish glorification of self-discipline than a system that made a surrender to passion so easy and inviting. Lincoln believed that slaveholding could only appeal "to the thoughtless and giddy headed young men who looked upon work as vulgar and ungentlemanly." He told Joseph Gillespie that you might have any amount of land, money in your pocket or bank stock and while traveling around no body would be any the wiser but if you have a darkey trudging at your heels every body would see him & know you owned slaves — It is the most glittering ostentatious & displaying property in the world and now says he if a young man goes courting the only inquiry is how many negroes he or she owns and not what other property they may have. The love for Slave property was swallowing up every other mercenary passion. Its ownership not only betokened the possession of wealth but indicated the gentleman of leisure who was above and scorned labour.

Slaveholding was a relationship that debased labor into vulgarity, and held the laborer up to the contempt of the planter class. "Mr. Lincoln was really excited," Gillespie remembered, "and said with great earnestness that this spirit ought to be met and if possible checked." Thus, even if he harbored much of the common racism of other white Americans, slavery still grated on Lincoln's Whiggism, and forced him into denouncing it as "a great & crying injustice" and "an enormous national crime."

But just as his Whiggism inflamed him against slavery, Whig politics also presented him with several practical obstacles to dealing directly with slavery. One of these was the federal Constitution, which (without actually using the word) gave legal sanction to slavery, through its mechanism for calculating the every-ten-year federal census, its prohibitions of emancipation for any fugitive "held to service or Labour in one state," and the restrictions that prevented federal interference in state affairs, including state laws allowing and regulating slavery. Short of amending the Constitution, there was no practical hope of ending black slavery in the states where legislatures had made it legal; and given the large block of Southern representation in Congress, there was even less hope of a constitutional amendment on slavery. "The Congress of the United States has no power, under the Constitution, to interfere with the institution of slavery in the different States," Lincoln explained in 1837, and no power even "to abolish slavery in the District of Columbia . . . unless at the request of the people of said District."

In that case, all the agitation raised on behalf of abolition would serve only to distract and divide the nation when it most required unity and when the Whig party most required solidarity for its grand market program. It was one of the things Lincoln pointed out for praise in Henry Clay, that although Clay "was, on principle and in feeling, opposed to slavery," Clay had no workable plan "how it could at *once* be eradicated, without producing a greater evil, even to the cause of liberty itself." On those terms, Lincoln might oppose slavery and "the increasing number of men, who, for the sake of perpetuating slavery, are beginning to assail and to ridicule the white-man's charter of freedom — the declaration that 'all men are created free and equal.'" But the Constitution and the Union gave him no choice other than, as he told Joshua Speed, to "bite my lip and keep quiet." Whatever his "first impulse," Lincoln assured Speed, who owned slaves in Kentucky, that "I also acknowledge *your* rights and *my* obligations, under the constitution."

By the same token, anxiety for the Union also made Lincoln pull shy of the abolitionists, "who would shiver into fragments the Union of these States . . . rather than slavery should continue a single hour." If racism had any real role to play in Lincoln's ambivalence toward black slavery, it was here, since Lincoln clearly did not believe that an immediate act of emancipation would accomplish any real good. Whites would not live contentedly beside their former slaves, nor would these slaves fit into white society. Like Clay, Lincoln "did not perceive, that on a question of human right, the negroes were to be excepted from the human race." But prejudice was a fact, and so the quietest procedure he could imagine was a non-confrontational program of "gradual emancipation," with financial compensation offered to slaveowners, and following that, repatriation back to Africa in American-sponsored colonies. "My first impulse would be to free all the slaves, and send them to Liberia, — to their own native land," Lincoln remarked in 1854. Once colonization began, its excellence as a solution would become self-evident: "many" of the freed slaves "will colonize and" for the young or the disabled "the South will be compelled to resort to" an "apprentice system," similar to Illinois's "indentured servants."

Just where Lincoln and Clay expected to get volunteers for gradual emancipation (even with financial compensation), colonization, and apprenticeship is a question neither answered. But by the 1840s, colonization schemes had become the standard Whig proposal for dealing with slavery, and Whigs like Clay were the chief movers in organizing the American Colonization Society in 1816 and in getting federal funding in 1818 to support the purchase of land on the west coast of Africa for the repatriation of freed blacks. Little enough came of the ACS's efforts, partly because free blacks showed scant enthusiasm for a return to Africa when some of their families had been in America longer than their white would-be benefactors, but even more because Southern Democrats were instantly alarmed at a proposal which, while it might leave a white America without blacks, would also leave an agricultural South without slaves. For all its racial condescension, colonization implied a real criticism of black slavery. Leonard Bacon, whose *Report of the Committee . . . to inquire respecting the black population of the United States* (1823) articulated the guiding philosophy of the ACS, was convinced that colonization "will ultimately be the means of exterminating slavery in our country" and "will eventually redeem and emancipate a million and a half of wretched men." Lincoln, who told Joseph Thompson in 1864 that Bacon "had much to do in shaping my own thinking on the subject of slavery," entirely agreed, and so he had no incentive to press too hard for its soon dismantling. "God will settle it, and settle it right," he assured Robert Browne, "but for the present it is our duty to wait."

The primary reason why he could wait was his confidence in the eventual triumph of the market and how it would eventually render slavery, like subsistence farming, obsolete as a labor system. Like many of his Whig contemporaries, Lincoln thought of slavery as a cumbersome relic of a past age which consumed resources faster than it could return long-term profits and which had no imaginable way of competing with Northern markets and Northern wage labor. If legalized slavery was confined to the Southern states where it was already on the books and denied any significant further expansion, Whigs had only to wait for economic asphyxiation to solve the problem of slavery for them, and without further antagonizing Northern whites by agitating for an immediate abolition, which they feared would inundate them with newly freed black labor. The option for "gradual emancipation of the slaves" and colonization could then be put in place, and (as Clay and the ACS calculated it) for less money than it cost Andrew Jackson to forcibly uproot and relocate the Cherokee Indians in 1838 or suppress the Seminole Indians in Florida. The future, in other words, could take care of itself; slavery would die of its own doctrine of necessity, and good Whigs need only take care (as Lincoln explained in 1845 to an abolitionist tempted to desert the Whig party) to "never knowingly lend ourselves directly or indirectly, to prevent slavery from dying a natural death — to find new places for it to live in, when it can no longer exist in the old."

But finding new places to live in was precisely what slavery turned out to be quite good at. Cotton agriculture destroyed soils, and the pages of *DeBow's Review*, the South's premier agricultural magazine, were filled with dire warnings that "our system is of the most exhausting character" and that Virginia, with "her ten thousand abandoned farms," would become a model for the South unless new ground could be broken for cotton. Why this was a cause of concern for anyone but the cotton nabobs might be worth wondering, until the moment when the planters reminded both Southern white farmers and Northern workingmen what the racial consequences might be if slavery declined and released a black workforce to compete with whites. And so, with the blessing of Democratic agrarians and Democratic proletarians alike, cotton began to move westward, to cross the Mississippi, to secure the Missouri lowlands, to persuade Illinois voters to legalize it, to inch toward the American republic's border with Texas, the northernmost province of Mexico.

This was not the script that Americans who hoped slavery would die out on its own had expected. "When our federal Constitution was adopted," Lincoln explained in 1852, "we owned no territory beyond the limits or ownership of the states . . . east of the Mississippi," and within those original boundaries the slave question had been pretty definitely settled. "But in 1803, we purchased Louisiana of the French; and it included with much more, what has since been formed into the state of Missouri." And in Missouri, "nothing had been done to forestall the question of slavery." When Missouri asked for admission to the Union as a slave state in 1819, the petition touched off a violent row in Congress, where Northern representatives resisted what they saw as the South's bid to secure a launching pad for its interests in the West. What made this confrontation so threatening was that, unlike "other questions" which "had their opposing partizans in all localities of the country and in almost every family . . . so that no division of the Union could follow such, without a separation of friends," slavery and

Missouri threatened to separate whole sections, and would "separate opponents only." The controversy was damped down in 1820 by Henry Clay, who cobbled together a compromise he believed would simultaneously put a lid on further slave expansion and prevent agitation over the slave question from disrupting the Union.

The difficulty with Clay's Missouri Compromise was that it looked more substantial than it really was. Missouri, Clay conceded, would have to be admitted as a slave state, but his Missouri Compromise would divide all the rest of the Louisiana Purchase along a line drawn at 36°30′. All new territories organized north of that line could be admitted only as free states, and all of them organized south of it could be admitted as slave states. On the map, this was a poor deal for the slave states, since the lower triangle of the Louisiana Purchase below 36°30′ offered the promise of organizing only one or two more states at best. But the northern tier of the Louisiana Purchase was generally understood in the 1820s to be little more than a wasteland, while it was assumed from the start that the American republic would continue to expand its southern and western borders into the northern provinces of the Mexican republic, which would then organize themselves as slave states.

That this was precisely what was liable to happen appeared as early as 1835, when American settlers in Mexican Texas erupted in rebellion against the Mexican government and successfully set up an independent slave republic there. The Texans would have preferred to join the American Union, and given the influence of the cotton South in the Democratic party in the 1830s, there was every reason to expect that Texas would be taken in as the next slave state (or perhaps subdivided into as many as five new slave states). But President Van Buren had more than enough on his hands with the collapse of the American economy in 1837 to worry about kindling another Missouri-style confrontation in Congress over Texas; and then, when William Henry Harrison and the Whigs succeeded Van Buren in 1840, all hope of a Texas annexation faded.

But Harrison's premature death in 1841 brought to the president's chair the turncoat Democrat John Tyler, and in an effort to ingratiate himself again with his old Democratic friends, Tyler paved the way for Texas to be received into the Union in 1845. The Mexican republic, which had been smoldering over its humiliation in the Texan revolution for a decade, announced that it would not recognize United States sovereignty over Texas. Tyler's successor in 1845, James Polk, read this as an opportunity rather than a warning, and in the spring of 1846, after American cavalry patrols clashed with Mexican cavalry on disputed ground near the Rio Grande River, Polk asked Congress for a declaration of war on Mexico. Even though President Polk insisted that he had never intended the war to become a vehicle for the expansion of slavery, it was obvious even before the war was over that the door to the greater Southwest below 36°30', all the way to California and the Pacific, stood open for slavery to enter.

A more subtle brand of expansion for slavery occurred in the way Southern slaveholders began to define slavery as a labor system in the 1840s. Few slaveholders before the 1830s would have disagreed with the Whig explanation for slavery's persistence: that it was little more than an unfortunate cultural holdover from the colonial past which economic necessity or the supposed intellectual backwardness of African-Americans compelled them, for some unforeseeable future, to maintain. But the escalating profitability of mass-market cotton exports gradually prompted Southerners to drop the apologetic pose. By 1810, 48 percent of Britain's cotton imports were coming from the American South; by 1860, Britain was importing 900 million pounds of cotton a year, well over 90 percent of all British cotton imports.

From that sprang a new line of argumentation, declaring slavery a "positive good," and perhaps even the superior of free wage labor. "The man who lives by daily labor, and scarcely lives at that, and who has to put out his labor in the market, and take the best he can get for it; in short, your whole hireling class of manual laborers and 'operatives' . . . are essentially slaves," jeered South Carolina governor James Henry Hammond.

> The difference between us is, that our slaves are hired for life and well compensated; there is no starvation, no begging, no want of employment among our people, and not too much employment either. Yours are hired by the day, not cared for, and scantily compensated, which may be proved in the most painful manner, at any hour in any street in any of your large towns. Why, you meet more beggars in one day, in any single street of the city of New York, than you would meet in a lifetime in the whole South.

It would be "a good and proper remedy" for these victims of wage-labor capitalism, recommended Edmund Ruffin in *The Political Economy of Slavery*, to contemplate the "enslaving of these reckless, wretched drones and cumberers of the earth . . . thereby compelling them to habits of labor, and in return satisfying their wants for necessaries, and raising them and their progeny in the scale of humanity, not only physically, but morally and intellectually."

Ruffin and Hammond did not proffer this advice because aggressive cotton entrepreneurs had discovered in slave agriculture some alternative economic organization to capitalism. Like their Northern mill-owning counterparts, Southern planters exhibited all the acquisitive instincts of capitalist entrepreneurs. "The large planters — the one thousand bale planters," observed one Mississippi newspaper, "sell their cotton in Liverpool, buy their wines in London and Havre; their negro clothing in Boston; their plantation implements and supplies in Cincinnati; and their groceries and fancy articles in New Orleans." Rather, it was because in slavery they had discovered an alternative labor system to wage labor which allowed them to have their agrarianism and yet still prosper within the transatlantic commodity markets.

This should have provoked the suspicion and opposition of the yeomen and workingmen who were the real critics of capitalism, and who formed the backbone of the Democratic party. But cotton capitalism had established an alliance with the yeomanry as early as Jefferson's own presidency, since the interests of both slaveowning cotton planters and upcountry rural farmers neatly coincided on a number of crucial points. Planters as well as yeomen saw the federal protective tariff system as rigged against their needs for cheap imported manufactures, both opposed the distribution of federally owned lands to the states (planters wanted the new lands held open for cotton, the yeomen wanted them for squatting), and both opposed the creation of federally supported internal improvement schemes (the planters because river transportation sufficed for much of the cotton South, the yeomen because they resented the levels of threatening taxation these schemes would involve, and both together because they feared that a government big enough to send railroads into the South would soon discover it had the authority to meddle with slavery in the South).

There was no mistaking the fact that the ultimate interests of planters who sold cotton on the Liverpool exchanges and yeomen who

135

grew wheat and potatoes to feed themselves were bound to diverge at some point along this path, and there might have been little even then to keep the agrarian yeomen from concluding that the cotton nabobs had more in common with New England bankers than with piney-woods farmers. The real glue in this relationship, therefore, had to be racial rather than economic; Jeffersonian farmers who feared the market feared blacks even more, and so cotton capitalism saw its opportunity for security in proposing an alliance with Jefferson's "cultivators" based on a mutual determination to keep the black slave a slave.

This also required from the planters an elaborate and highly risky game of pretense. They had, in order to rally nonslaveholders, to insist that cotton agriculture was not a capitalist enterprise at all, but simply a large-scale variation on subsistence agriculture. This allowed cotton planters like Jefferson Davis of Mississippi to declare that they ruled their plantations, not as profit-seeking entrepreneurs, but as precapitalist patriarchs who disdained "vulgar parvenus . . . vulgar landlords, capitalists, and employers." And yet they also had to avoid arousing the ire of yeoman farmers who wanted no part of aristocrats in the bottom lands. They had to insist again that slavery really served the interests of all whites in the South by imposing on blacks "the drudgery so essential for the sustenance of man, and the advance of civilization," thereby securing the political solidarity of the Southern electorate for slavery and King Cotton. But yet again they had to avoid provoking the rage of an upcountry agrarian workforce who regularly had to perform the same drudgery day in and day out.

Finally, they had to convince Northern urban workers to join them in opposition to Whig banking and Whig corporations by denouncing wage labor and the "harmony of interests" as no different from slavery itself, as George Fitzhugh did in *Sociology for the South* (1850) when he announced that "self-interest makes the employer and the free laborer enemies." And yet the planter class had to be careful not to suggest that their own slaves might, on the logic of such an equivalence, offer economic competition to Northern workingmen in the form of a slave-based industrial proletariat, or that slavery might just turn out to be capitalism's final solution to the problem of a stable and submissive labor force. This, as Leonidas Spratt explained in 1855, was by no means so far-fetched as it sounded: "Slave labor may well be employed in manufactures and in the preparatory departments of commerce." Still, if rightly managed, these pretenses meant that cotton planters could tout themselves as simple Jeffersonian farmers, striking hands with Northern urban workingmen as common Democratic critics of Northern urban wage labor.

Defenders of slavery thus came to draw a shrewd line of demarcation between their brand of capitalism and what could be found in the North. Northern wage labor was really "wage-slavery," in which propertyless whites were reduced to performing menial "mud-sill" work for uncertain and unpredictable pay. In the South, by contrast, the menial labor necessary to float cash-crop agriculture toward profitability was performed entirely by blacks. The whites of the Southern master-class could enjoy the fruits of a capitalist economy without degrading their fellow whites with "wage-slavery" and indulge a fantasy panorama of Jeffersonian agrarianism, while lower-class Southern whites could always be assured of white racial solidarity, or even be encouraged to secure their hold on agrarian property by acquiring a slave.

Both brands of slave expansion, geographic and ideological, threw down challenges to Lincoln's belief that black slavery would be best ended by being left alone. Lincoln had learned from Francis Wayland that free labor and wage labor were essentially the same thing, and that "wages are the result of a partnership, formed between the laborer and the capitalist." For that reason, wage labor could never be mistaken for slavery except in those cases where someone was already morally enslaved to "improvidence, folly, or singular misfortune." The transformation of slave labor into a species of labor security (as described by Ruffin and Hammond) made slavery out of what Lincoln believed was the best means of freedom, and nothing was more easily calculated to provoke an explosion from him. Herndon remembered how George Fitzhugh's *Sociology for the South*, which attacked the mobility of market societies as an "abyss of misery and penury," succeeded in arousing "the ire of Lincoln more than most pro-slavery books." What made this worse was the possibility that the Mexican War might give slavery just the second wind it would need by opening up an entire new western geography for slave agriculture. And if it succeeded in that respect, the new pro-slavery arguments Lincoln was starting to hear at the end of the 1840s darkly promised that a third form of expansion for slavery might be attempted: that slavery might try to invade the free states as a rival for the free labor that Abraham Lincoln had pegged his whole intellectual life to defending.

Abraham Lincoln was elected to Congress a little less than three months after the outbreak of the Mexican War, and at first he saw no particular connection between the problems concerning Texas and the war and the expansion of slavery. The line he drew for containing the expansion of slavery conceded Texas to slavery, and perhaps even a little more of the southwest. "Individually I never was much interested in the Texas question," Lincoln explained to a fearful Whig supporter. "I never could see much good to come of annexation . . . ; on the other hand, I never could very clearly see how the annexation would augment the evil of slavery." His primary concerns clustered around the conventional Whig demands for market development, and Lincoln poured most of his energies into demands for renewed federal sponsorship for a national banking system, for internal improvements, and for tariffs.

The Whigs were not likely to get much encouragement from President Polk, who had already relied on Democratic majorities in the Twenty-Ninth Congress to veto two internal improvements bills, reauthorize Van Buren's "independent Treasury" arrangements, and adopt lowered federal tariffs. But the off-year election in 1846 gave the Whigs a slight four-vote majority in the House of Representatives, and that raised Lincoln's hopes that federal money could be diverted to the rescue of his old internal improvements scheme in Illinois. Five months before leaving for Washington, Lincoln attended a national River and Harbor Convention in Chicago to pick up lobbying ammunition, and when he was sworn in as a member of the Thirtieth Congress on December 6, 1847, he was ready to "battle, and battle manfully" for "the question of improvements."

When he did manage to turn his attention to the Mexican War, it was the pretext for attacking President Polk's assumption of Jackson-style executive high-handedness in starting the war in the first place. Three weeks after being sworn into office, Lincoln joined with fellow Whigs in the House to demand that Polk certify that the war had, as Polk claimed, actually been triggered by Mexican aggression, "whether the particular spot of soil on which the blood of our *citizens* was shed . . . was or was not, *our own soil*." The "Spot Resolutions" Lincoln offered would not have altered the course of the war; in fact, by the time Lincoln arrived in Washington, the shooting part of the war was over and Mexico City had been captured by an American army under Winfield Scott. But he and the other Whig members of the House did hope to embarrass Polk and the Democrats politically, and restrain Polk from using "the exceeding brightness of military glory" to "catch votes" and make political war on the Whigs.

Rather than embarrassing Polk, the "Spot Resolutions" backfired on Lincoln, since the Democratic newspapers plastered the resolutions across the nation as an example of small-minded Whigs betraying the boys in uniform. Democrats gleefully hung the nickname "Spotty" around Lincoln's neck, and in Lincoln's home district, Democratic political rallies in Charleston, Peoria, and Jacksonville howled with delight over "Spotty" Lincoln's "case of spotted fever." Even anxious Illinois Whigs warned Lincoln that too much open opposition to the war would be electorally costly. "If the Whigs as a party join issue with Mr. Polk," warned Lincoln's old political friend Anson Henry, "I shall at the polls (but no where else) *sustain Mr. Polk.*"

But the Whigs fought patriotic fire with fire in 1848 by putting forward as their next presidential candidate Zachary Taylor, a Louisiana slaveholder and the general who won the greatest American victory of the war at Buena Vista. Lincoln declared for Taylor as early as February, 1848, and though Lincoln had to admit that Taylor was politically colorless, it was also true that he was highly electable. "I have to say I am in favor of Gen. Taylor as the whig candidate for the Presidency because I am satisfied we can elect him, that he would give us a whig administration, and that we can not elect any other whig." If the fact that Taylor was a slaveholder had any place in Lincoln's concerns, it was only for keeping Taylor mum on the question of whether the final peace treaty with Mexico should include the cession of Mexico's northern provinces to the United States, since that might "enlarge and agrivate the distracting question of slavery."

But Lincoln soon discovered that he could not wish the slave question away. In July of 1848, President Polk was able to sign a peace treaty with Mexico which fixed the Rio Grande as the American boundary with the Mexican republic, and extorted from Mexico the cession of 525,000 square miles in the American southwest. This set off new fears across the North that the west was being readied for slave

139

expansion, and when the Whig national committee dispatched Lincoln to campaign for Taylor in New England that fall, the "eloquent Whig" from Illinois got a full ear of New England Whig anxiety. Normally, a Whig candidate had little to fear in New England. But Taylor was a slaveholder, and Lincoln found himself well occupied in calming New England Whigs nervous at the prospect of the Mexican Cession being added to the Federal Union under the aegis of a slaveholding president. He found that it did no good to maintain "that Gen. Taylor occupied a high and unexceptionable whig ground . . . with regard to the Bank, Tariff, Rivers and Harbors, &c." He now had to promise that somehow "freedom would be easier and better attained by voting for Taylor."

That argument, as far as it went, was enough to get Taylor elected in November, 1848. But New England's complaints did not move Lincoln into any significant anti-slavery activism. All through the first session of the Thirtieth Congress, Lincoln voted consistently with the Whig majority against the Southern policy of tabling of anti-slavery petitions, then presented a petition from his own district calling for the abolition of the slave trade in the District of Columbia, and finally voted for an Oregon territorial bill that banned slavery. But he also voted for a bill to compensate a slaveholder for the loss of a slave to the British in 1814, and of the thirty-six major speeches made in the House on the slavery question, not a single one was delivered by Lincoln. When the lame-duck session of the Thirtieth Congress assembled in December, 1848, Lincoln again split his votes on slavery, supporting Pennsylvania congressman David Wilmot's Proviso to bar the introduction of slavery into the Mexican Cession, but also voting against the introduction of a bill to abolish the slave trade in the District if it did not allow the inhabitants of the District a vote of confirmation. He came off, in the eyes of the *New York Tribune* as "a strong but judicious enemy of Slavery," whose efforts were bent more toward the "very practical, if not always successful."

Only toward the end of the Thirtieth Congress, on January 10, 1849, did Lincoln announce to the House that he had a proposal of his own for abolishing slavery in the District of Columbia. The proposal, however, contained no dramatic surprises: it called for a referendum in the District to consider abolition, and still provided for a right-of-transit to slaveholding "officers of the government," for "apprenticeships" for minors, and compensation to District slaveowners from the Treasury for "the full value" of their slaves. This was not a particularly radical gesture, and in fact Lincoln never formally introduced the bill because he could not garner enough support among Whigs in the House for an anti-slavery measure even that mild — or perhaps too mild. Northern anti-slavery Whigs like Joshua Giddings offered to support it only because "it is as good a bill as we could get at this time." Southern Whigs, as Lincoln learned when he went the rounds of the mayor of the District, "senators, and others whom I thought best acquainted with the sentiment of the people," wanted nothing to do with it at all.

It would also be the only step he would take as a congressman in an anti-slavery direction. To his own disappointment, Lincoln had not particularly enjoyed congressional work. Members had no offices in the 1840s, and carried on all their work at small school-house desks on the House floor, with one drawer and single shelf to accommodate all business. (Lincoln was in the rear row of desks, twenty feet behind former president John Quincy Adams, who sat as a Massachusetts Whig until a fatal stroke in February 1848.) "I hate to sit down and direct documents," he wrote to Mary in April, 1848. "It has grown exceedingly tasteless to me." He took up bowling for amusement, and kept the House post office and the table at Mrs. Spriggs's boarding house in a continual uproar of funny stories. But there is no evidence that he ever went to any of Washington's thirty-seven churches, and most of his time outside the Capitol was spent "in this old room by myself."

Even before the first session was over, he had already decided that he would abide by the reciprocity agreement he had with the other Whigs of the Seventh District and allow Stephen Logan to run for his seat in 1848. "I thought at the time, and still think, it would be quite as well for me to return to law at the end of a single term," he told Herndon in January of 1848. "I made the declaration that I would not be a candidate again . . . from a wish to deal fairly with others, to keep peace among our friends, and to keep the district from going to the enemy."

What he did hope, even more than the opportunity to return to legal practice, was that his service in the House and his campaign work for Zachary Taylor would translate into a federal appointment by the president, preferably as Commissioner of the General Land Office. (David Davis had warned Lincoln that law practice in Springfield had only grown more competitive, and that it would be more lucrative to wait for some federal office from Taylor's hands.) The Land Office controlled the sales of all federally owned public lands, a subject for which Lincoln had long demonstrated a more-than-healthy interest, and it was also handsomely salaried (twice Lincoln's previous law income). Lincoln even went so far as to appeal directly to President Taylor for the position, boldly asking whether central Illinois's loyalty to the Whig cause meant "nothing? — that center which alone has ever given you a Whig representative?"

But Taylor had bigger mouths to feed than a one-term Whig congressman, and to Lincoln's almost uncontrollable anger, the Land Office went to an "old-hawker" Chicago Whig named Justin Butterfield. Lincoln was eventually offered the secretaryship, and then the governorship, of the Oregon Territory. And he might have taken the governorship, if he had been able to persuade Mary Lincoln to go, and Joshua Speed to come along as an assistant. "But," as Orville Hickman Browning observed, "Mary would not consent to go out there." The matter died, and in April, 1849, Lincoln was back in Springfield, ready to pick up the Lincoln-Herndon law practice for what promised to be the rest of a comparatively dull life.

4 The Fuel of Interest

Abraham Lincoln was no longer a part of the United States Congress when the postwar political storm over the Mexican Cession finally broke. The old Missouri Compromise line, which was supposed to govern federal policy on slavery in the west, ran well to the north of almost all of the Cession, and that seemed to suggest that the Cession was fair game for slavery. And so, even though the Missouri Compromise technically applied only to the Louisiana Purchase lands, the Mexican War was hardly over before Southern politicians began demanding free access for slavery in the Cession under the Compromise's terms. Some Southerners, more radical in their pro-slavery expectations, were unhappy even with the idea of appealing to the Missouri Compromise as the rationale for opening the southwest to slavery. Gathered around the South's aging and white-haired paladin, Senator John C. Calhoun of South Carolina, they argued that the federal government had no jurisdiction (whether through the Missouri Compromise or any other congressional enactment) over the kinds of "property" American citizens took into any of the Cession.

The trouble with these arguments was that they made sense to nearly no one outside the South. The Missouri Compromise had been understood for a generation as a gentleman's agreement for the re-

straint of slavery; and the idea that the federal government had no authority at all to prevent slave expansion into the Cession flew in the
face of long-standing precedents in congressional management of the
Northwest Territory and the Louisiana Purchase. Even if it was now
going to be conceded that the federal government might not have regulatory powers about slavery in the Cession, that still didn't mean that
no one else had such power. Michigan senator Lewis Cass, one of President Polk's most ambitious rivals for power in the Democratic party,
protested that even if Congress lacked regulatory authority over slavery in the Cession, the American citizens who moved into the Cession
themselves could, when they organized themselves as a United States
territory or when they petitioned Congress for admission to the Union,
exercise their own "popular sovereignty" to permit or to prohibit the
presence of slavery in the Cession.

But Cass, who plainly hoped that the "popular sovereignty" plan
would boost him as the obvious successor to Polk in the 1848 elections,
only ended up enraging the Calhounites on the one hand, and on the
other causing the small corps of committed anti-slavery Democrats in
the North to bolt the Democrats to form a Free-Soil party with the
comeouters of the Liberty party. This divisive infighting, together with
the bland political inoffensiveness of Zachary Taylor, cost the Democrats an election they should easily have won, and ushered Taylor and
the Whigs into the White House.

Taylor, as it turned out, had his own plan for dealing with the
Cession, and to nearly everyone's surprise (for a Southerner and a
slaveholder), Taylor advocated the immediate organization of large
chunks of the Cession — California and the neighboring territory of
New Mexico — for direct admission to the Union as free states. This
amounted to the frank exclusion of slavery from the Cession, and (to
the horror of the Calhounites) simply on the strength of federal authority. When the Thirty-First Congress assembled in December, 1849,
political war between Northerners and Southerners, Whig as well as
Democrat, exploded. Calhoun, so close to death that he could not read
his own speech, demanded not only "an equal right in the acquired
territory" for slavery but a constitutional amendment that would forever forbid any tampering with slavery in the Union. Otherwise, he
warned, "the Southern States . . . cannot remain, as things now are,
consistently with safety and honor, in the Union." As if on cue, a gen-

144

eral convention of the Southern states was called to meet in Nashville, Tennessee, to consider whether the time was at hand for the slave states to protect slavery by seceding from the Union entirely. "It is apparent, horribly apparent, that the slavery question rides insolently over every other everywhere," wrote Georgian Henry L. Benning. "I think then, 1st, that the only safety of the South from abolition universal is to be found in an *early* dissolution of the Union."

It fell to the 72-year-old Henry Clay, donning the mantle of the dispassionate Whig statesman, to take the floor of the Senate on January 29, 1850, and offer another Union-saving compromise which would guarantee an "amicable arrangement of all questions in controversy between the free and slave States." The plan Clay laid before the Senate asked that California be admitted for what it already was in fact, a free state; that the remaining Mexican Cession lands of Deseret (or Utah) and New Mexico be allowed to exercise the popular sovereignty principle in organizing themselves as territories; and, as a sop to hard-core Calhounites, that a new national Fugitive Slave Law be adopted to give slaveholders new legal rights in recovering runaway slaves from free states (this would demonstrate to the Calhounites that everyone in the Union was willing to respect the institution of slavery as it presently existed, even if they didn't sympathize with it).

It was a magisterial political gesture, calling for "mutual forbearance" from both North and South, and if Clay had not unwisely demanded that the whole plan be adopted as a piece, or if President Taylor had been less jealous of Clay's stature among the Whigs, it might have worked. But Clay could not construct a coalition in the Senate or the administration large enough to endorse the whole compromise plan, and in the end it fell to Abraham Lincoln's Democratic rival from the 1840 races, Stephen A. Douglas (who had been elected U.S. senator by the Illinois legislature in 1847) to pick up the banner of Clay's compromise, especially the provisions for popular sovereignty, and smooth its final passage through Congress in September. It helped, too, that the unyielding Zachary Taylor died suddenly in the summer of 1850, and left a Whig successor in Vice President Millard Fillmore who was quite happy to cooperate with Douglas in smothering the blow-fires of disunion.

The result of the Compromise of 1850 was that, at least for the moment, Congress was relieved of the fearful need to grapple directly with the slave-extension nightmare. Popular sovereignty would allow the people in the Cession to decide that for themselves. What was even happier for the Democrats was that, because the Compromise of 1850 appealed fully as much to the Democratic partiality for localism and diversity as it did to the Whig preference for national unity and conformity, the lion's share of the credit for the Compromise went to neither Clay nor Fillmore but to Stephen Douglas and to the Democratic leadership of Congress. In the national election of 1852, the Whigs vainly tried to repeat their 1848 triumph by running the sclerotic Mexican War hero, Major General Winfield Scott, as their candidate. But Scott carried only four states, and the White House passed triumphantly into the hands of a handsome Northern Democrat, Franklin Pierce.

Abraham Lincoln might well have predicted this, since his failure to secure the Land Office appointment from President Taylor in 1849 had convinced him that Taylor was a straw man and that the Whig national leadership was its own worst enemy. "I was then so disgusted" with the Whigs' nerveless confusion, that "I made up my mind to retire to private life and practice my profession." After 1849 he "was losing interest in politics" and had concluded to go "to the practice of law with greater earnestness than ever before." He told Herndon that he considered himself "politically dead" and "despaired of ever rising again in the political world." When the *Illinois State Journal* published an editorial in the summer of 1850 calling for Lincoln to run for his old Seventh District seat, Lincoln firmly declined. "I neither seek, expect, or desire a nomination for a seat in the next Congress," he wrote to the editors, and he forbade "the use" of his name "in that connection."

In the place of politics, as he explained to Henry Clay Whitney, Lincoln instead had "a good business, and my children were coming up, and were interesting to me," and so home and law, for the first time in his life, now became Lincoln's principal focus. And he could once more consume his spare hours in reading. Harriet Chapman, Lincoln's niece, who came to live with the Lincolns briefly, recalled that "when not engaged in reading law Books he would read literary works, and was very fond of reading Poetry and often when he would be or appeared to be in a deep Study" would "Commence and repeat aloud Some piece that he had taken a fancy to and Commited to Memory," like Knox's "Mortality" or Charles Wolfe's "The Burial of Sir John Moore." Julius Royce, a New Yorker with property and business dealings in Bloomington, came upon Lincoln in a hotel in Bloomington and found him preoccupied with a book. "I am reading Homer, the *Iliad* and *Odyssey*," Lincoln replied when Royce questioned him. "You ought to read him. He has a grip and knows how to tell a story."

Even more than books, there was a great deal in Lincoln's family life that needed attention in the 1850s. In December, 1849, Lincoln's second son, Edward Baker Lincoln, fell ill and died, after a fifty-two-day sickness, on February 1, 1850. "We miss him very much," Lincoln wrote to John D. Johnston. But this was an understatement. Mary Lincoln, who had lost her father to sudden death the previous July and her grandmother six months after that, went to pieces over Eddie's death, unable even to open her son's drawers lest she have to look at his clothing. To Lincoln, little Eddie had been an unusually warmhearted child, and like his older brother Robert, something of the "rare-ripe sort" who was almost too smart for his age. No matter: he was dead now, before his fourth birthday.

There was some consolation in the birth, ten months later, of another son, named William Wallace (for Lincoln's physician brother-in-law), and in the last of the Lincoln children, Thomas (or as he was better known, Tad), in 1853. And in contrast with the way he had left his children on the margins of his political ambitions, Lincoln now shamelessly spoiled his younger boys. One observer was amazed that Lincoln could sit with visitors, "and all the while, two little boys, his sons, clambered over [Lincoln's] legs, patted his cheeks, pulled his nose, and poked their fingers in his eyes, without causing reprimand or even notice." James Gourley recalled that "Lincoln would take his Children and would walk out on the Rail way out in the Country — would talk to them — Explain things Carefully." Unlike his own father, Lincoln apparently never physically punished his sons, no matter what their behavior. Instead, to William Herndon's despair, Lincoln often brought the boys to the law office and allowed them to run riot:

> It happened that sometimes Lincoln would come down to our office
> . . . with one or two of his little children, hauling them in the same little wagon, and in our office, then and there, write declarations, pleas, and other legal papers. The children — spoilt ones to be sure

147

— would tear up the office, scatter the books, smash up pens, spill the ink, and [piss] all over the floor. I have felt many and many a time that I wanted to wring their little necks, and yet out of respect for Lincoln I kept my mouth shut.

When Henry McPike and Lyman Trumbull came calling on Lincoln at the office one day, their meeting was interrupted by Tad, who "when he was about 6 feet away . . . jumped and caught his father around the neck. Lincoln wrapped his arms about the boy . . . both of them laughing and carrying on as if there was nobody looking at them."

Lincoln himself would pay no attention at all: "he would say nothing, so abstracted was he and so blinded to his children's faults." In his family, Lincoln explained, "Children have the first place," so much so that Herndon privately groused that "had they [shit] in Lincoln's hat and rubbed it on his boots, he would have laughed and thought it smart." "It is my pleasure that my children are free — happy, and unrestrained by paternal tyranny," he announced. "Love is the chain whereby to lock a child to its parent." Acting on this self-advice made Lincoln "the most indulgent parent" Joseph Gillespie "ever knew. His children literally ran over him and he was powerless to withstand their importunities."

Mary Lincoln was a different story. Without the help of the slave nurses and mammies she had grown up with, Mary found child-raising wearying and boring, and she once complained that "I have certainly been a slave for their interest the best part of my life." She responded to her sons' offenses as any quondam slaveowner might, as a species of deliberate resistance, and the Lincolns' hired girls remembered that Mary "would whip Bob a good deal." But then, she would spin erratically in the opposite direction and spoil them nearly as badly as her husband. Mary once brought home a new clock and warned the boys not to touch it. This was, of course, an invitation to mayhem, and in short order "two of them had taken the clock to pieces." Mary accordingly "whipped them." But almost immediately afterward she felt so sorry for what she had done she told the boys "to take the clock and do what they pleased with it."

In that way, Mary Lincoln took the death of Eddie with far more shattering intensity than her husband. She abandoned her infrequent and genteel attendance at St. Paul's Episcopal Church and began seeking the spiritual counsel of the newly installed pastor of Springfield's First Presbyterian Church, a Scotsman named James Smith. This selection was no accident. James Smith was born in Scotland in 1798, and the trajectory of his life bore some uncanny intellectual resemblances to that of the Lincolns: he had lost both parents in his youth, emigrated to southern Indiana in 1824, dabbled in merchandising, and was "led astray by the sophisms of Volney and Paine" to "the conclusion that Religion was a fraud contrived to govern mankind." Unlike the Lincolns, however, Smith was converted in a revival meeting in 1825, and in 1829 was ordained by the Cumberland Presbyterian Church, an ultra-New School Presbyterian splinter group. Smith eventually gravitated back to the Old School Calvinism of his forebears in the 1840s. Since the Presbyterian Church had formally split into New School and Old School general assemblies in 1837, Smith was received into the Old School General Assembly in 1845. Like most Old Schoolers, Smith was a Democrat, but a moderate rather than a rabid "Loco-Foco" Jacksonian. He had served for four years in Kentucky, and he brought to Springfield in 1849 precisely the mildly Southern but clearly anti-disunion attitude that Mary Lincoln would have found congenial. Smith, also like Abraham Lincoln, warmly supported temperance reform, although, like Lincoln again, he pulled shy of demanding any single method for achieving it. The only subscription list for a "discourse" by a clergyman that Lincoln ever signed was for Smith's "A Discourse on the Bottle — Its Evils, and the Remedy" in 1853.

Smith's most fundamental resemblance to Lincoln was intellectual, since Smith had thoroughly assimilated the Old School preference for religious argumentation based on reasonableness and probability rather than religious passions or "affections," an apologetical strategy that had been perfected by Smith's Old School peers, Archibald Alexander (whose *Evidences of the Authenticity, Inspiration and Canonical Authority of the Holy Scriptures* was published in 1836), Jacob Janeway (the author of *The Internal Evidence of the Holy Bible* in 1845), and Charles Pettit McIlvaine (whose *Evidences of Christianity* appeared in 1832). In 1841, Smith purchased a brief moment of national notoriety by facing down a popular lawyer and "champion of Deism," Charles G. Olmsted (the author of *The Bible Its Own Refutation*, a Paineite book Olmsted published in 1836), in a public debate on "the GENUINENESS, AUTHENTICITY and INSPIRATION of the Old Testament

Scriptures." The debate lasted over eighteen consecutive nights and featured Smith and Olmsted each speaking for two hours on alternate nights, with time for a half-hour rebuttal each night.

The whole text of Smith's arguments was published in 1843 as the 650-page *The Christian's Defense, Containing a Fair Statement, and Impartial Examination of the Leading Objections urged by Infidels Against the Antiquity, Genuineness, Credibility, and Inspiration of the Holy Scriptures,* and it aimed directly at the "judgment and reason" of "the better educated young men of the country" who had been "led astray by the assertions and sophisms of the adversaries of Christianity . . . Hume, Volney, Taylor, Paine, Olmsted, English and other Infidels." He did not intend to defend Christianity as "a question of sentiment" — that would make Christianity appear as though it were nothing more than an object for the passions — but by "the exercises of the understanding." This was, in effect, to challenge the deists and unitarians on their own ground, and to demand "that the arguments which are held decisive in other historical questions" should be allowed to settle this one, as well.

Which is what Smith then proceeded to do, walking his hearers and readers from "the existence and operations of minds" to the existence of spiritual substance, and from there to the existence of God, "an all-wise and all-powerful SPIRIT." Far from religious faith resting only on sentiment, "it is impossible to find another truth in the whole compass of morals which, according to the justest laws of reasoning, admits of such strict and rigorous demonstration." He worked his way inexorably through the Old Testament, conceding that the six days of creation in Genesis were not literal days but nonetheless insisting on a literal act of divine creation, drawing out parallels between ancient history and literature and the biblical record of the Israelite kings and prophets, and taking the resulting confidence that "the Seers of Israel were true prophets of God" to demonstrate that "the prophecies of Messiah [have] been fulfilled in the person of Jesus Christ." It was not an argument from faith, but from reason toward faith, and Smith prided himself on having "taken nothing for granted." He had "reasoned together, from the first line to the last," so that "Impartial reason should now render an honest verdict."

This was just the sort of rational argument most likely to ease Lincoln's skeptical discomfort with preachers. Lincoln "relied upon reason at all times," fellow-lawyer Charles Zane observed. "He never allowed his natural emotions or the emotions of the heart to become agitated, excited, broken up, or thrown out of their proper action." Thus, Smith, as a conservative Democrat, dwelt close enough to the cultural boundary line of the two parties to give Lincoln, as a secular Whig, little discomfort. And fragmentary as knowledge of Mary Lincoln's inner life must be, Smith must also have made a tremendous impression on the bereaved mother in 1850: it was Smith who was invited to conduct Edward Baker Lincoln's funeral in the Lincoln home, and less than two years later, Mary Lincoln appeared before the session of the First Presbyterian Church to be received as a member of the church "on examination" — which was to say that, having never belonged formally to any previous church, she was required to give a convincing statement of religious experience and conversion on her own, along with her promise of adherence to Presbyterian doctrine and organization. And she managed to persuade her husband to rent and then refurbish a pew in the First Presbyterian Church for the use of her family and began dragooning her children off to the First Presbyterian Sunday School.

But even with Smith at the helm, religion still involved commitments that Lincoln held aloof from, and though in 1860 his political supporters would find it useful to define Lincoln as "a regular attendant upon religious worship" and "a pewholder and liberal supporter of the Presbyterian Church in Springfield," not even the political necessity of portraying Lincoln as friendly to religion could ignore the fact that First Presbyterian was the church "to which Mrs. Lincoln belongs," and not Abraham Lincoln. His lawyer friends never heard from Lincoln "an expression which remotely implied the slightest faith in Jesus as the Son of God and the Saviour of men." David Davis afterward insisted that he "don't Know anything about Lincoln's Religion" and "don't think anybody Knew."

This silence was not from any want of understanding of Christianity on Lincoln's part. His speeches and public documents were littered with biblical allusions from the 1830s onwards, and he told John Langdon Kaine that "the Bible is the richest source of pertinent quotations." When one Presbyterian minister passed by a crowd where Lincoln was speaking, he good-naturedly hooted, "Where the great ones are, there will the people be." Lincoln instantly shot back, "Ho! *Parson*

151

a little more Scriptural; 'Where the carces is there will the eagles be gathered together'" (an allusion to Luke 17:37). Even some of his cele-brated jokes and stories betrayed a fairly sophisticated comprehension of the intricacies of Protestant Christian doctrine. He was amused by the Old School Presbyterian who objected to the arrival of a universal-ist preacher in town: "There comes one among us, preaching the salva-tion of all men. But brethren, let us hope for better things." He once told Abner Ellis that if anyone was right about baptism, it must be the Baptists: "that he thought Baptism by imertion [immersion] Was the true Meaning of the Word, for he said John Baptised the Saviour in the river Jorden because their was much Water & they Went down into it and Came up out of it." Yet he just as quickly joked that "he preferred the Episcopalians to every other sect, because they are equally indiffer-ent to a man's religion and his politics."

But if Lincoln could joke about the foibles of Christianity in the 1850s, there was also much less of a note of contempt in it than there had been fifteen years before, much less of what Matheny called Lin-coln's early "enthusiasm in his infidelity." James Smith, who had al-ready been dealing with the grief of Mary Todd Lincoln, thought that the death of Eddie Lincoln had also sobered Abraham Lincoln consid-erably on the subject of religion. "I found him very much depressed and downcast at the death of his son, and without the consolation of the gospel," Smith told a fellow Presbyterian minister. "Up to this time I had heard but little concerning his religious views, and that was to the effect that he was a deist and inclined to skepticism as to the divine origin of the scriptures, though, unlike most skeptics, he had evidently been a constant reader of the Bible." Not surprisingly, for a "fatalist" like Lincoln, "he was perplexed and unsettled on the fundamentals of religion, by speculative difficulties, connected with providence and revelation."

Lincoln did not doubt that there was some form of "providence" at work in the order of the universe; the question was what the nature of this "providence" actually was. "No man had a stronger or firmer faith in Providence," observed William Herndon, but this did not mean "that he believed in a personal God." Lincoln "had no faith in the Christian sense of that term — Had faith in laws, principles — causes & Effects — Philosophy." Herndon recalled that in 1854 "he asked me to erase the word God from a speech I had written and read to him for criticism because my language indicated a personal God, whereas he insisted that no such personality ever existed." In an unfinished note Lincoln penned in 1848 after viewing Niagara Falls, Lincoln attributed the power of the falls, not to some divine intention, but to the "vast power" of "five hundred thousand tons of water." Anyone who sat for a moment to add it all up would, of course, be "overwhelmed in the contemplation," but they would also recognize that "there is no mystery about the thing itself. Every effect is just such as any intelligent man knowing the causes, would anticipate, without it."

At its barest, providence was for Lincoln nothing more than the "necessity" imposed by cause and effect, just as the will responded automatically to motives and the call of self-interest. It satisfied Lincoln's need, in a universe governed by necessity, to ascribe all human events to some form of causation. "Lincoln's whole life was a calculation of the law of forces and ultimate results," Leonard Swett told Herndon. And even when Lincoln was willing to grant to providence some form of intelligence, purpose, or power as God, it was an idea that only dimly resembled the Presbyterian idea of God. "He went to the old school church," Charles H. Ray acknowledged, "but in spite of that outward sign of assent to the horrible dogmas of the sect, I have reason from himself to know that his 'vital piety,' if that means belief in the impossible, was of the negative sort." If Lincoln's concept of God looked like anything else on offer, it was not the orthodox trinitarian God of Father, Son, and Holy Spirit described by the Old School theologians, but a truncated one with God the Father — remote, austere, all-powerful, uncommunicative — and neither Son nor Spirit.

This seemed to some of his friends to place Lincoln as close to unitarianism as one could get, and Jesse Fell (himself a unitarian) believed that unitarians "were generally much admired and approved by him." Both Fell and Herndon, in fact, thought that Lincoln's nearest intellectual resemblance was to the radical Boston unitarian Theodore Parker. But unitarianism was, fully as much as it was a rejection of orthodox trinitarianism, a New England rebellion against the idea of predestination; and Lincoln could never reconcile his pervasive belief in "necessity" with unitarianism's defiant assertions of human free will. "In religious matters, Mr. Lincoln was *theoretically* a predestinarian," wrote Joseph Gillespie. "Mr. Lincoln once told me that he could not avoid believing in predestination." And although unitarianism prided itself on what William Ellery Channing called "the constant exercise of reason," even Channing (who warned against the disturbing influence of the "passions" in 1819) was rapidly broadening in the 1850s into appeals "addressed to the affections and to the conscience." Others believed that Lincoln's predestinarianism was precisely what located him close to universalism, another late-eighteenth-century New England revolt from Calvinism which preached the ultimate salvation of all human souls. Ever since his New Salem days, Lincoln had reasoned that if every human action was foreordained, then it was the deepest unfairness on God's part to punish anyone in the next world, and so Lincoln told William Hannah "That he never Could bring himself to the belief in Eternal Punishment." Hannah even claimed that "Mr. Lincoln told him he was a Kind of Universalist" in 1856, and Isaac Cogdal was convinced that "He was a Universalist, tap root & all in faith and sentiment" because "He did not believe in Hell — Eternal Punishment as the christians say."

But whatever resemblance he seemed to have to either unitarianism or the universalists, Lincoln neither joined them nor associated with them. He refused, for that matter, to join "any Society except it be for the Good of my Country." The idea of providence pulled him to the Presbyterians, while his love for rationality and his cautious mainstream Whiggism pulled him to Old School Presbyterians in particular, rather than to the reformers and revivalists of the New School camp. But even there, Lincoln kept his distance, and kept his definitions to himself. Leonard Swett thought that Lincoln "believed in God as much as the most approved Church members," yet "he had in my judgment very little faith in ceremonials or forms." And while he believed in providence fully as much as James Smith, "Yet he judged of Providence by the same system of great generalization as of everything else." Charles Ray thought that "orthodoxy, if that means the Presbyterian doxy, was regarded by him as a huge joke; but he was far too kindly and cautious to challenge any man's faith without cause."

However, much as providence and necessity gave a "fatalist" like Lincoln powers of "great generalization" in explaining events, they presented problems of their own in explaining the why-and-wherefore of specific tragedies. Moments like the death of Eddie could not be salved with generalizations, and they found no solution except in submission. The Calvinism of the Hard-Shell Baptists of Lincoln's youth had taught that this sense of submission was morally a good thing, since it could function as a divine catharsis and generate the monumental decision-making necessary to conversion and religious happiness. But even then, the actual gift of grace remained still the action of an inscrutable God, and for those who did not receive that grace, the blows of providence could just as easily produce swings into despair unless some mechanism could be found within the soul. "The preachers have preached and talked this 'miraculous conversion,'" Lincoln complained to Benjamin H. Smith, but "I have honestly at times doubted the whole thing."

Nor was Calvinism the only schoolroom Lincoln experienced for lessons in the immovability of "necessity." Lincoln confided to Herndon "about 1850" suspicions he had acquired from who-knows-where (probably his Hanks relatives, long before in Indiana) that his mother had been illegitimate, and Herndon later became convinced that Lincoln believed even his own legitimacy was not beyond question. Bastardy, like necessity, cursed its victims without hope of appeal or redress, and Herndon believed that the rumors of bastardy convinced Lincoln "that God had cursed and crushed him especially," so much so that Lincoln strictly forbade Herndon to breathe even a hint of this to anyone "while I live." Providence thus presented Lincoln on the one hand with requirements — for conversion, for respectability, for action — but with the other hand denied the grace or the means and ability for satisfying them, and even took from him his child.

It was not the smart-tongued "infidelity" of his New Salem days which, in the 1850s, kept Lincoln from following Mary Lincoln into a church fellowship that would otherwise have had every reason to welcome him with but few questions asked. It was Lincoln's sense of being helpless and unworthy in the estimate of the glowering Father who offered nothing but demands for a perfection Lincoln could not honestly claim for his own. This was far more terrifying than the passivity which is supposed to be the flip side of "necessity," and it is this which accounts for the new edge of plaintiveness that creeps into Lincoln's comments on religion in the 1850s. Joshua Speed believed that Lincoln "tried hard to be a believer, but his reason could not grasp and solve the great problem of redemption." He was even more revealing of this wistfulness to the family of Henry Rankin, when he told Rankin's mother that "probably it is to be my lot to go on in a twilight, feeling and reasoning my way through life, as questioning, doubting Thomas did."

If this kept him away from church, it still brought him within the orbit of James Smith's interest, who unlike most preachers, could at least get Lincoln to listen to him "preach and converse." (Smith once remarked to Lincoln, "You are a rising man. You will be President yet.") The Old School parson attempted to deal with Lincoln's "perplexity" through an appeal to Smith's own rationalist apologetics, and he urged Lincoln to work his way through *The Christian's Defense,* on the grounds that a man who could be persuaded that the Bible was truthful was not far from being persuaded that grace and redemption were nigh. Lincoln took at least some parts of Smith's advice: Ninian Edwards remembered Lincoln discussing "a work of Dr. Smith on the evidences of Christianity," and Thomas Lewis, one of the lay elders of the First Presbyterian Church, was convinced that Lincoln had been led "to change his views about the Christian religion" through Smith's influence. And as far as logic went, Lincoln was willing to admit that Smith's arguments "in favor of the divine authority and inspiration of the Scriptures was unanswerable."

This was not the same thing as saying that Lincoln believed them himself. Robert Todd Lincoln told Herndon years later that he never remembered "Dr. Smith's having 'converted' my father . . . nor do I know that he held any decided views on the subject as I never heard him speak of it." John Todd Stuart knew that Smith "tried to Convert Lincoln from Infidelity so late as 1858 and Couldn't do it." At best, Lincoln told Springfield postmaster James Keyes, he could believe

> in a Creator of all things, who had neither beginning nor end, who possessing all power and wisdom, established a principal, in Obedience to which, Worlds move and are upheld, and animal and vegetable life came into existance. A reason he gave for his belief was that in view of the Order and harmony of all nature which we behold, it would have been More miraculous to have Come about by chance than to have been created and arranged by some great thinking power.

But he could not be nudged by Smith into affirming that God the Creator had any necessary connection with Christ the Redeemer, or that

156

the Bible was more than a source of "pertinent quotations." Belief in Jesus Christ "had better be taken for granted," Lincoln told Keyes, but it came "in somewhat doubtful Shape" and was only worth acknowledging because "the Sistom [system] of Christianity was an ingenious one, at least — and perhaps was Calculated to do good." Herndon believed that Lincoln's only use for Smith's *Christian's Defense* was to shelve it in his office: "Lincoln brought it to the office, laid it down, never took it up again to my knowledge, never condescended to write his name in it, never spoke of it to me." (Herndon, like other Springfield lawyers with books that were generally shared around, usually wrote his name at four or five places in his books to prove possession.) Though Lincoln attended some services at First Presbyterian from time to time, he just as often whiled away Sunday mornings at "the railroad shop and spends the sabbath in reading Newspapers, and telling stories to the workmen," or in his office, allowing his sons' after-Sunday-school antics to drive Herndon into wordless furies. "Whether he went to Church once a month or once a year," remarked Leonard Swett, "troubled him but very little."

Curiously, this did nothing to hurt Lincoln's Whiggish reputation for probity, loyalty, and sincerity. "The framework of his mental and moral being was honesty," Herndon remembered, "open, candid and square in his profession, never practicing on the sharp or low." Judge Owen Reeves remembered that Lincoln "impressed court and jurymen with his absolute sincerity." That he could do so when, as one Springfield minister, G. W. Pendleton, observed, "he makes no pretensions to piety" made Lincoln a puzzle, but even Pendleton acknowledged "he is probably as moral as most persons who discard religion entirely in their practice." Despite Lincoln's falling "far short of the standard" of "Church Creeds and unexceptionable language," Leonard Swett was relieved to find that he "believed in the great laws of truth, the rigid discharge of duty, his accountability to God, the ultimate triumph of right, and the overthrow of wrong." What Pendleton, Swett, and Herndon missed was that Lincoln's moralism, far from puzzling, was driven precisely because he *was* "wholly wanting" in "piety." It was the mark of many Victorian unbelievers who came from pious Protestant households — like the novelist George Eliot, Harvard president Charles Eliot, or even the notorious agnostic Robert Ingersoll — to imbibe from those households a puritanical demand for

157

earnestness and relentless truthfulness and then turn it on their own Christianity. Duty became the moral surrogate of religion. And often, it was the very high-mindedness of their honesty which led them to reject Christianity as untrue or to lapse into unbelief if they felt they could not honestly describe themselves as Christians. The ethics of Protestant Christianity outlasted its theology, and almost as a compensation for the absence of faith, "infidels" like Lincoln redoubled their own pursuit of conscientiousness.

Nevertheless, Lincoln deliberately toned down the harshness of his "skepticism" in middle life. The toning-down was so noticeable that James Matheny mistook it for a political ploy, and it is not impossible that this played some role in it:

> Lincoln Knew he was to be a great man — was a rising man — was looking to the Presidency &c. and well Knowing that the old infidel, if not Atheistic charge would be made & proved against him and to avoid disgrace — odium and unpopularity of it tramped on the Christian toes saying — "Come and Convert me": the Elders — lower & higher members of the churches, including Ministers &c flocked around him & that he appeared openly to the world as a seeker.

Infrequent though his church attendance might be, Lincoln would now make an occasional acknowledgment of "a simple faith in God," even if it remained sufficiently "simple" as to pose no particular obligations. Speed remembered that "for a sincere Christian" Lincoln had "great respect," and Lincoln "often said that the most ambitious man might live to see every hope fail; but no Christian could live and see his hope fail, because fulfillment could only come when life ended." How much Lincoln intended his allusion to "the most ambitious man" to be self-referential is unclear, and it is for that reason almost impossible to disentangle poignancy from self-protecting disingenuity. But the note of poignancy is at least there, and it is something that was absent from his single-minded preoccupation with "infidelity" in his high-flying days as a state legislator.

That poignancy surfaced most clearly when Lincoln had to deal with his other great family crisis of the 1850s, the death of his father. Lincoln's ties to his father grew even more remote once he left his father's farm near Decatur in 1831, and nothing Thomas Lincoln did after that convinced his son that he had been wrong in departing. Thomas Lincoln had moved almost at once from Decatur, bought a new farm and tried unsuccessfully to operate a sawmill, and then finally in 1840 bought 160 acres in Coles County. He fell continually deeper into debt, and Abraham was forced to intervene in 1841 to save his father's property by buying forty acres of it for $200 and then letting the old man have it back for his own use. Even then Thomas Lincoln had to mortgage half of the property just to pay his school taxes in 1842. It should have been no surprise to anyone that when Abraham Lincoln married Mary Todd later that year, Thomas Lincoln was not invited. As Thomas Lincoln's strength declined in the late 1840s, he came more and more to lean, not on his son, but on his unreliable stepson, John D. Johnston, who was at the same time badgering his lawyer stepbrother with ever-mounting requests for loans and bailouts.

These requests increasingly came sandwiched with crying-wolf about Thomas Lincoln's health. In May of 1849, Johnston frantically wrote Abraham Lincoln that Thomas had been "atacken with a lesion of the Heart. . . . He is very anxious to See you before he dies & I am told that his Cries for you for the last few days are truly Heart-rendering." The alarm turned out to be a false one, and it must have grated all the harder on Lincoln for it being accompanied with Johnston's tearful reminders that Thomas Lincoln "thinks that ower Savour has a Crown of glory, prepared for *him*. . . ." That was what Thomas Lincoln could expect; Abraham Lincoln could not believe that God had any such good intentions for him, something which Johnston proceeded unwittingly to second by adding that Thomas Lincoln "wonts me to tell your wife that he Loves hure & wants hur to prepare to meet him at ower Savours feet" — her, and not necessarily Abraham. All of this is a major reason why, when Johnston began writing again a year and a half later with more warnings about Thomas Lincoln's deteriorating condition, Abraham Lincoln ignored him "because it appeared to me I could write nothing which would do any good."

When Lincoln finally replied to Johnston on January 12, 1851, it was to express a polite but firm unwillingness to make the trip down to Coles County. Mary was still unwell from the birth of William Wallace Lincoln, and, even more to the point, the distance between father and son had simply grown too great to be reconciled, even if the old man was at death's door. "If we could meet now," Lincoln told Johnston, "it is doubtful whether it would not be more painful than pleasant." And almost as if this mysterious inability to find reconciliation with his father reminded Lincoln of another equally painful inability, he dropped back into language from his boyhood which he must have known would be the substance of his father's religious hopes but which he could only acknowledge as a distant impossibility for himself:

> at all events tell him to remember to call upon, and confide in, our great, and good, and merciful Maker; who will not turn away from him in any extremity. He notes the fall of a sparrow, and numbers the hairs of our heads; and He will not forget the dying man, who puts his trust in Him. . . . if it is his lot to go now, he will soon have a joyous [meeting] with many loved ones gone before; and where [the rest] of us, through the help of God, hope ere-long [to join] them.

It is hard to imagine the "infidel" of the 1830s writing such advice, even if it was (as Herndon insisted it only was) designed largely as the dutiful sentiment a tactful but distant son might be expected to offer a dying father. Mixed up together with the sentimentality are all the old echoes of the Lincoln family's unbending Calvinism; and mixed together with that was Lincoln's inability to attach it to the hope of Christian redemption. What he was willing to acknowledge as grace for others he could not acknowledge for himself. It was "the help of God" the predestinating Father, not the mediation of Christ the redeeming Son, which was the best Lincoln could offer.

Thomas Lincoln died five days later. His son, his only son, did not attend the funeral, or mark the grave with a stone, or name a son of his own for him until two years after his death.

Abraham Lincoln's personal losses made no discernible mark on his legal practice, which, thanks to Herndon's tending of the store while Lincoln was in Washington, could be picked up again in 1849 almost without missing a beat. Between 1850 and 1855, the Lincoln-Herndon case load more than doubled, from 150 to just over 400 cases a year. Lincoln had never shown much aptitude for office-bound legal work, such as wills and estates, or for any significant number of criminal cases. (Criminal and probate work amounted to less than 5 percent of his practice at home in Sangamon County.) He preferred the personal and property litigation he found on the Eighth Judicial Circuit, and he had hardly resettled himself in Springfield in 1849 before resuming the rollicking progress of wandering lawyers from county courthouse to county courthouse. Grant Goodrich, a Chicago lawyer, invited Lincoln to move to Chicago in 1849 and enter into partnership with him there. But Lincoln replied "that he would rather go round the circuit . . . than to sit down & die in Chicago." As early as the fall term for 1850, Lincoln was "absent on the circuit seven weeks, only getting home [for] the election."

This incessant circuit riding posed less of a contradiction with the demands of his family than it had in the 1840s, since the steady spread of railroads across Illinois in the mid-1850s permitted Lincoln to return to Springfield over the weekends with greater frequency than before. By 1857, he could reach every county seat on the circuit by rail. The Eighth Circuit itself was shrunk by legislative redistribution to eight counties in 1853, and five in 1857, and anyway the bulk of his circuit work was now being done in Springfield for the rapidly expanding Sangamon County Circuit Court, where he handled over 3,200 cases (well over half of his entire circuit practice). It was all the more pleasant to discover that his massively corpulent friend, David Davis, had won election as the circuit judge in 1848, and Lincoln and Davis formed an association on the circuit so close that Davis occasionally deputized Lincoln to sit as judge in his place. "It was the habit of Judge Davis to frequently leave the bench when attacked with headache or indisposition and Call one of the principal attorneys to sit in his place for an hour or two," recalled Jasper Porter, the Champaign County clerk. "And he called upon Mr. Lincoln more than any one else to take his place, they being very warm and Close friends." In 1858 alone, Lincoln filled in as a judge for Davis in ninety-five cases. In between the two circuit sessions each year, he was handling an increasing number of cases in the Illinois Supreme Court in Springfield, in the federal district and circuit courts in Springfield, and (after 1855) in Chicago, where he took on 431 cases. He even served as attorney of record in six U.S. Supreme Court cases between 1849 and 1861.

He had by now acquired a certain seniority among the lawyers on the Eighth Circuit, and he emerged after 1850 as a mentor for a number of the younger lawyers who had just taken up practice there, like the elegant Maine-born twenty-four-year-old Leonard Swett (who emerged along with Lincoln and Davis as one of the most respected lawyers on the Eighth Circuit) or Henry Clay Whitney, who began practicing law in Urbana, in Champaign County, in 1854 (Whitney made his first motion in court before Lincoln as judge) or Lawrence Weldon, who moved to Illinois from Ohio in 1854 to practice law in Clinton. Just as in religion, time and experience had worked a smoothing-off of the abrasive confrontationalism that had marked Lincoln's early entrance into law. In contrast to the antagonistic witness-slayer of a decade before, "he was remarkably gentle with young lawyers becoming permanent residents at the several county-seats in the circuit where he had practiced for so many years." William Walker remembered, as a law student in Springfield, how Lincoln would drop in unannounced in Edward Baker's law office "and take up some text-book . . . and give us a close and rigid examination, laughing heartily at our answers, at times; and always made the hour he spent with us interesting and instructive." Lawrence Weldon remembered "with what confidence I always went to him because I was certain he knew all about the matter and would most cheerfully help me," and Henry Clay Whitney found Lincoln "so good natured & so willing to give advice that young lawyers went to him a great deal."

> I did not feel the slightest delicacy in approaching him for assistance; for it seemed as if he invited me to familiarity if not close intimacy at once; and this from no selfish motive at all — nothing but pure philanthropy and goodness of heart to a young lawyer just beginning his career.

However, much as he was willing to take younger circuit lawyers under his wing, Lincoln took on only a few students or clerks of his own to read under him in Springfield, partly because he preferred circuit work, partly because his own legal education inclined him to give short shrift to the day-by-day supervision of apprentices. "I am from home too much of my time, for a young man to read law with me advantageously," he told Isham Reavis in 1855; besides, "If you are resolutely determined to make a lawyer of yourself, the thing is more than half done already." He saw no reason to improve on his own self-taught methods: "Get the books, and read and study them till you understand them in their principal features; and that is the main thing." When Shelby Cullom applied to Lincoln to read law in the Lincoln-Herndon office, "Mr. Lincoln told my father that he could not give me the attention I ought to have, the catechising and directing of my studies, as he was then much engaged and a good deal absent."

Lincoln's seniority also allowed him to develop a large network of informal working partnerships with other senior lawyers on the circuit, most of which amounted to no more than verbal agreements to join forces whenever Lincoln came to town, "so there was Lincoln & Jones in this county and Lincoln & Smith in that; but the partnership was limited simply to Lincoln trying Smith's and Jones' cases, if they had any, and dividing fees with them." One of the closest of those partnerships was with Ward Hill Lamon, a thickset, walrus-mustached Virginian from Danville, in Vermilion County. Lamon and Lincoln were nearly as unalike in their ways as Lincoln and Herndon; but what Lincoln found in Lamon was the same ferociously reliable personal loyalty that Herndon gave him. Along with Lamon in Danville, Lincoln built an equally close relationship with the "Bloomington triumvirate" of David Davis, the Maine-born Leonard Swett, and Jesse Fell, a Pennsylvanian who had given up lawyering to make even more money in real estate. With these men around him Lincoln liked nothing so much as "the atmosphere of a court-house, and seemed to be contented and happy when Judge Davis was on the bench and he had before him the 'twelve good and lawful men' who had been called from the body of the county to 'well and truly try the issue.'"

Above all, seniority allowed him to assume the most prized of Whig cultural roles, that of elder statesman who rises above personal or political partisanship in the name of harmony, compromise, and reason. In a series of notes he compiled for a lecture on lawyering (perhaps as part of one of the Springfield lyceums' frequent lectures on the professions), Lincoln advised "young lawyers" to rest their cases more on solid beforehand research and preparation than on witness-badgering or emotional pleas before the jury. "Extemporaneous speaking should be practiced and cultivated" since "it is the lawyer's avenue to the public," but no aspiring lawyer could make "a more fatal error . . . than relying too much on speech-making." He began to encourage "compromise" as a goal in settling cases. In 1845, a more sharp-edged Lincoln had advised clients "not to compromise the case at any cost; but let them sue if they will." Ten years later, rather than turning courtrooms into verbal dueling matches, Lincoln urged beginning lawyers to "discourage litigation" and (like the Whig pattern, Clay) "Persuade your neighbors to compromise whenever you can." "Never stir up litigation" yourself, he warned. He advised a client in 1851 that, even with a strong case in hand, "still it is better to get along peaceably if possible," and he offered another client to "charge nothing" for his work in a case if "you will settle it" out of court. One client who criticized Lincoln's willingness to accept partial settlement of a debt was told "it is so much better to get the debt reduced by actual payments, than to push forward in sole reliance upon the law." Herndon watched him in the office warn clients with shaky cases, "You are in the wrong of the case and I would advise you to compromise, or if you cannot do that, do not bring a suit on the facts of your case because you are in the wrong and surely [will be] defeated and have to pay a big bill of costs." David Davis, observing him in court in the 1850s, thought that his friend "shrank from Controversy as a general rule — hated quarrell — hated to say hard & sharp thing of any man and never Stept beyond this Except that his duty — his honor or obligations — principles demanded it."

This did not, as Herndon noted, make Lincoln less formidable a courtroom opponent, but it did make him more evasive, more indirect, less predictable than a decade before. Behind the affability, there remained both the pervasive sense of melancholy and a distinct reserve that not even his closest friends and protégés could dispel or penetrate. "With all his awkwardness of manner, and utter disregard of social conventionalities that seemed to invite familiarity, there was something about Abraham Lincoln that enforced respect," wrote Donn Piatt. "No man presumed on the apparent invitation to be other than respectful." Henry Clay Whitney also found that there was in Lincoln "an indefinable *something* that commanded respect." It was a respect that invited, and sometimes even indulged, treatment as an equal, or even as a "brother." But that *"something"* also provided a curtain that the respectful found themselves unable and unwilling to penetrate. The young Adlai Stevenson remembered that "He was always addressed and referred to in Bloomington as Mr. Lincoln. People did not call him 'Abe' Lincoln." He was, David Davis said, "the most reticent, secretive man I ever saw or expect to see," and Herndon thought that Lincoln was a "terribly reticent, secretive, shut-mouth man."

> If a man came to see him for the purpose of finding out something which he did not care to let him know, and at the same time did not want to refuse him, [Lincoln] was very adroit. In such cases Lincoln would do most of the talking, swinging around what he suspected was the vital point, but never nearing it, interlarding his answers with a seemingly endless supply of stories and jokes. The interview being both interesting and pleasant, the man would depart in good humor, believing he had accomplished his mission. After he had walked away a few squares and had cooled off, the question would come up, "Well, what did I find out?" Blowing away the froth of Lincoln's humorous narratives he would find nothing substantial left.

The true elder was in the world but not of it, a man of the people but also a man apart. "Mr. Lincoln only revealed his soul to but few beings — *if any*," remarked Herndon, "and then he kept a corner of that soul from his bosom friends."

Lincoln not only practiced eldership, he came actually to wear it like a costume. Jane Martin Johns, who moved to the Macon County seat of Decatur in 1849, remembered him as neither an oafish ex-farm hand nor as a would-be Whig aristocrat, but as a simple old-fashioned gentleman. "When I first knew Lincoln, the ungainliness of the pioneer, if he ever had it, had worn off and his manner was that of a gentleman of the old school, unaffected, unostentatious, who 'arose at once when a lady entered the room, and whose courtly manners would put to shame the easy-going indifference to etiquette.'" James Ewing, a Bloomington lawyer, insisted that "Mr. Lincoln wasn't a sloven and he wasn't a buffoon." Judith Bradner remembered that "Mr. Lincoln was not so careless about how his clothes lookd as some people say," and while "His clothing did not fit him well . . . the material was of the best. His linen was always fresh and clean." Elihu Washburne, who first met Lincoln in 1847 in Chicago, was surprised to hear him described as "Old Abe" by Lisle Smith (even though Lincoln was only thirty-eight at the time) and he cheerfully accepted being addressed as "old Mr. Lincoln" in 1858. "They have been at that trick many years," Lincoln commented off-handedly. "They commenced it when I was scarcely thirty." Even in 1854, he wrote to a distant relative in Tennessee, "I can no longer claim to be a young man myself."

Leonard Swett, meeting Lincoln for the first time on the circuit in a Danville hotel, thought he was "certainly the ungodliest figure I had ever seen." But it was precisely Lincoln's willingness to concede his own "homeliness," rather than demanding the "degree of Deference" Swett had anticipated, which won Swett's loyalty to "this apparition." As in manner, so in dress: David Davis noticed that Lincoln preferred "an old-fashioned stiff stock which encircled his neck" rather than a necktie, and Henry Clay Whitney found himself charmed by the image of the celebrated Springfield lawyer whose hat "was brown and faded and the name invariably worn or rubbed off."

> He wore a short cloak and sometimes a shawl. His coat and vest hung loosely on his giant frame and his trousers were usually a trifle short. In one hand he carried a faded green umbrella with his name, A. LINCOLN, in rather large white cotton or muslin letters sewed on the inside. The knob was gone from the handle and, when closed, a piece of cord was usually tied round it in the middle to keep it from flying open. In the other hand he carried a literal carpet-bag in which were stored the few papers to be used in courts, and underclothing enough to last till his return to Springfield.

Lincoln's assumption of eldership was reinforced by his well-advertised reluctance to charge overly high fees in personal litigation, and his willingness to take on several well-publicized *pro bono* criminal cases. He was almost embarrassed at times to bill individual clients for fees, and delicately tried to hint to Andrew McCallen in 1851 that he was now owed a substantial sum of money. "I have news from Ottawa, that we *win* our Galtin & Saline county case," he wrote to McCallen. "As the dutch Justice said, when he married folks 'Now, vere ish my hundred tollars.'" In 1852, he rescued the property of William Florville, a free black barber in Springfield, when Florville became embroiled in a suit over the title to "certain town lots sold to him." In 1858, he undertook at no cost the defense of the young William "Duff" Armstrong, the son of his old New Salem wrestling rival and friend, Jack Armstrong, in Armstrong's trial for the murder of James Metzger.

Leading the principal witness into claiming that he had clearly recognized Armstrong as the killer by the light of a full moon, Lincoln was able to produce an almanac which proved that the moon had actually set earlier that evening, thus collapsing the only hostile testimony against Armstrong and winning the youth's release into the tearful arms of his aged and grateful mother. A year later, he appeared in defense of Quinn "Peachy" Harrison, who had fatally stabbed the grandson of Lincoln's old congressional rival, Peter Cartwright. Lincoln made a sensational plea to the jury based on the victim's deathbed forgiveness of Harrison, and despite the attempt by the judge to disallow the dying boy's testimony, Lincoln pulled the jury to acquittal.

But if the combativeness that marked Lincoln's early career underwent a maturing and stabilizing in the 1850s as he turned away from politics to his family and his profession, that did not mean that ambition had ceased to drive him. His circuit practice in the 1850s began to shift away from the petty litigation he had conducted as a junior partner for Stuart and Logan, and into ever-more-expensive land law cases. He still refused to follow Davis and his lawyer colleagues into large-scale land speculation, and he bitterly denounced as "a fiend" the sort of lawyer "who habitually overhauls the register of deeds in search of defects in titles, whereon to stir up strife, and put money in his pocket." Nevertheless, his practice earned him payment in the form of several town lots in Springfield and Bloomington in 1851 (which he resold for a healthy profit five years later), and in 1853, a new town north of Springfield on the line of the Chicago & Mississippi Railroad not only paid Lincoln for representing it with a town lot, but even named the new town for him. Characteristically, he warned the town fathers, "You'd better not do that, for I never knew anything named Lincoln that amounted to much"; just as characteristically, he did not refuse either the honor or the town lot.

It was the railroads he had once championed in the state legislature which became his most lucrative clients, usually in land cases. Between 1840 and 1860, railroad mileage in Illinois rocketed from twenty-six to nearly three thousand miles of track, and in 1850, at the height of its distraction over the great Compromise, Congress had authorized a long-desired sale of 2.5 million acres of federal lands in Illinois to underwrite the stalled Illinois Central Railroad project. The Illinois legislature, with the eager support of Governor William H. Bissell, passed an incorporation bill for the Illinois Central in February, 1851, but only after a month of ferocious debate and political jockeying (and with Lincoln acting as lobbyist for the railroad). Even then, it was clear that a substantial amount of land litigation was going to follow as the railroad sought to prove its title to land sections that had been occupied by squatters. Laid out to bisect Illinois from north to south, the Illinois Central arose as a single line from Cairo, at the junction of the Ohio River and Mississippi River, and then forked at Centralia, with one line heading for Galena in the far northwestern corner of Illinois and the other reaching northeastward for Chicago and the Great Lakes. Even more than the Illinois and Michigan Canal, which had finally opened its locks in 1848, the Illinois Central promised to free Illinois farmers from dependency on St. Louis or New Orleans, or anywhere else in the slave South, and to make Chicago the dominant commercial entrepôt of the state and the New York markets the principal point of exchange. It also promised to create a miasma of litigation that would keep Illinois lawyers well employed for the following decade.

Lincoln's defense of the Illinois Central fifteen years before, plus the experience and stature he had acquired through his term in Congress, together with the fact that the most contentious title cases for the railroad lay right through the Eighth Circuit, made Lincoln a highly desirable recruit for the railroad's legal interests. "He proves to be not only the most prominent of his political party," advised one Illinois Central company director, "but the acknowledged special advisor of the Bissell administration" on railroad matters. They would need him at once, too; in the spring of 1853, litigation begun by squatters in Champaign County concerning the railroad's right-of-way was already on appeal in the Eighth Circuit; and much more threatening, McLean County was trying to tax railroad property that the legislature had declared exempt. (The legislature's charter for the Illinois Central had levied an annual gross receipts tax on the railroad, in exchange for which the railroad was granted immunity from local property taxes for the first six years of its operation.) The first section of the railroad to be completed, in fact, lay between Bloomington and LaSalle in McLean County, and the county tried to levy property taxes on the railroad on the ground that the state had no business interfering in the counties' jurisdiction over property.

What this litigation amounted to in real terms was a contest over whether local communities had the authority to prevent the intrusion of large-scale corporations, and with them the larger network of the markets, into their domain, and so the railroad sued the county. On that point, there was no doubt where Lincoln's interest would lie. "The question, in its magnitude, to the Co. on the one hand, and the counties in which the Co. has land, on the other, is the largest law question that can now be got up in the State," he wrote. Lincoln was slightly embarrassed by the fact that Champaign County had beaten the railroad to the punch by suggesting the payment of a hefty retainer to Lincoln, possibly with a view toward keeping Lincoln out of the litigation entirely. But by October, the county had either failed to make the offer or had second thoughts on the whole proposition, and on October 3rd, Lincoln offered his services to Mason Brayman, the Illinois Central's general solicitor, for a retainer of $250.

This was only the beginning of a long and highly profitable relationship between Lincoln and the Illinois Central, which became his most important corporate client. Lincoln was not wrong when he told Illinois Central general counsel James F. Joy that "A great stake is involved" in the McLean County case, "and it will be fiercely contended for." The Eighth Judicial Circuit dismissed the Illinois Central's suit against McLean County almost immediately so that an appeal could be taken to the state supreme court in February, 1854, where a generally binding judgment for the entire state of Illinois could be issued. It dragged into hearing and rehearing before the supreme court until 1857, but in the end, the supreme court decided unanimously for the railroad and the state. (Lincoln, who had written the brief and argued the case alongside Joy, came away with a $5,000 fee as his reward.) In 1857, the six-year tax exemption ran out and the state auditor, Jesse Dubois, assessed the railroad's property at $13 million and proceeded to levy a business tax on it. The railroad protested disingenuously that its property was worth less than $8 million, and insisted that its charter limited the tax rate to 7 percent, and it then employed Lincoln to defend it. Lincoln did so, not only in the state supreme court (where Lincoln persuaded the court to accept the railroad's valuation of its property), but by brokering a deal with Dubois, an old political friend, which allowed the railroad to make a partial payment and to lobby the legislature for a revised statute to restrain future taxation.

Nor was this all. Between 1854 and 1859, Lincoln represented the Illinois Central's interests in over fifty cases (including eleven before the state supreme court), ranging from the eviction of squatters on lands granted by the federal government, to livestock owners who wanted the railroad held liable for inadequate fencing along rail lines and the loss of value their animals suffered during delays in market shipment. (He also continued to look out for the interests of old friends like John Todd Stuart, whom he assisted in buying up a section of prize railroad land the federal land office had previously closed for sale.) He became, by 1855, the Illinois Central's *de facto* agent on the Eighth Judicial Circuit, and the circuit's strategic sprawl across middle Illinois made Lincoln a key figure in the state's most ambitious internal improvements project. "Much as we deprecated the avarice of great corporations," Herndon chuckled, "we both thanked the Lord for letting the Illinois Central Railroad fall into our hands."

Lincoln eventually picked up the business of almost every other railroad that, in the 1850s, was seeking to lay track into the heart of Illinois, including the Tonica & Petersburg Railroad, the Alton & Sangamon Railroad (and its successor corporation, the Chicago & Mississippi), and the Ohio & Mississippi Railroad. (Years later, it would be rumored that in 1860 the New York Central Railroad had offered Lincoln the job of general counsel of the New York line.) But Lincoln, always willing to represent anyone able to pay fees, also took up suits against the railroads, as in a small suit for unpaid bills against the Sangamon & Morgan Railroad and the larger suits of big-time property owners whose land values were threatened by the encroachment of the Chicago, Burlington, & Quincy Railroad. But his most sensational railroad case was not, strictly speaking, a railroad case at all, but the civil suit that arose from the destruction of the Mississippi River steamboat *Effie Afton*.

In 1855, the Rock Island Railroad, which ran a spur line from the Illinois Central at LaSalle westward to the Mississippi River at Rock Island, created a subsidiary company, the Rock Island Bridge Company, to build a railway bridge across the Mississippi at Rock Island, so that the railroad could extend its connections into the new state of Iowa at Davenport. The Rock Island Railroad was, in effect, a long arm of the Illinois Central and the first beachhead of the northern market system on the west side of the river. The Rock Island Railroad not only promised to begin commercializing Iowa farming, but to pull Iowa's agricultural production toward Chicago, the Great Lakes, and the free North. For that reason, no one could miss what was at stake when, on May 6, 1856, the sidewheel steamboat *Effie Afton*, carrying freight and some two hundred passengers, struggled upstream beneath the newly constructed Rock Island railway bridge, only to have one wheel stall in the rapid rush of the current through the bridge's piers and spin the boat back against the bridge, where it collided with a bridge pier and caught fire. The captain, Jacob Hurd, and the owners of the *Effie Afton* promptly filed suit in federal court against the Rock Island Bridge Company, declaring that the bridge was a hazard to river navigation and demanding damages for the boat and its cargo. The real aim, of course, was to remove the bridge and the threat it posed to the supremacy of the Mississippi, and in Chicago it was rumored that St. Louis commercial interests had bribed the captain of the *Afton* to ram the bridge on purpose.

The railroad's counsel was joined by a local Rock Island attorney and by Lincoln, partly through his connections with the Illinois Central and partly through his experience in two other federal cases involving bridge obstructions. The trial began in the federal district court in Chicago in September, 1857, under the righteous eye of Supreme Court associate justice John McLean (a one-time Jacksonian Methodist turned Whig). It lasted through two sweatily contested and publicly debated weeks full of depositions, examination and cross-examination of expert witnesses, and a final two-day-long summation of the bridge company's defense by Lincoln.

If there was ever a finest hour for Lincoln as a lawyer, it was here, for Lincoln's summation bristled with his mastery of the details of the case. The one-time surveyor had taken the trouble to visit the site of the accident, measure distances and the volume of water flowing under the bridge, and get statements from witnesses the plaintiff had not bothered to look up, so that the boat's owners would find themselves resting, too late, on "the testimony of men who had made no experiment — only conjecture." He denied, based on the testimony of a civil engineer, that the bridge's construction posed any peculiar difficulty; he cited other witnesses to show that Captain Hurd had passed under the bridge knowing very well that his starboard engine was malfunctioning, thus taking all the chances of a collision on himself. Even

171

worse, the boat's river pilot, Nathaniel Parker, had never bothered to get "acquainted with the place" and had rashly nosed the *Afton* under the bridge to its destruction.

But the most intriguing aspect of Lincoln's defense was his attempt to transpose the entire case from being a mere civil suit into an epic contest of Northern and Southern interests, and of Democratic and Whig political cultures. It was clear, Lincoln argued, that the real plaintiffs were not the captain and the owners of the *Afton*, but the St. Louis Chamber of Commerce and the stranglehold that regionalism and sectionalism hoped to keep on Illinois's commercial development. In that case, what the plaintiffs were pleading for was not justice, but a special privilege for Southern river interests over the railroads, a privilege they did not merit. The behavior of the pilot, Parker, only confirmed the existence of a deliberate conspiracy, since Parker exhibited all the tell-tale marks of a Democratic political character: "He should have discarded passion," Lincoln argued, "and the chances are that he would have had no disaster at all" — as though the collision was an offense by Democratic reactionaries against the Whig railroad. And that may have actually been what lingered at the back of Lincoln's mind, too, since he cast an ominous shadow over the entire case by pointing out that a decision in favor of the plaintiffs was a decision, in the largest sense, for "a dissolution of the Union." After an afternoon's worth of instructions from the judge, the jury sat for four hours, and then came back, deadlocked, nine to three in favor of the bridge company. There were, of course, appeals and more appeals for almost another five years, all the way to the U.S. Supreme Court. But the bridge, and Lincoln, had triumphed.

Lincoln's growing successes as a lawyer brought him corporation business beside that of the railroads. Deep-pocket commercial clients also began to call on him, including Nicholas Ridgely's new Springfield gas works, at least nine banks in Sangamon, McLean, and Morgan counties, two insurance companies, and a venture capital firm in St. Louis. The same mind that had picked up surveying in the span of a few months and ran to "mathematical precision" of expression in jury pleadings found a particular pleasure in mechanical contraptions and, with them, patent cases. His railroad business was, after all, partly a homage to the triumph of machinery over the farm, and the only aspect of agricultural life that retained any interest for Lincoln once he left his father's farm was the development of agricultural machinery which would render the drudgery of subsistence agriculture conveniently obsolete. "The successful application of *steam power*, to farm work is a desideratum," he told one of his unlikeliest speaking venues, the Wisconsin State Agricultural Fair in September, 1859, and he admitted that "I have thought a good deal, in an abstract way, about a Steam Plow."

Indeed he had. He turned his hand in 1849 to patenting a cumbersome and never-manufactured device for floating stranded boats off river shoals (still trying, fifteen years after the event, to bring the *Talisman* up the Sangamon River), and he devoted two rare nonpolitical lectures in 1858 and 1859 to the praise of "Discoveries and Inventions." Invention, in these lectures, was an inbred trait of human nature. "Man is not the only animal who labors; but he is the only one who *improves* his workmanship," Lincoln began in the second lecture, "whereas all other creatures are feeders and lodgers, merely." The history of the human race was itself a history of improvements, starting from the original "Old Fogy," Adam. "There he stood, a very perfect physical man," and not coincidentally, entirely reminiscent of Lincoln's own father.

> He must have been very ignorant, and simple in his habits. He had no sufficient time to learn much by observation; and he had no near neighbors to teach him anything. No part of his breakfast had been brought from the other side of the world; and it is quite probable, he had no conception of the world having any other side.

The world had advanced from this "first of all fogies," first by the mastery of language, and then as a result of the self-discipline of *"observation, reflection and experiment."* The prime example of this, not surprisingly, was the development of steam power, but first in historical order was the creation of writing, followed by the printing press, the spinning jenny, transportation, and finally artificial power and "its application to mills and other machinery." He was also interested in how one invention leap-frogged the imagination to another. "The arts of writing and of printing" led to "the discovery of America, and the introduction of Patent-laws," and with each new development the time needed to produce the next grew shorter and shorter.

What Lincoln was describing, unreflectively, was a history cast in terms of ever-mounting stages of progress, culminating unapologetically in joint creation of the steam engine and the American republic. At the dawn of the age of print, people "were utterly unconscious, that their *conditions* or their *minds* were capable of improvement" and "they supposed themselves to be naturally incapable of rising to equality." But the easy availability of print, together with the discovery of America, fostered "an immancipation of thought, and the consequent advancement of civilization and the arts." Thus, the greater the material accomplishments, the greater the demand for self-advancement and liberty. The odd element in this story of progress was what Lincoln placed at its apex — "the Patent Laws." But this was, in Lincoln's case, a recognition that land had ceased to be the prime measure of wealth. *"Discoveries, Inventions,* and *Improvements"* were the real capital of the transatlantic markets, and the protection of those ideas through patent laws provided as fundamental a legal sanction for the new industrial age as the notion of contract itself. What moved people to experimentation, as it moved them to everything else in Lincoln's Benthamite reckoning, was "the fuel of *interest."* If interest could not be protected from piracy and intellectual theft, it would never spark "the *fire* of genius." History, then, was a story of progress, and a progress in which material acquisition and political liberation relied on each other to "immancipate the mind," to "break its shackle, and to get a habit of freedom of thought, established."

Unhappily for Lincoln, Whiggish lectures glorifying patent laws were not rewarded with tremendous audiences, and he found a better outlet for those ideas in taking on patent cases. His first case in the federal district court in Chicago in 1850 was a suit in which Lincoln defended Charles Hoyt against the charge that he had stolen the design of a waterwheel from the patent holder. The case consumed two weeks but Lincoln triumphed, and it became the pattern for a series of patent infringement suits he conducted in the federal district courts from 1851 till 1855.

His most important patent case arrived as a referral in 1855. Despite Lincoln's interest in "steam plows," no piece of machinery was more efficacious in transforming subsistence agriculture into cash-crop commercial farming than the mechanical reaper, and no mechanical reaper was more successful than the "Virginia Reaper" designed and manufactured by Cyrus McCormick in Chicago after 1847. Although McCormick easily dominated the market for mechanized farm equipment — over thirty thousand of his reapers were sold across the old Northwest by 1859 — McCormick kept a jealous eye on his competition, bankrupting them where he could by sharp competition (as he did with Baltimore's Obed Hussey) and driving them from the market by alleging patent infringements. John H. Manny, whose Rockford, Illinois, company produced a smaller but locally popular reaper in central Illinois, ran afoul of McCormick's acquisitive temper, and in 1854 McCormick brought an infringement suit against Manny in federal district court, asking for an injunction against further production of the Manny reaper and whopping compensatory damages of $400,000.

McCormick had a battery of nationally famous lawyers on retainer, but McCormick's resentful eastern rivals decided to use Manny's dilemma as a way of teaching the almighty McCormick a lesson, and so Manny's allies funded the acquisition of some equally high-powered legal talent of their own to defend Manny. Assuming that the case would be heard in the federal court in Chicago, Manny's chief counsel, the Philadelphia lawyer George Harding, began scouting for a reliable Illinois lawyer to add to the defense team, and as it turned out, both Isaac Arnold of Chicago and one of Lincoln's former law protégés, Ralph Emerson (who now worked for Manny as Manny's in-house counsel), recommended that Harding recruit Lincoln.

Lincoln set to the case with as much energy as he would later apply to the *Effie Afton* case, visiting Manny's Rockford plant and looking up the original depositions by the lawyers on both sides in Chicago. "I attended the U.S. Court at Chicago, and while there, got copies of the Bill and Answer," Lincoln reported to Peter Watson, another of Manny's lawyers. "During my stay in Chicago, I went out to Rockford, and spent half a day, examining and studying Manny's Machine." Harding had strongly implied that, since the case was expected to be argued in Chicago, Lincoln would probably be given the summation of the case before Justice John McLean. Unhappily, McLean instead announced that he would hear the case in Cincinnati, and when Lincoln arrived in Cincinnati, he discovered that Harding no longer needed an Illinois lawyer. Lincoln had to step back and allow another member of the team, a growly, contemptuous Pittsburgher named Edwin M. Stanton, to seize the role Lincoln had imagined for himself.

It did not help the atmosphere in the hallways that Stanton, a Democrat, treated Lincoln like the cornfield lawyer Lincoln never wanted to be mistaken for. Lincoln bitterly told Herndon afterwards that he had overheard the trumpet-voiced Stanton ask Manny why he had brought "that [damned] long armed Ape" from Illinois, since Lincoln did "not know anything and can do you no good." "Grieved and mortified" (according to Herndon), Lincoln quietly packed his bags and left Cincinnati after the close of the case, politely promising everyone that he would never come back to the Queen City (although he did in 1859). But contrary to Lincoln's embittered expectation that "he had lost his case," Justice McLean decided in favor of Manny, and Lincoln collected a $1,000 fee over and above his initial $400 retainer.

Even in defeat Lincoln was now dealing with clients who could pay hefty fees, and during the 1850s, his income reached an average of $3,000 a year (eight to ten times the average working-class income). R. G. Dun & Co., the New York credit-rating firm (and forerunner of Dun & Bradstreet), evaluated his total assets at about $12,000 and noted that he had no outstanding indebtedness. He was providing for his son Robert's education at private academies in Springfield, and in 1856, he paid $1,300 to have his one-and-a-half-story house raised to include an entire new second story. The simplicity of manner Lincoln cultivated as a Whig elder statesman thus sat oddly beside his increasing professional success as he turned into his mid-forties. But this only meant that he had become the perfect Whig conundrum, the scrupulously self-disciplined individual who would not stoop to the passion of getting and spending, but whose very self-discipline ensured that he would get quite enough to spend anyway.

In all of these labors for eldership, he never entirely lost his interest in politics, which in Lincoln's case meant almost exclusively the affairs of the Whig party. Although the early 1850s have often been portrayed, and largely with Lincoln's own words in mind, as a political wasteland for Lincoln, that was true only in the sense that he gave up hunting for serious political office and concentrated on making his living from law rather than politics. But he remained a key figure in the Whig party in Illinois. Lincoln (along with Stuart, Washburne, Gillespie, and Orville Hickman Browning) was one of the organizers of the Whig state convention in Springfield in 1851, and continued to supply the *Sangamo Journal* (which became the *Illinois State Journal*) with anonymous anti-Democratic journalism. When President Taylor died in July, 1850, Lincoln was asked to deliver the eulogy at a Whig memorial meeting in Chicago, praising Taylor for having offered the perfect solution to the slave extension question — "the one *great* question of the day" — and lauding the former general and slaveholder in unlikely terms as a model Whig "of a sober and steady judgment," who "indulged no recreations" and "visited no public places, seeking applause; but quietly, as the earth in its orbit, he was always at his post." When an aggressive Morgan County Whig, Richard Yates, proposed to recapture Lincoln's old Seventh District seat for the Whigs in 1850, Lincoln acted as his political adviser, and in 1852 he stumped the state on behalf of Winfield Scott's unsuccessful bid to keep the presidency in Whig hands.

The message was the same as it had ever been for Lincoln: "the inconsistency of the sham democracy on the question of internal improvements," the need for "a protective tariff," Scott's own platform promises "about the Public Lands," and the irrelevance of making "flings at the Whigs about free soil and abolition!" When the venerable Henry Clay died at the height of the campaign in 1852, Lincoln was asked to deliver yet another public eulogy to a Whig mass meeting in the state capitol in Springfield, and once again he turned it into a tribute not only to Clay but to the Whig character that Clay had embodied. Never mind that Clay had earned an unsavory reputation in his early days as a womanizer and cardsharp, or that he and John Quincy Adams still labored under the reputation of the "corrupt bargain" in 1824 — Lincoln focused preeminently on Clay's role as "that truly national man" whose devotion to liberty and equality led him to walk a middle path of compromise and national unity. "Whatever he did, he did for the whole country," Lincoln declared, rather than for the sake of local or sectional diversity. Clay "loved his country, but mostly because it was a free country . . . because he saw in such, the advancement, prosperity, and glory, of human liberty, human right and human nature." What Lincoln praised in "Harry of the West" was Clay's placing of ideology above the demands of people: "He desired the prosperity of his countrymen, partly because they were his countrymen, but chiefly to show to the world that freemen could be prosperous."

177

But Lincoln might just as easily have been describing the man he himself had become by 1852, not the fun-loving jokester of New Salem, but the silent, cautious lawyer and the Whig ideologue. Young Billy Thompson "met Mr. Lincoln on the street as I went to and from school" and noticed that he "was not an observant man on the street; in fact he hardly ever saw us unless we spoke to him. He walked along with his hands behind him, gazing upward and noticing nobody." John Todd Stuart found over time that Lincoln "loved principles and such like large political & national ones, Especially when it leads to his own Ends." Lincoln "had no idea — no proper notion or conception of particular men & women," Herndon complained. "He could scarcely distinguish the individual." In fact, Leonard Swett thought of Lincoln as "a trimmer, and such a trimmer as the world has never seen" when it came to "dealing with men." But "Lincoln never trimmed in principles — it was only in his conduct with men. . . ."

It never occurred to Lincoln that the Whig party was doomed, and not just to another routine electoral defeat, as Scott fell heavily before Pierce in the 1852 election. Even less could it have occurred to Lincoln that in just four years' time, the middle path of Whig nationalism would vanish beneath his feet.

The territory of Iowa was admitted as a state of the Union in 1846, and in the estimate of Stephen A. Douglas, it was about time. Although Missouri and Arkansas had been the first states organized out of the Louisiana Purchase in 1820 and 1836 under the restrictions of the Missouri Compromise, not a single other state had been organized in the old Purchase lands west of the Mississippi until Iowa. In the mind of the junior senator from Illinois, this was rubbish. "How are we to develop, cherish and protect our immense interests and possessions on the Pacific," Douglas asked, "with a vast wilderness fifteen hundred miles in breadth, filled with hostile savages, and cutting off all direct communication?" The chief culprit in this paralysis, for Douglas, was the Missouri Compromise itself, since the Compromise's restrictions on the introduction of slavery north of 36°30' in the old Purchase territories instantly chilled the interest of Southern immigrants, representatives, and developers. And needlessly, too, Douglas argued: the climate of the northern plains was naturally hostile to slave-based agriculture, and "whenever the climate, soil and productions preclude

178

the possibility of slavery being profitable, they will not permit it." The Missouri Compromise was therefore a gratuitous irritant, doing nothing more than Nature did to discourage slavery while doing everything possible to choke off Southern support for fresh territorial development.

The organization of New Mexico and Utah under the Compromise of 1850 had demonstrated for Douglas a better and less provocative means for organizing the territories, the doctrine of popular sovereignty, the "great fundamental principle of self-government upon which our republican institutions are predicated." Let the Missouri Compromise be set aside and popular sovereignty allowed to become the principle by which the old Louisiana Purchase lands could be organized, Douglas argued, and Southerners in Congress could back the territorial organization of the great plains without feeling humiliated, while Northerners in Congress could feel morally certain that slavery would never emerge there as a practical system. In fact, set aside the Missouri Compromise and allow popular sovereignty to rule the Louisiana Purchase as it was now ruling the Mexican Cession, and neither Congress nor the Democratic party need never again be at each other's throats over the vexing question of slavery, since Congress would hand all determinations about the future of slavery over to the people of the territories.

It was true, Douglas admitted to Kentucky senator Archibald Dixon, that tampering with the Missouri Compromise would probably "raise the hell of a storm." Three and a half decades had given the Missouri Compromise a sense of permanence, and to Northerners in particular it remained the bargain slavery and freedom had struck to keep slavery alive but subordinate. But in Douglas's mind, the storm was worth braving. "The slavery agitation which followed the acquisition of California and New Mexico . . . had an injurious effect by diverting public attention from the importance of our old territory [the Louisiana Purchase] and concentrating the hopes and anxieties of all upon our new possessions," Douglas explained. Popular sovereignty, by extending "the principle established by the Compromise measures of 1850" to the old Purchase territories, would "so far as the slavery question is concerned" pour oil on the troubled national waters and allow the opening of the west to proceed.

The question was brought directly to Douglas's doorstep as

chair of the Senate's Committee on Territories in late 1853, when the new settlements along the Kansas and Platte rivers sent delegations to Washington to ask Congress to provide territorial organization for the huge region they called Nebraska. Douglas had proposed organization bills for Nebraska as early as 1844, and in 1853 a fresh bill for organizing the Nebraska Territory under the old Missouri Compromise provisions had been taken up in the House of Representatives, only to die on the points of solid Southern truculence. With that lesson before him, Douglas devised a new Nebraska bill and brought it to the floor of the Senate in January, 1854. In its final form, it divided Nebraska's huge sprawl into two separate territories of Kansas and Nebraska, voided the Missouri Compromise, and left "the people thereof perfectly free to form and regulate their domestic institutions in their own way, subject only to the constitution of the United States."

Douglas soon discovered that he had been right about the "hell of a storm" his Kansas-Nebraska bill might generate. Popular sovereignty was denounced by Northerners as a sleight of hand for tearing down the fence of the Missouri Compromise and giving slavery a free shot on expansion into Nebraska. Northern newspapers raged at Douglas for going "down on his marrow-bones at the feet of slavery," and Northern politicians howled that "this is a bold bid of Douglas" to get Southern backing "for the next Presidency." Whigs like Missourian Edward Bates screamed that Douglas had scrapped the Missouri Compromise as "a pure electioneering trick" to bribe the South into nominating him for the presidency, while New York Whig senator (and former governor) William Henry Seward reminded Douglas that in making slavery a subject of popular choice he had forgotten that slavery presented a moral problem which could not be reduced merely to the decision of a popular majority. Seward warned that Douglas's pious desire to remove the debate over slave extension from the halls of Congress conveniently ignored the fact that "the slavery agitation you deprecate so much is an eternal struggle between conservatism and progress, between truth and error, between right and wrong." Free-Soil Democrats like Salmon P. Chase of Ohio and one-time "Conscience" Whigs like Charles Sumner of Massachusetts turned angrily on Douglas and published an "Appeal of the Independent Democrats," denouncing the Kansas-Nebraska bill as a gross violation of a sacred pledge; as a criminal betrayal of precious rights; as part and parcel of an atrocious plot to exclude from a vast unoccupied region, emigrants from the Old World and free laborers from our own States, and convert it into a dreary regime of despotism. Take your maps, fellow citizens, we entreat you, and see what country it is which the bill gratuitously and recklessly proposes to open to slavery.

A "Slave Power" — a shadowy conspiracy of slaveowners and slave-bought politicians — had hatched this "plot" and was even now preparing to "permanently subjugate the whole country to the yoke of a slave-holding despotism."

But Douglas was "not deterred or affected by the violence & insults of the Northern Whigs & abolitionists." He had the backing of President Franklin Pierce, and all the force of party discipline which Pierce could bring to bear on the Democratic majorities in Congress, and so the Kansas-Nebraska bill was jammed through the Senate in March and the House of Representatives in May. "The storm will soon spend its fury," Douglas assured Georgia senator Howell Cobb, "and the people of the north will sustain the measure when they come to understand it."

In fact, Douglas knew he had a rougher road before him in the North than he liked to admit, and when Congress adjourned in late August, 1854, Douglas immediately headed back to Illinois to face down the anti-Nebraska opposition in his own state. Douglas glumly remarked that he could have traveled from Boston to Chicago by night by the light of all his burning effigies on the way, and when he tried to address a crowd of eight thousand in Chicago on September 1st, two hours of hisses and booing finally silenced him. But Douglas was a fighter, and he needed to fight this fall in Illinois. The other Illinois Senate seat, held by Democrat James Shields, was up for election, and it would be necessary for Douglas to get pro-Nebraska Democrats elected to the state legislature to ensure Shields's re-election. But Douglas's persuasive powers were formidable, and so were the thumbscrews of the party's legendary internal discipline; and by the beginning of October, when Douglas arrived at the Illinois State Fair at Springfield to speak in the state capitol's Hall of Representatives, the catcalls were beginning to yield to cheers for Douglas's defense of "the right of all American communities to self-government," and Douglas could at last expect to see political daylight in his home state.

But not if Abraham Lincoln could help it. "In 1854, his profession had almost superseded the thought of politics in his mind," Lincoln wrote several years afterward, "when the repeal of the Missouri Compromise aroused him as he had never been before." This was not an exaggeration, although the reasons bound up with it were more complex than this sounds. On the practical level, the Kansas-Nebraska brouhaha offered Illinois Whigs like Lincoln a golden opportunity to divide the Illinois Democrats into self-destructive pro-Nebraska and anti-Nebraska factions, and the Whigs could stand to profit politically if the anti-Nebraska Democrats could be lured into supporting the Whigs. Since the Whigs had never yet managed to secure a permanent majority in the state legislature, and since Richard Yates was at risk in the Seventh Congressional District for re-election that fall, this was not a bad moment for Lincoln to wade back into the thick of Whig politics in Illinois.

Lincoln could also see the turmoil over the Kansas-Nebraska bill as an opportunity for his own personal advancement. "Lincoln saw his opportunity and Douglas's downfall" in the Nebraska agitation, Herndon wrote. A split in the Democratic majority in the legislature might translate into a split in James Shields's re-election supporters, and that might mean an opening for a Whig candidate to capture Illinois's junior U.S. Senate seat when the new legislature assembled in February. So, although he campaigned vigorously for Richard Yates that fall in the Seventh District, he also campaigned outside the district, and allowed his name once more to be put on the Whig ballot for the state House.

But Lincoln was motivated by infinitely more than just the bubble opportunities provided by the Kansas-Nebraska uproar. The whole bill — from the establishment of popular sovereignty to the dismantling of the Missouri Compromise — struck at the very heart of Lincoln's Whiggish complacency about slavery. All along, he had conceived of slavery as a blemish on the republic, but a blemish which Northerners and Southerners alike had agreed to let alone in the name of the Union, a blemish which time would cure on its own so long as slavery was contained within its current boundaries. But the removal of the Missouri Compromise, in Lincoln's mind, tore down the old understanding that slavery would not be spread into the territories —

tore up even the illusion that everyone agreed that slavery was a problem — and made the extension of slavery (not its containment) the
new price for Union. And what galled him most was that this was to
proceed under the fiction of democratic choice — of Douglas's "popular sovereignty." In an editorial he wrote for the *Illinois State Journal* in
September, Lincoln compared Kansas-Nebraska to

> a fine meadow, containing beautiful springs of water, and well-
> fenced, which John Calhoun had agreed with Abraham (originally
> owning the land in common) should be his. . . . John Calhoun then
> looks with a longing eye on Lincoln's meadow, and goes to it and
> throws down the fences, and exposes it to the ravages of his starving
> and famished cattle. "You rascal," says Lincoln, "what have you
> done? what do you do this for?" "Oh," replied Calhoun, "everything
> is right. I have taken down your fence; but nothing more. It is my
> true intent and meaning not to drive my cattle into your meadow,
> nor to exclude them therefrom, but to leave them perfectly free to
> form their own notions of the feed, and to direct their movements in
> their own way!"

Once popular sovereignty allowed slavery to establish itself in
the west, it would either spread the plantation system across the plains
or, worse still, pour slave labor into small-scale manufacturing and
commercial farming. This would not only turn the West into a Democratic stronghold, it would curtail the possibility of the Northern middle class and working class finding new opportunities for economic
mobility in the West, penning free labor into the existing "free" states
and cramping the hope of "self-improvement."

> The whole nation is interested that the best use shall be made of
> these territories. We want them for the homes of free white people.
> This they cannot be, to any considerable extent, if slavery shall be
> planted within them. Slave States are places for poor white people to
> remove FROM; not to remove TO. New free States are the places for
> poor people to go to and better their condition.

Worst of all, "popular sovereignty" might then become the basis of a
new argument that would tear up even the free-state statutes of the

North, and permit slave labor to emerge as a labor system everywhere in the United States, in the industrial capitalist North as well as the cotton South. "The compromises of the constitution we must all stand by," Lincoln conceded, "but where is the justness of extending the institution to compete with white labor and thus to degrade it?"

The possibility posed by Kansas-Nebraska that slavery might become available to lift gears in the North and harvest grain in the West as well as pick cotton in the South could well make a mockery of Lincoln's confidence and assurance that free markets would make the world safe for free labor, that material progress would always guarantee movement toward "immancipation of thought," and that the Northern factory worker could enjoy a "harmony of interests" with the factory owner based on the eternal right to rise. "This thing is spreading like wildfire over the country," Lincoln warned. "In a few years we will be ready to accept the institution in Illinois, and the whole country will adopt it." And so, in the summer of 1854, Lincoln's political pot began to simmer again, although no longer with the usual Whig agenda of banks, improvements, and public land distribution. It was slavery which now became his principal burden, and for the first time Lincoln began to sketch out speeches entirely devoted to the subject.

As slavery now assumed the demonic role once played in his Whiggish imagination by Jacksonian agrarians, his whole treatment of slavery began to undergo a transformation. No longer would slavery be merely a historical embarrassment that white people could joke about or dismiss as an antique on the way to dissolution. It would now become, for Abraham Lincoln, a moral offense, and *moral* to the degree that economic mobility represented for him a moral triumph over his own agrarian "slave" origins, *moral* to the extent that it represented an unthinkable reversal of the tide of progress, *moral* as from this moment the black slave now began to emerge in Lincoln's mind as a human being with the same Whiggish aspirations for escape and success as Abraham Lincoln.

5 Moral Principle Is All That Unites Us

It is a good measure of just how "aroused" Lincoln was about the Kansas-Nebraska bill that through most of the fall of 1854, he did virtually no legal work and devoted himself almost entirely to campaigning for Richard Yates throughout the Seventh District and to his own race for the state legislature, where he could put his personal vote in against James Shields. But in the long series of campaign speeches he made for himself and for others that summer, it was clear that Shields was only a straw target for Lincoln. Much as Shields had given Lincoln political offense by supporting Kansas-Nebraska in Congress, the real political enemy for Lincoln was the man behind Shields, Stephen Douglas, and the great object in obstructing Shields's re-election was the damage it could do to Douglas's political standing.

Only four of Lincoln's speeches from the 1854 campaign come down to us in anything close to full form (and three of them survive only because shorthand reporters took them down for local newspapers), but the same basic outline shows up in nearly every account of Lincoln's campaign appearances that summer and fall. The Founders, he began, had always opposed slavery: they had banned its spread into the old Northwest Territory, and they looked forward to seeing the West become "the happy home of teeming millions of free, white, prosperous people, and no slave amongst them." They could not avoid the unpleasant fact that slavery already existed in the Southern states of the Union, but they had regarded its existence as an anomaly and they tolerated its continuation there as an "argument of NECESSITY" for establishing the national Union. Even when Missouri won admission as a slave state in 1820, its slave status was only a concession; in fact the Missouri Compromise line explicitly restricted the further spread of slavery into the West. Even the Compromise of 1850 was only another extension of that bargain. "We never thought of disturbing the original Missouri Compromise line."

But now Kansas-Nebraska had broken this down, repealing the Missouri Compromise and making "the Kansas and Nebraska territories . . . as open to slavery as Mississippi or Arkansas were when they were territories." The specious excuse offered by Douglas in defense of this was the popular sovereignty doctrine, as though the settlers of the territory "cannot get along at all" without an opportunity to make themselves into slave states. But the real force behind Kansas-Nebraska was the selfishness of the "slave power." Slaveholders "had got all they claimed, and all the territory south of the compromise line had been appropriated to slavery; they had gotten and eaten their half of the loaf of bread; but all the other half had not been eaten yet . . . and the slaveholding power attempted to snatch that away." The bargain that had held the Union together from its founding was now being tossed away, and "at this time one party having exhausted its share of the bargain, demands an abrogation of the Compromise and a re-division of the property."

Lincoln dismissed out of hand Douglas's argument that the climate and soils of Kansas and Nebraska could never support slavery "and that therefore there is no need of any bother about it." This is a *"palliation,"* Lincoln snorted, *"a lullaby."* Missouri lay right along the Platte River country of Nebraska, "and slavery lost no time in marching right in and going to the utmost verge of that boundary. . . . Will it not go, then, into Kansas and Nebraska, if permitted? Why not? What will hinder?"

He took a strikingly different tack, however, in dealing with Douglas's other justification for Kansas-Nebraska: that slavery had to be given its chance in the territories because it was the right of free settlers to exercise their popular sovereignty in choosing their own kind

186

of government. "The doctrine of self government is right — absolutely and eternally right," Lincoln acknowledged, "but it has no just application as here attempted." In practical terms, popular sovereignty actually subverted the principle of self-government by giving allowance to a choice for slavery. Admit for a moment, Lincoln asked, that a black slave is a man, just as a white farmer is a man: Is not slavery "a total destruction of self-government, to say that he too shall not govern *himself*? When the white man governs himself that is self-government; but when he governs himself, and also governs *another* man, that is *more* than self-government — that is despotism." Popular sovereignty thus became a means for ending some men's freedom. It could be argued, in reply, that slaves are not men at all, and that "inasmuch as you do not object to my taking my hog to Nebraska, therefore I must not object to you taking your slave." But the truth was that no one really believed this. Otherwise, why did Southerners agree to ban the African slave trade and make it a capital offense? "The practice was no more than bringing wild negroes from Africa, to sell to such as would buy them. But you never thought of hanging men for catching and selling wild horses, wild buffaloes or wild bears."

But more than simply painting slavery as a practical contradiction of the very principle Douglas promised to defend, Lincoln now began to cast opposition to slavery as a moral argument. The great accomplishment of the American republic was that "we proposed to give *all* a chance; and we expected the weak to grow stronger, the ignorant wiser; and all better and happier together." If the black man, "upon soil where slavery is not legalized by law and sanctioned by custom, *is* a man, then there is not even the shadow of popular sovereignty in allowing the first settlers upon such soil to decide whether it shall be right in all future time to hold men in bondage there." Appeals to "the sacred right of self-government" cannot trump questions of morality. And slavery was a wrong, a moral wrong "made so plain by our good Father in Heaven" because it denied the morality of self-aspiration and self-improvement that had guided Lincoln's own life. The offense of popular sovereignty was that, by making the decision purely a matter of choice, "it assumes that there can be MORAL RIGHT in the enslaving of one man by another."

This was an odd argument for Lincoln to make, not because others were not making it, but because the selfishness of the "slave

187

power" was exactly the principle which he believed animated human decision-making anyway, and appeals to popular sovereignty, regardless of moral warnings, were precisely what Lincoln otherwise expected from human beings. But now, for this religionless, utilitarian man, opposition to slavery no longer made sense on purely liberal grounds. He had long disliked the hedonism associated with slaveholding, but this was a criticism limited to the slaveholders themselves rather than the slave system. He needed a morality with which to embarrass popular sovereignty's appeal to selfishness — not the chilly morality of duty, but the morality of natural law, even of natural theology. And so, for the first time, Lincoln began to speak, not in terms of motives, but in terms of certain natural moral relationships, which slavery violated. "Almost every man has a sense of certain things being wrong," Lincoln remarked. Even "the ant who has toiled and dragged a crumb to his nest, will furiously defend the fruit of his labor, against whatever robber assails him"; slavery, which similarly robbed the slave of the fruit of his labor, was just as much an outrage on the part of the human laborer. This was "so plain, that the most dumb and stupid slave that ever toiled for a master, does constantly know he is wronged." He even turned, in the style of James Smith's apologetics, to appeals to natural theology. "I think that if anything can be proved by natural theology, it is that slavery is morally wrong." It was as though Douglas had exposed the dark side of Lincoln's liberalism, "insisting that there is no right principle of action but *self-interest*," that in its effort to gain the maximum exercise of rights, liberalism could allow no single version of truth or the good to rule. Lincoln's struggle was now the ultimate struggle of all Whig liberals, to find some kind of moral containment to rights run amuck, without falling back into the rigidly contained society of the old Jeffersonians.

This did not mean, however, that he had lost any of his grim confidence that necessity still ruled political affairs. He had no war to declare on Southern slaveholders, simply because necessity had made them what they were. "Southern slaveholders were neither better, nor worse than we of the North, and . . . we of the North were no better than they. If we were situated as they are, we should act and feel as they do; and if they were situated as we are, they should act and feel as we do." The Founders, too, had yielded to the necessity of recognizing slavery in the states where it was legal, and he had no intention of turning into an outright abolitionist and interfering with slavery in the South. "It was 'in the bond' and he would live faithfully by it."

In fact, far from being an abolitionist, Lincoln actually had no good idea of what would be done with the South's slaves if slavery were to be abolished. "My first impulse would be to free all the slaves, and send them to Liberia, — to their own native land." But given the palpable impracticalities of this, "its sudden execution is impossible." Yet he certainly did not propose to "free them, and make them politically and socially, our equals." The black slave might be a man with the same "natural rights" as a white man, but that did not mean that he had an entitlement to civil or political equality in the American polity. "My own feelings will not admit of this; and if mine would, we well know that those of the great mass of white people will not." So, "with slavery as existing in the slave states at the time at the formation of the Union, he had nothing to do."

But "there was a vast difference between tolerating it there, and protecting the slaveholder in the rights granted him by the Constitution, and extending slavery over a territory already free, and uncontaminated with the institution." Kansas-Nebraska overthrew not only the Missouri Compromise, but the national assumption that slavery was an evil that "necessity" forced the American republic grudgingly to "tolerate," and publicly proclaimed that Americans cared not at all whether slavery could move freely as it willed across the North American continent. "I hate it because it deprives our republican example of its just influence in the world — enables the enemies of free institutions, with plausibility, to taunt us as hypocrites — causes the real friends of freedom to doubt our sincerity." The solution, then, was to "get the Compromise restored," if not by immediate congressional repeal of Kansas-Nebraska, then by the demand of "popular sentiment."

Lincoln bore these themes during the 1854 campaign to Winchester, to Carrollton, to Jacksonville, to Urbana, to Bloomington, to Peoria, to Quincy, even to Chicago (on October 27th). But at no place did he make a greater impression than in Springfield, where Douglas arrived on October 3rd to take advantage of the crowds in town for the State Fair to promote his drive for Kansas-Nebraska and pro-Nebraska Democratic candidates. Inclement weather forced Douglas indoors, and twenty-five hundred people crammed into the Hall of Representatives (and downstairs into the lobby) in the State Capitol to greet the

"Little Giant" with "loud cheers." One of them, though not with cheers, was Lincoln. "I will answer that speech without any trouble," Lincoln told Springfield banker John W. Bunn. "I can show that his facts are not facts, and that will refute his speech." From the stairs of the Capitol, Lincoln announced that either he or the anti-Nebraska Democrat Lyman Trumbull would reply to Douglas the next afternoon. He was not about to give away his opportunity to Trumbull if it could be helped, and so it was Lincoln who stood up at the dais the next day at two o'clock, and for three hours he hammered Douglas in "one of the ablest & most effective" speeches "of his life."

The most difficult problem Lincoln faced was the apparent naturalness of popular sovereignty, that the people have the power to set rules for themselves and their property any way they please. This was usually true, Lincoln explained, and it would be true concerning slavery, too, if "the slaveholder has the same right to take his negroes to Kansas that a freeman has to take his hogs or his horses," since no one thinks of interfering with any state or territorial right to restrict the movement of hogs and horses. But were "negroes . . . property in the same sense that hogs and horses are"? Lincoln replied, "It is notoriously not so." Blacks have "mind, feelings, souls, family affections, hopes, joys, sorrows — something that made them more than *hogs* or *horses*," and therefore their fate is no more the due object of "popular sovereignty" than any other human being. Rather, slavery itself, and not just its extension out of the South, is "universally granted to be, in the abstract, a gross outrage of the law of nature." So, instead of self-government being vindicated, the result would be that slavery would take a free ride into the territories on its back. And before the audience of world opinion, it would throw the principle of self-government into a shade, since the chief outcome of self-government in this case would be the extension, not of freedom, but of the destruction of freedom. In shielding slavery behind the will of a majority, Americans were

> descending from the high republican faith of our ancestors, to repudiate that principle and to declare by the highest act of our government that we have no longer a choice between freedom and slavery — that both are equal with us — that we yield our territories as readily to one as the other! This was ignoble teaching. We were proclaiming ourselves political hypocrites before the world, by thus fos-

tering Human Slavery and proclaiming ourselves, at the same time, the sole friends of Human Freedom.

But still, bad policy though it was, evil though it was, and embarrassment though it was, the wisest answer to slavery remained containment and not abolition. On the evening of October 16th, Lincoln followed a Douglas campaign speech in Peoria with a torchlight speech asserting that it was no business of his to interfere with slavery in the states where the constitution legalized it. "I wish to MAKE and to KEEP the distinction between the EXISTING institution, and the EXTENSION of it, so broad and clear, that no honest man" could confuse them. He was not even opposed to popular sovereignty in many respects. But "what I do say is, that no man is good enough to govern another man, *without that other's consent.* I say this is the leading principle — the sheet anchor of American republicanism," and "the relation of masters and slaves is, pro tanto, a violation of this principle."

In a foreshadowing of what would be his greatest utterance (less than a decade later), Lincoln told the Peoria audience, "Near eighty years ago, we began by declaring that all men are created equal; but now from that beginning we have run down to the other declaration, that for some men to enslave others is a 'sacred right of self-government.'" Instead of promoting slavery, it was time to admit that slavery was "fatally violating the noblest political system the world ever saw."

> Our republican robe is soiled, and trailed in the dust. Let us re-purify it. Let us turn and wash it white, in the spirit, if not the blood, of the Revolution. Let us turn slavery from the claims of "moral right," back upon its existing legal rights, and its arguments of "necessity." Let us return it to the position our fathers gave it; and there let it rest in peace. Let us re-adopt the Declaration of Independence, and with it, the practices, and policy, which harmonize with it.

And two days later, Lincoln foreshadowed yet another great speech in an editorial in the *Illinois State Journal*, predicting that, with the encouragement the Douglasites were giving to slavery, there could be nothing in the American future except "to become a nation of slaves or a nation of freemen."

For the moment, though, it would be a nation of Democrats. Lincoln won his legislative seat, but Richard Yates and the other Whig congressional candidates lost heavily to Democratic candidates. However, the Democrats who won those victories were largely anti-Nebraska men, especially in the state legislature, and even before the last ballots were counted, Lincoln grew hopeful that an alliance of Whigs and anti-Nebraska Democrats in the legislature might be persuaded to dump Shields and elect him as U.S. senator. "From his standing in the State and from the great service he had rendered in the campaign, it was agreed that if the . . . anti-Nebraska men should carry the Legislature, Mr. Lincoln would succeed General Shields," recalled Elihu Washburne. "I know that he himself expected it." This may have been in his plans as early as August, and once the election was over, he resigned his new legislative seat (Illinois law prevented sitting legislators from being candidates for United States senator), and began buttonholing Whig colleagues and disgruntled anti-Nebraska Democrats whom he knew could be persuaded not to vote for Shields.

Lincoln was actually able to assemble a coalition that included all but three votes of a majority, leading Shields (who had forty-one votes pledged) and Lyman Trumbull (who had five). "I can not doubt but I have more committals than any other one man," he wrote hopefully to Washburne on January 6th. But when the balloting in the legislature began on February 8th, the Douglasites pulled Shields out of the running and substituted the popular Democratic governor, Joel Matteson, as the pro-Nebraska Democratic candidate. Lincoln's following abruptly dropped to only fifteen. Rather than allow the Douglasites to elect Matteson, Lincoln bitterly fell on his own sword and instructed his loyalists to "drop me and go for" Lyman Trumbull. Better an anti-Nebraska Democrat like Trumbull than a Douglasite, Lincoln reasoned, although he must also have thought, better not to elect a Democrat at all. Publicly, he reassured his "condoling friends" that "it was all right, &c . . . I think the cause in this case is to be preferred to men." Privately, it was the old story of desertion again, of being (as he remarked to Joseph Gillespie) "wounded in the house of his friends." That night, at a post-election reception, Lincoln graciously congratulated Trumbull; but Mary Lincoln never spoke to Julia Trumbull for the rest of her life.

The speeches of the 1854 campaign not only marked out the platform Lincoln would stand upon for the next eight years, but also marked the appearance of some new and portentous additions to his political lexicon. Much as Lincoln could always fish up common biblical allusions on demand (even the bitter comment to Gillespie after the senatorial defeat was actually a citation from the minor prophets), those borrowings now took an alarmingly apocalyptic turn, as though his imagery and his politics had jumped to some new, ominous level. Kansas-Nebraska was "a woful coming down from the early faith of the republic" and had no "relish of salvation"; slavery extension was wrong at the heart, and so long as it was wrong "out of the abundance of his heart, his mouth will continue to speak"; while turning it back would save the Union so that, like the Virgin Mary, "millions of free happy people, the world over, shall rise up, and call us blessed, to the latest generations." Above all, the notion of purifying the republican robe of liberty in a sacrificial washing sounded eerily like the millennial imagery of the martyrs in St. John's Revelation whose white robes had been washed and made white "in the blood of the Lamb." It was also, characteristically, an image of judgment, not of reconciliation; Lincoln could not, even in allusions, tear himself free from the idea that God was a Judge who demanded the washing of tribulation and blood. "There is no peaceful extinction of slavery in prospect for us," he gloomily wrote to George Robertson in August of 1855. "Our political problem now is, 'Can we, as a nation, continue together *permanently — forever* — half slave and half free?'"

Just as surprising was the sudden appearance of the Declaration of Independence as a major rhetorical touchstone for Lincoln's arguments. Before the 1854 speeches, Lincoln had only twice made public reference to the Declaration, once in his 1838 lyceum speech and again in 1852 in his eulogy for Henry Clay. But this was not from any want of interest as a Whig. The Declaration, of course, was Thomas Jefferson's document, and throughout the 1780s and 1790s the Declaration was one of the public icons of Jefferson's party. But even before Jefferson's death in 1826, the Declaration was slowly becoming an embarrassment for the Democratic party, especially in the South. As the South grew more and more dependent on cotton agriculture, and as the Democratic party became more and more dependent on its Southern wing for leadership and finance, many Democrats began to give surprisingly short shrift to the Declaration. John C. Calhoun insisted that the Declaration had no binding significance for the United States after 1776: it was only "the declaration . . . made in the name, and by the authority of the people of the colonies, represented in Congress . . . declaring them to be — 'free and independent states'" and had no role in "merging their existence, as separate communities, into one nation." It was particularly the Declaration's "equality" clause — "that all men are created equal" — which gave Calhoun the most irritation, and he became convinced of the need to awaken to "the danger of admitting so great an error to have a place in the declaration of our independence," especially since it suggested "an utterly false view of the subordinate relation of the black to the white race in the South; and to hold . . . that the former, though utterly unqualified to possess liberty were . . . fully entitled to both liberty and equality. . . ."

It was the Whigs, and not their Jacksonian counterparts, who found a way to assimilate the Declaration into their political strategies, and they praised it, in conveniently Whiggish fashion, for creating a single unified nation, not the confederation of states that Calhoun found in the Constitution. No part of the Declaration had more appeal for the Whigs than the controversial "equality" clause, since equality in the Whig lexicon immediately translated into economic opportunism, and thus positioned the Declaration as an endorsement of the Whig political agenda. "We must preach the great truth of our Declaration of Independence, that all men are created free," announced the Whig-leaning Cleveland *Herald* in the 1850s, and to do so meant that "we must build a railroad from the Atlantic to the Pacific, build schools and churches — we must educate all." Kansas-Nebraska provoked even more Whig appeals to the Declaration. Richard Yates, in the 1854 campaign, attacked Kansas-Nebraska for contradicting "the sentiment of the Declaration of American Independence."

For Lincoln to begin appealing to the Declaration was a resort to a convenient Whig tactic. "I love the sentiments of those old-time men," Lincoln announced, and the sentiment he came back to most often in the Peoria speech was "Our Declaration of Independence" and its equality clause. "'All men are created free and equal,' says the Declaration of Independence," Lincoln declared in the Springfield speech, and that meant, "The theory of our government is Universal Freedom." What told most heavily against the admission of slavery into the territories was that "the author of the declaration of Independence" had drafted the "policy of prohibiting slavery in the new territory. . . . Thus, away back of the constitution, in the pure fresh, free breath of the revolution . . . the National congress put that policy in practice."

Lincoln read the Declaration as a document that transcended, not only the states' rights so vital to the Democrats, but even national boundaries. The Declaration "set up a standard maxim for free society, which should be familiar to all, and revered by all." Immigrants who read the Constitution, Lincoln argued, saw only the rules and regulations of a foreign country; but when they read the Declaration, they found principles and ideas that reached over the head of language or section or previous nationality and bound Americans together as Americans, seeking life, liberty, and the pursuit of happiness. "Half our people . . . have come from Europe — German, Irish, French and Scandinavian," Lincoln observed in 1858, people who had no personal or ancestral stake in the writing of the Constitution or the rights of the states. "But when they look through that old declaration of Independence," Lincoln believed, they find principles that rise above one's place of birth, whether another country or another state of the Union. "They find that those old men say that 'We hold these truths to be self-evident, that all men are created equal,' and then they feel that that moral sentiment taught in that day evidences their relation to those men . . . and that they have a right to claim it as though they were . . . flesh of the flesh of the men who wrote that Declaration."

Lincoln also read the Declaration as promoting the critical Whig demand for economic expansion. The foundation of any worthwhile idea of equality was economic "betterment," and that right was what Lincoln found first in the Declaration. "It was that which gave promise that in due time the weights should be lifted from the shoulders of all men, and that *all* should have an equal chance. This is the sentiment embodied in that Declaration of Independence." On those terms, it gave Lincoln no end of amusement to twist Democratic tails with the words of their own champion. "Those claiming descent from [Jefferson] have nearly ceased to breathe his name everywhere," and so long as he could confine Jefferson to the Declaration, and especially his own Whiggish interpretation of the Declaration, he was delighted to be a Whig who could yield "all honor to Jefferson."

He did not try to claim that Jefferson meant "that all men are equal in their attainments or social position." The civil or social rights that each society grants to its members will vary from society to society, and some societies may choose, rightly or wrongly, to restrict the civil or social rights of some groups within it. Blacks, Lincoln insisted, may have to tolerate some measure of inferiority in their civil or social rights in an overwhelmingly white society, and the probability that this would remain a permanent feature of American life kept Lincoln proposing gradual emancipation and colonization rather than abolition as the ultimate answer. But "no sane man will attempt to deny that the African upon his own soil has all the natural rights" the Declaration "vouchsafes to all mankind." Even if on American soil the African must suffer some measure of diminished social or civil rights, the natural rights established by Jefferson in the Declaration cannot be taken away.

And yet, there was a harder edge to Lincoln's handling of the Declaration than the conventional Whig political script. In his search for a moral theory from which to denounce slavery extension, the Declaration came to assume the role of a substitute scripture, and the Fathers the role of political patriarchs in creating what Lincoln called in 1838 a "civil religion." The Declaration was, like the Old Testament Proverbs, "*the* word, *'fitly spoken'* which has proved an 'apple of gold' to us." This meant that the Declaration's announcement of the natural equality of all men gave it force of natural law, and more. "To us it appears natural to think that slaves are human beings; men, not property," and therefore "that some of the things, at least, stated about men in the declaration of Independence apply to them as well as to us." In that case, the enslavement of blacks was a step away from the sacred document of the Founding, a step away from liberty and toward the enslavement of everyone. "Then we may truly despair of the universality of freedom, or the efficacy of those sacred principles enunciated by our fathers — and give in our adhesion to the perpetuation and unlimited extension of slavery."

And yet this would not resemble the passionate moralism of New School revivalists. Lincoln did not propose, as come-outer abolitionists had, to tear up the Constitution as though it represented a subversion of the Declaration. William Lloyd Garrison, appalled by the protection federal law granted to the pursuit and recapture of slave

196

runaways in the North, attacked the Constitution as the fundamental support of the evil. The design of the Founders, argued Garrison on the pages of *The Liberator* in 1844, was "union at the expense of the colored population of the country," and in that case it was better that abolitionists "declare the contract at an end, and refuse to serve under it." But Lincoln was convinced that any move to set the Constitution aside was the swiftest guarantee of the death of liberty for everyone. The Constitution, Lincoln insisted, incorporated rather than contradicted the Declaration's promises of liberty, and therefore deserved to be read as a document whose basic drift ineluctably faced against slavery. The Constitution, and the federal Union the Constitution created in 1787, "are the *picture* of silver, subsequently framed around" the apple of gold. True, "the picture was made, not to *conceal,* or *destroy* the apple; but to *adorn,* and *preserve* it," but that did not mean that the frame was disposable. Be "ever true to Liberty, the Union, and the Constitution," Lincoln warned, "true to Liberty, not selfishly, but upon principle — not for special classes of men, but for all men, true to the union and the Constitution, as the best means to advance that liberty."

Lincoln had no constitutional theory as such, not because theory had no attractions for him, but because he believed the original intent of the Founders was actually quite easy to discover in the text of the Constitution and the historical context of the Founders. If, as Garrison had been at pains to illustrate, there were discrepancies between the spirit of the Declaration and the practices sanctioned by the Constitution, this was only the discrepancy one had to expect between aspiration and reality. It was no different, Lincoln explained, than the biblical injunction to be perfect "As your Father in heaven is perfect."

> The Savior, I suppose, did not expect that any human creature could be perfect, as the Father in Heaven; but . . . He set that up as a standard, and he who did most towards reaching that standard, attained the highest degree of moral perfection. So I say in relation to the principle that all men are created equal, let it be nearly reached as we can. . . . Let us turn this government back into the channel in which the framers of the constutition originally placed it.

In the case of both perfection and politics, aspiration was a legitimate connection between present realities and ideal futures. To step

197

outside the Constitution to promote the ideal of the Declaration, even if it were "politically expedient, and morally right," would give up "all footing upon the constitution or law" and open up the "boundless field of absolutism." In 1848, Lincoln attacked proposals even to amend the Constitution as a mistake leading to ruin:

> No slight occasion should tempt us to touch it. Better not take the first step, which may lead to a habit of altering it. Better, rather, habituate ourselves to think of it, as unalterable. It can scarcely be made better than it is. New provisions, would introduce new difficulties, and thus create, and increase appetite for still further change. No sir, let it stand as it is. New hands have never touched it. The men who made it, have done their work, and have passed away. Who shall improve, on what *they* did?

Although the Constitution gave some measure of legal sanction to slavery, this was only because the choice in 1787 was between making those concessions and getting a national Constitution, or a descent into national anarchy and misrule; and because the authors who made those concessions made them in the expectation that slavery would gradually die out anyway on its own. "You may examine the debates under the Constitution and in the first session of Congress and you will not find a single man saying that Slavery is a good thing," Lincoln wrote. "They all believed it was an evil."

Unlike many anti-slavery Northerners, Lincoln would not demand an end to the obnoxious provisions of the Fugitive Slave Law of 1850, because however much he disliked the operation of it, it was guaranteed to the South under the Constitution. "I have neither assailed, nor wrestled with any part of the constitution," Lincoln claimed. "The legal right of the Southern people to reclaim their fugitives I have constantly admitted. The legal right of Congress to interfere with the institution in these states, I have constantly denied." But to argue that the Constitution therefore gave slavery the broad right to plant itself in new areas and sprout new dominions for itself under the shelter of Douglas's argument — that the Constitution made no moral judgments about what people did in those new dominions — was actually a denial of the whole intention of the Constitution. Much as he appealed to Douglas's followers to "Throw off these things, and come to the rescue of this great principle of equality," he also added, "Don't interfere with anything in the Constitution. That must be maintained, for it is the only safeguard of our liberties."

Lincoln could not assume that all Whigs were reading Jefferson the same way, and they were not. The Whig party had, in electoral terms, always been something less than an outstanding success at the polls, and those failures at election times meant that they never had the spoils of office at their disposal either to reward loyalty or to punish desertions; in fact, in their eagerness to distance themselves from the rigid party discipline of the Jacksonians, the Whigs suicidally proclaimed their aversion to party regimentation, on the grounds that political harmony (like the economic "harmony of interests") ought to emerge naturally from shared cultural assumptions, and scorned the opportunity to make presidential cabinet-making an exercise in party uniformity. This was expecting the political equivalent of loaves and fishes, and it guaranteed that once a hugely divisive issue like slavery appeared over the horizon, the Whigs would have no single national leader, and no single party mechanism, to whip Northern anti-slavery Whigs and Southern pro-slavery Whigs into a single political file.

The Democrats, of course, had to deal with the same fissures, as the defection of the Free-Soil Democrats had demonstrated in 1848. But the Democrats had better organization, a better history of toeing the party line, and more carrots to dangle on sticks before the party faithful. The Whigs, on the other hand, began to fracture even before the Compromise of 1850 had been implemented. The Whig party caucus in the Thirty-First Congress balked at endorsing the Compromise, even in the face of pleas from the dying Henry Clay; Whig state conventions in New York, Ohio, and Pennsylvania voted down endorsements of the Compromise by embarrassing margins; the Whig national convention that nominated Winfield Scott for president in 1852 took fifty-three ballots to settle on Scott, largely because of the underlying inability of the convention to come to agreement about the Compromise — which induced the hapless Scott carefully to remove any reference at all to the Compromise in his acceptance letter.

Kansas-Nebraska only worsened matters, since it actually demolished the one Compromise the Whigs had held up as a "sacred compact" and one of their historic achievements. "Sir, the very moment you pass this measure, you explode, not only the Missouri Compromise, but the adjustment of 1850, and the Baltimore Whig platform of 1852," warned Connecticut senator Truman Smith. "You blow the Whig party into ten thousand atoms. Another Whig national convention will be impossible."

Some of Smith's "atoms" would land in the American Party, a small nativist party originally organized in 1850, which appealed to the dark side of Whig nationalism by advocating restrictions on immigration and naturalization of immigrants as a means to stemming the political influence of the waves of European immigrants pouring at unprecedented rates into the United States in the 1840s. From little more than a secret hate-society in New York City, the American Party mushroomed in four years into a national organization popularly known by its nickname, the "Know-Nothings" (from the promise in the party's original membership ritual that they would rebuff all inquiries into the party's secrets with the moronic answer, "I know nothing"). Especially, their commitment to excluding Catholic immigrants from the political process drew New School Whigs to their ranks as the Whigs fell more and more into political paralysis.

Another solution, at least for disheartened Northern Whigs, would be the creation of "fusions" on the state level with equally disgruntled Northern Democrats. "Fusionists" hoped to make opposition to Kansas-Nebraska and slave extension in the territories the foundation for united political action. But fusion was a risky game for Whigs to play, since fusionists were immediately disowned by the national party and left to wander in the political wilderness; and the moment fusionist Whigs moved an inch beyond the Nebraska issue to talk about tariffs or internal improvements, Democrat fusionists would promptly desert them and return (as many of the Free Soilers had done after 1848) to the old Jacksonian bosom. What was more, Whig fusionists who concentrated on Kansas-Nebraska would have a hard time persuading the public that they were not simply johnny-one-notes on slavery, a difficulty made harder still by the certain clamor of abolitionists to join any such fusion and radicalize it in ways unacceptable to mainstream Whigs.

The risks of fusion politics were starkly illustrated in Illinois by the failure of Whigs and anti-Nebraska Democrats to form a successful fusion in the fall of 1854, when the anti-Nebraska outrage was at the boiling point. Following on Lincoln's clash with Douglas at the State Fair that October, Owen Lovejoy and Ichabod Codding, whose anti-slavery passion had made them too hot for either Whigs or Democrats to handle, called for the state-wide organization of "a party which shall put the government on a Republican tack" and oppose "the repeal of the Missouri Compromise and . . . the future expansion and consolidation of the slave power." They hoped to imitate the success that anti-Nebraska fusionists in Michigan that summer had in organizing a "Republican" party. But Codding and Lovejoy, reeking as they did of abolitionism, could not persuade Lincoln or any other important Illinois Whig to join them. Although a "Republican" state committee was formed and a set of resolutions condemning Kansas-Nebraska and the Compromise of 1850 were adopted, Lincoln explicitly refused the offer of a seat on the Republican state committee. "I suppose my opposition to the principle of slavery is as strong as that of any member of the Republican party," he explained to Codding in November, 1854, but he could not abandon "the old Whig party and must continue" to support it "until a better one arose to take its place."

The failed Senate election of 1855 forced Lincoln to reexamine his resistance to fusion and to ask whether, once again, his passion for loyalty had kept him loyal to a losing proposition. The Whig party alone had not been nearly enough to defeat Shields, and in fact it had taken a "fusion" of sorts in the legislature just to get Lincoln the votes he did actually get; and his decision to throw those votes at the end to an anti-Nebraska Democrat like Trumbull was a fusion gesture of its own. Lincoln struggled with these difficulties throughout 1855, even as he returned from "dabbling in politics" to business on the circuit. When Lovejoy urged Lincoln in August, 1855, to join a "fusion" movement in Illinois, Lincoln patiently explained that "not even you are more anxious to prevent the extension of slavery than I," but still "the political atmosphere is such, just now, that I fear to do any thing, lest I do wrong." Later that month, he told Joshua Speed that as far as he was concerned, "I think I am a Whig." But there were voices all around him which argued that "there are no whigs, and that I am an abolitionist," which was just the kind of radical association that any fusion movement was likely to taint him with.

One thing which was "certain," he told Speed, was that he was "not a Know-Nothing." Lincoln "opposed Know-Nothingism in all its phases, everywhere, and at all times when it was sweeping over the land like wildfire," Herndon remarked. As Lincoln had told Lovejoy, "I do not perceive how any one professing to be sensitive to the wrongs of the negroes, can join in a league to degrade a class of white men." Without any identifiable religion of his own, Lincoln shared none of the anxieties of Whig Protestants about "political Romanism," and found the Know-Nothings, even more than the Calhounites, a standing repudiation of what, "as a nation, we began by declaring that 'all men are created equal.'" That had not prevented the Know-Nothings from trying to recruit him in 1854 as a state legislative candidate, and rumors that he had secretly taken the Know-Nothing oath cost him at least one critical vote in the 1855 senatorial election. If this was the future of fusion, Lincoln was better off staying a Whig, for what that might be worth.

By the end of October, 1855, however, Lincoln was finally sidling toward fusion politics. In Danville (where he kept up a circuit partnership with Ward Hill Lamon), he accepted an "invitation of the fusionists here" to speak against Douglas and Kansas-Nebraska in a fashion which one Democratic critic snarled "just suits them." Four months later, with another presidential election looming up, Paul Selby, a Republican lawyer and organizer, and editor of the Morgan County *Journal*, hosted an invitational conference of anti-Nebraska editors at Decatur with a view to recruiting potential fusionists for the Republicans, and added Lincoln and Richard Yates to the invitation list.

An invitation to join an editors' meeting was less peculiar than it seems, since partisan newspapers editors usually wore a number of professional and political hats (as Selby himself did) and editors would usually assemble themselves as the preliminary organizing network for county or state political conventions. The surprising element was the deliberate absence of Lovejoy and Codding; in fact, of the fourteen editors who participated (including John Nicolay of the *Pike City Free Press* and E. L. Baker, who bought the *Illinois State Journal* from Lincoln's old supporter Simeon Francis) none were abolitionists and most were former Whigs. It was, in other words, a deliberate attempt by Republican organizers to court Lincoln on the terms he wanted. This time, Lincoln cautiously promised Selby that he would "try and have some business at Decatur at the time of the Convention." And "although he did not take part in the public deliberations" of the meeting, he allowed himself to sit with the meeting's Committee on Resolutions and "advise" it, so that he could, for all practical purposes, write out the terms on which he would join the Republicans.

And the terms were just what "an old Whig" would demand: reaffirmation of the Declaration of Independence, denunciation of Kansas-Nebraska, the containment of slavery and restoration of the Missouri Compromise, and the repudiation of Know-Nothing xenophobia in favor of "liberty of conscience as well as political freedom" — but no agitation for national abolition. At the dinner that concluded the conference, the editors began calling on Lincoln to speak, to run for governor, even to run for the Senate against Douglas when Douglas's term expired in 1858. Lincoln declined the suggestion about the governorship — that, he felt, would be better served by running an anti-Nebraska Democrat like William Bissell instead — but he liked the idea of breaking lances with Douglas, and "said, that he was very much in the position of the man who was attacked by a robber, demanding his money, when he answered, 'my dear fellow, I have no money, but if you will go with me to the light, I will give you my note'; and resumed Mr. L., if you will let me off, I will give you my note."

The Decatur editors' conference moved to call a state-wide fusion convention, to meet in Bloomington in May, 1856. And since the organizers of the Bloomington meeting (including Lincoln's partner, Herndon) also happened to share much of the leadership of the Illinois Republican party, Lincoln's "note" was, in effect, a promise to throw in his lot with the Republicans if they would support a run by him against Douglas for the Senate two years hence. And this they were more than willing to do. Lincoln allowed Herndon to sign his name to a published call to Sangamon County fusionists on May 10th to send delegates to the Bloomington convention, and when the Bloomington convention assembled on May 29th, the two hundred and seventy delegates enthusiastically endorsed Bissell as the fusionist candidate for governor (against Douglas's lieutenant and congressional floor manager, William Richardson) and a German immigrant, Francis Hoffmann, for lieutenant governor, while the platform (which had been written by Orville Hickman Browning) denounced Kansas-Nebraska as "an open and aggravated violation of the plighted faith of the states."

But the set-piece of the meeting occurred that night, after the fer-

203

vor of the convention had been whipped to a frenzy by one flaming anti-slavery speech after another, when the call went up through the hall for Lincoln. "Abraham Lincoln, of Sangamon, came upon the platform amid deafening applause," reported the *Alton Weekly Courier*, and there he proceeded to deliver, without notes, one of the most critical speeches of his life. There were no more doubts or hesitations about fusion: "He was here ready to fuse with anyone who would unite with him to oppose the slave power." Here also was his underlying economic argument about slavery: that the expansion of slavery outside the South would mean the substitution of slave labor and "white slavery" for free labor all through the country. Here again was the invocation of the Declaration and "the individual rights of man" which Douglas and the Democrats had renounced and which "he must stand there now to defend." And here also was a word for the South: that if they tried to force a settlement of the territories by threatening disunion, they would find that "We do not intend to dissolve the Union, nor do we intend to let you dissolve it."

But more than his argument, it was Lincoln's inner man which was now alight. "Now he was newly baptized and freshly born; he had the fervor of a new convert; the smothered flame broke out; enthusiasm unusual to him blazed up . . . and he stood before the throne of the eternal Right," marveled Herndon, who tried to take notes on the speech but gave up after fifteen minutes, "threw pen and paper away and lived only in the inspiration of the hour." Nor was Herndon alone: "the reporters dropped the pencils and forgot their work." Thomas Henderson remembered that Lincoln "stood as if on tip-toe, his tall form erect, his long arms extended, his face fairly radiant with the flush of excitement." The Chicago journalist John Locke Scripps could not keep his jaw from dropping open — "Never was an audience more completely electrified by human eloquence" — and Scripps marked Lincoln down as a coming force on the national stage.

Nothing in the Bloomington convention's deliberations actually mentioned the name *Republican*, but the Bloomington convention appointed delegates to attend the first national Republican nominating convention in Philadelphia three weeks later, and Lincoln's name was put forward by the Illinois delegation as a possible vice-presidential candidate. Although the actual nomination went to William Dayton, a New Jersey Whig, Lincoln was pleasantly surprised to learn that he had garnered a third of the votes cast, and only a little less happy to endorse Dayton, another Whig-turned-fusionist, as "a far better man than I for the position he is in." Lincoln had greater reservations about the Republican presidential nominee, John Charles Fremont, a celebrity soldier and explorer, an ex-Democrat from Missouri who was married to the daughter of Thomas Hart Benton, one of Andrew Jackson's most loyal political spear-carriers, and who was riding on the influence of one of Jackson's oldest political allies, Francis Preston Blair. Lincoln had originally hoped that the Republicans would nominate Justice John McLean, since McLean was a Whig whose "nomination would save every whig" for the Republicans. It was possible that disillusioned Whigs "would stand Blair or Fremont for Vice-President — but not more."

Nevertheless, he promised to support the Republican ticket "most cordially," and Republicans all across the old Northwest sent up calls for Lincoln's services as a campaigner for Fremont. Lincoln ended up devoting almost every waking hour between the close of the Eighth Circuit's summer term in June and election day in November to stump speaking on behalf of Fremont and Bissell. "I have never seen him so sanguine of success, as in this election," Herndon wrote to Lyman Trumbull. "Lincoln feels confident Freemont will carry the State." And no wonder: Franklin Pierce's four years as president had been riddled with corruption and mismanagement, and anti-slavery Democrats accused both Pierce and Douglas of selling their souls to the South. Philadelphian Oliver H. P. Parker denounced Pierce as "a weak-kneed, New Hampshire Loco Foco . . . which made Him a fit subject for the Slave Power to operate upon." Brooklyn Democratic editor Walt Whitman (whose *Leaves of Grass* had just appeared in its first edition the previous year) begged for the appearance of "the Redeemer President of These States" who "fullest realizes the rights of individuals, signified by the impregnable rights of The States, the substratum of this Union." What Whitman and Parker got instead of Pierce, however, as the nominee of the Democratic national convention in June, was James Buchanan — a colorless and inoffensive Pennsylvanian — and a party platform that gave a blanket endorsement to Kansas-Nebraska.

Even so, a Fremont campaign was not going to be as easy as it looked. When Buchanan's nomination was announced in Springfield in June, Lincoln warned Lyman Trumbull that "a good many whigs, of conservative feelings, and slight pro-slavery proclivities, withal, are inclining to go for him." His own speeches were a careful reprise of the 1854 anti-Nebraska speeches, reviewing again the anti-slavery intentions of the Founders (and "of that Declaration made to the world, by our Fore Fathers, 'That all men are born free and equal'"), the folly of Kansas-Nebraska in turning those intentions upside down, and the need for the restoration of the Missouri Compromise. But at the end of August, Henry Clay Whitney saw Lincoln heckled for half an hour in Petersburg by "cat-calls, whistles, tin horns filled with air" before he could make himself heard. At Olney, Illinois, he threw "up his hands in disgust and despair, said — 'Oh, I can't interest this crowd,' and left the stand." Democratic newspapers charged him with "niggerism" and claimed that "he would occasionally launch out and lead his hearers to think that the most ultra abolitionism would follow, when, under the old whig eyes . . . he would soften his remarks to a supposed palatable texture."

Lincoln found that too many anti-Nebraska Whigs in Illinois were clinging to the stern-rail of the Whig ship even as it was sinking. James Matheny refused to join the Republicans and was running as a Whig candidate for Lincoln's old Seventh District seat. Joseph Gillespie told Lincoln that his endorsement of the Bloomington convention was "a clean sell of the Whigs and true conservative men of the state." Fletcher Webster and James Clay, the sons of the great Whig figureheads, both publicly endorsed Buchanan. It especially galled Lincoln that a last-stand Whig national convention in Baltimore named as its presidential candidate Millard Fillmore, the only surviving Whig president, who had publicly taken the Know-Nothing oath in order to bind Whigs and Know-Nothings together, and that Gillespie had consented to serve as a Fillmore elector. Fillmore had little chance of winning the presidency, but Lincoln knew that he stood in a good way to prevent hesitant anti-slavery Whigs from deserting the party for the Republican fusionists, thus dividing the anti-Nebraska opposition and handing the election to the Democrats. In a circular letter to a Fillmore mailing list, Lincoln pleaded, "Be not deceived. *Buchanan* is the hard horse to beat in this race. Let him have Illinois, and nothing can beat him; *and he will get Illinois,* if men persist in throwing away votes upon Mr. Fillmore."

Personally, Lincoln had almost as many reservations about some of his fellow Republicans as did Matheny and Gillespie. "The party is newly formed," Lincoln wrote, "and in forming, old party ties had to be broken, and the attractions of party pride, and influential leaders were wholly wanting." He was anxious to keep Owen Lovejoy and the abolitionists out of the Republican vanguard, and he told Henry Clay Whitney in July that "it turned me blind" when Illinois Republicans in the Third District gave their endorsement for the congressional race to Lovejoy rather than to Lincoln's friend Leonard Swett. But he felt just as much queasiness over the anti-Nebraska Democrats who had bolted to the Republicans, some of whom carried their own destructive intra-party feuding with them into the new Republican ranks. Chicago's "Long John" Wentworth, who had moved into the Republican camp at the Bloomington convention, also had aspirations for Douglas's Senate seat in 1858; Wentworth, in turn, was nursing a mortal quarrel with Norman Judd, one of the anti-Nebraska state senators who had deserted Lincoln for Joel Matteson in the humiliating 1855 Senate contest; Judd, in turn, was loathed by David Davis, Orville Hickman Browning, and the other old stalwarts of central Illinois Whiggery. "The Republican party" was a "Composite — made up of all parties, associations, &c.," wrote Davis, and as Lincoln remarked in 1856, "Moral principle is all, or nearly all, that unites us." Lincoln eventually came to see it as his task to keep principle rather than personality before all of them, and keep the ex-Whigs away from Fillmore and the ex-Democrats away from Buchanan. "A union of our strength, to be effected in some way is indispensable to our carrying the State."

Lincoln's best arguments against both Fillmore and Buchanan were provided for him by the practical results of the Kansas-Nebraska Act. Settlers began pouring into Kansas as early as the summer of 1854, and as they did, they quickly sorted themselves out into pro-slavery and anti-slavery factions, each determined to see that they would exercise the popular sovereignty which would decide Kansas's future as a territory and a state. There was too much at stake for each side merely to rest content in the other's good political faith; and in short order, each was cutting the other's throats and rigging the elections for a territorial legislature. By the end of 1855, pro-slavery and anti-slavery Kansans had managed to create two rival legislatures with two rival territorial constitutions; meanwhile the level of violence escalated until, in May, 1856, a small pro-slavery army attacked and burned the anti-slavery capital at Lawrence. Nor did the violence stop at the Kansas border. The conflict in Kansas brought Northerners in Congress to their feet to denounce popular sovereignty as a bankrupt policy, Southerners to attack Northern immigrants to Kansas as abolitionist troublemakers, and on May 19, 1856, a Southern congressman named Preston Brooks caned Massachusetts senator Charles Sumner into unconsciousness on the floor of the Senate for Sumner's denunciation of "The Crime Against Kansas." The territory Stephen Douglas had dreamt of opening to a peaceful, democratic settlement of differences through popular sovereignty had instead become a "Bleeding Kansas."

If the maladroit President Pierce had been renominated as the Democratic candidate, the Kansas debacle might have set off precisely the stampede from the ranks of the Northern Democrats that Fremont needed for victory. James Buchanan, however, was unsullied with any connection to the Kansas outrages (he had been Pierce's minister to England and was out of the country), and given the infancy of the Republicans and their almost exclusively Northern political base, the Republican coalition had poor chances of tagging Buchanan as a proslavery puppet or Fillmore as unelectable, despite Lincoln's pleas to his old Whig friends in September that "every vote withheld from Fremont, and given to Fillmore, *in this state,* actually lessens Fillmore's chance of being President." And, he might have added, ensured Buchanan's. Early state elections in Pennsylvania and Indiana went to the Democrats, and in the November presidential election, although Fremont and Fillmore together polled over 2.2 million votes to Buchanan's 1.8 million, by dividing that majority the Fillmore-ites successfully handed the election to Buchanan.

Still, the size of Fremont's popular vote — 1.34 million, as opposed to Fillmore's 874,000 — was impressive for a first-time party, and suggested that the country as a whole was shifting its political center more and more toward the active containment of slavery. This would, in the long run, be bad news for the Democrats. The bulk of the votes which had elected Buchanan came more than ever from the South, and Buchanan would be beholden to Southern pressure to eliminate any containment on slave extension. And even though Illinois had gone for Buchanan, it had also elected Bissell as governor. A month after the election Lincoln addressed a Republican banquet in

Chicago, congratulating his fellow Republicans for having forced Franklin Pierce out of office and "elected a Republican State ticket." He also urged the Fillmore-ites to lay aside their suspicions of the Republicans and keep a "steady eye on the real issue . . . the good old 'central ideas' of the Republic . . . that 'all *men* are created equal.'" With that in view and a united anti-Kansas-Nebraska front, they could dump Buchanan at the next election in 1860. And in the meanwhile, Lincoln would have plans of his own for dumping Stephen A. Douglas from his Senate seat in 1858.

Abraham Lincoln's most important ally in that cause would be no one less than President James Buchanan himself. The great anxiety that had driven national politics on the subject of slavery for the previous ten years was the fear that any decision on slavery extension by Congress would prove so hot to handle that no imaginable peaceful resolution could possibly be achieved in Washington, and the Union might split over the results. Even the great Compromise of 1850 was really Congress's agreement not to settle the matter in Congress, but rather to let popular sovereignty in the Mexican Cession settle the matter a safe distance away. The Kansas-Nebraska Act was supposed to perform the same defusing of the problem by extending popular sovereignty to the Louisiana Purchase territories, as well. But "Bleeding Kansas" demonstrated in horrifying detail just how limited a solution popular sovereignty might be; the Sumner caning illustrated even more graphically what might result if the Kansas disaster threw the subject back into the lap of Congress.

And so, with grotesque political timing, the United States Supreme Court stepped in at this moment to protect Congress and the Union from itself, in the form of the case of *Dred Scott v. Sanford.* Dred Scott was a shrewd but illiterate Virginia-born slave who had been taken by his master, an army surgeon, from Missouri in 1834 to Illinois and then to the Wisconsin Territory. In 1842, Scott returned with his master to Missouri, and after his master died the following year, Scott sued for his freedom in the St. Louis County Circuit Court, on the grounds that residence in free territory had rendered him a free person. The Missouri Supreme Court eventually found against him, unwilling "to show the least countenance to any measure which might" invite other oft-moved slaves to file similar suits. But Scott appealed to the federal courts, and by 1856, the case was before the United States Supreme Court, and its Chief Justice, Roger B. Taney.

After thirteen years of winding its way up the appeals ladder, *Dred Scott v. Sanford* had acquired a good deal of legal notoriety, especially since part of Scott's appeal was based on his residence in a federal territory whose free-soil status was regulated originally by a federal statute, the Northwest Ordinance. A Supreme Court decision on Scott's freedom could be construed as a judicial decision on the persistent question of who, if anyone, had the power to determine the free or slave status of federal territories. Lincoln had enough legal business near St. Louis to be aware of the *Dred Scott* case, and in January of 1857, as it was being argued before the Court, he speculated on whether the Court might use the case to issue some declaration "as to the constitutional restriction on the power of a territorial Legislature, in regard to slavery in the territory."

Few could have expected, however, the dimensions of the decision until it was handed down by Taney himself on March 6, 1857, two days after Buchanan's inauguration as president. *Dred Scott v. Sanford* not only denied Scott legal standing on the grounds that blacks could never be considered citizens under the Constitution, but announced that the federal government had no authority to restrict the movement or the status in the territories of any citizen's property. "The Territory being a part of the United States, the Government and the citizen both enter it under the authority of the Constitution, with their respective rights defined and marked out; and the Federal Government can exercise no power over his person or property, beyond what that instrument confers, nor lawfully deny any right which it has reserved." This certainly removed slavery as a problem for the federal government to deal with, to the delight of the newly inaugurated James Buchanan; it also just as certainly enshrined John C. Calhoun's old argument that no one had the authority to ban slaveholders from transplanting slavery and struck down as unconstitutional not only the great Compromises, but even the authority of a territorial legislature elected under congressional supervision to exercise popular sovereignty in determining whether it should be free or slave. "No word can be found in the Constitution which gives Congress a greater power over slave property, or which entitles property of that kind to less protection than property of any other description." Taney, who had been appointed to the Court by Andrew Jackson after faithfully acting as Jackson's hatchet-man in destroying the Second Bank, congratulated himself on settling the controversy over slave extension once and for all.

Instead, it triggered another violent backlash all across the North. By opening the gates of all the territories to slavery without restraint, and decreeing that they must remain open, Taney had set up a principle which might, if a better case soon emerged, allow the Taney Court to strike down all the bans on slavery in the free states as well. Horace Greeley's *Tribune* denounced *Dred Scott* as a "collation of false statement and shallow sophistries"; the New York legislature defied the Court by extending new state voting rights to blacks and commissioning a report which prophesied that "the decision . . . will bring slavery within our borders against our will, with all its unhallowed, demoralizing, and blighting influences." The Albany *Evening Journal* sarcastically celebrated the triumph of "three hundred forty-seven thousand, five hundred and twenty-five Slaveholders in the Republic" in converting "the Supreme Court . . . into a propagandist of human Slavery." The Washington-based *National Era* screeched, "The Slaveholding Oligarchy have the Administration, the majority in the Senate and in the House, and the Supreme Court. What is left to the People?"

No one, however, had more to lose from *Dred Scott* than Stephen A. Douglas, not because Douglas had any particular sympathy for Scott, but because *Dred Scott* appeared to have put paid to popular sovereignty as a means of settling the problem of slave extension. If Congress could not forbid the movement of slaves into a territory, then a decision by a territorial legislature created by Congress, whether by popular sovereignty or anything else, was just as unconstitutional, and Douglas's prize political program was rendered null. What was worse for Douglas, President Buchanan received Taney's decision (and some said, actively conspired in its creation) with undisguised pleasure, and announced his intention of accepting, as the solution for Kansas most in harmony with *Dred Scott*, a pro-slavery territorial constitution composed by the pro-slavery rump legislature sitting at Lecompton, Kansas. If Douglas attempted to stand by popular sovereignty, not only would he have to find some way of reconciling it with *Dred Scott*, but he would be pitted squarely against the leadership of his own Democratic party just when his own re-election to the Senate was looming before him in the Illinois legislature. "The scheme is on foot," he was warned by a party insider, "to carry the Legislature against you at the next session — not by our enemies the Republicans — but by your enemies in our own ranks."

But Douglas, as his supervision of both the Compromise of 1850 and Kansas-Nebraska had indicated, was not easily discouraged. On December 9, 1857, at the opening of the Thirty-fifth Congress, Douglas lashed out at the Lecompton constitution as a "flagrant violation of popular rights in Kansas" which he would "resist to the last." And he insisted that slavery could still be excluded from the territories by popular sovereignty if the territorial legislatures withheld the necessary enabling and police legislation to keep it intact; in fact, on those terms, *only* a decision by this kind of popular sovereignty could keep slavery out. When Buchanan warned him that any bucking of the party line on Kansas would be met with the kind of party discipline meted out by Andrew Jackson, Douglas tartly informed Buchanan, "Mr. President, I wish you to remember that General Jackson is dead." Buchanan responded by lining up Douglas supporters — party workers, postmasters — for dismissal. "Old Buck has got the guillotine well greased and in full swing," grinned one anti-Douglas newspaper. The heads of Douglasites would be "falling into the basket as fast as the old machine can be made to work."

The prospect of a "*rumpus* among the democracy over the Kansas constitution" delighted Lincoln, since it (like the Kansas-Nebraska bill) would split the Illinois Democrats between Douglas's loyalists and the party faithful loyal to Buchanan. The one hitch in this scenario was the possibility that Douglas's defiance of Buchanan would attract so much sympathy from Republicans that they might be tempted to treat Douglas as a sort of honorary Republican, and throw the support of the party behind Douglas, a figure of unquestioned national stature, rather than behind Lincoln, the regional hero. And just as he feared, eastern Republican leaders, including New York's William Seward and the *Tribune*'s Horace Greeley, openly courted Douglas, and Republican money financed a mass printing of Douglas's anti-Lecompton speech. Lincoln noticed the threat in this movement as early as December, 1857, when he querulously asked Lyman Trumbull in Washington what eastern Republicans thought they were doing by "constant eulogising, and admiring, and magnifying Douglas. . . . Have they concluded that the republican cause, generally, can be best promoted by sacrificing us here in Illinois? If so we would like to know it soon; it will save us a great deal of labor to surrender at once." To Herndon he complained, "I think Greeley is not doing me, an old Republican and a tried antislavery man, right. He is talking up Douglas, an untrue and untried man, a dodger, a wriggler, a tool of the South once and now a snapper at it."

To the task of keeping the Illinois Republicans united, Lincoln added the job of keeping the Illinois Democrats divided. He tacitly encouraged Buchanan Democrats (the "Danites" or "Buchaneers") to run a rival field of candidates against Douglas's men and funneled Republican money to anti-Douglas newspapers. And in order to secure Republican unity, Lincoln and the Republican state committee decided not to wait (as Lincoln had done in 1855) until after the state legislative elections had taken place to announce his intentions as a senatorial candidate, but to call a state convention in the early summer that would commit the full strength of the Illinois Republicans to Lincoln at once and make the legislative elections a referendum-in-advance on Lincoln's challenge to Douglas. "He had become conscious that some of his party friends distrusted his ability to meet successfully a man whom, as the democrats declared and believed, had never had his equal on the stump," recalled Isaac Arnold.

When the convention, braving floods that had swollen the Mississippi and Illinois rivers, assembled in the state capitol's Hall of Representatives on June 16th, Lincoln's backers were ready to focus all the attention on Lincoln. Even Norman Judd, who had let Lincoln down so painfully in 1855, marched in at the head of the Cook County delegation with a banner blaring "COOK COUNTY IS FOR ABRAHAM LINCOLN," and it was one of Judd's delegates — Charles Wilson, the editor of the Chicago *Journal* — who rose after the report of the resolutions committee was adopted, to nominate Lincoln as "the first and only choice of the Republicans of Illinois for the United States Senate." This clearly set Greeley and the eastern Republicans on notice that Illinois would tolerate no dallying with Douglas. And when Lincoln appeared for the convention's evening session to give his acceptance speech, he was equally set on undercutting any claims of Douglas to anti-slavery votes, Republican or otherwise. He had worked on this speech with unusual care, reading it to friends behind closed doors to gauge their reaction, and its words were terse, precise, and cutting.

We are now far into the *fifth* year, since a policy was initiated, with the *avowed* object, and *confident* promise, of putting an end to slavery agitation. Under the operation of that policy, that agitation has not only, *not ceased,* but has *constantly augmented.* In *my* opinion, it *will* not cease, until a *crisis* shall have been reached, and passed. "A house divided against itself cannot stand." I believe this government cannot endure, permanently half *slave* and half *free.* I do not expect the Union to be *dissolved* — I do not expect the house to *fall* — but I *do* expect it will cease to be divided. It will become *all* one thing, or *all* the other. Either the *opponents* of slavery, will arrest the further spread of it, and place it where the public mind shall rest in the belief that it is in course of ultimate extinction; or its *advocates* will push it forward, till it shall become alike lawful in *all* the States, *old* as well as *new* — *North* as well as *South.*

Despite every promise that Kansas-Nebraska and the repeal of the Missouri Compromise would somehow pacify the slavery issue, the reality of "Bleeding Kansas" and *Dred Scott* had demonstrated that, left to Douglas's devices, slavery would never die out at all; it would persist for as long as Lincoln could foresee, and would swell and bloat until it either overran the North or until it forced the North to destroy it. And Lincoln deliberately cast the dilemma in the apocalyptic tones of the Gospels, of the "house divided against itself" whose inevitable end is not coexistence between the divisions, but destruction and collapse.

Nor was this *"crisis"* looming merely because Douglas was an inept politician. Lincoln proceeded to put the political history of the divided house from 1854 onwards into the context of the slave power conspiracy, a "complete legal combination" superintended from Washington by Buchanan, Pierce, Taney, and (however unbelievable) Stephen A. Douglas himself, to promote the nationalization of slavery. Whatever Douglas's seeming conflict with Buchanan, said Lincoln, Douglas had been hand-in-hand from the beginning with Taney, Pierce, and Buchanan to promote the triumph of slavery, not only in the territories, but all over the Union. "We can not absolutely *know* that all these exact adaptations are the result of preconcert," Lincoln disingenuously admitted,

But when we see a lot of framed timbers, different portions of which we know have been gotten out at different times and places and by

214

different workmen — Stephen, Franklin, Roger and James, for instance — and when we see these timbers joined together, and see
they exactly make the frame of a house or a mill, all the tenons and
mortices exactly fitting . . . in *such* a case, we find it impossible to not
believe that Stephen and Franklin and Roger and James all understood one another from the beginning, and all worked upon a common *plan* or *draft* drawn up before the first lick was struck.

Kansas-Nebraska had been the first timber, and the second timber,
Dred Scott, had been neatly timed to be "argued *in* the Supreme Court
of the United States . . . *before* the *then* next Presidential election." The
decision itself was delayed just long enough to get Buchanan inaugurated, so that Buchanan could suspiciously exhort "the people to abide
by the forthcoming decision, *whatever it might be*." The next timber,
Lincoln prophesied, will be "the revival of the African slave trade,"
and "how can [Douglas] resist it?" The moral of the story was clear:
unless Douglas is stopped, "We shall *lie down* pleasantly dreaming that
the people of *Missouri* are on the verge of making their State *free;* and
we shall *awake* to the *reality*, instead, that the *Supreme* Court has made
Illinois a *slave* State."

The convention went appropriately wild over the "House Divided" speech, and Herndon beamingly predicted that it would make
him president. But the reaction of newspaper readers across the state
made it clear that Lincoln had stumbled on the very threshold of his
campaign. His Republican backers had quietly "condemned the
speech in Substance & Spirit, and especially" the opening reference to
the "house divided," and other friends afterward told him bluntly:
"That foolish speech of yours will kill you — will defeat you in this
Contest — and probably for all offices for all time to come." John
Armstrong "could hear from all quarters in the crowd, Republicans
say — 'Damn that fool speech; it will be the cause of the death of Lincoln and the republican party." Lincoln soon learned why. The rhetoric
of divided houses was read throughout Illinois as Lincoln's confident
promise that civil war was the next step, and that since the "government cannot endure, permanently half *slave* and half *free*," he would be
in the forefront of a movement to make it all free, even if it required the
forced subjugation of the South.

"I am much mortified that any part of it should be construed so

215

differently from any thing intended by me," Lincoln wrote irritably to John Locke Scripps a week afterward. After all, he had been comparing the political situation posed by Kansas-Nebraska to a "house divided" ever since the 1854 campaign, and a month before the "House Divided" speech, he had actually used the phrase *"A house divided against itself cannot stand"* in a speech at Edwardsville to express his belief that "the government cannot endure permanently half slave and half free" — all without public horror. And in the "House Divided" speech he had stated clearly that "I do not expect the Union to be *dissolved* — I do not expect the house to *fall.*" He had wanted only to say in as strong terms as possible that the destruction of the Missouri Compromise by Douglas was the beginning of a nationalization of slavery, leaving Americans with only the choice between the patent impossibility of making the republic all free at once or the unpalatable but unavoidable choice of it becoming all slave.

No matter. It *sounded* like a call to sectional struggle. The solution he took for granted as the obvious conclusion of his remark was a restoration of the Missouri Compromise that would put slavery back on the old "course of ultimate extinction," not a civil war between North and South. And for this, no one could safely turn to Douglas. "He don't *care* anything about it." And those whose ears could not stop ringing from the "house divided" imagery were not helped by Lincoln's strange claim that James Buchanan and Stephen Douglas were really acting out a national charade. Perhaps Lincoln really believed that all Democratic disagreements were only charades to fool upright but gullible Whig-Republicans. What was certain was that Lincoln himself believed that only by placing himself on one side of a stark contrast, and only by putting Douglas unambiguously on the other side (even if it meant claiming that Douglas and Buchanan were really allies) could Lincoln keep Republicans in Illinois and elsewhere from softening toward Stephen Douglas and abandoning Lincoln.

At first, Douglas showed no interest in rising to Lincoln's challenge — no interest, in fact, in responding in any way that might give Lincoln the look of a serious rival. For three weeks after Douglas opened his appeal to the Illinois voters to elect Democrat legislators on July 9th, Lincoln was reduced to trailing after Douglas from rally to rally, looking for opportunities to set up his own soapbox to offer rebuttals. He attempted to keep alive the conspiracy theory, and he directly attacked the popular sovereignty doctrine as an illusion whose last hope had been smashed by *Dred Scott*. But all too much of his time was spent on parrying Douglas's blows at him, denying that the Republicans wanted interference with slavery in the South, denying that he wanted disunion and civil war, denying that he had been inciting people to defy the Supreme Court. When Lincoln tried to appeal to the fears of Illinois farmers about the extension of slavery into the free states under *Dred Scott*, Douglas easily outflanked Lincoln with even more radical appeals to the fears of Illinois whites about race and the prospect of a "black Republicanism" that would abolish slavery everywhere and open Illinois to a flood of free black immigrants. The Associated Press's coverage of the campaign gave another Douglas speech on July 16th a half-column of front-page coverage, but only five lines to Lincoln's reply. "Mr. Lincoln's course in following Senator Douglas is condemned even by his friends," the *New York Herald* sniffed. Very quickly Lincoln found himself and his campaign "now in need of money," and Herndon thought that Lincoln had become "gloomy — rather uncertain, about his own success."

July was very nearly over when Lincoln, after a hurried conference with Republican state leaders in Chicago, wrote to Douglas to suggest a series of formal debates "to divide time, and address the same audiences during the present canvass." It was not an idea Douglas welcomed: Douglas's campaign was already ahead and needed no debating to coast to victory. But perhaps because Douglas had indeed become so confident of the course of the campaign, or perhaps because he had no wish to look unwilling, he agreed to meet in the open with Lincoln "at one prominent place in each congressional district in the state, excepting the second and sixth districts, where we have both spoken." And in keeping with the code of the duel, Douglas chose the sites: "Freeport, Ottawa, Galesburg, Quincy, Alton, Jonesboro & Charleston."

Stephen Douglas symbolized many things to Abraham Lincoln, all of them bad. Lincoln had known Douglas now for over twenty years, ever since both of them had gone down to Vandalia as state legislators, and he had seen in Douglas virtually every Democratic principle he hated. In the mature years of the 1850s, diminutive five-foot-four

217

Douglas had gone from strength to strength as the "Little Giant" — a congressman, a judge, a senator — and the rumor hung thick in the Illinois air that Stephen A. Douglas ought to be the next Democratic candidate for president. By contrast, Lincoln had achieved almost nothing of what he wanted most from politics. "Twenty-two years ago Judge Douglas and I first became acquainted," Lincoln wrote dejectedly in December of 1856. "We were both young then; he a trifle younger than I. Even then, we were both ambitious; I, perhaps, quite as much so as he. With *me*, the race of ambition has been a failure — a flat failure; with *him* it has been one of splendid success."

He could not stanch his irritation over the symbolic incongruity of Douglas's physical stature (compared with Lincoln's own) and his national prominence, and he remarked bitterly in 1852 that once "Judge Douglas was not so much greater man than all the rest of us," but now Douglas "has outgrown me & [be]strides the world; & such small men as I, can hardly be considered as worthy of his notice." All through the campaign Lincoln would be cordial towards Douglas, but privately "Lincoln despised Douglas" (according to Henry Clay Whitney). Douglas might well be a great orator and "impossible to get the advantage of" in debate. But all the same, as Lincoln remarked to Thomas J. Henderson, "the truth is Douglas is a liar," and he told Clifton Moore that "Douglas will tell a lie to ten thousand people one day, even though he knows he may have to deny it to five thousand the next."

This campaign would give Lincoln his greatest opportunity to expose those lies. At twelve o'clock on the dusty summer afternoon of August 21, 1858, a special train seventeen cars long brought Lincoln into the crowded, cheering station at Ottawa, eighty miles southwest of Chicago, on the Illinois and Michigan Canal that Lincoln had done so much to create. A carriage decorated with evergreens was ready for Lincoln, and nudged its way through the packed hurrahing streets to a freshly hammered wooden platform on Washington Square where, under the merciful canopy of the old elms, Lincoln would face on equal terms the man who had become his ironic mirror.

Both candidates had planned their debating strategies well, and the hour-long speech Douglas led off with at Ottawa contained the basic outlines of the speech he would make everywhere else in the debates. It was his strategy "to drive" Lincoln "from a *conservative* position to one or the other extremes," and the "House Divided" speech would be his prime weapon. Moving quickly to the offensive, Douglas declared that Lincoln was a radical abolitionist, so radical that he had tried to subvert the "old Whig party" to abolition doctrines, and so radical that he was willing to call into question even the wisdom of the Founding Fathers on the subject of slavery. Did Lincoln believe the republic could not endure half-slave and half-free? Why couldn't it? Douglas replied. Hadn't the Founding Fathers created it that way? Contrary to Lincoln's reasoning, the American republic had actually been designed to endure half-slave and half-free: "They knew when they framed the Constitution that in a country as wide and broad as this, with such a variety of climate, production and interest, the people necessarily required different laws and institutions in different localities . . . and they, therefore, provided that each State should retain its own Legislature, and its own sovereignty with the full and complete power to do as it pleased within its own limits, in all that was local and not national."

Breaking down that design by abolishing slavery would, at best, unleash upon Illinois hordes of black migrants who would "cover your prairies with black settlements" and "turn this beautiful state into a free negro colony"; at worst, as the language of the divided house suggested, it could easily provoke a "dissolution of the Union" and "sectional warfare." He warned Illinoisans not to be fooled by Lincoln's appeals to the Declaration of Independence and its "equality" clause as an argument against slavery. The signers of the Declaration had never meant to include blacks under the heading of "equality," and Douglas, for his part, did "not regard the negro as my equal, and positively deny that he is my brother or any kin to me whatever." It was not that Douglas loved slavery, or necessarily wanted to ignore the black man's rights "in his life — in his person — in his property." But just what those rights were was up to each state to determine on its own. "We have no right to go further, but we must leave each and every other State to decide for itself." Far better to let each state have its own way on slavery, and by implication, each territory enjoy its own popular sovereignty in peacefully deciding its future about slavery — conclusions that could not be guaranteed by sending Lincoln to the Senate.

Lincoln's first instinct on the Ottawa platform was to drop back to the defensive again, to deny that he was an abolitionist, or that he intended to lead a crusade to rewrite the Constitution and interfere with the slave states, or that he intended to promote racial equality. "I have no purpose directly or indirectly to interfere with the institution of slavery in the States where it exists," Lincoln replied, and "no purpose to introduce political and social equality between the white and the black races." But this much was not the real issue of the year 1858 in Illinois — the real issue was whether Douglas, in designing the Kansas-Nebraska Act and nailing his flag to popular sovereignty even in the face of the *Dred Scott* decision, had actually promoted the expansion of slavery into the territories, and was laying the basis for it to spread back into the free states, and Lincoln soon remembered to swing back to the offensive. "We will not have peace upon the question until the opponents of slavery arrest the further spread of it, and place it where the public mind shall rest in the belief that it is in the course of ultimate extinction," something which the Kansas-Nebraska Act and Douglas's popular sovereignty had proven themselves disastrously unfitted to do. As it was now, "Popular Sovereignty, as now applied to the question of Slavery, does allow the people of a Territory to have Slavery if they want to, but does not allow them *not* to have it if they *do not* want it."

But the question of slavery required a higher answer than merely a discussion about the mechanics of confining and shrinking it, if only because slavery was more than a mere political inconvenience. Slavery was a violation of the most basic natural rights recognized by the American republic, and even if one allowed that blacks suffered from "a physical difference" that made "perfect equality" in political or social rights with whites impossible, "there is no reason in the world why the negro is not entitled to all the natural rights enumerated in the Declaration of Independence, the right to life, liberty and the pursuit of happiness," regardless of the wishes of legislatures. If in nothing else, then at least "in the right to eat the bread, without leave of anybody else, which his own hand earns" — a right which Lincoln held as his most fundamental political instinct — *"he is my equal and the equal of Judge Douglas, and the equal of every living man."*

This was a better reply than anything he had offered Douglas so far in the campaign, but it did not strike at Douglas's vulnerable quarrel with the "Buchaneers" of his own party. Joseph Medill urged Lincoln, "Don't act on the defensive at all. . . . Hold Doug up as a traitor and conspirator, a proslavery, bamboozling demagogue." Iowa Republican James Grimes advised Lincoln "that he should assume the aggressive & attack his adversary in turn, — that it was useless to defend himself against Mr. Douglas' charges, for, as one would be refuted another would be trumped up." Fired with these urgings, Lincoln arrived at Freeport, in the northwest corner of Illinois, on August 27th for the second debate with a wedge in hand that he hoped would make it impossible for Douglas to rally divided Democrats behind him. Under cloudy skies and before a packed audience of over 15,000, Lincoln laid out a series of four questions for Douglas, the second of which pinned Douglas to his own party's divisions — "Can the people of a United States Territory, in any lawful way, against the wish of any citizen of the United States, exclude slavery from its limits prior to the formation of a State Constitution?" — while the third tried to lure him into an admission that *Dred Scott* was simply the warm-up for the nationalization of slavery — "If the supreme court of the United States shall decide that states cannot exclude slavery from their limits, are you in favor of acquiescing in adopting and following such decision as a rule of political action?"

Good cross-examiner that he was, Lincoln knew that Douglas had in fact already more or less answered the second question "a hundred times from every stump in Illinois," and that the answer was *yes:* despite *Dred Scott,* and even more, despite the leadership of his own party, "it matters not what way the Supreme Court may hereafter decide as to the abstract question whether slavery may or may not go into a territory under the constitution, the people have the lawful means to introduce it or exclude it as they please, for the reason that slavery cannot exist a day or an hour anywhere, unless it is supported by local police regulations." What this accomplished was to keep Douglas's quarrel with Buchanan at center stage, where no Democratic voter or legislator could miss it, as well as to suggest that Douglas really had been a witless patsy to the slave power conspiracy behind Kansas-Nebraska and *Dred Scott.* The third question was even more damaging for Douglas. Much as he disliked *Dred Scott* as a decision, he could not repudiate it without furthering the Democratic split; yet, if another Taney decision broke down the anti-slavery statutes of the free states, Douglas could scarcely step back from it. The best answer he could make to Lincoln was a denial that such a second *Dred Scott* could ever happen. "Now I am amused that Mr. Lincoln should ask such a question," Douglas scoffed. "I tell him that such a proposition as that is not possible."

There was no way to keep score on the debates, but the newspapers awarded most of whatever points could be tallied from Freeport to Lincoln. "Let Mr. Douglas be one thing or another, fish, flesh or fowl, and not be dodging and skulking about," demanded the Republican *Chicago Tribune*, while its editor, Charles Ray, declared that "Douglas has been grossly overestimated as a debater." Douglas himself was feeling the heat of Lincoln's attack, and telegraphed an associate, "The hell-hounds are on my track. For God's sake . . . come and help me fight them." He did not like the rumor he heard from another political ally that "it will not be possible for me to sustain my position," and by the time Douglas faced Lincoln again in the southern Illinois town of Jonesboro after a three-week hiatus, Douglas was reaching for his own conspiracy theories. As before, he rang the changes on Lincoln's abolitionism, Lincoln's obsession with the social equality of negroes, Lincoln's lust for disunion and sectional war. But now, he disclosed, the opposition to Kansas-Nebraska was the work of "certain restless, ambitious and disappointed politicians," the chief of which was Lincoln, who "had a private arrangement" with Free-Soil Democrats like Lyman Trumbull to build up a great sectional party, and through its organization to "control the political destinies of the country." Three days later, when the debates finally moved onto Lincoln's old Eighth Circuit ground at Charleston, Douglas had upped the ante by announcing that "there is a conspiracy to carry this election for the Black Republicans by slander, and not by fair means," a conspiracy which Douglas peppered with suggestions that it was also intended to promote "negro equality and negro citizenship."

This might not have been good debating but it was shrewd politics, since no Illinois politician could hope to survive in the white racial supremacist climate of Illinois with those kinds of insinuations unanswered. To Douglas's delight, it sent Lincoln back on the defensive. Lincoln's reply at Jonesboro and his opening speech in Charleston were his lamest efforts in the whole debates, given over mostly to denying the charge of collusion with Trumbull and with the abolitionists. At Charleston, facing an audience in southern Illinois of Southern-born immigrants, Lincoln was almost too eager to demonstrate his opposition to "the social and political equality of the white and black races," specifying how "I am not nor ever have been in favor of making voters or jurors of negroes, nor of qualifying them to hold office, nor to intermarry with white women." This allowed Douglas to beat him with the charge of hypocrisy, with preaching near-abolitionism in Chicago and near-slavery in southern Illinois. It also allowed Douglas to return happily to his first argument at Ottawa, that there was no reason to suppose that the republic couldn't exist very well half-slave and half-free. "Why can we not thus continue to prosper? We can if we will live up to and execute the government upon those principles upon which our fathers established it."

The intentions of the Fathers, however, were precisely what Lincoln was best prepared to dispute. "I say when this government was first established it was the policy of the founders to prohibit the spread of slavery into the new Territories of the United States, where it had not existed." It was not the Republicans, but Douglas who had cast aside the intentions of the "fathers," since "Judge Douglas and his friends have broken up that policy and placed it upon a new basis by which it is to become national and perpetual." The Compromise of 1850, the Kansas-Nebraska Act, and even the Lecompton constitution had all been offered with the promise of settling "the slavery agitation," and the result was that "we can just as clearly see the end of the world as we can the end of this agitation." Consequently, "there is no way of putting an end to the slavery agitation amongst us but to . . . restrict it forever to the old States where it now exists." Unless, of course, one simply proposed "to surrender and let Judge Douglas and his friends have their way and plant slavery over all the States — cease speaking of it as in any way a wrong — regard slavery as one of the common matters of property, and speak of negroes as we do of our horses and cattle."

Speaking of slavery as "a wrong" in moral terms had been precisely what Lincoln had, up to Charleston, hesitated to do, and even then it was almost a passing comment. But when the debates shifted back to northern Illinois, to Galesburg, on October 7th, Lincoln's attack on the immorality of slavery moved to the center of his arguments. "Up to this time I have not found Judge Douglas . . . in favor of making any difference between slavery and liberty," Lincoln charged. "Every

223

thought that he utters will be seen to exclude the thought that there is anything wrong in slavery."

> I confess myself as belonging to that class in the country that be-lieves slavery to be a moral and political wrong. . . . I believe that slavery is wrong, and in a policy springing from that belief that looks to the prevention of the enlargement of that wrong, and that looks at some time to there being an end of that wrong. The other sentiment is, that it is no wrong, and the policy springing from it that there is no wrong in its becoming bigger, and that there never will be any end of it. There is the difference between Judge Douglas and his friends and the Republican party.

This prompted Douglas to renew his charge that Lincoln was hypocritically tuning his message to the ears that heard it in northern Illinois. But it is not clear whether northern Illinois whites were less enamored of white racial supremacy than southern Illinois whites; what is more likely is that Lincoln was still, as late as the fourth debate, fumbling for the right offensive weapon to use on Douglas. Once he found it, and found that the appeal against the immorality of slavery worked, it became the mountaintop of every speech he made. "The real difference between Judge Douglas and the Republicans," Lincoln claimed in Galesburg, "is that . . . every sentiment he utters discards the idea that there is any wrong in Slavery." When Lincoln and Douglas met in the Mississippi River town of Quincy a week later, he unrolled the argument more grandly by insisting that "the difference of opinion, reduced to its lowest terms, is no other than the difference between the men who think slavery a wrong and those who do not think it a wrong."

The fundamental reason it was wrong was that the Declaration of Independence had established that human beings of no matter what color had at least three natural rights secured to them — life, liberty, and the pursuit of happiness — with which slavery was incompatible. Douglas vehemently denied that Jefferson and the "fathers" had ever intended to secure these rights to any other than white people, and so they had no application to black slavery. That, Lincoln argued, was the slippery slope down which the republic was being rolled by Douglas toward nationalizing slavery. The campaign to "dehumanize the negro

— to take away from him the right of ever striving to be a man" was only done "to prepare the public mind to make property, and nothing but property, of the *negro in all the States of this Union*." He began his speech in the sixth debate at Quincy by reducing "the difference of opinion . . . to its lowest terms," which was "no other than the difference between the men who think slavery a wrong and those who do not think it a wrong . . . and so deal with it as in the run of time there may be some promise of an end to it." In the last debate at Alton two days later, Lincoln blended opposition to slavery with opposition to every principle of class privilege and exclusion that had roused his ire from his earliest days:

> That is the real issue. That is the issue that will continue in this country when these poor tongues of Judge Douglas and myself shall be silent. It is the eternal struggle between these two principles — right and wrong — throughout the world. They are the two principles that have stood face to face from the beginning of time; and will ever continue to struggle. The one is the common right of humanity and the other the divine right of kings. . . . No matter in what shape it comes, whether from the mouth of a king who seeks to bestride the people of his own nation and live by the fruit of their labor, or from one race of men as an apology for enslaving another race, it is the same tyrannical principle.

Douglas was aghast at Lincoln's proposal to turn a debate on public policy into a forum on morality. Citizens and communities, in Douglas's lexicon, were simply individuals possessing the right to do as they pleased with what property they pleased as a matter of choice, and questions of whether their choices were moral or not were not the business of anyone outside those communities. "Lincoln admits that all the domestic questions are left to each State under the Constitution in regard to all other questions except slavery, without the right to interfere with them. What right have we with slavery any more than with any other?" Where Lincoln complained "that I don't look forward to the time when slavery shall be abolished everywhere," Douglas did not see why he couldn't simply "look forward to the time when each State shall be allowed to do as it pleases." Questions of morality were purely personal and had no place on the public square of debate. If a state "chooses to keep slavery forever, it is its business, and not ours. If it chooses to abolish, very good, it is its business and not mine. I care more for the great principle of self-government — the right of the people to rule themselves — than I do for all the niggers in Christendom."

By the end of the debates, Lincoln's expectations had soared. At the end of September, he told the Springfield Republican Club that "wherever he has been the skies are bright and the prospects good," and a week after the last debate in Alton, he confided to Norman Judd that "I now have a high degree of confidence that we shall succeed." And if the actual popular vote on November 2nd had decided the senatorial selection, Lincoln would have found matters (as he explained them to Judd on October 24th) "*Tight*, with chances slightly in our favor." He had made some sixty speeches, traveled more than 4,300 miles around the state, and (together with Lyman Trumbull and other Republican campaigners) garnered for Republican state candidates over 125,000 votes as against the 121,000 cast for Douglasite Democrats and 5,000 for the Buchaneers.

But the Republican plurality was not evenly spread around the state, or in the state legislative races. Of the eighty-seven seats up for election in 1858, forty-six went to Democratic candidates and only forty-one to Republicans. Added to the thirteen seats in the state senate not up for re-election, the Democrats retained a 54-to-46 edge, and when the legislature assembled in January, a single party-line vote re-elected Stephen A. Douglas to the Senate.

Lincoln had known the jig was up the night of the legislative election. The voting news was dampened with "a cold, pelting rainstorm, one of the most uncomfortable in the whole year." As Lincoln stepped out into the rain in the evening, his path across a Springfield street was slick, and "my foot slipped out from under me, knocking the other one out of the way." But he managed to "recover myself and lit square," remarking that "It's a slip and not a fall." It seemed like a good metaphor for salving a political defeat that had cost him most of a year's legal business and left him "absolutely without money now for even household purposes." He would not allow himself to indulge discouragement. He wrote to one political supporter, "The fight must go on. The cause of civil liberty must not be surrendered at the end of *one*, or even, one *hundred* defeats." The "pile" of Republican votes was "worth keeping" and using in another election, he told Norman Judd, even if "in that day I shall fight in the ranks" rather than "at the head of a ticket."

6 An Accidental President

The Lincoln-Douglas debates did not get Lincoln elected, but they did get him noticed. "No man of this generation has grown more rapidly before the country than Lincoln in this canvass," the *New York Evening Post* announced, and Charles Ray, the editor of the *Chicago Tribune*, cheerfully informed him that "you are like Byron, who woke up one morning and found himself famous. . . . I have found hundreds of anxious inquirers burning to know all about the newly raised up opponent of Douglas." Prominent among those who wanted to know about Lincoln was Ray himself, who tried to tease Lincoln into writing an autobiographical outline by airing "my suspicion that Abe Lincoln was not born with a silver spoon in his mouth." (It said a great deal for Lincoln's lifelong efforts to disguise his agrarian origins that Ray was surprised to discover that Lincoln in fact had not been born with any form of spoon in his mouth, much less a silver one.) Jesse Fell reported that his east-coast business contacts were all asking, "'Who is this man Lincoln, of your state, now canvassing in opposition to Douglas?'" Fell was convinced that, despite the defeat, "you are getting a national reputation" and "can be made a formidable, if not a successful, candidate for the Presidency." Lincoln chuckled at Fell's enthusiasm. "Oh, Fell, what's the use of talking of me for the Presidency . . . nobody, scarcely, outside of Illinois knows me."

But this was not entirely true: the Lincoln-Douglas debates had not only been covered by the press, but had actually been transcribed word-for-word in their entirety by a quartet of shorthand-ready reporters working for the *Chicago Times* and the *Chicago Tribune*, and were usually printed in full within forty-eight hours in the Chicago newspapers. Eastern newspapers eager for copy on Douglas picked up the texts of both debaters and thus ensured, as Fell told Lincoln, that "your speeches, in whole or in part, have been pretty extensively published in the East." Lincoln was aware, by the time of the fifth debate, that "the speeches that I have made in Chicago, at Jonesboro and at Charleston" were "in print, and that all reading men might read them." In the Quincy debate, he remarked that "these seven joint discussions" had become "the successive acts of a drama . . . to be enacted not entirely in the face of an audience like this, but in the face of the nation." By the end of December, as Lincoln told Henry Clay Whitney, he was putting out feelers about publishing the complete text of the debates in book form.

Lincoln had also become a prize property for Republican electoral campaigns elsewhere in the midwest. He had to turn down pleas from Norman Judd to campaign for Republicans in the Chicago municipal elections because "my loss of time and business" during the 1858 campaign "bears pretty heavily upon one no better off in world's goods than I." He told Hawkins Taylor in the fall of 1859 that he had been "constantly receiving invitations . . . to go to Minnesota; and I now have two invitations to go to Ohio," and felt "compelled to decline" those, too, because of the financial strain it would impose "if I neglect my business this year as well as last." What eventually overcame his reluctance was the allure of crossing swords with Stephen Douglas again. The Ohio invitations were "prompted by Douglas' going there" to stump for Democrats in the October state elections. And so in September of 1859, Lincoln set off on a wide swing through Ohio and Indiana, speaking on behalf of local Republican candidates in Columbus, Hamilton, Cincinnati, Dayton, and Indianapolis, and then for Wisconsin Republicans in Beloit and Janesville.

He barely noticed the local candidates he was supposed to be cheering on. "It was almost impossible . . . to speak of politics without associating Judge Douglas with it," Lincoln remarked in Indianapolis, and Lincoln's 1859 campaign speeches read as though the 1858 debates had merely taken a recess. Overall, the same basic series of arguments Lincoln had developed in the debates were deployed in the Ohio, Indiana, and Wisconsin speeches. The Fathers (Lincoln argued) had struck a national bargain on slavery which provided that "the spread of slavery in the territories should be restrained," but Douglas and Kansas-Nebraska had wrecked that bargain. Worse, the old bargain was being replaced by an insidious effort to extend slavery across the nation, and popular sovereignty was simply a clever device of Douglas's to lull to sleep the people's resistance to that extension. Rather than guaranteeing freedom of choice, it would guarantee freedom for nothing. Despite Douglas's claim that popular sovereignty would allow the territories to refuse to enact the necessary slave codes, once slavery was in, no amount of popular sovereignty could ever expect to get it out. "Slavery comes gradually into territory where it is not prohibited without notice, and without alarming the people, until having obtained a foothold, it cannot be driven out," he insisted in Janesville. "Thus we see that in all the new states where slavery was not prohibited, it was established."

The only thing that had kept "the country north, free" was the explicit congressional legislation embodied in the Northwest Ordinance, banning the extension of slavery. "It was not the great principle of popular sovereignty." In fact, the logic of popular sovereignty would not only open both the territories and the free states to slavery, but would reopen the transatlantic African slave trade. "If any man can show how the people of Kansas have a better right to slaves because they want them, than the people of Georgia have to buy them in Africa, I want him to do it," Lincoln told a vast crowd on Market House Square in Cincinnati on September 17th. "I think it cannot be done."

But Lincoln pulled hardest in these speeches on two themes which the Douglas debates had taught him rang the loudest with midwesterners: the undiluted moral wrong of slavery, and the threat slavery posed to free labor. Whatever the technical policy flaws in popular sovereignty as a solution to the slave problem, the fundamental flaw in it was really one of morals. Douglas (Lincoln complained) had no real scruples, at least concerning slavery, and did not believe that moral questions ought to interfere with policy decisions. "The Judge never says your institution of Slavery is wrong; he never says it is right, to be sure, but he never says it is wrong." Lincoln could not have disagreed more, and he had behind him the long Whiggish propensity for uniting moral and political concerns. "If this principle is established, that there is no wrong in slavery, and whoever wants it has a right to have it . . . [that] it is a mere matter of policy; [that] there is a perfect right according to interest to do just as you please — when this is done, where this doctrine prevails, the miners and sappers will have formed public opinion for the slave trade." It was already "debauching" public "sentiment" to the point where, "five years ago no living man expressed the opinion that the negro had no share in the Declaration of Independence," whereas now Douglas was laughingly teaching people to think of negroes as "brutes" and "had got his entire party, almost without exception, to join in saying that the negro has no share in the Declaration."

Lincoln had barely brought his Whiggish economic liberalism into the Douglas debates, but in the 1859 speeches, he unfurled it full-length. Grant that "Labor is the great source from which nearly all, if not all, human comforts and necessities are drawn." There are only two ways to get someone to provide labor for you, "one is to hire men and to allure them to labor by their consent; the other is to buy the men and drive them to it, and that is slavery." There was no question in Lincoln's mind but that "hiring other people to labor" for wages "is right," since wage labor finds "men who have not of their own land to work upon, or shops to work in" and pays them out of the capital of the employer. "Thus a few men that own capital, hire a few others, and these establish the relation of capital and labor rightfully." He contrasted this sharply with sophisticated Southern arguments that capital and labor were actually in competition, that the only way labor could be kept at the low-level "mud-sill" tasks of life was by force — in this case, by the enslavement of a subhuman race that was only good for "mud-sill" work anyway. They believed that only independent agrarian ownership promised true freedom, and consequently even free whites who worked for wages as *hired* labor were really no better off than blacks. But the moment Southerners suggested that, they called into question the entire logic of Abraham Lincoln's life. "The speaker himself had been a hired man twenty-eight years ago," Lincoln remarked in Indianapolis. "He didn't think he was worse off

231

than a slave. He might not be doing as much good as he could, but he was now working for himself."

But if the 1859 speeches showed a more confident and well-focused Lincoln at work, there were still traces of defensiveness and self-apology left from the Douglas debates. He felt the repeated necessity of explaining the "House Divided" speech, and assuring audiences that it had nothing of the radical intentions that Douglas had hung around it during the debates. (And was still hanging around it, since Douglas cited the "House Divided" speech in his own Ohio campaign tour as proof that Republicans like Lincoln advocated disunion and civil war.) "I told him, on the question of declaring war between the different states of the Union, that I had not said I did not expect any peace upon this question until slavery was exterminated; that I had only said I expected peace when that institution was put where the public mind should rest in the belief that it was in the course of ultimate extinction," Lincoln explained in Cincinnati. "I assured him, as I assure you, that I neither then had, nor have, or ever had, any purpose in any way of interfering with the institution of Slavery where it exists." Far from sympathizing with disunion, Lincoln now began making his first warnings against Southerners who might be tempted to break up the Union to prevent interference with slavery. "I often hear it intimated that you mean to divide the Union whenever a Republican, or anything like it, is elected President of the United States," Lincoln bluntly addressed Kentuckians in his Cincinnati crowd. "Well, then, I want to know what you are going to do with your half of it? Are you going to split the Ohio down through, and push your half off a piece? . . . Will you make war upon us and kill us all?"

This question had a particular edge for Lincoln, since by the fall of 1859 a persistent trickle of admirers was telling him that he ought to think about being that Republican president. In November, 1858, the *Illinois Gazette* credited Lincoln for Republican victories across the state and announced "the wish of a large majority of the people that he should be the standard-bearer of the Republican party for the Presidency in 1860." The *Peoria Daily Message* noticed how "Republican journals in different sections of the Union are beginning to talk of him for Vice President, with Seward for President," while in the east, Republican newspapers in Pennsylvania and Connecticut noticed that

Lincoln "has been mentioned in various parts of the country, in connection with the highest post in the gift of the people."

Lincoln was not sure whether this would do more harm than help. He could not avoid being "very much pleased" at editorial flattery, but he tersely discouraged Peoria editor T. J. Pickett when Pickett offered to recruit other Republican editors to boost him for the presidential nomination. "I must in candor say I do not think myself fit for the Presidency," he replied to Pickett in April, 1859, and repeated the same disclaimer to Ohio editor Samuel Galloway in July. He warned another over-eager inquirer that "for personal considerations, I would rather have a full term in the Senate." Among those "personal considerations" was surely Lincoln's consciousness that his lack of formal education and administrative experience would make any presidential ambitions look like "a great piece of folly" once they were written up in the press. He was also conscious that he did not look the part of a presidential candidate. A hostile Cincinnati newspaper described him as "a tall, dark-visaged, awkward positive-looking sort of individual" who had been "originally a flatboatman, and one perceives in him the traces of his early life and profession." His twangy midwestern accent, together with his piercing high-pitched voice, made the same reporter wonder "whether he is speaking his own or a foreign tongue."

Even though Lincoln might be the favorite son of Illinois Republicans, he was still a minor political player next to Republican stars like William Henry Seward, the former Whig senator and governor of New York who had been an advisor to Zachary Taylor and who was now being nudged toward the Republican presidential nomination by his skilled political handler, Thurlow Weed. Lincoln also sat several steps below the Ohioan Salmon P. Chase, the righteous evangelical lawyer who had achieved national fame during the Kansas-Nebraska imbroglio for co-authoring "The Appeal of the Independent Democrats," and who finally went over to the Republicans to run for governor of Ohio. Even in the west, Lincoln was over-matched by other old Whig standard-bearers like Justice John McLean and the old Fillmore-ite Missourian Edward Bates, who (like Fremont in 1856) had the backing of the country's other great political manager, Francis Preston Blair. David Davis, who confessed that "I sh[oul]d like it, if Lincoln could be nominated," was convinced that the nomination was more likely to go to "Mr. Bates or Gov. Seward."

It was not merely that Lincoln lacked stature next to Bates or Seward. Although the core of the Republican party might be reliable old Whigs, its swing votes were not. The Republican party remained, even up to 1860, an anti-Nebraska fusion party, embracing a coalition of wide-eyed abolitionists at one end and anti-slavery Democrats at the other. "Much of the plain old democracy is with us," he explained to Anson Henry in November, 1858, "while nearly all the old exclusive silk-stocking whiggery is against us. I do not mean nearly all the old whig party; but nearly all of the nice exclusive sort." Any Republican presidential aspirant had to mind the long-term political animosities that bubbled beneath the anti-Nebraska surface of the Republican party, and Lincoln had earned more than his share of animosities over twenty-five years of Illinois politics. The feuds between Judd and Wentworth continued to splutter, as did their individual feuds with David Davis and the Bloomington circle. Lincoln had not only to convince them all that he was their friend (and he lavished numerous letters on Judd, assuring him that he did not plan to challenge Judd's favorite, Lyman Trumbull, in the 1860 Illinois Senate race), but that they had to be friendly enough to each other to win elections. He assured Trumbull in February, 1859, that whatever danger there was "of the old democratic and whig elements of our party breaking into opposing factions," it would not happen "if I can prevent it."

But rather than discouraging Lincoln, this actually gave him the prize Whig role of delf-denying, statesmanlike compromiser to play; and for the most part, compromise won. In speeches he made to Republican rallies in Illinois in the spring of 1859, Lincoln incessantly warned Republicans not "to allow ourselves to seek out minor or separate points on which there may be difference of views as to policy and right." For his old Whig allies, that meant staying away from the tariff issue, lest it "drive from it those who came to it from the democracy for the sole object of preventing the spread, and nationalization of slavery." For the abolitionists, it meant muffling opposition to the Fugitive Slave Law, and in June of 1859, Lincoln went so far as to write directly to Salmon Chase to protest the Ohio state Republican convention's decision to call for "a repeal of the Atrocious Fugitive Slave Law." Once the party became associated with that, "I assure you the cause of Republicanism is hopeless in Illinois." He began to see himself as offering perhaps the right electoral balance, an old Whig who could bind

234

the wandering Fillmore-ites of the 1856 election, and a Southern-born Illinoisan who could act as a "Southern man with Northern principles" and soothe Southern anxieties about Republican radicalism.

But worse than prickly Republican personalities, the greatest difficulty, in 1859, in the way of any Lincoln campaign for the presidency, was the public's image of the Republican party. On October 17, 1859, while Lincoln was making up his financial losses by carrying an unusually heavy case-load out on the fall term of the Eighth Judicial Circuit, a radical Connecticut-born abolitionist named John Brown led a mixed band of black and white anti-slavery guerrillas in a raid on the federal arsenal at Harper's Ferry, Virginia. Brown had earned an ugly reputation in Kansas in 1856 for settling disagreements with guns and broadswords, and he now hoped to raise a general slave insurrection with arms looted from the arsenal. He dallied long enough in Harper's Ferry to allow his men to be surrounded by the local militia, and the next day, a detachment of U.S. Marines stormed the arsenal and killed or captured almost all of Brown's band, including Brown himself. Put on trial for treason against the state of Virginia, Brown was hanged on December 2nd, but he raised a nightmare in the minds of Southern slaveholders of long-knived butchery in their beds. Brown's raid, warned the New Orleans papers, was the beginning of a Republican conspiracy against slavery all through the South.

It did not help matters that the most radical of the Republicans had, in fact, carelessly declared before the raid that they looked forward to the moment "when the torch of the incendiary shall light up the towns and cities of the South, and blot out the last vestiges of slavery." Four months after Lincoln's "House Divided" speech, William Seward had carelessly prophesied (and without Lincoln's caveats) that slavery and freedom were "antagonistic systems" which would result in "an irrepressible conflict between opposing and enduring forces," and compel the United States to become "either entirely a slave-holding nation, or entirely a free-labor nation." The *Nashville Union and American* declared that Brown "would never have dared the attempt at insurrection but for the inflammatory speeches and writings of Seward, Greeley, and the other Republican leaders." When the Thirty-Sixth Congress assembled on December 5, 1859 (three days after Brown was hanged), Southern representatives were on their feet to denounce "Black Republicans" for promoting "insurrectionary and hostile" literature, to call for a congressional investigation into the Brown raid, and (at the prompting of Mississippi senator Jefferson Davis) to introduce resolutions endorsing *Dred Scott* and the Lecompton constitution.

Lincoln's eagerness to remind people that, the "House Divided" notwithstanding, he was not a John Brown abolitionist, rose in tandem with his uncertain confidence that he might really have a chance at the Republican presidential nomination. In early February, the Republican state committee met in Springfield, and Norman Judd, who was nursing his own ambitions to run for governor in 1860, seriously urged Lincoln to allow his name to be put into nomination by the Illinois delegation at the next Republican national convention. "I am not in a position where it would hurt much for me to be nominated on the national ticket," Lincoln replied blandly, but he did admit that "it would hurt some for me to not get the Illinois delegates." But even to get that far, he needed to repel any suspicion of radicalism, and that might not be easy to do. The state Democratic newspapers had already announced that "Harper's Ferry is but the logical sequence of the teachings of Wm. H. Seward and Abraham Lincoln," and he continued to get letters from anxious correspondents who wanted him to clarify what he meant by the "House Divided" speech. ("If you, or any of you, will state to me some meaning which you suppose I had," Lincoln wrote back to one of them in exasperation, "I can, and will instantly tell you whether that was my meaning.") When he finally relented in late December, 1859, to Jesse Fell's request for an autobiographical outline Fell could use in lining up Illinois party support for a Lincoln nomination, Lincoln was careful to stress that he had been "always a whig in politics, and generally on the whig electoral tickets," and never mentioned slavery at all. When John Locke Scripps prevailed on him to write a longer autobiographical sketch for the *Chicago Tribune*, he cautiously explained his reentry into politics, not as a response to slavery, but to "the repeal of the Missouri compromise."

The most important opportunity he would have to establish himself nationally as an electable moderate came in October, 1859, when a committee of prominent New York Republicans invited Lincoln to address an open meeting at Henry Ward Beecher's celebrated Plymouth Church. Not only would this give Lincoln critical first-hand exposure to the east-coast Republican leadership, but it would happen in New

York City, where Republicans like Horace Greeley, David Dudley Field, and William Cullen Bryant were already complaining that Seward, New York's favorite son, might be too unstable to sustain the Republican banner in 1860. "The fame of ancient Abraham has extended even into foreign lands," joked Mason Brayman, and he found that, at least among Seward's Republican critics, Lincoln was "certainly becoming an object of attention."

Consequently, Lincoln prepared for this speech as he had prepared for no other in his life. Even as he was handling Illinois Central Railroad cases before the U.S. Circuit Court and the state supreme court, he ransacked the library in the State Capitol for specific citations to prove, contrary to Douglas, that the Founding Fathers had never intended that slavery continuously extend itself over the continent and, contrary to John Calhoun, that the Fathers had always assumed that the federal government had full jurisdiction over the organization of the territories and the migration of slavery into them. He also achieved a small victory over his own temperamental penny-pinching and lavished $100 on a new suit for the occasion, and when he arrived in New York on February 25, 1860, he booked himself into the regal Astor House and had his photograph — a full-length, standing portrait — taken at the Broadway studio of the celebrated Mathew Brady. A last-minute change in the schedule also worked to his advantage: rather than speaking at Plymouth Church, Lincoln was notified on February 9th that the Young Men's Central Republican Committee was folding Lincoln's speech into an ongoing series of speeches from western Republicans at the Cooper Union, and it would be there, in an even more prestigious political venue, that he would have his one moment to shift the axis of his career.

The weather turned foul the night of the speech, and snow descended on New York. For the fifteen hundred Republicans who braved the storm to fill the Cooper Union, the atmosphere inside the hall also chilled as William Cullen Bryant introduced what looked to New York eyes like "something weird, rough, and uncultivated." Even in the best broadcloth suit, Lincoln still looked gawky and clumsy, and his "peculiarly high-keyed voice" (almost squeaky with self-consciousness) and midwestern twang grated embarrassingly on New Yorkers, who twisted uncomfortably in their seats and wondered how this giraffe from the prairies had ever given five minutes' trouble to Stephen A.

Douglas. But Lincoln often started dryly in speeches: it was only after Lincoln had disposed of the usual opening pleasantries and posed the rhetorical question, "Does the proper division of local from federal authorities, or anything in the Constitution, forbid *our federal Government* to control as to slavery in *our Federal Territories?*" that a reporter for Greeley's *Tribune* noticed how "his face lights with an inward fire."

No one was surprised when Lincoln answered his own question with *yes.* This was the question with which he had begun every important political utterance he had made since the fall of 1854, and it led to his great point that the Fathers had never sanctioned slavery, but had always planned for its gradual extinction as part of the great national bargain on slavery. For this audience of elite New Yorkers, however, he pulled out all the legal stops, marshaling text after text, citation after citation, from Washington to Madison, to show that nothing and no one before Roger Taney and Stephen Douglas ever questioned the authority of "the Federal Government to control slavery in the federal territories." And yet, as before, he reiterated that he was not attacking the necessity or legality of the bargain which had permitted slavery to continue in the strongholds it always occupied. Slavery had "to be tolerated and protected," but this was "only because of and so far as its actual presence among us makes that toleration and protection a necessity," and only with the clear understanding that it was "an evil not to be extended. . . . For this Republicans contend, and with this, so far as I know or believe, they will be content." There would be no John Brown raids, no federal invasions, no abolitionist campaigns let loose in the South. What he wanted was the restoration of the original bargain — and no more slavery outside the states where it now existed.

What was new in this speech was how Lincoln next turned his attention, not to Douglas, but to the South. (He had done this once before, in Cincinnati, almost as an afterthought, from the large number of cross-river Kentuckians in the audience.) He rhetorically addressed "a few words to the Southern people," for he now wanted to speak (or at least be seen as speaking) nationally. He hoped that his assurances about non-intervention would mollify Southerners; or rather, he chided Southerners for not having been mollified by Republican assurances before this. "You charge that we stir up insurrections among your slaves. We deny it; and what is your proof? Harper's Ferry! John Brown!" Lincoln exclaimed. But "John Brown was no Republican; and you have failed to implicate a single Republican in his Harper's Ferry enterprise." Or else, Southerners accuse the Republicans of ignoring how "the Supreme Court has decided the disputed Constitutional question in your favor" in *Dred Scott*. But court decisions are not "a conclusive and final rule of political action," especially when they are "made in a divided Court" and "based upon a mistaken statement of fact." This was not so much an act of persuasion intended for Southerners as it was a map of the ground Lincoln believed Republicans needed to stand upon, and Lincoln had the sea of upturned faces "hushed for a moment to a silence like that of the dead." What will satisfy the South? "Simply this: We must not only let them alone, but we must, somehow, convince them that we do let them alone."

But he did not want Republicans to imagine that this effort to placate Southerners had no moral boundaries; if so, there was no reason why, as they almost had in 1858, they should not "dally" with Douglas. The moral boundary Lincoln established for conciliation was the line he had first drawn in the 1858 debates, and drew more boldly in the 1859 speeches: the evil of slavery, the wrong of it, and the impossibility of ever consenting to regard it as right. Republicans would respect slavery where it was, but only out of "necessity," and they would agitate for its restriction because they knew that, ultimately, it was a moral wrong. Whatever else could be offered to Southerners as mollifications, that moral conviction could never be yielded, and it was that conviction which undergirded the Republican resolve not to "allow it to spread into the National Territories, and to overrun us here in these Free States." By now, Lincoln "held the vast meeting spell-bound," and when he concluded with a vivid exhortation — "Let us have faith that right makes might, and in that faith, let us, to the end, dare to do our duty as we understand it" — the "house broke out in wild and prolonged enthusiasm." One listener told Noah Brooks, "When I came out of the hall, my face glowing with excitement and my frame all a-quiver, a friend, with his eyes aglow, asked me what I thought of Abe Lincoln . . . I said: 'He's the greatest man since St. Paul.'" The next morning the *Tribune* announced that "no man ever before made such an impression on his first appeal to a New-York audience."

That impression had been made just in time. There were only two and a half months remaining before the Republican national convention assembled, and if a dump-Seward movement was to succeed, it would have to move fast. However, despite the assurances of Norman Judd, Jesse Fell, and the Republican state committee, Lincoln still measured himself short against the formidable New York political mechanism of Seward and Weed. He wrote in March that it was important to "give no offence to others," so that if the party regulars are "compelled to give up their first love," he would be available. Despite assurances by "several gentlemen" in New York that "they thought my chances were about equal to the best," Lincoln refused to be drawn out publicly about his interest in the nomination on the grounds that "when a not very great man begins to be mentioned for a very great position, his head is very likely to be a little turned." To another inquirer in mid-April, he vaguely replied that, "as to the Presidential nomination," he should be willing to "be placed anywhere, or nowhere, as may appear most likely to advance our cause." Part of this was deliberate policy, since it would not be wise for him to publicly elbow his way to the head of the Republican table unbidden; another part was the practical realization that campaigning cost money, and money was what he did not have. "I could not raise ten thousand dollars if it would save me from the fate of John Brown," he wrote in mid-March.

But hesitation was not the same thing as indifference, and he remained very curious to see what the Democrats were doing for their own presidential nomination in 1860. Harper's Ferry propelled the Southern Democrats beyond all thought of compromise and concession, and they arrived at the Democratic national convention in Charleston, South Carolina, in April (with John Brown less than five months in his grave), bristling with demands for a platform which, in effect, legislated *Dred Scott* into federal policy — no federal authority over slavery in the territories, no territorial legislature permitted "to prohibit the introduction of slaves therein." This was, among other things, clearly intended as a slap to the face of Stephen A. Douglas and popular sovereignty, and to make a nomination of Douglas impossible by making the party platform indigestible to the Little Giant. But the Southern delegations could not muster the numbers to force their platform on the convention, and when they failed, the Alabama delegation, followed first by Mississippi, and then by Louisiana, South Carolina, Florida, Arkansas, Texas, and Georgia, all withdrew, loudly and with bare-knife speeches. The withdrawal of so many delegates wrecked the convention procedurally: although the remaining Northern Democrats would have happily nominated Douglas for president, they could not muster enough remaining votes to nominate him by the convention's rules, and they adjourned themselves in disarray.

The Democratic national convention reassembled in June, and after another flurry of Southern withdrawals, the convention managed to nominate Douglas for the presidency through a simple majority-vote resolution. But by then, all hope for keeping up a united Democratic front had disappeared. The renegade Southern delegates from Charleston assembled their own presidential convention in Richmond on June 11th with anti-Douglasite delegates from twenty-one states, and proceeded to nominate John C. Breckinridge, a Kentuckian and President Buchanan's vice president. In the meanwhile, yet another convention, this time of old Fillmore-ite Whigs who were immobilized between the damaged Democrats on the one hand and the "Black Republicans" on the other, nominated a geriatric Tennessee Whig, John Bell, for president. The Democratic party lay shattered, and everyone knew it. If there was to be a Republican moment, this was it.

Just how clearly Lincoln understood this became evident by April 29th, when he wrote to Lyman Trumbull that, since "Charleston hangs fire," he would "wait no longer" and would now admit that "the taste *is* in my mouth a little." And though he had little more than two weeks before the Republican convention opened, much of the ground had already been prepared by Norman Judd as the chair of the Illinois Republican state committee and by the vast network of lawyers and political friends whom he had cultivated over the long years of circuit-riding and stump-speaking. It was Judd, in particular, who did him what may have been the most critical service, first by persuading the Republican national committee to hold the convention in Chicago, rather than an east-coast city like New York or Philadelphia, where Seward could easily snatch the nomination, or St. Louis, where old Edward Bates might dominate the scene, and then by arranging the convention seating plan to isolate the Seward delegates from "the doubtful delegations." (Years later, Judd remarked to John Hay that "his two great political feats" were "getting the Convention at Chicago & then seating the Convention.")

But Judd was also pushing the buttons for the Illinois state Republican convention, which met at Decatur on May 9th. Judd had already badgered the Republican state legislative caucus back in the winter "to claim the Presidency" for Lincoln "and nothing less," and Lincoln ("with his characteristic modesty") had agreed that they might "consider him and work for him if we pleased for the Presidency." Now, the state convention had hardly opened before the chair, Richard Oglesby, picked out Lincoln from the floor as "one whom Illinois will ever delight to honor" and brought him, through an uproar of applause, to a seat on the platform. The meeting went on through a series of nominations for state offices, but only long enough for Oglesby to interrupt the proceedings with an even greater coup: "There is an old Democrat outside who has something he wishes to present to the convention," Oglesby announced. And in the doorway of the convention hall stood Lincoln's cousin, John Hanks, carrying on his shoulders two fence rails, one of locust, the other of walnut, bedecked with a banner which read:

ABRAHAM LINCOLN.
THE RAIL CANDIDATE FOR PRESIDENT IN 1860.
TWO RAILS FROM A LOT OF 3000 MADE IN 1830 BY
JOHN HANKS AND ABE LINCOLN — WHOSE FATHER
WAS THE FIRST PIONEER OF MACON COUNTY

Years before, Oglesby had "worked on a farm with Mr. John Hanks," and Oglesby had heard from Hanks how he and Lincoln had cleared land, split rails, and built the flatboat that carried Denton Offutt's goods to New Orleans. Oglesby seized on the information, and put Hanks up to purchasing some fence rails he thought he and Lincoln might have split thirty years before. As Hanks stood framed in the doorway with his banner, the convention went berserk with cries of "Receive it! Receive it!" Hanks carried the rails and the banner through the hall to the platform, and Lincoln laughingly admitted, "Well, the truth is, John Hanks and I did make rails in the Sangamon Bottom. . . . I made rails then, and I think I could make better ones than these now." In one stroke, Judd and Oglesby had identified Lincoln, not as the successful railroad lawyer that he really was, but as the heroic son of pioneer soil, as an old Whig (like William Henry Harrison and Zachary Taylor), as the rail-splitter. Privately, the rails symbolized everything that "troubled him, and, in his own judgement, detracted from his qualifications for the high office." But if escape from those reminders was what Lincoln wanted socially, he saw at once the popular appeal those rails had for making him, at least symbolically, into the common man's candidate. The next morning, John M. Palmer moved the meeting to instruct the Illinois delegates to the Republican national convention to give their votes as a block for a Lincoln nomination for the presidency.

The day after, Jesse Dubois and David Davis were in Chicago to meet with Judd and take in the lay of the land for the convention. The delegates would assemble in a newly constructed meeting hall at Market and Lake Streets known as the Wigwam, capable of seating a thousand convention delegates and ten thousand spectators. The large majority of them, as the Illinoisans knew, would come in the full expectation that the nomination was ready to be handed to Seward on the first ballot. As early as February, Weed scolded Joseph Medill of the *Chicago Tribune* for supporting Lincoln — "that prairie statesman" — and "gave me to understand that [Seward] was the chief teacher of the principles of the Republican party before Lincoln was known other than as a country lawyer of Illinois." And by the time Weed arrived in Chicago for the convention, he was certain that he had secured 150 delegate votes for Seward, with only 84 more needed (after favorite-son nominations had been cleared away) to clinch the nomination. Greeley, Seward's political scourge, was in the convention as an alternate in the Oregon delegation, but he was pumping for Bates. None of the New York papers had even mentioned Lincoln as a possibility, and the May 12th issue of *Harper's Weekly* barely mentioned him in passing after Seward, Salmon Chase, Bates, and seven others. Two political handbooks published in advance of the convention by John Savage and D. W. Bartlett included biographies of all the important front-runners, but neither of them had thought to add Lincoln. Lincoln himself would not attend the convention (although he had been tempted to do so) lest he give "the appearance of obtrusion"; neither for that matter would Seward.

Still, even with Seward's vast name recognition and resources, David Davis (as Jesse Dubois wrote Lincoln on May 13th) "is furious, never saw him work so hard and so quiet in all my life." The work that Davis and Dubois were performing was blunt political persuasion,

243

and their message was that Seward was unelectable: to Republican moderates, they whispered that Seward was too well known as a radical who was willing to trigger an "irrepressible conflict"; to antislavery radicals they explained that Seward was an unreliable trimmer; and to anyone with half a doubt in his mind they argued that Douglas could only be defeated by another westerner. "It was honestly felt that it was hazardous to present to them Seward or even Chase," recalled Edward L. Pierce. "The names left for a choice were Judge McLean, Bates, and Lincoln." Meanwhile, Medill and Ray of the *Chicago Tribune* were prepared to launch a pro-Lincoln paper barrage. The *Tribune* greeted convention delegates on May 15th with a lengthy editorial, extolling Lincoln as "radical up to the limit to which the party, with due respect for the rights of the South, proposes to go," but governed by "that wise conservatism which has made his action and his expressed opinions so conform to the most mature sentiment of the country on this question of slavery." And although Lincoln warned David Davis to make no promises of cabinet seats for the favorite sons of impressionable state delegations, deal-making was exactly what Davis resorted to when persuasion failed.

The first two days of the convention were given over to delegate credentials and the platform, and on the third day, the convention opened its nominating session with William Evarts of New York nominating Seward; almost at once, Norman Judd sprang up to nominate Lincoln, followed by nominations for William Dayton of New Jersey (who had bumped Lincoln out of the vice-presidential nomination under Fremont four years before), Simon Cameron of Pennsylvania, John McLean, Edward Bates, and Salmon Chase. To Thurlow Weed's delight, the first ballot gave Seward 173 1/2 votes. What was dismaying was that the same ballot also gave 102 votes, not to Chase or Dayton or Bates or McLean, but to Abraham Lincoln. Unshaken, the Sewardites called for a second ballot, and true to expectations, the favorite-sons began to dwindle away: Bates went down to thirty-five votes, Dayton to ten. But those votes did not transfer to Seward's column. Davis and Dubois had done their work the night before in the back rooms of the delegates' hotels quite well indeed, and the Pennsylvania, Indiana, and New Jersey delegations now veered to Lincoln.

At the end of the second ballot, Seward had gained eleven votes, but Lincoln's total had risen to 181. The call went up for a third ballot, and within four minutes, the Seward column began to tremble, and then to shed transfers to Lincoln, until Lincoln stood only two votes shy of nomination. For a long moment, the Wigwam held its collective breath; then "in about ten ticks of a watch," David Cartter of Ohio, nerved by a whispered promise from Joseph Medill that Salmon Chase could have "anything he wants" if Ohio swung to Lincoln, stood to announce that four Ohio votes desired to be moved from Chase to Lincoln. An uproar convulsed the Wigwam. "Imagine all the hogs ever slaughtered in Cincinnati giving their death squeals together," wrote Cincinnati journalist Murat Halstead. "I thought the Seward yell could not be surpassed; but the Lincoln boys . . . made every plank and pillar in the building quiver." An avalanche of hesitant delegates now screamed to transfer their votes to Lincoln, and in the end a hollow-voiced William Evarts took the floor to ask that the nomination of Lincoln be made unanimous. "The Seward men were terribly stricken down," wrote Halstead, "and walked thoughtfully and silently away from the slaughter house, more ashamed than embittered." Charles Coffin saw Thurlow Weed "press his fingers *hard* upon his eyelids to keep back the tears."

"WE DID IT GLORY TO GOD," sparked the telegraph wire to Springfield, where Lincoln had been waiting all day and reading bulletins in the office of the *Illinois State Journal,* the newspaper for which he had once written satirical political essays from Vandalia. Charles Zane, the *Journal's* editor, handed Lincoln the telegraph slip, and Lincoln quietly read it. "When the second ballot came, I knew this must come," he remarked simply. Stepping outside into a gathering crowd of cheering friends, Lincoln could only think to say, "Well, gentlemen, there is a little woman at our house who is probably more interested in this dispatch than I am; if you will excuse me, I will take the dispatch up and let her see it."

Once the euphoria had worn off, Lincoln realized that his nomination had been an upset, almost an accident. It was "from the fact of his having made a race for the Senate of the United States with Judge Douglas in the state of Illinois" that "his name became prominent, and he was accidentally selected" over Seward, Lincoln explained to former congressman Charles Morehead; he was not sure that he was "suited to the position," he told Philadelphian Samuel Hart, and accepted the nomination "because it had been thrown upon him" and he "considered it was my duty." Some of these comments were little more than the customary expressions of public humility any politician might make in 1860. The protocol of the presidential elections still required that candidates appear as simple Cincinnatuses at their plows, called by the people (and not their own ambitions) to public service. Lincoln, like every other presidential candidate before 1860, would not even campaign on his own behalf. But Lincoln was also being realistic: apart from the limelight he had shared briefly with Douglas in 1858, he was a question mark across much of the country. Gideon Welles remembered that "the nomination of Mr. Lincoln was . . . a general disappointment to active politicians." The *Toledo Blade* confidently asserted that Lincoln was "no new man" and then proceeded to misspell his name twice. Southern ultras were temporarily baffled by the nomination of a "moderate . . . of agreeable manners" and decided that this was "a master-stroke of political craft" to deceive and weaken Southern unity. Republican evangelicals, like the revivalist Charles Grandison Finney, were shocked that the Republicans would nominate a man whose "ground on the score of humanity towards the oppressed race was too low." Lincoln's debates with Douglas might have demonstrated "his intellectual ability and forensic powers" but, by the exacting standards of evangelical moralism, "did him no honor."

Nearly everyone between those two extremes was equally curious, not to say puzzled and apprehensive, about Lincoln. An official delegation from the convention arrived in Springfield on May 19th to inform him of the nomination with the hope of hearing some vigorous new statement of principles. Newspapers dispatched reporters to satisfy subscribers who wanted to know what Lincoln looked like and what Lincoln talked about. Anxious politicians, beginning with Thurlow Weed, descended on Springfield to make their peace or to make their point. Thirteen campaign biographies, including John Locke Scripps's rewriting of the material Lincoln had worked up for him, appeared during the summer, while a small flock of artists on hire from state Republican committees in the east showed up to paint his portrait, and seventeen new Lincoln photographs were made for magazine illustrators around the country to use as models for their lithographers. Despite the best efforts of the illustrators, there was not much which could be done to improve Lincoln's features. A group of "very earnest" New York Republicans expressed the "candid determination" that Lincoln "would be much improved in appearance, provided you would cultivate whiskers and wear standing collars" in order to "be the best looking as well as the best of the rival candidates." The *Charleston Mercury*, which was not going to be friendly to a Republican candidate anyway, was appalled to discover that Lincoln was a "horrid-looking wretch . . . sooty and scoundrelly in aspect; a cross between the nutmeg dealer, the horse-swapper, and the nightman." As one Georgia satirist described him,

> His cheekbones were high and his visage was rough,
> Like a middling of bacon, all wrinkled and tough;
> His nose was as long, and as ugly and big
> As the snout of a half-starved Illinois pig;
> He was long in the legs and long in the face,
> A Longfellow born of a long-legged race. . . .

Lincoln heard so much of this (even from a small admirer, eleven-year-old Grace Bedell, who told him "You would look a great deal better" if he grew a beard "for your face is so thin") that by November, he actually did yield and begin growing a set of jaw whiskers that not only softened the cadaverous hollows of his cheekbones but added a touch of the sober Presbyterian elder to his appearance. What he would not yield to, however, was the incessant demand of friends, politicos, newspapers, and Southern fire-eaters for some new statement of what his policies would be if elected president. "My published speeches contain nearly all I could willingly say," he replied to an over-curious New York abolitionist. He thanked the notification committee from the convention for their news, but carefully refused to make any political statement apart from affirming that the party platform "meets my approval; and it shall be my care not to violate, or disregard it, in any part." On the day of his nomination, he replied to a rally on his doorstep by referring "his numerous and enthusiastic hearers to his previous public letters and speeches."

Within weeks, the pile of eager requests for some new statement "on certain political points" had grown so high that Lincoln moved into a borrowed office in the state capitol, hired a secretary (a German-born Republican journalist named John Nicolay, who had first met

Lincoln in 1856 at the Decatur editors' conclave) and began sending out a form letter which politely informed inquirers that "his positions were well known when he was nominated, and that he must not now embarrass the canvass by undertaking to shift or modify them." Callers who tried to get at Lincoln personally in his temporary capitol office were screened first by Nicolay, who was told to schedule interviews only if "indispensable" and to "commit me to nothing." Lincoln did not even write to the vice-presidential nominee whom the convention had selected for him, Hannibal Hamlin, a former Maine Democrat, until mid-July.

This was not just Lincoln's usual taciturnity at work. Douglas had broken with precedent and taken to the road in an exhausting round of campaign speech-making through all of the free states and most of the South, and Lincoln asked the Republican national committee whether he ought to be doing likewise. But William Cullen Bryant warned him in June "to make no speeches, write no letters as a candidate" which could be twisted into causes for intra-party fighting or into rallying cries for Breckinridge or Douglas to gather hesitant voters. Lincoln discovered just how little fuel could make these pots boil when he remarked off-handedly to Samuel Haycraft that a visit to his Kentucky birthplace would probably get him lynched by local slaveholders. A few weeks later, the *New York Herald* was reporting that Lincoln believed that all of Kentucky was plotting to "do violence to me," and Lincoln had to move swiftly to get Haycraft and the Republican national committee to issue a denial before incensed Kentuckians dismissed any thought of voting for him. When he was invited to speak at a national fair in Springfield, Massachusetts, in August, he yielded to the advice of the Republican national committee not to accept. Far wiser, Bryant warned, to allow the Democrats to divide themselves and "allow yourself to be elected."

As early as July, it was becoming clear that this was exactly what was going to happen. "The prospect of Republican success now appears very flattering, so far as I can perceive," Lincoln wrote to Hannibal Hamlin. "It looks as if the Chicago ticket will be elected," he wrote to Anson Henry on the Fourth of July. "The election is ours now," George Fogg, the secretary of the Republican National Committee, assured him on August 18th. "The triumph is ours." Even Mary Lincoln "feels quite confident of her husband's election," and Robert

Lincoln was being sarcastically christened as "the Prince of Rails." There was a brief flutter of political nerves at the beginning of the autumn, when the first state elections in the North gave anxiously thin majorities to state Republican candidates or even (as in Rhode Island) defeats. But in October, Pennsylvania and Indiana elected Republican governors by substantial majorities, along with big Republican majorities in the state legislatures and in the state congressional elections. "It now really looks as if the Government is about to fall into our hands," Lincoln wrote Seward on October 12th.

The image of "falling" was more apt than Lincoln might have realized: the general election on November 6th gave Lincoln and the Republicans 1.8 million votes across the country, outdistancing Douglas's surprisingly strong showing of 1.3 million, the feebler pulse of Breckinridge's 850,000 Southern bitter-enders and John Bell's 588,000 old Whigs. This meant that Lincoln garnered only slightly less than 40 percent of the popular vote, much less than he might have hoped. Breckinridge and Douglas combined — an undivided Democratic party, in other words — would have beaten him by a substantial popular margin. (Only if all of Bell's voters had gone as a block for Lincoln could Lincoln have won a clear-cut victory over an undivided Democratic ticket.) But Breckinridge and Douglas had of course not combined, and even if they had, only in California and Oregon (among the free states) would combining Democratic forces have cost Lincoln the electoral votes of those states. Lincoln had scored his heaviest tallies in Northern states rich with electoral votes, and before the evening was over it was clear that Lincoln had won a heavy majority of the electoral vote. In the end, once the returns from the west coast were in, Lincoln had 180 electoral votes over 72 for Breckinridge, 39 for Bell (from Virginia, Kentucky, and Tennessee), and only 12 for Douglas (only Missouri and New Jersey).

Lincoln spent most of the day in his temporary office in the State Capitol, "quietly overlooking the outside proceedings," and about 3:00 P.M., went over to the courthouse and voted, and late in the evening set himself up in the Western Union telegraph office to monitor the news of the election. By midnight it was clear which way the tide was flowing, and Lincoln allowed himself to be pulled into a celebration supper. He returned to the telegraph office at 1:30 A.M. to make sure nothing had changed, and finally arrived home in the wee hours of the morning. He was too keyed up to sleep, though, "for I then felt as I never had before the responsibility that was upon me."

The South Carolina legislature had been waiting for this moment. All through the summer and autumn, as Democratic defeat loomed larger and larger, white Southerners began to take stock of what a Lincoln election might bring, and they did not like what they saw. Lincoln might have thought of containment as a middle ground between abolition and slave extension, but few in the lower South and even fewer in South Carolina saw containment as anything but a covert strike at slavery and Lincoln as anything other than a covert abolitionist. Even if Lincoln did not agitate for federal legislation to abolish slavery, he still possessed vast discretionary powers which could destabilize slaveholding everywhere in the South. The president and his party appointed federal postmasters, who could then become agents for spreading abolition propaganda; they appointed judges and marshals, who might refuse to pursue runaway slaves; they could use federal patronage to lure nonslaveholding Southern whites into hostility toward the planter class; they even distributed military commissions, and could turn federal army and navy installations into potential Harper's Ferries all through the South. Stymied slaveholders "in all Frontier States" would begin dumping their increasing slave population in the deep South, driving down the market value of slaves to "one hundred dollars each" and wiping out "four hundred and thirty millions of dollars" of capital investment. "They know that they can plunder and pillage the South, as long as they are in the same Union with us, by . . . every other possible mode of injustice and peculation," warned a New Orleans newspaper. "They know that in the Union they can steal Southern property in slaves, without risking civil war, which would be certain to occur if such a thing were done from the independent South."

South Carolina did not intend to linger to see this happen. "The terrors of submission," announced the *Charleston Mercury* even before the election, "are ten fold greater even than the supposed terrors of disunion." The legislature, called into special session by Governor William H. Gist on November 5th, voted to authorize a state convention "for the dissolution of the Union and the formation of a Southern Confederacy." The convention, when it met on December 17th, scarcely bothered to debate the question. An ordinance of secession was passed unanimously on December 20th in Secession Hall in Charleston, with instructions for bell-ringing and artillery-firing and the dispatch of commissioners to carry to every other slave state the secession ordinance and an appeal "to the people of the Slaveholding States" to join them in "a great slaveholding confederacy, stretching its arms over a territory larger than any Power in Europe possesses." The appeal was welcomed in Mississippi, whose secession convention lost only three weeks in voting 85 to 15 to withdraw from the Union; in Florida, which bolted on January 10th; and in Alabama, which followed the next day; and finally by Georgia on January 19th, by Louisiana on January 26th, and by Texas on February 1st. In six weeks, all of the lower South had severed its ties to the Union, and on February 4th, another set of commissioners from these states met in Montgomery, Alabama, to create a cooperative federation to be known as the Confederate States of America.

The secession fever triggered panicked responses. Northern financial markets trembled, as Northern lenders feared that secession would be an invitation for Southern borrowers to repudiate their debts. Depositors emptied out banks, and in Washington, Philadelphia, and New York, specie payments were suspended. Prophecies of "a *financial smash up* in this country" hung heavily in the air, and the by-now-recovered senator Charles Sumner wailed that "if there is not some speedy relief, more than half of the best concerns in the country will be ruined." President James Buchanan was fully as fearful of a political smash-up. When the Thirty-Sixth Congress assembled for its last session on December 3, 1860, Buchanan's annual message to Congress vigorously arraigned the North for its "long-continued and intemperate interference . . . with the question of Slavery in the Southern States," and asked that "the Slave States . . . be let alone, and permitted to manage their domestic institutions in their own way." Much as he deplored secession and regarded it as a legal impossibility, he would do nothing against it which might touch off a civil war between North and South. Congress, in his reading of the Constitution, had no "power to coerce into submission a State which is attempting to withdraw."

Buchanan hoped that this would be read as an assurance of good will, and so forestall secession. Others in Congress who had the same

hope of calming the secession enthusiasm also began offering concession packages — revive the Missouri Compromise, abolish the presidency and reorganize the Union into three equal executive districts,
and so forth. The most compelling of these proposals came from Kentucky's staunch old Whig senator, John J. Crittenden, who made his
own bid for the role of nation-saving Compromiser by calling on December 18th for a series of six constitutional amendments and four
standing resolutions that would permanently restore the Missouri
Compromise (over the head of the Supreme Court), forbid any congressional action on slavery in the slave states or the District of Columbia, block restrictions on the interstate slave trade, and provide financial compensation to the owners of runaways. The South, Crittenden
had warned, "has come to the conclusion that in case Lincoln should
be elected . . . she could not submit to the consequences, and therefore,
to avoid her fate, will secede from the Union." Only by sweeping "constitutional provisions — which shall do equal justice to all sections"
could these "serious and alarming dissensions" be "permanently qui-
eted and settled."

Neither Lincoln nor the Republicans would believe any of it. "Mr. Lincoln did not believe, could not be made to believe, that the South
meant secession and war," wrote Donn Piatt, an Ohio politician who
irritated Lincoln with the prediction that "in ninety days the land
would be whitened with tents." For one thing, it violated Lincoln's
utilitarian expectation that self-interest was the polestar of most human behavior. Secession could not possibly be in the interest of the
southern states; *ergo,* secession would not happen. This reasoning convinced Piatt that "this strange and strangely gifted man, while not at
all cynical, was a sceptic. His view of human nature was low" and
"this low estimate of humanity blinded him to the South." Besides, by
the beginning of February, less than half the slaveholding states had
actually passed secession ordinances; Missouri, Kentucky, Maryland,
Delaware, Virginia, Arkansas, Tennessee, and North Carolina still held
aloof in varying degrees, some (as in Delaware) by doing nothing, and
others (as in Virginia) by calling a state secession convention which
then proceeded to sit and wait on events. Secession, concluded many
Republicans, was only brinkmanship, an empty threat useful mainly
for frightening the Republicans away from their own political princi-

252

ples. Carl Schurz, the leader of the German-speaking Republicans in Wisconsin, joked that the South had threatened secession before, "went out, took a drink, and then came back." Now, they would secede, "take two drinks but come back again." The Southern secession conventions, declared Massachusetts Republican Henry Wilson, were simply one more production of the old "DISUNION FARCE" which the slave power trotted out whenever it wanted to "startle and appall the timid, make the servility of the servile still more abject," and "rouse the selfish instincts of . . . nerveless conservatism."

Lincoln (who moved his office out of the State Capitol in December to a rented second-floor suite across the square in order to make room for the new incoming governor and state legislature) refused to believe that the secession threat was real or that the Republicans should be hurried into ripping up their party platform. The notion of Southern secession had seemed ridiculous in his Cincinnati speech a year before, and it appeared no less ridiculous now. He told Herndon that "he could not in his heart believe that the South designed the overthrow of the government," and he wrote to John Fry that he had received "many assurances . . . from the South that in no probable event will there be any very formidable effort to break up the Union." He declined an invitation by former Connecticut senator Truman Smith to issue a public statement to calm the money markets on November 10th, since calming the markets was tantamount to admitting that they had something to be worried about. "I am not insensible to any commercial or financial depression that may exist," Lincoln wrote, "but nothing is to be gained by fawning around the *'respectable scoundrels'* who got it up." Any financier who really believed that secession rhetoric was the sign of the break-up of the Union had not read the sign rightly; the hotter the secessionists talked, the more likely it was that they were revealing their own desperation and that secession would never happen. "Disunionists . . . are now in hot haste to get out of the Union, precisely because they perceive they can not, much longer, maintain apprehension among the Southern people that their homes, and firesides, and lives, are to be endangered by the action of the Federal Government." He told a Philadelphia newspaperman only days before the South Carolina secession convention that "things have reached their worst point in the South, and they are likely to mend in the future," and a month later he was again confident that "the secessionists are already in danger of reaction."

Lincoln's obtuseness to the secession threat was probably the greatest political misjudgment of his life. But it was rooted in his conviction that the agitation for slave extension in the 1850s, and now the secession fever, were the work of the same planter oligarchy that had fashioned Kansas-Nebraska, and the same Democratic elites who had for so long misled and manipulated the ordinary nonslaveholding whites of the South. Lincoln had lived his entire political life among just such yeoman farmers who had migrated to Illinois, and he was convinced that they disliked the white plantation elites as much as the abolitionists. The only thing that kept them submissive to that elite was the usual Democratic political demagoguery, and once that wore thin, the white yeomanry of the South would assert themselves and the Union would be restored. "When the Union standard is raised in the South," predicted the young John Hay, "there will be more flock to it than secession leaders are at all aware of." Calls for new statements on the slavery issue were just "a trick" of the plantation aristocrats to whip up white fear in the South, as well as intimidate and "break down every northern man" as well. When Duff Green, a veteran Jacksonian journalist who had known Lincoln since his days in Congress, arrived in Springfield in December as a personal representative of President Buchanan, Lincoln refused all requests for a statement favoring concession and would do no more than repeat the party platform. They had his "old record" in print and had been unable to manipulate it; they only wanted a new "record" in the hope that he could be made to "appear as if I repented for the crime of having been elected, and was anxious to apologize and beg forgiveness."

This is also why, at first, he turned such a resolutely deaf ear to any of the concession proposals emerging in Congress. He wrote to Lyman Trumbull just after Congress convened for its lame-duck session, "The tug has to come, & better now, than any time hereafter." Similarly, let there be no tolerance for fire-eater folderol about secession. "The Union must be preserved," he told Richard Parsons, a political emissary from Salmon Chase. "Yes the Union must be preserved at all hazards." He knew of nothing in his political lexicon (he told Thurlow Weed) which suggested that any "state can, in any way lawfully, get out of the Union." Duff Green begged Lincoln "to come to

254

Washington" and use his influence as the Republican banner bearer to support "Mr. Crittenden's resolution, extending the Missouri Compromise," but Lincoln refused. Of course, he would not oppose the Crittenden amendments if the country as a whole wanted them. But the Crittenden give-aways were not what Lincoln defined as a good compromise. He told Orville Hickman Browning that "no concession by the free States short of a surrender of every thing worth preserving, and contending for would satisfy the South, and that Crittenden's proposed amendment to the Constitution in the form proposed ought not to be made." And in fact, when the Crittenden measures were finally put to a vote in select committees in both House and Senate in January, Lincoln abandoned his moratorium on policy discussions long enough to exercise "a strong influence through several sources" on congressional Republicans to defeat the Crittenden proposals.

It was not disunity in the nation so much as it was disunity in the Republican party that Lincoln feared, and it was there that Lincoln believed compromise was the order of the day. Lincoln had begun doodling with a cabinet list the night of his election, and amazingly, at the head of the list was the name of William Henry Seward. "A slouching, slender figure; a head like a wise macaw's; a beaked nose; shaggy eyebrows," Seward seemed the very embodiment of a politician. And indeed, despite the radicalism of the "irrepressible conflict" speech, the former Whig senator and governor thirsted after the reputation of nation-saving Compromiser even more than Crittenden. Despite Seward's hard feelings at the upset in the Wigwam in May, the New Yorker carried too much weight in the Republican party, and too much capacity for political mischief, to be left outside Lincoln's immediate oversight. Moreover, his experience in foreign affairs seemed to make Seward a natural candidate for secretary of state, and after a little self-flattering reluctance, Seward agreed to take the top cabinet post.

But then, Lincoln turned next to Salmon Chase. Tall, portly, self-consciously self-righteous, utterly "opposed to any concession or compromise," Chase was the Republican party's chief ideologue and Seward's temperamental opposite. "The introduction of Chase, a strong and active force, would destroy the unity of the Cabinet," wrote New York journalist William Thayer. (Seward actually tried to withdraw his acceptance of the State Department when he found he would have to share the cabinet with Chase, and Lincoln was beset by influential New

Yorkers almost on the eve of his inauguration to dump the dour Ohioan.) But Chase was the darling of the Republican abolitionists, and he had the added advantage, like Vice President-elect Hamlin, of being a former Free-Soil Democrat, which would bind up the Democrats west of the Appalachians who had deserted Douglas in 1860 to vote Republican. Chase had also been the rare Republican of national stature to unequivocally back Lincoln against Douglas in 1858, and Lincoln admitted to having "a kind side for him." To Chase would go the second office of the cabinet, the Treasury, while New England's anti-slavery advocates were appeased with the appointment of Gideon Welles, a Connecticut Democrat, as secretary of the navy.

Seward and Chase represented in varying degrees the sharp edge of the Republicans on slavery. On the other hand, even before he had word back from Seward, Lincoln was meeting with Edward Bates, the former Whig who had garnered a handful of votes at the convention, and with Bates's handler, Francis Preston Blair. With both Bates and Blair, Lincoln shared a reluctance to surrender to any radical agenda for a Republican administration; with both Bates and Blair, Lincoln was plainly trying to appeal to the Unionism of the border slave states, especially Missouri. He had even considered giving Bates, with whom he was politically more comfortable than Seward, the State Department if Seward refused, and in the end he appointed Bates as attorney general. As a further mark of his confidence that there was enough residual Unionism throughout the upper South to deflate secession, Lincoln appealed to Robert Scott of Virginia, Alexander Stephens of Georgia (who had energetically denounced secession before the Georgia legislature in November), and John Gilmer of North Carolina to enter the cabinet; all three were former Whigs and all three would be living demonstrations that secession was the policy of nothing more than a Bourbon minority in the South. He also picked out Montgomery Blair, the son of Francis Preston Blair, as postmaster general to represent the border states in general and the influence of the Blair family in particular.

And then there were the cabinet appointments he owed as plain political paybacks: Indiana and Pennsylvania had helped put him over the top in the Wigwam, and despite his protests that he would be bound by no horse-swapping at the convention, Lincoln eventually promised cabinet posts to Caleb Smith of Indiana and Simon Cameron of Pennsylvania. In Cameron's case, Lincoln had to hold his nose. A former Democrat and protégé of James Buchanan, Cameron had acquired an unsavory reputation for precisely the kind of corrupt logrolling politics that Lincoln deplored. But much as Lincoln shuddered at the thought of rewarding Cameron, "whose very name stinks in the nostrils of the people for his corruption," party loyalty, even under those circumstances, had to be served, and so the post of secretary of war would go to Cameron.

None of the Southern Whigs he had hoped to bring into the cabinet showed any interest in helping Lincoln. And instead of the secession virus consuming its own energies, a fresh source of contention offered itself. As each of the seceding states cut their ties to the federal government, it became a good question as to what should be done with the federal property and federal installations standing inconveniently on their soil. If secession meant anything more than bluster, none of the seceding states could honestly allow them to remain where they were; but no violent attempt to seize or occupy them could pass unnoticed by the Buchanan administration as a provocation close to war. In many cases, the situation was resolved simply by the personnel of the forts, mints, and customs houses quietly surrendering them to state control, and if every federal outpost had gone the same way, the new Confederate states might have had a completely unobstructed path to the independence they claimed. But a handful of federal forts resisted all calls to run down the flag and give themselves up. And the most aggravating of them all, Fort Sumter, sat in the middle of the ship channel of Charleston harbor, almost within artillery range of Secession Hall, beyond any hope of South Carolina to budge the small garrison of artillerymen by force.

Those artillerymen inside Sumter had never planned to be there. Their commander, Major Robert Anderson, was a Kentuckian and a slaveowner who had been sent down to Charleston at the first sign of trouble as a tacit pledge that the Buchanan administration would make no overt gesture to disturb the South Carolinians. In fact, when Anderson arrived to take charge of the artillery company that looked after the Charleston defenses, all but a handful of the artillerymen were quartered in shoreside Fort Moultrie, which it was assumed Anderson would cheerfully surrender the first moment South Carolina demanded it. But Anderson was a career regular officer who believed with his heart that "neither slavery nor any thing else should stand in the way of the preservation of the Union," and he had no intention of surrendering any federal garrison without express orders from his superiors. Six days after the South Carolina secession ordinance was passed, Anderson quietly collected his vulnerable little company and its baggage and rowed them out to the middle of Charleston harbor and the safety of the unoccupied, unfinished — but militarily untouchable — Fort Sumter, a squat brick pentagon on an artificial rubble spit in full, mocking view of the Charleston dockside.

When Charlestonians awoke on December 27th to discover that Anderson had holed himself up inside Sumter, their collective political furies erupted. Three South Carolina commissioners were dispatched to President Buchanan to accuse him of bad faith and demand that Anderson's garrison return to Fort Moultrie. Buchanan had indeed made promises early in December not to disturb the *status quo* in Charleston, and he had three Southern members of his lame-duck cabinet beseeching him to yield to the South Carolinians' ultimatum. But Buchanan also had before him three equally stubborn Northern Democrats in the cabinet — among them, as attorney general, Lincoln's one-time mocker in the McCormick reaper case, Edwin M. Stanton — and the private warnings of the army's senior major general, old Winfield Scott (the one-time Whig presidential candidate), that Anderson should be reinforced rather than evacuated. In the end, Buchanan refused to order Anderson to abandon Sumter. South Carolina responded by seizing the federal arsenal in Charleston, and when Buchanan sent an unarmed supply ship, the *Star of the West*, into Charleston harbor to restock Anderson's supplies, the artillery batteries that truculent South Carolinians had begun building around the harbor opened fire and forced the *Star of the West* to withdraw.

Lincoln had first been apprised of the potential for confrontation in Charleston harbor as early as September, 1860, and in December, General Scott privately notified Lincoln (through Illinois congressman Elihu Washburne) that the artillery company at Fort Moultrie and the undefended Fort Sumter were now in imminent danger of being overrun by the secessionists. Lincoln quickly passed word to Scott that "I shall be obliged to him to be as well prepared as he can to either *hold*, or *retake*, the forts, as the case may require, at, and after the inauguration." A day later, he replied to another confidential warning from another senior officer, Major David Hunter, that he could do little but "watch events" before the inauguration, but once in office, "if the forts fall, my judgement is that they are to be retaken." Although he promised Alexander Stephens that "a Republican administration would" never "*directly,* or *indirectly,* interfere" in the affairs of individual states, Lincoln drew the line at surrendering federal property to the secessionists.

Simply from the point of view of a Whig nationalist, the forts were federal property and represented an authority that no state could ever have sufficient sovereignty legally to assault. But even more, the longer even one bit of South Carolina stayed in federal hands, the more hollow the secession premise would appear. Disorganized Unionists in the Gulf States would find their hands strengthened and it would give an opportunity to what Edward Bates was calling "the real people" to "rebel against the traitors and compel a return to allegiance." Even "if Mr. B. surrenders the forts, I think they must be retaken," Lincoln advised General Scott. "I should regard any concession in the face of menace the destruction of the government itself, and a consent on all hands that our system shall be brought down to a level with the existing disorganized state of affairs in Mexico," Lincoln told a *New York Herald* reporter in mid-January, ten days after the *Star of the West* was turned back from Charleston harbor.

But this only meant for Lincoln how important it was to show no particular anxiety over the Sumter situation. He had, in fact, quite enough to do with the more mundane aspects of constructing a Republican administration after almost a decade of Democratic rule. With a Republican administration on the horizon, the Republican party faithful gathered for their portion of the spoils. "The offices are now sought for with avidity," observed the sardonic Amos Tuck, chairman of the New Hampshire state committee and himself a talked-about possibility for the cabinet. "A rush to reap where they have not sown is made by every slippery politician in the Republican party." Those who didn't actually queue up outside Lincoln's office suite across from the State Capitol belabored him by mail. By mid-January, the volume of letters aimed at Lincoln's political generosity had increased "so wonderfully" that John Nicolay had to carry each day's mail delivery from the post office in "a good-sized market basket."

Lincoln by this point had stopped reading it all. "So many callers and so much correspondence occupied his time," Lincoln told an Illinois journalist, that unless a letter-writer was someone Nicolay had been posted to recognize, a goodly proportion of the letters were "consigned to the stove without the least mercy." By the end of January, Nicolay had to prevail on Lincoln to hire an additional secretary, a sprightly, tart-tongued Brown University graduate named John Hay, who was at that moment reading law in the office of his uncle, Milton Hay, and Stephen Logan. "Aint you beginning to get a little tired of this constant uproar?" Robert Todd Lincoln wrote his parents from Philips Exeter Academy (where he had gone for a year's mental toughening-up before entering Harvard).

As the euphoria of the election wore off, and the prospect of leaving Springfield for Washington and his inauguration grew nearer, Lincoln lapsed into an unusually sentimental and unbuttoned mood. Ada Bailhache, the daughter of Illinois Central counsel Mason Brayman, was surprised that Lincoln could spend "nearly all the evening telling funny stories and cracking jokes. I could hardly realize that I was sitting in the august presence of a *real live president*." He slipped away from his hungry pursuers to Charleston, Illinois, at the end of January, and hired a buggy to visit John Hanks and the seventy-two-year-old Sarah Bush Lincoln. "I did not want Abe . . . elected," she later told Herndon, because she "felt it in my heart that something would happen [to] him." He gently brushed aside her fears: "No, no, Mama," he answered. "Trust in the Lord and all will be well. We will see each other again." To Herndon, Lincoln recollected all the arguments people had used to persuade Lincoln to drop him as a partner, and told Herndon to leave the *Lincoln & Herndon* shingle untouched. "If I live, I'm coming back some time," Lincoln promised, "and then we'll go right on practising law as if nothing had ever happened."

Memories of the old days in New Salem came rushing back over Lincoln, and for the first time in almost thirty years, Lincoln reminisced about his early love for Ann Rutledge. "It is true — true indeed I did," Lincoln replied when Isaac Cogdal asked him whether he had proposed to Ann Rutledge. "I have loved the name of Rutledge to this day." And almost as though Mary Todd Lincoln had never existed, he added, "I did honestly and truly love the girl and think often, often of her now." He escaped from one particularly grueling series of callers in the State Capitol by slipping into the office of Newton Bateman, the Republican state superintendent of education, and began uncharacteristically reflecting about religion. "I am not a Christian," he admitted. "God knows I would be one" if he could; what amazed him was that people who did profess to be Christians could actually defend slavery. "It seems as if God had borne with this thing until the very teachers of religion have come to defend it from the Bible."

He was careful to seem in no particular hurry to leave Springfield. James Conkling wrote on New Year's Day that "Mr. Lincoln takes the Secession troubles calmly — is patiently biding his time." Even though he told Joseph Gillespie that "I would willingly take out of my life a period in years equal to the two months which intervene between now and my inauguration," yet, when Seward, as his designated secretary of state and de facto representative in the capital, begged him "to drop into the city a week or ten days earlier" than the usual mid-February arrival of a new president, Lincoln made no move to depart for Washington. For one thing, Lincoln had no intention of being sucked into concession schemes emerging from Congress or Buchanan. Lincoln told William Jayne "that he would rather be hung by the neck till he was dead on the steps of the Capitol, before he would buy or beg a peaceful inauguration."

For another, as he told Seward, there were rumors of plots afoot in Washington. The capital remained, for all its being the national capital, very much a Southern city, surrounded on three sides by slaveholding Maryland and on another by slaveholding Virginia. At the mildest, he had been warned by Joseph Medill that the Southern congressional delegations in the House and Senate might absent themselves from the closing session of Congress in mid-February, when the electoral votes were officially counted before the assembled House and Senate, in order to prevent a quorum, then "prevent the counting of the electoral votes," and so short-circuit any legal confirmation of his election. At the worst, there were uneasy hints that the city's four militia companies might prove unreliable on inauguration day if Lincoln turned out to be an abolition demagogue. Governor Henry Wise of Virginia had been boasting that, in 1856, he had been prepared to lead the Virginia militia into Washington to prevent the possible inauguration of a Republican president, and might try to do so again if Lincoln showed up early enough to give him cause.

Lincoln could not wait forever, though. The representatives from the seven Confederate states, meeting in Montgomery, Alabama, published a new constitution for themselves on February 8th, and on February 18th they inaugurated former Mississippi senator Jefferson Davis as the provisional president of the Confederacy. What might have looked like caution in December would now look like indecision on Lincoln's part, and on January 27th, he announced that he would leave Springfield for Washington on February 11th, one day short of his fifty-second birthday. The house at Eighth and Jackson was rented out to a railroad official, the family's belongings were packed up and any furniture too big to be moved easily was either sold or put in storage. Seven hundred Springfielders crowded into the house for a farewell reception on February 6th, and almost a thousand packed into the railroad station on the rainy morning of the 11th to say good-bye.

He had deliberately kept his entourage small. Mary, with Willie and Tad, would leave separately and rendezvous with him the next day in Indianapolis. Lincoln's own party would include Robert, the secretaries Hay and Nicolay, a handful of political friends like Ozias Hatch, Newton Bateman, Jesse Dubois, Ward Hill Lamon, David Davis, Orville Hickman Browning, and Norman Judd, and a small military escort made up of Major Hunter, Colonel Edwin V. Sumner, and Captain John Pope, whose father Nathaniel had once been a circuit judge on the old Eighth Circuit. As the specially chartered train built steam, Lincoln stepped out onto the platform at the rear of the last car, and, one more time, the flood of reminiscence rolled over him. "No one, not in my situation, can appreciate the sadness of this parting," Lincoln said slowly and with tremendous feeling. "To this place, and the kindness of these people, I owe everything. . . . I now leave, not knowing when or whether ever I may return, with a task before me greater than that which rested upon Washington." He had told Herndon that "the sorrow of parting from his old associations was deeper than most persons would imagine," and James Conkling was surprised to see that Lincoln's rational "breast heaved with emotion and he could scarcely command his feelings sufficiently to commence."

He would say nothing new, however, about how he intended to manage that task. Lincoln was playing his cards so close that he would release the names of only two of his cabinet choices to the press,

Seward for State and Bates for attorney general. He had been working on his inaugural address ever since mid-January, but that he was guarding even more closely, and when Robert Todd Lincoln managed to lose the "gripsack" containing copies of the address in a pile of hotel luggage in Indianapolis, Lincoln flared out in irritation at him until it was found. The rail route to Washington had been laid out to allow Lincoln to speak in as many Northern state capitals as possible, beginning with Indianapolis and continuing through Columbus, Albany, Trenton, and Harrisburg, with a number of other points in between. But the speeches were often evasive: "I do not expect, upon this occasion, or any occasion, till after I get to Washington, to attempt any lengthy speech," he told a welcoming committee in Indianapolis. When he would speak about the secession crisis at all, it was usually in a dismissive tone: dismissive of Southern fears of "coercion" by the federal government, dismissive of secession as reducing the Union to "a sort of free-love arrangement," and dismissive of the entire "excitement at present existing in our national politics" as "altogether an artificial crisis."

If anything, he reversed his advice of the year before to Republicans to keep their attention on the slavery extension question, and now struggled to deflect attention onto the old Whig issues. He promised to abide by "all and every compromise of the constitution" (but not the Crittenden compromise), he advocated "an adjustment of the tariff" and the distribution of "the wild lands of the country . . . so that every man should have the means and opportunity of benefitting his condition," and pledged that (unlike Andrew Jackson), during the Lincoln presidency, "congress should originate, as well as perfect its measures, without external bias" from him. And as if to underscore his contention that the secession crisis was "artificial," he resolutely ignored the firing on the *Star of the West*, and in fact ignored the seizures of federal properties outside Charleston as though Sumter were the only place in dispute. Any thought, he explained to a delegation upon his arrival in Washington, that he had come to Washington to fan "the ill feeling that has existed between you and the people of your surroundings" could only have "depended, and now depends, on a misunderstanding."

On just the same terms, the inaugural address, as Lincoln delivered it from the East Portico of the federal Capitol on March 4th, was a deliberate mixture of the obvious and the hopeful, but without any proposal for concession to secessionists. Like Buchanan four months before, he repeated that secession from the Union was a legal impossibility. "Plainly, the central idea of secession is the essence of anarchy," since whenever any party to the Constitution rejects the decisions of the "constitutional majority" — as in his election — they must "of necessity, fly to anarchy or to despotism." On the other hand, he reiterated that federal intervention in the "property . . . and personal security" of the Southern states was, in his view, just as much a legal impossibility, and nothing was said about any determination to "retake" any "public property" now under the Confederate flag. In fact, he would "fully recognize the rightful authority of the people over the whole subject" if they wished to amend the Constitution in a national convention. And if the amendment which emerged from such a convention declared that Congress "shall never interfere with the domestic institutions of the States," he would "have no objection to its being made express, and irrevocable." But he would make no such gesture himself.

And why should he? There could be no serious cause for so drastic an act as secession, and no serious cause to challenge his determination to "hold, occupy, and possess the property, and places belonging to the government." There would be no "invasion" — and on that score, very likely no attempt to repossess the federal property already seized by the Confederates; he would even "forego" attempts to collect customs duties, perhaps even the federal delivery of mail. Such crisis as there was, was purely the creation of the Southern imagination. Only "in *your* hands, my dissatisfied fellow countrymen, and not in *mine* is the momentous issue of civil war." It was only "passion," the terrible mark of the Jeffersonian and Jacksonian temperament, and not sober reason which had "strained . . . our bonds of affection." "We are not enemies, but friends," Lincoln closed, and if North and South will only "think calmly and *well*, upon this whole subject" — if they would, in effect, subordinate Democratic passion to Whig reason — then "the mystic chords of memory, stretching from every battle-field, and patriot grave, to every living heart and hearthstone, all over this broad land, will yet swell the chorus of the Union. . . ."

Lincoln could square his pledge of no invasion with his earlier promise to hold and, if necessary, retake Fort Sumter largely because he thought the two promises would never come into conflict. Major Anderson was neatly cooped up in Sumter, and the longer Anderson sat there, the more time the Confederates would have to contemplate their folly, Lincoln's conciliation, and the refusal of the upper South to join them. "I think the Administration means peace," wrote William Thayer. "The tone of the Inaugural indicates an over-reaching desire for peace and conciliation, and where there is a will there is a way." But the day after the inauguration, these cards were dashed from Lincoln's hand. On February 28th, Major Anderson had written to Buchanan to advise him that the Sumter garrison had only six weeks' supply of food, and that sometime in mid-April, he and his men would have to evacuate the fort or starve. When Anderson's letter was delivered into Lincoln's hands by outgoing Secretary of War Joseph Holt after the inauguration, Lincoln at once realized that he no longer had the luxury of casually out-waiting the secessionists: if he waited too long, Sumter would be lost and both the Confederates and his own party would seize on it as proof of presidential weakness; but if he tried to reinforce or resupply Sumter, that would be taken as an aggressive gesture that belied the promises made in the inaugural address. He now faced a maddening choice between either concession or confrontation, and he was facing them at once.

Lincoln did not find much enthusiasm for confrontation in his cabinet. He sent his completed cabinet list to the Senate for confirmation on the day after the inauguration, and then met with his new cabinet on March 9th to get a clear sense of what to do. But when he polled the secretaries for their recommendations on March 15th, everyone except Montgomery Blair and Salmon Chase followed Seward in agreeing that Lincoln would have to surrender Sumter. Welles was sure Lincoln would cave in, and Blair was ready to resign his week-old office in protest. Nor was Lincoln helped by the military. General Scott, who had warned him for months about the need to hold Sumter and the other installations, responded on March 11th to a series of queries prepared by Lincoln on the Sumter situation that holding Sumter would require "A fleet of war vessels & transports, 5,000 additional regular troops & 20,000 volunteers." This was more men than the entire United States Army had on its rolls, "and to raise, organize & discipline such an army, would require new acts of Congress & from six to eight months." With such bleak prospects, Seward now counseled concession, insisting "that there was a strong Union party in the South — even in South Carolina," and if Lincoln would avoid a provocation over Sumter by evacuating the fort, Southern Unionism would have an opportunity to "stop the movement." In a memorandum drawn up on March 18th, weighing the pros and cons of intervention in Charleston, Lincoln began leaning toward evacuation, and by March 25th the prevalent rumor in Washington was that "the order for evacuation . . . is given."

Yet the struggle within Lincoln's mind over Sumter was by no means concluded. The next day, Lincoln met with Montgomery Blair, and Blair's brother-in-law, Captain Gustavus Fox, and at that point Lincoln suspended whatever decision he may have made concerning evacuation and dispatched Fox to Fort Sumter, and Stephen Hurlbut (an Illinois political acquaintance but a native Charlestonian) and Ward Hill Lamon to Charleston to take the Unionist temperature of the people. What these emissaries reported back by March 28th surprised Lincoln: not only had Hurlbut found no shred of Unionist sentiment in Charleston, but Fox had returned from Sumter convinced that even a modestly equipped expedition could force its way into the harbor to Sumter's relief. It did nothing to encourage Lincoln toward concession that a proposal he made to Virginia Unionist John B. Baldwin which would have traded the evacuation of Sumter for the permanent adjournment of the Virginia secession convention was "hardly treated . . . with civility" by Baldwin.

But nothing surprised him more than a memorandum General Scott submitted on March 28th, advising Lincoln to abandon not only Sumter but also Fort Pickens, in the harbor of Pensacola, Florida. "It is doubtful," Scott advised the president, "whether the voluntary evacuation of Fort Sumter alone would have a decisive effect upon the States now wavering between adherence to the Union and secession." That night, at the conclusion of the Lincolns' first state dinner, the president closeted himself with the cabinet and read Scott's memorandum "with evident emotion." There was no imaginable way this could be seen as anything but desertion, and desertion was the vice he most loathed in himself and others. "He could not, consistently with his conviction of his duty, and with the policy he had enunciated in his inaugural, order the evacuation of Sumter," he told Gideon Welles, "and it would be inhuman on his part to permit the heroic garrison to be starved into a

266

surrender without an attempt to relieve it." The next morning, he polled the cabinet again, and found that now only Seward and Smith favored surrendering Sumter. That afternoon, he ordered Welles and Cameron to prepare a naval expedition for Sumter by April 6th. On April 4th, Secretary of War Cameron notified Major Anderson that a supply expedition was on its way to restock his provisions "and, in case the effort is resisted . . . to re-enforce you."

Lincoln's decision appalled Seward, who was not only convinced that this would needlessly trigger civil war, but who had rashly promised Southern Unionists like Baldwin that a Sumter evacuation was certain. Concluding that this was an example of Lincoln's inexperience in policy matters, Seward took it on himself to derail the resupply effort, first by trying to persuade Lincoln on April 1st to surrender policy management to him, and then by crossing the wires of the resupply mission so that it started off for Charleston harbor without its armed escort. It was too late: once Lincoln's mind was made up, no one who mistook his long dallying for uncertainty could budge him. If there were decisions to make, "*I* must do it," Lincoln wrote in sharp reply to Seward, and Seward backed away whimpering. Lincoln did, however, offer one last-minute olive branch to the South Carolinians. State Department clerk Robert S. Chew was sent by Lincoln on April 6th to South Carolina governor Francis Pickens (Lincoln would not recognize that there was now a Confederate government which South Carolina belonged to) with the promise that the supply mission would bring in only food, not "men, arms, or ammunition," so that the *status quo* in Charleston harbor would only be prolonged rather than altered.

But prolonging the status quo was exactly what the authorities in Charleston did not want. The new Confederate commander in charge of the batteries ringing the harbor, General Pierre G. T. Beauregard, summoned Major Anderson to surrender on April 11th. Anderson refused, and at 4:30 A.M. the next morning, the Confederate batteries erupted in bombardment. Anderson's garrison was too weak to offer much response, and after thirty-four hours of pounding by the Confederate guns, Anderson wearily but gamely hauled down his flag. Oddly, Lincoln felt a moment of resigned relief. "All the troubles and anxieties of his life had not equaled those which intervened between [the inauguration] and the fall of Sumter," he told Orville Hickman Browning. Now, without himself having to take aggressive action, "they attacked Sumter. It fell and thus did more service than it otherwise would." War had been made inevitable; necessity had answered his doubts and questions. On April 15th, Lincoln issued a proclamation calling out 75,000 state militia and summoning Congress into special session.

7 War in a Conciliatory Style

Lincoln's first inclination, once Major Anderson had surrendered Sumter to the Confederates, was to strike back at Charleston as quickly as possible and retake the fort. He told John Hay on April 25th that he intended to provision and reinforce the garrisons at the two remaining federal installations in the South, Fort Monroe and Fort Pickens, then blockade the Confederate ports, secure the safety of Washington, and finally "go down to Charleston and pay her the little debt we are owing her." He was naive enough in his office to believe that this could be done without much more than a police action against the South Carolina secessionists. He assured Garrett Davis of Kentucky that "he intended to make no attack, direct or indirect, upon the institutions or property of any state, but, on the contrary, would defend them to the full extent with which the Constitution and laws of Congress have vested the president with the power." As late as April 26th, he still clung to the belief that "the last hope of peace may not have passed away."

But those hopes swiftly spiraled downwards. Pickens and Monroe could be restocked by sea, but the great navy yard at Norfolk, Virginia, was hastily abandoned and burnt by its commandant, and the federal arsenal at Harper's Ferry was occupied by Virginia militia on

April 18th. Lincoln issued his blockade proclamation on April 19th, threatening seizure, not only to vessels flying a Confederate flag, but any foreign ships trying to enter Confederate ports. But the U.S. Navy had only forty-two ships in commission for covering 3,500 miles of Southern coastline, and it would be almost a year before Navy Secretary Gideon Welles would be able to hire or build enough vessels to make the grip of the blockade tight enough to be believed. In the meanwhile, Lincoln would discover that blockades were regulated by international conventions whose tangled distinctions between blockade, closure of ports, and liability of ships to seizure would easily trigger international diplomatic incidents, especially with the British. As it was, British dependence on Southern cotton imports was so great that the imposition of a blockade might be enough to persuade Britain to intervene in the American war in order to safeguard its own economic interests. And on May 13th, the British government took what looked like the first step in that direction by extending recognition to the Confederacy as a belligerent power, and not merely an insurrection.

The problems of the navy were dwarfed by the problems Lincoln faced with the army. The U.S. Army in the spring of 1861 consisted of only 16,000 officers and men, and nine-tenths of them were scattered company-by-company in eighty-nine posts from Canada to Florida. None of the four overaged major generals of the army was really fit for field service, including the ponderous General Scott, while the lower echelons of the officer corps of the army were dominated by Southern-born men whose loyalties might be suspect. All through the 1850s, the army and the War Department had been a Southern preserve (Jefferson Davis had actually been President Pierce's secretary of war), and some of the most promising Northern officers to emerge from West Point in the 1840s and 1850s had been quietly shunted off into dead-end assignments or had handed in frustrated resignations from the service. There was no question about Scott's loyalties — Lincoln had been careful to sound that point long before leaving Springfield — but most of his fellow Southerners were another story. Scott's hand-picked favorite, Robert E. Lee of the 2nd Cavalry, was discreetly approached at Lincoln's prompting by old Francis Preston Blair about taking charge of a federal field army, but Lee refused. (Lee was already packing his bags for Richmond, where he would take command of the Virginia militia.) Georgia-born brigadier general David Twiggs surrendered the entire Department of Texas to Texas militia and in May accepted a commission as a Confederate major general. Lincoln was livid when artillery colonel John B. Magruder personally assured him on April 18th of his "loyalty and devotion," only to have Magruder hand in his resignation three days later and head south. By the end of August, 1861, almost one in three of the army's officers had resigned, most of them to join the Confederacy.

Nor could Lincoln easily find replacements for them. Congress was out of session (the Senate had remained in an extra session after the inauguration, but only until March 28th) and was not due to assemble with its new members from the past November's elections until December. Without congressional approval, Lincoln had no constitutional authority to expand the federal army, either by organizing new federal regiments or commissioning new officers for them. His April 15th proclamation called for Congress to assemble in special session for the purpose of adopting war measures, but he had been forced to set the date for the session forward all the way to July 4th to allow for the completion of late congressional elections in Tennessee, Kentucky, Maryland, and western Virginia, where he has hoping for strong Unionist turnouts. Until then, he had to promise that "he would make no attempt to retake the forts &c., belonging to the United States, which had been unlawfully seized . . . but would leave the then existing state of things to be considered and acted upon by Congress." After all, the only legal forces he had at his disposal beside the Regular Army were the state militias which the federal militia statutes permitted him to call out as part of the proclamation. Even so, the militias could never be much more than a stopgap. The statutes limited their service to only thirty days after the assembling of Congress, and the outraged refusal of some of the slaveholding states which had not joined the Confederacy (like Kentucky, Missouri, Virginia, and North Carolina) to contribute their militia made it unlikely that Lincoln would even get the 75,000 militiamen he had called for. Unless Lincoln was prepared to act unilaterally, he had no choice but to wait and make hopeful plans about retaking Charleston.

Time to wait for Congress, however, was exactly what the secessionists did not allow him. Although Virginia stood to one side through the secession crisis, Virginia's governor, John Letcher, denounced the militia call as a plot "to subjugate the Southern states."

On April 17th, the Virginia secession convention voted to secede and join the Confederacy, and it was followed by Tennessee and Arkansas in early May and North Carolina on May 20th. With Arkansas and Tennessee went a huge stretch of the Mississippi River; with Virginia went one entire side of the Potomac River and a border with the District of Columbia itself, so that Lincoln had no trouble peering through a telescope cross-river toward Alexandria and seeing secession flags sprouting on rooftops. Both Virginia and Tennessee promptly offered Richmond and Nashville as capitals for the new Confederacy, and on May 20th, the Confederate Congress voted to move to Richmond, only one hundred miles away from Washington. Meanwhile, the border slave states of Kentucky (and the entire Ohio River line), Missouri (and half of the Mississippi River up past central Illinois), and Maryland (which surrounded the District on its three other sides) also teetered in the balances.

Maryland was the most critical factor in the equation, since any move by Maryland to join the Confederacy would strangle the capital and probably force the surrender of the federal government for no more than the trouble of walking in and asking for the keys. Maryland governor Thomas Hicks refused to send the Maryland militia to Lincoln's aid, while Baltimore mayor George William Brown warned the president that any "passage of troops" through Baltimore to relieve the capital would result in "a fearful slaughter." The day following Brown's letter, the 6th Massachusetts regiment (bound for Washington) attempted to change trains in Baltimore, only to be surrounded by a mob which stoned them and provoked a volley of rifle fire that killed eleven of the rioters. For three days, Maryland militiamen and Baltimore police happily tore up the railway lines north of Baltimore to prevent further troop movements, seized federal military stores from Baltimore's President Street depot, and tried to plant a "protective" guard around Fort McHenry in Baltimore harbor. (The fort's commander politely declined the offer and promised to blow them all to perdition if they came anywhere within range of his guns.) "All the roads and avenues to this city were obstructed, and the capital was put into the condition of a siege," Lincoln recalled a year later. "The mails in every direction were stopped, and the lines of telegraph cut off by the insurgents. . . ."

In desperation, odds and ends of District militia and federal workers were rounded up as defense units, and gouty old General Scott ordered sandbag barricades banked up around the Treasury building as a last-stand citadel if the Virginia militia crossed over the river. With the virtual closure of Baltimore, Lincoln had no way of bringing reinforcements or supplies into the capital, or even knowing if they were coming. "I don't believe there is any North," he remarked helplessly to some volunteers in the Washington defenses on April 24th. "Rhode Island is not known in our geography any longer. You are the only Northern realities." "What is the North about?" he complained on April 25th. "Do they know our condition?" Two days later Governor Hicks nervously proposed to Lincoln that the British ambassador be asked "to act as mediator between the contending parties of our Country." The question had become, not whether Lincoln could retake Charleston, but whether Lincoln could even hold onto Washington.

Governor Hicks was not the only one to suggest a certain lack of confidence in Lincoln's abilities to resolve the crisis on his own. Not only was Lincoln younger than many of his predecessors in the presidency (younger in fact than most of his own cabinet), he was also substantially less experienced in management and military affairs. Lincoln himself admitted to Robert Wilson that "when he first commenced doing the duties, he was entirely ignorant, not only of the duties, but of the manner of doing the business." His only taste of military life had been as a militia captain thirty years before, and apart from one lackluster term in Congress, Lincoln had never served in any executive capacity, not even as mayor of Springfield. Up till his election he had never run any organization more complex than his law office. Kansan Addison Proctor, who had been a delegate at the Wigwam, believed that "Mr. Lincoln, although admitted by all to be a most adroit politician and wonderful in debate, had never been called upon to show that he possessed a single one of the qualities at that time most in demand." To many observers, Lincoln even *looked* disorganized. One New York financier wrote Lincoln in May to chide him for "your own personal manners," since "soldiers write home to their friends in this town with reference to their disappointment in your bearing and manners when reviewing them." Sentinels at the White House would present arms, only to have Lincoln walk past "apparently absorbed in thought." Bostonian Edward Pierce discreetly remarked that "Mr. Lincoln's manner and style of conversation" showed "that he was not profoundly in earnest."

Not only did he lack the experience, but he also seemed to lack the temperament for complex administration. Lincoln "had no organizing abilities," admitted John Todd Stuart. Pennsylvania congressman Edward McPherson thought Lincoln "too cautiously deliberate" to have much hope of success as "a first class executive officer," and even David Davis agreed that Lincoln had "no power of organization" and "no administrative ability." Even Nicolay thought Lincoln's "official habits . . . were reckless of all order, and gave his secretaries no end of trouble." His basic impulse with his cabinet was to treat them as he might have treated an assembly of law clerks rather than an administrative team. Salmon Chase found that becoming secretary of the Treasury was no particular honor, since Lincoln treated the cabinet as "only separate heads of departments, meeting now and then for talk on whatever happens to come uppermost, not for grave consultation on matters concerning the salvation of the country." He expected that each member would report to him on "the manner of conducting the affairs of his particular department," not put an oar into the shaping of policy, and when he came to conclusions, he wanted their "adhesion," not discussion. Even the colorless Caleb Smith complained "that Mr. Lincoln dont treat a Cabinet as other President's — that he decides the most important questions without consulting his cabinet." David Davis "asked him once about his Cabinet: he said he never Consulted his Cabinet. He said they all disagreed so much he would not ask them — he depended on himself — always." Leonard Swett "sometimes doubted whether he ever asked anybody's advice about anything. He would listen to everybody; he would hear everybody, but he never asked for opinions."

At times, Lincoln seemed to have not only to have no interest in the cabinet's advice, but no clear policy of his own to follow. Lincoln's handling of the Sumter crisis was full of mixed and uncertain signals, and he had not hesitated to assemble the cabinet, take polls of cabinet opinion, and then drop them all at the behest of the last person he had talked to. "The Sumter question was not absolutely decided in Cabinet," Simon Cameron recalled; in fact, "nothing was ever decided — there was general talk." Even after the fall of Sumter, he expected to use force on the secessionists, but then made vast exceptions to whom the force would be applied. "He did not organize by a solid plan," Davis remarked years later, "hence his Adm[inistration] didn't run smooth." To the exasperation of the over-diligent Chase, Lincoln announced that "I have never had a policy," and was passing his time "preventing the storm from blowing down the tent, and I drive in the pegs as fast as they are pulled up." When Ohio senator John Sherman introduced his brother, William Tecumseh Sherman, so that William could brief Lincoln on the seriousness of the secession situation in Louisiana, Lincoln dismissively replied, "Oh, well! I guess we'll manage to keep house." Outside, Sherman erupted in frustration to his politician-brother, "You have got things in a hell of a fix, and you may get out of them as best you can."

Some of this appearance of administrative madness on Lincoln's part actually had some method to it. The model of a Democratic presidency had, throughout Lincoln's life, been Andrew Jackson, whose passions and ambitions were unappeased by anything less than absolute power and desk-thumping demands for submission. A Whig-Republican presidency was supposed to stand poles apart from Jackson, to defer conscientiously to the will of Congress, to appoint impartially a cabinet chosen for its talents rather than its personal loyalty to the president, and to regard the use of the veto as the weapon of last political resort. His indifference to military niceties was also politically cultivated: in contrast to Jackson, "our President was not lost in his high admiration of brigadiers and major-generals, and had a positive dislike for their methods and the despotism on which an army is based." To have "no policy" was, in effect, to declare that he was entirely the servant of the people; and to appoint to his cabinet both Montgomery Blair and Salmon Chase, who represented both the most conservative and the most ultra factions of the Republican coalition, and who cordially detested each other, was the functional sign of Lincoln's superiority to mere political considerations.

But Welles was, all the same, not far from the mark in noticing Lincoln's initial managerial ineptness. Lincoln even had trouble establishing a daily routine. The White House, then as now, functioned as both office and home for the president, and the second floor of the White House was literally divided into the Lincoln family's private quarters (in the west wing) and the presidential office suite (in the east

275

wing). There was, unhappily, no private passageway between the two wings, so that Lincoln was constantly forced to emerge from the family quarters and then plunge into a crowd of office-seekers, petitioners, and visitors in the central hallway before being able to reach the sanctuary of his office. The office suite itself occupied five rooms in the east wing, with John Nicolay presiding as chief over a staff of male secretaries and guarding official access to Lincoln. (Nicolay's office, writing room, reception room, and the vestibule to the suite were all wrapped protectively around Lincoln's own office and cabinet room.)

But much as Nicolay and his assistant, John Hay, tried to control the flow of mail, newspapers, requests, and callers, Lincoln upset every effort of his staff to manage his time. "There was little order or system about it," recalled John Hay. "Those around him strove from the beginning to end to erect barriers to defend him against constant interruption, but the President himself was always the first to break them down." Lincoln initially insisted on conducting a personal "examination into the qualifications of each applicant" for office, and on handling all of his own correspondence, and was rather proud that he could tell a journalist in 1862 that "You are in error if you suppose any important portion of my correspondence escapes my notice." Only gradually did he yield to Nicolay and Hay's plan to sift out the irrelevant correspondence (and especially the crackpots and assassination threats) and prepare daily digests of the newspapers. Like many others who have found themselves suddenly elevated to responsibilities beyond their experience, Lincoln tried to compensate for that lack by sheer volume of effort. "He had immense physical endurance," Charles Dana remarked. "Night after night he would work late and hard without being wilted by it, and he always seemed as ready for the next day's work as though he had done nothing the day before." "His methods of office working were simply those of a very busy man who worked at all hours," remembered Robert Todd Lincoln.

This meant, of course, that Lincoln, who had taken such pleasure (and built such a formidable political following) from riding the Eighth Judicial Circuit, as president hardly ever stirred out of Washington. Unlike his Confederate counterpart, Jefferson Davis (who made several extended state trips through the Confederacy to rally Southern morale or consult with distant field commanders), Lincoln stayed close to his White House desk and the War Department tele-

graph center, and declined all but a handful of requests and invitations
to appear at mass political meetings or public demonstrations. He contemplated briefly an invitation in 1863 for a major midwestern Republican political rally, but in the end, he turned even that down.

Lincoln compensated for tying himself to Washington by turning
his office schedule into an open-season for callers, petitioners, inven-
tors, social-climbers, and what-not. "Nobody ever wanted to see the
President who did not," Seward remarked to John Hay. "There never
was a man so accessible to all sorts of proper and improper persons."
Ward Hill Lamon recalled that "Mr. Lincoln would let in People indis-
criminately — Members of Congress Could get to see him most any
time." Nicolay tried to screen out unwanted visitors (and earned the
wrath of large portions of Washington officialdom in the process), but
Lincoln insisted on lavishing large amounts of office time on them.
"He said that as a Republican government all men & women &
Children had a right to see the Presdt & State his grievances," David
Davis remembered. Lincoln also insisted on scheduling open-door
public levees, when callers without appointments could greet him in
one of the first-floor public rooms of the White House. "I call these re-
ceptions my public-opinion baths," Lincoln explained to a puzzled
staff officer, Charles Halpine. Whatever he lost in the way of public
contact by closeting himself in Washington, his mercilessly exhausting
open-door levees "all serve to renew in me a clearer and more vivid
image of that great popular assemblage, out of which I sprang." As a
result, "the House remained full of people nearly all day."

There was, nevertheless, one aspect of the new administration
which looked like anything but indecisiveness, and that was Lincoln's
handling of the federal patronage. Lincoln complained bitterly and
frequently about the time he was compelled to waste on the office-
seekers who lined the corridor outside his office and sometimes
queued all the way down the staircase to the front door of the White
House. He told Robert Wilson that "he was so badgered with applica-
tions for appointments that he thought sometimes that the only way
that he [could] escape from them would be to take a rope and hang
himself on one of the trees in the lawn south of the president's house."
Either that, or (as he once told William O. Stoddard, whom Nicolay
added to the secretarial staff in July, 1861) he ought to move his office
to a smallpox hospital. But then, he added, "they'd all go and get vac-

cinated, and they'd come buzzing back, just the same as they do now, or worse."

But for all his complaining, no one since Andrew Jackson played with the federal patronage system more vigorously than Lincoln. Of the 1,520 federal offices directly under presidential control, Lincoln emptied nearly 1,200 of them of Democrats after his election to replace them with Republicans. If he hesitated to appear as a "military chieftain," he had no qualms about appearing as a political one. Although "it had been the policy of successful administrations to make sweeping changes of opponents," Gideon Welles wrote, "the President and some of the Cabinet, particularly the Secretary of State, were disposed to go beyond others in these respects." The war would serve to quintuple the number of civilian patronage jobs in the government, from 40,000 in the entire network of federal employment to nearly 195,000 by the war's end, and all of them would become plums for Republican party loyalists.

As might be expected, Lincoln's Illinois Republican friends stood to benefit first: David Davis would be made a Supreme Court justice in 1862, Norman Judd was sent to Berlin as head of the American mission to Prussia, Gustave Koerner was appointed minister to Spain, Samuel Parks would obtain an appointment to the Supreme Court of the Idaho Territory, Archibald Williams would become a U.S. district judge for Kansas, Lawrence Weldon would become federal attorney for the southern federal district in Illinois, James Speed (the brother of Joshua Speed) would replace Edward Bates in the cabinet as attorney general in 1864, and even William Herndon was offered a small Treasury job (he declined). Patronage rewards were so much expected as the norm that Lincoln's friends felt free to complain bitterly if nothing they desired was cast their way. "I am sorely disappointed in all my expectations from Washington," Jesse Dubois wrote angrily to Lincoln in 1861, after Lincoln declined to appoint Dubois's son-in-law as superintendent of Indian Affairs, "I did feel as though I had some claims for the favors I asked for. But in all I have been disappointed."

Sometimes, the disposal of patronage offices was intended to placate Republican factions as much as to chastise Democrats. Montgomery Blair's appointment as postmaster general gave him (and the powerful Blair family) control over the largest network of patronage jobs in the country (some 22,700 appointments), and strategic city postmasterships were awarded to faithful campaigners and pro-Blair Republican moderates, although not necessarily in that order. On the other hand, Salmon Chase's Treasury Department controlled the most lucrative patronage network (some 4,000 customs-house and management posts), and Chase proceeded to fill that network with anti-slavery — and anti-Blair — loyalists. The Collector of the Port of New York, the fattest patronage plum in the country (worth over $6,000 a year in salary and probably another $20,000 in "pickings and fees") went to Hiram Barney, a loyal Lincoln man and a close friend of Salmon Chase.

The last word in patronage, however, remained Lincoln's. He intervened directly in numerous patronage appointments, overriding Chase, Blair, and other cabinet officers to demand the hiring of certain party faithful or to provide reliable incomes for party workers. In August, 1861, when one of Chase's lieutenants in charge of the Philadelphia mint hesitated to hire Elias Wampole, a loyal Lincoln campaigner in Illinois, Lincoln irritably insisted that a job be found for Wampole, even if it meant make-work. "You must make a job of it, and provide a place. . . . You *can* do it for me, and you *must*." If patronage petitions stretched Lincoln's patience, it was a stretching he asked for himself.

But even if Lincoln was lacking in experience as an executive, he could hardly avoid seeing how swiftly the Maryland situation was deteriorating. Governor Hicks called the Maryland legislature to meet in special session at Annapolis on April 26th, and it did not take prophetic powers to predict that a majority of the legislature would favor secession. Nicolay and Hay found Lincoln in a "state of nervous tension," pacing the White House floor, gazing out his office window toward the Potomac River, and breaking out "with irrepressible anguish" with the cry, "Why don't they come! Why don't they come!" Orville Hickman Browning pleaded with Lincoln that Baltimore "should be seized and garrisoned, or, if necessary to the success of our glorious cause, laid in ruin." Finally, on April 20th, Lincoln summoned Governor Hicks and Mayor Brown to the White House, and informed them that he intended to bring troops through Baltimore no matter what.

Almost as if on cue, Benjamin Butler, the brigadier general of the Massachusetts militia, arrived at Perryville, Maryland, on April 20th

279

to find the railroad bridge across the Susquehanna River burned and further railroad movement by Northern troops toward Washington impossible. Unfazed, Butler seized a river steamer, boarded it with the 8th Massachusetts regiment, and unloaded them the next day at the docks at Annapolis, the Maryland capital. Over the protests of Governor Hicks, Butler put Annapolis under martial law and proceeded to work his way over the railroad from Annapolis to Washington, repairing it as he went, until on April 25th, the first Northern reinforcements burst into the isolated capital. The Maryland legislature, collecting its wits but not its secessionist wind, assembled forlornly in Frederick, and voted not to secede. Meanwhile, Butler set off to deal with the problem of Baltimore, and on May 13th, he planted federal troops and artillery on Federal Hill, overlooking the resentful city, and cowed it into submission.

This secured most of the corridor northwards that Lincoln needed for the supply and defense of Washington, but it did not prevent isolated acts of arson and sabotage by Confederate sympathizers in Maryland, and that led Lincoln into an even more dramatic gesture. Ripping up telegraph lines and wrecking railroad lines were more like nuisances than outright acts of war, and could be dealt with by the civil courts. But it was another question as to whether the civil courts in Maryland would connive with secessionist saboteurs by refusing to convict the culprits. Any effort by the army to keep such saboteurs under indefinite arrest would sooner or later provoke some secessionist judge into issuing a writ of habeas corpus, the Constitution's one express guarantee that any citizen could demand a day in court.

On April 27th, in order to protect the railroad lines leading northwards through Baltimore, Lincoln authorized General Scott "to suspend the writ of Habeas Corpus for the public safety" — in effect, to authorize the arrest of suspected saboteurs and sympathizers by the federal army and refusal of any demand by the civil courts to turn them over to civil jurisdiction. Since Lincoln limited this authorization only to the "military line . . . between the City of Philadelphia and the City of Washington," this was hardly a wholesale suspension of civil liberties, and the Constitution did concede the power to suspend the writ whenever "rebellion or invasion" might imperil "the public safety." But Maryland was in neither a state of rebellion nor invasion, and the Constitution did not actually specify that the president alone had the power to authorize suspensions of the writ. When Maryland militia lieutenant John Merryman was arrested on May 25th by General George Cadwalader in Baltimore and jailed in Fort McHenry for secretly recruiting and drilling Marylanders for the Confederate army, Lincoln found himself staring at yet another challenge from an obstinate Marylander, in this case Supreme Court Chief Justice Roger B. Taney.

Chief Justice Taney — the same Taney who had served Andrew Jackson's death sentence on the Second Bank and authored *Dred Scott* — looked with skepticism on Lincoln's presidency from the start, and when Merryman's lawyer appealed directly to Taney (in his double capacity as federal circuit judge for Maryland) the eighty-three-year-old Taney lost no time in fashioning a stick to push into the spokes of Lincoln's war machinery. Assuming jurisdiction over the Merryman arrest, Taney issued a writ of habeas corpus to Merryman's jailers, ordering them to produce Merryman for civil trial, and sent a federal marshal to serve the writ at Fort McHenry. General Cadwalader refused to surrender Merryman, and on May 28th Taney announced Merryman was entitled to his freedom. Taney filed a lengthy opinion, *ex parte Merryman,* which attempted to use Lincoln's own Whiggish minimalism against him by declaring that suspension of the writ was a congressional, not a presidential prerogative. "The President has exercised a power which he does not possess under the Constitution," Taney declared. The writ could not be suspended even by Congress while the civil courts were open, and therefore Lincoln was threatening free government by allowing his military underlings to hijack civil liberty.

This, of course, was ridiculous. Taney himself had offered exactly the contrary opinion in 1849 in a Rhode Island case, and over the next two years a series of distinguished Northern jurists — including Horace Binney, New Hampshire chief justice Joel Parker (in the October, 1861, *North American Review*), Yale law professor Henry Dutton, federal district judge Peleg Sprague, and Lincoln's own attorney general, Edward Bates — offered detailed refutations of *ex parte Merryman* based on the common-sense proposition that, in time of war, judges should not be niggling about how the military conducted the war, any more than a concern for property rights should keep the fire company from dousing down a burning house. Yet American law offered little concrete direction about how to handle the problem. Joseph Story's *Commentaries* leaned toward confining the authority of suspension to Congress; James Kent's *Commentaries* was more expansive about suspension, but only in the context of foreign war. Binney reached for the loophole created by civil war and rebellion, admitting that the suspension of the writ was probably intended to be, "in the light of Parliamentary law in England," a prerogative of Congress. But this was "the merely legal and artificial argument"; the need to suspend the writ was "inseparably connected with rebellion or invasion," and that meant that suspension "is supplementary to the military power to suppress or repel" and so were "inseparable incidents of the Executive power. . . . Both the fact of the rebellion and what the public safety requires, to the defeat or suppression of rebellion, are of Executive cognizance and decision, and of execution also, to the whole extent of the lawful means of that department."

But the most powerful response to *ex parte Merryman* came from Lincoln himself, in the message he prepared for the Thirty-Seventh Congress when it finally assembled for its special session at noon on July 4th. The one allowance a Whiggish reading of the Constitution usually made for the broad exercise of presidential powers was in time of war, and although the Constitution described the war powers of the president in only the vaguest of terms — those of commander in chief of the army, navy, and serving militia — those terms were available to justify a free resort to powers and policies that no Whig under ordinary circumstances would ever have dreamt of claiming. And these, as Lincoln hardly needed to remind Congress, were anything but ordinary circumstances. In fact, as Lincoln remarked to Carl Schurz, "Looked at from a constitutional standpoint, the executive could do many things by virtue of the war power which Congress could not do in the way of ordinary legislation." The firing on Sumter meant that "no choice was left but to call out the war power of the Government," and Lincoln included under the rubric of "war power" the authorization "to suspend the privilege of the writ of habeas corpus."

Lincoln conceded Taney's point that his own presidential oath bound him to enforce the laws of the land, not suspend their operation in favor of military law. But "in nearly one-third of the States" those same laws were being resisted "and failing of execution," and Lincoln could not let all those laws go unenforced "when it was believed that disregarding" the restrictions on suspending the writ "would tend to preserve" the rest of the laws. Besides, he argued, the Constitution allowed the suspension of writ in cases of rebellion, and "it was decided that we have a case of rebellion, and that the public safety does require the qualified suspension of the privilege of the writ." In the face of that fact, it could be no more than a quibble as to who had the power to authorize the suspension, the president or Congress: "it cannot be believed the framers [of the Constitution] intended, that in every case, the danger should run its course until Congress could be called together."

But in Lincoln's mind, standing behind Taney's tedious Jacksonian constitutionalism was the larger issue of whose freedom, exactly, was being called into question by suspending the writ. The war "embraces more than the fate of these United States," Lincoln warned. "It presents to the whole family of man, the question, whether a constitutional republic, or a democracy — a government of the people, by the same people — can, or cannot, maintain its territorial integrity, against its own domestic foes." This cast the war into the same fundamental terms Lincoln had been debating since his earliest political days as a Whig, with Whiggism seeing the future of the American republic in cultural and national unity and the Democrats suspiciously glorifying individualism and states' rights. "We must settle this question now," Lincoln said, "whether in a free government the minority have the right to break up the government whenever they choose," because "if we fail, it will go far to prove the incapability of the people to govern themselves." To John Nicolay, Lincoln explained that the unity of the Republic trumped the right of any faction within it to dictate policy. "The very existence of a general and national government implies the legal power, right, and duty of maintaining its own integrity. This, if not expressed, is at least implied in the Constitution." Jacksonian constitutionalism was a perversion of the Constitution's intentions, a glorification of process over substance, and never was that more on display than in *ex parte Merryman*. The war was therefore a conflict of cultures, and he was quick to insist that the triumph of the Democratic culture, whether at the hands of Roger Taney or Jefferson Davis, would "practically put an end to free government upon the earth."

Or at least it would put an end to free government in the sense Lincoln had always construed freedom — as economic liberalism.

"This is essentially a People's contest," Lincoln announced, by which he meant a contest in which "the people" asserted their right to remake and transform themselves as they might, free from narrow little oligarchies, from provincialism and parochialism, from his own father's patriarchal demand for a lifetime of agrarian drudgery. "On the side of the Union, it is a struggle for maintaining in the world, that form, the substance of government, whose leading object is, to elevate the condition of men — to lift artificial weights from all shoulders — to clear the paths of laudable pursuit for all — to afford all, an unfettered start, and a fair chance, in the race of life." Setting the war as the ultimate ideological confrontation of the Whig and the Jacksonian, Lincoln dismissed Taney's obstructions as little more than the usual Democratic manipulation of the Constitution to the Constitution's own destruction. By October, Lincoln expanded the authority to suspend the writ all the way to Maine.

But Taney's opinion in *ex parte Merryman* did have at least this much success, in that it permanently saddled Lincoln, who had all along espoused the most cautious constitutionalism among the Republicans, with the reputation of a dictator-in-the-make, eager to shred recklessly the restraints of the Constitution in pursuit of the ideological goal of equality. It also made it easier, as the war trod upon the toes of a variety of civil liberties, to hang every violation of civil process around Lincoln's neck, as consistent with some vague disregard for law. "By whom hath the Constitution been made obsolete? By Abraham Africanus the First," accused an anti-Lincoln "catechism" in 1864. "To what end? That his days may be long in office — and that he may make himself and his people the equal of negroes." But most of the civil-liberties violations would turn out later to have involved criminal rather than civil arrests, or the detention of Southerner spies, the crews of captured blockade-runners, and at least seven violations of federal slave-trade laws on the high seas. Of the approximately 12,000 civil arrests that were linked in some way to political dissent, the largest majority occurred in the border states, where uncertain allegiances abounded. Against these arrests has to be balanced the absence on Lincoln's part of any effort to establish a personal government. Lincoln actually would end up exasperating members of his own party for his reluctance to act more aggressively outside the Constitution. Gideon Welles (a former Democrat with a sharp eye for Republican improprieties) concluded that "Mr. Lincoln . . . though nominally a Whig in the past, had respect for the Constitution, loved the federal Union, and had a sacred regard for the rights of the States." And the war, along with the legal complications of military arrests and trials, was "forced upon the Administration by the secessionists themselves, who insisted that slavery which was local and sectional should be made national."

There was another set of considerations governing Lincoln's dealing with Maryland beyond mere inexperienced hesitation, and that was his abiding fear that drastic steps taken in dealing with any one of the slave states still in the Union — Delaware, Kentucky, Missouri — might transfer them into the secession column. Maryland, by threatening to choke off the capital, left him with no choice but to resort to coercion, but even then, the suspension of the writ and the military arm-twisting of the Maryland state authorities amounted to substantially less than Lincoln might have done if he had aimed at becoming a "military chieftain." He could not afford to risk even that much with Kentucky and Missouri. If he provoked those two key border states into joining the Confederates, then the frontiers of the Confederacy would stand on the other side of the Ohio River, Illinois would be boundaried on two sides by slave states, and the West might be tempted, for the sake of its commerce, to coerce the North into striking a deal for peace and Southern independence.

From the first, then, the congressional delegations from the border states were generously assured of a hands-off approach. No federal troops would be used to occupy them, and the federal government would contemplate no plans for the abolition of slavery. He "regretted the necessity of marching troops across Maryland," and "if Kentucky made no demonstration of force against the United States, he would not molest her." In his July 4th message to the special session of Congress, Lincoln repeated his pledge to "have no different understanding of the powers, and duties of the Federal government, relatively to the rights of the States, and the people, under the Constitution, than that expressed in the inaugural address." Especially, he assured them, he had no designs on their slaves. For one thing, he had no constitutional authority to do so. "I did not consider that I had a *right* to touch the state institution of slavery until all other measures for restoring the Union had failed," he remarked. He also had no political mandate from the people to do so. "I should never have had votes enough to send me here if the people had supposed I should try to use my power to upset slavery." Besides, given his own Whiggish respect for property, he "did not wish to see rich men made poor by having their negroes freed."

And to the irritation of those who were impatient for Lincoln to deal dramatically with secession, the hands-off appeasement of the border states worked. Delaware, with a slave population of less than a thousand, was never much of a danger. Kentucky mistrustfully declared its neutrality of both the Union and the Confederacy on May 20th, and by studiously observing that neutrality, Lincoln calmed enough Kentucky fears to permit the election of a three-to-one pro-Union legislature on August 5th. Instead, it was the Confederates who impatiently resorted to force, and in September, Confederate troops crossed the Kentucky line from Tennessee and occupied the Cumberland Gap and the strategic town of Columbus, just below the confluence of the Ohio and Mississippi rivers. The amazed Kentucky legislature promptly ended its neutrality and on September 25th called out 40,000 volunteers for the federal army. Thereafter, Lincoln could congratulate himself on having saved the Ohio River and opened a direct route of support to the unsubdued Unionists of the eastern Tennessee mountains.

The same story prevailed in Missouri (although there, Lincoln's plans were very nearly upset by one of his own generals). Missouri was a slave state, but slaves made up less than a tenth of the population, and it was the only slave state that had given a decisive vote for Stephen Douglas in 1860. All the same, the governor, Claiborne Jackson, was determined to take Missouri out of the Union, and he cajoled the legislature into calling a secession convention in March, 1861. But Jackson's demands for secession were met with even firmer demands for staying put by the younger Francis Preston Blair (Montgomery Blair's brother, who had gone over to the Republicans in 1856 and garnered 17,000 votes for Lincoln in Missouri) and the overwhelmingly anti-slavery German population clustered around St. Louis. Not only did the Missouri convention fail to recommend secession, but Blair and Captain Nathaniel Lyon, the commander of the federal arsenal in St. Louis, disarmed and disbanded a threatening state militia encampment, and after a month-long flurry of political histrionics, chased Jackson and his secessionist militants into southern Missouri. Although Missouri secessionists would "declare" Missouri out of the Union and trouble the unhappy state with four years of civil-war-within-a-civil-war, keeping federal hands off Missouri had secured Missouri for the Union.

Lincoln not only had to keep Kentucky and Missouri placated; he also had a substantial Democratic opposition in the Northern states which, once the burst of patriotic solidarity over Sumter had dissolved, could also be extremely dangerous. The 1860 election had been an electoral disaster for the Democrats of the Northern states — Democrats were left holding only four governorships, three legislatures, and a pitiable forty-two seats in the House of Representatives and seventeen out of forty-eight senatorial seats — and the factionalism spurred on by the three-way party split over the presidential nomination left the Democrats organizationally weaker than at any time since Andrew Jackson. What was worse, Stephen A. Douglas, still the Northern Democrats' greatest figure, bravely urged Northern Democrats to support Lincoln and resist the secessionists. Jacob Dolson Cox heard him in Columbus, Ohio, just after the fall of Sumter, demanding that "the Union must be preserved and the insurrection must be crushed" and pledging "his hearty support to Mr. Lincoln's administration in doing this."

But it would have been unwise to count on the disappearance of an animosity so old and so ideological. Douglas fell ill in Chicago, and died suddenly on June 3, 1861, at age forty-eight, thus dispelling any guarantee of Democratic support for the war. And even with their poor electoral showing in 1860, the Democrats retained the loyalty of 45 percent of the northern voters. They gained back ground in local Northern elections in 1861, and their very presence in Congress allowed them the opportunity to question administration military policy, impute the most outrageous motives to administration actions, and begin training a new cadre of anti-Republican congressional leaders like Ohio's Clement Vallandigham and Indiana's Daniel Vorhees. Vallandigham, wrote John Hay, "is the object of no inconsiderable attraction. . . . Vallandigham is a man of respectable talents, a good lawyer, a finished scholar . . . and seldom makes a speech without attracting the entire attention of the House." He was, even as a lawyer, an agrarian and a sectionalist: "I became and am a Western sectionalist," Vallandigham wrote. Democrats like Vallandigham, Vorhees, and New York governor Horatio Seymour would agree with Republicans that the Union ought to be preserved, but they would soon raise persistent objections about how to do the preserving, what degree the containment or abolition of slavery should figure in that preservation, and how to treat public dissent from administration policies. In the end, the Democrats in Congress might have lacked enough votes to do more than (as a disgusted Republican put it) "oppose everything and propose nothing," but they had the capacity to generate electoral mischief, and Lincoln could not ignore them.

At the same time, Lincoln could not prevent large portions of the North and his own party from concluding that, because slavery had been the root of secession, secession was only going to be rightly dealt with by immediately extirpating slavery. "Some of our northerners seem bewildered and dazzled by the excitement of the hour," Lincoln remarked to John Hay; others seemed "to think that this war is to result in the entire abolition of Slavery," and still more urged "upon me most earnestly the propriety of enlisting the slaves in our army." For these critics, waging war merely to end secession, or even to contain slavery, left the fundamental threat, politically and economically, untouched and free to carry on its dark campaign by some other means. "The preservation of the Union with the Slave System of labor extending over one half of it, and the Free-Labor System over the other half, is, in the ordinary course of human affairs, an impossibility," declared Orestes Brownson. Only the outright destruction of slavery could strip the Slave Power of its political and commercial underpinnings, and the war over secession offered an opportunity for that extirpation which might never come again. "The Slave States, by their unprovoked rebellion, have given us an opportunity of performing an act of long delayed justice to the negro population of the Union, and of assimilating the Southern Labor system to ours," Brownson added. And with the expectation that Lincoln would actually take up this opportunity, one of the first acts of the July 4th special session was the adoption of a Confiscation Act which threatened rebels with the confiscation of any "property" used for war-related purposes — with the clear understanding that this "property" would include slaves put to work for the Southern war effort.

Some of the Republicans were not content with simple confiscation. Charles Sumner, the Republican party's walking martyr to the fury of the Slave Power, beseeched Lincoln immediately after the attack on Sumter to use "the war power . . . to emancipate the slaves." "Slavery is the cause of the present war," insisted the veteran abolitionist Lewis Tappan. "What then is the remedy? We unhesitatingly answer: IMMEDIATE AND UNIVERSAL EMANCIPATION." Ohio senator Benjamin F. Wade, a former farmer, schoolteacher, and Whig leader ("on whose rough face a smile never comes," wrote John Hay, "out of whose firm lips little praise ever issues"), grimly announced that the time had come to bury slavery, and if the war "continues thirty years and bankrupts the whole nation, I hope to God there will be no peace until we can say there is not a slave in this land." Zachariah Chandler, a wavy-haired, thick-lipped Detroit merchant who had entered the Senate to replace Lewis Cass in 1857, declared that the "rebel has sacrificed all his rights. . . . Everything you give him, even life itself, is a boon which he has forfeited." The implacable Thaddeus Stevens, who represented south-central Pennsylvania in the House and who now chaired the powerful House Ways and Means Committee, called for the Confederacy to "be laid waste, and made a desert," so that it could be reconstructed with free labor.

Few of these radical Republicans particularly liked Lincoln, whom they regarded as a political upstart and a part of the most "notoriously conservative . . . old fogy" wing of the old Whig party; and Lincoln, for his part, sometimes found them "almost fiendish" in their zeal to destroy slavery. (John Hay soon began labeling them as "Jacobins.") Lincoln's relation to the Republican Radicals was both politically and ideologically ambivalent. He naturally shared their admiration for free wage labor and their moral antipathy for slavery, and considered that at least on those general points they were "facing Zionwards" with him. He warned Missouri senator John Henderson that "Sumner and Wade and Chandler are right about" slavery. "We can't get through this terrible war with slavery existing," or at least not as it had been up till 1861. He held Sumner at arm's length through 1861 about emancipation, alternately infuriated and embittered at the florid Harvardian; yet he assured Sumner in November, 1861, that "the only difference between you and me on this subject is a difference of a month or six weeks in time." But the zeal of the Radicals for outright abolition by military force struck Lincoln as reckless, and reckless not only of the touchy political realities of the border states, but reckless in its use of abolition as a vehicle for a darker sectional hatred of the South. Recklessness of this dimension might lose the war by losing the border states; it might just as easily lose the peace by making any form of postwar reconciliation impossible, and lose postwar political control of the nation by making the Republican party an object of undying resentment by white Southerners. And politics aside, Lincoln simply could find no comfort in the Radical temperament, which resembled nothing so much as the purism of New School moralists, demanding action where Lincoln was inclined to calculate necessity.

Lincoln first discovered how much discomfort the Radicals could give during that first summer of the war. In order to back up young Frank Blair and his Missouri Unionists, Lincoln named as military district commander for Missouri John Charles Fremont. Fremont's appointment was, on paper, a shrewd move: a military man, the first Republican presidential candidate and the darling of the Radicals, as well as the son-in-law of Missouri's most famous politician, Thomas Hart Benton; it would have been hard to imagine a better choice to please all parties. Unhappily, among all these assets, Fremont did not possess wisdom. On August 10, 1861, only weeks after Fremont's arrival in St. Louis, Nathaniel Lyon and the Unionist Missouri militia were dealt a sharp defeat at Wilson's Creek, where Lyon was killed. Casting about for weapons to strike back, Fremont placed his entire district under martial law, promised the arrest, trial, and execution of any Missourians who had aided Claiborne Jackson's secessionists, and — most alarming of all — announced that "their slaves, if any they have, are hereby declared free men."

Confiscating slaves as the property of traitors was one thing; declaring them free was quite another. "He evidently considered himself clothed with proconsular powers," Gideon Welles sardonically remarked, and border state Unionists promptly rushed to warn Lincoln that "that foolish proclamation of Fremont . . . will crush out every vestige of a union party in the state." Lincoln, who had known nothing of Fremont's proclamation before reading it in the newspapers, immediately ordered Fremont to delete all references to shootings and emancipations. "I think there is great danger that . . . the liberating slaves of traitorous owners, will alarm our Southern Union friends, and turn them against us — perhaps ruin our fair prospect for Kentucky," Lincoln explained in a confidential letter to Fremont. He told Orville Hickman Browning that if Kentucky bolted to the Confederates, "we can not hold Missouri, nor, as I think, Maryland . . . and the job on our hands is too large for us." But Fremont was too obtuse to take hints: not only did he argue back in his own defense, but he sent his wife, Jessie Benton Fremont, to Washington to argue his case. An interview with the daughter of one of Andrew Jackson's most famous lieutenants was clearly not to Lincoln's liking, and when she arrived in Washington, Lincoln bluntly told her that her husband "should never have dragged the Negro into the war."

Conveniently for Lincoln, Fremont also proved as unwise a general as he was a politician. After a series of small-scale defeats at rebel hands in Missouri (which further seemed to confirm that emancipation declarations would only harden slaveowner resistance), coupled with reports of wholesale corruption and administrative ineptitude, Lincoln relieved Fremont of command in October, 1861, and gave the district to his old military informant, David Hunter, now a major general. But Hunter created very nearly the same problem for Lincoln only eight months later. In November, 1861, federal warships boldly steamed into South Carolina's Port Royal Sound and cleared the coastal islands in the Sound in order to establish a coastal supply base for the federal navy. The Confederates abandoned not only their weapons, but also their slaves. Hunter was placed in command of this tiny new department, and, in May, 1862, promptly proceeded to imitate Fremont by imposing martial law, and then declaring all "persons . . . heretofore held as slaves . . . forever free." Once again, an embarrassed Lincoln had to rein an officer in, and the proclamation was canceled.

The decision to boot Fremont and restrain Hunter placated border state anxieties, but it crystallized anger at Lincoln among the Radicals. "The proclamation of General Fremont," announced the *New York Times*, "though the first appeal to the law dissolving . . . the tie between master and slave, only states the inevitable result of the rebel war." In Congress, Ben Wade was so "disgusted with the slowness and inanity" of Lincoln in pressing down on slavery that he wondered out loud that more people do not "desert to Jeff. Davis, as he shows some brains; I may desert myself." But Lincoln would not budge. He toyed with the idea of vetoing the Confiscation Act, and when Secretary of War Simon Cameron coyly tried to bid for the sympathy of the radicals by including a recommendation in his end-of-the-year report for 1861 for emancipating and arming slaves, Lincoln curtly asked for (and got) his resignation. He replaced him, to the initial dismay of the Radicals, with a Democrat and one-time Buchanan appointee — and the lawyer who had so humiliated him in Cincinnati years before — Edwin M. Stanton.

"In considering the policy to be adopted for suppressing the insurrection, I have been anxious and careful that the inevitable conflict for this purpose shall not degenerate into a violent and remorseless revolutionary struggle," he told the Thirty-Seventh Congress when it at last assembled for its first regular session on December 3, 1861. For the moment, at least, Lincoln preferred to regard the war as a question of the preservation of the Union, and he would not "be in haste to determine that radical and extreme measures, which may reach the loyal as well as the disloyal, are indispensable." Let the war be won rightly, and secession closed off as a means of escaping from the bottle Lincoln had promised to cork by preventing the extension of slavery into the territories, and slavery would gradually eliminate itself.

It was not the hectoring of the Radicals which eventually pushed Lincoln out of the caution and hesitation that characterized so much of his first months in office, as it was the inactivity of the generals who turned out to be, for their own reasons, almost inert. General Scott seconded Lincoln's own cautious first instincts in May when he urged that the Confederates be cordoned off by a naval blockade along the Gulf and South Atlantic coasts and a secure defensive line along the Ohio and Potomac rivers, so that the Confederacy could be gradually starved to the point where Southern Unionists would gather strength and pull the Confederate regime down. The attraction of such a plan was, as Attorney General Bates suggested, that it would "give the least occasion for social and servile war, in the extreme Southern States, and to disturb as little as possible, the accustomed occupations of the people."

The great difficulty with it was that it had all the appearance of doing nothing, and doing nothing aroused the ire of Northern politicians, newspapers, and even a few impatient officers. At the end of April, a former Regular Army officer named George Brinton McClellan, who had been persuaded to accept a commission as brigadier general of volunteers by the governor of Ohio, offered a dramatic alternative to Scott's so-called "Anaconda Plan." He would invade western Virginia and "secure the destruction of the Southern Army," and then strike through Kentucky into Tennessee and finally to "Pensacola, Mobile & New Orleans." A month later, McClellan took his own advice and moved several regiments of Ohio troops across the Ohio River into western Virginia, where they successfully linked up with Virginia Unionists in the Allegheny Mountains, expelled a small Confederate force, and encouraged the western Virginians to organize a loyalist government of their own.

Not only McClellan's victories, but every other incident in the six weeks following the reinforcement of Washington seemed to suggest that the rebels would collapse at the first touch. On May 13th, delegates from the Unionist western counties of Virginia met in their own convention and created a "Restored Government of Virginia," and elected Francis Harrison Pierpont as the Unionist governor of "Virginia." On June 17th, a convention of Tennessee Unionists met in Greeneville and reaffirmed their loyalty to the Constitution. On May 24, federal troops boldly moved across the Potomac and seized Alexandria almost without resistance, and on June 15, Harper's Ferry was recaptured from withdrawing Virginia militia. (The only discordant note in these advances was the death of Elmer Ellsworth, colonel of the 11th New York Zouaves and a one-time clerk in the Lincoln-Herndon law office, whom Lincoln mourned "as a son.") These successes created unbearable pressure on Lincoln and Scott to do something with the militia around Washington before they were disbanded. On June 26th Horace Greeley's *Tribune* loudly drummed

FORWARD TO RICHMOND!
FORWARD TO RICHMOND!
The Rebel Congress Must Not be Allowed
to Meet There on the 20th of July
By That Date the Place Must be
Held by the National Army!

And Greeley ran the headline consecutively for a week to underscore popular impatience. Three days later, the *Chicago Tribune* took up the same cry, "THE NATION'S WAR CRY — FORWARD TO RICH-MOND."

Reluctantly, Scott appointed one of his staff officers, a newly minted brigadier general named Irvin McDowell, to take command of the 35,000 men now encamped around Washington, and on June 29, McDowell hesitantly laid before Lincoln and the cabinet a plan for a campaign into Virginia. It was not a plan McDowell had much confidence in, due to the inexperience of his troops, but Lincoln waved away the objection. "You are green, it is true, but they are green, also; you are all green alike." In fact, though, they were not entirely alike. The Confederates had gathered a modest army near Manassas Junction, a critical rail-crossing twenty miles southwest of Washington, and placed it under the command of Pierre G. T. Beauregard, who only a few months before had commanded the guns at Charleston that had pounded Fort Sumter into surrender. Not only did Beauregard have advance intelligence of McDowell's plans, but he had reinforcements near at hand by railroad from the Shenandoah Valley under the command of Joseph E. Johnston, who had until April been the quartermaster-general of the federal army. When McDowell's under-disciplined and disorganized army stumbled down the road from Washington on July 21st, they collided with Beauregard's Confederates across a small stream known as Bull Run, three miles above Manassas Junction. Johnston's reinforcements arrived off the train just in time to turn the battle against the hapless McDowell, and the federals collapsed into a shameful stream of whipped and demoralized soldiers, headed back to Washington in a gloomy and streaming rain.

"Today will be known as BLACK MONDAY," wrote New York lawyer George Templeton Strong in his diary the day after the battle at Bull Run. Lincoln spent all of the afternoon of the battle in the telegraph office of the War Department, whose building then sat across the green of the "President's Park" from the White House, and till past midnight he returned there "at intervals" to take in the awful news. The city went wild with rumors that the Confederates were at the heels of the retreating federals, that pro-Southern conspirators were about to turn the city over to Jeff Davis, and even old General Scott showed up at the White House at two in the morning to insist that Mary Lincoln, Willie, and Tad be bundled north to safety (she refused).

The finger-pointing began before Black Monday was over. Lin-

coln blamed McDowell and relieved him of command; Scott more indirectly blamed Lincoln for having pressured him into the Virginia invasion. "Your conversation seems to imply that I forced you to fight
this battle," Lincoln angrily responded, and bitterly remarked several
days later that Scott had actually been too optimistic about the invasion, that "he would insist that we couldn't be beat nohow, and that
was all there was of it." Across the North, newspapers clamored for
McClellan to be appointed in McDowell's place, and the *Philadelphia
Inquirer* wailed that "General McClellan is woefully wanted in the
neighborhood of Washington. . . . His ability, the military science, the
energy, and the lightening-like rapidity . . . are indispensable there
now."

To one administration staffer, Lincoln could only moan, "If hell is
any worse than this, it has no terror for me." But despite appearing
"tired, jaded and wretched," Lincoln did not lose either his energy or
his long-cultivated self-control. Two days after the Bull Run battle, he
drew up a new military plan to reorganize and regroup the defeated
federal forces, discharge "as rapidly as circumstances will permit" the
unreliable militia, and bring forward the training of "new volunteer
forces . . . as fast as possible." He personally toured the disheartened
encampments around Washington, and he yielded to the public
clamor to bring George McClellan to Washington and hand him the
job of organizing a new three-year volunteer army.

McClellan was thirty-four years old, and although he was a
Douglas Democrat by persuasion, his career had otherwise been all
that Lincoln could desire. A graduate of West Point (second in his class
of 1846), he had won one of the Academy's prestige commissions in
the Corps of Engineers, served with distinction under Scott in Mexico,
and been detailed as a military observer to the Crimean War.
McClellan had also found, like many other Northerners, that the ladder to promotion in the prewar army was clogged with Southerners
and pro-Southern prejudice, and when he stalled at the rank of captain, he resigned from the army to become chief engineer and then vice
president of the Illinois Central, and then (in 1860) Ohio district president of the Ohio and Mississippi Railroad. A Philadelphian by birth,
McClellan was promptly offered command of Pennsylvania's volunteers by Governor Andrew Curtin at the outbreak of the war. But his
business life had him living in Cincinnati in the spring of 1861, and an

even-more-prompt offer of command of Ohio's volunteers reached him from Governor William Dennison. Command in Ohio became McClellan's springboard for the invasion and redemption of western Virginia, and it was his successes there and the reputation he had won as a manager and administrator in the railroad business which led to the call to Washington on July 22nd.

At first, everything seemed to confirm the wisdom of putting the training of the new volunteer army into McClellan's hands. He was a tremendous organizer: almost like putting a railroad on a timetable, McClellan built up a series of protective fortifications around Washington, whipped the streams of newly uniformed and newly equipped volunteers and their untried officers into brigades and divisions, hand-picked commanders and created a working staff, and bestowed on this slowly coalescing new force the name that would stick with it throughout the war — the Army of the Potomac. The army returned the favor by cheering him as "Little Mac" and the "Young Napoleon," and no wonder: "His bow and smile seemed to carry a little of personal good fellowship even to the humblest private soldier," remembered one of his staff officers, "establishing a sort of comradeship between him and them."

Not only the soldiers, but official Washington swooned over him, and he was so quickly snowed with social calls that he "refused invitations to dine today from Genl Scott & four Secy's — had too many things to attend to." Installing himself in a townhouse on Pennsylvania Avenue, he was writing within a week of his appointment that with the "Presdt, Cabinet, Genl Scott & all deferring to me," he seemed "to have become *the* power of the land" and "could become Dictator or anything else that might please me." Soon enough, McClellan was privately whispering that "he wanted to undertake an offensive, but was thwarted by his superior, General Scott," and in November, Lincoln allowed the octogenarian veteran of the War of 1812 to retire quietly and turn command of all of the Union armies, from Missouri to Washington, over to McClellan.

Lincoln was not sure that McClellan would be better able to manage the heaving chaos of federal military mobilization than Scott had been, but once again, as in politics, Lincoln was too inexperienced in military matters and too intimidated by professional soldiers to impose himself directly on McClellan. This "will entail a vast labor upon you," Lincoln warned him, but McClellan only replied, "I can do it all," and Lincoln pressed the question no further. Lincoln was uneasy about leaving everything in McClellan's hands. "He did not pretend to know anything about the handling of troops . . . but he had common sense enough to know that celerity was absolutely necessary; that while armies were sitting down waiting for opportunities to turn up which might, perhaps, be more favorable from a strictly military point of view, the government was spending millions of dollars every day. . . ." But beyond that, he had little choice but to yield all practical control of the war to McClellan, and to put up with McClellan's increasingly dismissive attitude toward him. Lincoln confessed to Winfield Scott "that he knew nothing about the science of war, and it was very important to have just such a person to organize the raw recruits of the Republic around Washington." And since he "was not a military man, it was his duty to defer to General McClellan."

Much of Lincoln's willingness to "defer" was based on his expectation that McClellan genuinely required time and a free hand in organizing the army, and on the general agreement both men had about the war's objects. Like Lincoln, McClellan condemned slavery and swore that "when the day of adjustment comes, I will, if successful, throw my sword into the scale to force an improvement in the condition of those poor blacks." But this war was not the day of adjustment: "I am fighting to preserve the integrity of the Union & the power of the Govt," not to "fight for the abolitionists" or to confiscate and liberate slaves. To the extent that such voices were being heard in Washington, McClellan believed that they would alarm the border states and dampen the response of oppressed Southern Unionists who would, if the war was prosecuted in a restrained and respectful fashion, soon rise up and overthrow the fanatical secessionists running the Confederacy.

McClellan's chief strategic aim was "to display such an overwhelming strength, as will convince our antagonists, especially those of the governing aristocratic class, of the utter impossibility of resistance." "The contest began with a class," McClellan wrote in August of 1861, but "now it is with a people," and the aim of the war would be to divide the vast Unionist majority of the Southern people from the planter class who had deluded them into secession. It relieved McClellan that Lincoln was not pressing for an abolition war. "The president is perfectly honest & is really sound on the nigger question," McClellan wrote to New York Democratic politician Samuel Barlow in November, 1861. "I will answer for it now that things go right with him."

But they did not go right. As the summer of 1861 faded into the autumn, McClellan continued to drill and organize and fortify, but he did not lead a fresh movement into Virginia, or even divulge an over-all plan like the one he had offered in April for bringing the rebel armies across the Potomac and the Ohio to battle. "The autumn passed away in grand reviews and showy parades, where the young General appeared with a numerous staff composed of wealthy young gentlemen, inexperienced, untrained, and unacquainted with military duty," complained Secretary Welles, and "as time wore on and no blow was struck or any decisive movement attempted, complaints became numerous and envy and jealousy found opportunity to be heard." Congressional invitations to dinner changed into congressional inquiries about the Army of the Potomac's inaction. McClellan pled that the rebel army down at Manassas was still too strong to be challenged ("Beauregard probably has 150,000 men — I cannot count more than 55,000," he wailed in mid-August, 1861), and promised that he would be ready to move "without regard to season or weather" as soon as "I have an Army strong enough & well enough instructed to fight with reasonable chances of success."

But the day of readiness arrived no sooner than the day of adjustment for slavery, and McClellan's fears of Beauregard's numbers always mounted as fast as the number of his own recruits. Accordingly, McClellan was deeply embarrassed at the end of September when Confederate fortifications on the Virginia side of the Potomac below Washington were abandoned, only to be found full of dummy artillery — "Quaker guns" — made up from logs, and the criticism that blew his way from Congress was sufficiently heavy to nudge him into sending one of his most trusted subordinates, General Charles P. Stone, with a small Union force over the river on October 21st to brush back other Confederate outposts on the Potomac north of Washington. This time, however, the artillery was real: a federal brigade ran full-tilt into a waiting Confederate brigade at Ball's Bluff, and was knocked heavily back into the river, with the loss of over half the 1,700 men in the expedition. (Another casualty close to Lincoln: among the dead was Edward Dickinson Baker, Lincoln's old legislative ally and the friend for whom he had named his second son, shot through the head while leading a regiment of Pennsylvanians he had raised personally for the war.)

The debacle at Ball's Bluff convinced McClellan of the rectitude of his own caution, and no further actions were planned. But when the Thirty-Seventh Congress assembled for its first regular session in December, Radical Republicans drew exactly the opposite lesson, and darkly accused McClellan and Stone of using the dead of Ball's Bluff as a deliberate excuse for lassitude. Ben Wade and Zachariah Chandler grimly organized a joint House-Senate Committee on the Conduct of the War which became a prime engine for criticizing McClellan and, incidentally, arresting and imprisoning Stone as an object lesson. Even Secretary of War Stanton, who told Heman Dyer that he had been added to the cabinet in Simon Cameron's place largely as "the sincere and devoted friend of General McClellan," grew weary of the Young Napoleon. "Instead of an army stuck in the mud of the Potomac," Stanton erupted, "we should have . . . one hundred thousand men thrusting upon Nashville and sweeping rebellion & treason out of Kentucky with fire & sword."

Lincoln, unhappily, tried to have it both ways, alternately prodding McClellan for action, but backing off when McClellan bristled and shifting the blame for criticism onto "the Jacobins." When "the Jacobin club" demanded on October 26th that Lincoln push McClellan into action, "the President stood up for McClellan's deliberateness." But when Lincoln accosted McClellan, he gingerly told the general that he "deprecated this new manifestation of popular impatience but at the same time said it was a reality and should be taken into account." When McClellan refused, Lincoln hastily agreed, "General, you must not fight till you are ready."

This only convinced McClellan that he was better off digging his heels deeper, burying his own plans more defiantly in secrecy, and treating both Lincoln and the Republicans with mounting contempt. "I am becoming daily more disgusted with this administration — perfectly sick of it," McClellan wrote. "There are some of the greatest geese in the Cabinet I have ever seen." Lincoln soon became "an idiot" in McClellan's estimate. "I can never regard him with feelings other than those of thorough contempt — for his mind, heart, & morality."

One evening in November, McClellan walked past Lincoln as the president sat in the general's parlor, and went upstairs to bed. In late December, McClellan developed typhoid fever from the Washington drinking water and withdrew into his sickroom for two weeks.

As late as the end of the year, Lincoln still had difficulty nerving himself to challenge McClellan, or even demanding that McClellan finally lay out an operational plan for the war. Instead, he warned John Hay that "it was better at this time not to be making points of etiquette and personal dignity." But with every day burning up millions of Congress's wartime appropriations, Lincoln could not keep from throwing up his hands in frustration. "My distress is that our friends in East Tennessee are being hanged and driven to despair, and even now, I fear, are thinking of taking rebel arms for the sake of personal protection," he complained to one officer. To Quartermaster-General Montgomery Meigs he demanded: "General, what shall I do? The people are impatient . . . the General of the Army has typhoid fever. . . . What shall I do?"

The fact that Lincoln would even ask the question confirmed the suspicion of many observers that Lincoln was a mistake. "The Prest. is an excellent man, and, in the main wise," Attorney General Bates told his diary, "but he lacks *will* and *purpose*, and, I greatly fear he, has not *the power to command.*" "Lincoln himself seems to have no *nerve* or decision in dealing with great issues," Ohio Republican representative William Parker Cutler wrote in his diary; and Maine senator William Pitt Fessenden erupted, "If the President had his wife's *will* and would use it rightly, our affairs would look much better." Illinois Democrat William A. Richardson even used the floor of the House to announce that Lincoln "has not the will to stand up against the wily politicians who surround him and knead him to their purposes." When the members of the Joint Committee met with Lincoln and the cabinet on January 6th to plead for some kind of movement across the Potomac, Lincoln admitted that McClellan had confided no plans for an invasion to him, and that as the commanding general, McClellan had to be allowed to run his own show. "The spectacle," wrote George Julian, one of the committee's members, "seemed to us very disheartening."

But by January, Lincoln was sufficiently exasperated by McClellan's inaction that he began reaching for the limp reins of command himself. "If General McClellan did not want to use the army," Lincoln growled, "he would like to borrow it, provided he could see how it could be made to do something." Lincoln began telegraphing McClellan's department commanders — Henry Wager Halleck in Missouri, Don Carlos Buell in Ohio — for information on whatever plans McClellan had communicated to them. Fumblingly, they replied that no such plans had been sent them by McClellan, and so Lincoln began dispatching his own orders, first to Buell, then to Halleck, for an immediate movement into eastern Tennessee to rally Unionists in the Tennessee mountains. Caught between their inert commanding general and an irritated commander in chief, neither Buell nor Halleck would meet Lincoln's "request to name the DAY when they can be ready to move."

Lincoln got better responses when he turned to McClellan's immediate subordinates in Washington. Acting on the advice of Quartermaster-General Meigs, Lincoln called in two of the Army of the Potomac's division commanders, William Franklin and the unhappy Irvin McDowell, who already had a political and personal grievance with McClellan, and on January 10th Lincoln asked them for opinions and plans for new army operations. News of the consultation catapulted McClellan out of his sickbed and into an angry meeting with Lincoln on January 13th, but the ground had shifted decisively under McClellan's feet. On January 27th, Lincoln issued a "General War Order," mandating a general advance southwards by Halleck, Buell, and McClellan no later than Washington's Birthday. "From that time," wrote John Hay, "he influenced actively the operations of the Campaign. He stopped going to McClellan's and sent for the General to come to him."

McClellan reluctantly bestirred himself, and on February 3rd, submitted a comprehensive plan for taking the war onto Confederate territory which involved a more-or-less simultaneous movement to "push Buell either towards Montgomery, or to . . . Georgia" and "to throw Halleck southward to . . . New Orleans." With the Army of the Potomac, McClellan planned to bypass the Confederate "entrenched positions at . . . Manassas," and instead load the Army of the Potomac onto navy transports and sail down the Chesapeake Bay and to "a point of landing" at Urbanna on the lower Rappahannock River. "A rapid movement from Urbanna would . . . enable us to occupy Richmond before it could be strongly reinforced."

301

This was a remarkably good plan, as plans went, and Halleck demonstrated just how good it was in February by sending one of his officers, a former West Pointer from Illinois named Ulysses Simpson Grant, into Tennessee along the Tennessee River, where Grant's 15,000 Union infantry and a flotilla of gunboats easily reduced Fort Henry on February 6th and then Fort Donelson on the Cumberland River on February 16th. The entire western Confederate line collapsed like a pricked balloon, and Confederate troops hastily abandoned all of western Kentucky and western Tennessee and fell back in disorganization all the way to Corinth, in northern Mississippi. Buell occupied Nashville on February 25th, while on March 8th, an outnumbered federal force under General Samuel Curtis trounced 14,000 Confederates at Pea Ridge, Arkansas, and on March 14th, federal troops under General John Pope (who a year before had been one of Lincoln's escorts on the train to Washington) seized New Madrid on the Mississippi River and began laying siege to the Confederacy's most important obstacle in the upper Mississippi, the fort on Island No. 10. "Secesh is about on its last legs in Tennessee," predicted the victorious Ulysses Grant, and as Lincoln had so hopefully expected, Tennessee Unionists like the old Whig parson and newspaper editor William G. Brownlow jubilantly rallied to the old flag with assurances that "Secession is well-nigh played out — the dog is dead."

The one person who seemed to draw no enthusiasm from these successes was George McClellan, and Lincoln was now beginning to suspect why: "because most of the West Point men were Democrats" and were determined to keep the edge off the war so as to prevent either a Republican triumph or the shifting of the war's aim toward emancipation of the slaves and the "revolutionizing" of Southern society. In Congress, "it was asserted that the Army of the Potomac had been drilled into an anti-Republican engine & that not one in a thousand would vote for a Republican." At best, McClellan's preference for a joint naval expedition to the Rappahannock rather than an attack on Manassas was viewed as simply one more example of McClellan's wish to avoid a real confrontation with the Confederates; at worst, it represented a "traitorous intent of removing its defenders from Washington and thus giving over to the enemy the capital and the government thus left defenseless." McClellan was furious when Lincoln repeated this to him at a White House meeting on March 8th, though

Lincoln insisted that he was merely rehearsing "what others had said and that he did not believe a word of it."

What he *had* come to believe, though, was that McClellan had stacked the upper echelons of the Army of the Potomac with politically sympathetic officers, a suspicion which seemed to confirm itself when Lincoln polled McClellan's twelve principal commanders about the Urbanna plan and found that the eight youngest, who owed their advancement to McClellan, all lined up faithfully behind their chief. He was also sure that the Northern people were convinced "that the General does not intend to do anything," and that would sap Union civilian morale. "By a failure like this we lose all the prestige we gained by the capture of Fort Donelson," Lincoln scolded Randolph B. Marcy (McClellan's father-in-law and chief of staff) on February 27th. This was quite enough for Lincoln: at the end of day on March 8th, he issued an order reorganizing the Army of the Potomac into four corps, with each of the senior officers who had dissented from the Urbanna plan in charge of a corps.

If this was a signal to prod McClellan into advancing on Manassas, it did not work, although the actual results made McClellan look foolish. Rather than await a federal attack, the Confederates abandoned their entrenchments at Manassas on March 9th, falling back to the Rappahannock River over the next two days. McClellan cautiously probed the abandoned lines, only to discover that they had been held by less than 50,000 men (fewer than a third of what McClellan had estimated) and by still more phony "Quaker" artillery. The Joint Committee on the Conduct of the War was convinced "that McClellan was a failure" and toyed with presenting a resolution in the House "asking the President to relieve McClellan of command." Lincoln conceded the point, but only in a limited way: he relieved McClellan of his overall command of the Union forces and confined him to the Army of the Potomac, either in hope that this would finally galvanize him into action or in fear that the Army of the Potomac might mutiny if McClellan were removed from that command, too. As it was, McClellan was sufficiently embarrassed by the Manassas fiasco that on March 13th, he announced to a meeting of his corps commanders that he was now ready to begin his great proposed movement by water on the Chesapeake, and four days later, the first elements of the Army of the Potomac were embarked at Alexandria, Virginia.

They did not go to Urbanna, but to Fort Monroe, the stubbornly held federal toehold dominating Virginia's James River peninsula. The withdrawal of the Confederates to the Rappahannock forced McClellan, at the last minute, to shift his base of operations to the James River instead, although that actually put the Army of the Potomac even closer to the rebel capital at Richmond. But the closer McClellan was to Richmond, the more inexplicably slower he moved. Although McClellan's landing at Fort Monroe caught the Confederates napping and left them with only a thin screen of 15,000 men at Yorktown standing between McClellan and Richmond, McClellan convinced himself that a far larger rebel army was dug in at Yorktown, and so he dug himself in to observe the results and bombard Washington with requests for more troops and siege artillery. Lincoln upbraided him on April 9th: "I think it is the precise time for you to strike a blow. By delay the enemy will relatively gain upon you — that is, he will gain faster, by *fortifications* and *re-inforcements*, than you can by re-inforcements alone."

But McClellan did not feel ready to open an attack until May 3rd, by which time the Confederates simply evacuated the Yorktown lines and pulled back toward Richmond. Lincoln had lost so much faith in McClellan's abilities, not to mention McClellan's advice, that he and Salmon Chase came down to Fort Monroe themselves to inspect the situation. And as if to demonstrate how much McClellan's anxieties were the product of his imagination, both civilians directed a little military foray of their own across Hampton Roads which resulted in the recapture of Norfolk, as well as the navy yard which had been abandoned to the Confederates a year before.

Instead of profiting from these manifest signals of Lincoln's increasing independence of action, McClellan and the Army of the Potomac — now swollen to over 100,000 men — continued to crawl up the peninsula with abysmal slowness, until on May 31st, the Confederate army (now under Joe Johnston) launched a preemptive strike on McClellan at Seven Pines. The Confederates were badly bruised in the fight, and Johnston was so seriously wounded that he was put out of action and replaced by Robert E. Lee. But the battle at Seven Pines did nothing to feed McClellan's eagerness for combat, and on June 26th, with the Army of the Potomac still short of Richmond, Lee and the Confederates seized the initiative in a running series of battles known as the Seven Days. Although Lee was actually outnumbered by McClellan and paid a heavy price in casualties for his aggressiveness, McClellan panicked in the face of what he was sure was a Confederate army of overwhelming magnitude. "We are contending at several points against superior numbers," he telegraphed on June 27th, and telegraphed again that evening, "Have had a terrible fight against vastly superior numbers."

Clammy with fear at the prospect of defeat, the perfect general with the perfect managerial skills now began howling in self-pity and lashing out at everyone who had not made matters perfect for him. Past midnight on June 28th, he sent to Washington one of the most astounding messages an American soldier has ever visited upon a civilian administration: "I know that a few thousand men more would have changed this battle from a defeat to a victory — as it is the Govt must not & cannot hold me responsible for the result. . . . If I save this Army now I tell you plainly that I owe no thanks to you or any other persons in Washington — you have done your best to sacrifice this Army." And with that, McClellan pulled the Army of the Potomac back behind a defensive cordon around his supply base at Harrison's Landing, where gunboats in the James River could protect him.

One charge that Lincoln could not endure was the charge of desertion, and he at once sought to scrape together 25,000 men from Halleck's forces in the west for McClellan's army, and approved an appeal on June 30th to state governors for 150,000 men, and again on July 1st for 300,000 volunteers. But he would do nothing more for McClellan himself. "I expect to maintain this contest until successful, or till I die, or am conquered, or my term expires, or Congress and the country forsakes me," he told William Seward, and in an effort to impart some of this determination to McClellan, he again came down to McClellan's army on July 8th to confer with the general. But McClellan was bent upon doing the teaching, not receiving it, and he greeted Lincoln on board the vessel that had brought the president up the James River with a firm, polite, but ultimately defiant letter on what McClellan expected the overall aims of the war were about. With scarcely a glance back at his own defeats on the Peninsula, McClellan's letter proceeded to lecture Lincoln on why the war "should not be a War looking to the subjugation of the people of any state, in any event," and how "neither confiscation of property, political executions of prisoners, territorial organization of

305

states or forcible abolition of slavery should be contemplated for a moment." Any "declaration of radical views, especially upon slavery, will rapidly disintegrate our present armies."

The letter convinced Lincoln that "McClellan would not fight . . . that if by magic he could reinforce McClellan with 100,000 men today, he would be in ecstasy over it, thank him for it, and tell him that he would go to Richmond to morrow; but that when tomorrow came, he would telegraph that he had information that the enemy had 400,000 men and that he could not advance without reinforcements." What was even more evident, however, was that McClellan had persuaded himself that he and his army had been deliberately sacrificed on the Peninsula in the hopes that a defeat would disgrace the cause of moderation and restraint in the war and open the path for Radical Republican abolitionists to convert the war into a crusade for the destruction of black slavery and the white South. Democratic politicians like New York mayor Fernando Wood visited McClellan's headquarters to urge defiance of Lincoln and to "conduct the war in that inefficient conciliatory style."

In that light, McClellan did not feel that his defeats meant anything professionally embarrassing to himself, and his letter was therefore a veiled threat that any further conspiratorial hanky-panky by Lincoln's administration would have dire consequences. Lincoln left for Fort Monroe the next day, and proceeded to Washington where, almost as if to put McClellan firmly in his place, he invited Henry Halleck to leave St. Louis and come east to assume the command of all the federal forces, the position Lincoln had fired McClellan from in March. (Halleck, not McClellan, had been Winfield Scott's preferred choice as commander of the armies back in the previous fall.) And it was Halleck, at Lincoln's prompting, who ordered McClellan to evacuate Harrison's Landing on August 3rd and return to Washington. Lincoln would not take the chance of giving orders directly to McClellan; and he would not actually relieve McClellan of command. Instead, Lincoln and Halleck began feeding pieces of McClellan's army, as they pulled out of their James River base, into a new Army of Virginia, which had been placed under the command of the victor of Island No. 10, John Pope.

In addition to his victory at Island No. 10, Pope had the advantage of being as enthusiastic a Republican as McClellan was a Democrat, confident that the war had to bring an end to slavery and that "it was only a question of prudence as to the means to be employed to weaken it." Among those means were to be methods of dealing with the rebeldom of northern Virginia on a very different basis than McClellan's. He intended to "subsist upon the country," to compel civilians to repair damage done to rail lines by rebel guerrillas, and to confiscate the property — or rather, the slaves — of "disloyal male citizens." But Pope was something less than a military genius, and even his staff officers found him "irascible and impulsive in his judgements of men." And even without McClellan nearby, Pope still had to work with McClellan's division and brigade commanders, most of whom had no intention of working any too eagerly for Pope. "I regret to see," remarked one of McClellan's division commanders, Fitz-John Porter, "that General Pope . . . has now written himself down as what the military world has long known, an ass."

The result, as might have been expected, was a disaster. On August 29th, with substantial parts of the Army of the Potomac still in transit from the James River, Pope blundered into a trap laid by Robert E. Lee on the old Bull Run battlefield. Pope's army lost just over 16,000 men at what became known as Second Bull Run. Rumors flew wildly that the defeat had been an act of McClellanite sabotage. "It is honestly believed by many that a flat, persistent, long-continued failure to obey orders on the part of General McClellan alone prevented them from being . . . successful," wrote the *Cincinnati Gazette*'s premier Washington correspondent, Whitelaw Reid. "It is known that, with thousands of troops surrounding him, General McClellan even refused to send supplies to the suffering and fighting army ahead of him."

Rumors notwithstanding, Lincoln restored McClellan to full command of his troops. "It was humiliating, after what had transpired and all we knew, to reward McClellan and those who failed to do their whole duty in the hour of trial," Lincoln admitted wearily to Secretary Welles, but "personal considerations must be sacrificed for the public good." Lincoln needed to assure the defense of Washington from the rampaging Confederates, and passive defensive roles were at least one thing McClellan seemed competent for. Still, Lincoln strongly suspected that McClellan "wanted Pope defeated" and had dragged his heels in evacuating the Peninsula precisely in order to deprive Pope of enough men to meet Lee. He suspected even more strongly that

McClellan's lieutenants — Fitz-John Porter, in particular — had deliberately wrecked Pope's battle plans and (as he told Orville Hickman Browning) "occasioned our defeat and deprived us of a victory which would have terminated the war." (Porter was, in fact, court-martialed in January, 1863, after McClellan could no longer protect him, and Lincoln privately believed that "the case would have justified, in his opinion, a sentence of death.")

But even if Lincoln was certain that "there has been a design, a purpose in breaking down Pope," he also knew that "McClellan has the army with him." McClellan, in fact, had toyed half-seriously with the notion of "taking my rather large military family to Washington to seek an explanation of their course — I fancy that under such circumstances I should be treated with rather more politeness than I have been of late. . . ." Even if McClellan only fancied the idea, Lincoln had "no remedy at present" for dealing with him. There was also the problem of Robert E. Lee, who was now loose in Maryland, only thirty-five miles northwest of Washington, with 55,000 Confederate soldiers and the possibility that the crowds who had been cowed by federal soldiers the previous year would now rise in delirious joy to greet the Confederates and take Maryland out of the Union. McClellan was the only available alternative.

Happily for Lincoln, McClellan was blessed with the intelligence coup of the century on September 13th when two federal soldiers picked up a lost copy of Lee's campaign orders from the grass near Frederick, Maryland. Waving the lost orders with the promise that "If I cannot whip Bobbie Lee, I will be willing to go home," McClellan swung the reunited Army of the Potomac westward to face Lee, and cornered him between the Potomac and the Antietam Creek at Sharpsburg on September 17th. "Destroy the rebel army, if possible," Lincoln urged McClellan, and the all-day battle of Antietam that followed very nearly did that. By sundown, nearly 13,000 rebels were dead, wounded, or missing , and if McClellan had pressed the day, Lee would probably have been forced to surrender his entire army. But McClellan had also lost over 12,000 men, and with them, he had lost what little energy he had brought to the battle. Lee slipped across the Potomac back into Virginia, and McClellan slipped into a listless lethargy that not even another extended visit from Lincoln in early October could disturb.

308

Lincoln could scarcely believe McClellan's lassitude. "The army of the enemy should have been annihilated," Lincoln told Orville Hickman Browning, "but it was permitted to recross the Potomac without the loss of a man, and McClellan would not follow." That, as he told the *New York Tribune,* "was the last grain of sand which broke the camel's back." "Do you want to know when I gave him up?" Lincoln asked a reporter. "It was after the battle of Antietam." When Lincoln came up the Potomac to McClellan's headquarters in October, his grudging tolerance of McClellan finally collapsed into outright sarcasm. He warned McClellan "that he w[oul]d be a ruined man if he did not move forward, move rapidly & effectively." And as he wandered the borders of McClellan's encampment with Ozias Hatch, the Illinois secretary of state, Lincoln abruptly turned, spread out his arms, and asked Hatch what he saw spread before them.

"Why . . . I suppose it to be part of the grand army."

"No," responded Lincoln, "you are mistaken."

"What are they then?" asked Hatch.

Lincoln paused a moment and then added "in a tone of patient but melancholy sarcasm, 'That is General McClellan's bodyguard.'"

Three weeks later, when McClellan explained that he could not mount a new campaign because his cavalry horses were "absolutely broken down from fatigue," Lincoln savagely wired back, "Will you pardon me for asking what the horses of your army have done since the battle of Antietam that fatigue anything?" But McClellan never seems to have seen the sarcasm for the sign it was. "Mr. Lincoln was the last man to yield to the necessity of McClellan's removal," David Davis assured Leonard Swett. "He wished to give him every chance." But every chance had been squandered. "We are done throwing grass at the rebels," Lincoln had told the *Chicago Tribune*'s Washington correspondent in July; "henceforth he proposed trying stones."

Throwing stones, of course, would mean getting rid of McClellan first and foremost, which Lincoln finally did on November 5th, one day safely past the New York and New Jersey congressional elections in order to mute the potential political damage. Worse damage was likely to come if the Army of the Potomac responded badly to all this, perhaps in the form of a coup, perhaps a military dictatorship. One of his principal reasons for the October visit to McClellan's headquarters was "to satisfy himself personally without the intervention of any-

body, of the purposes, intentions, and fidelity of McClellan, his officers, and the army," which indicates just how much doubt there was in
Lincoln's mind about all three. He had already heard whisperings that
members of McClellan's staff were boasting that McClellan had deliberately halted pursuit after Antietam because "that was not the game,
that we should tire the rebels out, and ourselves, that that was the only
way the union could be preserved, we come together fraternally, and
slavery be saved." And when Major John J. Key, one of Halleck's staff
and brother of McClellan's judge advocate, was fingered as the source
of these rumors, Lincoln had Key cashiered, and later refused to hear
any appeal.

By dismissing McClellan, Lincoln was taking the greatest political risk of his life, and perhaps in the history of the republic. "I knew
that his dismissal would provoke popular indignation and shake the
faith of the people in the final success of the war," Lincoln admitted to
Noah Brooks; and Ozias Hatch warned Lincoln that letters had been
circulated to McClellan from "one of General Lee's aides . . . suggesting that Genl. McClellan turn his army around, march upon Washington . . . and take charge of the government." And all through the Army
of the Potomac, remembered one Pennsylvania officer, "there was considerable swearing indulged in, and threats of marching on Washington, should McClellan but take the lead." But for Lincoln it was a risk
for which there were no longer any alternatives. Lincoln had "tried
long enough to bore with an augur too dull to take hold." The months
of Lincoln's presidential apprenticeship, when the long deficit of experience had translated into deference and hesitation, were now over.

And besides, he now had assurances of success from another
quarter.

8 Voice Out of the Whirlwind

Lincoln was never again as confiding with his generals as he had been with Scott and McClellan at the start. For that matter, he was never again as confiding with his cabinet as he was during the Sumter crisis, and as for Congress, Thaddeus Stevens once snortingly claimed that Lincoln's only friend in the House was Isaac Arnold, the one-time Democrat from Chicago. The multiple disappointments and frustrations of his first year as an administrator taught him to retreat into the reticence of the circuit lawyer, increasingly unwilling to lay out large-scale plans even to his closest associates or to show that he was leaning to anyone else's. "Lincoln never confided to me anything," David Davis complained in later years, "He said he ran the machine himself." And while he "listened patiently to all that had an idea," he "asked no man advice" and "took no mans advice." If anything, he delighted in putting the over-curious off the track by painstakingly pointing out to them every sign of danger or dissonance in the path they were recommending, even though he personally planned to follow exactly that path. He preferred to keep up constantly the appearance of being led by the case rather than leading the jury, casting his real wishes as hypotheses and inviting his hearers to think of the unpleasant consequences if this or that should be the result, always avowing the most

311

minimal of intentions and yet always ending with a tantalizing, almost off-hand suggestion that some dramatic new development might be over the hill of the next argument. "He liked to feel that he was the attorney of the people, not their ruler," Noah Brooks wrote, "and I believe that this idea was generally uppermost in his mind." Davis took this reticence as a sign of Lincoln's contempt, but it was just as much a desire on Lincoln's part to keep his decision making free from the influence of others. He had criticized himself earlier for being too pliant, too willing to yield to the expertise of others. "It's a fortunate thing I wasn't born a woman," he quipped to Herndon, "for I cannot refuse anything, it seems." Now he backed into his own personal corner to be sure that what he was doing was really *his* doing. He had no "disposition to make my own personal will supreme," he explained to a Missouri delegation; he simply wanted to "preserve one friend within me, whoever else fails me, to tell me . . . that I have acted right."

Some people claimed to see great differences in him from the old days in Illinois. Brooks, who had known Lincoln briefly in Illinois and who arrived in Washington in 1862 to cover the capital for the *Sacramento Daily Union*, thought Lincoln was "grievously altered from the happy-faced Springfield lawyer of 1856. . . . His hair is grizzled, his gait is more stooping, his countenance sallow, and there is a sunken deathly look about the large, cavernous eyes, which is saddening to those who see there the marks of care and anxiety. . . ." Others were convinced that his trials as president had finally brought him to religion. Joseph Gillespie thought "his mind was unsettled on religious matters until his election . . . after that, it seemed to me that he became religiously inclined." Brooks claimed years later that Lincoln had developed "the habit of daily prayer," that after his election he had undergone "a process of crystallization" in religious faith. Even Lincoln's long-ago friend Joshua Speed (whom Lincoln now turned to as a listening-post for public opinion in the border states) thought that "after he was elected President, he sought to become a believer — and to make the Bible a preceptor to his faith and a guide for his conduct."

But these hopeful opinions were usually exaggerations, magnified by Lincoln's sudden prominence or a friendly desire to provide what seemed inexplicably absent in Lincoln's character. "Mr. Lincoln did not, to my knowledge, in any way change his religious ideas, opinions or beliefs from the time he left Springfield to the day of his death,"

John Nicolay firmly averred in 1865, and hardly anyone was in a better position to know than Lincoln's chief-of-staff. "I do not know just what they were, never having heard him explain them in detail; but I am very sure he gave no outward indication of his mind having undergone any change in that regard while here."

Especially for those who had not known Lincoln before the war, Lincoln's comfortable resort to biblical language made it easy to impute some form of piety to him. Stephen Douglas had complained in 1858 about Lincoln's "proneness for quoting Scripture," and Lincoln lost none of that penchant after becoming president. When William Speer wrote to Lincoln in 1860, hoping to draw out some new comment on Lincoln's policies, Lincoln told Speer that his opinions were "in print, and open to all who will read," and added pungently: "If they hear not Moses and the prophets, neither will they be persuaded though one rose from the dead." When he was greeted in Philadelphia on the route bringing him to the inauguration, he declared that "All my political warfare has been in favor of the teachings" of the revolutionary generation who had once gathered there: "May my right hand forget its cunning and my tongue cleave to the roof of my mouth, if ever I prove false to those teachings." To a disgruntled general who appealed to Lincoln to overrule his arrest and dismissal, Lincoln would only reply that "the permanent estimate of what a general does in the field, is fixed by the 'cloud of witnesses' who have been with him in the field." When he came upon a series of Henry Ward Beecher's impatient editorials in the *New York Independent*, criticizing his administration for timidity, Lincoln irritably asked out loud, "Is thy servant a *dog*, that he should do this thing?" He could even refer to Jesus as "the Saviour," as he had during the senatorial campaign against Douglas in 1858 ("The Saviour, I suppose, did not expect that any human creature could be perfect as the Father in Heaven . . .") and in his "Lecture on Discoveries" ("the language of the Saviour . . . indicates that, even in the populous city of Jerusalem . . .").

But he never spoke, in the language of evangelical Christianity, of Jesus as *my* Savior, and his repertoire of biblical citations was more a cultural habit rather than a religious one, to provide "lines to fit any occasion." He could respect the rationalism of Old School arguments for belief, and even admire the moral tone and self-transformative power that evangelical Protestantism could impart to a competitive society of upwardly mobile strivers. But he remained a Victorian child of the Enlightenment, of Paine and Burns and Mill — and, as the Old School apologists had unwittingly demonstrated to Lincoln, the Enlightenment could nestle quite comfortably inside the hollow shell of Lincoln's ancestral Calvinism. "He read the Bible quite as much for its literary style as he did for its religious or spiritual content," commented Julia Taft Bayne, who (with her brothers) provided playmate and baby-sitting services for the Lincoln children in the White House. "He read it in the relaxed, almost lazy attitude of a man enjoying a good book." Orville Hickman Browning, who often went to the New York Avenue Presbyterian Church with the Lincolns and then spent "the afternoon with him in the Library," could recall Lincoln frequently reading the Bible, "but never knew of his engaging in any other act of devotion. He did not invoke a blessing at table, nor did he have family prayers. What private religious devotions may have been customary with him I do not know. I have no knowledge of any."

At least the Bible Lincoln could take on his own terms. The preachers were another matter. He told Newton Bateman in 1860 that he expected few preachers to vote for him, either because they did not trust his religious preferences or because they were overwhelmingly pro-slavery. "I shall be vindicated," he told Bateman, "and these men will find that they have not read their Bibles aright." But even then, Lincoln could not entirely reconcile himself to the indifference the Bible displayed toward slavery. One of his rare written eruptions in the 1850s occurred after reading Old School Presbyterian Frederick Augustus Ross's *Slavery Ordained of God* (1857), a collection of Ross's addresses to the Old School Presbyterian General Assembly defending slavery as a beneficent institution. "Nonsense!" Lincoln scrawled. "Wolves devouring lambs, not because it is good for their own greedy maws, but because it is good for the lambs!!!" What little reading he did in theology in the White House was, not surprisingly, focused on the classics of rationalist apologetics. He "particularly liked Butler's Analogy of Religion," recalled Noah Brooks, "and he always hoped to get at [Jonathan] Edwards on the Will."

It was not preachers, but actors, humorists, and poets whose company Lincoln enjoyed. He loved the uproarious satires of fellow-Illinoisan David R. Locke (who wrote a syndicated humor column under the pseudonym *Petroleum Vesuvius Nasby*), R. H. Newell (who poked fun at Washington officialdom as *Orpheus C. Kerr*, the "office-seeker"), and Charles F. Browne (the creator of the semi-literate backwoods schemer *Artemus Ward*). "For the ability to write the queer, quaint and good things," Browne wrote in his Artemus Ward sketches, "I'd give up my office tomorrow." The radical poetry of his youth, especially Burns, remained dear to his heart, and Isaac Arnold remembered hearing Lincoln deliver "a lecture" on Burns "full of favorite quotations and sound criticism." He was still capable of reciting William Knox's "Mortality" by heart to Francis Carpenter, and Noah Brooks was surprised to discover that Lincoln "appeared to prefer [Thomas] Hood and [Oliver Wendell] Holmes . . . beyond any thing else which he read." When he found that Orville Hickman Browning had never read Hood's "The Haunted House," Lincoln "rang his bell — sent for Hood's poems and read the whole of it to me, pausing occasionally to comment on passages which struck him as particularly felicitous." (On the other hand, Lincoln remained too much the rationalist to have much relish for the arch-sentimentalist among American poets, Henry Wadsworth Longfellow; characteristically, he liked only Longfellow's hackneyed paean to duty, "A Psalm of Life," and his anticlerical satire, "The Birds of Killingworth.")

But Lincoln's greatest affection was reserved for the theater, and at no point was his real departure from the norms of evangelical Protestantism more clear. Both evangelical Protestants and even many secular Whigs were deeply suspicious of the theater, since they understood all too well that actors in nineteenth-century America were the principal rivals of preachers in setting out and legitimizing culture. Acting itself offered a rival form of personal transformation to evangelical conversion, and urban theaters were often raucous and vulgar, with prostitutes commonly plying their trade in the upper tier. For secular Whigs, the straining, thunderous style of antebellum actors like Edwin Forrest reeked too heavily of hedonism and self-display, and was too reminiscent of the passionate theatricality of Democratic political rhetoric for Whiggish comfort. The secular Whig answer was to transform the theater by the pressures of the market, enticing it into submission to middle-class tastes by the promise of large new middle-class audiences, and by the 1850s, the theater was becoming rapidly gentrified through the example of Moses Kimball's Boston Museum and P. T. Barnum's American Museum, which expelled the prostitutes, moralized the dramas, and disciplined the audiences. But evangelical hostility remained unmoved. The great Chicago Baptist E. J. Goodspeed denounced theaters as "royal roads to perdition" and refused to believe that actors could "be considered suitable companions for our children, or visitors in our homes." The greatest single cultural triumph of the evangelicals was Charles Grandison Finney's transformation of the notorious Chatham Garden Theater in New York City into the Chatham Street Chapel in 1832.

But Lincoln loved the theater, especially Shakespeare (who remained throughout the years before the war the most popular playwright among American audiences). "It matters not to me whether Shakespeare be well or ill acted," he remarked to Francis Carpenter, "with him the thought suffices." A good deal of that thought came easily to memory: he could quote Shakespeare with almost as much facility as the Bible, unself-consciously describing his proposals for gradually ending slavery as falling "as gently as the dews of heaven" *(The Merchant of Venice)*, and describing his own policies as "never having willingly planted a thorn in any man's bosom" *(Hamlet)*. Once in Washington, Lincoln took every opportunity to be a regular theatergoer, attending the opera nineteen times (for Bellini's *Norma* and Donizetti's *Fille du Régiment*), visiting Leonard Grover's National Theater on E Street twenty-one times, and John Ford's Theater (itself a converted Baptist church, rebuilt after a fire in 1863 as a "magnificent new Thespian temple") on 10th Street at least ten times during his presidency. There, without fear of serious interruption by office-seekers or generals, usually in the company of his secretaries or an invited politician or just his footman, Charles Forbes, Lincoln could indulge his passion for the stage. "I think nothing equals Macbeth," he wrote to the noted American Shakespearean, James Henry Hackett, in 1863. "It is wonderful." Leonard Grover, quick to notice that box-office receipts went up whenever it was known that the president would be coming to the theater, artfully invited Lincoln to suggest "any of the other plays of Shakespeare" he might like to have Grover produce, and Lincoln was on hand when Grover opened the National Theater in October 1863 with a new production of *Othello*.

He was just as willing to become his own theater, if needs be. One summer night in 1863, Lincoln "read Shakespeare" to John Hay, "the end of Henry VI and the beginning of Richard III till my heavy eye-lids

316

caught his considerate notice & he sent me to bed." He was not at all shy about requesting personal interviews with his favorite performers. The greatest American Shakespearean family of the day were the Booths — father Junius Brutus, and sons Edwin, Junius the younger, and John Wilkes — all of whom lionized the Washington stage. (John Wilkes Booth's performances in *The Merchant of Venice, Richard III*, and Charles Selby's *The Marble Heart* so impressed Lincoln that, according to George Alfred Townsend, Lincoln applauded him "rapturously" and sent an invitation to Booth to come up to the presidential box after an 1863 performance of *The Marble Heart*, "but Booth evaded the interview.") Lincoln also admired John McCulloch (whom Lincoln called up to the presidential box to talk Shakespearean shop after a sensational performance in *King Lear*) and Hackett, whose role as Falstaff Lincoln not only followed through *Henry IV Part 2* and *The Merry Wives of Windsor*, but whom Lincoln actually brought to the White House for a private performance. Even the popular comic Stephen Massett ("Jeems Pipes, of Pipesville," according to his stage name) gave Lincoln "a very informal and perfectly private" show in the Red Room.

Nor was Lincoln shy about testing his critical acumen. Anticipating an opportunity to see Edwin Booth in *Richard III*, Lincoln indulged a little theatrical criticism by informing Francis Carpenter that "the opening of the play of 'King Richard the Third' seems to me often entirely misapprehended," and after watching Edwin Forrest in *King Lear* at Ford's Theater in 1865, he allowed that he did have "one reproach to make of Shakespeare's heroes — that they make long speeches when they are killed." He told Hay that Hackett's "reading of a passage where Hackett said, 'Mainly *thrust* at me' . . . should be read 'mainly thrust at *me*,'" and criticized "the dying speech of Hotspur" as "an unnatural and unworthy thing — as who does not." Hackett saluted Lincoln's amateur criticism by sending Lincoln a copy of his own *Notes and Comments upon Certain Plays and Actors of Shakespeare*, and in reply Lincoln made another "small attempt at criticism" by suggesting that, "unlike you gentlemen of the profession, I think the soliloquy in Hamlet commencing 'O, my offense is rank' surpasses that commencing, 'To be or not to be.'" That soliloquy, Lincoln told Francis Carpenter, "always struck me as one of the finest touches of nature in the world."

317

Quoting alternately from the Bible and Shakespeare, Lincoln managed by small gestures to please and amuse both secular and evangelical Whigs, without alluding to the larger and more provocative fundamental problems behind them. He would not attack Christian denominations but he would not join them, either; he would quote Scripture, but more by way of proverb and illustration than authority; and he would pay pew rent in churches and occasionally turn up there on Sundays, but more as a matter of intellectual respect for any religion that painted the same backdrop of necessity, providence, and predestination which colored his own perceptions of the world. He remained, by any technical definition, an "infidel," but it was an infidelity with a darkly Calvinistic twist which convinced Lincoln that he had no will to embrace Christianity even if he had wanted to. "I never heard him pray or saw him in the attitude of prayer," Julia Taft Bayne recalled. "In that day many families conducted some sort of family worship . . . but I do not remember that the Lincoln family did."

That he could perform this straddling as easily as he did was due to a certain slipperiness that was already available in Protestant thinking, and especially in key concepts like *providence*. In the hands of Old School theologians, *providence* was a description of how God directly governed the universe; God not only creates the world, but superintends its activities at every successive point. "God not only sees the end from the beginning," wrote the doyen of Old School Presbyterianism, Charles Hodge, but "an infinitely wise, good, and powerful God is everywhere present, controlling all events great and small . . . so that everything is ordered by his will and is made to subserve his wise and benevolent designs." But *providence* might not necessarily mean that a self-conscious deity was superintending the works; the "infidel" writers whom the young Lincoln had so admired also spoke of *providence*, but instead used it to describe how natural processes worked generally to secure harmony and progress in the universe. The term *providence* had a certain politeness and orderliness to it which allowed Presbyterian theologians to affect an atmosphere of respectful restraint in describing the power of God, while allowing Paine-ite deists to pass for believers in some form of personal God. "Nothing is easier than to use the word, and mean nothing by it," John Henry Newman complained in 1852. If "you do but mean a Being who keeps the world in order, who acts in it, but only in the way of general Providence, who acts towards us but only through what are called laws of Nature, who is more certain not to act at all than to act independent of those laws . . . such piety is nothing more than a poetry of thought or an ornament of language."

Lincoln could, on those terms, speak quite freely about *providence* in the 1850s without seeming to cross the religious sensibilities of his neighbors — in fact, to flatter them — and yet without also committing himself to what his neighbors believed. "The providence of God" gave America Henry Clay, he said in the eulogy he delivered in Springfield after Clay's death in April, 1852, and he recommended that Clay's mourners "strive to deserve, as far as mortals may, the continued care of Divine Providence, trusting that, in future national emergencies, He will not fail to provide us the instruments of safety and security." But this might mean only that there was a kind of historical or material logic to human affairs which could be counted on, like Tom Paine's "vast machinery," to produce certain responses to certain needs. The only thing anyone knew for certain, as Jesse Fell told Ward Lamon, was that Lincoln "fully believed in a superintending and overruling Providence that guides and controls the operations of the world, but maintained that law and order, not their violation and suspension, are the appointed means by which this Providence is exercised." There is nothing to suggest that Lincoln saw personal will behind those operations. Back in 1850, when Stephen Douglas attributed the death of Zachary Taylor in office to "the hand of Providence," Lincoln mocked Douglas's sudden rise to religion and the idea of "special interference of Providence, against the people, and in favor of Locofocoism." Lincoln might say that "God rules," but the moral of that rule was not that God would hear prayer and appeals to his rule, but that "we should submit &c."

Little of this changed once he was elected president. The brief farewell speech that Lincoln gave on the morning he left Springfield movingly described "my feeling of sadness at this parting," a sadness made all the greater for realizing that the "task before me" would be "greater than that which rested upon Washington." And he added what was, for all practical purposes, a routine invocation of *providence:*

Without the assistance of that Divine Being, who ever attended him, I cannot succeed. With that assistance I cannot fail. Trusting in Him, who can go with me, and remain with you and be every where for good, let us confidently hope that all will yet be well. To His care commending you, as I hope in your prayers you will commend me, I bid you an affectionate farewell.

This said a great deal less than it seemed, and even the use of the term *Divine Being* was actually a bloodless way of speaking about God, on a par with the conventional deistic preference for speaking of God in gigantic circumlocutions — Great Mover, Almighty Architect, Almighty Hand, Great Disposer of Events. Little in the rest of his whistlestop progress toward the inauguration went beyond the political, apart from a handful of references to "that God who has never forsaken" the American people, and a peculiar self-description in a short address to the New Jersey senate as "an humble instrument in the hands of the Almighty, and of this, his almost chosen people." But Lincoln made no claim to any personal interest in the Almighty, and his inaugural address showed virtually no imprint of religious vocabulary, apart from two faint references to his constitutional oath "registered in Heaven" and the "better angels" who would touch the "mystic chords of memory" like some celestial harp. Even then, the "better angels" were the messengers "of our nature," not of God's.

Allusions to the superintendence of *providence* continued to surface in Lincoln's public papers through the first year of the war with some of the same ambiguity and conventionality as before, only now more frequently. When the historian George Bancroft told him of his confidence that the "civil war is the instrument of Divine Providence to root out social slavery," Lincoln politely acknowledged "the main thought" but added that it represented a matter "with which I must deal in all due caution, and with the best judgement I can bring to it." His first annual message to the new Congress in December, 1861, simply urged "a reliance on Providence, all the more firm and earnest," and he promised a visiting committee of Baltimore Methodists in May, 1862, that "By the help of an all-wise Providence, I shall endeavor to do my duty." To a delegation of evangelical Lutherans he reaffirmed the appeal of "this Government" to "the Divine Being who determines the destinies of nations that this shall remain a united people."

But far from this suggesting any increased religious sensibility on Lincoln's part, Nicolay was correct in seeing that Lincoln was only re-

320

establishing the same indifferent religious patterns in Washington as he had in Springfield, which was to say, a certain cultural friendliness as a Whig to religious morality and a vague willingness publicly to identify himself with Christian churches. Washington's First Presbyterian Church, which liked to advertise itself as the "church of the presidents" because Jackson, Polk, Pierce, and Buchanan had rented a pew there, offered Lincoln the use of the same pew as his predecessors, but sitting in the pew of the Jacksonians was not Lincoln's idea of comfort. "I wish to find a church whose clergyman holds himself aloof from politics," he told Montgomery Blair, but what he really meant was a church that would not brim with Democratic politics, and by mid-April, the Lincolns had gravitated toward the New York Avenue Presbyterian Church, where the Old School pastor, Phineas Densmore Gurley, was safely anti-slavery and anti-secession. There, the Lincolns rented a pew for fifty dollars a year on the right hand side of the center aisle.

A student of Charles Hodge and Archibald Alexander at Princeton Seminary, Gurley had impeccable, if unexciting, Old School credentials. He had first served Old School Presbyterian congregations in Indianapolis and Dayton, and had come to Washington in 1854 as pastor of the F Street Presbyterian Church. When the F Street Church combined with Second Presbyterian to form the New York Avenue Presbyterian Church in July, 1859, Gurley was retained as the pastor. There was much that Lincoln admired in Gurley's rhetorical gifts as a preacher, and he once remarked to John Hay that it had to be a good sign that Gurley's "faith in ultimate success" in the war was so vast. Gurley "spoke with an authoritative air of sincerity," and "his preaching was confined with remarkable closeness to the great central doctrines of the cross," but, happily, he also managed to stay away from politics. John DeFrees believed that Lincoln "had several conversations with the Rev. P. D. Gurley . . . on the subject of religion," and on at least three occasions Lincoln allowed Gurley to present petitions for pardons or appointments. Yet Lincoln never developed a particularly close relationship with Gurley, apart from inviting Gurley to the White House from time to time and allowing Gurley to be generally understood by Washington society as the Lincolns' pastor.

He was no more eager to welcome the delegations of clergymen who appeared in his White House office vestibule "almost daily" in the first year of the war, bold with confidence about what the will of God was for Abraham Lincoln to do. "I hope it will not be irreverent for me to say that if it is probable that God would reveal his will to others, on a point so connected with my duty," Lincoln twitted a group of Chicago divines in September, 1862, "it might be supposed he would reveal it directly to me." Another delegation "from the West," led by a "fault-finding" clergyman of "uncontrollable zeal," was dismissed out-of-hand by Lincoln: "The persons managing the ship of state in this storm are doing the best they can. . . . Keep silence, be patient, and we will get you safe across. Good day, gentlemen, I have other duties pressing upon me that must be attended to." An even more impatient delegation of Quakers from the Philadelphia Yearly Meeting who presented him with a highly critical petition were dismissed (according to Pennsylvania congressman William D. Kelley) "with an asperity of manner of which I had not deemed him capable." He even met the representatives of the Christian Commission in the East Room of the White House with a bit of Calvinistic counter-theology when he told them, "You owe me no gratitude for what I have done . . . and I, I may say, owe you no gratitude for what you have done" since "this has all been for us a work of duty."

And yet Lincoln still believed that religion, if not certain religious leaders, needed to play a public role in the formation of a Whiggish national culture. The "moral training" of evangelical religion and the "hopes and consolation of the Christian faith," Lincoln wrote in 1863, were the best cultural mechanisms for promoting "elevated and sanctifying influences." Where the Jeffersonians had regarded even the slightest hint of public support for religion as a contradiction of Democratic principles, Whigs — even secular Whigs — had welcomed the injection of moralism into public life and tended to favor virtually any sponsorship of public religion short of outright establishment by tax monies. So, whereas Democratic presidents resisted the appointment of chaplains for the army and the issuance of presidential thanksgiving proclamations, Lincoln had no hesitation in May, 1861, about expanding chaplaincy services and specifically asked Congress to approve his appointment of seven hospital chaplains who had not been provided for in the expanded army statutes. More symbolically, he issued calls for days of "Public humiliation, prayer and fasting" and proclamations for days of thanksgiving (the first, in November, 1861, was just for the District of Columbia; the others, in April, 1862, July and October, 1863, May and July, 1864, and September and October, 1864, were intended to be national days of thanksgiving and became the pattern for the modern November "thanksgiving" holiday). He also handed diplomatic posts to politically friendly clergymen, including James Smith, who had retired to Dundee, Scotland, and needed the Dundee consular stipend to live on. And almost as if in echo of the failed evangelical campaigns of the 1820s to get Sunday mail deliveries suspended, Lincoln issued a military directive in November, 1862, designating "the orderly observance of the Sabbath by the officers and men" as "the sacred rights of Christian soldiers and sailors." Sunday duties were to be limited to "the measure of strict necessity" so as to avoid "the profanation of the day or the name of the Most High." One of the infrequent occasions he took to participate in a public celebration outside the White House was the anniversary convention of the Christian Commission in February, 1864.

But none of this contained any suggestion that it represented Lincoln's personal predilections. Acknowledging the vigorous support his administration received from the million-and-a-half Northern Methodists, Lincoln told one delegation in 1864 that "We could never have gotten through this crusade without the steady influence of the Methodist Episcopal Church," but he showed no inclination to join it, or even to attend Methodist preaching. The Sabbath observance directive was predicated equally on "a due regard for the Divine will" and the more practical consideration of "a becoming deference to the best sentiment of a Christian people." (Nor was Lincoln entirely unique in this inspiration, since George McClellan twice issued Sabbath-observance instructions to the Army of the Potomac in the fall of 1861.) The expansion of the chaplaincy paid immediate dividends to Protestant clergy, but it was also partly designed to include Jewish chaplains. For the first year of the war, chaplaincy appointments were restricted to ordained clergy of "Christian denominations," but in December, 1861, Rabbi Arnold Fischel personally prevailed on Lincoln to open military chaplains' appointments to Jews, and he promised Fischel he would sponsor "a new law broad enough to cover what is desired by you in behalf of the Israelites." Which he did, and in July, 1862, the statutory restriction of the chaplaincy to Christian clergy was dropped in favor of a blander limitation to the clergy of "religious denominations." Even the thanksgiving proclamations were largely bland recognitions of the need to acknowledge "submission to the Divine Will" and "the watchful providence of Almighty God." (At least one of them, for 1863, was not even written by Lincoln at all, but by Seward.)

And as much as he might welcome chaplains in the army or thanksgiving in the home, he also had no demonstrable wish to see matters go further. Secretary of War Stanton took unusual liberties in instructing federal department commanders in Missouri, Tennessee, and the Carolinas to oust from their churches clergy sympathetic to the rebels, and replace them with loyalist ministers from the North. But in 1864, border state Methodists appealed Stanton's interference directly to Lincoln, and Lincoln ordered Stanton to desist. When Samuel McPheeters, the pastor of the Pine Street Presbyterian Church in St. Louis, was expelled from Missouri in 1862 by General Samuel Curtis for "unmistakeable evidence of sympathy with the rebellion," Lincoln canceled the order — not out of sympathy for Old Schoolers like McPheeters, but because "the U.S. government must not . . . undertake to run the churches . . . but let the churches, as such take care of themselves."

In 1864, the National Association for the Amendment of the Constitution proposed to Lincoln that the preamble of the Constitution be rewritten to recognize "the rulership of Jesus Christ and the supremacy of the divine law" and "the Lord Jesus Christ as the Governor among the Nations." Although the association had the backing of the Old School Presbyterian General Assembly, and managed to recruit the endorsement of eleven Methodist and Episcopal bishops and a future U.S. Supreme Court associate justice, William Strong, Lincoln received the association's petition coolly, and all the more so because their appeal had taken his proclamations as "pleasing evidence that God is graciously inclining the hearts of those who are in authority over us to recognize His hand in the affairs of the nation." Lincoln had no intention of allowing his own words to be quoted back to him: "The general aspect of your movement I cordially approve," Lincoln replied, but "In regard to particulars I must ask time to deliberate, as the work of amending the Constitution should not be done hastily." The time, of course, never came. His annual message to Congress in December, 1864, "did contain a paragraph calling the attention of Congress to the subject," but for the final version Lincoln had the government printer, John D. De Frees, eliminate it, "remarking that he had not made up his mind as to its propriety." Public endorsements of religion would be determined by political, not theological, considerations, which meant that on that score, Lincoln remained the sort of secular Whig that evangelical Protestants had always regarded as the weak link in the Whig chain.

But if Lincoln began his presidency still coolly balanced between promoting a civil religion of Whiggish morality and practicing a private nonreligion composed of "Laws" that "ruled everything, everywhere, both matter and mind from the beginning to the end, if there was a beginning and an end," the war would force on Lincoln the possibility of a providence which was more than a general cosmic process. One Sunday afternoon after First Bull Run, Orville Hickman Browning (who had been appointed by Illinois governor Richard Yates to fill Stephen A. Douglas's Senate seat) pressed him "substantially" to realize that "we can't hope for the blessing of God on the efforts of our armies, until we strike a decisive blow at the institution of slavery." But, Lincoln countered, "Browning, suppose God is against us in our view on the subject of slavery in this country, and our method of dealing with it?" Browning was "much struck" by Lincoln's odd reply, "which indicated to me for the first time that he was thinking deeply of what a higher power than man sought to bring about by the great events then transpiring."

More than that, it suggested that Lincoln's notion of providence was softening under the pressure of the war and its losses into something more personal and perhaps more inscrutable and infinitely less routine. This did not mean, as Joshua Speed hoped, that "Mr. Lincoln was a growing man in Religion," or as James Matheny had heard it rumored, "that Mr. Lincoln became a Christian." Leonard Swett was just as convinced in 1866 as Nicolay that Lincoln had not "changed his religious opinions towards the close of his life." But Lincoln was reaching backwards for an older concept of providence than the Enlightenment's mechanistic concept of necessity was liable to yield. He warned the importunate Quakers whom he had dismissed with such "asperity" in June of 1862 that "God's way of accomplishing the end which the memorialists have in view may be different from theirs," and in

325

October he replied to the English Quaker Eliza P. Gurney with the warning that if his efforts as president failed to save the Union, "I must believe that for some purpose unknown to me, He wills it otherwise . . . and we must believe that He permits it for some wise purpose of his own, mysterious and unknown to us; and though with our limited understandings we may not be able to comprehend it, yet we cannot but believe it, that he who made the world still governs it."

All of this might still be written down as simply more of Lincoln's prudent concessions to other people's religious sensibilities and vocabulary, were it not for a private memorandum Lincoln composed in September, 1862, after the debacle at Second Bull Run, when Washington again seemed likely to fall into Confederate hands and when Lincoln was staring at the unappetizing inevitability of reappointing George McClellan to command of the Army of the Potomac. As if in an effort to sort out on paper what his anxieties would not let him cope with otherwise, Lincoln began with a simple axiom: "The will of God prevails." That much no one disagreed with, no matter what their definition of God. That was followed by a second axiom: "In great contests each party claims to act in accordance with the will of God." That much, too, was an observable fact, both from what he knew of pro-slavery clergymen in the South and from the delegations that came parading through his office. By now, however, some inkling of which party was correct should have emerged, and every confidence Lincoln had in the inevitable necessities of history had led him to expect a victory of some sort for the Union. Leonard Swett remarked years later that Lincoln "believed the results to which certain causes tended, would surely follow; he did not believe that those results could be materially hastened, or impeded." This, after all, had been the logic of history he had assumed in his 1859 "Lecture on Discoveries" — science, literacy, progress all marched irresistibly upwards over time; the idea of slavery winning a permanent repeal of that progress was unthinkable. Hence, there should be no expectation that the war would turn out to be other than a vindication of freedom.

But this was not what had happened. Therefore, "in the present civil war," Lincoln had to confront the unsettling possibility that providence was guided by more than mere cause and effect, that a more mysterious and unpredictable purpose guided human events, that "God's purpose is something different from the purpose of either

party." The evidence that this might be the case stemmed from the simple fact that the war was allowed to continue, despite being waged in
the name of liberty, progress, and freedom, and especially to continue
to the very brink of destroying the Union. The continuity of history
which Lincoln confidently laid out in the "Lecture on Discoveries"
now dangled inexplicably in the balance, and the only explanation for
such an interruption had to be the intervention of an intelligent will. "I
am almost ready to say this is probably true — that God wills this contest, and wills that it shall not end yet." Much as God "could give the
final victory to either side any day," yet he had not. "The contest proceeds," and for Lincoln that opened the terrifying conclusion that the
war — and God — had another purpose than merely confirming that
the North (or the South) fully understood what they were doing, and
that one of them consequently was right.

The memorandum (Nicolay and Hay later gave it the title "Meditation on the Divine Will") ended there, but even on those short terms,
it contains the most radically metaphysical question ever posed by an
American president. Lincoln had come, by the circle of a lifetime and
the disasters of the war, to confront once again the Calvinist God who
could not be captured or domesticated into Tom Paine's Almighty Architect, who possessed a conscious will to intervene, challenge, and re-
shape human destinies without regard for historical process, the voice
out of the whirlwind speaking to the American Job. It did not mean
that he had given up hope for Union victory in the war. When his old
mentor, John Todd Stuart, visited him in 1865, Stuart assured him that
he believed "that Providence is carrying on this thing."

> Said he with great emphasis in reply:
> "Stuart that is just my opinion."
> Considering our manner of approaching the subject — the late-
> ness of the hour — the emphasis and evident sincerity of his answer,
> I think he meant and felt all he said — I am sure he had no possible
> motive for saying what he did unless it came from a deep and settled
> conviction.

But it did mean that whenever the victory came, it might have a different meaning for Lincoln than just an automatic endorsement of the
Union as perpetually and unarguably right, that it would have a pur-

pose "different from the purpose . . . either party" had carried into the war. When Iowa congressman James F. Wilson and the Iowa congressional delegation told Lincoln that he must do right so that God would give victory to the Union, Lincoln replied, "My faith is greater than yours. I not only believe that Providence is not unmindful of the struggle . . . but I also believe that he will compel us to do right . . . not so much because we desire them as that they accord with His plans of dealing with this nation. . . ."

Recognizing in *providence* the intervention of a divine personality rather than simply forces or laws did not relieve Lincoln's strained sense of distance from religion. If anything, it only reinforced for Lincoln personally the tremendous gap that yawned between himself and this mysterious God, and underscored the helplessness he felt in being reconciled to him. "He was deeply sensible of his need of Divine assistance," he told the Quakers, but he made no claims to having personally received any; he believed that he was "a humble instrument in the hands of our Heavenly Father," but being an instrument in the hands of a father had, in his experience, rarely if ever translated into affection and acceptance. Two Pennsylvania women who begged an interview with Lincoln thanked him and hoped to meet him in heaven. Lincoln "walked with them to the door — & said — I dont know that I will ever get to heaven."

This uncertainty was given an even keener edge by the death of William Wallace Lincoln. Willie, the replacement child for the dead Eddie, had become Lincoln's dearest favorite, the son who most resembled Lincoln himself in temperament, the "true picture of Mr. Lincoln, in every way, even to carrying his head slightly inclined toward his left shoulder." (One Springfielder remembered that Willie had his father's remarkable memory, and, like his father, "after he had heard a sermon . . . could repeat it almost word for word.") But in February, 1862, Willie Lincoln contracted typhoid fever (probably from the tainted Washington water system) and died after a tortured two-week illness. The distraught Lincoln invited Phineas Gurley to conduct the funeral, and "had several interviews with Rev. Dr. Gurley"; Mary Lincoln, whose own mental balance nearly tipped over after Willie's death, read it as a judgment on her for being "so wrapped up in the world, so devoted to our own political advancement." For months afterward she could not even bear to hear the Marine Band playing on the White House lawn, and Willie's playmates were never invited back to the White House to play with Tad. Other deaths also crowded in on the Lincolns: Elmer Ellsworth at Alexandria; Edward Baker at Ball's Bluff; Mary's half-brothers Sam (at Shiloh), David (at Vicksburg), and the family favorite, Aleck (at Baton Rouge) — all three fighting for the Confederacy. Both parents began to have bizarre dreams about the dead Willie; for Mary, Willie would show up in the company of little Eddie and Aleck. No less than the war, even Lincoln's personal tragedies bore the stamp of a providence that he could not comfortably dismiss as mere inevitability, or easily accept as a comfort.

Even at the theater, providence was never far from Lincoln's mind. His favorite soliloquy "O, my offense is rank," was the king of Denmark's agonizing meditation on the inability of human beings to choose, on their own, even the most desirable ends.

> Try what repentance can: what can it not?
> Yet what can it when one can not repent?
> O wretched state! O bosom black as death!
> O limned soul, that struggling to be free
> Art more engaged!

Just as the miserable king cannot find within himself the strength of will to repent of his brother's murder, Lincoln was haunted by the sense of his own foreordained inability to believe or to be content in his unbelief. "I have often wished that I was a more devout man than I am," he told the Baltimore Synod of the Old School Presbyterians when Phineas Gurley brought them to the White House in 1863. But the overarching providence which decreed all things that came to pass had not, at least as far as his own unsparingly honest self-inventory could discover, placed that within his power. He was only "a piece of floating driftwood," he told Herndon; to Josiah Blackburn, he explained that he had "drifted into the very apex of this great event." He thought of himself as an "accidental instrument" of providence and not a beloved son. Still, what providence would not perform for him, it might for others, and even if he could not be delivered from the bondage of his own will, there was another kind of bondage from which providence, and providence alone, could deliver.

Anyone who asked Abraham Lincoln at the end of 1861 what the war was about would have received a stock answer: it was about the restoration of the original federal Union, the United States being a perpetual arrangement that could not be broken up. "We didn't go into the war to put down slavery," Lincoln insisted in September, 1861, "but to put the flag back, and to act differently at this moment, would, I have no doubt, not only weaken our cause but smack of bad faith." The Confederates, in Lincoln's mind, should be viewed as nothing more than the attempt of the slave power to override the decision of the entire nation, which made "the insurrection . . . largely, if not exclusively, a war upon the first principle of popular government — the rights of the people." The Confederacy was therefore not a government but a *coup*, pulled off by the planter aristocracy and utterly unrepresentative of the Unionist loyalties of the larger Southern people. "It may well be questioned whether there is, to-day, a majority of the legally qualified voters of any State, except perhaps South Carolina, in favor of disunion," he assured the July, 1861, special session of Congress. "There is much reason to believe that the Union men are the majority in many, if not every one, of the so-called seceded States." What was necessary was to "liberate the union sentiment there, and then let the thing work; we must then rely upon the people getting tired and saying to their leaders — 'we have had enough of this thing.'" This was an attitude that even Northern Democrats could endorse. "The Southern Government is a military oligarchy," wrote Lincoln's old Illinois rival, James Shields, in January, 1862. "The head of the oligarchy is in Richmond, and when the head falls a Union sentiment will be bound to burst forth in the south, which will soon entomb the body of this foul conspiracy."

Lincoln at first said nothing about slavery itself, and indeed he could not afford to without sending the border states bounding into the arms of the Confederacy like jackrabbits. "Public opinion in them has not matured," Lincoln cautioned. "We must patiently educate them up to the right opinion." Kentucky, in particular, "is the key to the situation" and "must not be precipitated into secession." Also, any hint on slavery would quickly turn the hand of every Northern Democrat against him and against the war. "We are not for propagating philanthropy at the point of the bayonet," Massachusetts Democrat Robert Winthrop warned. "We are not wading through seas of blood in order to reorganize the whole social structure of the South." He also had to keep an anxious eye on the possible responses of his own generals. He told Charles Sumner, after McClellan's Harrison's Landing letter, that his "two objections" to immediate emancipation were "that half the army would lay down its arms" and "that three more states would rise — Kentucky, Maryland, Missouri." And personally, Lincoln had no wish to entangle slavery with the war. As an "old Whig," Lincoln had always spoken for the restriction of slavery, not for total abolition. He "did not pretend to disguise his antislavery feeling; that he thought it was wrong and should continue to think so, but that was not the question we had to deal with now." He had "always himself been in favor of emancipation, but not immediate emancipation, even by the states."

Behind this reluctance to commit himself to abolition also lay a sense of shared national guilt. "He believed the people of the North were as responsible for slavery as the people of the South, and if the war should then cease, with the voluntary abolition of slavery by the states, he should be in favor, individually, of the government paying a fair indemnity for the loss to the owners." What was more, abolition opened up questions for which he had no answer, especially about the future of the freed slaves in America, and the best solution he could imagine to American slavery would be some form of government-financed emancipation, stretched out over several decades, and then colonization. But these, at best, would have to be by-products, not deliberate goals, of his wartime policies. "Nothing now occurs," he told Congress at the end of 1861, "to add or subtract, to or from, the principles or general purposes" he had "stated and expressed" at the beginning of the war. And at least until 1862, he was confident that the inevitable processes of history would bring everyone to abolition sooner or later anyway, so that there was no need for dramatic exertions for abolition now. "He believed from the first," Leonard Swett remembered, "that the agitation of Slavery would produce its overthrow, and he acted upon the result as though it was present from the beginning."

But if this made philosophical sense, it also demanded from Lincoln a large measure of moral discomfort. Despite his willingness in the 1850s to support the Fugitive Slave Law as part of a legitimate constitutional compromise, Lincoln had no real stomach for returning fugitives to slavery once they had escaped it. "The slave of every rebel master who seeks the protection of the flag shall have it and be free,"

Lincoln pledged in September, 1861 — although he was soon to add that "the President does not mean, at present, to settle any general rule in respect to slaves or slavery, but simply to provide for the particular case under the circumstances in which it is now presented." He also had to contend with the increasing restlessness of the Radicals in his own party, who were eager to push him toward some active intervention in slavery. And they had both the votes and the organization to make Lincoln, as president, pay attention to them. Morton Wilkinson, who sat as one of Minnesota's senators throughout the war, was wide-eyed at the power of the Republican party caucuses in both the House and Senate: "The Republican Senators used to meet almost every day in caucus, and by caucus conference decide upon the action they would take on pending legislation, so as to leave no chance for hesitation, or division among themselves." Lincoln could not easily ignore such pressure. "Stevens, Sumner and Wilson, simply haunt me," he complained to John B. Henderson, "with their importunities for a Proclamation of Emancipation. Wherever I go and whatever way I turn, they are on my trail. . . ." Worse than that, Lincoln was convinced that, soon enough, "the Radicals would take the extreme step in Congress of withholding supplies for carrying on the war, leaving the whole land in anarchy. . . ."

Lincoln also had to deal with moral pressure from a more unexpected quarter, and that was from blacks themselves. The beginning of the war was greeted by Frederick Douglass with jubilation that "the keen knife of liberty" could at last be put to the throats of slaveholders, and across the North companies of free blacks were organized "to go forth and do battle in the common cause of the country." Unhappily, the same federal Militia Act under which Lincoln called out the first volunteers limited enlistment to whites, and Lincoln himself was convinced that "to arm the Negroes would turn 50,000 bayonets from the Loyal Border States against us that were for us." Whitelaw Reid, covering Washington in 1862 for the *Cincinnati Gazette* reported the threat of "several Kentucky Colonels . . . who have declared they would resign at once if Negro troops were sent into the field, and their whole regiments are declared to be imbued with the same feeling."

But if he found it necessary to hold off free Northern blacks, Lincoln could not dismiss so easily the appeal posed by the runaway slave. Despite loud proclamations that the Union armies were marching into the South only to restore the Union, slaves immediately read the invading federal armies as the vanguard of emancipation, and ran away to the Union lines in droves. Sympathetic Union officers declared such runaways "contraband of war" and refused to return them to their masters. But this was only postponing a day of political reckoning: If a slave is no longer a slave, does that make the slave a free person? The best peace Lincoln could make with himself was to try to deal as he could with slavery on a domestic-policy track, separate from the war. And that track would involve, as it might have under any circumstances, three elements: once-for-all congressional containment of slavery to those states where it was legal under state law, federal incentives to the border states to create gradual emancipation schemes, and the colonization of freed slaves somewhere abroad. "In my judgment, gradual, not sudden emancipation is better for all," Lincoln wrote in early 1862. Those "who are in favor of gradual emancipation represented his views better than those who are in favor of immediate emancipation," he explained to James Taussig, and he agreed with Browning in December, 1861, that "There should be connected with it a scheme of colonizing the blacks somewhere on the American continent."

Here, the enthusiasm of the Radicals helped rather than hindered him, since they were at least willing to support his calls for compensated emancipation as a first step toward their goal of total abolition. At the very opening of Congress in December, 1861, Massachusetts senator Henry Wilson immediately proposed a compensated emancipation bill for the District of Columbia to "strike [slavery] out from the national capital," with the striking cushioned by the Treasury's paying slaveowners in the District an average of $300 a head for their slaves. Wilson and the Radicals rode down efforts by the border-state congressional delegations and by appalled Northern Democrats to make colonization of the District freedpeople mandatory and to force a referendum on emancipation among District residents (oddly enough, both of which had been provisions of Lincoln's own unsubmitted District emancipation bill in 1849) and Lincoln signed it into law on April 16, 1862. He told Horace Greeley that the District emancipation bill had made him "a little uneasy" for not including the referendum, "not that I would be glad to see it abolished, but as to the time and manner of doing it." The ideal emancipation bill would have "three main features — gradual — compensation — and vote of the people."

333

Lincoln himself had begun to take a hand in designing compensated emancipation proposals for the border states, too. As early as November, 1861, he drafted a proposal for the Delaware legislature that looked to emancipate all of Delaware's 1,800 slaves by 1893, funded by $719,200 in government bonds, and in December he told Browning that he was contemplating "paying Delaware, Maryland, Kentucky, and Missouri $500 apiece for all the Negroes they had according to the census of 1860, provided they would adopt a system of gradual emancipation which should work the extinction of slavery in twenty years." On March 6, 1862, after meeting with the cabinet and with Charles Sumner, Lincoln sent a special message to Congress, recommending a joint congressional resolution which would offer "pecuniary aid" to any of the border states that would "initiate" a gradual emancipation plan. He bent over backwards to assure the border states that "such a proposition . . . sets up no claim of a right, by federal authority, to interfere with slavery within state limits, referring, as it does, the absolute control of the subject, in each case, to the state and its people, immediately interested." And he begged Maryland congressman John W. Crisfield at a meeting with the border state congressmen on March 10th to understand that he was merely arguing for a practical inevitability, not proposing a radical reorganization of Southern society. The war would "of necessity" bring the Union armies "into contact with slaves in the states we represented; that slaves would come to the camps and continual irritation was kept up"; why not resort to a compensated emancipation plan now, and ease the inevitable weathering of slavery by the war? Besides, the longer the border-staters clung to slavery, the more damage they were doing to the Union they had sacrificed their fellow Southerners to preserve. Every day the border states kicked against Lincoln's goads and "strengthened the hopes of the Confederates that at some day the border states would unite them and thus to prolong the war." Let the border states adopt even the most gradualized emancipation plan, and the Confederates would see the handwriting on the wall "and more would be accomplished towards shortening the war than could be hoped from the greatest victory achieved by the Union armies."

Lincoln's proposed joint resolution was passed by both House and Senate within a month, but none of the border-state legislatures ever responded. "Since I sent in my message," Lincoln complained, "about the usual amount of calling by the border-state congressmen has taken place; and although they have all been very friendly, not one of them has said a word to me about it." (Even the Delaware emancipation scheme died in the Delaware state senate on a tie vote.) Far from welcoming the gradualism of Congress or Lincoln's hands-off stance, Kentucky senator Garrett Davis complained bitterly about the incessant "introduction of the subject of *slaves* and *Slavery*" into Congress, while the only Maryland slaveholders who asked to confer with Lincoln in person came on May 19th to demand that Lincoln discipline James Wadsworth, the commandant of the Washington defenses, for sheltering fugitive slaves. "You can not if you would, be blind to the signs of the times," Lincoln pleaded, while at the same moment invoking the words of biblical apocalypticism: "May the vast future not have to lament that you have neglected it."

Just as Lincoln's hopes of nudging border-state slaveholders toward compensated emancipation in the border states were fizzling, so his hopes of a self-inflicted Southern collapse, too. The string of Union victories that had made the early spring of 1862 so promising came to a halt when an unlooked-for Confederate army nearly overwhelmed Ulysses S. Grant's cocksure Army of the Tennessee at Shiloh on April 6th. Grant survived and threw back the Confederate surprise, but the punishing two-day battle at Shiloh was waged with unprecedented ferocity and at the cost of killed and wounded on both sides — some 20,000 — whose sheer numbers illustrated the folly of imagining that Southerners had any inclination toward unionism and restoration. Grant, for one, now became convinced that the Confederates were deadly in earnest about the war and "gave up all idea of saving the Union except by complete conquest." As he set up a federal occupation of Tennessee, Grant also gave up any notion that the South was deep with latent Unionism that was only waiting for a federal advance to trigger. Even under occupation, Tennesseeans remained stubbornly loyal to the Confederacy and sheltered guerrillas who tore up occupation garrisons and troop supply lines.

Lincoln had something of the same epiphany that spring. "Things had gone from bad to worse, until I felt that we had reached the end of our rope on the plan of operations we had been pursuing," Lincoln told Francis Carpenter, "that we had about played our last card, and must change our tactics, or lose the game!" That fear was confirmed when he came down to Harrison's Landing in July to meet with McClellan, only to have his reluctant general present him with his demand not to expand the war further in the direction of emancipation. McClellan's letter had precisely the opposite effect on Lincoln: the Peninsula campaign, like Grant's near-disaster at Shiloh, had convinced Lincoln that slavery was what united the Southern people, not some residual Unionism, and slave labor not only supported the Confederate war effort by releasing white laborers for service in the rebel army but also provided the agricultural products that fed those armies and kept the war coffers full. "From his observances in that visit," Gideon Welles remembered, "he became convinced that the war must be prosecuted with more vigor, and that some decisive measures were necessary on the slavery question, not only to reconcile public sentiment and to consolidate and make uniform military action, but to bring the slave element to our aid instead of having it turned against us." What Lincoln would not do as an act of impatient New Schoolish moralism, he could give himself permission to do as a secular means of ending the war, and thus get the ultimate result he and the Radicals alike favored the end of slavery, without looking as though the Radicals had come to the point of running his administration for him. "I am a patient man," he replied severely to one Marylander, "but it may as well be understood, once for all, that I shall not surrender this game leaving any available card unplayed."

And ultimately, as he was learning in that summer of 1862, playing that card was the only way he could make sense of providence. If the war was only part of a natural law of progress, then it had no business turning out as it had; in fact, if the war was being fought for no other purpose than Union-saving, then the events of 1862 suggested that it was probably not going to be saved at all. Yet, God had obviously not willed that it be destroyed, either, since he had given the rebels no clear-cut success. There was no prediction in providence, and the war, as he found in his meditation on the divine will, had been let run on inconclusively for this long precisely to make an easy peace on the expected terms impossible, precisely to make an unbelievable alternative not only believable but unavoidable. *God wills this contest, and wills that it shall not end yet.* Here was the moral of the summer of 1862 for Abraham Lincoln: human events do not run on like machines, but by providential intervention; just so, the war would not run to a conclusion, nor the Union be saved, unless Lincoln himself took note of providence's whispering.

Returning to Washington, Lincoln made one last appeal to the border-state congressmen on July 12, 1862, and this time he abandoned all pretense that the war and slavery could be kept apart. If the border states "had voted for the resolution in the gradual emancipation message of last March, the war would now be substantially ended," Lincoln scolded them, because when "the states which are in rebellion see . . . that, in no event, will the states you represent ever join their proposed Confederacy . . . they can not much longer maintain the contest." Four months later, the war had now entered a new phase, and "if the war continue long, as it must . . . the institution in your states will be extinguished by mere friction and abrasion." Examples of that "friction" were already on hand, as Lincoln pointed to David Hunter's aborted attempt to emancipate by decree the slaves in his district on the Carolina coast. Lincoln had canceled that decree, but "in repudiating it, I gave dissatisfaction, if not offence, to many whose support the country can not afford to lose."

He could not forever hold off Hunter and Fremont and Grant from taking the steps they needed to take for victory; either they would act or he would act, and once they did he would have to support them and the ball would be rolling toward a general emancipation whether the border states liked it or not. He also could not hold off the impatient Radicals of his own party. Illinois's congressional odd-fellows, Isaac Arnold, the renegade Democrat, and Owen Lovejoy, the evangelical Radical, put up a bill to abolish slavery in the territories which finally passed the House on June 19th, over more tears and anguish from the border-staters. A second and more dramatic Confiscation Act was already being debated in Congress, which would now emancipate not just slaves employed by the rebel armies, but the slaves of any white slaveowner fighting in those armies, and it would include provisions that would permit Lincoln to employ blacks "in such manner as he may judge best for the public welfare" — in other words, as soldiers. "How much better to you, as seller, and the nation as buyer," Lincoln warned, to take the last chance for compensated emancipation, before the next bill took their slaves away from them without any compensation at all. And to give shape to his plea, Lincoln submitted a bill to provide federal funding for any state emancipation plan, "either immediately, or gradually."

It was all for nothing. Twenty out of the twenty-eight border representatives and senators politely declined to act on his plea. But the result must not have surprised him, because he had already been at work on an alternative. On July 17th, Congress passed the Second Confiscation Act. He had prepared a veto of the act in case the border-state men came around at the last moment, but after their lukewarm response, he signed the confiscation bill, sending back with it to Congress a memorandum of technical objections, but signed all the same. On its own terms, the Second Confiscation Act still fell short of radicalism: the slaves it freed were given no indication of what their status as free men was now to be, and even the provisions for recruiting them for "the public welfare" suggested that the freedpeople might only move into some form of wartime limbo, like impounded freight. But for Lincoln, it was radical enough. "Henceforth his policy should be as stringent as the most enthusiastic could desire," he told John Forney. "Hereafter there will be no restriction in the employment of all men to put down this rebellion." At the same time, once the border-state congressmen had "extinguished" what Gideon Welles called Lincoln's "remote and glimmering hope" for keeping slavery and the war apart, he began working on a new document. He would raise the ante of the Second Confiscation Act, and proclaim the immediate, uncompensated emancipation of all the slaves throughout the entire Confederacy.

Secretary of War Stanton lost an infant child, James Hutchison Stanton, in July, 1862. Lincoln went to the funeral on July 13th, and rode back in a carriage in company with Seward and Navy Secretary Gideon Welles, and he took the occasion to tip his hand to both of them on the subject of emancipation. "He had given it much thought and he had about come to the conclusion that we must free the slaves or be ourselves subdued," Welles wrote in his diary. He had given up on the border states, and further efforts with them would be "useless." He was certain that the country "was prepared for it," and even "the army would be with us." And on he went, as Welles and Seward listened in deepening surprise. Whenever emancipation had been brought up before, Lincoln had "been prompt and emphatic in denouncing any interference by the General Government with the subject." But the war, Lincoln argued, "had removed constitutional obligations and restrictions with the declared rebel communities." It had opened up an opportunity for that one avenue of Whig presidential initiative, the war powers of the president; and he told both secretaries that he "had about come to the conclusion that it was a military necessity, absolutely essential to the preservation of the Union." After all, the slaves were "undeniably an element of strength to those who had their service." Let the federal government declare its determination to free them, and "all, bond and free," would "desert those who were in flagrant war upon the Union and come to us."

The following week was taken up with the adjournment of the Thirty-Seventh Congress and the submission of the Second Confiscation Act, but Lincoln sent notices to the cabinet for a special meeting on Monday, July 21st. The special meeting struck Salmon Chase as a "novelty," and it was noteworthy only for Lincoln's announcement that he "had determined to take some definitive steps in respect to military action and slavery." What this seemed to refer to was a series of orders Lincoln had drafted for implementing the new Confiscation Act. But at the next day's regular cabinet meeting, Lincoln plainly showed that he had something more in mind: "The President . . . proposed to issue a Proclamation, on the basis of the Confiscation Bill, calling upon the States to return to their allegiance . . . and proclaiming the emancipation of all slaves within States remaining in insurrection on the first of January, 1863." Not merely the slaves of rebels in actual arms, but now all the slaves of the Confederate rebellion would be freed.

The cabinet at once erupted in disharmony. Montgomery Blair, who arrived late for the meeting, warned Lincoln afterwards in a lengthy written minute that an emancipation proclamation would be strongly opposed in the North, where the war would not be sustained if it was going to be detoured into a war to free black slaves. Caleb Smith actually threatened to resign "and go home and attack the administration" if Lincoln went forward with his proclamation. Stanton and Bates, on the other hand, urged "its immediate promulgation," while Salmon Chase, speaking with all the force of the Radicals, actually objected that the proclamation was too soft. (In one final gesture toward compromise in the proclamation, Lincoln also proposed to dangle the offer of compensation and a schedule for "gradual abolishment" of slavery if the rebel states would lay down their arms at once.)

Lincoln ignored them: characteristically, he had "resolved upon this step, and had not called them together to ask their advice, but to lay the subject-matter . . . before them." As Caleb Smith complained, "He only wanted their advice as to the particular form of it."

But on that score, he took some very sage advice indeed from Seward: issue the proclamation, but not just yet. The Peninsula campaign had spluttered to its unlovely finish, and the federal forces on the Mississippi were mired in occupation duties. An emancipation proclamation at this moment would "be viewed as the last measure of an exhausted government, a cry for help" — for a bloody slave insurrection, for John Brown and for the butchery of Southern civilians on their verandahs, a deliberate and reckless incitement for a race war to succeed the civil war that the government hadn't been able to win on its own, "the government stretching forth its hands to Ethiopia, instead of Ethiopia stretching forth her hands to the government" (in Seward's apt biblical simile). "While I approve the measure," Seward pleaded, postpone its issue, until you can "give it to the country supported by military success," or at least enough of a success that the proclamation would not look like "our last *shriek,* on the retreat." Lincoln at first demurred. But when Thurlow Weed showed up at the White House that night to argue Seward's point, Lincoln finally conceded and locked the document away again. He would wait for a victory.

He might never have gotten it out again, either, if he had relied solely on the events of the next few weeks. Rumors flew out of Washington, some of them strategically leaked by Lincoln to test public opinion. On August 19th, Horace Greeley, sniffing out the hint that Lincoln had composed an emancipation order, tried to force Lincoln's hand by publishing an impatient editorial in the *New York Tribune,* "The Prayer of Twenty Millions," charging him with coddling the border states and requiring — *requiring* — Lincoln "as the first servant of the Republic" to "EXECUTE THE LAWS . . . with regard to the emancipating provisions of the new Confiscation Act." A coldly irritated Lincoln replied (in a public letter published not in Greeley's *Tribune* but in John Forney's *Washington Chronicle* on August 22nd and later reprinted by Greeley on August 25th) as though he had had enough of the abolitionists. "My paramount object in this struggle *is* to save the Union, and is *not* either to save or to destroy slavery," he wrote to Greeley. "If I could save the Union without freeing *any* slave, I would

340

do it. . . ." And yet, tantalizing at the end, he closed the letter with an assurance of friendship for Greeley, and mysteriously insisting that this represented only "my view of *official* duty; and I intend no modification of my oft-expressed *personal* wish that all men, every where, could be free." At the end of August, John Pope's new-modeled Army of Virginia was chopped to pieces at Second Bull Run, forcing Lincoln to restore McClellan to command in Virginia. When a delegation of Chicago ministers headed by William Patton and John Dempster appeared on September 13th to present the resolutions of a mass emancipation meeting the week before, Lincoln impatiently asked them if they knew "What *good* would a proclamation of emancipation from me do, especially as we are now situated?" Perhaps even Seward was too optimistic.

But he did promise the Chicago delegation that "Whatever shall appear to be God's will I will do." What he did not tell them, or anyone else, was that he had also made another promise. Four days after Lincoln's meeting with the Chicagoans, McClellan grappled with Lee at Antietam, and although the result was less than a resounding victory, it was enough to move Lincoln to draw the papers out of his desk and write up another draft of the proclamation. Within a week, as the results of the Antietam battle became clear, Lincoln called the cabinet into yet another special session, and proceeded to deliver the most astounding remarks any of them had ever heard him make. "I think the time has come now" to issue the emancipation proclamation; admittedly, he could wish that "it were a better time" or that Antietam had provided "a better condition." But the rebels at least "have been driven out of Maryland," and he had determined two weeks before, that as soon as Lee "should be driven out of Maryland, to issue a proclamation of emancipation." He had said nothing about this determination to anyone; it was a promise he made only to "myself and" — here, Chase noted in his diary that Lincoln hesitated — "to my Maker." It was, as Welles described Lincoln's comments in his own diary, "a vow, a covenant, that if God gave us the victory in the approaching battle, he would consider it an indication of the divine will and that it was his duty to move forward in the cause of emancipation." This was the "something different" which Lincoln had concluded must be the will of God, and it had been confirmed by providence in the outcome of battle.

341

The contrast between the skeptical and infidel Lincoln of the pre-war days who spoke of God as a remote and impersonal cause of a universal Niagara Falls, and the Lincoln who now sat somewhat un-surely before a cabinet of sophisticated and thick-skinned politicians, offering as his reason for the most radical gesture in American history a private vow fulfilled in blood and smoke by the hand of God, is al-most too great to reconcile. Only once before in his life, at the end of the March 6th special message to Congress on compensated emancipa-tion, had he ever prefixed any name for God with the possessive *my*, as though some unprecedented personal reciprocity had been estab-lished. Even he had to concede that "it might be thought strange that he had in this way submitted the disposal of the matter when the way was not clear to his mind what he should do," and the slight catch the ever-vigilant Chase noticed in Lincoln's voice (Welles later recalled Lincoln's "somewhat subdued tone" as he spoke) underlined how in-congruous it felt for them to hear Lincoln say these "strange" things about covenants with God. But "circumstances had happened during the war," he told Joseph Gillespie, "to induce him to a belief in 'special providences.'" As he explained it to the cabinet, "God had decided this question in favor of the slaves." And strange or not, what was cer-tain was that this Providence now promised to shift the entire war on its axis. "It is a step in the progress of this war — a beginning, the re-sults of which will extend into the distant future," Welles jotted in a memorandum later that day.

The incredulity with which Lincoln's cabinet listened to this un-likely confession has been overmatched by the even greater incredu-lity with which later generations have read the Emancipation Procla-mation. In Richard Hofstadter's entirely-too-memorable phrase, the proclamation "had all the moral grandeur of a bill of lading," and the conventional wisdom has been that it really accomplished nothing at all. There is some technical truth in these criticisms: there are actually three Emancipation Proclamations, beginning with (a) the draft docu-ment Lincoln passed around to the cabinet in July, (b) the "prelimi-nary" Emancipation Proclamation he introduced to the cabinet on Sep-tember 22nd and subsequently published under his own authority as president with the warning that the South would have only till the end of the year before it was put into operation, and (c) the final Emancipa-tion Proclamation which Lincoln duly signed into effect on January 1,

342

1863. The July draft comes closest to Hofstadter's "bill of lading": it was only two paragraphs long, and could be read simply as an extension to *all* rebel-held slaves of the Second Confiscation Act. It was not based on any appeal to natural or civil rights, nor did it offer any extension of civil rights to those whom it freed. It still provided federal aid for gradual emancipation if the rebels surrendered. (As late as his annual message to Congress on December 1st, Lincoln was still urging the adoption of a compensated emancipation scheme, this time involving three amendments to the Constitution and "deportation," almost as though the real purpose of the Emancipation Proclamation had been, not to free anyone, but to prod slaveowners, North and South, into "gradual emancipation.") And although it freed slaves, it did not abolish the institution of slavery, so that it would not have been impossible to imagine slavery being reborn in the South, after the war, from the slaves in the border states who had not been freed.

The second, or "preliminary" proclamation, which was issued on September 22nd, sang very nearly the same hesitant song. It insisted that "as heretofore, the war will be prosecuted for the object of practically restoring the constitutional relation" of the states; it kept alive the offer of compensated emancipation to the border states and promised an "effort to colonize persons of African descent, with their consent, upon this continent, or elsewhere"; and it promised to declare "forever free" only the slaves in rebel territory, which was as much as to say that it actually emancipated no one except runaways from the Confederate states (who were already as good as gone). As he admitted to Admiral John A. Dahlgren, "he knew his proclamation would not make a single Negro free beyond our military reach." But even recognizing these limitations, both the draft and the preliminary proclamations made a dramatic shift in policy. Both Confiscation Acts had freed slaves, but did so selectively. Now, the proclamation was declaring that, not some slaveholders, not the Slave Power, but the entire Confederacy was in real rebellion, and beyond mild appeals to Unionism, and slavery itself, not just specific slaveholders, was the reason for it. And as if to confirm the finality of this recognition, the preliminary proclamation reiterated the language of the Confiscation Acts: that no fugitives would be surrendered back to slavery by the Union armies.

Still, the Emancipation Proclamation has been set down as a half-hearted effort, partly because it was, after all, not a declaration of national abolition, and partly because the authority the proclamation was predicated upon was only the military necessity of the war (which was, of course, why slavery in the border states was left alone — they had not legally put themselves in the way of Lincoln's military necessity). But it is hard to see how Lincoln could have done otherwise. Every jurist in the country knew that any proclamation, any congressional statute, any military gesture that crossed slavery, would be appealed to the federal courts, either after the war or while it was still being waged. And though it might be expected that the federal judiciary would be reluctant to hamstring Congress, the president, and the armed forces in the middle of a war, that was exactly what Chief Justice Taney had shown he was willing to do in *ex parte Merryman*. Any proclamation that failed to pay attention to the niceties of law, or indulged freely in flights of "moral grandeur," was liable to perish on Taney's legal spike, as would any emancipation measure that based itself on anything beside military necessity and the presidential war powers. "His own opinion was that as the proclamation was a war measure and would have effect only from its being an exercise of the war power, as soon as the war ceased, it would be inoperative for the future." This also offered yet another reason to leave the border states alone. By January, 1863, there was considerably less threat that the border states would actually be able to secede and upset the balance of power. But they also remained the most potent source of embarrassing legal challenges, as Taney (a Marylander) would manage to do later in 1863 in *Prize Cases*, a legal challenge to the validity of the naval blockade which came within one Supreme Court vote of rendering the federal blockade of the Confederacy illegal. It was best not to kick over the hornets' nest even if the hornets had gone to sleep.

If all this looked like hesitation later on, very few saw it that way then. Just as Seward had feared, the proclamation was commonly assumed in the fall of 1862 to be the spark that would touch off a slave uprising. The relentlessly anti-Lincoln London *Times* predicted that the proclamation would ignite "horrible massacres of white women and children, to be followed by the extermination of the black race in the South," and the British foreign secretary, Lord John Russell, urged British intervention in the war that October precisely to head off the "acts of plunder, of incendiarism, and of revenge" that would flow after the proclamation. Least of all did the Confederates take the three

proclamations lightly. "This will only intensify the war," wrote a Confederate War Department official. "Some of the gravest of our senators
favor the raising of the *black flag*, asking and giving no quarter hereafter." The "massacres," of course, did not happen, but a tidal wave of
runaways did. From 1863 onwards, up to 20 percent of the slave population of the Confederacy, bringing with them the hands and legs that
built up and supplied the Confederate armies and defenses, packed up
and fled to the Union lines, assured by the proclamation that they were
now free. In that sense, an uprising was exactly what the proclamation
caused, although in this case, it was an uprising and an up-moving toward the nearest Yankee picket line.

For Lincoln, any second thoughts or reconsiderations were understood to be out of his hands. On New Year's Day, Robert Lincoln
remembered, "my mother and I went in to his study, my mother inquiring in her quick, sharp way, 'Well what do you intend doing?'"
Lincoln simply looked heavenwards and replied, "I am under orders, I cannot do otherwise." The final version of the proclamation,
which embodied a flurry of last-minute alterations, declared the freeing of "all persons held as slaves within said designated States," and
added the announcement that "such persons of suitable condition"
would now be recruited into the "armed service of the United
States." And at the prompting of Salmon Chase, Lincoln added at the
end an invocation of "the considerate judgment of mankind, and the
gracious favor of Almighty God." After a lengthy morning public reception and three hours in formal hand-shaking with the diplomatic
corps and "several hundred people," he withdrew upstairs to his office, where Seward had delivered the formal copy of the proclamation, with all the last-minute corrections from the cabinet Lincoln
had asked for the day before. Three hours of hand-wringing in the
reception had made his wrist shaky, and he remembered that "I
could not for a moment control my arm." But he was not willing to
let anyone suppose that "he had some compunctions," and so he
bore down and signed it, as he only rarely did, with his full name,
Abraham Lincoln. "I never in my life felt more certain that I was doing
right than I do in signing this paper," he remarked to Seward. Across
town, at the Navy Yard, naval guns began to boom in celebration; a
mass meeting of African-Americans began singing, "I'm a Free Man
Now, Jesus Christ Made Me Free."

It was just as well that Lincoln had the confidence of Providence before him at the end of 1862, because the Emancipation Proclamation presented him with two enormous subsidiary problems: what to do with the African-Americans he had freed, and how to keep Northern whites fighting now that fighting was going to free more of them. Although he told Ohio congressman William P. Cutler that "he was troubled to know what we should do with these people — Negroes — after peace came," his first instinct for dealing with the freed slaves remained colonization. "Opposed to the whole system of enslavement, but believing the Africans were mentally an inferior race," wrote Welles, Lincoln "believed that any attempt to make them and the whites one people would tend to the degradation of the whites without materially elevating the blacks, but that separation would promote the happiness and welfare of each," and Welles noted that Lincoln considered emancipation and colonization "to be parts of one system, and that must be carried forward together." Edward Bates in fact had recommended "compulsory deportation — compelling the slaves when set free to leave the country." "Many of them will colonize," Lincoln predicted to T. J. Barnett in late 1862, and at the regular cabinet meeting that followed the unveiling of the preliminary proclamation, Lincoln assured everyone that "he thought a treaty could be made" with a friendly government in West Africa or Central America "to which the Negroes could be sent."

But he was wrong on both counts. Free blacks in the North had opposed colonization for decades; they had no intention of leaving the only country they had ever known, and when he tried to persuade a delegation of African-Americans headed by Edward M. Thomas of the Anglo-African Institute for the Encouragement of Industry and Art that "it is better for us both . . . to be separated," the response was anything but enthusiastic. Thomas consulted "with leading colored men in Phila., New York and Boston" and found them thoroughly cold to colonization. "Mr. Lincoln assumes the language and arguments of an itinerant Colonization lecturer," Frederick Douglass crisply complained, "showing all his inconsistencies, his pride of race and blood, his contempt for Negroes and his canting hypocrisy." Never mind: almost as though he was still a manager of the American Colonization Society, Lincoln plunged ahead with plans to erect free black colonies at Chiriqui (on the Gulf Coast of Central America) and on the Ile de

Vaches off the coast of Haiti. But he got few volunteers — only 453 for the Chiriqui settlement by April, 1863 — and those whom he was able to recruit for both experiments were unable to make the tiny colonies self-sufficient.

Rather than colonization, what Douglass and the Radical Republicans wanted Lincoln to do was to begin recruiting freed blacks into the federal armies and turning them back against their former masters. The path toward black enlistments had been cleared in June, 1862, when Congress rewrote the national militia law to eliminate its ban on black volunteers, and in the provisions of the Second Confiscation Act in July. But even then Lincoln had restrained the War Department from accepting anything more than "colored laborers" for hauling and digging. Nor, it has to be said, were the Radicals actually much further ahead of Lincoln on this point. Some of them were quite willing to accept colonization as the outcome of immediate emancipation, and the Second Confiscation Act only recognized the likelihood of blacks receiving "all the rights and privileges of freemen" once they had been transported some place else. But all the same, enlistment meant granting African-Americans a stake in the preservation of the Union, and from there it would be nearly impossible to deny men who had risked their lives for that Union the reward of full civil rights in it. "Once let the black man get upon his person the brass letters, U.S.," Frederick Douglass predicted, "and there is no power on earth which can deny that he has earned the right to citizenship" — which was, ironically, exactly the reason Lincoln anticipated white resistance. Lincoln also had to admit that once "let the Negroes fight," then Douglass was right: "When you give the Negro these rights, when you put a gun in his hands," Lincoln told Josiah Grinnell, "it foretells that he is to have the full enjoyment of his liberty and manhood."

If he could not have colonization, Lincoln would have no choice but enlistment, or risk the drifting of thousands of newly freed blacks through the Union lines into northern territory, where they would begin competing for the jobs of absentee soldiers and create precisely the racial conflicts Stephen Douglas and the Democrats had all along predicted. And if Northern whites disliked the idea of enlisting blacks because it might lead ineluctably to black citizenship, they might be persuaded to look more favorably on black soldiers if they were advertised as reinforcements or even substitutes for white soldiers. As

347

Lincoln explained to Andrew Johnson, the military governor of Tennessee and a former Jacksonian Democrat, "The colored population is the great *available* and yet *unavailed* of, force for restoring the Union." In terms of sheer numbers, black recruits, for whatever purpose, would free the hands or spare the lives of untold numbers of white soldiers to dig the Confederacy's grave still deeper. So, even before the publication of the preliminary proclamation in September, Lincoln decided finally to allow the organizing and arming of black volunteers by General Rufus Saxton on the Carolina coast (where in May Lincoln had expressly forbidden David Hunter from doing much the same thing). In May, 1863, the War Department centralized the direct recruitment of blacks into federal service by creating the United States Colored Troops, a series of all-black regiments with white officers. By the end of the war, 180,000 blacks had been mustered into federal service, approximately 8 percent of all federal army enlistments.

Lincoln braced himself for a white eruption. Richard Yates, the governor of Illinois, warned him that Illinois volunteers "have laid down their arms and gone home, swearing they will not fight to free the negroes," much less fight beside them. Other white soldiers predicted that "if they were to be brought up face to face with the former white masters — they would break and . . . run like Sheep." But the eruption was milder than Lincoln had anticipated. By 1863, white soldiers in the federal armies had learned the same lesson Lincoln had learned about the incorrigibility of the Confederates. "I had thought before that God had made the Negro for a slave for the whites," wrote a teenage soldier in the 14th Wisconsin, but once in the South "my views on slavery took a change." In the end, white soldiers were willing, even if hesitantly, to turn their hands to any weapon that might strike at the heart of the rebellion. "I wish they would arm all the slaves there is in the south and set them on & spat their hands and holler ateboy," wrote one soldier in the 8th Vermont. "They are ready to go at the rebels like a mess of blood hounds." By June, 1863, Whitelaw Reid could snort, "What a change! Scarcely six months ago, to advocate the arming of a Negro was to horrify all the respectable conservatives of the Union party"; now, "the day for raising a panic over Negro enlistment has passed. . . ."

It helped enormously that the blacks who were recruited into the federal colored regiments and the six state volunteer regiments like the

1st South Carolina (recruited from runaways and freedpeople on the occupied Carolina coast) and the 54th and 55th Massachusetts (which were actually recruited from across the North) performed in combat far above the expectations that racial prejudice had set. In Louisiana, the federal colored regiments fought bravely at Milliken's Bend and Port Hudson in May and June, 1863; the 54th Massachusetts took the lead in a failed assault on Fort Wagner, outside Charleston, in mid-July, 1863, which cost them 40 percent of the regiment in casualties. Before the end of 1863, a Wisconsin cavalryman could admit, "I never believed in niggers before, but by Jesus, they are hell in fighting." This admiration for black bravery was not, of course, unmixed with self-interest. "My doctrine is that a Negro . . . will do as well to receive Rebel bullets and would be likely to save the life of some white men," wrote an Ohio officer in the United States Colored Troops. A popular ditty celebrated "Sambo's Right to be Kilt":

> Some tell us 'tis a burnin' shame
> > To make the niggers fight;
> And that the threat of bein' kilt
> > Belongs but to the white;
> But as for me, upon my soul!
> > So liberal are we here,
> I'll let Sambo be murdered instead of myself
> > On every day in the year.

Whatever the reasoning, opposition to black enlistments never assumed serious proportions, and a Rhode Island artilleryman could write in September, 1863, that, "The prejudice against Negro troops is fast wearing away and will vanish entirely in a few months."

From reluctance, Lincoln swung by mid-1863 to near-enthusiasm over the promise of black soldiers. He toyed with the idea of retaking Fort Sumter so "that he would man it with Negroes," and alternately considered employing "African troops to hold the Mississippi River and also other posts in the warm climates, so that our white soldiers may be employed elsewhere." Rather than worrying that Northern whites would disapprove, Lincoln now fixed on how unnerved white Southerners would become at the prospect of the former slaves, armed and turned on them. "The bare sight of fifty thousand armed, and

349

drilled black soldiers on the banks of the Mississippi, would end the rebellion at once," Lincoln optimistically told Andrew Johnson. It also delighted Lincoln to discover that the freedpeople in occupied Carolina had turned to raising their own crops on their former masters' land, and were turning a handy profit from their own cotton-planting. They were beginning, in other words, to look a lot like Lincoln himself, looking for upward mobility, and Lincoln could not deny those aspirations without making nonsense of his own. When Frederick Douglass arrived at the White House in August, 1863, to meet Lincoln for the first time, he expected to meet a "white man's president, entirely devoted to the welfare of white men." But he came away surprised to find Lincoln "the first great man that I talked with in the United States freely who in no single instance reminded me of the difference between himself and myself, or the difference of color." The reason, Douglass surmised, was "because of the similarity with which I had fought my way up, we both starting at the lowest rung of the ladder." This, in Douglass's mind, made Lincoln "emphatically the black man's president."

By the end of 1863, Lincoln had "sloughed off the idea of colonization" as "a hideous & barbaric humbug." But notwithstanding Douglass's improved estimate of him, Lincoln remained reluctant to confront the contradiction of employing blacks as soldiers without also pushing ahead toward the granting of civil rights to blacks. Technically, the Constitution gave the federal government no power to define citizenship, leaving voting rights largely to the decision of individual states, and Lincoln was minded to evade the question for the duration of the war, and even then "to let that question remain as it stood before the war." Even in Southern states where federal occupation troops now ruled the political scene, Lincoln could hardly issue decrees about black civil rights when Northern states like New Jersey and Illinois still stubbornly refused them to their own free black populations. It went almost without saying, too, that emancipation had been enough of a pill to force the Southerners to swallow, without the prospect of deepening a bitter Southern resistance by the promise of black equality in a postwar world. He hoped, according to Hugh McCulloch, that once the war was over, the Constitution could be amended so as to eliminate the notorious "three-fifths" clause, which gave the Southern states added representation in Congress based on three-fifths of their slave populations; this would induce "the recent slave States, for the purpose of increasing their Congressional influence and power, to give the ballot to black men as well as white." But to take so monumental a second step now, Lincoln would need an even greater revelation of the will of providence than the one that had been given him at Antietam. And this time, providence might be much more inscrutable.

9 Whig Jupiter

The first weeks after the publication of the preliminary Emancipation Proclamation were not good ones for Lincoln. Much as he told Methodist leader John McClintock that he was convinced that the proclamation "was right," he still "feared its effects upon the border states." And, sure enough, in east Tennessee, Unionist leader Thomas Nelson renounced his support of Lincoln and called for resistance to Lincoln's "infamous" proclamation. Even within the cabinet, there was apprehension. "It imparted no vigor but rather depression and weakness to the North," grumbled Gideon Welles. From there things only proceeded to get worse. "It is six days old," Lincoln wrote to Hannibal Hamlin on September 28, 1862, "and while commendation in newspapers and by distinguished individuals is all that a vain man could wish, the stocks have declined, and troops come forward more slowly than ever. This, looked soberly in the face, is not very satisfactory."

Still more bad news, based on popular discontent with "the management of the War and of the Finances, the treatment of Gen. McClellan, and the general inefficiency and incapacity of the Administration," came in October and November. The debacle on the Peninsula was blamed by the New York newspapers, not on McClellan, but on Secretary of War Stanton. State elections installed Democratic governors in New Jersey and New York and Democratic majorities in the state legislatures in Pennsylvania, Ohio, Indiana, and Illinois, jeopardizing the election of Republican senators. The congressional midterm elections slashed Lincoln's majority in the next House by thirty votes. This was not, on the whole, quite as bad a jolt as it might have been, since the Republicans clung to majority control of both houses of Congress. But the resurgent Democrats made it feel bad enough. George Boutwell, a congressional Radical, noticed how Democrats in the House now became "confident and aggressive." The new Democratic governor of New York, Horatio Seymour, used his inauguration to launch a carefully prepared attack on Lincoln's suspension of habeas corpus. In Lincoln's old home district John Todd Stuart (now a Democrat) trounced Lincoln's circuit associate, Leonard Swett, for the district congressional seat, while another Lincoln friend, Orville Hickman Browning, was dumped from his U.S. Senate seat by the new Democratic majority in the Illinois legislature. One Republican congressman who had survived the election warned Lincoln that even Republicans in his district "would be glad to hear some morning that you had been found hanging from the post of a lamp at the door of the White House."

The rumblings of no confidence increased immediately after the elections, when Lincoln finally dismissed McClellan for good. Not only was the Army of the Potomac full of mutterings — "Lead us to Washington, General, we'll follow you," men called out as McClellan reviewed his army for the last time on November 10, 1862 — but Lincoln appointed as McClellan's successor General Ambrose E. Burnside, a floridly side-whiskered Rhode Islander who turned out to be substantially less than the sum of his parts. No one was more aware of Burnside's shortcomings than Burnside himself. He had twice rebuffed quiet offers of command of the army, both because he was a personal friend of McClellan's and because he doubted his own capacities to manage things as well as McClellan had. But he had acquired a reputation for success in combat, based on his command of a major coastal clearing operation he had supervised in the Hatteras Sound back in the early spring of 1862, and his long partnership with McClellan would ensure that he could dampen the mistrust of the officer corps of the Army of the Potomac.

In fact, he managed to deal neither with the rebels nor the

McClellanites. Burnside gathered up the army in mid-November and attempted to strike directly at Richmond by crossing the Rappahannock River at Fredericksburg before Robert E. Lee and the Confederates could get there to stop him. But he did not get his army across the river until mid-December, by which time Lee was fully and immovably entrenched on the heights above Fredericksburg. Burnside then proceeded to hammer futilely at Lee's lines, with 12,600 of his men killed and wounded in the process. At the end, Burnside had not budged Lee an inch, and he withdrew blankly to the northern side of the Rappahannock. When the news of the defeat finally trickled back to Washington, one Ohio Republican congressman wrote, "To human vision *all is dark* — & it would seem that God works for the Rebels — & keeps alive their cause." Confederate satirists boldly hooted,

> The days are growing shorter,
>   The sun has crossed the line,
> And the people are all asking,
>   "Will Abraham resign?"

In the White House, Lincoln groaned to Browning, "We are now on the brink of destruction." Providence had hidden itself again. "It appears to me the Almighty is against us, and I can hardly see a ray of hope."

Burnside's appointment had not been popular in Congress, and as the Thirty-Seventh Congress assembled for its third and final session on December 1, 1862, there was mounting anxiety, especially among the Radicals, that something had to be done, and quickly, before a new and more unpredictable Congress came in. "The feeling of utter hopelessness is stronger than at any time since the war began," wailed Joseph Medill, Lincoln's old Illinois newspaper ally. "The terrible defeat of our brave army . . . leaves us almost without hope." A good deal of the anxiety centered on Lincoln: the disaster at Fredericksburg looked like a piece with McClellan's campaigns, and seemed to underscore Lincoln's inability to cope with the disloyal foot-dragging within the Army of the Potomac. On the other hand, Lincoln had put himself on the side of the angels with the preliminary Emancipation Proclamation, which suggested that the real problem was not the intentions of the president but the poor advice he was getting for implementing those intentions from his cabinet. "Mr. Stevens thought that all the trouble was with the cabinet," wrote one member of the House Republican caucus, while James Ashley of Ohio "proposed to go further & agree upon a new cabinet."

Or if not an entire new cabinet, then certainly a new secretary of state. William Seward had been suspected from the start by abolitionists like Horace Greeley as an undependable faint-heart, and he had been particularly blamed for the dismissal of Fremont and the cancellation of David Hunter's black recruitment proclamation. Seward helped himself not at all at the end of 1862, when the first volume of his official diplomatic correspondence was published, containing some choice barbs aimed at the Radicals. But far more damaging was the anti-Seward gossip leaked out of the cabinet to the Radicals by Seward's arch-rival, Treasury Secretary Salmon Chase. According to Chase, Seward was "the unseen hand" who suppressed all useful debate within the cabinet and made all the decisions, the "mesmerist" who had reduced Lincoln to a puppet, an "evil genius" who had perverted Lincoln's good intentions. This, of course, was a wild exaggeration: it was not that Lincoln listened to Seward rather than Chase, but that Lincoln tended to listen to no one at all in the cabinet. Nevertheless, by setting up Seward as the caucus's target, Chase hoped to pave his own way to increased control and perhaps to the presidential nomination he had been denied in 1860. "Chase is at work night and day laying pipe," John Hay recorded in his diary. Chase's "head," quipped Lincoln, "was so full of Presidential *maggots* he would never be able to get them out."

The Fredericksburg debacle galvanized the Republican senatorial caucus into action. Ben Wade convinced himself, and others, that Seward was the "back stairs & malign influence which controlled the President," and that Lincoln needed to appoint "a Lieutenant Genl with absolute and despotic powers, and said he would never be satisfied until there was a Republican at the head of our armies." On December 17th, all but one of the thirty-two Republican senators agreed to demand "a change in and partial reconstruction of the cabinet" beginning, it was understood, with Seward, but mainly operating to the greater promotion of Salmon Chase. A committee headed by old Jacob Collamer of Vermont was deputized to present the caucus's demands to Lincoln. Seward, catching wind of the caucus at the State Department, immediately offered to fall on his sword and resign to spare Lin-

355

coln a potentially explosive confrontation with his own party. But Lincoln saw this at once as a challenge to his own authority, not Seward's. If he could only have a cabinet that the caucus approved, he might as well hand over most of his administration into their control or, even worse, hand over the powers they were vaguely accusing Seward of exercising to Chase. Lincoln needed the caucus and he needed Chase, but he had no intention of letting them wrench the reins of the executive branch out of his hands. "It was very well to talk of remodelling the Cabinet, but the caucus had thought more of *their* plans than of *his* benefit," Lincoln remarked, and he promised Browning that he would teach them "that he was master."

His plan for that lesson was brinkmanship raised to the most dizzying degree. On the evening of December 18th, Lincoln received Collamer's committee and a three-hour bill of complaints which ran the gamut from Ben Wade's sandpapery demand that Lincoln sack all Democrat generals to William Pitt Fessenden's allegations (fed by Chase's tales-out-of-cabinet) that Seward was running the war out of his own office. Lincoln listened, then dismissed them with the request that they meet with him again the next evening. The following morning, Lincoln called the cabinet together in special session to report on Seward's resignation and the charges that had been leveled against him, most of which, whether they liked Seward or not, the cabinet recognized as fabrications. Lincoln then asked them, also, to meet with him that night — so that at 7:30 P.M. the senatorial committee and the cabinet both found themselves in Lincoln's White House office. He had one major object: to cut the ground out from under Chase without actually provoking a confrontation with the Radicals. Turning to the cabinet, Lincoln asked them if it were true that the cabinet was divided in its loyalty to the war effort, if it was true that Seward kept them all in the dark and suppressed discussion. "Decisions had, so far as he knew, received general support after they were made." It might be true that not much collaborative decision-making went on in the Cabinet, but that was his policy, not Seward's (Lincoln explained), and "He thought Mr. Seward had been earnest in the prosecution of the war, and had not improperly interfered — had generally read him his official correspondence, and had sometimes consulted with Mr. Chase." While Chase looked on, clammy-faced, his cabinet colleagues all agreed that "most questions of importance had received a reasonable discussion" and that there had not been "any want of unity." Even Chase, in front of the most direct witnesses, could not pretend that Seward had been "undertaking the control of the whole Admn."

With that flat contradiction of Chase's backstage whisperings, the committee's case against Seward collapsed, and their rage was transferred to Chase. Going out the door, Lyman Trumbull stopped to tell Lincoln that "the Secretary of the Treasury had held a very different tone the last time he had spoken with him." Collamer was more blunt: asked by Orville Hickman Browning how Chase could have said those things about Seward, Collamer grunted, "He lied." The next day, Chase offered Lincoln his resignation, which Lincoln had expected. "I can dispose of this subject now," he snapped, and jointly refused the resignations of both Seward and Chase. There would be no question after this who was in charge of Lincoln's cabinet.

On the surface, Lincoln had handled the Radicals with ease, even with "urbanity." He told Hay, "I do not see how it could have been done better." Privately, Fredericksburg and the caucus, coming on the heels of McClellan and the midterm elections, had nearly driven him to distraction. "They wish to get rid of me," he told Browning on the day Collamer's committee came calling, "and I am half disposed to gratify them." He groaned to Samuel Wilkeson the same day that "if there was any worse Hell than he had been in for two days, he would like to know it." He remarked to Hay after the cabinet crisis, "If I had yielded to that storm & dismissed Seward the thing would all have slumped over one way & we should have been left with a scanty handful of supporters."

Nor was there any relief in the months that followed, months that Horace Greeley called "the darkest hours of the National Cause." The resurgent Democrats found in New York's Fernando Wood and Horatio Seymour and Ohio's Clement Vallandigham several dangerously persuasive voices of opposition to the war. Vallandigham was especially skillful in casting the suspension of habeas corpus and the Emancipation Proclamation as outrages on civil liberties and the constitutional process which made Southern secession look mild. "The organization and integrity of the Democratic party give us an ancient and still admirable machinery wherewith to rally the masses and to save the Constitution and public and private liberty," Vallandigham wrote, "and I hope — it is the desire of my heart — to restore the

Union, the Federal Union, as it was forty years ago" — in the heyday of Andrew Jackson. Even former president Franklin Pierce used a Fourth of July speech to make a bitter public attack on Lincoln.

Lincoln was particularly embarrassed when Vallandigham himself was arrested and imprisoned by a military commission. This was the perfect confirmation of all of Vallandigham's accusations, and turned Vallandigham into a martyr for civil liberties. Lincoln shrewdly commuted Vallandigham's sentence to expulsion into the Confederacy, but the uproar was so great that in June, 1863, he issued a major public letter, addressed in reply to a petition from New York Democrat and railroad magnate Erastus Corning. Lincoln hotly denied that he had "knowingly employed" anything other than "constitutional and lawful measures to suppress the Rebellion. The very idea that he, of all people, intended violence on the Constitution was absurd, and the only thing that approached it in absurdity was the blindness of Democrats like Corning to Vallandigham's cynical appeal to civil liberties as a shield for "a most efficient corps of spies, informers, suppliers, and aiders and abettors of their cause in a thousand ways." Could not Corning see that "Ours is a case of rebellion," that "the Constitution is not, in its application, in all respects the same, in cases of rebellion or invasion involving the public safety"? Or, in more personal terms, "Must I shoot a simple-minded boy who deserts, while I must not touch a hair of a wily agitator who induces him to desert?" Clearly not, and "the Constitution itself makes the distinction; and I can no more be persuaded that the Government can constitutionally take no strong measures in time of rebellion . . . than I can be persuaded that a particular drug is not good medicine for a sick man, because it can be shown not to be good food for a well one." If anything, Lincoln complained, "In view of these and similar cases, I think the time not unlikely to come when I shall be blamed for having made too few arrests rather than too many."

Written with one eye on being "the best Campaign document we can have," the Corning letter was a great public success, and 50,000 copies were distributed by the *New York Tribune*. But the impact of the Vallandigham arrest, and the uncertain reception of the Emancipation Proclamation, continued to weigh so heavily on Lincoln that in August, 1863, he issued another public letter, this time addressed to his longtime Illinois friend James C. Conkling, who was organizing a statewide pro-administration rally in Springfield. Conkling had invited Lincoln to address the rally personally, and Lincoln took the opportunity seriously enough to toy with the idea. In the event, he sent the letter instead, but with careful instructions to Conkling, not only about the contents, but even about how Conkling should read it to the rally. Although Conkling's rally was decidedly friendlier than Corning's petition, the tone of worry and defensiveness still shone through Lincoln's letter. "You dislike the emancipation proclamation," Lincoln wrote. "You say it is unconstitutional — I think differently." The Constitution authorizes the president to employ the means for carrying on a war; very well, freeing the South's black slaves and arming them will "constitute the heaviest blow yet dealt to the rebellion." Even if "you say you will not fight to free negroes," there was nothing that demanded that anyone enlist solely for the purpose of liberating slaves. "Fight you, then, exclusively to save the Union," and we will all be thankful together. But even while doing so, why object to using any means — including black soldiers — to save the Union? If it is emancipation one objects to, then regard emancipation simply as the price one needs to pay for inducing black men to enlist and winning the war." Keeping in mind "the doctrine of necessity," Lincoln reminded the rally that "negroes, like other people, act upon motives." If we want them to fight for the Union, "they must be prompted by the strongest motives — even the promise of freedom."

For all his persuasiveness, not even Lincoln could be "over-sanguine of a speedy final triumph." The state elections in the early spring of 1863 nearly cost the Republicans control of New Hampshire and Rhode Island, and a nationally watched election for governor in Connecticut saw the Republican incumbent, William Buckingham, squeak back into office on less than 3,000 votes. Burnside tried to stir the Army of the Potomac to a new offensive, only to have it bog down under torrential rains in the half-frozen Virginia mud, and a rash of ugly finger-pointing began among his division commanders. Burnside, who had been so reluctant to take command of the Army of the Potomac, now struggled desperately to save it for himself by blaming the failures of his subordinates. This quickly translated into blaming subordinates who were McClellan favorites, and Burnside was soon currying the favor of the Joint Committee on the Conduct of the War. But Burnside had lost so much credibility by this time that nothing could really save him, and on January 25, 1863, Lincoln replaced him with General Joseph Hooker.

Hooker was a throw-back to John Pope, in the sense that Hooker had not only earned an enviable reputation as a hard-hitting and aggressive officer (the newspapers had dubbed him "Fighting Joe" Hooker), but had been openly, almost insubordinately, critical of McClellan and Burnside, and was known in some quarters to have endorsed Wade's call for a "dictatorship." Aggressiveness, however, was one thing, skill another. There was some doubt in Lincoln's mind whether Hooker had the leadership to piece the battered and demoralized Army of the Potomac back together again, especially since Hooker himself was partially responsible for the demoralization by fanning the blaze of gossip that consumed Burnside. Hooker seemed careless and overconfident, and his reputation also included rumors of hard drinking and womanizing, neither of which endeared him to Lincoln. "He can fight — I think that point is pretty well established," he observed to Lyle Dickey, "but whether he can 'keep tavern' for a large army is not so sure."

Actually it turned out to be exactly the opposite. Hooker spent the spring of 1863 doing a superb job of reorganizing and re-equipping the Army of the Potomac, but when he led it south across the Rappahannock in May, 1863, a Confederate army under Lee numbering not much more than half Hooker's 73,000 men stopped him at Chancellorsville and then delivered a staggering blow to Hooker's unprotected right flank which sent the federals stumbling back across the Rappahannock, minus some 17,000 casualties. It was the most complete federal defeat of the war, and Lincoln received the news with something close to desperation. "My God," he cried when Secretary of War Stanton brought him the news. "Our cause is lost! We are ruined — we are ruined; and such a fearful loss of life! My God! This is more than I can endure!" Hooker himself was nearly one of those casualties. As he leaned against a pillar of the Chancellor House's porch, a Confederate cannon ball smashed into the pillar and left Hooker temporarily dazed. But Lincoln wasted no sympathy on him. "If Hooker had been killed by the shot which knocked over the pillar," Lincoln acidly remarked to Gideon Welles, "we should have been successful." Hooker begged for another chance to take the army across the Rappahannock, but with Lee and the Confederates moving swiftly to invade Maryland and Pennsylvania, Lincoln would take no more chances on "Fighting Joe." Hooker knew enough to understand his position, and resigned.

And yet, through all the terrible string of political and military struggles from the late autumn of 1862 to the early summer of 1863, Lincoln's political resolve, especially concerning the Emancipation Proclamation, seemed to strengthen rather than weaken. "I am a slow walker," he remarked, "but I never walk back." He told Charles Sumner that he "is hard to be moved from any position which he has taken"; and three weeks before signing the final version of the Emancipation Proclamation, he urged the last session of the Thirty-Seventh Congress in his annual message not to draw back from supporting him. "We — even *we here* — hold the power, and bear the responsibility," he warned them. "In *giving* freedom to the *slave,* we *assure* freedom to the *free* — honorable alike in what we give, and what we preserve. We shall nobly save, or meanly lose, the last best, hope of earth." He assured an abolitionist delegation headed by Wendell Phillips in January, 1863, that although he had seen no "sudden results" from the proclamation, he was convinced that it "has knocked the bottom out of slavery."

Much as the battlefield defeats sent him into agonies of self-reproach, the peculiar resiliency bred into him by the years of constant win-and-lose in law and politics in Illinois time and again brought him back to center. The capacity to bend and recover was continuously fed by the books and storytelling he loved so well, or simply by turning to the Whiggish solution of "work, work, work." He knew that the jokes and stories put people off, and he also grew aware over time that he was acquiring a public reputation as a jokester. But he needed "these stories — jokes — jests" as "the vents of my moods and gloom"; and he assured onlookers that his "moods and gloom" were matters of temperament, not signs of despair. "You flaxen men with broad faces are born with cheer, and don't know a cloud from a star," Lincoln explained to anti-slavery Iowa congressman Josiah Grinnell. "I am of another temperament." Another part of his capacity to absorb tremendous amounts of political punishment was his Whiggish aversion to passion. He was determined to be governed by reason, and reason forced him to look beyond the viciousness and disappointments. "I believe in short statutes of limitations in politics," he told John Hay when Hay could not believe his forbearance with a former Radical critic. When all else failed, Lincoln could draw strength by appealing to providence. "If he was elected, he seemed to believe that no person, or class of persons could ever have defeated him," Leonard Swett remembered, "and if defeated, he believed nothing could ever have elected him."

As Lincoln's determination hardened, his skills in presidential management deepened. State Department clerk George Baker had been disappointed in Lincoln's lack of experience "as an Executive" in 1861, but by 1863 there was "a marked improvement in his executive ability." His shrewd handling of the senatorial caucus in December, 1862, revealed a firmer grasp of the intricacies of congressional power politics than he had ever before displayed, while nicely defending his own presidential prerogatives in time of war. "It is interesting and curious to observe how the President has grown morally and intellectually since he has been at the White House," Noah Brooks agreed. "Take his messages and read them . . . and you will see his advancement in ability, logic, and rhetoric, as evident as in the letters of a youth at school." Attorney General Bates, who quietly disapproved of emancipation, still thought that "the more he saw of Mr. Lincoln the more was he impressed with the clearness and vigor of his intellect and the breadth and sagacity of his views." The hesitations Lincoln felt in 1861 as an untried Illinois Republican in the face of long-service Washington legislative veterans like Stevens, Chase, and Seward were vanishing, and when Stevens tried to bully him into dismissing Montgomery Blair, he retorted, "Am I to be the mere puppet of power? . . . It would degrading to my manhood to consent to any such bargain — I was about to say it is equally degrading to your manhood to ask it." When Chase warned him that Congress was not likely to agree with Lincoln's views on the postwar status of the Confederate states, Lincoln asked, "Then I am to be bullied by Congress, am I? I'll be damned if I will."

Evenhandedly, as he shook off the attempts of the Radicals to push him ahead, he shook off the attempts of the hesitant to pull him back. When old Frank Blair pleaded with Lincoln to keep McClellan in command, Lincoln would only reply, "I said I would remove him if he let Lee's army get away from him, and I must do so. He has got the slows,

Mr. Blair." By 1863, Montgomery Blair was complaining that "his father had not, of late, been admitted, as much as he desired, to private conferences with the President." The fact was that Lincoln had stopped taking anyone's advice, and not just Frank Blair's. "The President's mind was so original and self dependent, that he fairly scorned all adventitious support and external auxiliaries," wrote one Connecticut congressman. He was now securely in control of his own executive patronage network, and used patronage appointees to enforce his wishes in local situations. The Radical Indiana congressman George W. Julian counseled his colleagues against any more quarrels with Lincoln because Lincoln's mastery of the patronage system was making him "the virtual dictator of the country." He was also more willing now to reach out and influence members of Congress for legislation he wanted enacted. His meetings with the border-state delegations were only the beginning of a more interventionist role for Lincoln in Congress, and by 1863, White House and cabinet staffers were being deployed as the regular summoners of congressmen to the presidential office, or else the bearers of discreet instructions on how to vote. Close associates from the old days in Illinois (like Leonard Swett) were drafted as confidential emissaries to hot situations or doubtful personalities, and among the White House secretaries, Hay and William Stoddard wrote anonymous pro-administration journalism for the New York and mid-western newspapers. "He handled and moved men *remotely* as we do pieces upon a chessboard," Leonard Swett remarked. "This was not by cunning, or intrigue in the low acceptation of the term, but by far seeing, reason and discernment."

At the same time, Lincoln was able to loosen his hand on parts of the executive machinery where before he had lavished entirely too much time and attention. Early in the war, he had taken his constitutional role as commander in chief to mean literally that he would give direct oversight to all military matters, and as if to make up in determination what he lacked in experience, he read up on military textbooks borrowed from the Library of Congress, issued field orders, and in the case of the recapture of the Norfolk navy yard in 1862, actually tried to direct some military operations as if he were a sort of co-general. It seemed odd to Hay that "nearly every evening" Lincoln used to trudge "over to McClellan's headquarters, sometimes picking up Seward by the way," and talk "war for an hour or more." Worse than

363

merely odd, William Howard Russell thought Lincoln looked pathetic, "trying with all his might to understand strategy, naval warfare, big guns, the movements of troops, military maps, reconnaissances, occupations, interior and exterior lines, and all the technical details of the art of slaying." Most of that had disappeared by mid-1863. Few of the ideas he developed from the textbooks were worth much, anyway, and the one persistent military theme generally applauded as an example of Lincoln's strategic insight — that Lee's army and not Richmond was the principal object of the Army of the Potomac — was really only a by-product of his residual political conviction that Jefferson Davis's government was a military dictatorship which would be overthrown by Southerners the moment the Confederate armies began to lose battles. (In the event, it would not be the pursuit of Lee's army which exhausted the rebels, but the capture of key Confederate cities like Atlanta, Chattanooga, Vicksburg, and Richmond.)

Similarly, Lincoln's cabinet now began to find that Lincoln's early awkwardness in failing to use his cabinet as a decision-making body had been converted into a conscientious and highly effective policy of allowing cabinet secretaries only the amount of leash they required for their jobs. "Each member of the cabinet was responsible for the manner of conducting the affairs of his particular department," Lincoln explained to the Missouri Radical James Taussig in May, 1863. "There was no centralization of responsibility for the action of the cabinet anywhere, except in the president himself." As a result, "No President ever leaned so lightly upon his Cabinet," wrote Connecticut congressman Henry Deming. "No man reproduces less in official documents, the argument and thought which he imbibes at consultations, and it is a marvelous fact that no sentence is to be found in any of his state papers, which suggests the suspicion of any other impress but that of his own mint. . . ." Republican newspaper publisher John W. Forney marveled at Lincoln as "that great, wonderful mysterious inexplicable man: who holds in his single hands the reins of the republic: who keeps his own counsel: who does his own purpose in his own way no matter what temporizing minister in his cabinet sets himself up in opposition to the age."

One reason why Lincoln could relax his grip even as he gained greater control over the helm was the growing sense of his own popularity across the North, and a large part of that popularity grew out of the skill with which Lincoln himself managed the newspapers. He departed from the conventional presidential practice of designating one Washington newspaper as a house organ, and instead played for broad press coverage by doling out tidbits of critical information to eager newspapermen like John W. Forney of the *Washington Chronicle* and Simon Hanscom of the *Washington National Republican.* To both Hanscom and Forney, Lincoln would deliberately leak hints, news, and trial balloons, allowing Hanscom to open up an "official Intelligence" column in the *Republican* and encouraging Forney to expand the *Chronicle* from a weekly into a daily. But by denying either of them official status, he also kept them subservient. Much as Forney thought Lincoln "the most truly progressive man of the age," he was exasperated by the number of times he had waited on Lincoln, hoping to pick up some publishable scoop, only to be asked, "What is the last good joke I have heard." Lincoln was more indulgent, but no less cautious, with the bureau reporters of the dozen national newspapers who kept permanent staffers in Washington. Lincoln never held formal press meetings — like his predecessors, Lincoln preferred to issue public letters to the Washington newspapers whenever he had a new policy goal to announce or an old one to defend — but William Stoddard remembered that Lincoln always liked "to have them come, and meets them cordially." The majority of them, like Noah Brooks of the *Sacramento Daily Union,* were young, well-educated adventurers, like Hay and Nicolay, and were just the sort of surrogate sons Lincoln liked to surround himself with. To them all, he became the ideal Whig elder: affable, diligent, compassionate, suffering.

Lincoln achieved the same image with the army as well. The failures of Burnside and Hooker had the oddly beneficial effect of weaning the loyalty of the Army of the Potomac off its generals and onto Lincoln. Just before jumping off toward oblivion at Chancellorsville, Joe Hooker invited Lincoln to come down to the army's encampment at Falmouth for a three-day grand review, and the soldiers who a few months before had been urging McClellan to lead them on Washington now "hailed" Lincoln "with hearty cheers" as "our revered President." The somber and burdened lines of his face seemed to speak of a sympathy with the soldiers, and "he appeared like a man overshadowed by some deep sorrow," as if he "was manifestly touched at the worn appearance of our men." He had become *Father Abraham.* And in defiance of the old law of familiarity breeding contempt, Lincoln even won the same loyalty from his closest staff, as well. John Hay was convinced "there is no man in the country, so wise, so gentle and so firm. I believe the hand of God placed him where he is." To Hay, Lincoln had become a "backwoods Jupiter" who "sits here and wields . . . the bolts of war and the machinery of government with a hand equally steady & equally firm."

Through it all, Lincoln remained a workaholic. He took no vacations, and although he sent Mary off to New England during the summer's heat, the only escape he permitted himself from Washington's oppressive weather was the use of the large, rambling presidential retreat at the Soldiers' Home, up the Seventh Street Road on the outskirts of Washington. Even then, he insisted on commuting to his White House office almost every day, an escort of cavalrymen jangling about his carriage. "While other men were taking recreation through the sultry months of summer," wrote one of the White House staff, "he remained in his office attending to the wants of the nation. He was never an idler or a lounger. Each hour he was busy." By mid-1863, there was no question about the skill with which Lincoln was now managing the presidency. "The Tycoon," as Hay called him, "is in fine whack. I have rarely seen him more serene & busy. He is managing this war . . . foreign relations, and planning a reconstruction of the Union, all at once. I never knew with what tyrannous authority he rules the Cabinet, till now. The most important things he decides and there is no cavil."

None of this might mean anything at all unless Lincoln could get his generals to beat the rebels, and in June of 1863, he was running perilously short of generals who might be able to do that. Lee and 75,000 cocky, hollow-eyed rebels poured across the Potomac, through Maryland, and into south central Pennsylvania, and Lincoln hastily turned to a dependable and politically colorless old Regular Army officer, George Gordon Meade, to take command of the Army of the Potomac and shield Philadelphia, Baltimore, and Washington. Despite having only three days to take up his balky command, Meade managed to find Lee before Lee found him, at the critical crossroads town of Gettysburg, and for the first three days of July, Meade successfully held off a vicious Confederate pounding. Drained by the loss of nearly a third of his army, Lee attempted to retreat back into Virginia, only to face a rain-swollen Potomac River at Williamsport, threatening to pin him on the ropes for a final knock-down blow from Meade. But the caution that had won Meade the battle at Gettysburg pulled the punch Meade might have delivered, and during the night of July 13th, Lee slipped away across the river, on a newly constructed pontoon bridge.

Lincoln was at first jubilant over the Gettysburg victory. He had hardly gotten the telegram in his hands from Meade on the morning of July 4th before announcing "that news from the Army of the Potomac . . . is such as to cover that Army with the highest honor, to promise a great success to the cause of the Union, and to claim the condolence of all for the gallant fallen." As late as July 11th, Hay found him "very happy in the prospect of a brilliant success." But that jubilation crested when Lincoln learned that Meade had issued a congratulatory order to the army, urging them to "greater efforts to drive from our soil every vestige of the presence of the invader." *Drive from our soil?* Lincoln erupted, "This is a dreadful reminiscence of McClellan. . . . Will our generals never get that idea out of their heads? The whole country is our soil." He now began to suspect that, like McClellan, Meade was going to be content "to get the enemy across the river again without a collision," when "to have closed upon him would . . . have ended the war." Frantic to prevent Lee's escape, Lincoln ordered Meade to attack the cornered Confederates at once, ready or not, and let the blame for any ill consequences fall on himself. It did no good. The news of Lee's escape left him inconsolable. Robert Lincoln, home from Harvard, came into his father's office at the end of the day to ride with him out to the Soldiers' Home, and found him "leaning upon the desk in front of him, and when he raised his head there were evidences of tears upon his face." He bitterly complained to John Hay that "Our army held the war in the hollow of their hand, and they would not close it."

Still, as he also added to Hay, he was "very grateful to Meade for the great service he did at Gettysburg." He assured General Oliver O. Howard, one of Meade's subordinates who had caught wind of Lincoln's disappointment from the Washington newspapers, that "Gen. Meade has my confidence as a brave and skillful officer, and a true man," and he told Melville Landon of the *New York Tribune* that "Lee's Pennsylvania campaign was a providential thing for us." And he was buoyed still more by even better news from the west. On July 4th, after a frustrating campaign of over seven months, Ulysses S. Grant had taken Vicksburg, the fortress city that dominated the lower Mississippi, opening the great Mississippi Valley water systems from Pittsburgh to northern Missouri and south to New Orleans. The news was brought into Lincoln's office on July 7th by Secretary of the Navy Welles, who had taken a telegram from Grant's naval support commander, David Porter, off the wires at noon, and at no time in the war did Lincoln become so elated. "What can we do for the Secretary of the Navy for this glorious intelligence? He is always giving us good news. I cannot, in words, tell you my joy over this result. It is great, Mr. Welles, it is great!" In one of his rare impromptu speeches, Lincoln addressed a crowd of well-wishers that night at the White House by asking, "How long ago is it? — eighty-odd years — since on the Fourth of July for the first time in the history of the world a nation by its representatives, assembled and declared as a self-evident truth that 'all men are created equal.'" Now, "when we have a gigantic Rebellion, at the bottom of which is an effort to overthrow the principle that all men were created equal," it could not be more appropriate that the same Fourth of July witnesses "the surrender of a most powerful position and army." In 1863, as much as in 1776, "on the 4th the cohorts of those who opposed the declaration that all men are created equal, 'turned tail' and ran."

Grant had not only taken Vicksburg, but bagged a rebel garrison of 30,000 men, and all on the strength of a campaign plan that even Lincoln had privately thought improbable. "Where is there anything in the Old World that equals it?" Lincoln joyously asked a Philadelphia journalist. "It stamps him as the greatest general of the age, if not the world." It also stamped him as the most available general. Not only was Grant demonstrably successful, but he was also politically friendly. Although a Douglas Democrat in 1860 and "never . . . an Abolitionest, not even what could be called anti slavery," Grant prudently shifted his political tack the higher he rose on the military ladder, and he was careful to discourage any talk of political ambitions. "The disaffected are trying to get him to run, but I don't think they can do it," Lincoln observed with relief. By August, Lincoln was "in very good spirits." He began to hope that "the rebel power is at last beginning to disintegrate," and that once again the Confederacy was proving to be nothing but a military faction tyrannizing a Union-loving people. "If that were crushed the people would be ready to swing back to their old bearings."

That fall, the elections ran back again. Pennsylvania returned the Republicans to control of the legislature and gave Governor Andrew Curtin a 15,000-vote re-election majority (despite the fact that his rival, Judge George W. Woodward, had been publicly endorsed by George McClellan). In Ohio, Republican John Brough coasted to an over-whelming victory over Clement Vallandigham, while in New York, Horatio Seymour's hand-picked candidate for secretary of state was beaten by a Republican with a plurality of 30,000 votes. In November, Grant took charge of a besieged federal army in Chattanooga, Tennes-see, handily broke up the siege, and sent the Confederates fleeing into northern Georgia. Through all the clouds, providence had contrived once again to smile.

Just how much providence remained on Lincoln's mind in the fall of 1863 became evident when he was invited by David Wills, who had been deputized by the governor of Pennsylvania to lay out a formal cemetery at Gettysburg for the "fallen heroes" of the battle, to partici-pate in the dedication ceremonies and "formally set apart these grounds to their Sacred use by a few appropriate remarks." The main oration of the day was dealt to Edward Everett, former president of Harvard and one-time Whig governor of Massachusetts. The invita-tion to Lincoln actually did not arrive until less than three weeks be-fore the ceremonies were scheduled. But Ward Hill Lamon had been in touch with Wills months before, so that Lincoln was aware that the in-vitation was coming, and he set to work on his "remarks" weeks in ad-vance, as though it were a major state paper. He had not quite finished them to his satisfaction by November 18th, when he boarded the train that took him to Gettysburg, and only the next morning, just before the procession to the new cemetery was to form up, did he write out the fi-nal draft of his "remarks."

Since he was only making the dedication, Lincoln was expected to be short (Edward Everett's main oration would last for two and a half hours, a remarkably eloquent rehearsal on its own terms of the events of the war up to that point), and short he was. What became known as Lincoln's "Gettysburg Address" (Lincoln only gave it the ti-tle "Address delivered at the dedication of the Cemetery at Gettys-

369

burg" in a copy made for Alexander Bliss in 1864) was only 272 words long, and it was over so quickly that "there was but slight applause at its conclusion." He spoke "in a most deliberate manner . . . with a hand on each side of his manuscript," wrote a student observer, but even speaking slowly, he was finished before most people realized it, and "there was surprise that his speech was so short." But what it lacked in length, it more than supplied in Lincoln's characteristic terseness of expression.

His fundamental message, beginning with an unconscious echo of his little July 7th speech, was this: the American republic was founded in 1776 around the principle of human equality, and we are now fighting a civil war which tests whether that was a particularly good foundation; here, we are dedicating a cemetery to those who have fallen in that war, but in fact the real dedication must be a dedication of ourselves to seeing that the war is won and that the principle is vindicated. But more than met the eye was packed into this little address. For one thing, it was yet another opportunity for Lincoln to establish the Declaration of Independence as the moral spirit animating the Constitution, and to see the war as a struggle for that moral spirit, rather than merely an overgrown dispute about certain procedural niceties of the Constitution. The opening line — *Four score and seven years ago, our Fathers brought forth on this continent a new nation, conceived in liberty and dedicated to the proposition that all men are created equal* — fixed at one stroke the foundations of the republic in 1776, not 1789, and around a moral principle, not a question of process. Yet, at the same time, this was not the dedication of a moral fanatic, like John Brown. The equality to which the republic was dedicated was a *proposition,* which was something very different indeed from what Thomas Jefferson had intended when he spoke of the equality of "all men" as the first of a series of "self-evident truths." In the language of the moral philosophers, like Wayland, Alexander, and Hodge, self-evidence was the result of the mind's instinctive judgment or recognition of truth, without any shade of relativism or social context cast over it. But the utilitarian cast of Lincoln's legal thinking recognized no such intrinsic judgments: people were motivated by selfishness, as Bentham and Mill had warned, and the only avenue that offered any semblance of escape from the dominance of selfishness was the triumph of "reason" and "all-conquering mind." "Equality," then, was a *proposition*, like one of the Euclidean theorems he had worked his way through in the 1850s, to be demonstrated and defended by reason rather than accepted as the voice of an instinctive common moral sense.

This did not put equality in a particularly hopeful light. Jeffersonian self-evidence assured everyone that equality was an undeniable discovery of every person possessing a moral sense, but reducing "equality" to a *proposition* opened up the risk that a perverted or uninstructed reason might miss "equality" entirely. And this, as Lincoln had argued years before, was exactly what had happened within Jefferson's own party. "One would start with great confidence that he could convince any sane child that the simpler propositions of Euclid are true," Lincoln wrote in 1859, but what if that child simply denied that their truth was self-evident? "He would fail, utterly, with one who should deny the definitions and axioms." Similarly, Jefferson might have thought *equality* self-evident in 1776, but "the democracy of to-day holds the *liberty* of one man to be absolutely nothing," and the axiom of "equality" is "denied, and evaded, with no small show of success. One dashingly calls them 'glittering generalities' . . . and still others insidiously argue that they apply only to 'superior races.'" The unhappy experience of a free people — in this case, the people of the Confederacy — submitting themselves to the yoke of Jefferson Davis's planter tyranny, and for the sake of protecting their own tyrannization of another race, made equality a *proposition,* a thing to be reasoned out, defended, argued over, protected, and not left to the happy assumption that it would always be "self-evident." Self-evidence does not require proof; but propositions do. And the war was, in that case, going to be the proof *whether that nation, or any nation so conceived and so dedicated, can long endure.* Ominously, Lincoln did not offer any confident prediction of how that proof — that *great civil war* — was going to turn out.

That would depend on the dedication and persistence of the ones offering the proof. Because it was a *proposition* — and one that would require a war to demonstrate — equality was also something to which men must be *dedicated,* and it was to an eloquent exhortation to dedication that Lincoln devoted the largest part of the address. Dedication, in Lincoln's sense, consisted of several separate parts. One was *humility,* an acknowledgment that the dedication of the grounds was actually only a pale shadow of the dedication manifested by the costly sacrifice of soldiers' lives in the battle, that the world *would little note nor long remember* even *what we say here.* Another is *devotion,* taking for ourselves the example of those who sacrificed themselves, even to the *last full measure of devotion.* Yet another is *resolution:* the fixing of the will so that the sacrifice will lead, not only to the proving of the proposition, but to the permanent establishment of the only government compatible with equality, a *government of the people, by the people, for the people.* Significant by its absence was any expression of anger, of vengeance, of fault-laying or righteous justification — in a word, of Democratic passion. Even in its final cadence (which was a direct echo of Daniel Webster's crushing "Reply" to Hayne in 1830, that the United States was not a mere assembly of state legislatures but "the people's government, made for the people, made by the people, and answerable to the people"), the address had the thumbprint of "an old Henry Clay Whig."

This suggested a sense of the republic as more than a diverse association of groups or communities or states. The very word "diversity" was with Lincoln a synonym for division and selfishness: "On the distinct issue of Union or no Union," Lincoln remarked a year later, "the politicians have shown their instinctive knowledge that there is no diversity among the people." Lincoln's favorite metaphors for the republic were familial, where differences and conflicts were to be sunk in the name of honor and a transcendent common identity, and in the address he dropped all allusion to the republic as a *Union* in preference to calling it a *nation.* Democratic critics saw this almost at once, and very nearly the first thing upon which hostile Democratic newspapers focused during the next week (when the proceedings of the dedication were published in pamphlet form and in most of the national weeklies) was Lincoln's substitution of *nation* for *Union.* This, objected the virulently antiwar *Chicago Times,* was "a perversion of history so flagrant that the most extended charity cannot view it otherwise than willful." What was less noted, but just as Whiggish in its vocabulary, was Lincoln's heavy interlacing of the address with Whig evangelicalism. Two years before, his lexicon in the first inaugural had been chaste of all religious reference except for a fairly tepid allusion to providence ("Him, who has never yet forsaken this favored land"). But his off-the-cuff pilot version of the address on July 7th ("How long

372

ago is it? — eighty odd years . . .") had begun with his wish to "most sincerely thank Almighty God for the occasion on which you have called." Now, it rolled out in a long biblical flourish, *Four score and seven years ago*, conjuring up at once association with the 90th Psalm's declaration that the human lifespan was "threescore years and ten." At that time, *our fathers*, like the biblical patriarchs, *brought forth on this continent, a new nation, conceived in Liberty* as though the republic were one with the woman of St. John's Revelation who "brought forth a man child, who was to rule all nations" and "fled into the wilderness, where she had a place prepared of God."

Less noticeable in the Address were the omissions. The proposition of *equality* was nowhere defined by Lincoln — did it mean civil equality, social equality, racial equality, or the equality of economic opportunity which was his favorite way of reading Jefferson's Declaration? Similarly, if Democratic passion was absent from the address, there was also more than just "all-conquering Reason." Dedication to the proposition of equality was a rational act, but its ultimate result would be a transformation that rose above both reason and passion in *a new birth of freedom*, the most vivid form of evangelical transformation. Reason might sustain dedication under normal circumstances, but slavery and secession had constituted a moral recision from the republican faith that, in the situation, could only be recovered by the transcendent impact of a *new birth*, trumping both passion and reason at a single divine stroke. Lincoln might not claim any such *new birth* in evangelical terms for himself, but it was still plain to him that only an experience of this caliber would be sufficient to renew the republic for the *great task remaining before us*, a task that Lincoln (in his one departure on the speaker's platform from his written text) decided to locate *under God*.

But if Lincoln felt freer to borrow the vocabulary of Christian rebirth as the scaffolding for the new national rededication, there was characteristically no effort on his part to import any formal recognition of Christian theology into that rededication. The Address is as personally aloof from Christian profession as Lincoln himself, prescribing *new birth* as a restorative for others but not reaching out, or else remaining convinced that in a world of "necessity" he was powerless by himself to reach out, for it himself. Even the structure of the Address owes more to the classical speeches he memorized out of the readers and orators he had borrowed in his youth, to Pericles' great ode on the Athenian dead, to Gorgias and Lysias, than to Moses or Paul. It was peculiar, too, that Lincoln chose to make freedom the goal of equality, rather than the other way round; true to the Whig political order, Lincoln urged that the fields be leveled, that opportunities abound, and then freedom would emerge in a new and greater birth.

He went home from Gettysburg late that evening, after attending an Ohio memorial meeting at Gettysburg's First Presbyterian Church, and came down, first with a headache, then with varioloid, a mild but contagious form of smallpox which required him, for the only time in the White House, to shave off his jaw-whiskers. "Since he has been President," the *Chicago Tribune* quoted him from his sickbed, "he has always had a crowd of people asking him to give them something, but . . . now he has something he can give them all."

Lincoln did not confine his residual Whiggism to the Gettysburg cemetery dedication. The republic to which he expected Americans to dedicate themselves anew was still the Whig republic he had tried to construct in Illinois, the republic of small manufacturers, commercial agriculture, and free wage labor, under the auspices of a benevolent and encouraging national government. The din and thunder of the civil war have usually drowned out in most narratives the significance of Lincoln's domestic policies, but looked at broadly, Lincoln's executive and legislative agenda amounted to nothing less than a repeal of six decades of Democratic dominance of the federal government, and would have made his presidency as controversial as Jackson's, even if there had been no civil war. "Whilst Democrats had in good faith . . . cast aside party feelings," complained the Indiana Democratic state committee in 1862, Lincoln and the Republicans had struck "down at one dash all the labor of Gen. Jackson for the last four years of his administration."

Lincoln turned his attention first to what had once been the centerpiece of the Whig "internal improvements" schemes, the development of railroad networks that could link isolated agricultural communities with east-coast commercial markets. Chief among these proposals was the construction of a transcontinental railroad to the Pacific. Discussions about a transcontinental railroad had sprung up in Congress even before the Mexican War was over. But Democratic reluctance to spend federal money on internal improvements, together with sectional rivalry over whether the railroad should follow a northern, southern, or central route westward through the territories, mired debate hopelessly. Lincoln told Grenville Dodge in 1859 that "There was nothing more important before the nation than the building of the railroad to the Pacific," and the demand for a Pacific railroad, funded by the federal government, was a plank in the 1860 Republican national platform. So it fell to the first full session of Lincoln's first Congress, unencumbered now by Southern Democrat opposition, to begin work on a Pacific railway bill, and by April, 1862, the House was ready to debate a comprehensive transcontinental railway proposal.

Like the old Illinois Central, the Pacific railroad would be built by private interests, the Union Pacific and Central Pacific Railroads, with the land for the track across the territories deeded over by the federal government. Funding for the construction would be provided by granting 15.5 million acres of public land to the railroad companies in alternate sections on either side of the proposed rail line, and dispensing government bonds the railroads could use to raise immediate cash. Lincoln signed the final version of the Pacific Railroad Act on July 2, 1862, and the Central Pacific began laying track from Sacramento, eastwards, on January 8, 1863, followed on December 3rd by the Union Pacific's construction start at Omaha, heading westward. When sales of the land grants failed to generate enough revenue, Lincoln announced that he "was perfectly willing to have the law changed so that the government should take the second mortgage and the promoters of the road should take the first," and in June, 1864, Congress passed an additional appropriation that doubled the size of the land grants and authorized the companies to issue their own first mortgage bonds. All told, the government funded the Pacific railroad project to the tune of nearly half a billion dollars.

Nor was the Pacific railroad the only beneficiary. Unlike the Confederate government in Richmond, which permitted the militarization of private rail lines by generals who mostly ran them into the ground, Lincoln's administration struck a general deal with private railroad companies in the North which established uniform rate formulas and subsidized the standardization of track gauges, rail connections, and new acquisitions, but which left management and ownership in corporate hands. Where Lincoln could not get direct congressional funding for railroad projects, he found ways of justifying federal grants and expenditures by means of his war powers. "The Nation, in time of peace, will derive great advantages from these Roads," Lincoln wrote as a justification for "the construction of certain rail roads concentrating upon the City of Washington" in early 1863, "and they will be invaluable to the government in time of war. Their want has been, and is severely felt in suppressing the present rebellion." Not only were the railroads invaluable to the government, they were an asset to the wartime economy: by 1865, Northern railroads as a whole were paying stockholders dividends of over $36 million.

Canal-building, too, enlisted Lincoln's support. "Enlarging the capacities of the great canals in New York and Illinois" was a matter of "vital, and rapidly increasing importance to the whole nation, and especially to the vast interior region," he told Congress in his December, 1862, annual message. And although a cash-strapped Congress balked at still further government spending for what amounted to private commercial interests, Lincoln authorized funding for an engineering survey to enlarge the Erie and Oswego Canal (justified on the grounds that this would determine whether naval vessels could navigate the canals), and in the summer of 1863 he dispatched Vice President Hamlin to preside at a new harbor-and-canal convention in Chicago (similar to the one he himself had attended in 1847) to promote the expansion of his old Illinois legislative project, the Illinois and Michigan Canal.

The markets he hoped to build by means of the railroads and canals would also require the national tariff protection Henry Clay had once made the foundation of the "American System" during Lincoln's political apprenticeship as a Whig in the 1830s. "In the days of Henry Clay I was a Henry Clay-tariff-man," Lincoln wrote in May, 1860, "and my views have undergone no material change upon that subject." He tried to touch "the tariff subject" only "lightly" during the election to avoid antagonizing anti-slavery Democrats who might otherwise throw their votes to him, but even before his inauguration, he returned to suggesting that "a tariff is necessary . . . for the protection of home industry," and promised that "no subject should engage your representatives more closely than that of a tariff." Even with the threat of civil war looming over him, Lincoln was still saying in 1860 that "the old question of tariff" was "a matter that will remain one of the chief affairs of national housekeeping to all time" and "will have to be attended to by whatever party has the control of the government."

Republicans in Buchanan's last Congress, in fact, did not even wait for Lincoln's inauguration before they took advantage of the withdrawal of the Southern representatives to enact a new tariff drawn up by Vermont senator Justin Morrill (and passed on March 2, 1861), and renewed and revised it in June and August, so that average tariff rates rose from 19 to 36 percent. Congress overhauled the tariff yet again in July, 1862, and twice in 1864, increasing the list of imported goods covered by tariffs and pumping the rates still further, until average tariff rates stood at the all-time high level of 47 percent, more than two and a half times what they had been in 1860. Democrats read this as an assault on agriculture — "the most outrageously burdensome law," according to the Indiana Democratic committee, "grinding, pressing upon the agriculturalist" — and as a shield for domestic manufacturing, since (as it had for Southern plantation owners) it increased the costs of farmers who bought imported goods and indirectly subsidized New England factory owners. The tariff was "that ass' jawbone by which the Yankee manufacturers have slain their millions of Western agriculturists." Democratic editor Samuel Medary believed that "The West has been sold to eastern manufacturers by the politicians; the tariff is not a war measure, but a New England protective measure by which she expects to lay the great agricultural West tributary at the feet of her cotton and woolen mills." Ohio Democrat Samuel S. Cox erupted, "New England manufacturers are getting richer every day. . . . They are getting all the protection of the Government." But the tariffs had both Lincoln's blessing and a healthy Republican congressional majority behind them. The high tariff rates of the Lincoln administration not only signaled a decisive break with the Democratic past in terms of federal economic policy, but remained largely untouched by furious Democratic criticism until well into the next century.

Old-time Democrats were just as unhappy with another leaf from Lincoln's Whiggish book, and that concerned the distribution of the public lands. The Pacific railway legislation already committed the federal government to a massive distribution of public land in the west, but this was followed by two other major land-grant bills in 1862: the Homestead Act and the Land Grant College Act. Three times in the 1850s, Congress had debated homestead legislation; each time, the legislation had been blocked by Southern Democratic majorities in Congress and by Presidents Pierce and Buchanan, all of whom argued in good Jacksonian fashion that the revenue from land sales was what made revenues from tariffs unnecessary. Lincoln, in his days as a state legislator, saw public land sales as a major source of funding for internal improvements. But more than merely generating revenue, cheap western lands helped underwrite the Whig "harmony of interests," since unhappy wage laborers could always find a way forward economically on government land. Also, with slavery barred from the federal territories by nearly the first of the Thirty-Seventh Congress's enactments, a homestead bill that could quickly settle the territories with free-soil farmers would be further insurance against any future Dred Scott decisions, a kind of economic popular sovereignty.

With so many Republican goals wrapped into one, homestead legislation went directly into the Republican platform in 1860, and Lincoln pledged his own support to "cutting up the wild lands into parcels, so that every poor man may have a home." The Thirty-Seventh Congress had hardly seated itself before a homestead act, with the lavish promise of 160 acres for the cost of nothing more than five years' residence and a ten-dollar registration fee, was reported out of the Committee on Public Lands. It passed the House by a resounding majority of 107 to 16, and the Senate by 33 to 7, and was signed into law by Lincoln on May 20, 1862 (even while McClellan was still crawling up the Peninsula toward Richmond). Over 26,000 migrants took up the offer, claiming over 3.4 million acres, before the end of the Civil War.

Nothing in this policy guaranteed that the land being offered was really worth anything — a good deal of it in the northern plains remains to this day some of the most difficult agricultural soil on the continent — and the stream of settlers that it sent into Nebraska, Minnesota, and the Dakotas helped trigger nearly three decades of Indian warfare on the frontier and disgruntled Grange politics. And given Lincoln's personal indifference to agricultural life, the "controlling influence" which he believed public land distribution would exercise on the "national domain" sits somewhat curiously beside the other elements of his "Old Whig" agenda. But the Homestead Act carried strong ideological attractions for Lincoln, overriding his more customary unconcern with agrarian interests. The same ideological motivation also hovers over the other major agricultural legislation of Lincoln's administration, Senator Justin Morrill's Land Grant College Act, which was passed with whopping majorities in both houses of Congress in June, 1862, and signed by Lincoln on July 2nd (the same day he signed the Pacific Railroad Act). The bill provided for the establishment of a series of agricultural colleges, once again subsidized by the sale of federal lands, which would instruct farmers' sons in "laboratory tillage." Unlike subsistence agriculture, agricultural colleges were dominated by models of "scientific" husbandry, which not only clearly identified them with commercial production but also with market-oriented attitudes governed by experimentation, rationality, and "improvement." The Morrill Act, in other words, described an agriculture Lincoln could respect, the same agriculture he had praised at the Wisconsin State Agricultural Fair in 1859 when he urged "deeper plowing, analysis of soils, experiments with manures, and varieties of seeds" and even the "application of *steam power*, to farm work." Not only agricultural colleges, but a new federal Department of Agriculture was established in 1862, which won rare praise from Lincoln for "the development of a correct knowledge of recent improvements in agriculture." Spurred by the influx of land-sale cash and the prodding of Lincoln's new department, twenty-two states added land-grant agricultural colleges or programs to their state educational systems, funded by the sale of 140 million acres of public land. Taken together, all of the land-grant bills spelled more than "improvements"; they marked the end of the subsistence farmers who had been Thomas Jefferson's chosen people.

Lincoln's most decisive departure from Democratic policy came, as might be expected, with Republican proposals for the revival of a national banking system in 1863. At the outbreak of the war, federal monetary policy was still governed by the same "Independent Treasury" scheme Lincoln had fought in 1840, which meant that the Treasury warehoused all its own funds and conducted all its business in specie. Managing all the financial exchanges of the government might have been almost unbearably cumbersome for the Treasury had not successive Democratic administrations ridden herd on federal expenditures in the 1850s and made the job of the Treasury comparatively minimal (in 1861, the federal budget amounted to no more than 2 percent of the gross national product, and federal revenues barely exceeded $40 million). No one was prepared for what the war might do to these arrangements. The initial appropriation Congress made for war expenses in its special session in July, 1861, seemed generous (it was actually ten times greater than the regular revenues of the federal government in the previous fiscal year) and even prudent, especially since it would be largely funded by a modest income tax enacted before the close of the session and by the sale of government bonds.

And if this had been all that was necessary for paying the war's bills, no one would have been happier than Salmon Chase, not only because it would have made his task as secretary of the Treasury all the more easy, but because Chase had come to the Republicans from the Free-Soil Democrats in the 1850s and still clung tightly to Jacksonian notions of political economy. "I do not believe in a high tariff, in a Bank of the United States, or a system of corporate banking," Chase wrote in 1846, and even after converting to the Republicans on the slavery issue, he was still assuring dubious Democratic friends that he loathed protectionism and believed that only specie — "a currency of coin" — could be considered real money. But events galloped away from both Chase and Congress. The federal army marched on Bull Run rather than Richmond, and by the end of 1861, the market for government bonds was evaporating; on December 28th, New York banks voted to suspend all payments in specie. "Chase has no money, and he tells me he can raise no more," Lincoln complained in January, 1862. "The bottom is out of the tub." Chase agreed: "Immediate action is of great importance. The Treasury is nearly empty."

The most immediate action Chase might have had in mind was an exit from the cabinet. But Chase's presidential ambitions (and the Treasury's patronage network which supported them) trumped whatever of the Jacksonian ideology was still in him, and over the next year Chase and Congress introduced a revolution in government finance which left loyal Jacksonians spluttering in disbelief. Faced with flagging sales of government bonds, Chase turned to a Philadelphia financial entrepreneur, Jay Cooke, who transformed government bond sales into a mass-market enterprise. By the end of the war, Cooke had enticed one out of every four Northern households to buy war bonds and flushed millions of private dollars into the war effort. This kind of mass borrowing put fresh cash into the hands of the government for paying soldiers, contractors, and creditors; but, of course, it only put off the day when the public would demand redemption of the bonds, and Chase could foresee that such a redemption would take more specie than the Treasury had ever had. The solution, therefore, was to create an alternative currency to specie, and in February, 1862, Congress passed the Legal Tender Act, which authorized the sale of $500 million in 6 percent bonds, and (under the strong hand of Thaddeus Stevens as chair of the House Ways and Means Committee) mandated the issue of $150 million in federal paper money — the so-called "greenbacks" — as a legal medium for paying off debts and conducting transactions. No other administration measure up till this point had worn such a radical profile; none caused so much hesitancy and soul-searching even among the Republican congressmen who eventually supported it. "It shocks all my notions of political, moral, and national honor," wrote William Pitt Fessenden, who also happened to be the chair of the Senate Finance Committee, "but to leave the government without resources at such a crisis is not to be thought of."

Lincoln indulged no such torments. He wryly told one Treasury official that "a committee of great financiers from the great cities" had come to tell him that "by approving this act, I have wrecked the country." And in raw truth, resorting to paper money helped inflate the cost of living in the North by nearly 80 percent. But the economy grew nonetheless: even with the subtraction of the Southern states, the gross national product still rose from $3.8 billion to $4 billion by 1864. And the inflationary impact of the paper money was cushioned, first by the fact that only $450 million in greenbacks was ultimately issued over the course of the war, and then by two even more dramatic departures from Jacksonian orthodoxy: a steep increase in taxes and a comprehensive national fiscal reorganization. The initial income tax passed by Congress in the summer of 1861 had been a flat-rate 3 percent tax on all incomes over $800 a year; its novelty was not in who was taxed, since the average American annual income at mid-century stood at anywhere from $300 to $500, but in the fact that it was a direct tax on citizens by the federal government, bypassing the states. It brought in only a trickle of revenue, however, and in July a new Internal Revenue Act introduced a progressive income tax which generated $55 million for the two years it was in operation. Still more money was raised by sales taxes and value-added taxes, and by the end of the war Chase was supplementing those revenues from the sale of high-priced confiscated Southern cotton. The new taxes were widely resented by the Northern public, but they helped take some of the inflationary steam out of the greenbacks. Above all, the largest recipients of the greenbacks were the soldiers, who then circulated their military pay back into the home economy.

A national bank would have helped monitor the circulation of the greenbacks, and by the end of 1862, not even Chase could resist the necessity for some means of fiscal centralization. He would not, after all, consent to a simple revival of the "Monster Bank," but in February, 1863, a National Banking Act did something very close to that by offering to franchise a series of "national" banks that would act as the handlers of the successive issues of federal greenbacks, as well as their own "national" banknotes. "As to the National Banks," Chase admitted, "I do not regard them as *perfect institutions*," but it was what "the commercial wants of the country" demanded, and the long-term result was to stabilize the Northern wartime economy and set the stage for reintroducing the sort of uniform national fiscal policies the Jacksonians had dreaded. The first of the new banks opened in Philadelphia on June 20, 1863, followed by banks in New Haven, Youngstown, Chicago, and Cincinnati. Four were established in New York City alone. Amost on cue, the *Cincinnati Enquirer* editorialized that this was the revenge of the Whigs: "The enormity of this bill is sufficient to make General Jackson, who killed the old Bank of the United States, turn over in his coffin. . . . The design is to destroy the fixed institutions of the States, and build up a central moneyed despotism."

Chase grudgingly regarded this as "a war necessity," but Lincoln thought otherwise. "Finance will rule the country for the next fifty years," Lincoln prophetically observed to Illinois Republican William Pitt Kellogg. He singled out the bank legislation for praise as "a valuable support of the public credit," and he was not shy about personally intervening in fiscal policy. Much as he liked to tease Chase by suggesting that the secretary pay government bills by giving "your paper mill another turn" — much, in fact, as he liked to tell Chase that he "don't know anything about '*money*'" and was going to leave Treasury policy entirely in his hands because "you understand these things; I do not" — Lincoln managed Chase more carefully than any other cabinet member besides Seward. Although he preferred to leave "to Mr. Chase exclusive control of those matters falling within the purview of his department," he believed "Chase's banking system rested on a sound basis of principle, that is, causing the Capital of the country to become interested in the sustaining of the national credit," in just the same way that Alexander Hamilton and Henry Clay had rationalized the creation of the first two Banks of the United States. Chase had "frequently consulted him in regard" to the creation of the new banking system, and the National Bank Act became "the principal financial measure of Mr. Chase, in which he had taken an especial interest."

Chase was not the only one who felt Lincoln's prodding on fiscal and monetary policy. Much as Lincoln, in good Whiggish fashion, tried to steer clear "about saying or doing anything which can be construed as Executive interference with the independence of the legislature," he strong-armed at least three senators (including Senate Finance Committee chairman Fessenden) into providing the key votes for the first National Banking Act when it came before Congress in February, 1863. One of only three vetoes he delivered during his administration was of a clumsily written bill that would have crippled the circulation of paper currency, and he warned (in almost the same words he had used twenty years before to defend the Illinois state bank) that "during the existing war it is peculiarly the duty of the national government to secure to the people a sound circulating medium." Such a currency — "a uniform currency," and not just state bank paper — in which "taxes, subscriptions to loans, and all other ordinary public dues, as well as all private dues may be paid, is almost, if not quite indispensable," he noted in January, 1863, while openly lobbying for Chase's "banking associations."

All of this amounted to nothing more than "centralization and meddling," according to New York's disgusted Democratic governor, Horatio Seymour. "It has loaded us down with debt and taxation. It has put back religion, temperance, and virtue by dragging them into political strife, and by the passage of laws which tend to make them odious in the minds of the people." But Lincoln proposed to "meddle" even further in 1863 by resorting to federal military conscription to fill the ranks of the federal armies. The Confederates had already legislated a compulsory military draft as early as the beginning of 1862; it was not until July, 1862, that Congress, in the process of revising the federal militia ordinance, also required the states to create lists of eligible males in the event that a draft would be needed. The proposal was not a severe one, especially since draftees could buy their way out of serving for a commutation fee of $300 or hiring a substitute, and local draft pools sprang up to provide commutation fees for any of their participants who might be drafted. But it was a draft all the same, and by asserting the authority of the nation over even the futures and wishes of individual citizens, it was another blow at the Jacksonian glorification of personal choice.

In March, 1863, Congress moved to begin its own federal enrollment plan, which this time touched off draft-resistance riots in several Northern cities. But even with the federal conscription plan, no more than 50,000 men were actually conscripted into the army, and the draft laws acted mostly as incentives to spur volunteering that filled up the draft quotas before actual conscription was needed. The draft might not make Horatio Seymour happy, as Lincoln acknowledged in a sharp reply to Seymour's demand on August 3, 1863, that Lincoln suspend conscription and submit the draft legislation to the review of Roger Taney and the Supreme Court. But conscription was, in Lincoln's mind, "just and constitutional" in the face of an enemy "who, as I understand, drives every able-bodied man he can reach, into his ranks, very much as a butcher drives bullocks into a slaughter-pen." Even more, it was "practical" — practical, in terms Lincoln knew would prick Seymour's Democratic sensibilities — for "maintaining the unity, and the free principles of our common country."

They had all heard this sort of language before. Lincoln "belongs to the old Whig party," grumbled one congressman, "and will never belong to any other."

Like emancipation, no single piece of this agenda would be safe without military victory, since failure on that score would send disgruntled and war-weary voters to the polls without any discrimination between Lincoln's war record and his domestic policies. It was true that Ulysses S. Grant's victories in the west had brought renewed hope that the war might be taking a quick turn for the better: all of the Mississippi Valley down to New Orleans was now in federal hands, Tennessee was under federal occupation and a federal military governor, the blockade was strangling the Confederacy's access to outside war supplies, and even if Lee's army had escaped destruction after Gettysburg, the myth of its invincibility was now in ruins. A solid hammer-blow in Virginia now might shiver the Confederacy into pieces, and with that as the goal, Lincoln brought Grant east in February to take charge of all the federal armies, and especially of the Army of the Potomac.

Grant had in mind more than a single strike into Virginia. He proposed "a very extensive Spring Campaign" to coordinate an advance by the Army of the Potomac into Virginia with a thrust into Georgia by a western army under Grant's capable lieutenant, William Tecumseh Sherman, and a move on the Gulf Coast from occupied New Orleans by General Nathaniel Banks. "Oh, yes! I see that," Lincoln delightedly approved. "As we say out West, if a man can't skin he must hold a leg while somebody else does." Never before had Lincoln felt such confidence in a general; never before had a general exuded such "perfect coolness and persistency of purpose"; and never "before Grant took command of the eastern forces" had he been able to "sleep at night here in Washington."

Never before, either, did a campaign seem to bog down so hopelessly. Grant jumped off into Virginia on the track Joe Hooker had followed across the Rappahannock the year before, and was stopped by Lee in a savage two-day melee in a tangle of desolate scrub forest known as the Wilderness. Rather than pull back as the other federal generals had done, Grant instead tried to slip eastwards around Lee's right flank, sidling steadily down toward Richmond, colliding violently with Lee's divisions at a string of country courthouses and crossroads across eastern Virginia. But by mid-June, all that Grant had to show for it was a horrendous casualty list and a settlement into a siege around Richmond and Richmond's rail junction, Petersburg, that showed no signs of going anywhere. The same story repeated itself with Sherman in Georgia: an advance, slowed and contested at every point by careful Confederate defensive actions, and finally a resultless siege of Atlanta. A heavy Confederate raid struck briefly across the Potomac and even into the District of Columbia, while Grant's Gulf Coast operation never even materialized. Popular opinion, weary but inflated by the optimism of Grant's accomplishments in the west, now plunged deeper than ever before into exhaustion. Even Horace Greeley advised Lincoln that "Our bleeding, bankrupt, almost dying country . . . longs for peace — shudders at the prospect of fresh conscriptions, of further wholesale devastations, and of new rivers of human blood."

These failures sank Lincoln in the summer of 1864 into his second great depression over the war since the McClellan crisis of two years before. "The people promised themselves when General Grant started out that he would take Richmond in June," Lincoln told Schuyler Hamilton that August. "He didn't take it, and they blame me." And this time the consequences were likely to be severer than merely public disapproval. Lincoln was now staring a re-election campaign in the face in November, and unless he resorted to martial law to cancel the election (something he never seems to have seriously considered at any moment), he might conceivably lose it to a Democratic candidate who would settle for peace at any price. "You think I don't know I am going to be beaten," Lincoln warned Hamilton, "but I do, and unless some great change takes place, *badly beaten.*"

The Confederates were only part of Lincoln's equation of misery that summer. Another major factor was Salmon Chase. The Treasury secretary's campaign to drive Seward from the cabinet in 1862 had been fueled by the assumption that Chase would step into whatever power vacuum Seward's removal created and thus boost him toward a presidential nomination in 1864. The failure of that gambit ruined Chase in the eyes of most of the congressional Republican caucus. But he remained the darling of the Radicals, and he still controlled, as secretary of the Treasury, the largest patronage network in the federal government (some 11,000 wartime Treasury workers nationally and 1,200 alone in the New York customs house). Gideon Welles was sure that he intended to use "the Treasury machinery" to "press his pretensions as a candidate" by organizing "Chase clubs" and dominating delegate elections to the next Republican convention. "There is no doubt but that Mr. C. is desperately bent on supplanting the President," Republican national chairman George Ashmun wrote. "You may rely upon the ripest state of inflammation between Mr. L. and Mr. C."

Despite the "inflammation," Lincoln resolutely "determined to shut his eyes to all these performances" through 1863 because "Chase made a good secretary." But Chase was a source of mounting aggravation, and not to the president alone. Chase and Montgomery Blair had represented the most radical and the most conservative voices in the cabinet from the start, and those differences had ripened into a blood feud by the fall of 1863. On October 3rd, Montgomery Blair decided to launch a preemptive strike against Chase's presidential plans in a withering speech to an "Unconditional Union Meeting" at Rockville, Maryland. "Rowdy" and "blackguard" were some of the kinder things Blair said about Chase and Charles Sumner, and he did not mind claiming that Chase was "no whit better than Jefferson Davis" for "amalgamating the black element with the free white labor of our land." The Radicals found Blair's slashing indictment of Chase and Sumner "so vulgar, so infamous" that Thaddeus Stevens wanted the caucus to demand that Lincoln dismiss Blair or resign himself. But Lincoln quietly turned away both demands — "the controversy between the two sets of men, represented by him and by Mr. Sumner, is one of mere form and little else," he told John Hay — and both Blair and Chase stayed in the cabinet.

Chase also found a way to stick the pin of annoyance inside the Lincoln family. A widower, Chase brought his beautiful and sociable eighteen-year-old daughter Kate to preside over his household in Washington, and Kate Chase quickly seized control over wartime Washington's social life from Mary Lincoln's untried hands. Mary's "personal vanity" and her expectations that her bluegrass Kentucky upbringing would command immediate respect in Washington were cruelly dashed at the very beginning by Washington's grand Southern dames, who regarded her instead as a déclassé westerner; and when Kate Chase wed Rhode Island governor William Sprague in October, 1863, Mary Lincoln refused to attend, and left her husband to represent them both at the ceremony. The year that Mary spent in mourning for Willie further distanced her from Washington social life, and long before the great Sprague wedding, she had acquired an unpleasant reputation for "meanness . . . beyond belief." Even the White House secretaries dreaded her: Nicolay referred to her as "Her Satanic Majesty," and Hay as "the Hell-Cat." Only the charming young William O. Stoddard got along well with Mary, and Nicolay and Hay cheerfully assigned him the task of dealing with Mary Lincoln's mail.

Benjamin B. French, the commissioner of public buildings in Washington, thought that Mary sought to compensate for Washington's snobbery by putting "on the airs of an Empress." But far from this establishing a position of superiority, it only made Mary Lincoln notoriously vulnerable to flatterers and confidence men, like Henry Wikoff, who used her to obtain patronage appointments from the president or as a leak of privileged information. This, in turn, brought on mounting friction with her husband. Where he continued to be indulgent towards his children's misbehavior even in the White House, Mary became an even harsher disciplinarian, "often short-tongued and bitter-tempered." Where Lincoln thought the White House was "sufficiently gorgeous for a prince," Mary saw only the peeling paint and mildewed wallpaper, and when she wildly overspent the congressional appropriation for White House maintenance, Lincoln accused her of a "monstrous extravagance" for "*flub dubs* for this damned old house." She dressed extravagantly, and more in the style of a debutante than a mother of four. "She . . . wore her dresses shorter at the top and longer at the train than even fashions demanded," wrote Alexander McClure, so much that Oregon senator J. W. Nesmith wrote that "Her only ambition seems to be to exhibit her own milking apparatus to the public gaze." Even Lincoln had to chide her that her dresses "would be in better style . . . if some of that tail was nearer the head." After Willie's death, Mary unwisely brought spirit mediums into the White House to hold seances so that she could contact her dead son, and what was worse, she also brought several of her displaced Todd relatives into the White House, despite their close connections to the rebels. It was not that Mary ever entertained any lingering loyalties for the South (when Aleck Todd was killed in 1863, she refused to mourn him: "He decided against my husband [and] through him against me"). But the tongues wagged anyway, and the Democratic newspapers filled with gossip about Mary Lincoln's supposed rebel sympathies, even while Radical papers brimmed with praise of Kate Chase and her fashionable and wealthy new husband. Still more unpleasant comparisons with the Chases surfaced when Robert Lincoln graduated from Harvard in 1864, and pled to be allowed to join the army, only to meet with Mary's adamant refusal to allow another son to be put at risk. While this spoke favorably of Mary's maternal instincts, her husband realized it was a political mistake, with so many of the country's other sons volunteering or being drafted, and in 1865 Lincoln persuaded Mary to allow Robert to join Grant's staff "with some nominal rank." Lincoln was left to talk to Orville Hickman Browning about "his domestic troubles," and Browning heard him say "several times" that "he was constantly under great apprehension lest his wife should do something which would bring him into disgrace."

Chase in the cabinet and Mary in the White House were distraction enough, but by 1864, Lincoln was under renewed pressure from the Radicals in Congress, this time over the problem of what to do with the newly reconquered districts of Louisiana, Arkansas, and Tennessee. It had been Lincoln's argument before secession that secession was actually a legal impossibility. As Confederate regimes were driven out by federal troops and Confederate territory recovered for the Union, it seemed logical to Lincoln to re-install the usual political mechanisms in the rebel states (only this time replacing the rebels with loyalists) as fast as possible and get the country back on the road to the gradual anti-slavery future he had seen for it in 1860. But after the Bull Run fiasco and the failure of Southern Unionists to stage any major overthrow of the Confederates, Congress lost its appetite for so easy a reconciliation. When Unionist districts in eastern Tennessee and western Virginia attempted to send representatives to Congress in December, 1861, Thaddeus Stevens denounced their elections as "a mere mockery" and the House Committee on Elections refused to seat them. Far from welcoming the Unionists, Radical Republicans like Stevens and Sumner now began to talk openly about the Confederate states having committed "state suicide," and the need to treat reconquered Confederate territory as though they were new territories requiring direct federal oversight and reconstruction.

"Territorialization" would, in Lincoln's mind, only inflame Southern resistance. Still worse, it would seem to give recognition to the fact of secession, and force him in the direction of making abolition the war's supreme aim (after all, if secession were a legal fact, one could scarcely confine the aims of the war to the suppression of a legal fact). "The President," reported Noah Brooks, "has never recognized by word or deed, written or spoken, that there is or was such a being in existence" as the Confederacy, "a thing which he holds to be a moral impossibility." Lincoln tried to forestall the formation of a Radical policy toward reconstruction in March, 1862, by appointing "military governors" for the occupied portions of Tennessee, Arkansas, Louisiana, and North Carolina, beginning with Andrew Johnson of Tennessee, the only senator from a Confederate state who had defied his own state government and remained in his seat in Washington. There was, of course, no legal precedent for "military governors" anywhere in American law, and Congress only half-heartedly agreed to the idea by confirming Johnson's commission as a brigadier general. The genius of the plan was that it would concede the Radicals' demand that rebel states not be re-admitted until some interim period of political sorting-out had taken place, while ensuring that the sorting-out would take place under Lincoln's war authority, rather than under the more unpredictable guidance of Congress.

But rule by military governors proved to be no more predictable in its results than rule by Congress would have been. Andrew Johnson quarreled with the federal military commanders in Tennessee, while the real center of Unionism in eastern Tennessee remained stubbornly under Confederate control. John S. Phelps was appointed military governor for Arkansas in July, 1862, but Phelps never managed to get a viable state government organized, and Lincoln finally cancelled the appointment. Edward Stanly, who was appointed military governor for North Carolina (or actually, the coastal region of North Carolina occupied by Burnside in early 1862), quickly angered Lincoln by tamely returning runaway slaves to their masters and closing down two schools in New Bern opened for the education of black children. When Stanly tried to sponsor the election of a Unionist congressional candidate in late 1862 so that North Carolina could be re-admitted without having to embrace the Emancipation Proclamation, only 800 voters turned out for the election, and the House refused to seat Stanly's candidate. Finally, in January, 1863, Stanly resigned in protest over the proclamation, and Lincoln appointed no more military governors. Only in Louisiana, where the federal navy seized New Orleans in April, 1862, did much hope surface for a worthwhile military governorship. There, military governor George F. Shepley managed to organize congressional elections in December that sent two unambiguously anti-slavery representatives, Benjamin Flanders and Michael Hahn, to Congress, and for once, the House voted to seat them.

Lincoln refused to debate theories of reconstruction with Congress, almost as if a discussion begun at that level would concede too much of the opening gambit to the Radicals. He told John Hay that "the question whether these States have continued to be States in the Union, or have become territories, out of it, seems to me, in every present aspect, to be of no practical importance." At the same time, he did not propose to be paralyzed by the failures of the military governors or the reluctance of Congress. On December 8, 1863, as part of his annual presidential message to the new Thirty-Eighth Congress, Lincoln issued a formal series of reconstruction guidelines in a "Proclamation of Amnesty and Reconstruction." The proclamation permitted the reconstruction of loyal state governments whenever 10 percent of the 1860 voting population had taken an oath of loyalty (which included submission to "all proclamations of the President made during the existing rebellion having reference to slaves," just to make sure that emancipation remained part of the agenda), and allowed them to write new state constitutions, hold elections, and send representatives back to Washington. This proposal, Lincoln hoped, would speed the reconstruction process, and perhaps even soften the fighting morale of the other rebel states, while wedging an oath to support the Emancipation Proclamation and the Confiscation Acts into the new state constitutions.

The first reaction of Congress was elation. "Men acted as if the Millennium had come," John Hay wrote in his diary. "Chandler was delighted, Sumner was beaming." "Depend upon it," declaimed Greeley's *Tribune*, "this Proclamation . . . will go far to break the back of the Rebellion. . . . Ninety of every hundred Rebels may be restored to every right to-morrow without sacrificing or relinquishing any particle of their property; while nine-tenths of the residue are required to relinquish nothing but their right to oppress and sell their fellow men." But once the Radicals had examined the proclamation in detail, their enthusiasm faded. For one thing, Lincoln's plan kept supervision of the reconstruction process firmly in his own hands, not Congress's. It also nettled the Radicals that Lincoln's only security for emancipation was the loyalty oath prescribed by his plan: provisions in the new state constitutions for making freedom a matter of permanent state law or for providing civil rights for freed slaves were described only mildly as acts that "will not be objected to by the national Executive." This left "the large landed proprietors of the South still to domineer over its politics," complained the abolitionist Wendell Phillips, "and makes the negro's freedom a mere sham." What McClellan was on the battlefield — "Do as little hurt as possible" — Lincoln was proving to be "in civil affairs — 'Make as little change as possible.'" Lincoln, said Phillips, was only a "half-converted, honest Western Whig, trying to be an abolitionist."

This was a serious shortchanging of Lincoln's intentions. The amnesty proclamation was not a blank check for automatic re-admission, and he did not offer his 10 percent plan as a final means of dealing with a conquered Confederacy. It was simply that a reconstruction based on carrots rather than sticks, and which subtly got the states to embrace emancipation for themselves rather than by military imposition, and as quickly as possible before the urgency of federal bayonets dissipated, would get the war over with under Republican oversight, and thus might get more of what the Radicals wanted than it seemed. Above all, he made it clear that whatever the mild appearances of his offer, emancipation was not an element on which he would tolerate shilly-shallying. "There have been men who have proposed to me to return to Slavery the black warriors of Port Hudson . . . to their masters to conciliate the South," Lincoln remarked to Judge Joseph T. Mills in August, 1864. "I should be damned in time & in eternity for so doing. . . . No human power can subdue this rebellion without using the Emancipation lever as I have done."

Even so, the president's plan got few takers. John Hay, sent as Lincoln's emissary to occupied Florida to administer loyalty oaths, became gradually convinced that "we cannot now get the President's 10th & that to alter the suffrage law for a bare tithe would not give us the moral force we want." In Louisiana, a state convention called in April, 1864, under the terms of the 10 percent proposal to write a new state constitution actually petitioned Congress for compensation for freed slaves. Similar misshapen plans from Arkansas and Tennessee emerged, and when Kentucky joined the din by refusing to allow federal draft officers to enroll male slaves, the Radicals became convinced that Congress needed to take matters into its own hands. It did no good for Lincoln to warn Kentucky's emissaries, Governor Thomas Bramlette, Senator Archibald Dixon, and newspaper editor Albert G. Hodges, that leaving Kentucky's slaves untouched would ensure "the wreck of Government, country, and Constitution, altogether."

Instead, Ben Wade and, in the House, Henry Winter Davis devised their own congressional reconstruction plan in early 1864, "the main object of which was to counteract the mild and tolerant policy of the Administration," and negotiated it towards adoption by both Houses on July 2, 1864. The Wade-Davis bill increased the threshold of oath-taking citizens in Lincoln's plan from 10 percent to at least 50 percent, excluded from participation in a new constitutional convention any former Confederate officials, and established a vague mandate for civil equality — all of which was, in effect, to make the reconstruction of the old state governments virtually impossible, since finding half of any Confederate state's population untainted under the Wade-Davis bill would be a difficult chore under any circumstances. Lincoln would have none of it: Congress adjourned on July 4th, and Lincoln let the Wade-Davis bill die by pocket-veto, without action. He was not, he explained in a proclamation released four days later, prepared to recognize "a constitutional competency in Congress" to reconstruct the South, or for that matter to be "inflexibly committed to any single plan of restoration."

Still, Lincoln held out the offer that the Wade-Davis plan was perfectly acceptable "for the loyal people of any State choosing to adopt it" on their own. But this fell far short of satisfying the Radicals. On August 5th, Wade and Davis defiantly issued a manifesto of their own, denouncing even Lincoln's allowance for state initiative as a "studied outrage on the legislative authority." Other Radicals had already taken the debate over reconstruction as a signal for a direct challenge to Lincoln. In May, 1864, abolitionist *ultras*, with the blessing of Wendell Phillips, bolted ahead to call a small convention in Cleveland and nominate as their presidential candidate Lincoln's most impatient emancipator, John Charles Fremont. Fremont enthusiastically accepted the nomination, denouncing "the imbecile and vacillating policy of the present Administration in the conduct of the war," and embracing a platform which declared that "the Rebellion must be suppressed by force of arms, and without compromise" and "that the question of the reconstruction of the rebellious States belongs to the people, through their representatives in Congress, not the Executive."

By July Lincoln was disheartened enough by these challenges that he sanctioned clandestine efforts on the part of the *New York Tribune*'s Horace Greeley to open peace negotiations with three Confederate representatives on neutral ground at Niagara Falls. It was effort more curious than serious — he assured James Ashley privately that "nothing will come of it," and nothing did — but Lincoln's anxiety over his political future had deepened sufficiently that he could not afford *not* to be curious about any proposal for ending the war on his terms rather than the Radicals'. The next month, Henry Raymond, editor of the rival *New York Times*, also personally begged Lincoln to open peace negotiations, and Lincoln broke down far enough to draft a let-ter to Jefferson Davis for Raymond to deliver to Richmond — only at the last minute to collect himself and cancel the mission as tantamount to surrender to the rebels. Greeley concluded that "Mr. Lincoln is al-ready beaten," and even Seward, the optimist of the cabinet, confessed on August 8th that he was "not altogether able to dispel this popular gloom from . . . my own mind." Orville Hickman Browning, though "personally attached to the President," had come to "fear he is a fail-ure." On August 23rd, Lincoln's spirits dipped so low that he asked the cabinet to endorse a pledge to "save the Union between the elec-tion and the inauguration," given that "this morning, as for some days past, it seems exceedingly probable that this Administration will not be re-elected."

But Lincoln turned out to be in less political jeopardy than he feared. Salmon Chase conveniently arranged his own political self-destruc-tion in February, 1864, when his principal congressional promoter, Kansas senator Samuel Pomeroy, imprudently published a dump-Lin-coln pamphlet, *The Next Presidential Election*, and then followed it with a "strictly private" circular to Republican party backers, naming Chase as the better candidate. This clumsy attempt to undermine the party's sitting president was more than even the Radicals could stomach, and it covered Chase with embarrassment. Montgomery Blair's brother, Francis Preston Blair, Jr., rose in the House of Representatives to charge Chase with corruption in his management of the Treasury. Lin-coln refused even to read the Pomeroy circular, and also refused Chase's resignation when, once again, it was offered. But Chase was finished as a serious presidential contender, and in June, when he crossed Lincoln again over a patronage dispute, Lincoln no longer felt the need to accommodate the sadly diminished Ohioan, and accepted Chase's resignation. In October, 1864, old Roger Taney finally died, and Lincoln named Chase to his place as chief justice so that, as Lin-coln sardonically observed, he could enforce the constitutionality of the national banking legislation he had so reluctantly authored. From his original high estimate of Chase's anti-slavery integrity, Lincoln had come to detest Chase, and Montgomery Blair believed that Chase "was the only human being that I believe Lincoln actually hated."

Then, at the end of August, the military situation suddenly

brightened. Confederate general John Bell Hood took his rebel army out of its trenches around Atlanta and threw them vainly at Sherman's besiegers, costing Hood almost 15,000 casualties. A month later, Sherman drew him out again by feinting southward towards Jonesboro, where Hood was badly beaten again. This time, Hood abandoned Atlanta, setting fire to the city as he withdrew. Almost at the same time, David Farragut sailed a federal squadron into the entrance of Mobile Bay, pounding the Confederate forts there into silence and forcing their surrender on August 23rd. In September, Philip Sheridan, Grant's irrepressible cavalry commander, pursued the rebel raiders who had threatened Washington in July and, by October, had eliminated them for good as a serious military threat. "These tidings revived at once, as if by an electric charm, the previously drooping spirits of the people," wrote Gideon Welles. "Do you know," an elated Lincoln quipped to Ward Hill Lamon, "that we have met the enemy and they are ourn? I think the cabal of obstructionists am busted! I feel certain that if I live, I am going to be re-elected."

The certainty only grew stronger once the Republican nominating convention met in Baltimore and easily nominated Lincoln on the first ballot. In September Fremont withdrew and a Radical plan to replace Lincoln on the ticket with Chase was sunk by the Radical leadership itself. James Ashley attacked the Fremont boom as "foolish and ruinous," and slammed Fremont himself for "a natural affinity for scoundrels." "If it was only Abe Lincoln, I would say go to —— in your own way," grunted Zachariah Chandler, "but it is this great nation with all its hopes for the present and future" which was at stake, and even Chandler and Wade took the stump for Lincoln. With the Radicals securely in tow, Lincoln reached out to war Democrats by restyling the Republican ticket as a "National Union" campaign and accepting the addition of Andrew Johnson, Tennessee's military governor and one-time Democrat, as his new running mate and proof of the future of reunion. "The loyal element in the Democratic party had rendered us great assistance in their unselfish devotion to the Union," Lincoln insisted, "and it was but just that they should be recognized." By the fall, state elections in Indiana, Pennsylvania, and Ohio had given Union candidates sumptuous majorities, and the election was now beginning to be a question, not of *if* but of *how much*.

The ultimate electoral gift, however, came from the Democratic national convention, which met in Chicago at the end of August. The Democrats adopted a platform describing the war as "four years of failure" and calling for "immediate efforts . . . for a cessation of hostilities," but then nominated as its presidential candidate no one less than George B. McClellan, who announced that he had no intention of negotiating for any peace which was not built on the return of the Confederate states to the Union. With the Democrats once again divided and the Republicans grudgingly closing ranks to prevent McClellan's election, Lincoln and Johnson won 55 percent of the popular vote, while regaining almost all the ground lost in Congress by the 1862 midterm election. "Judging by the recent canvass and its result, the purpose of the people, within the loyal states, to maintain the integrity of the Union, was never more firm, nor more nearly unanimous, than now," Lincoln told the last session of the old Congress in his annual message a month later.

And yet, Lincoln still interpreted even his re-election as a work that lay somewhere out of his own hands. To Hugh McCulloch, who took over Chase's job as secretary of the Treasury the following spring, Lincoln stressed how little he felt he had to do with it. "I am here by the blunders of the Democrats," he explained. "If, instead of resolving that the war was a failure, they had resolved that I was a failure and denounced me for not more vigorously prosecuting it, I should not have been re-elected." Even in victory, it was the mystery of necessity, rather than political strategy, that had told the tale.

The morning after the election, Edward Neill, who had been hired in 1864 by Nicolay to help process the incoming mail in the White House, stopped in at "the mansion earlier than usual" while everyone else was recovering from the previous night's celebrations. As he passed the door of Lincoln's office, "I saw that he was at his table and engaged in official work." Not even a major electoral triumph could distract Lincoln from his paperwork, and years afterward Neill remarked to Nicolay "that a man who could go back to his office and resolutely take up the dull routine drudgery of his post with such equanimity, on the morning after a triumphant re-election to the Presidency under the peculiar and exciting circumstances then existing, must be a man full of the elements of greatness, and one who would not lose his self-possession in any probable emergency."

10 Malice Toward None

The Civil War answered the question of slavery with such finality that it hardly seems thinkable to ask whether it might have turned out any other way. But that finality was by no means obvious to Lincoln. "He had always himself been in favor of emancipation," he insisted, and he believed that the doom of slavery had been written the moment a Republican Congress was in a position to end slavery's expansion into the territories. But he had never imagined that he would now be decreeing "immediate emancipation," and he admitted as late as 1865 that he would probably not have done that without having been "compelled by necessity to do it to maintain the Union." And even then, as he explained to Albert Hodges, he could not quite silence the voice of his own misgivings. "I was not entirely confident," he added to Hodges, "that the gain would be greater than the loss from such a move."

Still, Lincoln had always been willing to be brought along by providence. "At the beginning of the war," he explained to the last lame-duck session of the Thirty-Eighth Congress in December, no one had seriously contemplated abolishing slavery or arming black soldiers. But "upon a clear conviction of duty I resolved to turn that element of strength to account; and I am responsible for it to the Ameri-

397

can people, to the christian world, to history, and on my final account to God." He candidly told Hodges that the decision to emancipate the Confederacy's slaves involved no "compliment to my own sagacity," since "events have controlled me." As he told a delegation from the United States Christian Commission, whatever credit, or whatever blame, "God alone can claim it."

This was more than just an excuse to decoy insistent critics; it was an instinctive intellectual device for resolving his own hesitations and perplexities. And by every sign at the end of 1864, Lincoln had not been wrong to let himself "drift" into emancipation. "We have *more* men *now* than we had when the war *began* . . . we are not exhausted, nor in process of exhaustion . . . we are *gaining* strength, and may, if need be, maintain the contest indefinitely." The war brought unprecedented prosperity to the railroads, to food supply industries, to war-related textile production, and to banking; the inflation caused by the issuance of Chase's greenbacks (and the government bounties paid to soldiers) enabled debtors to pay off lenders in cheap money and deliver themselves from dependence. As Cyrus McCormick disgustedly remarked, Lincoln had allowed debtors to "pursue their creditors in triumph" with war-cheapened greenbacks "and pay them without mercy." A good measure of this prosperity would prove to be purely temporary, but from Lincoln's vantage-point, the wonder was, after three years of war, that it was there at all. "The national resources, then, are unexhausted, and, as we believe, inexhaustible."

Especially with the resounding endorsement of the 1864 elections behind him, Lincoln could at last let himself believe that "we can now see the bottom" of the war. But a successful end to the war was not an end to his problems. He wanted the end of the war, not just to come, but to come *quickly*, before more lives and treasure were washed away and before a protracted and vicious conclusion would endlessly embitter the South. He told Thomas Duval shortly before the Gettysburg cemetery dedication that "while the destruction of slavery was a necessary incident of war, he was well aware that its sudden extinction would be attended with great ruin," and Gideon Welles heard him "frequently" express apprehension that "unless immediately attended to . . . the civil, social, and industrial relations" of the South would "be worse after the rebellion was suppressed."

Yet Lincoln could not afford to have peace come too quickly, either, and the reason behind that horn of his dilemma had to do with emancipation. The Emancipation Proclamation, as Lincoln never tired of reminding people, was a wartime measure, issued on his authority as wartime commander in chief. Much as he assured white and black alike that he would never retreat from the proclamation, the authority that underlay the proclamation ran not one minute longer than the war itself. "The Executive power itself would be greatly diminished by the cessation of actual war," he acknowledged to Congress in December; once that happened, the question of whether or not the Emancipation Proclamation would continue to be binding "will be a question for the courts." And remembering that the Supreme Court's last word on the subject of slavery had been *Dred Scott,* there was no guarantee that the Court might not simply throw the proclamation out on the first peacetime challenge.

Some of Lincoln's anxiety on this subject was eased in October, 1864, when Chief Justice Taney — bitter to the end in his opposition to Lincoln — finally died. But a far better solution would be to keep nudging the border states and the reconstructed Southern state governments toward writing some form of emancipation into their state constitutions. And as the war swung more and more toward the Union, and gave the border states less and less leverage in their dealing with Lincoln, the president increased his pressure for state emancipation. Lincoln's new vice president-elect, Andrew Johnson, used his last months as military governor of occupied Tennessee to sponsor a state constitutional convention that abolished slavery there. In January, a Unionist constitutional convention in Missouri not only abolished slavery but also began recognizing a series of black civil rights. Even Maryland, where Union military occupation had simply drained slaves out of their masters' control, finally saw, too late, what Lincoln had called "the signs of the times" and adopted a new state constitution abolishing slavery on November 1, 1864. "It was a victory worth double the number of electoral votes of the state," Lincoln exulted to White House staffer Charles Philbrick, "because of its moral influence." Even Frederick Douglass, returning to Baltimore for the first time since he had run away twenty-six years before, rejoiced that "the revolution is genuine, full and complete."

But in each case, these new state constitutions were written within a ring of federal bayonets. Let the war end, and the constitutions could be amended once again. Almost to the end of the war, Kentuckians from the governor on down continued to pepper Lincoln with demands for the return of slaves who enlisted in the Union army, and there was no telling what the rebel states of the Confederacy might decide to do in the event a peace settlement came suddenly and reunited them with the North. Would the Emancipation Proclamation become at once a military dead letter? Would the slaves emancipated by it actually stay enslaved by the ex-Confederates while the reconstructed rebels besieged the federal courts with appeals?

The one single method for closing off any further life for slavery in the American republic was to amend the federal Constitution, and put the abolition of slavery beyond both the courts and the states. A thirteenth amendment to the Constitution to abolish slavery unilaterally throughout the nation would be, as Lincoln put it, "a King's cure for all the evils." And in fact a proposal for such an amendment had been introduced into the Senate as early as January, 1864, a one-sentence resolution modeled by Lyman Trumbull on the wording of the old Northwest Ordinance: "Neither slavery nor involuntary servitude, except as a punishment for a crime whereof the party shall have been duly convicted, shall exist within the United States, or any other place subject to their jurisdiction." But despite the two-thirds endorsement of the Senate in April, the proposed amendment failed to get a similar two-thirds majority in the House when it came to a vote on June 15, 1864. Too many House Democrats in the long summer of 1864 saw no reason to concede anything to Lincoln, and they denounced the amendment as "unwise, impolitic, cruel and unworthy of the support of civilized people."

The elections of November, 1864, changed that. When the next Congress assembled in December, 1865, there would be more than enough Republican votes to guarantee the amendment's passage. But Lincoln was unwilling to wait even for that. A sudden end to the war, say in the spring of 1865, would terminate the military authority of the Emancipation Proclamation and leave months of political dead time before Congress met, a time in which nearly anything could happen. "A question might be raised whether the proclamation was legally valid," Lincoln warned. "It might be added that it only aided those who came into our lines and that it was inoperative as to those who did not give themselves up, or that it would have no effect upon the children of the slaves born hereafter." And so he appealed in December to the last session of the Thirty-Eighth Congress to change its mind before dissolving. "It is not claimed that the election has imposed a duty on members to change their views or their votes," he admitted, but still the election was "the voice of the people," and they would do well to hear it. On January 6, 1865, Radical Republican James Ashley of Ohio called for a reconsideration of the amendment, and Lincoln now moved his own engines of influence into high gear.

This time, the Radicals could scarcely oppose him, and so the amendment offered him the rare opportunity to seize the initiative from them. But resistance could certainly be anticipated from Northern Democrats and border-state hold-outs. So, the secretaries were sent on their usual discreet embassies to unsure congressmen, while the more truculent border-staters were brought to the White House for personal interviews with the president. "You and I were old Whigs, both of us followers of that great statesman, Henry Clay," Lincoln cajoled Missouri congressman James S. Rollins, "and I have sent for you as an old Whig friend to come and see me, that I might make an appeal to you to vote for this amendment." His appeal to the unconvinced wasted no time on idealism. To Rollins, he argued frankly that "The passage of this amendment will clinch the whole subject; it will bring the war, I have no doubt, rapidly to a close." Others held out for more lucrative rewards, and got them. "Two of them wanted internal revenue collector's appointments," Charles Dana remembered, while another "wanted a very important appointment about the custom house of New York . . . worth perhaps twenty thousand dollars a year." And they all got them. "The greatest measure of the nineteenth century," remarked the canny Thaddeus Stevens, "was passed by corruption, aided and abetted by the purest man in America."

It was also aided and abetted by the collapse of Northern Democratic morale after the election. Why not "strengthen ourselves . . . by throwing off the *proslavery* odium?" a dejected Democratic stalwart asked during debate on the amendment. "Then & only then can we hope for Democratic ascendancy." A third of the House Democrats defected to Lincoln and, when the reconsidered amendment came to a vote on January 31, 1865, it sailed through the House with seven votes to spare. "I wish you could have been here the day the constitutional amendment was passed forever abolishing slavery in the United

401

States," Charles Douglass wrote to his father, Frederick. "Such rejoicing I never before witnessed, cannons firing, people hugging and shaking hands, white people I mean, flags flying. . . . I tell you things are progressing finely. . . ."

But if the Thirteenth Amendment represented a triumph for Lincoln's policy on emancipation, there still remained continuing battles to be fought with Congress and the Radicals in his own party over what shape postwar reconstruction in the South should assume. Most of those questions came to center on the political future of the newly freed slaves. Despite Lincoln's veto of the Wade-Davis bill, the Radicals hardly saw themselves as a defeated army, and now that the demand for emancipation had been fulfilled, a number of them were only too happy to take up black civil rights as the issue that would allow them to mount yet another campaign for control of the reconstruction process. "What is freedom?" asked Ohio congressman James A. Garfield. "Is it the bare privilege of not being chained? . . . If this is all, then freedom is a bitter mockery." Despite the sorry record of Southern Unionism, Lincoln saw the future of the South (and the future of the Republican party in the South) in the white nonslaveholders who had been duped by the plantation system into secession and war, but who could now become the basis for a new free-labor future in the South. But every evidence from occupied Louisiana's stumbling embrace of emancipation and the violent divisions within its Unionist ranks reinforced Radical suspicions that the political future of the South was better built upon enfranchisement of the former slaves. "I do not believe," wrote the implacable Wendell Phillips, "in an English freedom, that trusts the welfare of the dependent class to the good will and moral sense of the upper class." Writing to John Bright, Charles Sumner insisted "that the rebel States shall not come back except on the footing of the Decltn of Indep. with all persons equal before the law, & govt. founded on the consent of the governed."

"Mr. Lincoln," Sumner added, "is slow in accepting the truth." Years after the war, Benjamin Butler would claim that as late as 1865 Lincoln was still playing with colonization schemes; this is very unlikely, but it still points toward a known reluctance on Lincoln's part to move any discussion of the issue of black freedom the next step to a campaign for black civil rights. Once colonization was ruled out, the only next step Lincoln was at first willing to discuss was some ill-defined form of apprenticeship for freed slaves, something based on cash wages but hedged in by restrictions that confined ex-slaves to the plantation work they had always known. But when experiments in "apprenticeship" were implemented by Union generals in Louisiana and Mississippi, the results were almost uniformly embarrassing. Union general Nathaniel Banks imposed a compulsory sharecrop system on Louisiana freedmen and provoked an outcry in New Orleans, which in prewar days contained 11,000 free *gens du couleur* and the closest thing to a free black middle class in the South. In the spring of 1864, a petition drive for voting rights by upper-crust Louisiana blacks jolted Lincoln into recognizing that he was dealing with more than a collection of illiterate field hands. "If the recognition of black men as having a right to vote was necessary to close the war, he would not hesitate," he assured the black Louisiana petitioners on March 3, 1864; and ten days later he asked Michael Hahn, the new free-state governor of Louisiana, "whether some of the colored people may not be let in" to voting rights, "as, for instance, the very intelligent, and especially those who have fought gallantly in our ranks." But as much as he was willing to concede to Ward Hill Lamon "the justice of the measure," he wondered whether "it is of doubtful political policy." He mentioned no method for determining who the "very intelligent" were, and his suggestion to Hahn was really a constitutionally cautious hint that black civil rights were something that state governments, not the federal government, must settle. And he did nothing to rewrite a proposed reconstruction constitution for Arkansas that excluded blacks from voting and office-holding. In the end, as he remarked to John Hay in December, 1864, he simply had no "cast iron policy in the matter" to offer as yet.

The danger in this was that presidential uncertainty might be a bad signal to Radicals who by 1864 were eager to make determinations about civil rights a federal matter, and in so doing make them the ultimate solution for Southern treason. In March, 1864, Charles Sumner pushed onto the floor of the Senate a bill establishing a Bureau of Freedmen's Affairs, which would effectively take the freed slaves under the Treasury Department's wing (at a time when the Treasury Department was still under Chase's direction) and distribute food, clothing, and land, arbitrate labor differences, and investigate various rights violations. This was a voyage by the national government into what had, for the most part, been the confusing preserve of diverse state jurisdictions, and with the erratic Sumner as its author, the bill was so badly written that it had to be dragged through several rewrites. But when a House-Senate conference committee in February, 1865, reported out the overhauled bill, they had traveled quite a distance: the bill proposed nothing less than the creation of a new cabinet-level department for the freedmen and an aggressive program of land redistribution. This shocked all but the most extreme of the Radicals, and the bill was subsequently toned down before adoption so that it would at least be palatable to Lincoln, who signed it on March 3, 1865. But even in its milder form, it represented a tactical Radical victory, and in fact the Freedmen's Bureau would become, after the war, one of the principal agents of Radical reconstruction in the South.

The same uneasy jockeying between Lincoln and Congress for control of the postwar process dominated two other major questions in the last weeks of the congressional session. In the wake of the Wade-Davis debacle, Lincoln greeted Congress's last session in December, 1864, with a suggestion of a halfway reconstruction offer: his 10 percent plan had been in operation for "a full year," but "the time may come — probably will come — when public duty shall demand that it be closed; and that, in lieu, more rigorous measures than heretofore shall be adopted." A week later, James Ashley introduced a new reconstruction bill which gave congressional sanction to the 10 percent plan for Louisiana (thus assuring that Louisiana's free-state representatives could now be seated in Congress and the state's readmission to the Union finalized) but which leaned toward the Radicals by applying the Wade-Davis requirements to other still-rebellious Confederate states — provided that this time freed blacks could be counted as "male citizens" toward the Wade-Davis 50-percent requirement. States would, in other words, still do the deciding about civil rights for blacks, but they would be forced to see that decision as a way to avoid the hard hand of Radical reconstruction.

Lincoln at first hesitated over Ashley's new bill, confessing to Ward Hill Lamon that he thought "the question of universal suffrage to the freedman in his unprepared state is one of doubtful propriety . . . and may rebound like a boomerang not only on the Republican party, but upon the freedman himself and our common country." Ordinary Confederate soldiers — the white Southern yeomanry who would be

404

the most important political bloc of the postwar South — "would not return to their homes to accept citizenship under a hated rule; and with nothing but desolation and want throughout the South, the disbanded Confederate soldiers would be tempted to lawlessness and anarchy." But eventually, "with the exception of one or two things" in the bill, he finally declared to Hay "that he liked it."

Ashley, in the spirit of accommodation, made a few concessions of his own, rewriting parts of the bill to limit black voting rights to veterans of "the military or naval service of the United States." But nothing associated with Louisiana was acceptable to the Radicals. Swapping Louisiana for the promise of stricter reconstruction elsewhere was, according to Ben Wade, "a poor way to prevent wrong-doing, and a poor record to make for the future." Ashley was forced to accept fresh amendments which reclaimed Louisiana for the Wade-Davis requirement of 50 percent of the *prewar* citizenship, and that in turn chilled Lincoln's enthusiasm. In the end, the bill became acceptable to no one, and was tabled by the House on February 21, 1865, never to rise again. When the free-state Louisiana government tried to report its electoral votes in February, Congress refused to recognize that a "valid election for President and Vice President" had occurred there. A last-ditch effort, prompted by Lincoln and managed by Lyman Trumbull, to get the Louisiana congressional delegation seated by resolution collapsed at the end of February under a rain of rhetorical blows from Ben Wade. "No bill providing for the reorganization of loyal State government in the rebel States," admitted James Ashley, "can pass this Congress."

This intransigence placed Lincoln between fearing that the war would end so quickly that emancipation could be hung out to dry, and fearing that if it lasted too long, he would lose control over the reconstruction process. Although each had its own peculiar bitterness, the latter fear clearly spelled the greater danger. For that reason, he was cheered by a series of resounding military successes that winter which raised his hopes that the end might actually be only weeks away. In November, 1864, William Sherman jumped off from Atlanta with 62,000 hardened Union veterans on a gigantic raid that eviscerated central Georgia and ended with the capture of Savannah, just in time for Sherman to present it to Lincoln as a Christmas present. What was left of the Confederate army in the west tried to divert Sherman by feebly launching a raid of its own into occupied Tennessee. But Sherman had left another 60,000 federal troops behind him under George Thomas to deal with such contingencies, and on December 15-16, 1864, Thomas tore the Confederates to bits in a frigid two-day battle south of Nashville. In January, a joint army-navy expedition captured Fort Fisher, guarding the approaches to Wilmington, North Carolina, and closed the last major Confederate port of entry on the Atlantic coast. And in March, 1865, a large-scale cavalry raid under James H. Wilson ripped up the heart of the Confederacy from the Tennessee River to Selma, Alabama.

And yet, the last and most dangerous of the Confederate armies, under Robert E. Lee, still lay securely entrenched around Richmond and Petersburg, and by all appearances, there did not seem to be much that could budge the rebels in a hurry. It was at moments like these, when solutions remained remote and the consequences of delay were serious, that Lincoln's old lawyerly instinct for compromise reasserted itself.

For three years, Lincoln had resolutely turned away from any suggestion that he negotiate with the Confederates. Any such negotiations would only discourage the army and strengthen the Democratic opposition, not to mention setting the Radicals ablaze to impeach him. He had yielded in the summer of 1864 to Horace Greeley's hare-brained peace-talks scheme at Niagara Falls because the likelihood of his re-election seemed so remote then and because he was reasonably certain that nothing he had to offer the Confederates would ever be acceptable. He had even gone so far as to draft the letter for Henry Raymond to lay before Jefferson Davis, but then cancelled it. But proposals for peace talks kept popping up after the election, and the longer the stalemate at Petersburg dragged on, the more Lincoln became willing to listen. With the Confederacy visibly beginning to stagger, peace discussions could now only weaken the rebels; and with every day of the war costing millions of dollars, a swiftly negotiated peace would lift the back-breaking strain of the war. Since the Thirteenth Amendment was safely on its way to the state legislatures for ratification, the question of slavery was finished; peace talks now might be an opportunity to seize control of the reconstruction process from the Radicals by arranging a peace settlement on his own terms.

This was obvious, not only to Lincoln but to Northern Democrats and conservative Old-Whig Republicans, several of whom obtained permission from Lincoln to use their own political connections to send peace feelers to Richmond. The most important of these was no one less than old Francis Preston Blair, who had begged Lincoln for months to open contact with Jefferson Davis but who had been prevented by Lincoln from doing so until after the congressional vote on the Thirteenth Amendment was securely in the bag. Lincoln relented in mid-January, giving Blair a pass for what Blair told everyone was merely an effort to recover some family papers that had fallen into Confederate hands during the rebel raid in Maryland the past summer. Blair instead visited Davis and brought back a letter from the Confederate president expressing interest in talks that might lead to peace between "the two countries." Lincoln gagged on any suggestion that there were *two* countries involved, but he sent Blair back to Davis again, indicating that he would be pleased to receive any emissaries Davis cared to name, and on January 30, 1865, he issued a safe-conduct for a delegation the Confederates might send "for the purpose of an informal conference." Davis chose three commissioners and sent them through the Petersburg lines to meet with Seward on board the steamer *River Queen*, anchored near Fort Monroe in Hampton Roads. On February 2, 1865, after an appeal from Grant not to let the commissioners return to Richmond without talking with him, Lincoln himself quietly slipped out of Washington to join Seward on the *River Queen* and meet the Confederates himself.

Davis shrewdly named as the chief of the three-man Confederate group his vice president, Alexander H. Stephens, a former Whig and former congressional colleague of Lincoln's from his lonely term in the House eighteen years before. Stephens more than justified Davis's choice by adroitly sidestepping the "two countries" issue and opening the discussions with a Whiggish appeal to Lincoln to restore harmony and peace "between the different States and Sections of the country." Without rebuffing Stephens, Lincoln nevertheless made it clear that there were several conditions for such "harmony," about which he was not prepared to dicker: first, the Confederate armies must lay down their arms; second, the Emancipation Proclamation would not be recalled; and third, the Confederate states would have to submit to the authority of the federal government, rather than looking for a negotiated peace settlement. "His opinion was that when the resistance ceased and the national authority was recognized, the states would be immediately restored to their practical relations to the Union." Re-union, in short, would have to happen first, and only then could the talking begin.

But once it did, nearly anything was possible, and that included the manner in which slavery might be ended in the Confederacy and any prospect for black civil rights afterwards. Much as he would not recede from the proclamation "in the slightest particular," Lincoln con-ceded that there was no guarantee that in any postwar settlement the proclamation might not be set aside by the courts, and "he should leave it to the courts to decide." True, a constitutional amendment to abolish slavery was presently in the ratification process, and he would expect that the Southern states would join in this ratification. The war, and especially the black soldiers, had pushed things far beyond any hope of a return to the status quo. "Slavery must be abolished," he in-sisted. But if the rebels surrendered now, he would see to it that the im-plementation of abolition would be arranged selectively. "Stephens, if I were in Georgia," Lincoln advised the Confederate vice president, "I would go home and get the governor of the state to call the legislature together . . . and ratify this constitutional amendment *prospectively,* so as to take effect, say, in five years. Such a ratification would be valid in my opinion." That way, Lincoln explained, Southerners "will avoid, as far as possible, the evils of immediate emancipation." In fact, in order to sugar-coat the pill, Lincoln offered to create a special tax "to remu-nerate the southern people for their slaves." After all, the Southerners were no more guilty in reality than Northerners, and "the people of the North were as responsible for slavery as the people of the South," and therefore a "fair indemnity" to slaveholders could not be com-plained about.

A proposal from Lincoln to qualify the abolition of slavery, and, after the loss of hundreds of thousands of lives, to pay off the slave-holders whose secession had triggered the war in the first place, seems so bizarre in February of 1865 that the natural reaction might be to question whether Lincoln could ever really have made it. But all the evidence, from Seward as well as Stephens, suggests that this is pretty much what Lincoln did. And it makes sense only if it is understood how eager Lincoln was to bring the war to an end (both to cut costs and to cut off the Radicals), how much residual faith he had in the importance of achieving Whig-style national compromises, and how little expectation he had of making black civil rights into a federal crusade. The proof of the seriousness with which he made this proposal surfaced on February 5th, after his return to Washington, when he summoned the cabinet to a special evening meeting and briefed them on the Hampton Roads negotiations. "The President had matured a scheme which he hoped would be successful in promoting peace," recorded a dumbfounded Gideon Welles in his diary; more than a "scheme," Lincoln had actually drafted a joint resolution which he wanted to present to both houses of Congress for their adoption. It proposed, quite seriously, to offer all the slaveholding states, including the border states, $400 million in government bonds, half payable by April 1st if "all resistance to national authority shall be abandoned and cease" and the other half payable once the Thirteenth Amendment was ratified. This was, in other words, the resurrection of compensated emancipation, the carrot of compensation being held out to mitigate the stick of abolition.

But he could not have been entirely confident of the practicality of this settlement, if only because he uncharacteristically offered it to the cabinet for discussion. And no one in the cabinet, not even Seward, had the slightest enthusiasm for it. "I think his heart was so fully enlisted in behalf of such a plan that he would have followed it if only a single member of his Cabinet had supported him in the project," remembered Interior Secretary John P. Usher. Even more uncharacteristically, Lincoln pleaded with them for agreement: the war will last "at least a hundred days" more, and cost "three millions a day, besides all the blood which will be shed," whereas the compensation plan "will equal the full amount I propose to pay, to say nothing of the lives lost and property destroyed. I look upon it as a measure of strict and simple economy." He looked around at his advisers and found no support, and after only ten minutes, Lincoln "sighed and said in his sad manner, 'You are all against me.'" And the last peace proposal was put away for good.

This had been a war of surprises, with what had seemed like perfectly obvious questions — secession, treason, states rights, emancipation — turning out to have few direct answers. "We hoped for a happy termination of this terrible war long before this; but God knows best, and has ruled otherwise," Lincoln wrote, for the second time in the war, to the English Quaker Eliza P. Gurney in September, 1864. And lest this sound too much like cheap piety, he added, "The purposes of the Almighty are perfect, and must prevail, though we erring mortals may fail to accurately perceive them in advance. . . . We shall yet acknowledge His wisdom and our own error therein."

He was aware that less temperate voices were offering, and demanding, less measured explanations, and those voices only grew angrier and more self-righteous as the war wore on. In the Confederacy, the long-standing Democratic suspicion of public moralism had long divided public political speech from private religious dialogue, but the outbreak of the war broke that distinction down, as Southern clergy rushed to claim a divine sanction for the Confederacy. "God has given us of the South today a fresh and golden opportunity — and so a most solemn command — to realize that form of government in which the just, constitutional rights of each and all are guaranteed to each and all," preached one Richmond clergyman after first Bull Run. "We are engaged in one of the grandest struggles which ever nerved the hearts or strengthened the hands of a heroic race," announced the Episcopal bishop of Georgia, "to drive away the infidel and rationalistic principles which are sweeping the land and substituting a gospel of the stars and stripes for the gospel of Jesus Christ." The fanaticism of the abolitionists, explained the South's preeminent Presbyterian theologian, James Henley Thornwell, had transformed Northerners into "Atheists, Socialists, Communists, Red Republicans, Jacobins," while the Confederacy had the task of defending "order and regulated freedom." Even more to the point, Benjamin Palmer announced in November, 1861, that God had "providentially committed" the Confederacy to the preservation of "the institution of domestic slavery as now existing."

But the secular weight of Democratic political culture told heavily against Confederates who wanted to make the Confederacy into God's cause. For one thing, many Southern intellectuals like Thornwell privately harbored deep unease about reconciling slavery and Christianity. "Upon an earth radiant with the smile of heaven, or in the Paradise of God, we can no more picture the figure of a slave than we can picture the figures of the halt, the maimed, the lame, and the blind," Thornwell admitted. "That it is inconsistent with a perfect

410

state, that it is not absolutely a good, a blessing, the most strenuous defender of Slavery ought not to permit himself to deny." And on the eve of the war, Thornwell confided to his closest friend that "he had made up his mind to move . . . for the gradual emancipation of the negro, as the only measure that would give peace to the country." The fiery Presbyterian general, "Stonewall" Jackson, owned slaves himself, but also maintained and funded a black Sunday School in his hometown of Lexington, Virginia, that forced him to violate state laws against teaching slaves to read. "His interest in that race was simply because they had souls to save," his wife explained; but the conviction that slaves actually had souls undermined the absolutism of the slave system, and led "some of the Bourbon aristocracy" of Lexington "to threaten prosecution." Robert Lewis Dabney, next to Thornwell in theological stature among Southern Presbyterians and a major propagandist for the Confederacy, privately disbelieved that "we ought to rest contented that slavery should exist forever, in its present form." Southerners "must be willing to recognize and grant in slaves those rights which are a part of our essential humanity"; otherwise slavery "cannot be defended."

With religious friends like this, the Confederacy needed no enemies, and the secular Confederate press gradually cranked up its criticisms of religious patriotism to the point where the *Richmond Examiner* complained that "though it is well that a government should pay proper respect to the religious ceremony, that has been done and overdone by the Confederacy." Confederate officials were outraged when Georgia Baptists blamed the Confederacy's failures in 1864 on the failure of Southern slaveholders to respect the divine sanction of marriage among slaves. Confederate propagandists would continue to praise the personal piety and virtue of individual Confederate leaders like Robert E. Lee and "Stonewall" Jackson as evidence of the moral worthiness of the Confederate cause. But increasingly through the war the Democratic tradition of sharply separating church and state worked itself into justifying the Confederacy more through its dedication to pure republican politics or the classical political models of Athens and Sparta, rather than appeals to Providence. If anything, complained Edward Porter Alexander (Lee's chief of artillery), "It was a serious incubus upon us that during the whole war our president and many of our generals really and actually believed that there *was* this mysterious

411

Providence hovering over the field . . . and that prayers and piety might win its favor from day to day."

But if there was division within the Confederate mind about religion's role in the slave republic, there was just as much division in secular minds over what the political aims of the war should be. For Alexander H. Stephens in 1861, the war's goal was simple and straightforward, and it was the preservation of slavery. "Our Confederacy is founded upon . . . the great truth that the negro is not equal to the white man," Stephens told a Savannah audience in 1861. "Our new government is the first in the history of the world, based upon this great physical and moral truth." Others, like Thornwell, who shrank from such a frank embrace of slavery, tried to explain the war as the defense of a special Southern culture, of Jeffersonian agrarianism, of a "higher sentimentalism, and its superior refinements of scholarship and manners." Still others were more practical: an independent Southern republic would allow Southerners to escape the restraints of tariffs and federal taxes for internal improvements, and allow cotton capitalism to compete freely on world markets. The Confederacy was thus left to sort out its purposes even as it was fighting for its breath, and competition between these various definitions of Southern nationhood generated internal political strife which the Confederate government could ill afford.

The North, with its sizable Democratic population, experienced its own dangerous political divisions, and the loose anti-slavery coalition that made up the Republican party could barely be managed by anyone — including Lincoln, Sumner, Wade, or Chandler — even in the best of times. But unlike the Democrats, the Republicans were built on a core of old Whiggery which had no reluctance about mixing religion and politics into a single public agenda. Unlike strict Southern separationists, Henry Ward Beecher seemed to one observer like "a stump speaker who has mistaken his way and stumbled into a church." That produced a rhetoric of religious interpretation which was as overweening in its claims about the war as its Confederate counterpart had been hesitating and disenfranchised. Northern Methodists "saluted the stars and stripes as next in our prayers and affections to the very Cross of the Redeemer." Boston's great evangelical bastion, Park Street Church, rang with exhortations to "Strike for Law and Union, for Country and God's great ordinance of Government."

412

Robert Stanton's *The Church and the Rebellion* asked in 1864, "How can any believer in God's Providence, which extends to *all* things — in whose hand are the hearts of all people — fail to see in these events the inevitable designs of God? How can he fail to read in them the doom of slavery?" The New School Presbyterian General Assembly hailed the Union cause in 1862 as "the final theater" for solving "the final problems of history." There are occasions, wrote Charles Hodge (Thornwell's distinguished counterpart as a theologian among Northern Presbyterians) "when political questions rise into the sphere of morals and religion; when the rule for political action is not to be sought in the consideration of state policy, but the law of God."

The law of God in this case not only mandated the suppression of rebellion, but a new national order emerging from the ashes of the war, a new republic "to spread Scriptural holiness over these and all lands." This millennial republic conveniently resembled Whig political culture — "the bondman everywhere a freeman; the degraded white man everywhere educated and ennobled; the diverse elements in the national composition fused and welded inseparably together . . . the extremities of the country drawn into a closer relationship; its physical resources developed; a schoolhouse and church in every district" — but that only underscored how easily Republican Protestants could weld religion and politics together into an expectation that the war would consecrate the United States "to Jehovah as a national Israel and servant of the Lord, fit for her Master's use." Even liberal Unitarians and Congregationalists like Horace Bushnell and William Henry Furness hailed the war as the advent of a new world, "arrayed in millennial splendor, wherein the distinctions of race, which have always been such active causes of contempt and hatred and war shall be obliterated, and men shall live together in the relations of Christian brotherhood" in "a living, moral Union." Where the Confederacy had congratulated itself on the private piety of its leaders, but then excluded that piety from a public role, the Republicans brought religion directly onto the public square, without inquiring whether its leaders possessed that piety in their private moments. And of course no better example of this existed anywhere in the Republican party than Abraham Lincoln.

This religious policy-mongering, which culminated in 1864 with the drive for the "Bible Amendment," generated deep suspicions among

413

Northern Democrats, who believed that millennial fervor was a threat rather than an asset in managing the war. Northern Democrat elites shuddered with contempt when the United States Christian Commission organized 5,000 agents to travel with the federal armies, distributing religious tracts and preaching abolition, and they organized a rival United States Sanitary Commission to provide a secularized, and less impassioned, counterpart. But even among Republican intellectuals, there were moments of hesitation about too-eagerly identifying the North as the seat of unqualified righteousness and the South as the cave of unqualified evil. Charles Hodge, who had left Whiggism in 1856 to vote for Fremont and then Lincoln, agreed that "This war touches the conscience in too many points to render silence on the part of religious men either allowable or possible." But Hodge was hesitant about "the popular view of the subject," which assumed that praise and blame for the war could be easily identified and distributed to North and South. History was not judicial, Hodge warned, and the victories or defeats logged by either side do not necessarily represent the judgments of God. "Do not the Scriptures and all experience teach us, that God is a sovereign, that the orderings of his providence are not determined by justice, but by mysterious wisdom?" Hodge asked that question in 1863, when it was not at all clear whether the great Confederate victories at Second Bull Run and Chancellorsville were some form of divine message of judgment against the North. Oddly, Abraham Lincoln had begun asking the very same question, and coming to much the same conclusion as Hodge, at about the same time. And he was still asking that question in the spring of 1865 as he pondered the content of his second inaugural address.

Composing this second inaugural speech posed an interesting challenge of its own to Lincoln, since he was the first president since Andrew Jackson actually obliged to deliver a second inaugural, and he might have excused himself from offering little more than a reiteration of his December, 1864, message to Congress. He showed "a roll of manuscripts" to the artist Francis Carpenter and a congressional delegation on February 26th which "will be called my 'second inaugural,'" but he remarked that it would contain only "about six hundred words," and he locked it away in a desk drawer "until I want it." In the event, the address actually came out to seven hundred and three words, and in it he saw "less occasion for an extended address than there was at the first" inaugural. "Public declarations have been constantly called forth on every point and phase of the great contest," and so "Little that is new could be presented." But instead of this dispensing with the need for any address, the lack of news freed him to turn his address away from politics and toward the larger, more haunting, question of the war's meaning. And he would, in the process, not only manage to outdistance even his own customary rhetorical grace, but introduce into an American political address an element of religious speculation which, it is safe to say, none of the founders of the republic could ever have foreseen as the living concerns of an American president.

There was nothing in the way the inaugural was carried out that portended anything especially sublime. Congress had kept its dissension over reconstruction policy bubbling until the wee hours of inauguration day, March 4th, when the Thirty-Eighth Congress finally adjourned itself into history. Lincoln arrived at the Capitol hours in advance of the inauguration in order to sign the last flurry of bills, and he was too distracted by these last responsibilities to join the inauguration parade up Pennsylvania Avenue. (This was just as well for Lincoln, since the weather turned raw and gusty and the huge procession moved so slowly that Mary Lincoln had the White House carriage detour out of line to take a short-cut to the Capitol.) At noon, the gavel in the Senate chamber fell, the doors were opened to members of the House of Representatives and visitors, and Lincoln and the cabinet appeared from a side door and moved to seats in the diplomatic gallery to watch the swearing-in of his new vice president, Andrew Johnson.

Andrew Johnson was an odd number in this new administration. Running the war as military governor in his native Tennessee as though it were a war on the planter aristocrats more than secession, Johnson was one of the few successful exhibits of Southern Unionism, and Lincoln believed that his nomination as vice president was "calculated to give more strength to the ticket." All the same, he had pulled shy of forcing Johnson on the party, and he allowed the 1864 nominating convention to draft Johnson on their own motion. In January, Johnson wrote to Lincoln, asking to be excused from the inaugural ceremonies so that he could preside over the first meeting of the new free-state legislature of Tennessee, which would meet "& resume all the

415

functions of a state in the Union." If Lincoln had known what would happen next, he might have granted Johnson's request, since Johnson had reluctantly arrived in Washington nursing the effects of a bout with typhoid and had doused himself with whiskey the night before to clear his head. The alcohol had precisely the opposite effect, and Johnson proceeded to deliver an inaugural address of his own which wandered boozily from pillar to post, and ended only after outgoing Vice President Hannibal Hamlin forcibly tugged at Johnson's coattails to get him to stop. The whole assembly murmured in horror and embarrassment, and as the hall rose to move outside onto the Capitol's east portico for Lincoln's swearing-in, John Henderson overheard Lincoln instruct the marshal of ceremonies, "Don't let Johnson speak outside."

A wooden platform had been built out over the portico steps, with ranks of seats for the cabinet, the Supreme Court, and the rest of the government dignitaries, while "a literal sea of heads, tossing and surging, as far as the eye could reach," milled below. A single spindly dais stood at the front of the platform, and to this Lincoln stepped with a single large sheet of paper in his hand. The wind and drizzle had stopped and the umbrellas had come down as the inaugural party moved outside, and propitiously, "just at that moment" (wrote newspaperman Noah Brooks) "the sun, obscured all day, burst forth in its unclouded meridian splendor, and flooded the spectacle with glory and with light. Every heart beat quicker at the unexpected omen."

Lincoln began with a brief paragraph explaining what he was *not* going to say. "The progress of our arms, upon which all else chiefly depends, is as well known to the public as myself," and needed no rehearsal now. He had a larger agenda to pursue in this address, and that was his own inquiry into the meaning of the war, an inquiry he had been conducting almost since its beginning. For Lincoln, that meaning was linked to its causes, and unlike the first inaugural, he was not reluctant to finger slavery as the fundamental cause. "These slaves constituted a peculiar and powerful interest," Lincoln explained, and "All knew" — despite their denials — "that this interest was, somehow, the cause of the war." The precise method by which slavery caused the war was, as he had been saying since 1854, the determination of slaveholders "to strengthen, perpetuate, and extend this interest" into the western territories, "while the government claimed no right to do more than to restrict the territorial enlargement of it." And if Lincoln had wished to conclude matters at that point, he would already have said a great deal, laying the onus of war entirely on slavery and making its eradication the single object of the war.

But Lincoln had long before seen the war galloping away from the comparatively limited Enlightenment parameters of cause and effect. "Neither party expected for the war, the magnitude, or the duration, which it has already attained," Lincoln continued. "Each looked for an easier triumph, and a result less fundamental and astounding." Actually, Lincoln had anticipated "astounding" results for quite some time. Back in the summer of 1861, speaking to the hastily assembled special session of the Thirty-Seventh Congress, he had spoken of the war as a "people's contest," a war between popular government and a slave aristocracy, and at Gettysburg he had described it as a test of whether or not republics, which had no kings to decide public questions by force, were doomed to tear themselves apart over divisive political issues. But now, he had come to see in the war the most "astounding" result imaginable, something that transcended its causes, a kind of divine weighing of the republic — not just the South, but South and North together — in which the war's losses were the wages of national sin, payable by both in life and treasure.

And again, if Lincoln had stopped *here*, he would still have been saying a great deal, although it would have sounded very much like mere moral equivalence. "Both read the same Bible and pray to the same God; and each invokes His aid against the other" — and, Lincoln might have added, both have called the pitch wrong and are deserving of the same treatment. No doubt Lincoln had a weakness for such arguments: in a universe where "there was no freedom of the will" and where "men are made by conditions that surround them," it was easy for Lincoln to believe that even the deepest convictions were only the product of circumstances and self-interest, and conferred no particular superiority on one side or the other. "I have no prejudice against the Southern people," Lincoln once said back in 1854. "They are just what we would be in their situation."

But Lincoln did not believe that North and South were simple moral equivalents. The fact that, in 1854, they might be "no more responsible for the origin of slavery, than we," did not make slavery right, or the defense of it indifferent. North or South, he found it "strange that any men should dare to ask a just God's assistance in

417

wringing their bread from the sweat of other men's faces," and he held the South liable at least for having decided to "*make* war rather than let the nation survive," while the North only insisted that it "would *accept* war rather than let it perish." The North might not be perfect, but it was clearly on the side of the angels. In that light, then, North and South were to be weighed and judged *in spite* of the seeming moral superiority of slavery's opponents. All of which, in the human terms Lincoln had so far been discussing things, made no sense whatsoever.

To find sense in such a situation meant leaving behind the ordinary calculations of praise and blame. Granted that slaveholders were wrong, *why* should both North and South be punished together? For that, Lincoln had no other answer but an appeal to the inscrutability of God, the sovereign providence whom he had long before decided could not be anticipated, but only yielded to. As he had told Eliza Gurney months before, "The Almighty has his own purposes," and those purposes do not always coincide with what we expect historical justice and right to be. He did not disagree that slavery was an "offense"; yet he could not argue that "this terrible war" had not been given alike to both North and South, "until all the wealth piled by the bond-man's two hundred and fifty years of unrequited toil shall be sunk, and until every drop of blood drawn with the lash, shall be paid with another drawn by the sword." There was no other answer for why justice should bleed as freely as injustice except "the providence of God." And if that surrendered the whole problem to inscrutability, should that surprise anyone? "Shall we discern herein any departure from those divine attributes which the believers in a Living God always ascribe to him? . . . As was said three thousand years ago, so still it must be said, 'the judgments of the Lord, are true and righteous altogether.'"

This, of course, had been Charles Hodge's argument two years before, and it is no accident that Lincoln, the quondam predestinarian Baptist and "mechanist," and Hodge, the Old School Whig Presbyterian, had tracked each other's intellectual positions on slavery with some surprising degree of parallel since the 1830s. (Hodge and Lincoln shared Whig politics and Whig moralism; both refused to declare slaveholding an outright sin; both of them underwent a steady shift toward abolition of slavery, Lincoln in the 1850s, Hodge during the war.) Where the two parted in outlook was that Lincoln looked upon this inscrutable God purely as a Judge, and a Judge so remote that his most crucial decisions could only be unfathomable. There was no hint in the inaugural that the terrible bloodletting could in some way reflect a redemptive purpose, that God the Judge might also be perceived as God the Redeemer. Far away, in the white-shrouded confines of her father's homestead, Emily Dickinson, another of Calvinism's cast-offs, also flailed helplessly in search of redemption in the war.

> At least to pray — is left — is left
> Oh Jesus — in the Air —
> I know not which thy chamber is —
> I'm knocking — everywhere —
> Thou settest Earthquake in the South —
> And Maelstrom, in the Sea —
> Say, Jesus Christ of Nazareth —
> Hast thou no arm for Me?

But Christ the Redeemer was an apprehension of God that Lincoln had never found enough acceptance or grace or religious peace to embrace. The view of God that appears in the second inaugural as the core of his speculation on the war's meaning could only be God the Judge, who was simply an extension of the God who numbered the hairs of his dying father's head in 1851 and who took off three-year-old children in death without offering either rhyme or reason. What the war brought for him was the same reckoning of judgment — a far-seeing and comprehensive judgment that played no favorites and made no exemptions even for those who opposed slavery, but still only judgment.

However limited this view might be, it did have some advantages to confer. Given that the ultimate meaning of the war was thus bound up in inscrutability, there was no opportunity for Northerners to presume that they had the full answer to the war's questions and were thereby entitled to prescribe the solution: not the celebrity preachers and certainly not the Radicals in Congress. And hereby lies the basic political strategy of the second inaugural. For the address was not only a theological invocation which it is past imagining for any but a Whig-Republican and an old Calvinist to have uttered in public, but it was also an appeal against the Radicals, and anyone else so full of themselves as to think both the questions and answers obvi-

419

ous — an appeal to an authority not even the Radicals were brazen enough to defy. The man who had once suffered from having the religion card played against him, now played it against Sumner, Chandler, and Wade with the consummate skill of a theologian.

What was the proper set of mind for Northerners, looking for the "bottom" of the war? The last paragraph of the address was Lincoln's answer, simple, supple in its words, with the grace of a benediction, as if he were once again miming the sermons of preachers to perfection. "With malice toward none; with charity for all; with firmness in the right as God gives us to see the right." Inscrutability, like the doctrine of necessity, was not an excuse for passivity, but was rather a call for chastity of purpose. One should move with firmness in the right, but with the caution that not every right we think we see is necessarily the right as God sees and reveals it. And the right we could be sure of practicing was described in biblical, not political terms: "to bind up the nation's wounds; to care for him who shall have borne the battle, and for his widow, and his orphan — to do all which may achieve and cherish a just, and a lasting peace, among ourselves, and with all nations." As inscrutability teaches a humility of ultimate intentions, so it also teaches a humility of policy.

The applause and cheers were polite, not from want of agreement, but from the sheer prophetic solemnity of the last rolling cadences. And then the chief justice — with poetical appropriateness, it was Salmon Chase — stepped forward to administer the oath of office, and at the conclusion, Lincoln bent down and kissed the open Bible on which the oath was sworn. It read, from the fifth chapter of Isaiah, *None shall be weary nor stumble among them.*

But Lincoln *was* weary. Walt Whitman saw him at the reception afterwards at the White House, "drest all in black, with white kid gloves and a clawhammer coat, receiving, as in duty bound, shaking hands, looking very disconsolate, and as if he would give anything to be somewhere else." He posed for a visiting Massachusetts photographer on March 6th, and the resulting image shows Lincoln haggard and thin, with his jaw-whiskers now shaved to a wiry tuft at the chin. A series of photographs taken a month later by Alexander Gardner reveal a gaunt, hollowed face, his hair beginning to fleck with white. When his old friend Joshua Speed called on him at the end of February, he confessed, "I am very unwell. My feet and hands are always cold. I suppose I ought to be in bed." And in fact on March 13th, Lincoln was "quite sick to-day, and has denied himself to all visitors," even going to the extreme of hosting a cabinet meeting in his sickroom. A note of congratulation came to him from Thurlow Weed for the short message Lincoln had sent to Congress after the official notification of his re-election. Lincoln took it as congratulations for the inaugural address as well, and piquantly expressed his anticipation that the address would not be well received in some quarters. "Men" — and especially the Radicals — "are not flattered by being shown that there has been a difference of purpose between the Almighty and them. To deny it, however, in this case, is to deny that there is a God governing the world." The best evidence of God's hand in human affairs would be the incomprehensibility of what that hand wrought.

Lincoln expected in February that the war could not possibly end before the early summer. But by mid-March, Sherman had thrust upwards from Savannah into the Carolinas, brushing aside the annoyance provided by the last organized wreckage of the western Confederate army, and Grant was becoming more and more convinced that one good hard blow at Petersburg might flatten Lee's hemorrhaging army. "The rebellion has lost its vitality and if I am not much mistaken there will be no rebel Army of any great dimensions a few weeks hence," Grant wrote to his father on March 19th. If Grant was anxious about anything now, it was that Lee might slip out of the Richmond and Petersburg lines and "we would have the same army to fight again farther south — and the war might be prolonged another year." The next day, Grant telegraphed Lincoln from his headquarters at City Point, Virginia, asking whether Lincoln could come down for "a day or two?" He was guarded about his reasons. "I would like very much to see you and I think the rest would do you good," was the terse explanation Grant offered. But the truth was that Grant wanted to hear directly from Lincoln how to handle any potential surrender situation, and to that end Grant also sent for Sherman to come by steamer from the Carolinas to join the consultation. Lincoln, who was back in his office routine but still feeling unwell, immediately leapt at Grant's invitation, and on March 23rd Lincoln, along with Mary and Tad and a small staff chartered the *River Queen* and puffed off down the Chesapeake Bay with a naval escort for the James River and City Point.

421

It was as pleasant an excursion as any trip into a war zone could be, and while everyone waited for Sherman's arrival, Lincoln insisted on being given as close a view of the Petersburg siege lines as safety would permit. He reviewed Sheridan's cavalry, a division of infantry, a naval flotilla, and went to a review where Mary created an embarrassing scene by accusing the wife of General Edward Ord of flirting with her husband. And then, on the afternoon of March 27th, Sherman arrived at City Point, and that evening Grant, Sherman, and Admiral David Dixon Porter closeted themselves in the large after-cabin of the *River Queen* to decide how, without benefit of the Radicals, the war should be ended.

And it was quite clear by now that it would be ended by them. Congress would not reassemble to organize itself until December, which left Lincoln an almost entirely free hand in setting the terms on which the Confederates could surrender and the rebel states be received back into the Union. "He thought it providential that this great rebellion was crushed just as Congress had adjourned," Gideon Welles recalled, "and there were none of the disturbing elements of that body to hinder and embarrass us." The next eight months would leave just enough time to get the war finished quickly, even if it meant making some concessions to the Confederates. Both Grant and Sherman were convinced that the armies "would have to fight one more bloody battle," but Lincoln hoped to avoid even that. And when the Confederates finally did face eventualities, he encouraged his officers to "get the men composing the Confederate armies back to their homes, at work on their farms and in their shops," and even to grant recognition to the rebel "State governments then in existence, with all their civil functionaries," at least "till Congress could provide others." That way, "we should reanimate the states and get their governments in successful operation, with order prevailing and the Union reestablished, before Congress came together in December."

What to do with the Confederate leadership became a case in point: Lincoln wryly suggested that they simply be allowed to disappear. He believed that "we could not have peace or order in the South . . . while they remained there with their great influence to poison public opinion," but if they could be scattered then the loyal Southern farmers and middle class could assume their rightful control of the Southern states. "Scare them out of the country by having our generals inform them that if they stay, they will be punished for their crimes," Lincoln had told Schuyler Colfax, "but if they leave, no attempt will be made to hinder them." He would not go so far as to extend a pardon to Jefferson Davis or any other top rebel officials, but "if he had his way, he would let him die in peace on his southern plantation," or at least turn a blind eye if Davis wanted to discreetly scamper off into exile. "I hope he will mount a fleet horse," Lincoln had told Edward Neill, "reach the shores of the Gulf of Mexico, and drive so far into its waters that we shall never see him again." Davis's fate would thereby embitter none of his former followers, and Davis himself would never become a stick with which the Radicals could beat reconstruction into a more vengeful shape.

The discussions continued the next morning, and Sherman recalled that Grant sat throughout the hour-and-a-half second round without saying very much at all. Part of the reason lay in the plans Grant had been privately hatching to deliver his great hammer-blow at Petersburg while Lincoln was still at City Point. The next morning, the Army of the Potomac was on the move, its left arm curling around the end of Lee's paper-thin lines at a crossroads called Five Forks. On April 1st, the federals overran Five Forks and threatened to cut off any westward escape route Lee might hope for. The next day, on Lee's advice, the Confederate government hurriedly abandoned Petersburg and Richmond, piling desperately onto the last trains headed for Danville and safety; in the afternoon, Lee began skillfully withdrawing from his siege lines, collecting what remained of his skeletal army, and preparing to dash westward toward Amelia Court House, hoping to put enough distance between himself and Grant to slide southward and link up with the last remnant of Confederate forces in the Carolinas. Grant ordered a major bombardment of the Confederate trenches at Petersburg for five in the morning on April 3rd, to be followed an hour later by a general assault all along the lines. But by that time Lee had already escaped. Grant had only the consolation of telegraphing Lincoln back at City Point that Richmond was now open to federal occupation, and would the president like to come up to see the city?

Lincoln was loitering at City Point under the suspicion that Grant had been preparing just such an attack. "Do you know, general, that I have had a sort of sneaking idea for some days that you intended to do something like this?" he replied. He came up to Petersburg with

Tad and an escort early on April 3rd, and the next day the gunboat *Malvern* transported Lincoln, Tad, and a guard of sailors up to a deserted Richmond wharf on the James River. The evacuating Confederates, in an attempt to destroy military supplies, had let fires rage almost out of control, and now the city wore a deserted, sullen, emaciated look. Richmond's blacks, uncertain but eager, recognized Lincoln almost at once as the president and his escort fanned out into the deserted streets, and black dock workers came crowding along, hailing Lincoln as their messiah, trying to break through the cordon of sailors to touch his hand, his feet. "Don't kneel to me," Lincoln said. "That is not right. You must kneel to God only, and thank him." An escort of New York infantrymen arrived to conduct him to the improvised headquarters of General Godfrey Weitzel, who would be responsible for the occupation of Richmond, and Weitzel, in turn, took Lincoln over to the mansion Jefferson Davis had, until only two days before, used as his version of the White House. He sat at Davis's desk, ate a light lunch, and then toured other parts of the city through ever-more-jubilant crowds of blacks. And when he was asked what he thought federal occupation policy ought to be toward the city, he would only say in a few words what he had explained at such great length to Grant and Sherman a week before: "If you were in my place, you would not press them."

Just how easy he intended the pressing to be appeared the next day, when a delegation of Virginia officials, headed by Judge John A. Campbell (who had been one of the Hampton Roads commissioners) came calling at Weitzel's headquarters to learn what Lincoln's intentions might be for Virginia. There was no talk now about delaying the abolition of slavery: "the executive action on the subject of slavery, so far as it had been declared in messages, proclamations, and other official acts, must pass for what they are worth." But at the same time, just as he had directed Grant and Sherman the week before, there was no talk further than that, and he would give Campbell every chance to call "the Virginia legislature that had been sitting in Richmond together" and get them to "vote for the restoration of Virginia to the Union," call home the Virginia troops and effectively collapse what was left of Confederate military resistance. Unfortunately, this was less easy to do than it looked, since a provisional Virginia Unionist government had actually been sitting in Alexandria all through the war under Francis Pierpont, claiming to represent the *real* Virginia. But rump military governments like Pierpont's were the relics of an earlier stage in Lincoln's thinking on reconstruction, and Lincoln now assured Campbell that the Pierpont government actually had no real jurisdiction "and he did not desire to enlarge it." Turning to General Weitzel, Lincoln directed him to let Campbell publish a call for "the gentlemen who have acted as the Legislature of Virginia" to convene. But at the same time, Weitzel was to make sure that the Virginians did just what Lincoln wanted and no more. Any foolish defiance of federal authority, and they were to be dispersed and, if needs be, arrested.

Having warned Grant and Sherman about the need to be prepared for a Southern military surrender, Lincoln was himself caught unprepared by the suddenness of Campbell's request for direction in reconstructing Virginia. He went back to City Point and began working out a proclamation that would specify the details of the new Virginia settlement and found that it "gave me more perplexity than any other paper I ever drew up"; it kept him up till one in the morning "before I got it to suit me." As it turned out, it suited no one else. After lingering until April 8th to see if Grant could bring the fleeing Lee to bay for a surrender, Lincoln finally agreed that he could be absent no longer from Washington. Word had come on April 5th that William Seward had been dangerously injured in a carriage accident, and Lincoln needed to call together the cabinet to consult on the Campbell proposal.

But when the cabinet gathered on April 11th, "the subject . . . caused general surprise." Promises had been made to the Pierpont government which some of them felt could not be betrayed; others were far from convinced that any Virginia legislature called together under such circumstances would cooperate; and of course the agreement left hanging in mid-air any understanding of what was to happen to the former slaves. Besides, argued Gideon Welles, "as we had never recognized any other of their organizations as possessing validity during the war, it would be impolitic, to say the least, to now recognize them and their government." This disagreement "was annoying him greatly," and he claimed that he actually was not thinking of recognizing the Campbell legislature as "a real Legislature" but merely as a sort of convention that could pull the plug on Virginia's support for the Confederates and ensure a peaceful transition to civil government.

Nevertheless, "perhaps it was best the proceeding should be abandoned."

And as if to confirm the cabinet's misgivings, Lincoln received from Weitzel the next day a warning that Campbell was already beginning to describe the Virginia legislature as some form of equal negotiating partner in a separate peace settlement, that the Emancipation Proclamation was no longer in effect, that the South Carolina legislature should act together with the Virginians. This was enough. Lincoln angrily wired back an order to Weitzel to cancel Campbell's assembly. He had agreed to deal with the Virginia legislature "to do a specific thing, to wit, 'to withdraw the Virginia troops, and other support from resistance to the General Government,'" but if they had more ambitious aspirations, that was their mistake. Besides, he no longer really needed them. On April 9th, while Lincoln was still on board the *River Queen* heading back to Washington, Grant had finally cornered Lee's staggering remnant at Appomattox Court House, and Lee had surrendered. "Since Lee's army has surrendered," he remarked to Schuyler Colfax, "it became needless" to deal with Campbell. The surrender terms for Lee's soldiers were as generous as Lincoln had intended them to be: paroles to all the Confederate troops, no arrests of Confederate officers (including General Lee), even an allowance for officers to keep their side-arms and ordinary soldiers to claim an army horse or mule for themselves. The end had come.

Perhaps more ends than just Lee's had come, too. Washington went wild with joy over the news, late on April 9th, of Lee's surrender, and two nights later, Lincoln delivered an unusual public address to a huge crowd with "bands and banners" on the north lawn of the White House. Military victory, he explained, had pressed the question of reconstruction "much more closely on our attention," and it was a question which he acknowledged "is fraught with difficulty." Among those difficulties was the plain fact that "we, the loyal people, differ among ourselves as to the mode, manner, and means of reconstruction." His own plan for reconstructing Louisiana, for instance, despite being "distinctly approved by every member" of the cabinet, had been bitterly opposed in Congress, and all on the basis of distinctions about whether the Confederate states were still to be considered states, and whether the states alone should be responsible for the civil rights of the freedmen. This was "a merely pernicious abstraction": What did it

426

matter what the status of Louisiana had been in rebellion, so long as it was now willing to resubmit to federal authority? "Finding themselves safely at home, it would be utterly immaterial whether they had ever been abroad."

But it was true, he admitted, that Louisiana was not perfect. Certainly it would be better if Wade and Davis's 50 percent of the voters had taken the oath rather than just 10 percent; and with yet another experience immediately behind him of how unreliable Southern Unionism might be as the basis for a political future, perhaps it would be better if the new Louisiana constitution did confer voting rights on "the very intelligent" freedmen, "and on those who serve our cause as soldiers." But why, when Louisiana had at least abolished slavery and ratified the Thirteenth Amendment, destroy all of this good work simply because it was not a perfect work? "Concede that the new government of Louisiana is only to what it should be as the egg is to the fowl, we shall sooner have the fowl by hatching the egg than by smashing it." Besides, the Thirteenth Amendment required approval by three-fourths of the states, according to the Constitution; rejecting Louisiana also meant rejecting "one vote in favor of the proposed amendment" and thereby jeopardizing the whole abolition project.

Having met with so much frustration in trying to bring Louisiana (and by implication, Arkansas, Tennessee, and other occupied rebel states) back into the Union, it was now time "to make some new announcement to the people of the South." What it was, he would not say, but "I am considering, and shall not fail to act, when satisfied that action will be proper." He was being deliberately cryptic, but the fact that he was nurturing some "new" plan meant that neither the original 10 percent plan nor the embarrassing spectacle of the recalled Virginia legislature would be the models for future action. "This was not the sort of speech which the multitude had expected," Noah Brooks recalled, but the crowd was "loud and enthusiastic" anyway.

All, at least, but one in the mass of spectators on the White House lawn, a clandestine Confederate agent, now adrift, masterless and bitter in the rejoicing all around him. A Marylander by birth, he had never made any effort to conceal his Southern sympathies, but only a handful knew about his secret career as a Confederate informant, smuggler of medical supplies, and plotter. He was much better known

427

throughout the North and in Washington theater circles as the actor, John Wilkes Booth.

No high official in the government of the United States had ever been killed as retribution for his actions while in office, although one demented attempt had been made on the life of Andrew Jackson. Lincoln did not believe that he would be an exception to this rule. "Assassination of public officers is not an American crime," Lincoln assured Benjamin Butler in 1863. But he believed this in spite of a volume of threats and hate mail that frightened nearly everyone else close to him. "Soon after I was nominated at Chicago," Lincoln admitted to the artist Francis Carpenter, "I began to receive letters threatening my life. The first one or two made me a little uncomfortable, but I came at length to look for a regular installment of this kind of correspondence in every week's mail, and up to inauguration day I was in constant receipt of such letters." It was not that he dismissed any possibility of dying in office. In 1860, he had experienced an unusual double vision of himself in a mirror, one image vivid and the other pale, and he saw "the lifelike image betokening a safe passage through his first term as president; the ghostly one, that death would overtake him before the close of the second." But the death he expected, as he told Owen Lovejoy, was from sheer overwork rather than murder: "This war is eating my life out; I have a strong impression that I shall not live to see the end."

Still, the assassination threats only increased over time, as disgruntled Democrats, Southern sympathizers, and an assortment of unhinged crackpots for whom the stress of war had been too great came to see in Lincoln the incarnation of all their torments. Rumors of a plot to murder him along his inaugural route to Washington in 1861 were so convincing that his train schedule had to be rerouted to bring him through Baltimore to Washington by night, and old General Scott had carpeted the inaugural procession with sharpshooters and artillery to snuff any plot to assault Lincoln. Hate mail continued to pour in, threatening that "you will be a dead man in six months" or that "Abe must die, and now." Eventually, there was so much of it that the secretarial staff quietly destroyed the worst letters. Even so, enough of it crossed his desk for Lincoln to set aside a pigeonhole marked "Assassination" in his stand-up desk, and the threats preyed on his mind so much that he began to experience dreams about the murder of presidents and funerals in the East Room of the White House.

Publicly, however, Lincoln refused to take the threats seriously. "The way we skulked into this city in the first place has been a source of shame and regret to me; for it did look so cowardly," he complained to Ward Hill Lamon in 1862, and he did not propose to give his political critics further ammunition by behaving in office as though he was guilty of some crime deserving death. Besides, he rationalized, there was very little one could do in his position as president to forestall a really determined assassination attempt. "I cannot discharge my duties if I withdraw myself entirely from danger of an assault," he told John Nicolay. "I see hundreds of strangers every day, and if anybody has the disposition to kill me he will find opportunity. To be absolutely safe I should lock myself up in a box." To Jim Lane, he explained in May, 1864, "that while every prominent man was more or less exposed to the attacks of maniacs, no foresight could guard against them." During the first year of the war, the White House itself was protected by little more than the civilian staff, and Charles Halpine was amazed to discover that it was quite possible to walk right through the front door "as late as nine or ten o'clock at night," and ascend the stairs to the second floor living quarters "without seeing or being challenged by a single soul."

Eventually, once Lincoln began spending the summers at the Soldiers' Home, he was prevailed upon by Secretary of War Stanton to accept an escort (although he grumbled to Halpine that he was more afraid of being "shot by the accidental discharge of one of their carbines or revolvers" than by an assassin), and by 1863, Stanton had decided to station several hand-picked companies of infantry and cavalry from Ohio and Pennsylvania on the White House grounds. Lincoln was not even supposed to cross the lawn from the White House to the War Department without a bodyguard. Nevertheless, Lincoln often amused himself devising ways of eluding his protectors. When Major General Christopher Augur tried to beef up the White House escort detail with an extra company of cavalry in July, 1864, Lincoln sent their captain back with "a verbal order that the men were not wanted." A week later, as Confederate raiders struck at Fort Stevens, outside Washington, Lincoln insisted on being driven out to see the fighting and standing on the fort's parapet, in full view of rebel snipers whose bullets kicked up fountains of dirt near him. And Lamon (whom Lincoln regarded as "a monomaniac on the subject of my safety") was shocked to learn in December, 1864, that Lincoln "went unattended to the theatre" except for the company of Charles Sumner and "a foreign minister, neither of whom could defend himself against an assault from any able-bodied woman in this city."

Lincoln's lethal indifference to his safety sat oddly beside an often-repeated confession that he was not a particularly good example of physical courage. He once told Francis Carpenter that he regarded himself as "a great coward physically, and was sure that he would make a poor soldier . . . and run at the first symptom of danger." Noah Brooks heard him say that he "was sure that he would make a poor soldier, for, unless there was something in the excitement of a battle, he was sure that he would drop his gun and run at the first symptom of danger." And yet, as president and (constitutionally) commander-in-chief of the army, he had to assume responsibility for feeding hundreds of thousands of unknown lives into the maw of the war, and for the last two years of the war he was oppressed with the thought "of the sacrifices of life yet to be offered and the hearts and homes yet to be made desolate before this dreadful war . . . is over." He felt sometimes "like hiding in deep darkness," especially when he had to review, not just casualty lists, but courts-martial records and military death sentences. He waved Leonard Swett out of his office one afternoon, saying, "Get out of the way, Swett; tomorrow is butcher day, and I must go through these papers and see if I cannot find some excuse to let these poor fellows off." In time, Lincoln became notorious among his own generals for wholesale approval of pardons or remissions of sentences that were appealed to him as commander in chief (although in many cases, his pardons were simply ratifications of recommendations coming up from prior levels of appeal). For a man who had looked so often since 1862 for providence to vindicate his decisions — for a man for whom judgment and expiation were the underpinnings of his mental universe, rather than redemption — it would be irresistible to look for some further vindication, beyond his own powers of pardon, for the horrendous bloodletting of the war by exposing himself to the judgment of a bullet.

Lincoln had no way of telling just how much risk he was actually running. Anyone who actually took the trouble to write a death-threat letter was probably not going to do much more than that. Nor did the rebels seem to promise much in the way of bodily harm to Lincoln at first, since Jefferson Davis discouraged all talk of plots aimed personally at Lincoln. This changed, however, as the last year of the war spelled greater desperation for the Confederates, and after a failed Union cavalry raid on Richmond in February, 1864, turned up documents that appeared to authorize an assault on Davis himself. From that point on, retaliatory plots to kidnap Lincoln and deliver him to Richmond as a super-hostage for peace negotiations began to take on serious shape within the Confederate secret service, and the focus of those plots became John Wilkes Booth.

The Booth family, in addition to being the greatest acting family in America, were Marylanders whose loyalties were bitterly divided in the war. John Wilkes Booth, born in 1838 and the youngest son of Junius Brutus Booth, easily promised to add further laurels to the Booth family name, joining a Philadelphia acting company at age nineteen and making his first great debut as a Shakespearean in *Richard III* in New York in 1862. He was already being compared to his older brother Edwin, and Washington theater impresario John Ford thought that Booth was on his way to becoming "the greatest actor of his time." But Booth had other interests than just the stage. He loved the South, treated blacks with contempt, and viewed the coming of the war as a dark abolitionist plot. "My soul, life and possessions are for the South!" he declared to his sister, Asia, and from 1863 on, he became part of a network of Confederate agents stretching from Richmond to Montreal, passing information and contraband medical goods across the Potomac.

Sometime late in 1864, Booth began recruiting and funding a cell of conspirators in the Washington area for what he explained as a plan to kidnap Lincoln in Washington, spirit him out of the city along a pre-arranged route into northern Virginia where Confederate partisan units would be stationed, and pass him through to Richmond where he could be used to force a general release of Confederate prisoners or perhaps even a negotiated peace. The plan took various forms as it evolved, but all of them were based on Lincoln's notorious distaste for close escorts (Booth at one point even contemplated kidnapping him from a theater). The quality of Booth's recruits varied. The most reli-

431

able was John Surratt, a Confederate spy whose mother's boarding house in Georgetown became a headquarters for the plot, followed by Lewis Paine, a former Confederate soldier; less predictable but still useful were several Southern sympathizers Booth enlisted from stagehands he knew in the Washington theaters. Oddest of all was a halfwit named Davy Herold, whose chief credentials were his devotion to Booth and his knowledge of the Potomac countryside. Booth lavished money on the plot ($10,000 of his own funds, according to John Ford), but what he lacked was time. By March of 1865, the Confederacy was crumbling, and with it, Booth's rage and fury at Lincoln swelled to frantic proportions. Kidnapping now would be pointless; to dismiss his conspirators and confess failure was unacceptable. And so Booth's mind turned to assassination.

According to Edward Neill, the White House staff had actually been tipped off to "Booth's desire to do evil" by an anonymous letter-writer sometime early in 1865, but the effect of the warning had been lost in the torrents of nonsense that tumbled every day out of the White House mailbag. Lincoln certainly had no thought about assassination when he convened the cabinet's regular weekly meeting on Good Friday, April 14th. "His whole appearance, poise, and bearing had marvelously changed," recalled Iowa senator James Harlan. Congressman Elihu Washburne thought Lincoln "was in perfect health and in exuberant spirits." The surrender of Lee had lifted the cross of war from his shoulders, and he began the meeting by relating a dream he had, a dream in which he found himself on a ship, heading toward an ill-defined shore. It was a dream he had seemed to have whenever good news was about to break, and he expected in this case that this meant he would soon hear that Sherman had secured the surrender of the last bits of Confederate army in the Carolinas. He had other reasons to be jovial, too: Robert Lincoln was home from the war, and along with him into the cabinet meeting came Robert's commander, General Grant, to report on the surrender of Lee.

Only the troubles about reconstruction clouded the horizon. The Virginia legislature fiasco had forced Lincoln to wonder whether he "had perhaps been too fast in his desires for early reconstruction," and he invited Stanton to review for the cabinet a reconstruction plan that would return to the idea of using interim military governors to oversee the defeated Confederate states and guide the rebuilding of their governments until they were ready for full reintegration into the Union. Given the mild terms laid down to Lee by Grant, this might signify that Lincoln would use the army to make that kind of a peace the basic model for reconstruction. But military government might also signal the final abandonment of reliance on Southern white Unionism; in fact, if Lincoln had begun at last to entertain the idea of enfranchising blacks rather than Southern Unionists, resorting to military occupation of the South might be the most direct and unarguable way to achieve that. "He wished they had permitted negroes who had property, or could read, to vote" in the Louisiana constitution; yet at the same time he still clung to the belief that "this was a question" the reconstructed states "must decide for themselves." Perhaps the only point which was clear was that military government would leave his options for either direction open, and keep control of the reconstruction process firmly in his own hands as president. At any rate, as Noah Brooks thought, "before the present Summer closes there will be some order brought out of the chaotic mass, which Congress would have taken hold of arbitrarily and compressed into State Government forthwith. . . ."

Lincoln would not be going to any Good Friday services in the Washington churches. The Episcopal bishop of New Hampshire, Carlton Chase, had written to him in March to ask that Good Friday "be observed as a day of fasting and Prayer throughout the United States." But in his April 11th speech at the White House, Lincoln promised instead "a call for a national thanksgiving" sometime soon, and celebration rather than fasting occupied his mind (especially since April 14th was the fourth anniversary of the surrender of Fort Sumter). In that festive mood, John Ford had sent tickets to the White House for the Lincolns to attend veteran actress Laura Keene's benefit performance of Tom Taylor's comedy of manners, *Our American Cousin,* at Ford's Theater, with the delightful Keene and the slapstick Harry Hawk in the lead roles. At Mary's pleading, Lincoln had agreed to go, and after dismissing the cabinet, he and Mary took a lengthy carriage ride, came home to eat, and then set off for Ford's Theater, picking up Clara Harris (the daughter of New York senator Ira Harris) and her fiancée, Major Henry Rathbone, to make up the theater party.

Ford was delighted that the President was coming that night, since Lincoln's presence would surely boost ticket sales for his 2,500-seat theater. Notices went out hurriedly to the Washington papers for their afternoon editions, and the theater staff buzzed with anticipation — which meant, of course, that it also came to the embittered ear of John Wilkes Booth, who lived at a nearby hotel but who picked up his mail at Ford's. The news that Lincoln would be in the "state box" (just off the dress circle at stage left) that night galvanized Booth. Here was the opportunity he had sought to revenge the South; here was the perfect venue for his greatest role. Within hours he had collected his conspirators and assigned to them their new objectives: he would murder the president before the eyes of the entire audience at Ford's that night, while the others would fan out in pairs and assassinate Vice President Johnson, Secretary of State Seward (whose carriage accident had immobilized him at home in a neck brace), and General Grant. Together, they would bolt across the Potomac, link up with the chain of agents who had been recruited for the original kidnapping plan, and escape to safety somewhere in the South.

The Lincolns arrived at Ford's slightly late, but the packed house went wild with enthusiasm and interrupted the performance when Lincoln appeared at the rail of the theater box. The comedy rollicked along in fine fashion, with the actors ad-libbing "many pleasant allusions to him in the play, to which the audience gave deafening responses, while Mr. Lincoln laughed heartily and bowed frequently to the gratified people." But even though he laughed at the actors' ripostes, he could not keep his mind from straying in other directions. He was thinking about the future, about life after the presidency, and presently he told Mary that he would like to "visit the Holy Land," that "there was no city on earth he so much desired to see as Jerusalem."

Strange as this conversation must have seemed on Good Friday in a theater (and it has only one testimony to substantiate it), there is more sense to it than it seems. "Moving & travelling" had been on Lincoln's mind since the re-election, and he had been hinting to Mary that "when he was through with his Presidential terms to take me and family to Europe," and then "intended to return and go to California — over the Rocky Mountains and see the prospect of the Soldiers &c digging [out] gold to pay the National debt." But plans "to visit the Holy Land" involved a very different kind of travel. Christian pilgrimages to the Holy Land, especially from Protestant countries, had become a small industry in the nineteenth century, first for confirmed believers, but also for doubters tortured by their doubts and hoping that the reality of the holy places might somehow become an anchor by which they could arrest their drift from faith. Herman Melville, Nikolai Gogol, Charles Gordon, Alphonse de Lamartine all went in search there of a tangibility in the geography of the sacred places that they had not found in faith. Few of them would find what they wanted, but what is surprising is how many skeptics made the search. That Lincoln, who spent his life in the same search for religious truth, should have the same idea once he could put the presidency behind him, is far from strange. It would be one more chapter in his struggle for a way to be "more devout than I am."

Shortly after ten o'clock, Booth climbed the winding staircase of Ford's Theater from the lobby to the dress circle, and made a minor nuisance of himself by sidling past the back row toward the door of the president's box, forcing the annoyed spectators sitting in the cheap seats to push their chairs back and forth "to permit him to pass." Just as Booth had anticipated, Lincoln had brought along only two escorts, a Washington policeman named John Parker who was now sitting at the front of the dress circle in order to better see the play, and Charles Forbes, the White House footman. Booth flashed a card at Forbes, and Forbes, "after looking at it, allowed him to go in." Lincoln, after all, was partial to actors, and it would not have been the first time that Wilkes Booth had been invited up to the presidential box.

The box was a shallow rectangle, and to get to it, Booth had to pass an outer door and enter a small passageway, then stop before a smaller inner door that opened directly into the box. Lincoln was seated closest to the inner door, with Mary in a chair beside him and Major Rathbone and Clara Harris on a small sofa at the far end. Once inside the passageway, Booth wedged the outer door shut. Then, he had only to open the inner door softly and take one step to come beside and behind Lincoln on the president's left, place a single-shot derringer behind Lincoln's head, just behind the left ear, and fire. (Since the bullet traversed the head from left to right, Lincoln may have been "looking down at a person in the orchestra," according to James Ferguson, or in the dress circle; or he may have noticed Booth's

435

entrance at the last second and was turning his head to see who was there.) Lincoln lurched forward from the impact, and Major Rathbone rose in surprise, struggling to grab at Booth and instead being slashed from shoulder to elbow by a seven-inch hunting knife Booth now drew. In a single theatrical leap, Booth bounded over the rail of the box, landing on the stage, eleven feet below. Brandishing the bloodied knife, he cried aloud *Sic semper tyrannis* — the state motto of Virginia but, more important, the classic line of Brutus in assassinating the tyrant, Caesar. He then turned and disappeared through the scenery to the backstage door, leapt onto a horse he had tethered there, and galloped off into the Washington night.

"The whole occurrence, the shot, the leap, the escape — was done while you could count eight," wrote one onlooker the next morning. Several thought the noise of the shot was the accidental discharge of the revolver of "some soldier or drunken man," and for a long moment the entire house was stunned. "Then all rose up trying to recover themselves," while Mary stood up at "the front of the box with loud cries & screams," and suddenly it was clear what had happened, "that Mr. Lincoln had been assassinated." Frantic hands hammered on the wedged outer door of the box, which was opened by the blood-soaked Major Rathbone, and an assistant army surgeon, Dr. Charles Leale, who had been sitting in the dress circle, cried out to be admitted. Leale found the president slumped over on his right side in his chair, unconscious and breathing irregularly, "supported by Mrs. Lincoln who was weeping bitterly." Leale had Lincoln laid out on the floor of the box, and found the head wound behind Lincoln's ear. It was clear to Leale, whose specialty was gunshot wounds, "that it was a mortal wound," and as two other doctors from the audience crowded into the box, Leale now tried to find some way to move Lincoln. Several of the army provost marshal's guard, who were in the theater to check soldiers' passes, cleared the box and the dress circle, while several others, along with the three doctors, lifted Lincoln's limp body and gingerly carried him across the back of the dress circle and down the twenty-six steps of the staircase, the captain of the guard opening a passage through the crowd in the lobby "with the flat of my sword."

Once in the lobby, Leale vetoed the idea that Lincoln should be taken back to the White House, "being fearful that he would die as soon as he would be placed in an upright position." But then a boarder

436

in a house across the street belonging to one William Peterson shouted for them to come across, and so with little more than impulse for a guide, the fumbling bearers, surrounded by an appalled crowd in the street, carried Lincoln across the fifty feet of Tenth Street, up the semi-circular front steps of the Peterson house, and into a back room, where the long form of the president was laid out across a too-short bed. The word of the assassination flew madly, hysterically, across the city; the city garrison was turned out; Secretary of War Stanton arrived together with Secretary Welles, followed by Secretary of the Interior Usher, Schuyler Colfax, Surgeon General Joseph Barnes; and of course there was Mary Lincoln, in continuous and convulsive sobs, beseeching her husband to open his eyes, having to be led away so that Leale and the other doctors could try to keep Lincoln alive (and unobtrusively change the blood-drenched pillow cases). Couriers came and went; Vice President Johnson appeared in a daze. Phineas Gurley came from the New York Avenue Presbyterian Church, prepared to pray; Robert Lincoln wept openly on Charles Sumner's shoulder. The news which came into the Peterson house by fits and starts confirmed that an attack had been made on Seward, too, and Stanton now set an army corporal to taking down testimony in the back parlor from the actors and stagehands at Ford's, testimony which confirmed that Booth was the assassin of the president.

In the back bedroom, Leale watched as Lincoln's life ebbed away. It had been Leale's experience in similar cases that victims of these kind of wounds often regained a brief flutter of consciousness just before the end, and all through the night Leale held Lincoln's right hand "so that in his darkness he would know he had a friend." Gideon Welles sat quietly beside Leale through the night. "The giant sufferer lay extended diagonally across the bed," Welles wrote in his diary. "His features were calm and striking. I had never seen them appear to better advantage than for the first hour, perhaps, that I was there." But as the night wore one, Lincoln's "right eye began to swell and that part of his face became discolored." Around 1:00 A.M., "both pupils became widely dilated and remained so," and the doctors could only keep his pulse and respiration steady by repeatedly breaking up the clots that formed at the entrance to the wound.

Dawn came, damp and overcast, and still Lincoln breathed. But at 6:25 A.M., the breathing became shallower and uneven; by 6:40 A.M.

437

the "expirations" were "prolonged and groaning"; by 7:00 A.M. the breathing was only coming in "long pauses." The end was clearly near, and Surgeon General Barnes now fingered Lincoln's carotid artery to mark the pulse. Finally, at 7:22 A.M. on the morning of April 15, 1865, even that stopped, and Barnes folded Lincoln's hands across his chest, and said, "He is gone; he is dead." There was silence for what seemed like five minutes, and then Gurley offered a prayer, while Stanton — who was not noted for great depths of any public emotion except irritation — cried like a child in pain. And then, when Gurley closed his prayer with *Thy will be done, amen,* Stanton raised his head and said quietly, "Now he belongs to the ages."

A few minutes later, a chill rain began to fall outside.

Epilogue: The Redeemer President

Lincoln's death struck the nation with almost physical force. "You can scarcely imagine the feeling that pervades Washington," wrote one army clerk on Sunday. "The sorrow & Mourning are indescribable. It is not considered a shame or weakness to weep over the foul & horrid crime. Nor is it rare to see eyes streaming with tears. I cried like a child myself today. . . ." A Massachusetts soldier in the Washington garrison wrote home, "We all felt as though we had our father murdered"; Garth Wilkinson James, an officer in the black 54th Massachusetts (and brother of Harvard philosopher William James), wrote that his regiment had "been talking him over and over ever since we heard of his death, and such a crowd of heart-broken young men you would never see again." In city after city, the streamers and bunting that had celebrated Lee's surrender were haltingly pulled in and replaced by abject festoons of black crepe, and flags sank ashamed to half-mast. On Wall Street, "the excitement . . . was intense; so much so that business was stopped & many houses entirely closed. . . . By noon all of Broadway was draped in mourning." In Cincinnati, a mob gathered outside the hotel where Junius Brutus Booth was staying, howling for his blood, and it was several days before Booth was able to slip out of the city. Southern sympathizers and paroled Confederate soldiers were beaten

439

in the streets of New York, Rochester, and Washington; newspapers in Philadelphia and San Francisco pleaded for restraint and public order. Far away in Springfield on Saturday morning, church bells tolled, businesses shut down, and the "whole city presented a funereal aspect." William Herndon sat in the old law office, unable to concentrate on the papers before him. "The news of his going struck me dumb, the deed being so infernally wicked . . . that it was too large to enter my brain." Jane Addams, who was a four-and-a-half-year-old child in Cedarville, Illinois, when Lincoln died, recalled "my father's tears, and his impressive statement that the greatest man in the world had died," and she "dimly caught the notion of the martyred President as the standard-bearer to the conscience of his countrymen."

Martyrdom quickly became the dominant word, as clergymen across the country quietly put away the sermons they had prepared for Easter Sunday and struggled to give some kind of meaningful shape to the national horror. That Sunday became "Black Easter," and from pulpit to pulpit, Lincoln was eulogized as "one of the most faultless examples of true manhood ever prominently exhibited to the world." He was honest, sincere, charitable; he was a genuine man of the people, "a true type of the America of to-day"; he was compared to Washington, to Moses. And almost irresistibly, he was compared to Jesus Christ. Had not Lincoln come to set his people free? Had he not entered into Richmond in the same triumphant spirit, close to Palm Sunday, that Jesus had entered Jerusalem? Had he not been slain on Good Friday? "As Christ entered into Jerusalem, the city that above all others hated, rejected, and would soon slay Him," wrote Methodist Gilbert Haven about Lincoln's Richmond visitation, "so did this, His servant, enter the city that above all others hated and rejected him, and would soon be the real if not intentional cause of his death." And for Joel Bingham what followed the week after was nothing less than an offering of "a bloody sacrifice, upon the altar of human freedom" which "wrought out the painful salvation of the Republic." Lincoln's death, said the Hartford Baptist C. B. Crane, was "the aftertype of the tragedy which was accomplished on the first Good Friday, more than eighteen centuries ago, upon the eminence of Calvary in Judea." There was nothing blasphemous to Jesus, in Crane's estimate, in declaring "the fitness of the slaying of the second Father of our Republic on the anniversary of the day on which he was slain. Jesus Christ died for the world, Abraham Lincoln died for his country." He had become Whitman's Redeemer President, redeeming the political community of the republic from the sin of slavery and corruption in his own blood and pronouncing forgiveness to all offenders. "What Mr. Lincoln achieved, he achieved for us," intoned Massachusetts journalist Josiah Gilbert Holland at a mass memorial service in Springfield, Massachusetts, on April 19th. "He left as choice a legacy in his Christian example, in his incorruptible integrity, and in his unaffected simplicity, if we will appropriate it, as in his public deeds."

There were, of course, some difficulties to surmount in constructing this interpretation of Lincoln. The first and most obvious was that Lincoln's fatal wound had occurred in an embarrassingly unhallowed place for redeemers and martyrs: a theater. The Presbyterian George Duffield would have preferred "that he had fallen elsewhere than at the very gates of Hell — in the theater." Justin Fulton told Boston's Tremont Temple that "It was a poor place to die in. It would not be selected by any of you as the spot from which you would desire to proceed to the bar of God." But both Fulton and Duffield quickly found reasons for excuse in Lincoln's case which kept the image of the Redeemer President intact. "If ever any man had an excuse to attend a theater, he had," Fulton assured his congregation. "The cares of office were heavy upon him." Duffield was sure that Lincoln had only gone "reluctantly" and "through persuasion," and claimed that the real judgment lay on the "demoralizing" theater, not on Lincoln. "Mr. Lincoln went to the theater not to please himself, but to gratify others," agreed Josiah Holland. "He went with weariness into the crowd, that the promise under which that crowd had assembled might be fulfilled."

What was infinitely more difficult to reconcile with the image of the Redeemer President was his lack of any professed belief in Christianity. "It is to be bitterly regretted that he did not make a public profession of . . . faith in the Lord Jesus Christ," conceded the Illinois Presbyterian Samuel C. Baldridge, and in Springfield's First Presbyterian, a guest preacher from St. Louis noted disapprovingly that Lincoln's "name had never been enrolled on your list of communicants, and that he had never here been known as a professor of religion." But as with the theater problem, a host of likely explanations rose up: that Lincoln was someone who lived the Christian life in an "experimental" rather than a "theoretical" way, by practical precept rather than by doctrine; or that Lincoln had actually experienced Christian conversion after Willie's death in 1862, or after Gettysburg in 1863, or sometime that no one could fix with precision but which Lincoln had privately described to them. Josiah Holland, following on the success of his April 19th oration, was commissioned to produce the first full-length biography of Lincoln, and determined as he was to portray Lincoln as "eminently a Christian president," Holland took up testimony from Newton Bateman that in 1860, Lincoln had confessed to Bateman that "I know there is a God, and that he hates injustice and slavery. . . . I know that liberty is right, for Christ teaches it, and Christ is God." Noah Brooks told a Congregational clergyman, Isaac Langworthy, "For myself, I am glad to say that I have a firm belief in Mr. Lincoln's saving knowledge of Christ; he talked always of Christ, his cross, his atonement; he prayed regularly, cast all his cares on God and felt inexpressible relief thereby."

In fact, there was no concrete evidence for any of these claims. Brooks offered no transcript of Lincoln's prayers, and the ambitious newspaperman, like his peers, Forney and Hanscom, had a well-known weakness for exaggerating his intimacy with Lincoln. Bateman was dismissed by Lincoln's friends as "naturally sly" and over-eager to shine as a Lincoln confidant. No one was more contemptuous of these testifiers than William Henry Herndon, since the idea that Lincoln had undergone some secret conversion implied that Lincoln had secretly embraced Christianity but publicly concealed it, so that Lincoln became a hypocrite of the oddest but most distasteful sort. "Do you suppose for an instant," Herndon erupted when one hapless correspondent asked him his opinion of Lincoln's religion after the publication of Holland's *Life of Abraham Lincoln* in 1866, "that if Mr. Lincoln was really a converted man to the faith of three Gods, Revelation, Inspiration, Miraculous Conception, and their necessity, etc., as some of the Christian world pretend to believe of Mr. Lincoln, that he *would not have boldly said so and so acted like a deeply sincere man and an honest one fearlessly of that mob furor?*" Still, Holland stuck by Bateman's testimony, and Brooks and others could always reply that Lincoln in Washington had become someone very different from the Lincoln Herndon had known in Springfield, and so the enraged Herndon now embarked on his own plans for a biography, and began his own exhaustive round of personal interviews and testimony-gathering, which would keep straight a record about Lincoln's life that the pious were bent on distorting.

What Herndon found surprised even the bohemian attorney, who realized by 1866 that the spiritual life of the man he had worked with for over a decade really had been a closed book. While none of Herndon's informants went so far as to agree with Holland or Brooks, there were wild fluctuations in what even Lincoln's closest friends thought his religion, if any, had been like. David Davis and Robert Todd Lincoln told Herndon that the president had never been known to discuss the subject, while others like Isaac Cogdal and Jesse Fell claimed that Lincoln's religion was a bare form of deism or universalism, and still others like Francis Carpenter and Joshua Speed insisted that Lincoln had undergone some form of "crystallization" and had become "a growing man" in religion while president. "I can but think if you could have resumed your old intercourse with him at the end of his four years," Carpenter loftily informed Herndon, "you would have found his religious sentiments more fixed, possibly more *christian*." What was just as surprising to Herndon was to discover how little was certain about many other aspects of Lincoln's life. Interviewing old residents of New Salem, he stumbled across the story of Lincoln's early love for Ann Rutledge and how he had gone nearly insane after her death; other interviews in Indiana convinced him that Lincoln was possibly illegitimate and that embarrassment over this had tormented Lincoln all his life, that he had been trapped into his marriage with Mary Todd, that he was "a fatalist, denied the freedom of the will," that he wrote a "little book" on infidelity, asserting that "the Bible was not God's revelations; and secondly, that Jesus was not the son of God."

Herndon might have made more of an impression with his research if he had been able to follow Holland's best-selling *Life* with his own planned biography a year or two later. Instead, Herndon became obsessed with the research itself, spending over two years and nearly $2,000 on interviews and correspondence which he accumulated in three large, leather-bound volumes. He made the disastrous tactical mistake of casting the most sensational of his discoveries about Lincoln into a series of lectures in Springfield late in 1865 and 1866. The lectures were long, rhetorically bloated, and unflattering in their portrayal of Lincoln's depressions and his "cold," rational aloofness. The final lecture, delivered in November 1866, was the most sensational of all, since Herndon had reserved his final word for Lincoln's early love for Ann Rutledge in New Salem and how Ann Rutledge had been the only sincere love of Lincoln's life. With boundless naivete, Herndon supposed that his lectures would deepen understanding and appreciation for "the subjective Lincoln." Instead, the public reaction to his revelations bordered on revulsion. Francis Carpenter upbraided Herndon for what "seemed to me an invasion of a sacred *chamber*." Grant Goodrich, who had once invited Lincoln to practice law with him in Chicago, irritably asked Herndon whether he "did not realize what an injury and injustice you did to the memory of your dear friend, & mortification you caused his friends, but especially his widow and children." And from retirement in Scotland, the aged James Smith blistered Herndon for suggesting that Lincoln "was worse than a dishonest man" for marrying a women he did not love. "Was it not enough that she should be overwhelmed and stricken to the earth by the dreadful blow which had fallen upon her, in the Cruel death of her husband, but you must Come on the Scene and mingle your poisoned chalice into that cup of woe which she must drink to the dregs. . . ." And while Smith did not cross Herndon's claim that Lincoln was not a Christian, he retaliated with the declaration that "Mr. Lincoln did avow his belief in the Divine Authority and Inspiration [of] the Scriptures."

Herndon fought back, but every blow he tried to strike only damaged his own credibility. His law practice had gone to dust during his years of research, and by 1869, he was so short of cash that he sold his "Lincoln Record" materials to Ward Hill Lamon, who was also planning the first volume of a two-part biography which would paint a frank, and obligingly Herndonesque, view of Lincoln. Lamon, in fact, did far worse. Employing as a ghost writer Chauncey Black, the son of James Buchanan's one-time attorney general, Lamon's *Life of Abraham Lincoln* not only luridly played up Lincoln's bastardy and "atheism," but portrayed the Lincoln administration as a set of ambitious political fanatics, and expressly attacked Holland's use of Newton Bateman's narrative. The overall picture was so dark that Lamon's publisher, James Osgood of Boston, actually forced Lamon and Black to delete the final chapter and much of what Black thought were "the most interesting parts" of the others. When volume one of Lamon's *Life* was published in May, 1872, it met with almost universal condemnation by reviewers, and the publisher dropped all plans for publishing a second volume. Josiah Holland not only impaled the book in a review in *Scribner's Magazine,* but the following year published a lecture in *Scribner's* by James A. Reed (then the pastor of the First Presbyterian Church in Springfield) containing testimony from John Todd Stuart, Noyes Miner, Noah Brooks, Ninian Edwards, and James Matheny that, whatever "infidelity" Lincoln had espoused as a young man, "in later life . . . he was a firm believer in the Christian religion."

The knowledge that Lamon's work was based on Herndon's materials guaranteed that Herndon would also come in for renewed criticism, and Leonard Swett advised Herndon to self-censor any subsequent writings of his own on Lincoln. "Lamon's book fell flat, every body connected with it lost money & the public have not yet forgiven him for making it," Swett warned, "because it stated things which the public did not want to hear of its heroes." When Herndon at last finished his long-planned biography of Lincoln in 1889 (with the assistance of Jesse Weik), Springfielders cold-shouldered it as though Herndon had betrayed some peculiar familial trust. John Todd Stuart's granddaughter remembered that it was "anathema in our family," and "Herndon himself was thought to be a most reprehensible person."

What the public wanted to hear was that Lincoln had been Holland's "true Christian." More cautious and admiring biographers, like Isaac Arnold (in his *Life of Abraham Lincoln* in 1884), eased their way around the Rutledge romance as a "story made rather too tragic" by Herndon and Lamon or else half-heartedly acknowledged that Lincoln was not "orthodox," but was still the most "reverent Christian" who had ever "sat in the executive chair." The Newton Bateman narrative in Holland's *Life* set a pattern for supposed revelations of Lincoln's closet Christianity which persisted for years afterward. He had secretly attended prayer meetings at Henry Ward Beecher's Brooklyn church (a claim made after Beecher's death by his wife, but never made by Beecher himself); he had been secretly baptized (this story was passed on by Mariah Vance, the Lincoln family's washerwoman in Springfield, but only orally through a third party and never during the lifetime of any of the Lincoln family); he had been converted to Christianity after the death of Willie

(Francis Carpenter implied this, despite the fact that his account of the events in Lincoln's schedule around this conversion is inaccurate), or after the battle of Gettysburg (according to James Rusling in 1895 and General Daniel Sickles in 1911); he was a Mason (according to Dr. L. D. Carman in 1914, although Lincoln expressly denied ever joining any secret society); he had been converted in a Methodist revival in 1839 (on the word of Col. John F. Jacquess, who had been part of one of the failed peace missions in 1864, and who retailed the revival story in 1897); he would be ready to join a church (he supposedly told Connecticut congressman Henry Deming) whenever "any church will inscribe over its altar, as its sole qualification for membership, the Savior's condensed statement of the substance of both law and gospel, 'Thou shalt love the Lord thy God with all thy heart, and with all thy soul, and with all thy mind, and thy neighbor as thyself.'" (It never occurred to Deming that it would have been difficult to find such a church in nineteenth-century America, and that if Lincoln actually said this, he was probably putting Deming off with another of his notorious *if* scenarios.) Lincoln was not only made into a Christian, but he acquired a peculiar following among Christian preachers. Two of the most important Lincoln scholars in the generation after the passing of those who had known Lincoln, William E. Barton and Louis A. Warren, were Protestant clergymen.

What was curious in all of this was that none of the preachers and devout layfolk who wanted so badly to Christianize Lincoln in death ever penetrated to the real heart of Lincoln's personal religious anguish, the deep sense of helplessness before a distant and implacable Judge who revealed himself only through crisis and death, whom Lincoln would have wanted to love if only the Judge had given him the grace to do the loving. Like Herman Melville, Lincoln could "neither believe or be comfortable in his unbelief; he is too honest and courageous not to try to do one or the other." By transforming Lincoln into a political redeemer, the sermons of "Black Easter" became an exercise in the most cruel of ironies, since Lincoln did not believe in the possibility of redemption for himself. But rather than calling this failing to the attention of the nation, the well-nigh unanimous rush of the clergy was not to criticize Lincoln, but to baptize him posthumously.

Few seemed interested, either, in asking a more critical question, whether the religion Lincoln *did* seem to have had made any impact at all on the war. The preachers and evangelical religious organizations who had hoped to have the most direct influence on the war's results turned out, in the end, to have made little large-scale impact on the war. And in the conventional reckoning of the liberalism Lincoln espoused, that was largely what was expected, and in some cases desired. But Lincoln's own peculiar providentialism, his Calvinized deism, in fact played a controlling role in the outcome of the Civil War. In the most general sense, his appeal to the mysteries of providence in the fall of 1862 gave him permission to ignore the manifest signs on all hands that the Union was playing the war to no better than a draw, and that any resort to emancipation was folly. But in the most specific instance, providence was what allowed him to overrule the moral limitations of liberalism. To do liberalism's greatest deed — the emancipation of the slaves — Lincoln had to step outside liberalism and surrender himself to the direction of an overruling divine providence whose conclusions he had by no means prejudged.

What this resulted in, of course, was the prolonging of the conflict long past the possibility of negotiation, past the long-term physical and economic devastation of the South, past the horrendous casualty lists of Fredericksburg, Chancellorsville, Gettysburg, the Wilderness, and all the other battles that had to be fought in a war which Lincoln believed providence had designed. From any other man (from Salmon Chase, for instance), such appeals of policy to providence might have been written off as a species of fanaticism. But no one could hang the charge of religious fanaticism around the neck of Abraham Lincoln, the cool religious skeptic, the Old School Whig. And what was more, providence's directions during the war also produced freedom for the slaves and the preservation of the Union as a significant political entity, a price that balanced the redemptive shedding of blood in the reckoning scales of public opinion. Nor did providence stop giving after Lincoln's death. In a world where no free will existed, it was irrational for mere men to make judgments about charity and malice. Judgment belonged to God, Lincoln knew, and to God alone. But as a result, for twelve years after Appomattox the government dithered away its opportunity to remake the South in the national image and, in the end, gave up entirely. Rarely if ever, in a secular liberal republic, has so much public good and ill come from one kind of religious decision.

For all the struggle to merge Lincoln with redemption that Easter, the one religious quality that Lincoln would have most easily recognized in the public rhetoric was the one he most dreaded. Alfred Patton, a Baptist minister in Utica, New York, angrily declared, "Plainly, God is saying to us, by his providences to-day, what he said to his people of old, 'Execute judgment upon them speedily, whether it be unto death, or to banishment, or to confiscation of goods, or to imprisonment.'" "We have lost all sentiment of clemency," declared one New York City Episcopalian; and his Presbyterian counterpart, William Adams, believed that the "mawkish sentimentalism" (which arose from "a denial of future punishment, and arguing for universal salvation against the explicit assertion of the Scriptures") had to be set aside in favor of judgment. In Chicago, E. J. Goodspeed accused the Confederate leadership of backing Booth's plot, and Orville Hickman Browning heard one preacher suggest that "the President might have been removed because he was too lenient, and trusted that we now had an avenger who would execute wrath." Nor was the cry for judgment limited to the preachers. Lincoln's most important midwestern journalistic cheerleader, the *Chicago Tribune*, announced that "Yesterday we were with the late President, for lenity; he had been so often right and wise; he had so won our confidence that we were preparing to follow and support him in a policy of conciliatory kindness; today we are with the people for justice." William Lloyd Garrison, a pacifist among the abolitionists, called for the hanging of Jefferson Davis. The *Washington Star* agreed; "His unscrupulous hand has guided the assassin's trigger and dagger."

The canonization of Lincoln as martyr and redeemer proceeded in such flamboyant fashion that few wished to notice that it disguised an undercurrent of ambiguity and dissimulation about Lincoln. Southerners, fearing that the assassination would make a generous reconstruction impossible, rushed preemptively to claim that they deplored the assassination as much as any Northerner, and that Booth, far from acting as a Confederate agent, had been nothing more than a solitary and "irresponsible madman." But all too often, former Confederates who rushed to tie crêpe to their doorknobs were doing so to "save their homes" from angry federal occupation forces. Former Confederate War Department clerk John B. Jones described in his diary how he cautioned "those I met to manifest no *feeling*, as . . . the Federal soldiers

. . . might become uncontrollable and perpetuate deeds of Horror on the unarmed people." Under the watchful eyes of federal armies, Southern newspapers were careful to denounce Booth's deed, but in places where the last fragments of Confederate authority still held out (as in Texas) Booth was praised as a hero, and one defiant Houston newspaper claimed a week after the assassination, "From now until God's judgement day the minds of men will not cease to thrill at the killing of Abraham Lincoln."

Nor were the secret rejoicings limited to Southerners. In Princeton, New Jersey (which had given its votes to McClellan in the 1864 election), Charles Hodge was infuriated "almost to madness" when he found "that some of the Democrats" in Princeton "openly rejoiced when the news of Mr. Lincoln's murder arrived." But more grating were the ill-concealed expressions of satisfaction from the Radicals of Lincoln's own party. George W. Julian was convinced that Lincoln had shown himself all along to be too lenient in dealing with the Confederates and that "the accession of Johnson to the Presidency would prove a godsend to the country." As an old Jacksonian yeoman with no love for the planter aristocrats and a successful and vigorous occupation governor, Johnson promised to make treason "odious," and Ben Wade jubilantly congratulated Johnson with the promise, "Johnson, we have faith in you. By the Gods, there will be no trouble now in running the government." Julian was confident that the "influence of the War committee with Johnson, who is an ex-member, will powerfully aid the new administration in getting on the right foot." The sun had not set on the day of Lincoln's death before the Republican senatorial caucus was meeting to develop "a line of policy less conciliatory than that of Mr. Lincoln."

The most obvious person to whom judgment would be applied was John Wilkes Booth. Stanton quickly identified Booth as the assassin from the testimony he took down from actors and spectators at Ford's Theater, but no one seemed to have any idea where Booth had disappeared to once he vanished from the alley behind Ford's. Stanton posted a gigantic $100,000 reward for the capture of Booth, and not for Booth only. On Monday morning, April 17th, three members of Booth's conspiracy ring were picked up, and that evening War Department officers not only arrested Mary Surratt (the owner of Booth's headquarters boarding-house) but also bagged Lewis Paine, who had conducted the assault on Seward and who had chosen that untimely moment to show up at Mrs. Surratt's for shelter. Booth himself disappeared from Washington with remarkable ease, in the company of one of his co-conspirators, Davy Herold, and managed to elude capture for more than ten days after the assassination with the assistance of a network of Confederate sympathizers in Maryland and northern Virginia. It was not until April 26th that Booth was tracked down and shot to death by federal pursuers in a tobacco barn near Port Royal, Virginia, along the old route he had once proposed using for kidnapping Lincoln. The other conspirators were tried, not by a civil court, but by a military commission assembled under Stanton's aegis and Johnson's signature (on the grounds that the conspirators had killed the commander in chief of the army and navy in time of war). Four of the conspirators, including Herold, Paine, and Mrs. Surratt, were hanged on July 7, 1865, behind the walls of the old prison at the Washington Arsenal; three others were sentenced to imprisonment for life at Fort Jefferson, on a barren coral reef in Florida's Dry Tortugas.

Long before the conspiracy trial began, the body of Abraham Lincoln began a journey of its own. Despite appeals to bury Lincoln in Washington, or even beside Washington himself at Mount Vernon, Mary Lincoln made it clear from the inconsolable seclusion of her mourning in the White House that her husband was to be buried in Illinois, although she puzzled nearly everyone by proposing that he be buried in Chicago, rather than Springfield, near the grave of his old adversary, Stephen Douglas. "Robert Lincoln told me his mother did not wish to go back to Springfield," Orville Hickman Browning wrote in his diary, "and did not want his father's remains taken there, but to Chicago, if any where in Illinois." This brought protests from the governor of Illinois, Richard Oglesby, and after a week Mary finally agreed that he would be buried in Springfield, after all. But, to the annoyance of Springfielders, she insisted that the burial take place in the city's rural cemetery, Oak Ridge, rather than where the city fathers wanted Lincoln buried, in a tomb constructed near the city center where Lincoln in death (as he had in life) could continue to promote the city's visibility. Convinced that an Oak Ridge burial was a mistake, the city proceeded to purchase ground near the governor's mansion and built a receiving tomb. But Mary was adamant, and threatened to return to the Chicago plan if her wishes were ignored. Grudgingly, Springfield relented. He would be buried in Oak Ridge.

First, however, there were the more grisly aspects of Lincoln's remains to be dealt with. The body was brought back to the White House on an improvised hearse later in the morning of Lincoln's death, and, using the second-floor guest room of the White House as a temporary morgue, Surgeon General Barnes presided over an autopsy of the body "upon a rough framework of boards." The undertakers then went to work embalming the corpse, and the body was dressed in the suit Lincoln had worn at his second inaugural and laid in a lead-lined walnut coffin. An eleven-foot-high catafalque was constructed in the East Room (where William Henry Harrison and Zachary Taylor, the two other short-lived Whigs in the White House, had lain in state) and the coffin was carried downstairs for public viewing on Tuesday morning. On Wednesday, April 19th, Phineas Gurley and three other prominent Washington clergymen (including Methodist bishop Matthew Simpson, whom Lincoln had admired as an orator) conducted a formal funeral service for six hundred people, including Robert Todd Lincoln, President Johnson, and General Grant. Gurley would preach the sermon, praising Lincoln's honesty, benevolence, judgment, and "thorough, all-pervading, all-controlling, and incorruptible . . . integrity," but delicately avoiding any hint about Lincoln's personal religion apart from Lincoln's "calm and abiding confidence in the overruling providence of God." That afternoon, a gigantic procession of thirty thousand bore the coffin up Pennsylvania Avenue to the Capitol "with crape-enshrouded banners, and muffled drums, and arms reversed, and cannon shrouded, and mournful martial music," and Lincoln lay in state in the great Rotunda of the Capitol through Thursday for yet more thousands to view.

Then, on Friday, the body was borne to the Baltimore & Ohio station, where a railroad car that had been built for Lincoln's use during the war would now carry him back along the same path he had used to come to Washington in 1861. (Along with Lincoln's body, and filling several more passenger cars behind the coffin, were David Davis, Ward Hill Lamon, a "Guard of Honor" under Major General David Hunter, and a sizable congressional delegation.) First, the train would go to Baltimore, where ten thousand people passed by Lincoln's opened coffin; then to Harrisburg, where thousands more passed in a double line through the state House of Representatives to see the body, and another forty thousand lined the streets to see the coffin carried once again to the train; and then to Philadelphia, for a two-day lying-in-state in Independence Hall which counted three hundred thousand people somberly treading past the pale, hard face. Out along the tracks of the funeral train, still more of the great and the small gathered in silence to watch the coffin pass. James Buchanan waited in his carriage at the edge of a crowd at Lancaster to see his successor's last train drawn slowly along the line; standing at the Lancaster tunnel, Lincoln's bitter Radical critic Thaddeus Stevens awkwardly doffed his hat. "At Paoli and all the stations to Philadelphia," wrote a reporter on the train, "we found the same demonstrations, the same tokens of grief, the same quiet groups, the uncovered heads, the dead silence speaking an eloquence that could not be uninterpreted."

And it was the same in New York (where the only surviving photograph of Lincoln in his coffin was taken), in Albany, in Buffalo, in Cleveland, in Columbus, Indianapolis, and Chicago. On the evening of May 2nd, the funeral train departed Chicago for the last stage of the journey along the Illinois Central, arriving at Springfield the next morning for the final lying-in-state in the Hall of Representatives in the State Capitol, where almost seven years before he had delivered the "House Divided" speech. Nature was not cooperating by this point; Lincoln had been dead for over two weeks, and even the best efforts of the undertaker and embalmer who accompanied the funeral train had not been able to disguise a steady discoloration of the skin and a deep bruising under Lincoln's right eye. Old friends of Lincoln's from the prewar years found his face "black and shrunken almost beyond recognition," and years afterward Ida Tarbell spoke with Springfielders who would "weep as they recalled the scene, and heard them say repeatedly, 'If I had not seen him dead; if I could only remember him alive.'" But "the most pathetic sight" to one of the officers in the military escort "was the intense grief manifested by the colored people, thousands of whom had journeyed for days in order to be in Springfield at the funeral. . . . They well knew that their greatest friend was passing to his rest and the future seemed dark to their vision."

But the ghastly journey now was almost complete, and at noon on May 4th, a vast procession of soldiers, citizens, fire companies —

some 150,000 people, according to the *Illinois State Journal* — and the sole representative of the immediate family, Robert Todd Lincoln, passed through the town, past the house at Eighth and Jackson, out to the cemetery and over the twin ridges that gave it its name, to the cemetery's receiving vault, set into the side of one of the ridges, where Lincoln's coffin would stay until a proper and more elaborate tomb could be built. The pallbearers, walking beside a hearse borrowed from St. Louis for the occasion, were all the old friends, Jesse Dubois, Stephen Logan, John Todd Stuart. Dr. Gurley and Bishop Simpson were again in charge of the services, this time with Simpson preaching and Gurley delivering the benediction. Like Gurley, Simpson sidestepped any question about the exact substance of Lincoln's religion. "As to his religious experience, I cannot speak definitely, because I was not privileged to know much of his private sentiments," Simpson said, adding only the harmless allowance that "I think he was sincere in trying to bring his life into harmony with the principles of revealed religion." (Unlike Gurley, Simpson echoed the call for judgment on the South and "a traitor's death" for the rebel generals, but Simpson had always had greater sympathies for the Radicals.)

Finally it was over, and the whole throng joined in singing a funeral hymn Gurley had written for the occasion. Then the doors of the vault were swung shut, and "the great multitudes returned to their duties." Beside Lincoln's coffin in the vault, and with him all along the journey from Washington, was another, smaller coffin. It was that of Willie, the son who had so resembled him in every way, the child whom he had mourned more than any of his other losses, now come home with his father in the last and final gesture of loyalty.

The sheer magnitude of Lincoln's accomplishment as president has always tended to obscure the intellectual materials from which it was constructed. Lincoln had succeeded, under the most trying circumstances imaginable in the history of the republic, in holding together the Northern free states and the border slave states against a massive defection by the slave South, and then grinding the South into submission. At the same time, he managed to hold together his own party, and gradually sorted out the military leadership of the Union armies, so that together they could complete the grinding. As a result, the nature of the republic as a nation, not merely a loose association based on "self-interest," was confirmed. Almost as a by-product, he oversaw the liberation of an entire race of enslaved people, and though he died without giving clear direction as to what American society now proposed to do with the freedpeople, the emancipating of them was the first and most forbidding achievement. And while the nation was convulsed in civil war, Lincoln managed to shift the political economy of the republic off the Jeffersonian track and onto the liberal track of wage labor and high development, where it would (for all practical purposes) stay for another seventy years until the advent of Franklin Roosevelt and the resurgence of a revitalized Democratic ideology. Above all, Lincoln managed all of this without once breaking or panicking himself, even if from time to time he could display anger and occasionally vindictiveness. His self-control showed even in his prose: terse and lawyerlike to begin with, Lincoln never indulged in the "high diction" one finds in his counterpart, Jefferson Davis, or in so many of his contemporaries, when the patriotic feelings seemed almost to bring a speaker to the point of histrionics. It may be the greatest mark of Lincoln's achievement as president, that it is so difficult to imagine any of his peers — Seward, Chase, Sumner — being able to speak or write or lead nearly so well in Lincoln's place. In fact, the string of presidents in Lincoln's political generation, from 1840 till 1890, are so relentlessly undistinguished by comparison that Lincoln could have outshone them purely on the basis of his domestic agenda.

And yet, his accomplishments always had an air of the unpredictable, and sometimes the incomplete. He delivered, with the single stroke of the Emancipation Proclamation, a seismic shift in American social and economic relations; yet the proclamation came slowly from Lincoln, and was drawn out of him in the end by a mystical deference to providence, and it remains one of the stinging questions in American history just what Lincoln really intended as the future of blacks in America. Hardly less important, Lincoln made all thought of state secession and states' rights as a solution to political controversy in the Union an impossibility; yet he resisted any suggestion that the seceding states had lost their constitutional identity through attempting to secede. He presided over the greatest centralization of political authority ever seen in the American republic, from national finance to transcontinental railroads; yet he established no mechanism whereby this centralization would be made permanent, and in fact much of it crumbled away once the wartime emergency passed. "Born & educated a whig, a notoriously conservative party, called a fossil or old fogy party, wherein did he show himself radical?" asked "Long John" Wentworth in 1866. "What new measure did he start? Where did he show progress?" He was, as Helen Nicolay (the daughter of John Nicolay) wrote in 1912, "no prophet of a distant day. . . . His early life was essentially of the old era."

The sheer drama of the war — the management of the conflict, the liberation of the slaves — also cast into the shade the long ideological roots of those policies in liberal political economy. Like Cobden and Bright in England, and de Tocqueville in France, Lincoln was an intellectual child of the Enlightenment, the Enlightenment of Hobbes, Locke, and Montesquieu. He believed that reason, rather than inheritance, should govern human societies, that rights were the foundation of status (rather than the other way round), that individuals rather than communities were the primary units of society (hence, the importance of a national government to restrain communities from invading individual liberty of action), and that all of these principles represented the inevitable progress of human societies. Like the liberal Enlightenment again, he was more interested in humanity than in religion, but he did concede that religion might be an important factor in providing the self-restraint and moral discipline needed to keep liberal societies from disintegrating into mere hedonism.

But — and this has been the difficult point to grasp about Lincoln — there was more than one Enlightenment. Or rather, there has been a common base of Enlightenment assumptions about humanity and society from which two very different and antagonistic streams of American political ideology have sprung. While American politics has been united in its devotion to the Enlightenment, and with it the rule of equality and liberty, it has remained bitterly divided over which Enlightenment stream it ought to embody, the rational individualism of Locke or the passionate communal relativism of Rousseau, which was so determinedly expressed by both Thomas Jefferson and Andrew Jackson. The Whigs, in varying ways, existed as an embodiment of the Lockean Enlightenment, as did Lincoln, an intellectual positioning which underlies his lifelong antipathy to the Jacksonian Democracy. For all of Lincoln's willingness to quote Jefferson to his own purposes, it was the Jefferson of the common Enlightenment they shared which he quoted, not the Democratic Rousseauian political culture which Jefferson spoke for and which Lincoln condemned from his earliest political awareness. In that sense, American politics, which was once defined by Vernon Louis Parrington as a conflict between Jefferson and Hamilton, might be better defined as a division between Jefferson and Lincoln, with American culture and religion in both their rational and passional forms uncertainly divided between them.

Missing the distinctions that divide the two streams has posed a problem for Lincoln interpretation; in fact, missing these distinctions has played a major role in failing to integrate the public and the private Lincoln, since so much of what he was politically reflected and was built upon the cultural values that structured his inner life. Lincoln's earliest biographies — Holland's *Life,* Arnold's *Life* and his earlier and more hasty *The History of Abraham Lincoln and the Overthrow of Slavery* (1866), and even Lamon's ill-fated monstrosity — were so taken up with the theme of emancipation as the great labor of Lincoln's life that his political identity as "an old Henry Clay Whig" dissolved into thin air. Holland waved away Lincoln's Whiggism in one paragraph and passed quickly to his role as Great Emancipator; Arnold, an anti-Nebraska Democrat turned Republican, almost failed to avoid mentioning that Lincoln was a Whig, while Lamon allowed Chauncey Black to portray Lincoln as perversely sympathetic to conservative Northern Democrats and only a mild Whig at best.

Time also played its role in obscuring Lincoln's ideological origins to his biographers. By 1890, when John Hay and John Nicolay brought out what was supposed to be the authoritative biography of Lincoln, *Abraham Lincoln: A History,* the Whig party had been dead and gone for an entire political generation, and both men were more interested in concentrating on Lincoln's presidency than his prewar political career as a Whig. Hay, in particular, was too young to have ever identified himself with the Whigs, and he concentrated instead on turning *Abraham Lincoln: A History* into what Michael Burlingame has called a million-and-a-half-word Republican campaign tract for the '90s. Albert Beveridge's great *Abraham Lincoln, 1809-1858* (posthumously published in 1928) was so thorough and professionalized a biography that he might have incorporated more of Lincoln's Whiggish political roots into his work; but Beveridge, a Republican progressive and former senator from Indiana, had become so disillusioned with his own party that he actually found very little to admire in Lincoln as a politician. J. G. Randall, the first professional historian to turn his hand to Lincoln, was a Wilsonian Democrat who surprised his readers by praising George McClellan, and who unwittingly recapitulated Lamon and Black by portraying Lincoln as an almost-Democrat.

It did not help, either, that political ideology itself came under a cloud in the 1920s, with the rise of pragmatism as both a social and a political philosophy. Science, not the triumph of political theory, was promoted by John Dewey and George Herbert Mead as the solution to the problems of mass industrialization and corporate consumerism, while political theory, with its strong echoes of ethical conflict, was allowed to languish. The pragmatic tradition in the writing of American political history, over time, acquired considerable power, producing as its legacies works as various as Louis Hartz's *The Liberal Tradition in America* (which argued that all Americans inherited a common liberal tradition and that party ideologies were merely incidental modifications of that consensus) and Lee Benson's *The Concept of Jacksonian Democracy* (which reduced American political conflicts in the nineteenth century to contests of ethnic and religious origins). What was common to both Hartz and Benson was an indifference to ideology, almost as though it was an act of cultural treason to admit (especially in the face of the Cold War) that Americans had ever experienced ideological conflict within their own system. This was in turn reflected in the way successive Lincoln biographers unwittingly de-Whigged him. Ida Tarbell wrote off the political contests of Lincoln's early career as "almost purely personal"; Albert Beveridge dismissed the Whig party as a mere collection of issues, with its "chief practical asset" being the "popular idolatry" of Henry Clay. Even as late as 1993, political journalist Garry Wills could win a National Book Award for portraying Lincoln as a stealth Democrat.

But Lincoln was a deeply committed Whig, with an intense and ideologically driven loyalty to the anti-Jeffersonian liberalism the Whigs loved so well. "This aspect of Lincoln's behavior in the political arena" seems to modern pragmatists "particularly unappealing and not squaring with a devotion to a simple, heroic frontiersman's path to greatness," wrote Joel Silbey, in a provocative analysis in 1986 of Lincoln's party loyalties, but "this antiparty and antipolitician outlook, overlooks some essential points and fails to grasp some important distinctions about the American political nation in the antebellum years."

> He was a partisan [of] Whig ideology and spokesman for his party's cause in campaign and legislative debate, he was a party technician — an organization builder and political manager — and he remained loyal, committed and disciplined to the Whig cause. His partisanship was deeply important to his party and to himself. His Whiggery impinged on everything else he became and did.

If Jefferson and Jackson saw political life as a dark struggle of "haves" and "have-nots," Lincoln and the Whigs saw the Democrats — Jeffersonian, Jacksonian, and Douglasite alike — as an irrational and power-hungry elite, as the real "haves" trying to play the "have-nots" off against the bourgeois "have-somes" in order to lock American politics into a static system where they would always possess a monopoly on authority. Every issue Lincoln spoke for as a legislator — the railroads, land grants, tariffs — and every rhetorical gesture, from his abusive early political journalism to the refinement of the Gettysburg Address, was undergirded by his unwavering allegiance to the Whig ideology, to the reading of Mill, Wayland, and Carey, to the formation of an optimistic and socially mobile bourgeoisie who would guarantee an equal opportunity that "the weights should be lifted from the shoulders of men," "that every man can take care of himself," "to give *all* a chance," to "improve one's condition."

Lincoln's greatest political accomplishment was not that he centralized a previously weak federal government, but that he made the idea of the nation — a single people, unified rationally, not around a Rousseauian General Will but around certain propositions that transcended ethnicity, religious denominationalism, and gender — into the central political image of the republic. As George Templeton Strong confided to his diary after the end of the war, "The people has (I think) just been bringing forth a new American republic — an amazingly large baby — after a terribly protracted and severe labor, without chloroform." In the summer of 1865, in a tribute to Lincoln, Charles Hodge wrote, "Another consequence of the war . . . has been the development of the sentiment of nationality. . . . No one can doubt that this sentiment is stronger and more general now than it ever was before."

Nor is Lincoln's great economic victory the notion first advanced by Southern bitter-enders like E. A. Pollard and turned into sophisticated history by Charles and Mary Beard — that the war was deliberately transformed by Lincoln into a Republican weapon for forcing a precapitalist Southern economy into submission to Northern capitalist domination. Both North and South already were capitalist economies, the South almost more so than much of the North for dealing in the transatlantic world's prize commodity, cotton. But a capitalist economy is not necessarily a liberal one, as modern state-capitalist systems like China have all too easily demonstrated; and what Lincoln wanted was not so much a triumph of capitalism as the victory of free wage labor as the labor system of capitalism. "Lincoln's main argument against the expansion of slavery rested on the free labor ideal," writes Michael Sandel, and he "led the North to war in the name of free labor and the small, independent producer."

From the other side of post-industrialism and global free trade, all of this has a touchingly naive ring to it. The painful irony Sandel finds in Lincoln's achievement is the "lack of fit" between the ideal of free wage labor and the realities of the postwar economy, when the United States entered fully into the development of a mass industrial state. Within two decades of Lincoln's death, industrial wage labor had become "a system of slavery as absolute if not as degrading as that which lately prevailed at the South." Lincoln has often been forgiven this short-sightedness on the grounds that he had no real experience of the sort of mass industrial proletariat, politically free but economically powerless, which would make genuine social mobility remote. Still, Lincoln was not entirely blind to the possibility that mobility could become wedded to the pursuit of selfishness and exploitation. Selfishness, harsh as it sounds, it was the only alternative the liberal Enlightenment could offer as an explanation of why, in a world no longer governed by the supernatural, people should bother to work or associate. Lincoln himself abundantly agreed that "sooner or later the snaky tongue of selfishness" would emerge as the explanation for human conduct, and he agreed also that government existed largely to protect people in the pursuit of self-interest. Where Jefferson looked for occult commonalities in the yeomen, or where Southern aristocrats appealed to the mystical unities of race, as the basis for a social order, Lincoln frankly endorsed, and practiced, enlightened self-interest. "I believe there is a genuine popular sovereignty," he wrote in 1859, "that each man shall do precisely as he pleases with himself, and with all those things which exclusively concern him." When Richard Hofstadter conjured up the possibility of a Lincoln who survived assassination in 1865, only to become disillusioned by 1885 over the robber barons he had let loose, Hofstadter dramatically underestimated what Henry Clay Whitney recognized as Lincoln's cheerful unaverseness to serving the interests of "a great soulless corporation."

At the same time, however, Lincoln also recognized that societies founded on self-interest have little about which to boast, much less little ground upon which to establish systems of punishment or reward. "Insisting that there is no right principle of action but *self-interest*," as Lincoln admitted in the Peoria speech of October, 1854, could easily end up causing "the real friends of freedom to doubt our sincerity." Rousseau's (and Jefferson's) great appeal to the popular imagination has always been a human awareness of the disappointments and dividedness of the self-interested life and its failure to promote commonality, harmony, and pleasure. Loss of the common good was always one of the principal anxieties of the Enlightenment, all the way back to Locke and Adam Smith; and the solution in both Rousseau's and Jefferson's case was to find a new ground for society in something other than the artificialities of self-interested reason. The American Whigs — and particularly secular Whigs like Lincoln — strove to shore up this weakness by harping on the need for public moralism and appeals to natural law, and, ultimately, by forging a strategic political alliance with middle-class Protestant evangelicals.

Hardly any of the Whigs was in a better position to support this alliance than Lincoln. He might profess no particular Christian creed, but he did recognize both in his law practice and in Washington the need for Whigs to be beyond moral question, and he felt a certain distanced commonality with the rational apologetics and predestinarianism of Old School Presbyterianism. Hence, the lifelong cultivation of an image of honesty and transparency in all his doings, of polite encouragement of public religious gestures (but not favoritism of any particular religious denomination), even the repetitious citations of Scripture. This much, though, any conscientious Whig, or even any canny politician, could have been found doing, and among Lincoln's friends and enemies there were veiled suggestions that this was indeed the case. But Lincoln actually had reason to feel even more keenly than most of his political contemporaries the need to reach some form of religious plateau. Intersecting the ideological demand for moral appearances was a deeper personal conflict over religion, a conflict that stretched back far into his Calvinist childhood. It was a conflict generated in part by adolescent rebellion, and in part by the long Enlightenment anticlericalism one finds in Paine-ite and Benthamite propaganda; but it was fed all through Lincoln's adult life by the overweening moral rigorism of Victorian evangelicalism, which demanded such absolute self-honesty that the practitioners of it might, ironically, never honestly feel themselves worthy of forgiveness and grace. If Lincoln chose infidelity over piety, it was in the long run because piety made the choice so hard.

This imparted to Lincoln a deep, pervasive sense of the helplessness of human choice, and situates him within a long line of Victorian contemporaries whose turn to duty or reason or to withdrawal was generated at its root by the propensity of evangelicalism to give a stone rather than a loaf. The pathos with which Lincoln spoke of God in the second inaugural as the Judge who took back with the sword all the wealth that had been piled up by the lash, or as the unrevealing Mover of the "Meditation on the Divine Will" who could have ended the war with a thought, betrays the hand, not so much of a peculiar "religion of Lincoln" as of an evangelical religious culture that had turned the human situation into a "rungless ladder" to heaven, inculcating the most absolute and disinterested sincerity as the price for social mobility and market participation, and then stranding people with it. "The honesty of Mr. Lincoln appeared to spring from religious convictions," wrote Noah Brooks, who had no idea how much ambiguity dangled from the word *convictions*. "And it was his habit, when conversing of things which most intimately concerned himself, to say that, however he might be misrepresented by men who did not appear to know him, he was glad to know that no thought or intent of his escaped the observation of that Judge by whose final decree he expected to stand or fall in this world and the next." Like Emily Dickinson, who yearned for God to be her Father but only found the God of Amherst Congregationalism to be an "Eclipse," there is pain and desertion and remoteness, but not outright skepticism, in the mature Lincoln. "Cer-

461

tainly there is no contending against the will of God," Lincoln had written in 1858, "but still there is some difficulty in ascertaining, applying it to particular cases."

Lincoln often wished "that I was a more devout man than I am," but the ruthless self-honesty of evangelical Protestantism had early-on denied him the consolation of worthiness, and instead substituted a crushing sense of worthlessness. Even his early "work on infidelity" in New Salem was, as Herndon once remarked, "a blast, Job-like, of despair," written with "the thought and idea that God had forsaken him." Add to this desertion the trauma of family deaths, of Ann Rutledge, of his own mother, and Lincoln found himself hemmed in by a world in which his own choices meant nothing. Lincoln reminded Herndon, not of a brash unbeliever but "a blind intellectual Samson, struggling and fighting in the dark against the fates," and it seemed to Herndon that "God rolled Mr. Lincoln through His fiery furnace *specially*." But it was the agony of that "rolling" which Lincoln transmuted into the extraordinary gold of a charity for all, a malice toward none.

Lincoln was a typical Victorian doubter, born in the Enlightenment, shaped by classical liberalism, and nurtured in angst when the Enlightenment's confidence in its own optimistic solutions proved illusory. Yet Lincoln had this difference from Francis Newman or George Eliot or T. H. Green, that Lincoln's doubts ran backward, which is to say that for him the mystery of historical events called from him faith in divine superintendence rather than the incredulity over pain, death, and aimlessness one picks up from so many of the Victorians who could not reconcile infant mortality and the randomness of war with a loving God or the best of all possible worlds. Lincoln's pass through the furnace left him at the end wanting more, not less, to believe. "I should be the veriest shallow and self-conceited blockhead upon the footstool [of the earth]," he said to Noah Brooks on election day in 1864, "if, in my discharge of the duties which are put upon me in this place, I should hope to get along without the wisdom which comes from God and not from men." He did not know, he told Maine senator Lot Morrill, "but that God has created one man great enough to comprehend the whole of this stupendous crisis and transaction from beginning to end and endowed him with sufficient wisdom to manage and direct it."

Yet he could not come the whole way to belief. *He did not know* if there was a God who had made him, deliberately, with conscious interest and good will, like a father, for "the whole of this stupendous crisis." Similarly, he never succeeded in reconciling the optimism and self-confidence in the future which was so much a part of the Enlightenment frame of mind with his dark ancestral conviction that all choices were foreordained. He might have done so by retreating into passivity or by settling for a less demanding, more easily satisfied free-will evangelicalism (of which there were increasing versions on offer to complement the liberal mind). But perhaps it was the tension between his Calvinistic "melancholy" and his bourgeois aggressiveness which acted as the best mutual restraint, which gave him the depth and resiliency that everyone who knew him from the 1850s onward remarked upon as his greatest resources, and which became his most valuable character assets during the war. His confidence in the direction of providence kept his determinism from collapsing into helplessness in the darkest hours of the war, and it was his determinism that prevented his bourgeois optimism from soaring into arrogance in victory. "This purifying process," wrote Herndon, "gave Mr. Lincoln charity, liberality, kindness, tenderness, toleration, a sublime faith, if you please, in the purposes and ends of his Maker."

Perhaps, in the end, he hoped to find some beginning of an answer after the presidency was laid down, in Jerusalem or some other place of pilgrimage. But it is more likely, as Lincoln confessed to Aminda Rankin in 1846, that "probably it is to be my lot to go on in a twilight, feeling and reasoning my way through life, as questioning, doubting Thomas did." Those words make him something very different from the scoffer or deist or infidel in New Salem in 1831. But neither were they the confession of a convert or a prophet. They were, instead, the lonely murmur of abandonment, deathlike in the leafless trees.

A Note on the Sources

Any modern inquiry into the life and mind of Abraham Lincoln must begin with the Roy P. Basler's monumental edition of *The Collected Works of Abraham Lincoln*, published jointly by Rutgers University Press and the Abraham Lincoln Association in 1953 in eight volumes (with two further supplement volumes in 1974 and 1990 and an electronic version in 1999). Beside the *Collected Works* as standard references should also be E. S. Miers's three-volume *Lincoln Day-by-Day: A Chronology, 1809-1865* (rept. 1991) and Mark E. Neely's *The Abraham Lincoln Encyclopedia* (1984), although the Neely volume is now in need of revision and updating. The imminent publication of the Lincoln Legal Papers, in both paper and electronic formats, will add yet another important reference resource.

Odds are that the *Collected Works* will probably disappoint the casual reader, first, because nine-tenths of the Lincoln "works" are little more than day-to-day ephemera, and, second, because much of what is commonly identified as Lincoln's comes down to us only in the recollections of others, not in his own hand. For that reason, two necessary adjuncts to the *Collected Works* must be Rodney O. Davis and Douglas L. Wilson's *Herndon's Informants: Letters, Interviews, and Statements about Abraham Lincoln* (Chicago, 1998), which reprints the most important materials collected by William Herndon and Jesse Weik of direct recollections of Lincoln by his earliest acquaintances, and Don and Virginia Fehrenbacher's *Recollected Words of Abraham Lincoln* (Stanford, 1997), which offers a major compilation of Lincoln "sayings," culled from over 600 reminiscence works by Lincoln contemporaries. In addition to these, Michael Burlingame has edited a series of reminiscence collections in *An Oral History of Abraham Lincoln: John G. Nicolay's Interviews and Essays* (Carbondale, 1996) and *A Reporter's Lincoln* (Lincoln, NE, 1998), which reprints Walter B. Stevens's 1916 interview collection, along with newspaper interviews of Stevens's that were not included in the published book.

Firsthand reminiscence of Lincoln's sayings and doings, along with collections of documents, played a major role in Lincoln biography right from the beginning, starting with Lincoln himself, who prepared two autobiographical sketches of himself in 1859 and 1860. These, and direct interviews with Lincoln acquaintances, became the basis for a series of campaign biographies in the presidential elections of 1860 and 1864, the best of which came from William Dean Howells, John Locke Scripps, Henry J. Raymond, and James Barrett. The Raymond and Barrett volumes also added speeches and documents in almost equal proportion to biographical narrative. Before Lincoln's first term was over, William M. Thayer's *The Pioneer Boy* (1863) was also pieced together (with some imaginary dialogue supplied by Thayer) from reminiscence material, some of it gathered, apparently, by Lincoln's direction.

The first full-dress biographies of Lincoln were available almost within weeks of his assassination, starting with reprints of the Barrett and Raymond volumes that hurriedly tacked accounts of Lincoln's death onto their narratives. By February, 1866, the first purpose-written biography, Josiah Gilbert Holland's *Life of Abraham Lincoln*, was being sold by subscription across the country (it was a best-seller and made Holland, a well-known journalist, a wealthy man), to be followed by Isaac Arnold's *The History of Abraham Lincoln and the Overthrow of Slavery* (1866). Both Holland and Arnold told the story of Lincoln's life as a political history, with time and words bestowed chiefly on Lincoln's recruitment in the 1850s for the Republican party and his subsequent presidency (although Holland, with surprising energy for a journalist facing a deadline, dug out a substantial quantity of reminiscence material, too). The greatest of these political histories, how-ever, came in 1890, with the publication of John Nicolay and John Hay's masterwork, *Abraham Lincoln: A History* (followed in 1894 by the first critical collection of Lincoln letters and papers, overoptimistically titled in only two volumes, *The Complete Works of Abraham Lincoln*). Hay and Nicolay had the advantage not only of personal association with Lincoln in the White House but of access to Lincoln's private pa-pers, which had been removed from Washington after Lincoln's death by Robert Todd Lincoln. But the Nicolay-Hay biography found a wor-thy rival in Albert Beveridge's 1928 classic, *Abraham Lincoln, 1809-1858*. Cut short of completion by Beveridge's death, the biography had its own political advantage from having been written by a practicing politician, and even more from having personal access to the sprawl-ing collection of letters and interviews originally assembled by Wil-liam Herndon and kept under lock by Herndon's associate, Jesse Weik.

Herndon had always wanted to write a Lincoln biography him-self, but he had no interest in writing a political history. He was fasci-nated, as he told Josiah Holland in 1865, by "the *subjective* Mr. Lincoln — 'the inner life' of Mr. L.," which included Lincoln's intellectual life, his religion, his temperament, and his marriage. To that end, Herndon embarked on a series of self-financed journeys across Illinois and Indi-ana, interviewing (or soliciting correspondence) from Lincoln's old ac-quaintances from Little Pigeon Creek, New Salem, and early Spring-field. In the process he ruined his law practice, and he never managed to push any of the multitudes of firsthand materials he collected into print except in a series of lectures he gave in Springfield — lectures which revealed so much of the private Lincoln (especially the Ann Rutledge romance) that Herndon found himself ostracized by Spring-field society and hated by the Lincoln family. He eventually sold his materials to Ward Hill Lamon, who employed a ghostwriter to com-pose the "subjective" biography Herndon had always wanted. But when Lamon's *The Life of Abraham Lincoln* appeared in 1872, it was greeted with the same furious contempt nationally, and only the first of the projected two volumes of Lamon's biography ever appeared in print. It was not until an ambitious young Indianan named Jesse Weik presented himself to Herndon as an associate in the 1880s that Herndon finally was bestirred to complete his *Herndon's Lincoln: The True Story of a Great Life* (1889). By then, the battle lines over the veracity of Herndon and his long-dead informants had already been drawn. Weik himself conducted a series of follow-up interviews with the handful of survivors who had direct recollection of Lincoln, and published his own contribution to the "inner" Lincoln in *The Real Lincoln* (1922). The last Lincoln biographer to have, like Weik, the opportunity to take down new recollection material from Lincoln survivors was the muck-raking journalist, Ida Tarbell, whose articles on Lincoln in *McClure's Magazine* eventually blossomed into a major two-volume biography of its own in 1900. In the meanwhile, memoirs that touched in varying degrees on Lincoln (or else represented their authors' attempt to cash in on purported associations with Lincoln) appeared from Henry Clay Whitney, Henry B. Rankin, and a host of others.

The passing of the generation that remembered Lincoln, and the death of Albert Beveridge, rounded off an era when Lincoln biography lay chiefly in the hands of amateurs for whom the use of reminiscence posed no issue. In 1922, James Garfield Randall published *Constitutional Problems Under Lincoln,* and, with Randall, Lincoln was captured by the academics. For the next fifty years, between Randall and the publication of Stephen B. Oates's *With Malice Toward None: The Life of Abraham Lincoln* (1977), Lincoln biography became the preserve of university-based historians, and largely as a reaction against the amateurism of Herndon, Weik, and the "subjective" Lincolnites, the face of Lincoln biography wore an overwhelmingly political cast. Randall set the tone for the "politicization" of Lincoln with his multi-volume *Lincoln the President* (1945-53, finished in 1955 by Richard Current), which not only treated reminiscence — and especially Herndon's reminiscence material — cautiously, but which made clear that Lincoln's presidency was the only proper focus for Lincolnian biography. On Randall's cue, a series of outstanding political studies of Lincoln's presidency emerged, most notably T. Harry Williams on *Lincoln and His Generals* (1952) and *Lincoln and the Radicals* (1941), William F. Zornow's *Lincoln and the Party Divided* (1954), Herman Belz, *Reconstructing the Union: Theory and Policy During the Civil War* (1969), Harry Carman and Reinhold Luthin, *Lincoln and the Patronage* (1943), and LaWanda Cox, *Lincoln and Black Freedom: A Study in Presidential Leadership* (1981). Only Harry Jaffa's *Crisis of the House Divided: An Interpretation of the Issues of the Lincoln-Douglas Debates* (1959) strayed seriously from the presidential focus, although, in the process, Jaffa wrote what was incontestably the greatest Lincoln book of the century. Yet another great political history, this time focussed on political ideology, necessarily touched on Lincoln. This was Eric Foner's *Free Soil, Free Labor, Free Men: The Ideology of the Republican Party Before the Civil War* (1970), which laid a lonely path toward a reconsideration of Lincoln at the center of Whig/Republican ideas on political economy. Even into the 1990s, interest in the politics and presidency continued to be the benchmark of good academic Lincoln scholarship, something that was seen in Philip Shaw Paludan's *The Presidency of Abraham Lincoln* (1994), J. David Greenstone's *The Lincoln Persuasion: Remaking American Liberalism* (1993), and Mark Neely's 1992 Pulitzer Prize–winning study of Civil War–era civil liberties abuses, *The Fate of Liberty: Abraham Lincoln and Civil Liberties.* Ironically, what remains the finest one-volume survey biography of Lincoln, Benjamin Thomas's *Abraham Lincoln: A Biography* (1952), was written by a nonacademic, the executive secretary of the Abraham Lincoln Association from 1932 to 1936, associate editor of the *Abraham Lincoln Quarterly,* and editorial advisor to Roy Basler in assembling the *Collected Works.*

The academics' doubts about reminiscence, and their tendency to concentrate on the public documentary record of Lincoln's presidency, only got stronger as the amateurs grew more outrageous. In 1926, the Illinois-born poet Carl Sandburg published *Abraham Lincoln: The Prairie Years,* the first of what became a multi-volume Lincoln biography. Sandburg's *Lincoln,* in addition to meandering dreamily in and out of Lincoln's life, also made utterly uncritical use of any and all reminiscence sources, nothing seeming too ridiculous if it allowed Sandburg to wax bard-like. That, and the maddening popular acclaim for Sandburg's *Lincoln,* only drove the contempt of the academics for the "inner" Lincoln higher. It was the brave, and usually the nonacademic, soul who attempted to keep Herndon's candle burning. Two of these faithful were clergymen, Louis A. Warren (who, as director of the Lincoln National Life Insurance Company's Lincoln museum in Indiana, wrote a carefully pieced-together account of Lincoln's Indiana years in *Lincoln's Youth*) and William E. Barton (who in thirteen years, between 1920 and 1933, managed to turn out no less than eight substantial Lincoln studies, including the most serious and balanced investigation of Lincoln's religion in *The Soul of Abraham Lincoln*). But the quality of such work varied dangerously. Two other religious thinkers who attempted explorations of Lincoln's religion, the Quaker Elton True-blood (in *Abraham Lincoln: Theologian of American Anguish*) and William Wolf (in *Almost Chosen People*) were superficial in their conclusions and undistinguished in their research. A selection of the Herndon-Weik materials was edited and published by Emmanuel Hertz as *The Hidden Lincoln* in 1937, but the transcriptions were sometimes embarrassingly botched, and represented only a small fraction of the overall Herndon-Weik Papers.

Perhaps it was the result of the shattering of public confidence in politics during the Vietnam War and Watergate, but in the 1970s the volume of interest in the political Lincoln waned, and academic historians turned their attention inward for the first time, beginning with two psycho-biographies, George Forgie's *Patricide in the House Divided: A Psychological Interpretation of Lincoln and His Age* (1977) and Charles Strozier's *Lincoln's Quest for Union: Public and Private Meanings* (1982). Forgie and Strozier were excessive and often fanciful in their conclusions, but they signalled a dramatic reversal of priorities in Lincoln research. Even among the resolutely political, interest in Lincoln's politics shifted to his congressional and legislative service (as in Donald Riddle's *Lincoln Runs for Congress*, Paul Simon's *Lincoln's Preparation for Greatness: The Illinois Legislative Years*, Paul Findley's *A. Lincoln: The Crucible of Congress*, and Donald Fehrenbacher's *Prelude to Greatness: Lincoln in the 1850s*). But the real movement back toward the "subjective" Lincoln would come in 1990, with the publication of almost-simultaneous articles by John Y. Simon and Douglas Wilson, rehabilitating the reliability of Herndon and his informants and eventually shifting the center of Lincoln studies to the pre-presidential years.* This rehabilitation was helped along dramatically by Michael Burlingame's *The Inner World of Abraham Lincoln* (1994), which unapologetically swam back into the stream of the "subjective" Lincoln but also displayed a magisterial critical command of the Lincoln reminiscence literature to back it up.

In *The Inner World of Abraham Lincoln* and in a series of text editions

---

*On the use of the Herndon reminiscence material, see Douglas L. Wilson, "Editing Herndon's Informants," in *Lincoln Herald* (1993), 115-23, and Rodney O. Davis, "William Herndon, Memory, and Lincoln Biography," in *Journal of Illinois History* (1998), 99-112.

of the diary and wartime journalism of John Hay, and of John Nicolay's manuscript interviews with Lincoln informants, Burlingame exhumed new collections of Lincoln reminiscence material from sources that lay only a question or two away from even the simplest researcher. Like nearly everyone who has ever composed a footnote, Burlingame realized that few scholars, much less biographers, ever use more than a fraction of the research material they amass. A great deal of the excess goes into wastecans or, in the case of prominent writers, into collections of the writer's papers in college or university archives. It occurred to Burlingame that this was probably no less true of Lincoln's biographers than anyone else's, and so he began checking various archives in search of the cast-offs of Nicolay, Tarbell, and other Lincolnites. What he found were small gold mines in out-of-the-way places, such as the Tarbell Papers at Allegheny College, Tarbell's *alma mater,* and the newspaper interviews Walter Stevens had never bothered to include in the original *A Reporter's Lincoln.* Nor was Burlingame alone in this pursuit. Harold Holzer, in addition to pioneering work on Lincoln iconography, also found new gold in old mines with a fresh edition of the Lincoln-Douglas debates (based on the texts printed in the opposition newspapers of the two debaters) and revealing selections of letters addressed to Lincoln in *Dear Mr. President* (1994) and *The Lincoln Mailbag* (1998). Douglas Wilson and Rodney Davis revisited the vast jumble of the Herndon-Weik reminiscence materials, metriculously transcribing, editing, and organizing it, and publishing a generous selection of Herndon's interview transcripts and solicited reminiscences in *Herndon's Informants* in 1997. Wilson then built on that work to produce another landmark in the new "inner Lincoln" literature, *Honor's Voice: The Transformation of Abraham Lincoln* (1998), which was, in large measure, a series of essays focussed almost entirely on the formation of Lincoln's character from New Salem to Lincoln's marriage to Mary Todd.

Reminiscence and subjectivity have not been the only factors pressing the Lincoln presidency into the back seat. In 1977, Gabor Boritt, in *Lincoln and the Politics of the American Dream,* revived inquiry into Lincoln's Whig party allegiance and deciphered many of the meanings of the long-obscure economic debates that had consumed virtually all of Lincoln's political attention before 1854. Boritt did so just as historians of the early American republic were turning the historiography of that period toward "the market revolution" as the interpretive key for the Jefferson-Jackson years. This culminated in 1991 with the publication of Charles Sellers' *The Market Revolution: Jacksonian America, 1815-1848*. Sellers, alongside Harry Watson in *Liberty and Power: The Politics of Jacksonian America* (1990) and Daniel Feller in *The Jacksonian Promise: America, 1815-1840* (1995), made the impact of Whig capitalism on Jeffersonian pre-capitalist subsistence farmers the main story line of the early Republic and therefore of Lincoln's youth. Although Sellers made no direct connection with Lincoln, the opportunities to do so were obvious. At the same time, the evolution of traditional American intellectual history in the style of Perry Miller, Ralph Gabriel, and Merle Curti (who had little or no interest in middle-brown consumers of intellectual culture like Lincoln) into a broadly based inclusion of cultural history offered Daniel Walker Howe the opportunity, in *The Political Culture of the American Whigs* (1979) and *Creating the American Self: From Jonathan Edwards to Abraham Lincoln* (1997), to situate Lincoln in the heart of a Whig "culture," as well as Whig political economy.

What will become important in Lincoln studies over the next decade (leading as it does to the Lincoln bicentennial in 2009) will be the integration of the old political Lincoln with the revived subjective Lincoln, in the overall context of the Whig culture that formed the backdrop for Lincoln's life. In the green old age of Lincoln studies, this "intellectual biography" attempts to be a model for just such an effort. Reminiscence material will continue to carry pieces of controversy along with it, but it will seem very much a fixture of Lincoln studies; and, indeed, the only question will be where the newest sources of reminiscence material are likely to be unearthed.

The following annotations do not, in line with both the purposes of this book as an extended essay and with the series for which it is intended, attempt to be comprehensive. Rather, they are content to identify primary Lincoln-related citations, and whatever secondary citations may be absolutely necessary. The following abbreviations will be followed throughout:

ALQ   *Abraham Lincoln Quarterly*
CW   *The Collected Works of Abraham Lincoln*, ed. Roy P. Basler (New Brunswick, NJ, 1953), nine volumes, plus two supplements

CWH   *Civil War History*

HI   *Herndon's Informants,* eds. Douglas Wilson and Rodney O. Davis (Urbana, IL, 1997)

HW   William H. Herndon and Jesse Weik, *Herndon's Lincoln: The True Story of a Great Life* (New York, 1917), two volumes

JALA   *Journal of the Abraham Lincoln Association*

RW   *Recollected Words of Abraham Lincoln,* eds. Don and Virginia Fehrenbacher (Stanford, CA, 1996)

THL   *The Hidden Lincoln,* ed. Emmanuel Hertz (New York: Viking Press, 1937).

Introduction: The Strife of Ideas

The letter from Lincoln to Chester is in *CW*, 4:11-12. Lincoln's "hatred" for Jefferson is in Herndon to Lamon, March 3, 1870, in W. H. Lamon Papers, Library of Congress. Agrarian culture is described in Harry Watson, *Liberty and Power: The Politics of Jacksonian America,* and Christopher Clark, *The Roots of Rural Capitalism* (Ithaca, 1990), while the Randolph comment is in Robert Dawidoff, *The Education of John Randolph* (New York, 1979), 30. The church statistics are from Jon Butler, *Awash in a Sea of Faith: Christianizing the American People* (Cambridge, 1990), 270. On Jefferson and Rousseau, see Conor Cruise O'Brien, *The Long Affair: Thomas Jefferson and the French Revolution, 1785-1800* (Chicago, 1996), 11-12. On self-improvement, see "The Emerging Idea of Self-Improvement," in Howe, *Making the American Self: Jonathan Edwards to Abraham Lincoln* (Cambridge, 1997); on religion and civic virtue, see James Kloppenberg, "The Virtues of Liberalism: Christianity, Republicanism, and Ethics in Early American Political Discourse," in *The Virtues of Liberalism* (New York, 1998). On evangelicals being nine out of ten, see Carwardine, *Evangelicals and Politics in Antebellum America* (New Haven, 1993), 3-17. On "living Scripture," see Kazin, *God and the American Writer* (New York, 1997), 127.

On Victorian print culture, see Brewer, *The Pleasures of the Imagination: English Culture in the Eighteenth Century* (New York, 1997), and Newsome, *The Victorian World Picture* (New Brunswick, 1997). The "speculative tradition" comes from Bruce Kuklick, "Charles Hodge,

Scottish Realism and the American Philosophical Tradition" (unpublished manuscript, 1997). Royce's comment on the "typical American" is in Royce's "On Certain Limitations of the Thoughtful Public in America" (unpublished manuscript in the Royce Papers [HUG1755.5/ vol. 71, 31-33], Harvard University Archives). The Victorian propensity for seeing the loss of faith as a tragedy rather than a triumph is discussed in A. N. Wilson, *God's Funeral* (New York, 1999), 10-11, 151. Rorty's remark on disengaging discussion is in "The Priority of Democracy to Philosophy," in *The Virginia Statute for Religious Freedom: Its Evolution and Consequences in American History*, eds. M. D. Peterson and R. C. Vaughan (Cambridge, 1988).

Chapter One: The American System

On the Lincoln migrations, see Tarbell, *Life*, 1:1-3, 6; Tarbell, *In the Footsteps of the Lincolns* (New York, 1924), 1, 11, 30, 39, 46; and Beveridge, *Lincoln*, 1:6-7, 9, 10, 11. Uncle Mord is in Fehrenbacher, *RW*, 299. Land titles are discussed in Olivier Fraysse, *Lincoln, Land, and Labor: 1809-60* (Chicago, 1994), 9-14. Thomas and Sarah Bush Lincoln are described in *HI*, 41, 82, 99, 106, 113, 134, 176. AL's autobiography is in *CW*, 4:60-67. The silver half-dollars are described in Francis Carpenter, *Six Months at the White House with Abraham Lincoln* (New York, 1867), 96-98, and in Fehrenbacher, *RW*, 454. AL's reading list is in *HI*, 41, 105-6, 112, 121, 126, 146-47, and in Louis A. Warren, *Lincoln's Youth: Indiana Years, 1816-30* (Indianapolis, 1959, 1991), 28-32. On the Calvinist Baptists of Appalachia, see Tarbell, *In the Footsteps*, 108-9, and Warren, *Lincoln's Youth*, 13, 112-16, and more generally Peacock and Tyson, *Pilgrims of Paradox: Calvinism and Experience Among the Primitive Baptists of the Blue Ridge* (1989), and John G. Crowley, *Primitive Baptists of the Wiregrass South: 1815 to the Present* (1999). On slavery in Illinois, see Paul Finkelman, "Slavery, the 'More Perfect Union,' and the Prairie State," in *Illinois Historical Journal* 80 (Winter 1987), 248-69. The flatboat is described in Erastus Wright's interview of John Hanks, July 3, 1865, in Josiah G. Holland Papers, New York Public Library; and in Walter B. Stevens, *A Reporter's Lincoln*, ed. Michael Burlingame (Lincoln, NE, 1998), 125. AL's reading is listed in Stevens, *Reporter's Lincoln*, 280, *The Lincoln Papers*, ed. David C. Mearns (Garden City, 1948), 1:154-56, and *HI*, 10, 80,

172, 179, 374, 426, 498-99. AL's religious skepticism is described in Stevens, *Reporter's Lincoln*, 12, 250, and *HI*, 441, 458, 472, 576-77. The book on "infidelity" is in *HI*, 24, 61-62, 432, 441, 545, 577. On Al's proximity to the Owenites, see C. G. Vannest, *Lincoln the Hoosier: Abraham Lincoln's Life in Indiana* (St. Louis, 1928), 117-18, 120. AL pilots the *Talisman* in Beveridge, *Lincoln*, 1:118-19, and Paul M. Angle, *"Here I Have Lived": A History of Lincoln's Springfield, 1821-1865* (Chicago, 1971), 36-38. AL announces for the legislature in Paul Simon, *Lincoln's Preparation for Greatness: The Illinois Legislative Years* (Norman, 1965), 10, and *An Oral History of Abraham Lincoln: John G. Nicolay's Interviews and Essays*, ed. Michael Burlingame (Carbondale, 1996), 35. For AL as an old Whig, see *RW*, 37.

Chapter Two: The Costs of Union

AL's election handbill is in *CW*, 1:5-9, and his Pappsville speech, in *HI*, 7, 16-17, 203; *Oral History*, 20. AL's surveying and speech making, appearance, and "stiff" in Whig doctrine are in *Oral History*, 10, 30, 36, and in *HI*, 201-2. AL on public lands is in *CW*, 1:32; AL in caucus, in *Oral History*, 21; AL writing editorials, in *HI*, 431. An inventory of AL's legislative documents is available at www.sos.state.il.us/depts/archives/lincdocs.html. AL on distribution and the State Bank, in *CW*, 1:48, 61-69, and Gabor Boritt, *Lincoln and the Economics of the American Dream* (Memphis, 1977), 19-47. AL as manager, in *Oral History*, 30, and Francis F. Browne, *The Every-Day Life of Abraham Lincoln* (Minneapolis, 1887), 126. AL's entrance into law and legal reading are best covered by Mark E. Steiner in "Abraham Lincoln and the Antebellum Legal Profession" (unpublished Ph.D. dissertation, University of Houston, 1993); on the use of a legal form book, see *HI*, 170. Early Springfield is described in Angle, *Here I Have Lived*, 11, 45, 100, 102, 196-97; Springfield fighting over AL is described in *THL*, 123. AL's circle is described in *Oral History*, 27, and in Wilson, *Honor's Voice: The Transformation of Abraham Lincoln* (New York, 1998), 186-99. On Lincoln's infidelity in Springfield, see *HI*, 156, 167, 171, 432, 472, 501, 519, 529. For Lincoln on the circuit, see *HI*, 46, 390, Weik, *The Real Lincoln: A Portrait* (1922), chs. 11 and 14, and Arnold, *Life of Abraham Lincoln* (Chicago, 1884), 84. On AL's memory and quotations, see *HI*, 30, 93, 519; on the recollection of

Clardy Barnett, see *CW*, 2:312. On the "independent Treasury" speech and the 1840 campaign, see *CW*, 1:155-56, 157-58, 159-79, 184, 209-10, Wilson, *Honor's Voice*, 199-200, and *HI*, 181, 388, 342, 347. On AL and women, see *HI*, 91, 131, 170, 455. On Lincoln and Rutledge, see *HI*, 13, 205, 236, 325, 557, *RW*, 110-11, 522, and the articles by Simon, "Abraham Lincoln and Ann Rutledge," *JALA* (1990), 13-33, and Wilson, "Abraham Lincoln, Ann Rutledge, and the Evidence of Herndon's Informants," in *CWH* (1990), 301-24, as well as John E. Walsh, *The Shadows Rise: Abraham Lincoln and the Ann Rutledge Legend* (Chicago, 1993). On Mary Owens, see *HI*, 256-262, 530-531, and AL's letters in *CW*, 1:78, 94. On AL's "engagement," see Wilson, *Honor's Voice*, 216-52, and "Abraham Lincoln and 'That Fatal First of January'" in *Lincoln Before Washington: New Perspectives on the Illinois Years* (Chicago, 1997). On the marriage as a "policy match," see *HI*, 65, 251, 464, and *Oral History*, 2-3. AL's letters on "misery" are in *CW*, 1:229, 268, 282. On election from the new district, see *CW*, 1:306.

Chapter Three: The Doctrine of Necessity

AL's comments to Speed on bankruptcy and on his marriage are in *CW*, 1:305, 306, 324, 325, 328. AL and property transactions are in Harry E. Pratt, *The Personal Finances of Abraham Lincoln* (Springfield, 1943), 32. On AL and "aristocracy," see *HI*, 251, and *CW*, 1:320. AL and college education is in *RW*, 160. On AL's advice reading, see Chandler, *The Elements of Character* (3rd ed., Boston, 1855), 45; AL allegedly made marginalia in a copy of Chandler originally in the Oliver Barrett collection, and recopied by Ida Tarbell in her own copy of Chandler. On AL's and Herndon's reading, see *THL*, 116-17, and Stevens, *Reporter's Lincoln*, 154; on reading geology, see Mearns, *Lincoln Papers*, 1:159. On AL's "melancholy," see *THL*, 15, 51-52, 64-65, 110-11, 121, 124, 198, 204, and Herndon, "Analysis of the Character of Abraham Lincoln," in *ALQ* (1941), 341-83, 403-41. On other aspects of AL's temperament, see *HI*, 88, 193, 205, 236, 238, 243, 251, 266, 342, 432, 445, 446, 518, 556, and *Oral History*, 2, 37-38. On the Lincoln marriage, see *HI*, 453, 465-67, 597, 692, 729; on tipping domestics, see Stevens, *Reporter's Lincoln*, 193-94, and *HI*, 407, 597. On Whig political activities, see *CW*, 1:203-6, 244-49, 261-62, 264, 309-18. AL's perception that irreligion was costing him votes is in *CW*, 1:106, 320. AL's handbill on "infidelity" is in *CW*, 1:382; on Lincoln's "fatalism," see Allen C. Guelzo, "Abraham Lincoln and the Doctrine of Necessity," *JALA* (1997), 57-81. AL as a "slave" is in *RW*, 383, and Stevens, *Reporter's Lincoln*, 35. For AL on mobility and labor, see *CW*, 2:364, 3:477-78, 4:24-25, 5:52; also, James A. Stevenson, "Abraham Lincoln on Labor and Capital," in *CWH* (1992), 197-209, and John Ashworth, "Free Labor, Wage Labor, and Slave Power: Republicanism and the Republican Party in the 1850s," in *The Market Revolution in America: Social, Political and Religious Expressions, 1800-1880*, eds. M. Stokes and S. Conway (Charlottesville, 1996), 128-46. AL's letter to John Johnston is in *CW*, 2:15-16. On Springfield and slaves, see Richard Hart, "Honest Abe and the African-Americans," in *Illinois Times* (February 12, 1998), 6-11. The joint protest with Stone is in *CW*, 1:75. The Matson slave case is discussed in Steiner, "Abraham Lincoln and the Antebellum Legal Profession," ch. 5. AL on "stropping" is in Mearns, *Lincoln Papers*, 1:169; the two letters on the slaves in transit are in *CW*, 1:260 and 2:320; on John Hanks and AL's sight of slavery in New Orleans, see *RW*, 61, 198, 528. For AL's linking of slavery and hedonism, see *HI*, 183. AL on the influence of Leonard Bacon is in *RW*, 446. AL on the "Spot Resolutions" is in *CW*, 1:420-22, 431-42. AL's New England speeches and support of Taylor are in *CW*, 1:449, 452, 454, 501-16, and 2:1-9. AL's refusal of the Oregon governorship is in *Oral History*, 15.

Chapter Four: The Fuel of Interest

AL's refusal to run is in *CW*, 2:79, and the comments on his political "death" are in *CW*, 3:512 and 4:67. AL's reading is in *HI*, 407, and *RW*, 387. The behavior of AL's sons is described in *HI*, 453; Beveridge, *Lincoln*, 1:506-7; Weik, *Real Lincoln*, 55, 90-91, 102-3; *THL*, 129; Mrs. Benjamin Edwards in Stevens, *Reporter's Lincoln*, 162; and Donn Piatt, in A. T. Rice, *Reminiscences of Abraham Lincoln by Distinguished Men of His Time* (New York, 1886), 480. Charles P. McIlvaine, unlike Alexander and Janeway, was an Episcopalian bishop, but was trained by Old School Presbyterians at Princeton Theological Seminary. Charles Zane and David Davis are in *HI*, 348, 489. Langdon Kaine is cited in *RW*, 273; the comments on Baptists and Episcopalians are also in *RW*, 151, 160. James Smith's observations on AL's melancholy are in William E.

Barton, *The Soul of Abraham Lincoln* (New York, 1920), 162-63. AL's comments on providence are in *HL*, 409, and *HI*, 162, 529; his unbelief in a personal God is in *HW*, 2:156. AL's fragment on Niagara Falls is in *CW*, 2:10. Charles Ray is in Ward Hill Lamon, *Life of Abraham Lincoln* (1872), 489-90. On AL's resemblance to Theodore Parker, see Fell in *HI*, 578-80. For Joseph Gillespie on AL's predestinarianism, see *RW*, 168; for Swett, Hanna, and Cogdal on AL's unitarianism and universalism, see *HI*, 167, 441, 458, and *RW* 2, 110, 191, 198, 278, and 411. On AL and James Smith, *HI*, 524, 576. On AL's poignancy, see Henry B. Rankin, *Personal Recollections of Abraham Lincoln* (New York, 1916), 320-26; on reading Smith's book, see *RW*, 149, 296, 411. For James Keyes, see *RW*, 278, and *HI*, 464; on Smith's prophecy of AL's presidency, see *HI*, 484. The description of AL's non-attendance at church is in *Oral History*, 155; see Swett in *HI*, 167, and Reeves in Stevens, *Reporter's Lincoln*, 48. On AL not reading Smith, see *HL*, 77. On the ethical uprightness of Victorian unbelievers, see Ian Bradley, *The Call to Seriousness: The Evangelical Impact on the Victorians* (New York, 1976), 198-202, and James Turner, *Without God, Without Creed: The Origins of Unbelief in America* (Baltimore, 1985), 211-17, 222-25. Matheny's accusation is in *HI*, 577. John Johnston's letters are in Mearns, *Lincoln Papers*, 1:178-79, 180; AL's reply to Johnston is in *CW*, 2:96-97.

AL's law practice is described in *Lincoln Legal Briefs* #44 (October/December, 1997) and #46 (April/June, 1998); his Sangamon County practice is summarized in the LLB Annual Report for 1995. Goodrich and Chicago are mentioned by Davis in *HI*, 349. AL's practice on the circuit is described in Tarbell, *Life*, 1:246-50, and in Beveridge, *Lincoln*, 1:529-60. AL's reply to Isham Reavis is in *CW*, 2:327; Shelby Cullom is in Stevens, *Reporter's Lincoln*, 154. His injunctions to students to read are in *CW*, 2:327, 535, and in 4:121. AL's associates on the circuit are described in Beveridge, *Lincoln*, 1:511-15; his circuit partnerships and the Bloomington "triumvirate" are described in Stevens, *Reporter's Lincoln*, 33, 35. AL as judge is in *HI*, 600, 630, 634. AL's law lecture notes are in *CW*, 2:81-82; his advice to William Martin is in *CW*, 2:102. AL's advice to clients is in *THL*, 429; his overall role as a peacemaker is described in Mark E. Steiner, "The Lawyer As Peacemaker: Law and the Community in Abraham Lincoln's Slander Cases," *JALA* (1995). On AL's appearance, see Stevens, *Reporter's Lincoln*, 60, 94, 166, and Weik, *Real Lincoln*, 190-91. On AL's "presence," see Burlingame,

The Inner World of Abraham Lincoln (Urbana, 1994), 11-13, and Rice, *Reminiscences,* 493; on AL's secretiveness, see *HI,* 348, and *HW,* 2:2-3. Washburne on "Old Abe" is in Rice, *Reminiscences,* 16, and *RW,* 467. AL's appeal to the "dutch justice" is in *CW,* 2:106. The Lincoln town name is in Beveridge, *Lincoln,* 1:518. AL's defense of William Florville (or Fleurville) is in *CW,* 2:159. The Harrison trial is covered in Tarbell, *Life,* 1:273-74, and Beveridge, *Lincoln,* 1:550-61; the Armstrong trial is covered in Tarbell, *Life,* 1:270-73, and in Beveridge, *Lincoln,* 1:561-69. AL's interest in the McLean County tax case is in *CW,* 2:209, and the case is abstracted in *Lincoln Legal Briefs* #48 (October/December, 1998). The Rock Island Bridge case is covered in Tarbell, *Life,* 1:275-78; Beveridge, 1:598-605; and Weik, *Real Lincoln,* 177-87; AL's summation is in *CW,* 2:415-22. AL's idea for a "steam plow" in mentioned in *CW,* 3:476; his lectures on discoveries and inventions are in *CW,* 2:437-42 and 3:356-63. The McCormick Reaper case is covered in Tarbell, *Life,* 1:260-66, and Beveridge, *Lincoln,* 1:575-83; AL's examination of Manny's reaper is in *CW,* 2:315. Stanton's derogatory comments are in *RW,* 246, and *HW,* 2:22-24. AL's credit rating for 1857 is in Illinois vol. 198, p. 163, in the R. G. Dun credit ledgers, in the Special Collection of the Baker Library, Harvard Business School (my particular thanks to Scott Sandage for directing my attention to this). On AL's income, see Tarbell, *Life,* 1:267, and Pratt, *Personal Finances,* viii. On the Whig convention, see *CW,* 2:113. AL's Scott speeches are in *CW,* 2:135-39; his Clay eulogy is in *CW,* 2:121-32. Thompson on AL is in Stevens, *Reporter's Lincoln,* 98; Stuart and Swett are in *HI,* 65, 165. AL's arousal at the repeal is in *CW,* 4:67. His editorial on the Kansas-Nebraska Act is in *CW,* 2:230.

Chapter Five: Moral Principle Is All That Unites Us

The texts of the four principal 1854 campaign speeches are in *CW,* as follows: Bloomington, September 12 (2:230-33), Bloomington, September 26 (2:234-40), Springfield, October 4 (2:240-47), and Peoria, October 16 (2:247-83). Slavery tolerated as a necessity is in *CW,* 2:266, 274, 275. The South exhausting its share of the bargain, in *CW,* 2:241. Popular sovereignty a palliation, in *CW,* 2:262. Self-government eternally right, in *CW,* 2:265. Slaves are men, not animals, in *CW,* 2:264-65. Enslavement not a moral right, in *CW*, 2:274. Slavery as an outrage on natural law, in *CW*, 2:222, 245; 4:3, 9. Restoring the Missouri Compromise, in *CW*, 2:247, 272-73. Moral equivalence of Northerners and Southerners, in *CW*, 2:255. Incapability of political equality, in *CW*, 2:256. Coloniza- tion to Liberia, in *CW*, 2:255. Deprives example, in *CW*, 2:255. AL to Speed, in *CW*, 2:318.

AL to Bunn is in *RW*, 70. Descending from republican faith is in *CW*, 2:242. The distinction between existence and extension is in *CW*, 2:248. Sheet anchor of republicanism, in *CW*, 2:266. Republican robe soiled, in *CW*, 2:276. Washburne's comment on AL's eligibility for Sen- ate is in Rice, *Reminiscences*, 21. AL on vote-gathering to Washburne, in *CW*, 2:303. AL to Gillespie on Trumbull is in *HI*, 183. On AL's gracious- ness, see *Oral History*, 40; on Julia Trumbull and MTL, see Jean Baker, *Mary Todd Lincoln: A Biography* (New York, 1987). 150. AL's biblical al- lusions are in *CW*, 2:243, 270, 276; no peaceful extinction of slavery, *CW*, 2:318. On the Whigs and the Declaration, see Kenneth Stampp, *The Imperilled Union: Essays on the Background of the Civil War* (New York, 1980), 31-32, 153-54. AL on the sentiments of the old-time men, in *CW*, 2:267; on the Declaration transcending national origins, see *CW*, 3:468-69. The Declaration as economic opportunism, in *CW*, 4:438, 6:24-25, and J. David Greenstone, *The Lincoln Persuasion: Remaking American Liberalism* (Princeton, 1993), 30, 233-35, 250. The African upon his soil is in *CW*, 3:79. AL's description of the Declaration as an apple of gold, and the Constitution as pitcher of silver is in *CW*, 4:69. Black rights natural, in *CW* 4:16. AL's comments on the Constitution are in *CW*, 1:488, 2:366, 475, 501, 3:334, 496, 6:428-29. Truman Smith is in Thomas Brown, *Politics and Statesmanship: Essays on the American Whig Party* (New York, 1985), 227. AL to Codding is in *CW*, 2:288, and to Lovejoy, in *CW*, 2:316. AL on remaining a Whig is in his letter to Speed, in *CW*, 2:322-23, and in *RW*, 21. On the Decatur editors' meeting see Don E. Fehrenbacher, *Prelude to Greatness: Lincoln in the 1850's* (Stan- ford, 1962), 43-47. AL on comparing himself to the victim of a robber is in *CW*, 2:333. AL's Bloomington speech has not survived except in a brief newspaper abstract (in *CW*, 2:341) and in later reconstructions, which are surveyed in Elwell Crissey, *Lincoln's Lost Speech: The Pivot of His Career* (New York, 1967), 158-233. Herndon on AL's speech is found in *HW*, 2:53; Thomas Henderson is in Stevens, *Reporter's Lincoln*, 46. Herndon to Trumbull on the 1856 campaign is in *Concerning Mr.*

Lincoln, ed. Harry E. Pratt (Springfield, 1944), 5. AL's preference for McLean is in *CW,* 2:342-43. Parker on Pierce is in Mearns, *Lincoln Papers,* 1:283; Whitman's "Redeemer President" editorial is in David S. Reynolds, *Walt Whitman's America: A Cultural Biography* (New York, 1995), 351. AL on Buchanan, in *CW,* 2:342. Lincoln's campaign speeches for 1856 are as follows: Springfield, June 10 (*CW,* 2:344-45), Princeton, July 4 (*CW,* 2:346-47), Chicago, July 19 (*CW,* 2:348-49), Galena, July 23 (*CW,* 2:353-55), Paris, August 6, and Shelbyville, August 9 (*CW,* 2:359), Kalamazoo, August 27 (*CW,* 2:361-66), Petersburg, August 30 (*CW,* 2:366-68), Jacksonville, September 6 (*CW,* 2:368-73), Bloomington, September 12 (*CW,* 2:375), Vandalia, September 23 (*CW,* 2:377-78), Peoria, October 9 (*CW,* 2:379), and Belleville, October 18 (*CW,* 379-80). Heckling at Olney is in *CW,* 2:376. Gillespie and others on the Republicans, in Beveridge, *Lincoln,* 2:382, 401, 411, 420; AL on the Republicans, in *CW,* 2:347, 352, 391; Davis on the Republicans, in *HI,* 350; on Republican factions, see Don E. Fehrenbacher, "Lincoln and the Mayor of Chicago," in *Lincoln in Text and Context: Collected Essays* (Stanford, 1987), 33-43. AL on Fillmoreites, in *CW,* 2:358, 374. AL's Chicago speech is in *CW,* 2:383-85. AL's anticipation of *Dred Scott* is in *CW* 2:387-88. The "rumpus" among the Democracy is mentioned in *CW,* 2:427. AL's anger at east-coast Republicans is in *CW,* 2:430, 456-57, and *THL,* 114. Arnold's comment on AL is in Arnold, *The Life of Abraham Lincoln* (1884), 146-47.

The text of the House Divided speech is in *CW,* 2:461-69. Condemnation of the speech is in *HI,* 575. On AL's anger at misconstruction, see *CW,* 2:471, 514, and Rice, *Reminiscences,* 283. AL's invitation to Douglas is in *CW,* 2:522; Douglas's reply is in *The Letters of Stephen A. Douglas,* ed. Robert W. Johannsen (Urbana, 1961), 423-24. AL's contempt for Douglas is in *CW,* 2:136, 382, and *RW,* 5, 169. The standard text of the debates appears in the *CW,* vol. three, as follows: Ottawa, August 21 (1-37), Freeport, August 27 (38-76), Jonesboro, September 15 (102-44), Charleston, September 18 (145-201), Galesburg, October 7 (207-44), Quincy, October 13 (245-83), and Alton, October 15 (283-325). On blacks as the economic equal of Douglas, see AL in *CW,* 3:16; for the Freeport questions, see *CW,* 3:43. On AL's backtracking on black civil rights at Charleston, see *CW,* 3:145-46. On slavery as a moral and political wrong, see *CW,* 3:225-26. AL's definition of the "real issue" is in *CW,* 3:315. AL's estimate of chances is in *CW,* 3:332. AL on the "slip" is in *Inside Lincoln's White House: The Complete Civil War Diary of John Hay*, eds. Michael Burlingame and J. R. T. Ettlinger (Carbondale, 1997), 244. "The fight must go on" is in *CW*, 3:336-37.

Chapter Six: An Accidental President

AL after debates is in Tarbell, *Life*, 1:322; Charles Ray's letters are in Mearns, *Lincoln Papers*, 1:217, 218. Fell's comments are in his contribution to *The Lincoln Memorial: Album-Immortelles*, ed. Osborn Oldroyd (New York, 1883), 473-74. AL on the debates is in *CW*, 3:219, 221; on the face of the nation, see the version in *The Lincoln-Douglas Debates*, ed. Harold Holzer (New York, 1993), 288. For AL on publishing the debates, see *CW*, 3:347, and Mearns, *The Lincoln Papers*, 1:226. On AL's invitations, see *CW*, 3:337, 400; for Douglas and politics see *CW*, 3:463. From AL's 1859 campaign speeches, see *CW*, 3:485, 447, 442, 423, 444, 459, 468, 439, 454. For newspapers promoting AL's nomination and the 1859 speeches, see *Abraham Lincoln: A Press Portrait*, ed. Herbert Mitgang, 130, 131, 140; AL's responses to Pickett and Galloway are in *CW*, 3:377, 394. David Davis's comment on Bates and Seward is in Pratt, *Concerning Mr. Lincoln*, 23. AL to Anson Henry is in *CW*, 3:339, and to Trumbull, in *CW*, 3:356. For AL on Republican unity, see *CW*, 3:366, 486; on AL to Salmon Chase, see *CW*, 3:384. For AL as a Southern man, see *CW*, 3:397. On Judd and the nomination, see *HW*, 2:163, and *HI*, 247; for AL to Judd on the nomination, see *CW*, 3:517. AL's autobiographies are in *CW*, 3:511-12 and 4:60-67. The New York letters of invitation are in Mearns, *Lincoln Papers*, 1:227, 229. Mason Brayman's letter is in Carl Sandburg, *Lincoln Collector: The Story of Oliver R. Barrett's Great Private Collection* (New York, 1960), 160. AL's Cooper Union address is in *CW*, 3:522-50. On AL's impact, see Brooks's comment in his *Abraham Lincoln* (1888), 186-87, and New York *Tribune*, February 28, 1860. AL on reluctance to grasp for nomination is in *CW*, 4:33, 34, 36, 43. To Trumbull on the "taste" is in *CW*, 4:45. Judd's comment on the Chicago convention is in *Inside Lincoln's White House*, 116. On the Decatur Convention and Oglesby's part in bringing in John Hanks, see Rice, *Reminiscences*, 208; *Lincoln Among His Friends: A Sheaf of Intimate Memories*, ed. R. R. Wilson (Caldwell, 1942), 191-94; and James Hickey, "Oglesby's Fence Rail Dealings and the 1860 Decatur Convention," in

Journal of the Illinois State Historical Society (1961), 29-48. The Chicago *Tribune* editorial is in Mitgang, *Press Portrait*, 164-67. On AL's lack of political visibility before Chicago, see Tarbell, *Life*, 1:341-42. On "obtrusion," see *CW*, 4:49. Dubois on Davis is in Mearns, *Lincoln Papers*, 1:233. Pierce's comments are in *HI*, 683. Halstead's comments are in Robert S. Harper, *Lincoln and the Press* (New York, 1951), 52, and Mitgang, *Press Portrait*, 174; Weed weeping over AL's nomination is in Rice, *Reminiscences*, 167. Zane's report is in *RW*, 511. Morehead's reminiscence is in *RW*, 334. Samuel Hart's recollection is in a letter written by his son to Herndon, in *HI*, 223. On Welles's response, see "Nomination and Election of Abraham Lincoln," in *Lincoln's Administration: Selected Essays by Gideon Welles*, ed. A. Mordell (New York, 1960), 17. The Toledo paper's misspelling is in Harper, *Lincoln and the Press*, 54. Southern editorial response is from the New Orleans *Bee*, May 21, 1860, in *Southern Editorials on Secession*, ed. D. L. Dumond (New York, 1931), 104-5. On Finney's response, see *Oberlin Evangelist*, May 23, 1860. On AL's appearance, see Mearns, *Lincoln Papers*, 1:291, and Robert W. Johannsen, *Lincoln, The South and Slavery: The Political Dimension* (Baton Rouge, 1991), 112; the Georgia satire is E. P. Birch's "The Devil's Visit to Old Abe," at www.wfu.edu/Library/rarebook/broads/devils.jpg. On AL's refusal to offer statements, see *CW*, 4:50, 52, 60, 130, 132-33, 134, 138, 182. AL's instructions to Nicolay are in *CW*, 4:83. The correspondence of AL and Haycraft is in *CW*, 4:70, 97, 99, and Mearns, *Lincoln Papers*, 1:274-75. Bryant and Fogg on the election are in Mearns, *Lincoln Papers*, 1:258, 273. AL to Hamlin and Henry, in *CW*, 4:82, 84. AL to Seward is in *CW*, 4:126-27. MTL's confidence and RTL's christening are in a letter to Clinton Conkling from his mother, October 20, 1860, in Pratt, *Concerning Mr. Lincoln*, 25. On the election night, see *RW*, 39; on his realization of responsibility, see *Diary of Gideon Welles*, ed. E. T. Welles (Boston, 1911), 1:81-82.

The Southern newspapers on secession are in Dumond, *Southern Editorials*, 408. Buchanan's message to Congress is in *The Secession Crisis, 1860-1861*, ed. P. J. Staudenraus (Chicago, 1963), 39-46. Piatt on AL is found in *Memories of the Men Who Saved the Union* (New York, 1897), 33, and Rice, *Reminiscences*, 480-81. Schurz on secession is in David M. Potter, *Lincoln and His Party in the Secession Crisis* (1942; Baton Rouge, 1995), 12. On AL's skepticism about Southern intentions, see *HW*, 2:183, *CW*, 4:95, 138, and *RW*, 6. The Union standard is described in

Lincoln's Journalist: John Hay's Anonymous Writings for the Press, 1860-1864, ed. Michael Burlingame (Carbondale, 1998), 56. On his "old record," see *CW*, 4:151-52. On AL's refusal of concessions, see *CW*, 4:150, and *RW*, 353. On Duff Green's plea for AL to support Crittenden, see David E. Woodard, "Abraham Lincoln, Duff Green, and the Mysterious Trumbull Letter," in *CWH* (1996), 219. AL's comment to Browning is in *The Diary of Orville Hickman Browning*, eds. T. C. Pease and J. G. Randall (Springfield, 1925-33), 1:453. The description of Seward is in Burton Hendrick, *Lincoln's War Cabinet* (New York, 1946, 1961), 176. On Thayer, see Martin Crawford, "Politicians in Crisis: The Washington Letters of William S. Thayer, December 1860-March 1861," *CWH* (1981), 232. On AL's "kind side" for Chase, see *CW*, 3:395. On AL's invitation to Gilmer, see Charles M. Segal, *Conversations with Lincoln* (New York, 1961), 61. On AL's opinion of Cameron, see *RW*, 333.

On Anderson's loyalty, see R. C. Anderson to Gen. J. C. Davis, April 20, 1876, in private hands (Abraham Lincoln Book Shop Catalog #139). On AL's intention to hold the forts, see *CW*, 4:137, 157, 159, 160, 162, 164, and Mearns, *Lincoln Papers*, 1:277-78, 295-99, 314 and 2:344-45, 350-52. On AL's correspondence, see Harold Holzer, "Introduction" to *Dear Mr. Lincoln: Letters to the President* (Reading, MA, 1993), 5-6. RTL to MTL, in Sandburg, *Lincoln Collector*, 163. Ada Bailhache's letter is in Pratt, *Concerning Mr. Lincoln*, 32. AL's last meeting with Sarah Bush Lincoln is in *HI*, 108, 137. On Herndon and the law practice, see *HW*, 2:193-94. On Isaac Cogdal, see *HI*, 440. On the Bateman interview, see Josiah G. Holland, *Life of Abraham Lincoln* (Springfield, MA, 1866), 236-39. On departing slowly from Springfield, see Conkling in Pratt, *Concerning Mr. Lincoln*, 34. William Jayne is in *Concerning Mr. Lincoln*, 47. Medill's warning is in Mearns, *Lincoln Papers*, 1:356. The three versions of AL's farewell speech are in *CW*, 4:190-91. The train list is in Weik, *Real Lincoln*, 309, and in *Lincoln's Journalist*, 24; John Pope actually joined the escort in Indianapolis, in *The Military Memoirs of General John Pope*, ed. Peter Cozzens and R. I. Girardi (Urbana, 1998), 176. On the sorrow of parting, see *HW*, 2:194; on AL's emotion, see Conkling in Pratt, *Concerning Mr. Lincoln*, 50. On the near-loss of the First Inaugural, see Nicolay, "Some Incidents in Lincoln's Journey from Springfield to Washington," in *Oral History*, 108-10. From the speeches along the train route, see *CW*, 4:193-94, 211, 214, 216, 238, 247. The First Inaugural is in *CW*, 4:262-71. Thayer on desire for peace is in Thayer letters,

CWH (1981), 246. Scott's replies to AL's queries are in Mearns, *Lincoln Papers*, 2:477-78. AL's March 18th memorandum is in *CW*, 4:288-90. Baldwin's incivility was described by AL to John Minor Botts, in *RW*, 37. AL on desertion of Sumter is in "Fort Sumter," in *Civil War and Reconstruction: Selected Essays by Gideon Welles*, ed. A. Mordell (New York, 1959), 47. Scott's advice to abandon the forts is in *The War of the Rebellion: A Compilation of the Official Records of the Union and Confederate Armies*, Series One (Washington, 1888-1901), vol. one, 200-201. AL to Seward on policy, *CW*, 4:316-17. Chew's orders are in *CW*, 4:323-24; AL to Browning on Sumter, *Diary*, 1:476.

Chapter Seven: War in a Conciliatory Style

AL on Charleston is in *Inside Lincoln's White House*, 11. AL to Garrett Davis, and on last hope of peace, are in *RW*, 8, 133. AL's blockade proclamation is in *CW*, 4:338-39. AL's anger over Magruder is in *Inside Lincoln's White House*, 5, and *RW*, 432. The April 15th proclamation is in *CW*, 4:331-32. AL's promise to Garrett Davis not to retake is in *RW*, 133. Brown's and Hicks's protests are in Mearns, *Lincoln Papers*, 2:566-67, 583; AL's response is in *CW*, 4:340-42. AL's despondency over Washington's isolation is in *RW*, 1, *Inside Lincoln's White House*, 11, and Nicolay and Hay, *Abraham Lincoln: A History* (New York, 1890), 4:151-52. Addison Proctor in Stevens, *Reporters' Lincoln*, 200. New Yorker chiding AL is in Mearns, *Lincoln Papers*, 2:607; sentinels are in Robert W. McBride, *Personal Recollections of Abraham Lincoln* (Indianapolis, 1926), 33-43. Edward Pierce, J. T. Stuart, Edward McPherson, and David Davis on organization are in *HI*, 64, 230, 351, 678. AL on adhesion, in *RW*, 443. Davis on cabinet, in Pratt, *Concerning Mr. Lincoln*, 97. Davis and Swett on advice, in *HI* 165, 167, 346. Cameron on Sumter in the cabinet, in *Oral History*, 42; Davis on smoothness, in *HI*, 484. AL driving in the pegs and not having a policy are in *RW*, 269, 351. Sherman's interview with AL is in *Memoirs of General William T. Sherman* (1875; Library of America, 1990), 186. AL's opinion of the military is in Piatt, *Memories of the Men Who Saved the Union*, 37. John Hay on the White House system is in "Life in the White House in the Time of Lincoln," in *Addresses of John Hay* (New York, 1909), 323-24. On Nicolay and Hay sifting AL's correspondence, see *HI*, 331; on no item escaping AL, see

CW, 5:333. On AL's appointments, see *HI*, 206. Dana's recollections of AL's all-hours work is in *Recollections of the Civil War* (New York, 1898), 173. RTL on AL's work habits is in RTL to Isaac Markens, February 13 and June 18, 1918, in *A Portrait of Abraham Lincoln in Letters by His Oldest Son*, ed. Paul Angle (Chicago, 1968), 56, 62. On seeing AL, see Davis and Lamon in *HI*, 346, 466. AL's comment to Charles Halpine is in *Baked Meats of the Funeral: A Collection of Essays, Poems, Speeches, Histories, and Banquets by Private Miles O'Reilly* (New York, 1866), 106. On badgering with appointments, see *HI*, 207. AL's comment to Stoddard is in *RW*, 425-26. Welles on patronage is in *Lincoln's Administration*, 40, 42. On the growth of patronage jobs, see Philip S. Paludan, *The Presidency of Abraham Lincoln* (Lawrence, 1994), 35-36. Dubois is in Holzer, *Dear Mr. Lincoln*, 143. AL on Elias Wampole is in *CW*, 4:485.

On AL's frustration, see Tarbell, *Life*, 2:40; Browning's advice on Baltimore is in Mearns, *Lincoln Papers*, 2:582. AL's direction to General Scott on the writ of habeas corpus is in *CW*, 4:344, 347. Motley, Parker, and Binney on the suspension of the writ are in *Union Pamphlets of the Civil War, 1861-1865*, ed. Frank Freidel (Cambridge, 1967), 34, 37-38, 41, 48, 63-64, 240; on Binney see C. C. Binney, *Life of Horace Binney* (Philadelphia, 1903), 347-58. AL's comment to Schurz on the war powers is in Schurz, *Reminiscences of Carl Schurz* (New York, 1908), 3:104. AL's July 4, 1861, message to Congress is in *CW*, 4:421-41; see also *RW*, 206, 394. On civil liberties violations, see Mark E. Neely, *The Fate of Liberty: Abraham Lincoln and Civil Liberties* (New York, 1991), 133-50. Welles is in *Lincoln's Administration*, 72-73. AL's regret over Maryland is in *RW*, 134. On AL's reluctance to touch slavery, see Carpenter, *Six Months in the White House*, 76, *RW*, 295, and *HI*, 58. On Douglas, see Jacob Dolson Cox, "War Preparations in the North," in *Battles and Leaders of the Civil War* (1887; New York, 1956), 1:87. For Hay on Vallandigham, see *Lincoln's Journalist*, 74-75; on Vallandigham's sectionalism, see *Speeches, Addresses, and Letters of Clement L. Vallandigham* (1864), 211. On the bewilderment of abolition, see *Inside Lincoln's White House*, 19. Brownson and Tappan are in Freidel, *Union Pamphlets*, 104, 136, 138, 156; Sumner is in David Donald, *Charles Sumner and the Coming of the Civil War* (New York, 1966), 388; Wade, Chandler, and Stevens are in T. Harry Williams, *Lincoln and the Radicals* (Madison, 1941), 10-12; Hay's comment on Wade is in *Lincoln's Journalist*, 277. AL's comments on Radicals are in Edward Bates, *The Diary of Edward Bates*, ed. H. K. Beale (Washington, 1933), 333, and *Inside Lincoln's White House*, 101. AL to John Henderson is in Stevens, *Reporter's Lincoln*, 171; AL to Sumner on six months' time is in *RW*, 433. AL to Fremont is in *CW*, 4:506, and to Browning, in *CW*, 4:532. AL to Jessie Fremont is in *RW*, 164. Fremont's proclamation as inevitable is in New York *Times*, September 3, 1861. Wade on AL is in Bruce Tap, *Over Lincoln's Shoulder: The Committee on the Conduct of the War* (Lawrence, 1998), 16. AL's December 3, 1861, message to Congress is in *CW*, 5:35-53.

Bates on war plans is in Mearns, *Lincoln Papers*, 2:555; McClellan's war plan is in *O.R.*, Series 1, vol. 51 (Part One), 338-39. AL on green troops is in William C. Davis, *Battle at Bull Run* (Garden City, 1977), 77. AL's retort to Scott is in *RW*, 381; his remark on Scott is in Henry C. Whitney, *Life on the Circuit with Lincoln* (Boston, 1892), 502. The "want" of McClellan is in the Philadelphia *Inquirer*, July 23, 1861. AL's complaint to John DeFrees is in *RW*, 136. AL's reorganization plan is in *CW*, 4:457-58. McClellan's spell over the soldiers is in Jacob Dolson Cox, *Military Reminiscences of the Civil War* (New York, 1900), 1:243. For McClellan on deference, see *The Civil War Papers of George B. McClellan: Selected Correspondence, 1860-1865* (New York, 1989), 70. McClellan's reply to AL is in *Inside Lincoln's White House*, 31. AL on strategy is in *RW*, 179, 338-39, and in Edward D. Neill, *Abraham Lincoln and His Mailbag*, ed. T. C. Blegen (St. Paul, 1964), 28. For McClellan on emancipation, see *Correspondence*, 71, 72, 128, 132. Welles on grand reviews is in *Lincoln's Administration*, 63. McClellan on numbers is in *Correspondence*, 87, 128. Stanton to Dyer is in *Records of an Active Life* (New York, 1886), 452. AL's unwillingness to push McClellan is in *Inside Lincoln's White House*, 28-29, 32. AL as an idiot is in McClellan, *Correspondence*, 85, 106. AL to Meigs is in *RW*, 328. Richardson is in Segal, *Conversations*, 127. AL to Buell and Halleck, in *CW*, 5:91-92, 94. AL's meeting with Franklin and McDowell is in Segal, *Conversations*, 150-53. AL's war order is in *CW*, 5:111. AL's stopping deferring to McClellan is in *Inside Lincoln's White House*, 35. McClellan's operational plan is in *O.R.* (Series 1) vol. five, 42-45. AL on West Pointers as Democrats is in *RW*, 400. The army as an anti-Republican engine is in Allan Bogue, "William Parker Cutler's Congressional Diary of 1862-63," in *CWH* (1987), 323. AL confronting McClellan is in *McClellan's Own Story* (New York, 1887), 195-96. On the effects of McClellan's inaction, see *RW*, 346, and *CW*, 5:149. For AL on the need to strike a blow, see *CW*,

5:125. McClellan on the Seven Days battles is in *O.R.* (Series 1), vol. eleven (Part 3), 264-65, and vol. eleven (Part 1), 61, and *Correspondence*, 321. McClellan's letter on war policy is in *O.R.* (Series 1), vol. eleven (Part 1), 73-74. AL to Browning on reinforcements is in Browning, *Diary*, 1:563. Fernando Wood visiting McClellan is in *Inside Lincoln's White House*, 231. Reid on McClellan is in *A Radical View: The "Agate" Dispatches of Whitelaw Reid, 1861-1865*, ed. J. G. Smart (Memphis, 1976), 1:223. AL to Welles on McClellan's reappointment is found in *RW*, 472; on McClellan and Pope's defeat, see *Inside Lincoln's White House*, 37, Browning, *Diary*, 1:589, *RW*, 298, and Welles, *Diary*, 1:113. AL to McClellan before Antietam, in *CW*, 5:426. AL's disappointment to Browning, in *Diary*, 1:590, and *RW*, 380. Hatch's comment is in *Oral History*, 16. AL to McClellan on horse fatigue is in *CW*, 5:474. Davis to Swett on McClellan is in Pratt, *Concerning Mr. Lincoln*, 96. AL done with throwing grass, in *RW*, 9. AL's visit to McClellan concerning dictatorship, in *Oral History*, 16. On treason in the Army of the Potomac, see *CW*, 5:442 and *Inside Lincoln's White House*, 41, 232. For AL on McClellan's dismissal, see Brooks, *Washington in Lincoln's Time* (New York, 1895), 16, and Hatch, *Oral History*, 16, 137. The Pennsylvania officer was Amos Judson; see his *History of the 83rd Regiment of Pennsylvania Volunteers* (1865; Dayton, 1986), 98. AL comparing McClellan to a dull augur is in *RW*, 32.

Chapter Eight: Voice Out of the Whirlwind

On Isaac Arnold and AL, see Alexander McClure, *Lincoln and Men of War-Times* (Philadelphia, 1892), 125-26. Davis on AL's reticence is found in *HI*, 346, 348; AL to Herndon on not refusing, in *RW*, 249. AL on preserving a friend within is in a note of John Hay's on the meeting, September 30, 1863, in Nicolay Papers, Illinois State Historical Library. Brooks's comments are in *Lincoln Observed: The Civil War Dispatches of Noah Brooks*, ed. Michael Burlingame (Baltimore, 1998), 13, 211. Gillespie is in *The Lincoln Memorial*, 457; Speed and Nicolay are in *HI*, 6, 156. Douglas's complaint is mentioned by AL in *CW*, 2:252; AL's biblical allusions are in *CW*, 4:130, 6:383, 2:501, and 2:442; AL's irritation at Beecher is in Carpenter, *Six Months*, 230, and in Beecher in Rice, *Reminiscences*, 249. The Bible as lines for occasions is in *RW*, 273. On AL reading the Bible, see Julia Taft Bayne, *Tad Lincoln's Father* (Boston, 1931), 184; on AL's religious habits, see Browning to Isaac Arnold, November 25, 1872, in Arnold Papers, Chicago Historical Society. AL's comment to Bateman is in Bateman to J. G. Holland, June 19, 1865, in Holland Papers, New York Public Library. AL's interest in Butler, Edwards, and Locke is in Brooks, *Lincoln Observed*, 219, 278. AL's recitations of Burns, Knox, and Hood are in Arnold, *Life*, 444, Carpenter, *Six Months*, 60-61, Brooks, *Lincoln Observed*, 219, and Browning, *Diary*, 1:542-43. AL on Shakespeare is in Carpenter, *Six Months*, 49-52, *HI*, 156, *CW*, 6:392, and *Inside Lincoln's White House*, 76. AL witnesses Booth on stage in George S. Bryan, *The Great American Myth: The True Story of Lincoln's Murder* (1940; Chicago, 1990), 99, and in *Inside Lincoln's White House*, 110, 325-26. Stephen Massett is in Holzer, *Dear Mr. Lincoln*, 294. AL's Shakespeare criticism is in Carpenter, *Six Months*, 50-51, *Inside Lincoln's White House*, 127-28, *RW*, 276-77, 294, and *CW* 6:392. On family worship, see Bayne, *Tad Lincoln's Father*, 183.

Fell to Lamon on providence is in *HI*, 579; AL mocking Douglas is in *CW*, 2:150. Submitting to providence is in *HI*, 426. AL's invocations of providence are in *CW*, 4:190, 204, 236, 271; 5:26, 213, 215. On Gurley, see Edgar DeWitt Jones, *Lincoln and the Preachers* (New York, 1948), D. R. Barbee, "President Lincoln and Doctor Gurley," *ALQ* (1948), 3-24, and David Hein, "A Sermon Lincoln Heard: P. D. Gurley's 'Man's Projects and God's Results,'" in *Lincoln Herald* (1987), 161-66. On Gurley's involvement with AL, see *HI*, 497, *Inside Lincoln's White House*, 70, and Burlingame, *Inner World*, 207-8. AL's responses to delegations of clergy are in Segal, *Conversations*, 199, W. H. Lamon, *Recollections of Abraham Lincoln* (1895; Chicago, 1911), 93, *CW*, 5:278-79, Kelley, in Rice, *Reminiscences*, 282, and Holland, *Life*, 439. AL on moral training is in *CW*, 7:47-48 (although there is evidence that AL did not write these words). AL's calls for days of thanksgiving and prayer are in *CW*, 4:482, 5:186, 6:332, 7:333, 432, 533, 8:55. AL on the Sabbath is in *CW*, 5:497; on the Christian Commission's convention, see *The Lincoln Mailbag: America Writes to the President, 1861-1865*, ed. Harold Holzer (Carbondale, 1998), 140. See also Lucas E. Morel, "The Role of Religion in Abraham Lincoln's Statesmanship" (unpublished Ph.D. dissertation, Claremont Graduate School, 1994), 91-96. AL to Arnold Fischel is in *CW*, 5:69; AL on the McPheeters incident is in *CW*, 6:33-34. AL's response to the Bible Amendment is in *HI*, 497. AL's reliance on laws is in *THL*, 143. AL's interview with Browning is in *Oral History*, 5; his notions of providence are in *HI*, 167, 476, 582, *CW*, 5:278-79, 478. The "Memorandum" is in *CW*, 5:403-4. AL's comment to Stuart on providence is in *Oral History*, 14-15. AL's response to James Wilson is in *RW*, 500. AL on not getting to heaven is in *HI*, 31, 157. Willie Lincoln is described in *Intimate Memories of Lincoln*, ed. R. R. Wilson (Elmira, NY, 1945), 136-37, and Stevens, *Reporter's Lincoln*, 216; Browning on AL and Gurley is in Browning's letter to Arnold, idem. On MTL's response to Willie's death, see Baker, *Mary Todd Lincoln*, 222-23. AL's wish to be more devout is in *CW*, 6:535. For AL as driftwood, see Segal, *Conversations*, 336.

For AL on the purpose of the war, see *RW*, 295, *HI*, 405, and Cutler diary, *CWH* (1987), 319. For AL on the border states, see *RW*, 370, and A. H. Markland in Rice, *Reminiscences*, 318; on gradual emancipation, see *RW*, 122, 421, 422, *CW*, 5:49, and *HI*, 162. On not returning fugitives, see *RW*, 9. On the Republican caucus and the Radicals, see *Oral History*, 61, Segal, *Conversations*, 180, and Julian in Rice, *Reminiscences*, 62, 533. On black soldiers, see *RW*, 199, and Reid, *Dispatches*, 2:75-76. For AL on colonization and gradual emancipation, see *CW*, 5:145, *RW*, 443, and Browning, *Diary*, 1:512. AL's ideal emancipation bill is in *CW*, 5:169, and Browning, *Diary*, 1:541. On AL's compensation schemes, see *CW*, 5:29-30, 144-46, and *RW*, 121-22. AL to Maryland slaveholders is in *CW*, 5:222. AL on changing tactics is in Carpenter, *Six Months*, 20-21, and in Welles, "The History of Emancipation," in *Civil War and Reconstruction*, 235. AL's last appeal to border state congressmen is in *CW*, 5:317-19. AL's federal funding plan is in *CW*, 5:324; his comments on the Second Confiscation Act are in *CW*, 5:328-31. For AL to Forney, see *RW*, 162. AL's conversation with Welles and Seward is in Welles, *Diary*, 1:70, and in *Civil War and Reconstruction*, 237-40. AL in the cabinet meeting is in Chase, *Inside Lincoln's Cabinet: The Civil War Diaries of Salmon P. Chase*, ed. David Donald (New York, 1954), 97-100. On Seward's objection, see Carpenter, *Six Months*, 22. Leaks of the Proclamation are mentioned in James Gilmore, *Personal Recollections of Abraham Lincoln* (Boston, 1898), 75-76. Greeley's "Prayer" is in Holzer, *Dear Mr. Lincoln*, 156-61. The text of AL's interview with Dempster and Patton is in Segal, *Conversations*, 197-203. AL's covenant is described in *Inside Lincoln's Cabinet*, 149-53, and in Welles, *Diary*, 1:142-45. On *my* God, see *CW*, 5:146. AL's resort to special providences is in Gillespie, in *Lincoln Memorial*, 457. The three versions of the Emancipation Proclamation are in *CW*, 5:336-37, 433-36, 6:28-30. AL to Dahlgren is in *RW*, 129; on the legality of emancipation, see *RW*, 421. For AL's constitutional amendment proposal, see *CW*, 5:530-36. RTL's recollection of AL under orders is in Mrs. F. L. Stanley, *Christian Science Monitor*, September 23, 1937 (my particular thanks to Michael Burlingame for directing my attention to this). Welles on the last-minute changes to the final Proclamation is in *Civil War and Reconstruction*, 251; Chase as the source of the invocation is in Rice, *Reminiscences*, 91. AL on colonization after emancipation is in Cutler diary, *CWH* (1987), 330, *RW*, 23, and *CW*, 5:370-75. Douglass's protest is in David Blight, "The Bugbear of Colonization," in *Frederick Douglass' Civil War: Keeping Faith in Jubilee* (Baton Rouge, 1989), 122-47. AL to Grinnell on black civil rights is in *RW*, 187. AL to Andrew Johnson on black soldiers is in *CW* 6:149. Reid on acceptance of black soldiers is in *Dispatches*, 2:97. AL's proposals for the use of black soldiers are in *RW*, 163, 435, and *CW*, 6:150. Douglass on AL is in Rice, *Reminiscences*, 186, 193, and in Michael Burlingame, "'Emphatically the Black Man's President': New Light on Frederick Douglass and Abraham Lincoln," in *Lincoln Ledger* (1996), 1-5, citing Douglass's little-known December, 1865, eulogy of AL in the Frederick Douglass Papers, Library of Congress. AL sloughing off colonization is in *Inside Lincoln's White House*, 217. On state grants of civil rights, see McCulloch in Rice, *Reminiscences*, 422. David Lightner and LaWanda Cox offer views of Lincoln more aggressive in his commitment to black civil rights, in Lightner, "Abraham Lincoln and the Ideal of Equality," *Journal of the Illinois State Historical Society* (1982), 289-308, and in Cox, *Lincoln and Black Freedom: A Study in Presidential Leadership* (Columbia, 1981), 116-21; inclining to a more pessimistic view are Don E. Fehrenbacher, "Only His Stepchildren," in *Lincoln in Text and Context*, 95-112, and George M. Frederickson, "A Man but Not a Brother: Abraham Lincoln and Racial Equality," *Journal of Southern History* (1975), 40-58.

Chapter Nine: Whig Jupiter

AL to McClintock is in *RW*, 314; Welles is in *Civil War and Reconstruction*, 249; AL to Hamlin is in *CW*, 5:444. Army cheers for McClellan are in Bruce Catton, *Mr. Lincoln's Army* (New York, 1951), 329. God working for the rebels is in the Cutler diary, *CWH* (1987), 326; AL on no ray of hope is in Browning, *Diary*, 1:600. Medill is in T. Harry William, *Lincoln and the Radicals* (Wisconsin, 1941), 236, and in Hendrick, *Lincoln's Cabinet*, 386. Wade on dictatorship is in Segal, *Conversations*, 213; reconstruction of the cabinet is in Browning, *Diary*, 1:596-99. Accounts of the cabinet crisis and meetings are in Francis Fessenden, *Life and Public Services of W. P. Fessenden* (Boston, 1907), 1:239-40, 243-46, in Welles, *Diary*, 1:194-99, and Bates, *Diary*, 268-70. On Trumbull's comment to AL, see Nicolay and Hay, *Abraham Lincoln*, 6:267. On disposing of the subject, see Browning, *Diary*, 1:603. AL to Wilkeson is in *RW*, 496; AL to Hay on the cabinet crisis, in *Inside Lincoln's White House*, 104. Greeley on the darkest hour is in *The American Conflict* (Hartford, 1867), 2:484. The text of the Corning letter is in *CW*, 6:260-64; the text of the Conkling letter is in *CW*, 6:406-10. AL to Dickey on Hooker is in *Oral History*, 50. AL's lament to Stanton over Chancellorsville is in *RW*, 416. AL's comment on Hooker and the cannon shot is in Welles, *Diary*, 1:336.

On AL's political resolve on emancipation, see Segal, *Conversations*, 215, *RW*, 435, and *CW*, 6:518-37. The meeting with Phillips is described by Moncure Conway in Segal, *Conversations*, 238, but AL's comment on knocking the bottom out of slavery only appears in a later account Conway gave in 1885, in *RW*, 120. AL to Grinnell on temperament is in *RW*, 186; short statutes of limitations in politics are mentioned twice in *Inside Lincoln's White House*, 125 and 249. Swett on AL is in *HI*, 163. On AL's increasing grasp of the presidency, see *HI*, 160, Brooks, *Lincoln Observed*, 155, and Titian Coffey in Rice, *Reminiscences*, 245. AL's refusal to be bullied by Congress is in *Oral History*, 67, 78. AL on McClellan's slows is in *RW*, 32. Deming on AL's originality is in *Eulogy of Abraham Lincoln* (Hartford, 1865), 17. On AL's control of the patronage, see Henry Carman and Reinhold Luthin, *Lincoln and the Patronage* (New York, 1943), 228-29; Julian on AL as virtual dictator is in William C. Harris, *With Charity for All: Lincoln and the Restoration of the Union* (Lexington, 1997), 241. Swett on AL's handling of men in *HI*, 168. AL on his desire to accompany McClellan into battle is in *Inside Lincoln's White House*, 29. Hay on AL's visits to McClellan is in *Lincoln's Journalist*, 130. Russell is in *My Diary North and South*, ed. E. Berwanger (New York, 1988), 317. AL to Taussig on the cabinet is in *RW*, 443; Deming is in *Eulogy*, 17. Forney's comments were remarks to John Hay, in *Inside Lincoln's White House*, 113, 135. On AL and the Washington press, see Louis Starr, *Bohemian Brigade: The Civil War's Newsmen in Action* (New York, 1954), 152-63. On AL and the soldiers, see William C. Davis, *Lincoln's Men: How President Lincoln Became Father to an Army and a Nation* (New York, 1999), 140-45. Hay on AL as the Tycoon and Jupiter is in Segal, *Conversations,* 271.

AL's rejoicing and disappointment over Gettysburg are in *CW,* 6:314, in *Inside Lincoln's White House,* 61, 62, 64-65, and in *Oral History,* 88. AL's gratitude to Meade is in *CW,* 6:341, and in *RW,* 293. AL's joy over Vicksburg is in Welles, *Diary,* 1:364. AL's White House speech is in *CW,* 6:319-20. AL on Grant is in *RW,* 11; AL's hopes that the Confederacy might be collapsing are in *Inside Lincoln's White House,* 70-71. On the Gettysburg cemetery invitation, see Frank L. Klement, "These Honored Dead: David Wills and the Soldiers Cemetery at Gettysburg," in *The Gettysburg Soldiers' Cemetery and Lincoln's Address* (Shippensburg, PA, 1993), 3-19; on the distinction between propositions and self-evident truths, see Glen E. Thurow, "Abraham Lincoln and the American Political Religion," in *The Historian's Lincoln: Pseudohistory, Psychohistory, and History* (Urbana, 1988), 125-43. The Chicago *Times* editorial on the dedication remarks is in Mitgang, *Press Portrait,* 360. On AL's quip about smallpox, see *RW,* 13. The evidence that AL briefly shaved his beard due to complications from varioloid stems from Henry H. Cross's "beardless" AL portrait of 1863 and Cross's claims that AL had shaved "it off on account of a rash which had attacked his face"; see Harold Holzer and Lloyd Ostendorf, "The Long Lost Lincolns," in *Civil War Times Illustrated* (1979), 32-41.

General surveys of AL's domestic agenda are in: Paludan, *Presidency of Abraham Lincoln,* 107-18, 210-12, and *A People's Contest: The Union and the Civil War, 1861-1865* (New York, 1988), 103-197; Heather Cox Richardson, *The Greatest Nation of the Earth: Republican Economic Policies During the Civil War* (Cambridge, MA, 1997), 31-208; Richard F. Bensel, *Yankee Leviathan: The Origins of Central State Authority in America, 1859-1877* (Cambridge, 1990), 68-85; and Gabor S. Boritt, *Lincoln and the Economics of the American Dream* (Memphis, 1977), 195-221. AL to Grenville Dodge is in *RW,* 143. AL's directions on railroads are in *CW,* 6:68-69, on canals in *CW,* 5:526, and on tariffs in *CW,* 4:14, 49, 119, 125, 211-15. On Democratic criticisms, see Frank L. Klement, *Lincoln's Critics: The Copperheads of the North* (Shippensburg, PA, 1999), 43-63. On homesteaders, see Paludan, *People's Contest,* 135; on agricultural colleges, see Paul W. Gates, *Agriculture and the Civil War* (New York, 1965), 251-71. AL on the land-grant colleges is in *CW*, 5:526. On Chase having no money, see *RW*, 328. On the greenbacks, see Paludan, *Presidency of Abraham Lincoln*, 211, 216. AL to Kellogg on finance, in *RW*, 277. AL to Chase on his mill is in *Oral History*, 90; on management, see Chase, *Inside Lincoln's Cabinet*, 440. On AL's supervision of Chase, see *Inside Lincoln's White House*, 133. AL on the currency is in *CW*, 6:61. AL to Seymour on the draft is in *CW*, 6:370.

On holding "a leg" is in Grant, *Personal Memoirs of U. S. Grant* (Library of America, 1990), 456. AL on Grant, in *RW*, 148. AL to Hamilton on election, in *RW*, 196-97. Ashmun on Chase and AL is in Pratt, *Concerning Mr. Lincoln*, 110. On AL's refusal to notice Chase, see *Inside Lincoln's White House*, 93. On Blair's Rockville speech, see Williams, *Lincoln and the Radicals*, 298; AL's comment on Blair and Sumner is in *Inside Lincoln's White House*, 105. French on MTL's overspending is in *Witness to the Young Republic: A Yankee's Journal, 1828-1870*, eds. D. B. Cole and J. J. McDonough (Hanover, NH, 1989), 382. McClure and Nesmith on MTL are in Burlingame, *Inner World*, 298. MTL on Aleck Todd is in Baker, *Mary Todd Lincoln*, 223. AL on RTL's staff appointment is in *CW*, 8:223-24. AL's anxiety over MTL is in *Oral History*, 3. AL's refusal to recognize secession is in Brooks, *Lincoln Observed*, 177. On the military governor's scheme, see Herman Belz, *Reconstructing the Union: Theory and Policy During the Civil War* (Ithaca, 1969), 71-74, and Harris, *With Charity for All*, 40-71. AL's reconstruction proclamation is in *CW*, 6:36-53, 53-56. The delight over the proclamation is recorded in *Inside Lincoln's White House*, 122-23; the *Tribune*'s editorial is in Mitgang, *Press Portrait*, 365. AL to Joseph Mills is in Segal, *Conversations*, 340. Hay on AL's 10 percent plan is in *Inside Lincoln's White House*, 173. AL to Hodges, Bramlette, and Dixon is in *CW*, 7:281. The Wade Davis Bill and the subsequent Manifesto (which was published in Greeley's *Tribune*) are in *The Radical Republicans and Reconstruction, 1861-1870*, ed. Harold Hyman (Indianapolis, 1967), 128-34, 137-47. AL's veto is explained in *CW*, 7:433-34. AL's dismissal of Greeley's Niagara Falls mission is in *RW*, 19. AL's pledge is in *CW*, 7:514.

AL on the nomination of Chase is in *RW*, 94. On the revival of AL's fortunes, see Welles, *Lincoln's Administration*, 206; and Lamon, *Recollections*, 207-8. Ashley is quoted by Hay in *Inside Lincoln's White*

House, 195. On Chandler and the rallying of the Radicals to AL, see W. F. Zornow, *Lincoln and the Party Divided* (Norman, 1954), 145-48. AL's December, 1864, annual message to Congress is in *CW*, 8:136-52. AL to Hugh McCulloch is in *RW*, 330. Edward Neill on AL is in *Oral History*, 83.

Chapter Ten: Malice Toward None

AL not in favor of immediate emancipation is in *RW*, 421; for AL to Albert Hodges, see *CW*, 7:282. AL's estimate of Union strength is in *CW*, 8:151. AL on the ruin of the South to Duval and Welles is in *RW*, 146, and *Civil War and Reconstruction*, 182. On the weakness of the Proclamation, see *CW*, 8:152. AL to Philbrick is in *RW*, 355. Douglass is in Blight, *Frederick Douglass' Civil War*, 186. The Thirteenth Amendment as the King's cure is in *CW*, 8:254. On the validity of the Proclamation, see *CW*, 7:149, 8:254. AL's pressure on Rollins is in Arnold, *Life*, 280, and in *Lincoln Memorial*, 491-95. Dana's comment actually refers to the prior admission of Nevada as a state so that AL would have the necessary free-state votes for ratification of the amendment; see *Recollections*, 175-77. Sumner to John Bright, March 13, 1865, is in *Selected Letters of Charles Sumner*, ed. Beverly Wilson Palmer (Boston, 1990), 2:273. Butler's claim that AL was still entertaining plans for colonization is in Rice, *Reminiscences*, 149-54. AL on black civil rights is in *RW*, 14; *CW*, 7:243; Lamon, *Recollections*, 242; and in *Inside Lincoln's White House*, 253. AL on the possible closure of the 10 percent plan in *CW*, 8:152. AL to Lamon on the Ashley bill, in Lamon, *Recollections*, 242; and to Hay, in *Inside Lincoln's White House*, 253. For Lincoln on the Blair exchange, see *CW*, 8:188, 220-21; on AL's response to Stephens, see *CW*, 8:250-51. Other accounts of the Hampton Roads Conference are in Stephens, *A Constitutional View of the Late War Between the States* (1870), 2:598-619, and in John A. Campbell, *Reminiscences and Documents Relating to the Civil War* (1887), 11-17. AL's joint resolution after Hampton Roads is in *CW*, 8:260-61. On AL's rebuff by the Cabinet, see John P. Usher in *Oral History*, 66, and in Rice, *Reminiscences*, 98.

AL to Eliza Gurney is in *CW*, 7:535. Charles Hodge on "The War" is in *Biblical Repertory and Princeton Review* (January 1863), 141, 142-43, 145-47. AL shows the manuscript of the Second Inaugural to Carpenter in *Six Months*, 234. The text of the Second Inaugural is in *CW*, 8:332-33. AL on Andrew Johnson is found in *Inside Lincoln's White House*, 199. Johnson's letter to AL is in Holzer, *Lincoln Mailbag*, 212. On not letting Johnson speak, see *RW*, 235. On the delivery of the Second Inaugural, see Brooks, *Lincoln Observed*, 167, 168, and *Washington in Lincoln's Time*, 239. On the Bible opened to Lincoln after his oath, see Arnold, *Life*, 402. AL's appearance to Walt Whitman is in "Specimen Days," in *The Portable Walt Whitman*, ed. M. Van Doren (New York, 1945), 562. AL to Speed on ill-health is in *HI*, 157; on AL's exchange with Weed, see Holzer, *Dear Mr. President*, 138 and *CW*, 8:356. Grant to Jesse Grant, March 19, 1865, is in Grant, *Memoirs*, 1081. AL's relief that Congress was out of session is in Welles, *Civil War and Reconstruction*, 190, and Brooks, *Lincoln Observed*, 184. On the City Point conference, see Browne, *Every-Day Life*, 812-13, and Sherman to Isaac Arnold, November 28, 1871, in Arnold, *Life*, 423, *RW*, 114, 339. AL to Grant in Grant, *Memoirs*, 711. On AL's arrival in Richmond, see Segal, *Conversations*, 387, *RW*, 366, 466, 724, and Browne, *Every-Day Life*, 691. AL to Weitzel on Campbell is quoted in Weitzel's letter in *O.R.* (Series 1), vol. 46 (Part 3), 636; AL on Campbell is also in *RW*, 77, *CW*, 8:389, and Segal, *Conversations*, 388-90. AL's proclamation for Campbell is described in *RW*, 359; the text is in *CW*, 8:386. Welles's protest against the Campbell proclamation is in *Civil War and Reconstruction*, 186-88. AL to Weitzel cancelling the Campbell arrangement is in *CW*, 8:406-7. AL to Colfax on no longer needing Campbell is in *RW*, 114. AL's final speech is in *CW*, 8:399-405; on the reception by the crowd, see Brooks, *Lincoln Observed*, 183.

On AL discounting assassination, see *RW*, 73, and Carpenter, *Six Months*, 62. On the ghostly image, see Carpenter, *Six Months*, 163, Brooks, *Lincoln Observed*, 205-6, and Lamon, *Recollections*, 112-13. On threats to AL, see Holzer, *Dear Mr. President*, 345, 348. AL's complaint about skulking into Baltimore is in Lamon, *Recollections*, 266. AL to Jim Lane, in *Inside Lincoln's White House*, 195. On an unguarded White House, see Halpine, *Baked Meats of the Funeral*, 107. AL's order to disperse the cavalry is in Holzer, *Lincoln Mailbag*, 162. Lamon as monomaniac on AL's safety is in Lamon, *Recollections*, 280; Lamon's letter to AL is also in Holzer, *Lincoln Mailbag*, 195-96. AL's self-estimate as a physical coward is in Brooks, *Lincoln Observed*, 205. AL oppressed with the thought of further loss of life, in *RW*, 3. AL to Swett on butcher day is in *HI*, 166. Between 1862 and 1865, nine out of ten of the pardons AL issued to deserters were confirmations of recommendations made by lower courts-martial and by Judge Advocate General Joseph Holt; see Thomas Lowry, *Don't Shoot That Boy! Abraham Lincoln and Military Justice* (Mason City, IA, 1999), 260. Ford on Booth as greatest actor, and Booth on the South, are in Bryan, *Great American Myth*, 92, 111. Neill on Booth is in Holzer, *Dear Mr. President*, 338. Washburne on AL's health, in Rice, *Reminiscences*, 43. On AL's ship dream, see Welles, *Diary*, 2:282-83; and *RW*, 398. On AL's last cabinet meeting, see Welles, *Civil War and Reconstruction*, 189-93, and *Inside Lincoln's Cabinet*, 268. Brooks on the expectation of a new policy in the summer is in *Lincoln Observed*, 184. Bishop Chase's recommendation to AL on observing Good Friday is in Holzer, *Dear Mr. President*, 68-69. AL to MTL on seeing Jerusalem is in *RW*, 297, and *HI*, 359 (AL had also mentioned an interest in seeing California to Noah Brooks, in *Lincoln Observed*, 195, and to Schuyler Colfax, in *RW*, 113-14).

On Booth's entrance to AL's box, see Capt. Thomas McGowan in *We Saw Lincoln Shot: One Hundred Eyewitness Accounts*, ed. T. S. Good (Jackson, MI), 80. Rathbone, Sanford, and Leale are all in *We Saw Lincoln Shot*, 44, 48, 59-62. On AL's death, see D. M. Kunhardt and P. B. Kunhardt, *Twenty Days* (Secaucus, NJ, 1977), 79-80, and Welles, *Diary*, 2:286-88. On the rainfall, see William A. Tidwell, "April 15, 1865," in *CWH* (1996), 220.

Epilogue: The Redeemer President

On immediate reactions to AL's assassination: John Pierce, April 15, 1865, in *Yankee Correspondence: Civil War Letters Between New England Soldiers and the Home Front*, eds. N. Silber and M. Stevens (Charlottesville, VA, 1996), 52; Garth Wilkinson James, in *The James Family*, ed. F. O. Mattheisen (New York, 1947), 265; Thomas Reed Turner, *Beware the People Weeping: Public Opinion and the Assassination of Abraham Lincoln* (Baton Rouge, 1982), 27; W. W. Glenn, *Between North and South: A Maryland Journalist Views the Civil War*, ed. B. E. Marks and M. N. Schatz (Teaneck, NJ, 1976), 10; David Donald, *Lincoln's Herndon* (New York, 1948), 165; Jane Addams, *Twenty Years at Hull House* (Signet, 1981), 33.

On the sermon literature: Haven and Bingham, in *"No Sorrow*

Like Our Sorrow": Northern Protestant Ministers and the Assassination of Lincoln (Kent, OH, 1994), 106; Crane, in Lloyd Lewis, *Myths After Lincoln* (New York, 1941), 95; Holland, *Eulogy on Abraham Lincoln* (Springfield, MA, 1865), 18; Duffield and Fulton in Chesebrough, *No Sorrow Like Our Sorrow*, 32-33; Duffield in Lewis, *Myths*, 104; Holland, in *Eulogy*, 15-16; Baldridge, in Chesebrough, *No Sorrow Like Our Sorrow*, 29; Holland, *Life*, 237. On Bateman, see Julian Sturtevant to William E. Barton, March 8, 1920, in W. E. Barton Papers, University of Chicago. Herndon on Holland is in *THL*, 45. Carpenter on AL's religious sentiments is in *HI*, 521; Herndon on AL's disbelief, in *THL*, 65. Rebukes to Herndon from Carpenter, Goodrich, and Smith are in *HI*, 494, 511, 547-50. On Lamon's biography, see Benjamin P. Thomas, *Portrait for Posterity: Lincoln and His Biographers* (New Brunswick, 1947), 46. On James Reed's lecture, see Barton, *Soul of Abraham Lincoln*, 135-39. Swett's advice to Herndon on self-censorship is in *HI*, 636-37; on John Todd Stuart's contempt for Herndon, see Elizabeth Ide Brown, in *Autobiography of Christopher C. Brown* (privately printed, Edwards Brown, Jr, 1973), 68. AL's excuse to Deming for not joining a church is in Deming, *Eulogy*, 42. On the fascination of clergymen for AL, see Merrill D. Peterson, *Lincoln in American Memory* (New York, 1994), 219-20. On Melville, see Kazin, *God and the American Writer*, 91. Adams and Goodspeed are in Chesebrough, *No Sorrow Like Our Sorrow*, 41, 54. Browning on hearing a retribution sermon is in *Diary*, 2:21. On Southern responses to AL's assassination, see Carolyn L. Harrell, *When the Bells Tolled for Lincoln: Southern Reactions to the Assassination* (Macon, 1997), 61, 85; and Jones in *A Rebel War Clerk's Diary*, ed. E. S. Miers (New York, 1961), 536. Hodge's anger at Democratic responses to AL's assassination is in Charles Hodge to Hugh Hodge, April 15, 1865, in Charles Hodge Papers, Box 12, File 3, Firestone Library, Princeton University. On the Radicals' enthusiasm for Andrew Johnson, see Hans Trefousse, *Benjamin Franklin Wade: Radical Republican from Ohio* (New York, 1963), 249-50, and Tap, *Over Lincoln's Shoulder*, 242-43.

On RTL's and MTL's wishes, see Browning, *Diary*, 2:20. On crowds at Paoli and into Philadelphia, see the Philadelphia *Inquirer*, April 22, 1865. On the appearance of AL's corpse in Springfield, see Tarbell, *Life*, 2:250. The mourning of black people in Springfield is in Stevens, *Reporter's Lincoln*, 190. The crowds in Springfield for the funeral are described in James T. Hickey, "Springfield, May, 1865," in

Journal of the Illinois State Historical Society (1965), 87. Wentworth on AL as a fossil is in *HI*, 195. Helen Nicolay on AL is in *Personal Traits of Abraham Lincoln* (New York, 1912), 381. On Nicolay and Hay's biography, see Michael Burlingame, "Nicolay and Hay: Court Historians," *JALA* (1998), 2. AL's partisan Whig loyalties are analyzed in Silbey, "'Always a Whig in Politics': The Partisan Life of Abraham Lincoln," in *Papers of the Abraham Lincoln Association* (1986), 21-42. AL and free labor is discussed by Michael Sandel in *Democracy's Discontents: America in Search of a Public Philosophy* (Cambridge, MA, 1996), 181. Whitney on AL and corporations, in *HI*, 733. AL's honesty and religious convictions are in Brooks, *Lincoln Observed*, 209. AL on the will of God is in *CW*, 3:204. On AL's sense of being forsaken by God, see Herndon in *THL*, 36, 43, 52; and on how this translated from melancholy to charity, see also *THL*, 34, 46. AL to Brooks and Morrill is in *RW*, 336, and *Lincoln Observed*, 145. AL to Aminda Rankin is in Henry B. Rankin, *Personal Recollections*, 324.

Index